# Lecture Notes in Computer Science 16231

Founding Editors

Gerhard Goos
Juris Hartmanis

The series Lecture Notes in Computer Science (LNCS), including its subseries Lecture Notes in Artificial Intelligence (LNAI) and Lecture Notes in Bioinformatics (LNBI), has established itself as a medium for the publication of new developments in computer science and information technology research, teaching, and education.

LNCS enjoys close cooperation with the computer science R & D community, the series counts many renowned academics among its volume editors and paper authors, and collaborates with prestigious societies. Its mission is to serve this international community by providing an invaluable service, mainly focused on the publication of conference and workshop proceedings and postproceedings. LNCS commenced publication in 1973.

Romain Laborde · Joaquin Garcia-Alfaro ·
Guillermo Navarro · Jordi Herrera-Joancomartí ·
Hannes Hartenstein · Sokratis Katsikas ·
Frédéric Cuppens
Editors

# Computer Security

## ESORICS 2025 International Workshops

DPM 2025, CBT 2025, CyberICPS 2025
Toulouse, France, September 25–26, 2025
Revised Selected Papers, Part I

 Springer

*Editors*
Romain Laborde (iD)
IRIT, Université de Toulouse
Toulouse, France

Guillermo Navarro (iD)
Universitat Autònoma de Barcelona
Bellaterra, Barcelona, Spain

Hannes Hartenstein (iD)
Karlsruhe Institute Technology (KIT)
Karlsruhe, Germany

Frédéric Cuppens (iD)
Polytechnique Montréal
Montréal, QC, Canada

Joaquin Garcia-Alfaro (iD)
SAMOVAR, Télécom SudParis
Palaiseau, France

Jordi Herrera-Joancomartí (iD)
Universitat Autònoma de Barcelona
Bellaterra, Spain

Sokratis Katsikas (iD)
Norwegian University of Science
and Technology - NTNU
Gjøvik, Norway

ISSN 0302-9743          ISSN 1611-3349  (electronic)
Lecture Notes in Computer Science
ISBN 978-3-032-16088-1          ISBN 978-3-032-16089-8  (eBook)
https://doi.org/10.1007/978-3-032-16089-8

# Preface

The 30th edition of the European Symposium on Research in Computer Security (ESORICS) was held in Toulouse, France, during September 22–26, 2025. In addition to the main conference, 13 workshops were organized and held in the same time period.

This volume includes the accepted contributions to three of these workshops, as follows:

- the 20th International Workshop on Data Privacy Management (DPM 2025);
- the 9th International Workshop on Cryptocurrencies and Blockchain Technology (CBT 2025);
- the 11th International Workshop on the Security of Industrial Control Systems and of Cyber-Physical Systems (CyberICPS 2025).

While each of the workshops had a high-quality program of its own, the organizers opted to publish the proceedings jointly; these are included in this volume, which contains 31 revised papers. The authors improved and extended the accepted papers based on the reviewers' feedback as well as the discussions at the workshops.

We would like to thank each and every one who was involved in the organization of the ESORICS 2025 workshops. Special thanks go to respective Program Committees of each workshop, who contributed to making the ESORICS 2025 workshops a real success. We would also like to thank the ESORICS 2025 Organizing Committee for supporting the day-to-day operation and execution of the workshops.

November 2025

Romain Laborde
Joaquin Garcia-Alfaro
Guillermo Navarro-Arribas
Jordi Herrera-Joancomartí
Hannes Hartenstein
Sokratis Katsikas
Frédéric Cuppens

# Preface to the Proceedings of DPM 2025

This volume contains the post-proceedings of the 20th International Workshop on Data Privacy Management (DPM 2025), which was organized as a part of the 30th European Symposium on Research in Computer Security (ESORICS 2025). The DPM series started in 2005 when the first workshop took place in Tokyo (Japan). Since that inaugural meeting it has been held in different venues: Atlanta, USA (2006); Istanbul, Turkey (2007); Saint Malo, France (2009); Athens, Greece (2010); Leuven, Belgium (2011); Pisa, Italy (2012); Egham, UK (2013); Wrocław, Poland (2014); Vienna, Austria (2015); Crete, Greece (2016); Oslo, Norway (2017); Barcelona, Spain (2018); Luxembourg (2019); Guildford, UK (2020); Darmstadt, Germany (2021); Copenhagen, Denmark (2022); The Hague, The Netherlands (2023); and Bydgoszcz, Poland (2024).

The 2025 DPM event was held in Toulouse, France on September 25th as a part of the ESORICS 2025 workshops. All presentations were in person, and the workshop was structured to allow for a thorough presentation of each contribution's key ideas and allowed for subsequent discussion from attendees that provided new insights on the contributed work and facilitated nascent directions for subsequent work.

We received 27 submissions. All papers were assigned to at least three program committee members to provide commentary about each paper, and we are thankful to our PC members who returned all reviews in a timely way. Each submission was evaluated based on its significance, novelty, and technical quality. The program committee performed a thorough single-blind review process, undertook consensus discussions, and selected 8 regular papers for presentation at the workshop, complemented by 6 short papers and 1 invited keynote by Bart Preneel from KU Leuven on privacy technology and policy. The keynote was a joint keynote with the CBT and CyberICPS workshops.

We extend our sincere gratitude to all DPM 2025 Program Committee members, additional reviewers, and, above all, to the authors who submitted their work. We also thank all workshop participants for fostering a friendly and engaging atmosphere, and express our special appreciation to Ken Barker for chairing a session and contributing to greatly enriched discussions and overall experience during the workshop.

We would also like to thank everyone who helped with the event organization, including all the members of the organizing committees for both ESORICS 2025 and DPM 2025. Our gratitude goes to Vincent Nicomette and Abdelmalek Benzekri, General Chairs of ESORICS 2025, Romain Laborde, Workshop Chair of ESORICS 2025, and everyone in the ESORICS 2025 organization.

We also thank our sponsors for providing support in different forms: Institut Polytechnique de Paris, Universitat Autònoma de Barcelona, Cybercat, Plan de Recuperación, Transformación y Resiliencia funded with Next Generation EU funds through the project DANGER INCIBE-C062/23; Spanish Ministry SECURING/NET PID2021-125962OB-C33, and SAFE/BLOCKCHAIN PID2024-156914OB-C43; Catalan AGAUR SGR2021-00643.

We believe that the papers presented at DPM 2025 and the discussions held at the workshop will advance our understanding of how to effectively address the increasingly complex challenges faced by all those who value privacy.

November 2025

Joaquin  Garcia-Alfaro<br>
Guillermo  Navarro-Arribas

# Preface to the Proceedings of CBT 2025

This volume contains the post-proceedings of the 9th International Workshop on Cryptocurrencies and Blockchain Technology (CBT 2025), held in conjunction with ESORICS 2025 in Toulouse, France, on September 25, 2025. Since its first edition in 2017, CBT has provided a forum for researchers and practitioners to present advances and discuss open challenges in cryptocurrencies, distributed ledgers, and related security and privacy technologies.

The scope of CBT 2025 encompassed, among other topics: blockchain protocols and scalability; consensus mechanisms; blockchain analytics and forensics; cryptographic primitives for decentralized systems; privacy-enhancing technologies; smart-contract security and verification; DeFi analysis and risk; network-layer security; measurements and empirical studies; interoperability and cross-chain designs; and applications beyond finance.

This edition received 18 submissions. After a rigorous peer-review process that included at least three expert reviews for each submission, and discussion phase using a double-blind process, 8 papers were accepted as regular papers. The final program was complemented by an invited keynote, delivered in a joint session with the DPM and CyberICPS workshops, from Bart Preneel (KU Leuven).

The Program Committee comprised 22 members from 20 institutions across 12 countries. We are deeply grateful to the CBT 2025 Program Committee members and external reviewers for their careful and timely evaluations, to the authors for their high-quality submissions and camera-ready revisions, and to all the workshop attendees. We also thank the keynote speaker for sharing his insights and stimulating discussions.

We would also like to thank everyone who helped with the event organization, including all the members of the organizing committees for both ESORICS 2025 and CBT 2025. Our gratitude goes to Vincent Nicomette and Abdelmalek Benzekri, General Chairs of ESORICS 2025, Romain Laborde, Workshop Chair of ESORICS 2025, and everyone in the ESORICS 2025 organization.

Finally, we acknowledge our sponsors for the many forms of support they provided: Universitat Autònoma de Barcelona, Cybercat, Plan de Recuperación, Transformación y Resiliencia funded with Next Generation EU funds through the project DANGER INCIBE-C062/23; and Spanish Ministry project SECURING/NET PID2021-125962OB-C33.

November 2025

Hannes Hartenstein  
Jordi Herrera-Joancomartí

# Preface to the Proceedings of CyberICPS 2025

This book contains revised versions of the papers presented at the 11th Workshop on Security of Industrial Control Systems and Cyber-Physical Systems (CyberICPS 2025). The workshop was co-located with the 30th European Symposium on Research in Computer Security (ESORICS 2025) and was held in Toulouse, France, on September 25th, 2025.

Cyber-physical systems (CPS) are physical and engineered systems that interact with the physical environment, whose operations are monitored, coordinated, controlled, and integrated by information and communication technologies. These systems exist everywhere around us, and range in size, complexity, and criticality, from embedded systems used in smart vehicles, to SCADA systems in smart grids, to control systems in water distribution systems, to smart transportation systems, to plant control systems, engineering workstations, substation equipment, programmable logic controllers (PLC), and other Industrial Control Systems (ICS). These systems also include the emerging trend of Industrial Internet of Things (IIoT) that will be the central part of the fourth industrial revolution. As ICS and CPS proliferate, and increasingly interact with us and affect our lives, their security becomes of paramount importance.

CyberICPS 2025 brought together researchers, engineers, and governmental actors with an interest in the security of ICS and CPS in the context of their increasing exposure to cyberspace, by offering a forum for discussion on all issues related to their cyber security. CyberICPS 2025 attracted 16 high-quality submissions, each of which was assigned to three referees for review; the single-blind review process resulted in nine papers being accepted to be presented and included in the proceedings. The chairs and members of the Program Committee had no involvement with or visibility of the reviewing process of submissions authored or co-authored by them. The accepted papers cover topics related to many aspects of cyber security in cyber-physical and industrial control systems, ranging from threats, to risks that such systems face, to cyber-attacks that may be launched against such systems, to ways of detecting and responding to such attacks.

We would like to express our thanks to all those who assisted us in organizing the event and putting together the program. We are very grateful to the members of the Program Committee for their timely and rigorous reviews. Thanks are also due to the ESORICS Workshop Chairs and to the ESORICS Organizers. Last, but by no means least, we would like to thank all the authors who submitted their work to the workshop and contributed to an interesting set of proceedings.

November 2025

Sokratis Katsikas
Frédéric Cuppens
Nora Cuppens
Costas Lambrinoudakis

# Organization of DPM 2025

## Program Committee Chairs

| | |
|---|---|
| Joaquin Garcia-Alfaro | Institut Polytechnique de Paris, France |
| Guillermo Navarro-Arribas | Universitat Autònoma de Barcelona, Spain |

## Program Committee

| | |
|---|---|
| Abderrahim Ait Wakrime | Université Mohammed V de Rabat, Morocco |
| Ken Barker | University of Calgary, Canada |
| Elisa Bertino | Purdue University, USA |
| Alessandro Brighente | University of Padua, Italy |
| Jordi Casas-Roma | Universitat Autònoma de Barcelona, Spain |
| Jordi Castellà-Roca | Universitat Rovira i Virgili, Spain |
| Depeng Chen | Anhui University, China |
| Mathieu Cunche | University of Lyon/Inria, France |
| Frédéric Cuppens | Polytechnique Montréal, Canada |
| Sabrina De Capitani di Vimercati | Università degli Studi di Milano, Italy |
| Jose Maria de Fuentes | Universidad Carlos III de Madrid, Spain |
| Josep Domingo-Ferrer | Universitat Rovira i Virgili, Spain |
| Lorena González Manzano | Universidad Carlos III de Madrid, Spain |
| M. Emre Gürsoy | Koç University, Turkey |
| Guy-Vincent Jourdan | University of Ottawa, Canada |
| Florian Kammueler | Middlesex University London & TU Berlin, UK and Germany |
| Bruce Kapron | University of Victoria, Canada |
| Sokratis Katsikas | Norwegian University of Science and Technology, Norway |
| Christophe Kiennert | Télécom SudParis, France |
| Hiroaki Kikuchi | Meiji University, Japan |
| Evangelos Kranakis | Carleton University, Canada |
| Romain Laborde | Université de Toulouse, France |
| Patrick Lacharme | École nationale supérieure d'ingénieurs de Caen, France |
| Giovanni Livraga | University of Milan, Italy |
| Brad Malin | Vanderbilt University, USA |
| Lukas Malina | Brno University of Technology, Czechia |

| | |
|---|---|
| Zoltan Mann | University of Halle-Wittenberg, Germany |
| David Megías | Universitat Oberta de Catalunya, Spain |
| Gerardo Pelosi | Politecnico di Milano, Italy |
| Cristina Pérez-Solà | Universitat Autònoma de Barcelona, Spain |
| Ruben Rios | University of Málaga, Spain |
| Julián Salas | Universitat Autònoma de Barcelona, Spain |
| Pierangela Samarati | Università degli Studi di Milano, Italy |
| Vicenc Torra | Umeå University, Sweden |
| Alexandre Viejo | Universitat Rovira i Virgili, Spain |
| Isabel Wagner | University of Basel, Switzerland |
| Jens Weber | University of Victoria, Canada |
| Nicola Zannone | Eindhoven University of Technology, The Netherlands |

## Additional Reviewers

Sergio Martinez
Pablo Sanchez-Serrano
Carles Anglès-Tafalla
Cristofol Dauden-Esmel
Rami Haffar

# Organization of CBT 2025

## Program Committee Chairs

Hannes Hartenstein — Karlsruhe Institute of Technology, Germany
Jordi Herrera-Joancomartí — Universitat Autònoma de Barcelona, Spain

## Program Committee

Daniel Augot — INRIA Saclay-Île-de-France & LIX, France
Lennart Ante — Blockchain Research Lab, Germany
Arasu Arun — New York University, USA
Artem Barger — IdeaDLT, Israel
Alex Biryukov — University of Luxembourg, Luxembourg
Jeremy Clark — Concordia University, Canada
Vanesa Daza — Universitat Pompeu Fabra, Spain
Joshua Ellul — University of Malta, Malta
Co-Pierre Georg — Frankfurt School of Finance, Germany
Ghassan Karame — Ruhr-University Bochum, Germany
Pedro Moreno Sánchez — IMDEA Software Institute, MPI-SP, Spain
Shin'ichiro Matsuo — Virginia Tech and Georgetown University, USA
Guillermo Navarro-Arribas — Universitat Autònoma de Barcelona, Spain
Mariusz Nowostawski — Norwegian University of Science and Technology, Norway
Cristina Pérez-Solà — Universitat Autònoma de Barcelona, Spain
Weidong Shi — University of Houston, USA
Hitesh Tewari — Trinity College Dublin, Ireland
Dimitrios Vasilopoulos — University College Cork, Ireland
Edgar Weippl — SBA Research, Austria

## Additional Reviewers

Dimitrios Vasilopoulos
Annika Wilde
Jannik Albrecht
Anna Piscitelli
Pablo García Fernández

# Organization of CyberICPS 2025

## General Chairs

Costas Lambrinoudakis     University of Piraeus, Greece
Nora Cuppens     Polytechnique Montréal, Canada

## Program Committee Chairs

Sokratis Katsikas     Norwegian University of Science and Technology, Norway
Frédéric Cuppens     Polytechnique Montréal, Canada

## Publicity Chair

Aida Akbarzadeh     Norwegian University of Science and Technology, Norway

## Program Committee

Habtamu Abie     Norsk Regnesentral, Norway
Irfan Ahmed     Virginia Commonwealth University, USA
Aida Akbarzadeh     Norwegian University of Science and Technology, Norway
Cristina Alcaraz     University of Málaga, Spain
Ahmed Walid Amro     Norwegian University of Science and Technology, Norway
Marios Anagnostopoulos     Democritus University of Thrace, Greece
Victor Bolbot     Aalto University, Finland
Joaquin Garcia-Alfaro     Institut Polytechnique de Paris, France
Joe Gardiner     University of Bristol, UK
Vasileios Gkioulos     Norwegian University of Science and Technology, Norway
Dieter Gollmann     Hamburg University of Technology, Germany
Martin Gilje Jaatun     SINTEF, Norway

| | |
|---|---|
| Georgios Kavallieratos | Norwegian University of Science and Technology, Norway |
| Marina Krotofil | Information Systems Security Partners, Canada |
| Daisuke Mashima | Singapore University of Technology and Design, Singapore |
| Weizhi Meng | Lancaster University, UK |
| Simin Nadjm-Tehrani | Linköping University, Sweden |
| Aybars Oruç | Tallinn University of Technology, Estonia |
| Nikolaos Pitropakis | Edinburgh Napier University, UK |
| Rodrigo Roman | University of Málaga, Spain |
| Indrakshi Ray | Colorado State University, USA |
| Georgios Spathoulas | University of Thessaly, Greece |
| Gabor Visky | Tallinn University of Technology, Estonia |

# Contents


**20th International Workshop on Data Privacy Management (DPM 2025)**

How Worrying are Privacy Attacks Against Machine Learning? . . . . . . . . . . . . . . 3
*Josep Domingo-Ferrer*

Lost in the Averages: Reassessing Record-Specific Privacy Risk Evaluation . . . . 16
*Nataša Krčo, Florent Guépin, Matthieu Meeus, Bogdan Kulynych, and Yves-Alexandre de Montjoye*

Membership Inference Attacks Beyond Overfitting . . . . . . . . . . . . . . . . . . . . . . . . . 32
*Mona Khalil, Alberto Blanco-Justicia, Najeeb Jebreel, and Josep Domingo-Ferrer*

"Why is the Sky Blue?" – On the Feasibility of Privacy-Friendly
Conversational LLM Smart Toys . . . . . . . . . . . . . . . . . . . . . . . . . . . . . . . . . . . . 49
*Valentyna Pavliv, Luigj Lazri, Jan Büchele, and Isabel Wagner*

Win-k: Improved Membership Inference Attacks on Small Language
Models . . . . . . . . . . . . . . . . . . . . . . . . . . . . . . . . . . . . . . . . . . . . . . . . . . . . . . . . . 66
*Roya Arkhmammadova, Hosein Madadi Tamar, and M. Emre Gursoy*

Advanced Electronic Signatures and GDPR: Reconciling the Concepts . . . . . . . . 79
*Paweł Kostkiewicz, Mirosław Kutyłowski, and Gabriel Wechta*

Invisible Encryption . . . . . . . . . . . . . . . . . . . . . . . . . . . . . . . . . . . . . . . . . . . . . . . . 97
*Shahzad Ahmad, Stefan Rass, and Zahra Seyedi*

Eliminating Exponential Key Growth in PRG-Based Distributed Point
Functions . . . . . . . . . . . . . . . . . . . . . . . . . . . . . . . . . . . . . . . . . . . . . . . . . . . . . . . . 116
*Marc Damie, Florian Hahn, Andreas Peter, and Jan Ramon*

A Pseudo-inverse Matrix-Based LDP for High-Dimensional Data . . . . . . . . . . . . 125
*Hiroaki Kikuchi*

Using Prior Knowledge to Improve GANs for Tabular Data Without
Compromising Privacy . . . . . . . . . . . . . . . . . . . . . . . . . . . . . . . . . . . . . . . . . . . . . 137
*Sonakshi Garg, Marcel Neunhoeffer, Jörg Drechsler, and Vicenç Torra*

Lessons from a Robotaxi: Challenges in Selecting Privacy-Enhancing
Technologies .................................................... 154
    *Ala'a Al-Momani, David Balenson, Christoph Bösch,
    Zoltán Ádám Mann, Sebastian Pape, and Jonathan Petit*

Performance Analysis of Lightweight Transformer Models for Healthcare
Application Privacy Threat Detection ...................................... 171
    *Jude E. Ameh, Abayomi Otebolaku, Alex Shenfield, Augustine Ikpehai,
    and Dauda Sule*

The Bitter Pill: Tracking and Remarketing on EU Pharmacy Websites ......... 188
    *Zahra Moti, Kimberley Frings, Christine Utz,
    Frederik Zuiderveen Borgesius, and Gunes Acar*

PADOME: Adaptive Privacy Assistant for the Internet of Things ............. 206
    *Edward Rochester and Ken Barker*

**9th Cryptocurrencies and Blockchain Technology Workshop (CBT
2025)**

Fast Off-Chain Payments with Second-Layer Privacy ....................... 221
    *Sven Gnap, Kari Kostiainen, and Ghassan Karame*

AUPCH: Auditable Unlinkable Payment Channel Hubs ...................... 242
    *Pedro Moreno-Sanchez, Mohsen Minaei, Srinivasan Raghuraman,
    Panagiotis Chatzigiannis, and Duc V. Le*

Threshold Signatures for Central Bank Digital Currencies ................... 259
    *Mostafa Abdelrahman, Filip Rezabek, Lars Hupel, Kilian Glas,
    and Georg Carle*

Blockchain-Based Lotteries via Single Secret Leader Election ............... 277
    *Tegrid Fettuh and Oğuz Yayla*

Towards E-Voting Systems on Resource Based Blockchains ................. 293
    *Ricardo Lopes Almeida, Fabrizio Baiardi, Constantin Cătălin Drăgan,
    Damiano Di Francesco Maesa, Laura Ricci, and Nishanth Sastry*

Analysing the Adoption of the Terms-of-Use Field in EBSI Digital Wallets .... 311
    *Stefano Bistarelli, Chiara Luchini, and Francesco Santini*

Selfish Mining in Multi-attacker Scenarios: An Empirical Evaluation
of Nakamoto, Fruitchain, and Strongchain ................................. 328
    *Martin Perešíni, Tomáš Hladký, Jakub Kubík, and Ivan Homoliak*

`EVMpress`: Precise Type Inference for Next-Generation EVM
Decompilation ........................................................ 344
    *Jung Hyun Kim, Soomin Kim, Jaeseung Choi, and Sang Kil Cha*

**11th Workshop on the Security of Industrial Control Systems and of
Cyber-Physical Systems (CyberICPS 2025)**

Salty Seagull: A VSAT Honeynet to Follow the Bread Crumb of Attacks
in Ship Networks ...................................................... 363
    *Georgios Michail Makrakis, Jeroen Pijpker, Remco Hassing,
Rob Loves, and Stephen McCombie*

Signals and Symptoms: ICS Attack Dataset From Railway Cyber Range ...... 382
    *Anis Yusof, Yuancheng Liu, Niklaus Kang, Choon Meng Seah,
Zhenkai Liang, and Ee-Chien Chang*

Designing and Testing a Low-Cost Electromagnetic Spectrum Attack
Threat Monitoring System ............................................. 403
    *Vasileios Andrianopoulos, Panayiotis Kotzanikolaou,
and Christos Douligeris*

Detecting Anomalous Resource Consumption in EdgeAI-Based MQTT
Brokers .............................................................. 423
    *Phi Tuong Lau and Stefan Katzenbeisser*

CRLF: A Sim2Real Reinforcement Learning Environment for Automated
IT/OT Pentesting ..................................................... 442
    *Marc-Antoine Faillon, Julien Francq, Nora Boulahia-Cuppens,
Frédéric Cuppens, and Reda Yaich*

From Words to Wires: Toward Rapid ICS Cyber-Range Construction
Using LLMs ........................................................... 462
    *Tommy Helland Berg, Ahmed Amro, Aida Akbarzadeh,
and Georgios Kavallieratos*

In Numeris Veritas: An Empirical Measurement of Wi-Fi Integration
in Industry .......................................................... 482
    *Vyron Kampourakis, Christos Smiliotopoulos, Vasileios Gkioulos,
and Sokratis Katsikas*

Using Dual Algorithm Certificates in TLS: Enabling Rapid Transition
to Post-Quantum Cryptography with Backward Compatibility ............... 503
    *Tobias Frauenschläger and Jürgen Mottok*

Secure and Efficient Attribute-Based Signature Scheme for Substation
Automation Systems ............................................... 523
*Mohammed Ramadan, Moritz Gstür, Pranit Gadekar, Ghada Elbez,
and Veit Hagenmeyer*

**Author Index** ..................................................... 541

# 20th International Workshop on Data Privacy Management (DPM 2025)

# How Worrying are Privacy Attacks Against Machine Learning?

Josep Domingo-Ferrer[1,2(✉)] 

[1] Department of Computer Engineering and Mathematics, CYBERCAT-Center for Cybersecurity Research of Catalonia, Universitat Rovira i Virgili, Av. Països Catalans 26, 43007 Tarragona, Catalonia, Spain
`josep.domingo@urv.cat`
[2] LAAS-CNRS, Université de Toulouse, 7 Av. du Colonel Roche, 31400 Toulouse, France

**Abstract.** In several jurisdictions, the regulatory framework on the release and sharing of personal data is being extended to machine learning (ML). The implicit assumption is that disclosing a trained ML model entails a privacy risk for any personal data used in training comparable to directly releasing those data. However, given a trained model, it is necessary to mount a *privacy attack* to make inferences on the training data. In this concept paper, we examine the main families of privacy attacks against predictive and generative ML, including membership inference attacks (MIAs), property inference attacks, and reconstruction attacks. Our discussion shows that most of these attacks seem less effective in the real world than what a *prima facie* interpretation of the related literature could suggest.

**Keywords:** Machine learning · privacy · discriminative models · generative models · membership inference attacks · property inference attacks · reconstruction attacks

## 1 Introduction

The main regulations in the EU that affect the development of AI are the General Data Protection Regulation (GDPR) and the EU Artificial Intelligence Act. Both were conceived before the boom of generative AI in 2022. Furthermore, the EU has announced the implementation of a Code of Practice for general purpose AI models [29]. Outside Europe, in 2023 President Biden had signed Executive Order 14110, which committed the USA to a strong regulation of the development and use of AI along similar lines as the European regulation. However, in 2025 President Trump has signed Executive Order 14179, which basically revokes Biden's order and removes all AI regulations, allegedly to "remove barriers to American leadership in artificial intelligence".

Given the above situation and the fact that Chinese regulations on AI are more focused on protecting the government than the citizens from AI, the EU


R. Laborde et al. (Eds.): ESORICS 2025, LNCS 16231, pp. 3–15, 2026.
https://doi.org/10.1007/978-3-032-16089-8_1

remains the world's only major economic bloc committed to trustworthy AI. At the same time, the EU lags behind the USA and China from the AI technology point of view.

For the European AI industry to be able to catch up with its competitors in spite of a more strict regulatory framework, it is extremely important to make sure that regulations are not more strict than required to preserve the values of trustworthy AI, and in particular privacy. Unfortunately, this does not seem to be the case today. The EU regulations assume that *any* disclosure might cause a breach of privacy. In particular, there is an implicit assumption that the disclosure of a trained machine learning (ML) model entails a privacy risk for any personal data used in training comparable to the direct release of those data.

This overcautious approach is probably due to the rushed inclusion of generative AI in the legal texts, and it may lead to adopting countermeasures that increase the training overhead and decrease the accuracy of models. For example, differential privacy [12] is a commonly proposed countermeasure that can cause two-digit drops in model accuracy if applied with meaningful privacy parameters. This seriously compromises the performance and competitiveness of the models and might be *unnecessary* if risks can be demonstrated to be overestimated.

### Contribution and plan of this article

There is a fundamental privacy difference between releasing an ML model trained on personal data and directly releasing those training data. If only the trained ML model is disclosed, it is necessary to mount a *privacy attack* to make any inferences on the training data. In this paper, we discuss how effective the privacy attacks proposed in the literature against predictive and generative ML are in *real-world* conditions. Specifically, we cover membership inference attacks (MIAs), property inference attacks, and reconstruction attacks.

Our assessment concentrates on the disclosure potential of those attacks at the conceptual level, rather than on the analysis of the internals of the various attack techniques. We aim to uncover fundamental limitations of privacy attacks.

Section 2 gives a background on privacy disclosure. Section 3 is devoted to membership inference attacks. Section 4 discusses property inference attacks. Section 5 deals with reconstruction attacks. Conclusions are drawn in Sect. 6.

## 2    Background on Privacy Disclosure

For many years, the literature on database privacy [17] has used the notion of disclosure risk, in order to measure to what extent the release of data sets and statistical output puts sensitive information at risk of being disclosed. This notion remains relevant in the machine learning domain.

Two types of disclosure have usually been considered [17]:

- *Identity disclosure* means that the attacker is able to link some unidentified piece of data released with the subject (individual) to whom it corresponds. This linkage is also called *re-identification*.

– *Attribute disclosure* means that the attacker can determine the value of a confidential attribute (*e.g.*, income, diagnosis, etc.) for a target subject with great precision *after* seeing the released data.

In tabular data, reidentification occurs trivially if the released data contain *personal identifiers* (such as passport numbers). That is why identifiers should never be released. However, re-identification is also possible by *quasi-identifiers* (for example, gender, job, zipcode, age) that do not uniquely identify the subject, but whose combination may because they may be present in public identified databases such as electoral rolls. Finally, *confidential attributes* (income, diagnosis, etc.) reveal sensitive information about subjects when they can be unequivocally linked to them.

Identification and attribute disclosure can occur independently. A record can be reidentified but, if it contains no confidential attribute, no attribute disclosure occurs. Similarly, if the attacker can only determine a set of $k > 1$ records that might correspond to the target subject, but there is a confidential attribute whose values over those $k$ records are very similar, then attribute disclosure has occurred without reidentification.

*Membership disclosure* has been proposed as a third type of disclosure in machine learning [26]. Its purpose is to determine whether a given data point was included in the data set used to train a certain ML model. Thus, in a membership inference attack (MIA), the attacker does not try to discover to whom the point corresponds (which would be reidentification) or to find the value of any confidential attribute about the subject to whom the point corresponds (which would be attribute disclosure).

Thus, it can be argued that membership disclosure is weaker than identity or attribute disclosure. However, *if all subjects included in the training data set are known to share a sensitive condition, attribute disclosure can result from membership disclosure.* For example, if all subjects whose data are used for training suffer from a certain disease, then discovering membership for a target subject leads to attribute disclosure: the target suffers from that disease. Note that this is true even if there was no explicit attribute 'Disease' in the training data set.

## 3    Membership Inference Attacks

MIAs are the most common attack employed to assess the privacy of training data in machine learning. Rather than analyzing the operation of specific MIAs proposed in the literature, in this section we will focus on the disclosure potential of a generic MIA depending on the data used to train the model under attack.

Let us introduce a running example. Assume that an attacker Alice wants to perform an MIA on an ML model to determine whether the attacker's neighbor Neil was a member of the data used to train the model.

Two properties of the training data are simultaneously required for the MIA to allow unequivocal inferences:

- *Exhaustivity.* Unless the training data were an exhaustive sample of a population (which is very rare), membership inferences cannot be unequivocal. In other words, the membership revealed by an MIA to a non-exhaustive training set could be plausibly denied. In the running example, if Alice finds that one or several records containing the same quasi-identifier values known to her about Neil were members of the training data, she cannot be absolutely sure that Neil was a member. The reason is that perhaps Neil was not included in the training data, and the putative members she found are just people sharing Neil's quasi-identifier values. Hence, Neil could plausibly deny being a member. On the other hand, if the training data set is exhaustive, membership is trivial and no MIA is really needed: every existing record (and Neil's in particular) is a member.
- *Non-diversity of unknown attributes.* Since inferring membership to an exhaustive sample is not a real discovery, let us examine whether at least it can bring attribute disclosure. If there are several member records matching the attribute values known to the attacker, and the unknown attributes among those records differ significantly, then no attribute disclosure occurs. In the running example, if Alice finds that two or more records containing the same quasi-identifiers known to her about Neil were members of the (exhaustive) training data, but the confidential attribute Income unknown to Alice take clearly different values on those records, then Alice cannot unequivocally learn Neil's income.

In summary, the training data must be exhaustive for Alice to be sure that at least one of the putative members she has found who share Neil's quasi-identifiers is really Neil. On the other hand, since membership inference to an exhaustive sample is of little value, if Alice turns to attribute inference, she can unequivocally infer a confidential attribute value for Neil only if all putative members sharing Neil's quasi-identifiers share the same (or similar) values for that confidential attribute. In looking at the literature on MIAs, most attacks are demonstrated using training data sets that are not exhaustive and that may contain diverse values for unknown attributes.

The two conditions have long been studied in the statistical disclosure control (SDC) literature [17]:

- The protective effect of non-exhaustive samples is the principle of a well-known SDC method called sampling, in which a sample is released instead of the entire surveyed population. To evaluate the protection provided by sampling, it is relevant to compute the probability that a record is unique in the population $(PU)$ given that it is unique in the sample $(SU)$, that is, $\Pr(PU|SU)$. In [27] it was shown that this probability decreases with the sampling fraction, that is, the smaller the sample, the more plausible membership deniability.
- The protective effect of diversity against confidential attribute disclosure is the principle behind privacy models such as $l$-diversity [21] and $t$-closeness [19, 28]: both seek to prevent attribute disclosure by making sure there is enough

diversity of confidential attribute values within each set of records sharing quasi-identifier values.

In fact, it is relatively easy for a model trainer to benefit from the above two protections against MIAs. It is easier to get non-exhaustive than exhaustive training data, and the latter can always be made non-exhaustive by sampling. On the other hand, confidential attributes are naturally diverse and, if there is not enough diversity, it can be enforced by $l$-diversity or $t$-closeness.

Beyond studying the generic limitations of MIAs due to the data used to train the attacked ML models, one can examine the specifics of the model under attack and the attack method. That is, what else is needed for an MIA to succeed in the case when the training data happen to satisfy exhaustivity and non-diversity.

In [18], the effectiveness of MIAs on discriminative machine learning (ML) models is assessed by checking four requirements: i) the model under attack should not be overfitted (overfitted models are an easy MIA target, but they do not generalize well in their main tasks); ii) the model under attack must have a competitive test accuracy (attacking an uncompetitive model is not very interesting); iii) the attack must yield reliable membership inference; iv) and the attack must have a reasonable computational cost. Among the many MIA attacks reviewed by these authors, none can satisfy these four requirements simultaneously.

In fact, focusing only on overfitting, [9] had previously observed that MIAs on well-generalizable models suffer from practical limitations that reduce their practicality. Overall, it would seem that the privacy risks of machine learning may have been overstated in the literature as far as membership inference attacks are concerned.

## 4   Property Inference Attacks

A property inference attack seeks to infer a sensitive *global* property of the data set used to train an ML model, that is, a property $P$ of the data set that the model producer did not intend to share. This class of attacks was first presented for classifiers in [1]. They have also been formulated for deep neural networks in [15].

In [1], a meta-classifier was trained to classify the target classifier depending on whether it has a certain property $P$ or not. To do this, the attacker trains several *shadow classifiers* on the same task as the target classifier. Each classifier is trained on a data set similar to that of the target classifier, but constructed explicitly to have the property $P$ or not. Subsequently, the meta-classifier is trained on the sets of parameters of the shadow classifiers.

In [15], it is argued that the above meta-classifier training strategy does not work well for deep neural networks, due to their complexity and thousands of parameters. The authors explore different feature representations to reduce the complexity of the meta-classification task. However, the high-level structure of the attack is the same as in [1]. In [32], a property inference attack against generative adversarial networks (GANs) is presented. Instead of training shadow classifiers like in the previous papers, here shadow GANs are trained.

From the point of view of privacy, property inference attacks do not entail a significant risk, because *they aim to infer a general property of the training data set rather than a property specific to a particular target subject.* That is, *property inference attacks are not attribute inference attacks* trying to infer the value of a confidential attribute for a target subject. By way of illustration, an example of $P$ mentioned in [1] is whether "Google traffic was used in the training data", an example mentioned in [15] is whether "the classifier was trained on images with noise", and an example mentioned in [32] is whether "a GAN is mainly trained with images of white males".

Even if disclosing such properties was not intended by the model producer and may cause some embarrassment to them, the general nature of those properties can hardly disclose private information on any of the specific individuals whose data may have been used for training. The most obvious strategy to mount an attribute inference attack in machine learning is through a battery of MIAs each of which hypothesizes a candidate value for the target subject's confidential attribute (*e.g.*, was the target subject's record with "Disease=AIDS" a member of the training data set? was the target subject's record with "Disease=Cancer" a member of the training data set?, and so on).

A scenario where property inference attacks may be more privacy-disclosive is federated learning, in case they are used to infer properties of the training data set used by a certain client and those training data refer to just one or a few subjects. Imagine the client is a smartphone and the client's training data are health measurements on the smartphone owner at different times; in this specific case, inferring a property of the training data set can yield a property/attribute of the smartphone owner.

## 5   Reconstruction Attacks

### 5.1   Reconstruction Attacks Previous to ML

Dinur and Nissim (DN from now on) developed a formal theory of database reconstruction from a set of query responses in 2003 [8]. The authors assume that a database is an $n$-bit string, that is, it contains records each of which takes values 0 or 1. They further assume all queries to be of the form "How many records in this subset are 0's?" or "How many records in this subset are 1's?". In their setting, the response to every query is computed as the true answer to the query plus an error $E$ bounded in an interval $[-B, B]$ for some $B > 0$. Thus, the assumption is that query answers are protected by output perturbation with strictly bounded noise.

According to DN, a database reconstruction is a record-by-record reconstruction of the original values such that the distance between the reconstructed values and the original values is within specific accuracy bounds. DN considered two types of attackers, one that can ask an exponential number of queries and one that can only ask a polynomial number of queries, and gave results for the reconstructions achievable by those attackers as a function of $B$ and the number of queries allowed. Although such a theoretical framework for database reconstruction provides very relevant insight, it does not mean that every database can be uniquely reconstructed. In fact, for a given set of statistical outputs, there may be several (or even a large number) of database instantiations compatible with those outputs [22, 24].

## 5.2 Reconstruction Attacks and Overfitting in ML

The problem of reconstructing the data set used to train an ML model bears some similarities to the database reconstruction problem just described. During machine learning, sometimes the model memorizes parts of its training data [13]. This in turn enables attackers to extract points from the training data set when given access to the trained model. Successful reconstruction attacks have been reported for face recognition models [14, 31] and neural language models [6, 7]. Although there is no formal framework in the DN style for reconstruction in ML, bounds on the risk of reconstruction have been proven [16].

In fact (partial) reconstruction of training data is greatly facilitated if the model is overfitted because, in that case, it memorizes training data. Beyond being problematic for privacy, overfitting is also a great problem for utility, since overfitted models usually perform poorly regarding validation (the process of testing how well a trained model labels new, unseen data).

Regarding potential defenses against overfitting and, hence, reconstruction, [6] mention that

> "such memorization [of training data] is *not* due to overtraining: it occurs early during training, and persists across different types of models and training strategies [...] Furthermore, we show that simple, intuitive regularization approaches such as early-stopping and dropout are insufficient to prevent unintended memorization. Only by using differentially-private training techniques, we are able to eliminate the issue completely, albeit at some loss of utility."

Overtraining means training a model for too many iterations. It may result in overfitting, which occurs when the model exactly learns the training data set but is unable to correctly label new, unseen data. However, overfitting may also occur in the early stages of training, that is, without overtraining, such as when a very large model is trained on a small data set.

In [3], it was concluded that standard anti-overfitting techniques such as regularization and dropout could outperform DP and achieve a better utility/privacy/efficiency trade-off in ML training. The explanation of this seeming contradiction with [6] lies in the details:

- [3] tried several combinations of regularization/dropout and took the one with the best trade-off between utility, measured as test accuracy, and privacy, measured as the attacker's (little) advantage in the standard MIA implementation in TensorFlow Privacy.

– In contrast, [6] tried several anti-overfitting techniques (regularization, dropout, weight quantization, etc.) but without attempting to find the best-performing parameterizations. Also, they measured utility as (little) validation loss and privacy as preventing the recovery of randomly chosen "canary" sequences inserted into the models' training data.

Regarding utility, note that test accuracy and validation loss are two independent metrics. Whereas the former counts the number of mistakes/misclassifications, the latter is the distance between the true labels and the labels predicted by the model. Low test accuracy means many errors, whereas large validation loss means large errors.

Regarding privacy, the two above papers and a good deal of the related literature use MIA-based metrics. There are two important factors that influence the success of MIAs: (i) whether the target points whose membership is to be inferred are outliers or not and (ii) how good the MIA techniques employed are. Now, the random "canary" target sequences inserted by [6] in the training data are likely to be outliers due to their randomness, and hence their membership may be easy to discover, which gives a pessimistic privacy evaluation. The TensorFlow Privacy MIA implementation used by [3] does not rely on the inserting of random target points into the training data: it just uses the predictions of the trained model on the target points to deduce their membership [4].

## 5.3   On the Effectiveness of Reconstruction in ML

Using MIAs to assess the effectiveness of reconstruction attacks may seem reasonable if the training data are tabular. Let $\mathbf{D}$ be a training data set with attributes $A_1, A_2, \ldots, A_d$. Note that in the computer representation of any attribute $A_i$, the number $|A_i|$ of potential values can be considered finite, even for numerical attributes, due to limited length and precision. Still, $|A_i|$ can be quite large, especially for numerical attributes. We can give the following information-theoretic argument to illustrate the complexity of exhaustively trying all possible values. Assume that the information content of an item $X$ (record in the case of tabular data, but also unstructured text, image, etc., for non-structured data) one wishes to reconstruct is $H(X)$ bits, where $H$ is Shannon's entropy. Then discovering $X$ by exhaustive search is equivalent to discovering a random cryptographic key of $H(X)$ bits. If $H(X)$ is, say, 64 or more bits, this is known to be computationally infeasible.

This gives two scenarios:

1. *Total reconstruction.* Assume that the attacker has unlimited resources or, better, that the number of potential values $|A_i|$ of every attribute $A_i$ is relatively small. In this case, the attacker could mount an MIA for each possible combination of attribute values, to check whether that combination was part of $\mathbf{D}$. After $\prod_{i=1}^{d} |A_i|$ MIAs have been performed and if they are effective, the attacker has reconstructed the entire training data set $D$.
2. *Partial reconstruction.* If the attacker's resources are insufficient to pursue total reconstruction, then they can select a subset of possible combinations

of attribute values and mount MIAs only for those combinations. This can be viewed as a *guessing exercise* that may lead to a partial reconstruction of **D** (if the guesses, that is, the candidate combinations of attribute values, are classified as members and are really members of **D**). The attacker would favor those combinations deemed to be the most likely from the semantics of attributes, *e.g.* if there is an attribute *Age* and an attribute *Job*, the only plausible combination of *Age*=10 is with *Job*='student'. Note that betting on the most common combinations gives less interesting reconstruction results for the attacker: outlier combinations are more privacy-sensitive and thus interesting to the attacker than very common combinations.

It must be taken into account that state-of-the-art MIAs offering the best membership detection, such as LiRA [5], require training several shadow models to estimate the distribution $\Delta_{in}$ of models trained on data sets containing the target point and the distribution $\Delta_{out}$ of models trained on data sets *not* containing the target point. Thus, each MIA incurs a substantial computation cost.

Furthermore, especially in generative ML, training data are often non-tabular. For example, they are unstructured text or multimedia. Clearly, for non-tabular training data such as images or unstructured text, mounting an MIA to test whether each potential image or each potential unstructured text was part of the training data set **D** seems quite unreasonable. In the case of generative AI, one can resort to prompting for certain personal data or copyrighted content rather than mounting MIAs, in order to find out whether the model saw those items at training time. But in fact, this prompting amounts to a guessing exercise like those described above under partial reconstruction. The empirical study [1] shows that MIAs on pre-trained LLMs are barely better than random guessing, even though fine-tuned LLMs are far more vulnerable to MIAs. That is, MIAs are more effective at inferring membership on the data used for fine-tuning than on the data used for pre-training. Regarding cost, although guess prompting is almost free on the user's side, the computational cost is high in terms of LLM inference on the LLM manager's side.

In [20] a systematic evaluation of data reconstruction attacks and defenses is presented, where the reconstruction attacks considered are no longer MIAs, but *gradient inversion attacks*. Gradient inversion attacks [30] attempt to recover training points from gradients. They are mostly designed for federated learning (FL), because they require knowledge of the gradients computed during training. In fact, in FL, the server receives the gradients from the clients and can mount a gradient inversion attack and try to reconstruct the local training data for one or more clients [25]. If all clients receive all gradients, then clients can also behave maliciously and mount a gradient inversion attack to reconstruct the local data of a certain target client. The study [23] reviewed gradient inversion attacks against FL, as well as potential defenses based on mixed precision and quantization, gradient pruning, and differential privacy. They concluded that some of these defenses are effective and involve only slight accuracy drops. In centralized learning, where the attacker only sees the trained model, gradient inversion attacks are not applicable.

If reconstruction based on MIAs is problematic for the reasons above, reconstruction without MIAs suffers from a major weakness: *there is no numerical decision criterion in a realistic case in which the attacker has no access to the actual training data.* In other words, whereas in an MIA there is some kind of threshold that allows deciding whether a target point is a member or a non-member (although this decision may be in error), in a reconstruction attack there is no objective criterion to decide whether the putative reconstructed data belong to the training data set. For example, the fact that a gradient inversion attack produces a meaningful image does not necessarily mean that this image was part of the training data. Also, what "meaningful" means is debatable. One could certainly use an MIA to decide whether the putative reconstructed data were really in the training data, but this has the drawbacks of MIAs enumerated in Sect. 3.

Admittedly, there are situations in which it may be easier to make a decision on putative reconstructed data. This is the case for reconstruction attacks on machine unlearning. In unlearning, a trained model is updated to cause it to "forget" one or more data points, *e.g.*, to implement the right to be forgotten enshrined in the GDPR, or because those data points are subject to copyright. In [2], a reconstruction attack is described for the case in which the trained model is a simple one. The attack exploits the model updates to estimate the unlearned data point. However, even if the attack is quite successful according to the experiments reported in [2], success is determined by comparing against the ground truth of the unlearned data point, which would not be available to an attacker in a real world situation. Possible defenses are discussed in [10].

## 6    Conclusions

Our analysis casts doubts on the effectiveness of privacy attacks against ML in real-world conditions:

- MIAs suffer from limitations due to the data the target models have been trained on (non-exhaustivity, diversity of confidential attribute values). In addition, they may also suffer limitations that arise from the nature of the attacked models and the attack methods.
- Property inference attacks aim to infer a general property of the training data set, rather than a property specific to a particular data subject. For that reason, they do not achieve attribute disclosure for any particular subject and hence do not pose substantial privacy risks to subjects, except in specific federated learning scenarios where all of a client's training data refer to one or a few subjects. These attacks are more relevant to audit the potential biases or insufficiencies of the training data used by the model producer.
- Reconstruction attacks based on MIAs have a very significant cost, as they involve mounting an MIA for each data point whose membership in the training data is to be decided. Thus, they are only practical for tabular training

data where attributes have a limited range of potential values, and even in that case they are more suited for partial than total reconstruction. Besides, MIA-based reconstruction is also subject to the shortcomings identified for MIAs themselves.

– Reconstruction attacks based on gradient inversion are those that are used when training data are multimedia or unstructured text, as is the usual case in generative ML. However, such attacks are applicable only when the attacker has access to the gradients computed by the victim during the learning process. In practice, this restricts the applicability of these attacks to federated or otherwise decentralized learning. Furthermore, deciding whether a putative reconstructed data point was really a member of the training data is difficult if the attacker does not have access to the original training data (which is the usual case in the real world). Certainly, MIAs can be used to make this membership decision, but this inherits the shortcomings of MIAs described above.

All in all, the current real-world privacy risks incurred by machine learning seem less serious than what is usually assumed in the literature. Therefore, privacy defenses that entail severe utility loss, such as differential privacy, may be often unnecessary. The good side of all this is that trustworthy machine learning may be easier to implement than assumed so far, at least with respect to privacy. This is good news for jurisdictions like the European Union that struggle to reconcile strong AI regulations with the competitiveness of their AI industry.

**Acknowledgments.** This work was partly funded by the Centre International de Mathématiques et d'Informatique de Toulouse (CIMI), the Government of Catalonia (ICREA Acadèmia Prize to J. Domingo-Ferrer), MCIN/AEI/ 10.13039/501100011033 and "ERDF A way of making Europe" under grant PID2021-123637NB-I00 "CURLING", and INCIBE and European Union NextGenerationEU/PRTR (project "HERMES" and INCIBE-URV Cybersecurity Chair).

# References


1. Ateniese, G., Mancini, L.V., Spognardi, A., Villani, A., Vitali, D., Felici, G.: Hacking smart machines with smarter ones: How to extract meaningful data from machine learning classifiers. Int. J. Secur. Netw. **10**(3), 137–150 (2015)
2. Bertran, M., Tang, S., Kearns, M., Morgenstern, J., Roth, A., Wu, Z.S.: Simple models are vulnerable: Reconstruction attacks on machine unlearning. Adv. Neural. Inf. Process. Syst. **37**, 104995–105016 (2024)
3. Blanco-Justicia, A., Sánchez, D., Domingo-Ferrer, J., Muralidhar, K.: A critical review on the use (and misuse) of differential privacy in machine learning. ACM Comput. Surv. **55**(8), 1–16 (2022)
4. Boenisch, F.: Attacks against machine learning privacy (part 2): membership inference attacks with TensorFlow Privacy. https://franziska-boenisch.de/posts/2021/01/membership-inference/ (2021). Accessed 14 May 2025

5. Carlini, N., Chien, S., Nasr, M., Song, S., Terzis, A., Tramer, F.: Membership inference attacks from first principles. In: 2022 IEEE Symposium on Security and Privacy (SP), pp. 1897–1914. IEEE (2022)
6. Carlini, N., Liu, C., Erlingsson, Ú., Kos, J., Song, D.: The secret sharer: evaluating and testing unintended memorization in neural networks. In: 28th USENIX security symposium (USENIX security 19), pp. 267–284 (2019)
7. Carlini, N., et al. Extracting training data from large language models. In: 30th USENIX Security Symposium (USENIX Security 21), pp. 2633–2650 (2021)
8. Dinur, I., Nissim, K.: Revealing information while preserving privacy. In: Proceedings of the Twenty-second ACM SIGMOD-SIGACT-SIGART Symposium on Principles of Database Systems, pp. 202–210 (2003)
9. Dionysiou, A., Athanasopoulos, E.: Sok: Membership inference is harder than previously thought. In: Proceedings on Privacy Enhancing Technologies (2023)
10. Domingo-Ferrer, J., Jebreel, N., Sánchez, D.: Defenses against membership inference attacks on unlearned data. In: Modeling Decisions in Artificial Intelligence (MDAI 2025). Springer (to appear), (2025)
11. Duan, M.: Do membership inference attacks work on large language models? arXiv preprint arXiv:2402.07841 (2024)
12. Dwork, C., McSherry, F., Nissim, K., Smith, A.: Calibrating noise to sensitivity in private data analysis. In: Theory of Cryptography: Third Theory of Cryptography Conference, TCC 2006, New York, NY, USA, March 4-7, 2006. Proceedings 3, pp. 265–284. Springer (2006)
13. Feldman, V.: Does learning require memorization? a short tale about a long tail. In: Proceedings of the 52nd Annual ACM SIGACT Symposium on Theory of Computing, pp. 954–959 (2020)
14. Fredrikson, M., Jha, S., Ristenpart, T.: Model inversion attacks that exploit confidence information and basic countermeasures. In: Proceedings of the 22nd ACM SIGSAC Conference on Computer and Communications Security, pp. 1322–1333D (2015)
15. Ganju, K., Wang, Q., Yang, W., Gunter, C.A., Borisov, N.: Property inference attacks on fully connected neural networks using permutation invariant representations. In: Proceedings of the 2018 ACM SIGSAC Conference on Computer and Communications Security, pp. 619–633 (2018)
16. Guo, C., Karrer, B., Chaudhuri, K., Van der Maaten, L.: Bounding training data reconstruction in private (deep) learning. In: International Conference on Machine Learning, pp. 8056–8071. PMLR (2022)
17. Hundepool, A., et al.: Statistical Disclosure Control. Wiley, Chichester UK (2012)
18. Jebreel, N., Sánchez, D., Domingo-Ferrer, J.: A critical review on the eïñĂectiveness and privacy threats of membership inference attacks. In: 31st European Symposium on Research in Computer Security (ESORICS 2026). Springer (2026, to appear)
19. Li, N., Li, T., Venkatasubramanian, S.: $t$-Closeness: privacy beyond $k$-anonymity and $l$-diversity. In: 2007 IEEE 23rd International Conference on Data Engineering, pp. 106–115. IEEE (2006)
20. Liu, S., Wang, Z., Chen, Y., Lei, Q.: Data reconstruction attacks and defenses: A systematic evaluation. arXiv preprint arXiv:2402.09478 (2025)
21. Machanavajjhala, A., Kifer, D., Gehrke, J., Venkitasubramaniam, M.: $l$-Diversity: Privacy beyond $k$-anonymity. ACM Trans. Knowl. Discov. Data (tkdd), 1(1):3–es (2007)
22. Muralidhar, K., Domingo-Ferrer, J.: Database reconstruction is not so easy and is different from reidentification. J. Off. Stat. **39**(3), 381–398 (2023)

23. Ovi, P.R., Gangopadhyay, A.: A comprehensive study of gradient inversion attacks in federated learning and baseline defense strategies. In: 2023 57th Annual Conference on Information Sciences and Systems (CISS), pp. 1–6. IEEE (2023)
24. Sánchez, D., Domingo-Ferrer, J., Muralidhar, K.: Confidence-ranked reconstruction of census records from aggregate statistics fails to capture privacy risks and reidentifiability. Proc. Natl. Acad. Sci. **120**(18), e2303890120 (2023)
25. Shi, Y., Kotevska, O., Reshniak, V., Singh, A., Raskar, R.: Dealing doubt: Unveiling threat models in gradient inversion attacks under federated learning, a survey and taxonomy. arXiv preprint arXiv:2405.10376 (2024)
26. Shokri, R., Stronati, M., Song, C., Shmatikov, V.: Membership inference attacks against machine learning models. In: 2017 IEEE symposium on security and privacy (SP), pp. 3–18. IEEE (2017)
27. Skinner, C.J.: Disclosure avoidance for census microdata in Great Britain. In: Proceedings of the 1990 Annual Research Conference, pp. 131–143. US Bureau of the Census (1990)
28. Soria-Comas, J., Domingo-Ferrert, J.: Differential privacy via t-closeness in data publishing. In: 2013 Eleventh Annual Conference on Privacy, Security and Trust, pp. 27–35. IEEE (2013)
29. European Union. General-purpose ai code of practice. https://digital-strategy.ec.europa.eu/en/policies/ai-code-practice 2025. Accessed on 26 May 2025
30. Zhang, R., Guo, S., Wang, J., Xie, X., Tao, D.: A survey on gradient inversion: Attacks, defenses and future directions. arXiv preprint arXiv:2206.07284 (2022)
31. Zhang, Y., Jia, R., Pei, H., Wang, W., Li, B., Song, D.: The secret revealer: generative model-inversion attacks against deep neural networks. In: Proceedings of the IEEE/CVF Conference on Computer Vision and Pattern Recognition, pp. 253–261 (2020)
32. Zhou, J., Chen, Y., Shen, C. and Zhang, Y.: Property inference attacks against gans. arXiv preprint arXiv:2111.07608 (2021)

# Lost in the Averages: Reassessing Record-Specific Privacy Risk Evaluation


Nataša Krčo[1], Florent Guépin[1], Matthieu Meeus[1], Bogdan Kulynych[2], and Yves-Alexandre de Montjoye[1(✉)]

[1] Department of Computing and Data Science Institute, Imperial College London, London, UK
{n.krco23,florent.guepin20,m.meeus22,deMontjoye}@imperial.ac.uk
[2] Lausanne University Hospital (CHUV), Lausanne, Switzerland
bogdan.kulynych@chuv.ch



**Abstract.** Synthetic data generators and machine learning models can memorize their training data, posing privacy concerns. Membership inference attacks (MIAs) are a standard method of estimating their privacy risk. The risk of individual records is typically computed by evaluating MIAs in a record-specific privacy game. We analyze the privacy game commonly used for attackers under realistic assumptions (the *traditional* game)—particularly for synthetic tabular data—and show that it averages a record's privacy risk across datasets. We show this implicitly assumes the dataset a record is part of has no impact on the record's risk, providing a misleading risk estimate when a specific model or synthetic dataset is released. Instead, we propose a novel use of the leave-one-out privacy game, so far used exclusively to audit differential privacy guarantees, and call this the *model-seeded* game. We formalize it and show that it provides an accurate estimate of the privacy risk for a record in its specific dataset. We instantiate and evaluate the state-of-the-art MIA for synthetic data generators in both privacy games, and show across multiple datasets and models that they indeed result in different risk scores, with up to 94% of high-risk records being overlooked by the traditional game. We further show that records in smaller datasets tend to have a larger gap between risk estimates. Taken together, our results show that the model-seeded setup yields a risk estimate specific to a released synthetic dataset or model and in line with the standard notion of privacy leakage from prior work, meaningfully different from the dataset-averaged risk provided by the traditional privacy game.

**Keywords:** membership inference · synthetic data · differential privacy


---


An extended version of this work including appendices and additional results is available at https://arxiv.org/abs/2405.15423.

# 1   Introduction

Models ranging from synthetic data generators (SDGs) to machine learning (ML) models have been shown to memorize their training data, potentially allowing attackers to tell whether specific records were used for training [2,18,20,22,31, 41,46] or even reconstruct entire training examples [5,21,49,53]. As models are increasingly trained on personal and sensitive data—particularly in domains such as healthcare, law, and finance [7,10,37]—concerns about their implications for privacy continue to grow.

Membership inference attacks (MIAs) have become the standard approach for empirically estimating the privacy risk of synthetic data and ML models [8, 28,40,44,46]. MIAs aim to determine whether a target record was included in the training dataset of a given model. They can pose a direct privacy risk, and also provide an upper bound on the performance of other attacks such as attribute inference or data reconstruction [43]. MIAs can be developed under varying assumptions, ranging from black-box access to the target model and no knowledge of the training dataset, to very strong attackers leveraging white-box access to the model and knowledge of all training records but the target.

MIAs are evaluated in a controlled privacy game between an attacker and a data owner [46,55]. We here study the record-specific privacy games used in existing literature, which estimate how well an attacker can distinguish between models trained on one specific target record and those not. Record-specific privacy games are most often used in setups where the state-of-the-art attacks leverage record-specific information, such as for synthetic data generators [22,31,46], and for auditing formal privacy guarantees [3]. In contrast, model-specific privacy games estimate the ability of an attacker to distinguish between records used to train one target model and those not. This type of privacy game is often used to evaluate MIAs against ML models [8,11,20,42,45,56].

*Contributions.* We analyze the *traditional* privacy game commonly used to evaluate record-specific MIAs under realistic attacker assumptions [19,22,31,46]. We show that, by using dataset sampling as a source of randomness, it averages the risk across datasets, implicitly assuming that a record's privacy risk is independent of the dataset it belongs to.

We instead formalize and propose a novel use of the leave-one-out game, here called the *model-seeded* privacy game, to evaluate an MIA under realistic attacker assumptions. This approach is consistent with the standard notion of differential privacy [14,15], which captures a record's risk with respect to a specific dataset. Unlike the traditional game, we fix the target dataset and use only the model seed as a source of randomness. We show that the attack success rates computed using this privacy game converge to what we call the record's *differential privacy distinguisher* (DPD) risk—which is consistent with the standard notion of privacy leakage in existing literature—whereas the traditional game results in a dataset-independent estimate.

We instantiate the state-of-the-art record-specific MIA for synthetic data and evaluate it in both the traditional and model-seeded privacy game across 2 datasets and 2 synthetic data generators, replicating the setup used by Meeus et al. [31]. We observe significant differences between the risk estimates given by the model-seeded and traditional privacy games. For instance, 94% of high-risk records are misidentified by the traditional privacy game for the Adult dataset and Synthpop generator, and the root mean squared deviation (RMSD) is 0.07 between the two estimates. We obtain similar results across experimental setups.

Finally, we show the gap between the traditional and model-seeded risk estimates to be generally higher for small and medium datasets (fewer than $10,000$ records), as often used in tabular synthetic data [19,31,46], and lower for large datasets, typically used for ML tasks [8].

Taken together, our results show that the traditional game can yield misleading estimates by averaging the risk across datasets. We propose to use instead the model-seeded privacy game which provides more accurate risk estimates, aligning with differential privacy.

## 2    Background

### 2.1    Synthetic Data Generation

We consider the setting of statistical learning over the space of records $\mathbb{D} \subseteq \mathbb{R}^d$, sampled from a probability distribution $\mathcal{D}$. A dataset $D \in \mathbb{D}^n$ is i.i.d. sampled: $D \sim \mathcal{D}^n$. Using $D$, we train a model via a randomized training algorithm $\mathcal{A} : 2^{\mathbb{D}} \to \Theta$. The resulting synthetic data generator (SDG) defines a distribution $\mathcal{D}_\theta$ that mimics statistical properties of $\mathcal{D}$. A trained SDG with parameters $\theta = \mathcal{A}(D)$ can generate a synthetic dataset $D_{\text{syn}} \sim \mathcal{D}_\theta^n$, where we set $|D_{\text{syn}}| = n$.

SDGs include probabilistic models such as Bayesian networks [57] and deep generative models such as GANs [52]). We focus on tabular SDGs [35,57], where record-specific evaluation is crucial as attacks for this setting are inherently record-specific (see Sect. 2.2).

### 2.2    MIA Development

For a *target model* $\theta = \mathcal{A}(D)$, an MIA aims to infer whether a target record $x$ was in $D$ (member) or not (non-member). For a fixed target record $x$, we denote by $\phi_x : \Theta \to [0, 1]$ an MIA against target record $x$ and target model $\theta$. We drop the subscript $x$ when the target record is clear from context.

*Threat model.* By *threat model*, we refer to the assumptions made about the attacker's capabilities. We distinguish between *dataset-level* and *model-level* assumptions. Dataset-level access can range from no access to real data from $\mathcal{D}$ [19], access to data drawn from the same distribution [22,31,46], or full access to $D$ except for the knowledge of membership of $x$, as considered for the strong differential privacy attacker [3,23]. Model-level access can be black-box (query access) [8,44], or white-box (full parameter access) [12,33,42].

We assume a standard **realistic record-specific attacker** [19,22,31,46] in the context of tabular synthetic data, with access to an *auxiliary dataset*

$D_{\text{aux}} \in 2^{\mathbb{D}}$ drawn from the same distribution as $D$ but disjoint from it. The attacker has black-box query access to target model $\theta$. We assume the attacker to have full knowledge of the exact training process used to obtain $\theta = \mathcal{A}(D)$.

*Shadow Modeling.* Shadow modeling is a technique used to develop MIAs by simulating the target model's training process. The attacker samples *shadow datasets* $\{D_{\text{shadow}}^{(i)} \mid i = 1\ldots, N_{\text{shadow}}\}$ from $D_{\text{aux}}$, of the same size as $D$. The attacker then explicitly constructs 'in' shadow datasets that include the target record $x$ ($x \in D_{\text{shadow}}^{(i)}$) and 'out' shadow datasets that exclude it ($x \notin D_{\text{shadow}}^{(i)}$). The attacker trains *shadow models* $\{\mathcal{A}(D_{\text{shadow}}^{(i)}) \mid i = 1, \ldots, N_{\text{shadow}}\}$ using the knowledge of the training procedure of the target model. Thus, the attacker constructs a controlled set of models with known membership of the target record, which they can use to develop and refine the MIA.

*Computing a Membership Score.* The membership prediction of an MIA is typically in the form of thresholding a *membership score* $s_x : \Theta \to \mathbb{R}$. We denote the attack as $\phi_x(\theta) = \mathbb{1}[s_x(\theta) \geq \gamma]$ for some given threshold $\gamma \in \mathbb{R}$.

Existing MIAs against SDGs extract features from generated data using statistical queries [22,31], or training membership meta-classifiers per record [46]. These scores are inherently *record-specific*, driving the development and evaluation of MIAs tailored to individual records.

## 2.3   Differential Privacy and Its Hypothesis-Testing Interpretation

Differential privacy (DP) is a formal privacy guarantee that limits the contribution of any single record in statistical learning. A randomized training algorithm $\mathcal{A}(D)$ is differentially private if the inclusion or exclusion of any single record in $D$ will not significantly modify the resulting model distribution [15]:

**Definition 1.** *A randomized training algorithm $\mathcal{A}(D)$ satisfies $(\varepsilon, \delta)$-DP if for any measurable subset $E$ of the model space $\Theta$ and any partial dataset $\bar{D}$ and any record $x \in \mathbb{D}$, we have:*

$$\Pr[\mathcal{A}(\bar{D}) \in E] \leq e^\varepsilon \Pr[\mathcal{A}(\bar{D} \cup \{x\}) \in E] + \delta$$
$$\Pr[\mathcal{A}(\bar{D} \cup \{x\}) \in E] \leq e^\varepsilon \Pr[\mathcal{A}(\bar{D}) \in E] + \delta$$

The classical definition (Definition 1) has been shown to have an interpretation in terms of hypothesis testing [13,25,50], or equivalently, in terms of success rates of worst-case MIAs [26]. Consider the following MIA setting in which an adversary with access to a partial dataset $\bar{D}$, the target record $x$, and a model $\theta$, aims to tell whether $\theta$ comes from $\mathcal{A}(\bar{D})$ or $\mathcal{A}(\bar{D} \cup \{x\})$:

$$H_0 : \theta \sim \mathcal{A}(\bar{D}) \quad H_1 : \theta \sim \mathcal{A}(\bar{D} \cup \{x\}). \tag{1}$$

We omit the analogous case of $H_0$ corresponding to $\mathcal{A}(\bar{D} \cup \{x\})$ and $H_1$ to $\mathcal{A}(\bar{D})$. Given a *distinguisher* $\phi : \Theta \to [0, 1]$ which outputs 1 to guess the membership of $x$ in the training dataset ($H_1$), and 0 to guess its non-membership ($H_0$), we can characterize its success by its false positive rate (FPR) $\alpha_\phi$ and false negative rate (FNR) $\beta_\phi$:

$$\alpha_\phi = \mathbb{E}_{\theta \sim \mathcal{A}(\bar{D})}[\phi(\theta)], \quad \beta_\phi = 1 - \mathbb{E}_{\theta \sim \mathcal{A}(\bar{D} \cup \{x\})}[\phi(\theta)] \tag{2}$$

To analyze the privacy guarantees within this setting, we can consider the worst-case distinguisher $\phi_\alpha^*$ which achieves the lowest FNR at a given level of FPR $\alpha$:

$$\phi_\alpha^* = \arg \inf_{\phi: \; \Theta \to [0,1]} \{\beta_\phi \mid \alpha_\phi \leq \alpha\}. \tag{3}$$

Such an optimal attack always exists and can be constructed via Neyman-Pearson's lemma [13]. An algorithm $\mathcal{A}(\cdot)$ satisfies $(\varepsilon, \delta)$-DP if and only if the FNR of the optimal attack is lower bounded as follows:

$$\beta_{\phi_\alpha^*} \geq \min\{0, \; 1 - e^\varepsilon \alpha - \delta, \; e^{-\varepsilon}(1 - \alpha - \delta)\}, \tag{4}$$

for any given level of FPR $\alpha \in [0, 1]$, any $\bar{D} \in 2^{\mathbb{D}}$ and $x \in \mathbb{D}$ [13].

We refer to the trade-off curve, i.e., the set of all attainable $\alpha_\phi, \beta_\phi$, which is equivalent to the ROC curve of the worst-case MIA, as the *differential privacy distinguisher (DPD) risk* of attack $\phi(\cdot)$, following the prior terminology [43]. As DP is a standard notion of privacy leakage in statistical learning, we consider DPD risk an appropriate measure of privacy risk in our settings.

## 3   Record-Specific MIA Evaluation

In this section, we formalize the traditional and model-seeded privacy games and their estimations of attacker success.

### 3.1   Traditional Privacy Game

We refer to the privacy game commonly used in previous work [19,22,31,46,54] for record-specific evaluation of adversaries under realistic assumptions as the *traditional* game. An attacker's success at inferring a target record's membership is evaluated over multiple runs of the attack, each using a freshly sampled target dataset and the same target record $x$. We denote by $R^{\mathrm{T}}$ resulting risk estimate.

**Definition 2 (Traditional record-specific privacy game).** *For target record $x$, dataset size $n$, training algorithm $\mathcal{A}(\cdot)$, and attack $\phi(\cdot)$:*

1. *The challenger samples dataset $\bar{D} \sim \mathcal{D}^n$ from the distribution with a fresh random seed.*
2. *The challenger draws a secret bit $b \in \{0,1\}$ uniformly at random with a fresh random seed.*
3. *If $b = 1$, the challenger adds target record $x$ to dataset $\bar{D}$ to form the target dataset $D = \bar{D} \cup \{x\}$. Otherwise, $D = \bar{D}$.*
4. *The challenger trains the target model $\theta \leftarrow \mathcal{A}(D)$ on dataset $D$ with a fresh random seed.*
5. *The adversary outputs a guess $\hat{b} = \phi(\theta)$.*

## 3.2   Model-Seeded Privacy Game

We now formalize the *model-seeded* privacy game. Here, each run of the game uses the same target record and target dataset, and samples a fresh seed for training the target model. We denote the resulting risk estimate as $R^{\mathrm{MS}}$.

**Definition 3 (Model-seeded record-specific privacy game).** *For target record $x$, partial dataset $\bar{D}$, training algorithm $\mathcal{A}(\cdot)$, attack $\phi(\cdot)$, and number of runs $N$:*

1. *The challenger draws a secret bit $b \in \{0,1\}$ uniformly at random with a fresh random seed.*
2. *If $b = 1$, the challenger adds target record $x$ to $\bar{D}$ to form the target dataset: $D = \bar{D} \cup \{x\}$. Otherwise, $D = \bar{D}$.*
3. *The challenger trains the target model $\theta \leftarrow \mathcal{A}(D)$ on dataset $D$ with a fresh random seed.*
4. *The adversary outputs a guess $\hat{b} = \phi(\theta)$.*

In contrast with the traditional privacy game, this game results in an estimate of the target record's risk within a specific target dataset. By using only the model seed as a source of randomness and eliminating dataset sampling, the ability of the MIA to infer the presence of the target record $x$ in models trained on $D$ is evaluated. To the best of our knowledge, this privacy game has so far been used exclusively to evaluate the worst-case attack, where the adversary is assumed to have full knowledge of the target dataset apart from the membership of the target record [3,17], and never used to evaluate adversaries under realistic assumptions, e.g., with access only to auxiliary data.

## 3.3   The Relationship Between the Games and Privacy Risk

Consider $N > 1$ runs of either the model-seeded or traditional game with different random seeds, resulting in a set of guesses $\{\hat{b}_i\}_{i\in[N]}$ with corresponding secret bits (i.e. membership labels) $\{b_i\}_{i\in[N]}$. Let us denote the empirical FPR and FNR obtained in an evaluation using a privacy game for a given attack $\phi : \Theta \to [0,1]$:

$$\hat{\alpha}_\phi = \frac{\sum_{i=0}^{N} \mathbb{1}\{\hat{b}_i = 1 \wedge b_i = 0\}}{\sum_{i=0}^{N} \mathbb{1}\{b_i = 0\}}, \quad \hat{\beta}_\phi = \frac{\sum_{i=0}^{N} \mathbb{1}\{\hat{b}_i = 0 \wedge b_i = 1\}}{\sum_{i=0}^{N} \mathbb{1}\{b_i = 1\}} \tag{5}$$

We use $\hat{\alpha}_\phi^{\mathrm{T}}$ or $\hat{\alpha}_\phi^{\mathrm{MS}}$ to denote the empirical error rates computed using the traditional (T) and model-seeded (MS) game, respectively, and analogously for $\hat{\beta}_\phi^{\mathrm{T}}$ and $\hat{\beta}_\phi^{\mathrm{MS}}$. We show that, with a sufficiently large number of repetitions of the game with freshly drawn seeds, the empirical FPR and FNR obtained using the model-seeded game converge exponentially fast to the DPD risk as defined in Sect. 2.3 for any given attack $\phi$ and record $x$:

**Proposition 1 (Model-seeded game converges to DPD risk).** *For any fixed target record $x$, partial dataset $\bar{D} \in \mathbb{D}^{n-1}$, training algorithm $T(\cdot)$, and attack $\phi(\cdot)$, we have w.p. $1 - \rho$ for $\rho \in (0,1)$ over $N$ random coin flips, i.e., fresh seed draws, in the model-seeded game:*

$$|\hat{\alpha}_\phi^{MS} - \alpha_\phi| \le \sqrt{\frac{\log(2/\rho)}{2N}}, \ |\hat{\beta}_\phi^{MS} - \beta_\phi| \le \sqrt{\frac{\log(2/\rho)}{2N}} \tag{6}$$

*Proof (Proposition 1).* Consider the set of *in* models $\{\theta_{\text{in}}^{(i)}\}_{i=1}^N$ and the set of *out* models $\{\theta_{\text{out}}^{(i)}\}_{t=1}^N$ obtained in the model-seeded game. Let us define $X_i$ for $i \in [N]$ as $X_i = \mathbb{1}[\phi(\theta_{\text{out}}^{(i)}) = 1]$. The set $\{X_i\}_{i=1}^N$ is a set of independent Bernoulli random variables. Let $\bar{X} = \frac{1}{N}\sum_{i=1}^N X_i$. Then $\hat{\alpha} = \bar{X}$. Moreover, we have that $\alpha = \mathbb{E}[\bar{X}]$, where the expectations are over sampling $\{\theta_{\text{out}}^{(i)}\}_{i=1}^N$. By the Chernoff-Hoeffding inequality, for any $\gamma > 0$:

$$\Pr[|\bar{X} - \mathbb{E}[\bar{X}]| \ge \gamma] \le 2e^{-2N\gamma^2} \tag{7}$$

Thus, with probability at least $1 - 2e^{-2N\gamma^2}$:

$$|\bar{X} - \mathbb{E}[\bar{X}]| < \gamma. \tag{8}$$

Setting $2e^{-2N\gamma^2} = \rho$, we get:

$$\gamma = \sqrt{\frac{\log(2/\rho)}{2N}}, \tag{9}$$

which yields the sought statement. We get analogous results for $\beta$.

In contrast, empirical error rates obtained in the traditional privacy game converge *average* attack success rates over i.i.d. dataset resamples:

**Proposition 2 (Traditional game converges to average privacy risk).** *For any fixed target record $x$, dataset size $n > 1$, training algorithm $T(\cdot)$, and attack $\phi(\cdot)$, we have w.p. $1 - \rho$ for $\rho \in (0,1)$ over $N$ random coin flips, i.e., fresh seed draws, in the traditional game:*

$$|\hat{\alpha}_\phi^T - \mathbb{E}_{\bar{D}\sim\mathcal{D}^n}\alpha_{\phi,\bar{D}}| \le \sqrt{\frac{\log(2/\rho)}{2N}}, \ |\hat{\beta}_\phi^T - \mathbb{E}_{\bar{D}\sim\mathcal{D}^n}\beta_{\phi,\bar{D}}| \le \sqrt{\frac{\log(2/\rho)}{2N}}, \tag{10}$$

*where we explicitly use $\alpha_{\phi,\bar{D}}$ and $\beta_{\phi,\bar{D}}$ to emphasize the dependence of $\alpha_\phi$ and $\beta_\phi$ on $\bar{D}$ in the definition of the hypothesis test in Eq. (2). The proof is analogous to Proposition 1.*

Thus, the model-seeded game serves as an estimator of the DPD risk of an attack, as opposed to the traditional game, which estimates an average risk over hypothetical dataset re-samples.

## 3.4    Practical Implementation of the Privacy Games

Algorithm 1 outlines our implementation of the traditional and model-seeded privacy games. In both setups, we construct $\frac{N_{\text{eval}}}{2} = 500$ 'in' and 'out' datasets each. In the traditional setup, we sample 'out' datasets from the evaluation pool $D_{\text{eval}}$, and ensure $x$ is included in exactly half. In the model-seeded setup, the 'in' datasets are equivalent to the full target dataset $D$. To maintain an equal dataset size across runs, we construct the 'out' datasets by replacing $x$ with a randomly sampled record $x_r \sim \text{Unif}[D_{\text{eval}} \setminus D]$.

---

**Algorithm 1.** Practical privacy game implementation

---

**Input:** Target record $x$, target dataset $D$, target training algorithm $\mathcal{A}(\cdot)$, evaluation pool $D_{\text{eval}}$, partial evaluation pool $\bar{D}_{\text{eval}} = D_{\text{eval}} \setminus \{x\}$, MIA $\phi_x$ with membership score function $s_x$, attack thresholds $\gamma \in \{\gamma_1, \ldots, \gamma_m\}$, number of runs $N_{\text{eval}}$, and privacy game flag ($T$ for traditional, $MS$ for model-seeded).

**Output:** Empirical error rates $[\hat{\alpha}_{\phi,1}^{PG}, \ldots, \hat{\alpha}_{\phi,m}^{PG}]$ and $[\hat{\beta}_{\phi,1}^{PG}, \ldots, \hat{\beta}_{\phi,m}^{PG}]$ for each attack threshold $\gamma$, and summary risk metric $R^{\text{PG}}$ computed as the ROC AUC of attack $\phi_x$.

1: **for** $i = 0, 1, \ldots, \frac{N_{\text{eval}}}{2}$ **do**
2:     **if** PG $= MS$ **then**  `// model-seeded game`
3:         $D_{\text{in}} \leftarrow D$
4:         Sample reference record $x_r \sim \text{Unif}[D_{\text{eval}} \setminus D]$.
5:         Construct $D_{\text{out}} \leftarrow D \setminus \{x\} \cup \{x_r\}$.
6:     **else**  `// traditional game`
7:         Sample $\bar{D}_{\text{in}} \sim \text{Unif}[\bar{D}_{\text{eval}}]^{|D|-1}$
8:         $D_{\text{in}} \leftarrow \bar{D}_{\text{in}} \cup \{x\}$
9:         Sample $\bar{D}_{\text{out}} \sim \text{Unif}[\bar{D}_{\text{eval}}]^{|D|}$
10:    **end if**
11:    Train evaluation model $\theta_{\text{in}} = \mathcal{A}(D_{\text{in}})$ with fresh random seed.
12:    Train evaluation model $\theta_{\text{out}} = \mathcal{A}(D_{\text{out}})$ with fresh random seed.
13:    **for** $\gamma_j \in \{\gamma_1, \ldots, \gamma_m\}$ **do**
14:        Compute attack prediction $\phi_x(\theta_{\text{in}}) = \mathbb{1}[s_x(\theta_{\text{in}}) \geq \gamma_j]$
15:        $\hat{b}_{i,j} \leftarrow \phi_x(\theta_{\text{in}})$
16:        Compute attack prediction $\phi_x(\theta_{\text{out}}) = \mathbb{1}[s_x(\theta_{\text{out}}) \geq \gamma_j]$
17:        $\hat{b}_{i+\frac{N_{\text{eval}}}{2},j} \leftarrow \phi_x(\theta_{\text{out}})$
18:    **end for**
19:    $b_i \leftarrow 1, b_{i+\frac{N_{\text{eval}}}{2}} \leftarrow 0$
20: **end for**
21: Compute empirical FPR $\hat{\alpha}_{\phi,j}^{PG}(\{\hat{b}_{i,j}\}_{i=1}^{N_{\text{eval}}}, \{b_i\}_{i=1}^{N_{\text{eval}}})$ for each $\gamma_j \in [\gamma_1, \ldots, \gamma_m]$
22: Compute empirical FNR $\hat{\beta}_{\phi,j}^{PG}(\{\hat{b}_{i,j}\}_{i=1}^{N_{\text{eval}}}, \{b_i\}_{i=1}^{N_{\text{eval}}})$ for each $\gamma_j \in [\gamma_1, \ldots, \gamma_m]$
23: Compute summary privacy risk $R^{\text{PG}} = \text{AUC}(\{\hat{\alpha}_{\phi,j}^{PG}\}_{j=1}^{m}, \{\hat{\beta}_{\phi,j}^{PG}\}_{j=1}^{m})$

---

## 4 Experimental Results

### 4.1 Experimental Setup

*Datasets.* We use the Adult [6] and UK Census [36] datasets, commonly tabular datasets used in previous work concerning privacy-preserving synthetic data [19, 31,46]. Both are de-identified samples of census data containing categorical and continuous demographic features. We partition each dataset into $D_{\mathrm{aux}}$, used for MIA development, and $D_{\mathrm{eval}}$, used for evaluation. We perform the partitions so that $|D_{\mathrm{aux}}| = 2 \times |D_{\mathrm{eval}}|$. We consider $|D| = 1000$, $D \subset D_{\mathrm{eval}}$, a common setting in previous work concerning MIAs against synthetic data.

*Target Models.* We use Synthpop [35] and Baynet [57] in our main experiments, using the implementations available in the reprosyn [1] repository. We select these generators as they are widely-used, established models.

*MIA Methodology.* We use extended-TAPAS, the state-of-the-art query-based attack for SDGs, as originally introduced by Houssiau et al. [22], and extended by Meeus et al. [31]. We train the attack for each target record using auxiliary dataset $D_{\mathrm{aux}}$ to sample 1000 shadow datasets. TAPAS operates under black-box model access with auxiliary data, but no access to the training data of the target model. We use AUC ROC as a summary metric for privacy risk.

We use the following metrics to compare the traditional and model-seeded risk estimates.

*Miss rate* is the fraction of records classified as high-risk in the model-seeded setup, which are classified as low-risk in the traditional setup. We define a high-risk threshold $t$ for the MIA AUC, and consider records for which the attack reaches AUC above $t$ to be high risk. For a subset of records in the target dataset $S \subseteq D$ and high-risk threshold $t$, we compute the miss rate as: $\mathrm{MR}(S) = \frac{|\{x \in S \mid R^{\mathrm{T}}(x) \leq t \wedge R^{\mathrm{MS}}(x) > t\}|}{|\{x \in S \mid R^{\mathrm{MS}}(x) > t\}|}$.

*Root Mean Squared Deviation (RMSD)* measures the deviation between traditional and model-seeded risks. For $S \subseteq D$, we compute the RMSD between the two risk estimates as $\mathrm{RMSD}(S, \phi) = \sqrt{\frac{1}{|S|} \sum_{x \in S} (R^{\mathrm{T}}(x) - R^{\mathrm{MS}}(x))^2}$.

### 4.2 Difference Between $R^{\mathrm{MS}}$ and $R^{\mathrm{T}}$

Figure 1 shows the traditional and model-seeded risks to indeed differ substantially. Figure 1a shows the traditional and model-seeded risks for all 1000 records in $D$ for the Adult dataset and $\theta$ Synthpop. This shows that 94% of high-risk records for high-risk threshold $t = 0.8$ would be incorrectly classified as low-risk when using the traditional setup. Using the traditional setup leads to an RMSD of 0.07, for a value that empirically ranges roughly from 0.5 to 1. Figure 1b shows a histogram of absolute differences between the two risk estimates across records, showing that the estimate would be off by more than 0.1 for 15% of records when using the traditional setup, and could go up to 0.26. Table 1 shows that these results are consistent across setups. The miss rates are consistently high, ranging from 0.73 to 0.94, showing that high-risk records are being incorrectly identified.

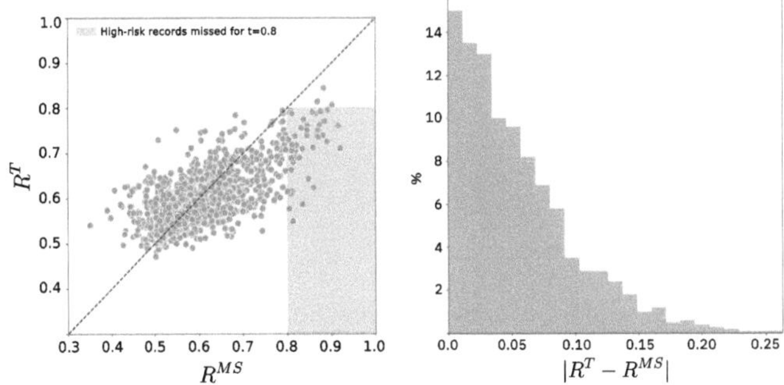


**Fig. 1.** Risk for all 1000 records in $D$ sampled from the Adult dataset (Synthpop). (a) per-record model-seeded and traditional risks. The shaded area marks all the high-risk records missed in the traditional setup for high-risk threshold $t = 0.8$. (b) histogram of per-record absolute differences between the model-seeded and traditional risks.

The majority of the records that are highly vulnerable will thus be incorrectly considered low-risk if MIAs are evaluated using the traditional setup. RMSD ranges from 0.04 to 0.11, a significant error for risk estimated using AUC.

**Table 1.** Miss rate and RMSD across different datasets and target synthetic data generators. We use a high-risk threshold of $t = 0.8$.

| Dataset | Model | RMSD | MR |
|---|---|---|---|
| Adult | Synthpop | 0.07 | 0.94 |
| | Baynet | 0.05 | 0.73 |
| Census | Synthpop | 0.11 | 0.94 |
| | Baynet | 0.04 | 0.75 |

*Different High-Risk Threshold t Values.* Fig. 2a shows that, for all high-risk thresholds, the miss rates are substantial, reaching values above 20% for all setups for $t = 0.6$ and up to 80% for $t = 0.9$. Using the traditional setup for MIA evaluation thus leads to high-risk records being incorrectly classified as low-risk, regardless of the threshold choice. Notably, we find that the miss rate increases with larger threshold values $t$. Identifying high-risk records becomes more difficult as the threshold becomes more strict, and the traditional setup fails to detect an increasing fraction of them.

*Dataset Size.* In Sect. 4.2, we consider target datasets $D$ of size 1000. We now study how varying $|D|$ influences the gap between traditional and model-seeded risks. For 20 records from the Adult dataset and with $\theta$ Synthpop, we compute the risk in both setups for $|D| =\in \{200, \dots, 10000\}$.

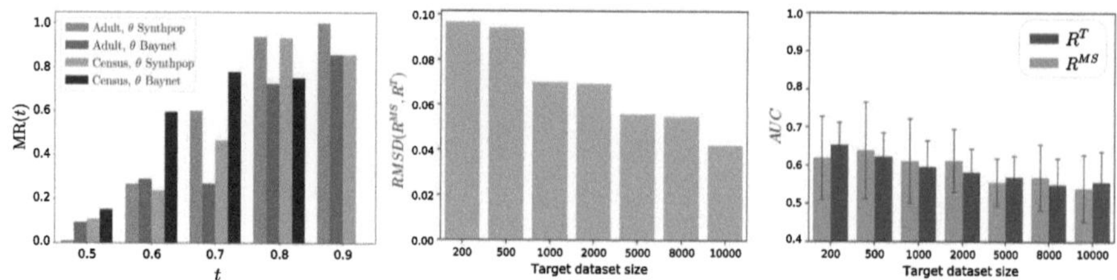

**Fig. 2.** (a) Miss rate for different high-risk thresholds $t$ for SDG setups. Note that for Census and Baynet, there are no records with $R^{\text{MS}} > 0.9$, therefore the miss rate is not defined. (b) RMSD between model-seeded and traditional risk per target dataset size. (c) Model-seeded and traditional risk values per target dataset size. For both figures, values are computed across 20 target records.

Figure 2b shows that the RMSD to decreases with dataset size, but remains non-negligible even at $|D| = 10,000$. Figure 2c shows the MIA AUC computed in both setups, averaged across the target records. MIA performance decreases, though it remains better than random, for larger datasets, naturally decreasing the gap. Yet, highly vulnerable records are present even in large datasets, and the two risk estimates do not converge to the same values, showing the importance of using the model-seeded game regardless of dataset size.

### 4.3   Evaluating One Record's Risk Within Different Datasets

We use the Adult dataset and the Synthpop model to illustrate an example of the potential negative impact of using the traditional instead of the model-seeded setup. We compute the risk of a single target record in the traditional setup. Then, we compute its model-seeded risk in 15 randomly selected datasets sampled in the traditional setup. As shown in Fig. 3, the model-seeded risk $R^{\text{MS}}$ varies from approximately 0.5 (random guess) to 0.8 (high risk), depending on the dataset. The traditional risk is $R^{\text{T}} = 0.62$, underestimating the DPD risk by up to 0.2 in the worst case.

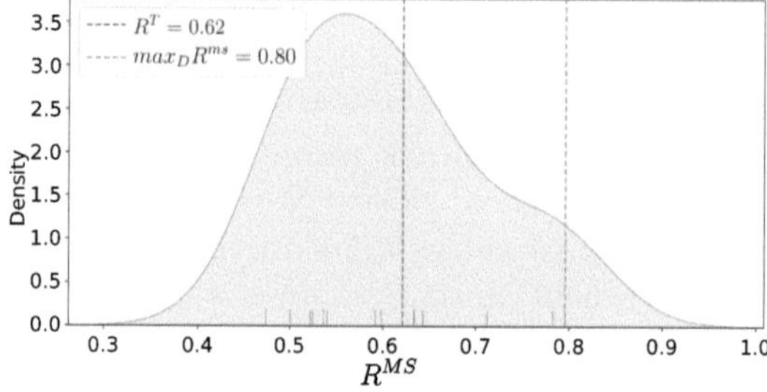

**Fig. 3.** Model-seeded risks of one target record within 15 different datasets and its traditional risk.

# 5   Related Work

*Membership Inference Attacks (MIAs).* Shokri et al. [44] introduced the first MIA against ML models, using model predictions and the *shadow modeling* technique, where multiple models including and excluding the target record are trained to approximate its impact. Various attacks based on shadow modeling have since been proposed [42,45,51,54,56], typically relying on model loss as the membership signal. The current state-of-the-art attack for ML models, introduced by Carlini et al. [8], uses a likelihood ratio test between loss distributions of models trained with and without the target record.

Tabular synthetic data generators model a dataset as a whole, learning feature distributions and sampling synthetic records [35,39,57]. They do not have a notion of per-record loss, rendering standard ML-focused MIAs inapplicable. Instead, specialized record-specific attacks that rely on shadow models and the generated data to assess a record's influence on synthetic outputs have been proposed [22,31,46]. Stadler et al. [46] train meta-classifiers on statistical features from the synthetic data. Houssiau et al. [22] extend this with $k$-way queries that count exact matches on random feature subsets, and Meeus et al. [31] further include range-based queries for continuous features.

*Threat Models.* A threat model specifies an attacker's access to the model and data. For synthetic tabular data, most attacks assume black-box access to model outputs [22,31,46], though some ML-focused attacks also assume access to predicted probabilities [8,45,56] or even labels [11]. White-box attackers have access to model internals, and are more common in vision tasks [4,12,20,30,38].

Data access defines the data available to the attacker and its relationship to the target data. Attackers are often assumed to access auxiliary datasets drawn from the same distribution as the target [8,22,31,46]. Guépin et al. [19] show this assumption can be relaxed using synthetic data, with performance tradeoffs. Privacy auditing literature typically considers a strong *leave-one-out* adversary with knowledge of all training records except the target [23,34,48].

*MIA Evaluation.* MIAs are typically evaluated in a *privacy game* between an attacker and a challenger [8,24,41,46,55]. Ye et al. [54] distinguish between *model-specific* and *record-specific* privacy games. The former evaluates an attacker's ability to distinguish between records included or excluded from the training data of one model [8,30,32,45,56], while the latter distinguishes between models trained with and without a specific record, and is standard for evaluating tabular synthetic data attacks [22,31,46].

Ye et al. [54] define a privacy game for a *fixed worst-case record and dataset*, typically used to test differential privacy guarantees with a very strong *leave-one-out* attacker [3,23,34,48]. To the best of our knowledge, this privacy game has never been used for weaker attackers or attacks against synthetic data. The model-seeded game is applicable to any attack, regardless of assumptions. The goal of the model-seeded game is to measure the DPD risk for *any* attacker, rather than only the worst-case attacker.

# 6   Discussion and Conclusion

We show that the model-seeded privacy game provides an unbiased estimate of a record's risk, whereas the traditional game averages risk across datasets. Empirically, we show the difference to be significant: the traditional setup results in 85% of high-risk records being misclassified. This confirms that assuming a record's risk is independent of the dataset is optimistic and can obscure vulnerabilities. Although larger datasets reduce this gap, the model-seeded game consistently offers a more accurate risk estimate and should be preferred.

The exact impact of the dataset on a record's risk remains open. Prior work suggests that outliers—records with rare or underrepresented features—are more at risk [9,16,27,31,46]. These characteristics are dataset-specific: a record may be an outlier in one sample but not another, especially in small or high-dimensional data. Larger datasets may better preserve such outlier status, making $R^{\mathrm{MS}}$ and $R^{\mathrm{T}}$ more aligned, but not interchangeable.

By formalizing and empirically validating the model-seeded game, we provide a practical and principled tool for assessing privacy risk. We hope this work helps organizations handling sensitive data, such as in healthcare [29] and finance [47], better assess data leakage risks and maintain high privacy standards when releasing synthetic data.

# References


1. Alan Turing Institute. 2022. Reprosyn
2. Annamalai, M.S.M.S., Gadotti, A. and Rocher, L.: A linear reconstruction approach for attribute inference attacks against synthetic data. In: USENIX Security (2024)
3. Annamalai, M.S.M.S., Ganev, G., De Cristofaro, E.: "What do you want from theory alone?" experimenting with tight auditing of differentially private synthetic data generation. In: USENIX Security (2024)
4. Azadmanesh, M., Ghahfarokhi, B.S., Talouki, M.A.: A white-box generator membership inference attack against generative models. In: ISCISC (2021)
5. Balle, B., Cherubin, G., Hayes, J.: Reconstructing training data with informed adversaries. In: IEEE S&P (2022)
6. Becker, B., Kohavi, R.: Adult. UCI Machine Learning Repository (1996)
7. Cao, Y., Chen, Z. and Quan, Z.[n. d.].: Assessing Insurer's Litigation Risk: Claim Dispute Prediction with Actionable Interpretations Using Machine Learning Techniques. SSRN 5126964 ([n. d.])
8. Carlini, N., Chien, S., Nasr, M., Song, S., Terzis, A., Tramer, F.: Membership Inference Attacks From First Principles. In: IEEE S&P (2022)
9. Carlini, N., Jagielski, M., Zhang, C., Papernot, N., Terzis, A., Tramer, F.: The privacy onion effect: Memorization is relative. In: NeurIPS (2022)
10. Chhikara, H., Chhikara, S., Gupta, L.: Predictive analytics in finance: leveraging ai and machine learning for investment strategies. In: Utilizing AI and Machine Learning in Financial Analysis. IGI Global Scientific Publishing (2025)
11. Choquette-Choo, C.A., Tramer, F., Carlini, N., Papernot, N.: Label-only membership inference attacks. In: ICML (2021)

12. D Cretu, A.M., Jones, D., de Montjoye, Y.A., Tople, S.: Investigating the effect of misalignment on membership privacy in the white-box setting. In: PoPETS (2024)

13. Dong, J., Roth, A., Su, W.J.: Gaussian differential privacy. J. Royal Stat. Society: Series B (Statistical Methodology) (2022)

14. Dwork, C.: Differential Privacy. In: ICALP (Lecture Notes in Computer Science) (2006)

15. Dwork, C., Roth, A., et al.: The algorithmic foundations of differential privacy (2014)

16. Feldman, V.: Does learning require memorization? a short tale about a long tail. In: ACM SIGACT Symposium on Theory of Computing 2020

17. Georgi Ganev, Meenatchi Sundaram Muthu Selva Annamalai, and Emiliano De Cristofaro. 2025. The Elusive Pursuit of Reproducing PATE-GAN: Benchmarking, Auditing, Debugging. *TMLR* (2025)

18. Guan, V., Guépin, F., Cretu, A.-M., de Montjoye, Y.-A.: 2024. A zero auxiliary knowledge membership inference attack on aggregate location data, PoPETS (2024)

19. Guépin, F., Meeus, M., Creţu, A.-M., de Montjoye, Y.A..: Synthetic is all you need: removing the auxiliary data assumption for membership inference attacks against synthetic data. In: ESORICS (2023)

20. Hayes, J., Melis, L., Danezis, G., De Cristofaro, E.: LOGAN: membership inference attacks against generative models. In: PoPETS (2019)

21. He, Z., Zhang, T., Lee, R.B.: Model inversion attacks against collaborative inference. In: Computer Security Applications Conference (2019)

22. Houssiau, F., et al.: Tapas: a toolbox for adversarial privacy auditing of synthetic data (2022)

23. Jagielski, M., Ullman, J., Oprea, A.: Auditing differentially private machine learning: how private is private SGD?. In: NeurIPS (2020)

24. Jayaraman, B., Wang, L., Knipmeyer, K., Gu, Q., Evans, D.: Revisiting membership inference under realistic assumptions. In: PoPETS 2021 (2021)

25. Kairouz, P., Oh, S., Viswanath, P.: The composition theorem for differential privacy. In: ICML (2015)

26. Kulynych, B., Gomez, J.F., Kaissis, G., Calmon, F., Troncoso, C.: Attack-aware noise calibration for differential privacy. In: NeurIPS (2024)

27. Kulynych, B., Yaghini, M., Cherubin, G., Veale, M., Troncoso, C.: 2022. Disparate Vulnerability to Membership Inference Attacks, PoPETS (2022)

28. Kumar, S., Shokri, R.: ML Privacy Meter: Aiding regulatory compliance by quantifying the privacy risks of machine learning. In: Workshop on Hot Topics in Privacy Enhancing Technologies (HotPETs) (2020)

29. Lotan, E., et al.: Medical imaging and privacy in the era of artificial intelligence: myth, fallacy, and the future. J. Am. Coll. Radiol. (2020)

30. Matsumoto, T., Miura, T., Yanai, N.: Membership inference attacks against diffusion models. In: IEEE S&P Workshops (SPW) (2023)

31. Meeus, M., Guepin, F., Creţu, A.M., de Montjoye, Y.A.: Achilles' heels: vulnerable record identification in synthetic data publishing. In: ESORICS (2023)

32. Meeus, M., Wutschitz, L., Zanella-Béguelin, S., Tople, S., Shokri, R.: The Canary's Echo: Auditing Privacy Risks of LLM-Generated Synthetic Text (2025)

33. Nasr, M., Shokri, R., Houmansadr, A.: Comprehensive privacy analysis of deep learning: Passive and active white-box inference attacks against centralized and federated learning. In: IEEE S&P (2019)

34. Nasr, M., Song, S., Thakurta, A., Papernot, N., Carlini, N.: Lower Bounds for Differentially Private Machine Learning. In: IEEE S&P, Adversary Instantiation (2021)
35. Nowok, B., Raab, G.M., Dibben, C.: synthpop: Bespoke Creation of Synthetic Data in R. J. Stat. Softw. (2016)
36. Office for National Statistics. 2011. Census Microdata Teaching Files
37. Osuala, R., Lang, D.M., Riess, A.: Enhancing the utility of privacy-preserving cancer classification using synthetic data. In: Artificial Intelligence and Imaging for Diagnostic and Treatment Challenges in Breast Care. Springer Nature Switzerland (2025)
38. Pang, Y., Wang, T., Kang, X., Huai, M., Zhang, Y.: White-box Membership Inference Attacks against Diffusion Models (2025)
39. Ping, H., Stoyanovich, J., Howe, B.: DataSynthesizer: Privacy-Preserving Synthetic Datasets (SSDBM). In: ACM (2017)
40. Pollock, J., Shilov, I., Dodd, E., de Montjoye, Y.A.: Free Record-Level Privacy Risk Evaluation Through Artifact-Based Methods. arXiv preprint arXiv:2411.05743 (2024)
41. Pyrgelis, A., Troncoso, C., De Cristofaro, E.: Knock Knock, Who's There? Membership Inference on Aggregate Location Data. (2018)
42. Sablayrolles, A., Douze, M., Schmid, C., Ollivier, Y., Hervé Jégou.: White-box vs black-box, Bayes optimal strategies for membership inference (2019). In: ICML (2019)
43. Salem, A.: SoK: Let the privacy games begin! A unified treatment of data inference privacy in machine learning. In: IEEE S&P (2023)
44. Shokri, R., Stronati, M., Song, C., Shmatikov, V.: Membership inference attacks against machine learning models. In: IEEE S&P (2017)
45. Song, L., Mittal, P.: Systematic evaluation of privacy risks of machine learning models. In: USENIX Security (2021)
46. Stadler, T., Oprisanu, B., Troncoso, C.: Synthetic data–anonymisation groundhog day. In: USENIX Security (2022)
47. Synthetic Data Expert Group, Financial Conduct Authority. 2024. Report: Using Synthetic Data in Financial Services (2024)
48. Tramer, F., Terzis, A., Steinke, T., Song, S., Jagielski, M., Carlini, N.: Debugging Differential Privacy, A Case Study for Privacy Auditing (2022)
49. Wang, Z., Song, M., Zhang, Z., Song, Y., Wang, Q., Qi, H.: Beyond inferring class representatives: User-level privacy leakage from federated learning. In: IEEE INFOCOM 2019-IEEE Conference on Computer Communications (2019)
50. Wasserman, L., Zhou, S.: A statistical framework for differential privacy. J. Amer, Statist, Assoc (2010)
51. Watson, L., Guo, C., Cormode, G., Sablayrolles, A.: On the importance of difficulty calibration in membership inference attacks. In: International Conference on Learning Representations
52. Lei, X., Skoularidou, M., Cuesta-Infante, A., Veeramachaneni, K.: Modeling tabular data using conditional gan, In: NeurIPS (2019)
53. Yang, Z., Zhang, J., Chang, E.C., Liang, Z.: Neural network inversion in adversarial setting via background knowledge alignment. In: ACM CCS
54. Ye, J., Maddi, A., Murakonda, S.K., Bindschaedler, V., Shokri, R.: Enhanced membership inference attacks against machine learning models. In: ACM CCS (2022)
55. Yeom, S., Giacomelli, I., Fredrikson, M., Jha, S.: Privacy risk in machine learning: analyzing the connection to overfitting. In: IEEE Computer Security Foundations Symposium (2018)

56. Zarifzadeh, S., Liu, P., Shokri, R.: Low-cost high-power membership inference attacks. In: ICML (2024)
57. Zhang, J., Cormode, G., Procopiuc, C.M., Srivastava, D., Xiao, X.: Private Data Release via Bayesian Networks, PrivBayes (2017)

# Membership Inference Attacks Beyond Overfitting


Mona Khalil[1]([✉]), Alberto Blanco-Justicia[1], Najeeb Jebreel[1],
and Josep Domingo-Ferrer[1,2]

[1] Universitat Rovira i Virgili, Department of Computer Engineering and
Mathematics, CYBERCAT-Center for Cybersecurity Research of Catalonia, Av.
Països Catalans 26, 43007 Tarragona, Catalonia
`{mona.khalil,alberto.blanco,najeeb.jebreel,josep.domingo}@urv.cat`
[2] LAAS-CNRS, Université de Toulouse, 7 Av. du Colonel Roche, 31400
Toulouse, France



**Abstract.** Membership inference attacks (MIAs) against machine learning (ML) models aim to determine whether a given data point was part of the model training data. These attacks may pose significant privacy risks to individuals whose *sensitive* data were used for training, which motivates the use of defenses such as differential privacy, often at the cost of high accuracy losses. MIAs exploit the differences in the behavior of a model when making predictions on samples it has seen during training (*members*) versus those it has not seen (*non-members*). Several studies have pointed out that model overfitting is the major factor contributing to these differences in behavior and, consequently, to the success of MIAs. However, the literature also shows that even non-overfitted ML models can leak information about a small subset of their training data. In this paper, we investigate the root causes of membership inference vulnerabilities beyond traditional overfitting concerns and suggest targeted defenses. We empirically analyze the characteristics of the training data samples vulnerable to MIAs in models that are not overfitted (and hence able to generalize). Our findings reveal that these samples are often outliers within their classes (*e.g.*, noisy or hard to classify). We then propose potential defensive strategies to protect these vulnerable samples and enhance the privacy-preserving capabilities of ML models. Our code is available at https://github.com/najeebjebreel/mia_analysis.

**Keywords:** Machine learning · Privacy · Membership inference attacks


## 1 Introduction

Machine learning (ML) has demonstrated remarkable performance across a wide range of tasks [9,15,27]. This success is mainly attributed to the availability of


**Supplementary Information** The online version contains supplementary material available at https://doi.org/10.1007/978-3-032-16089-8_3.

large and diverse data for training, along with advances in learning algorithms and computational capabilities.

However, training data often contain sensitive information related to individuals, such as personal photos [20], confidential texts [6], clinical records [21], and financial details [30]. Unauthorized access to or leakage of such data can lead to significant privacy risks and adverse consequences for affected individuals.

Trained ML models can memorize and inadvertently reveal sensitive information about their training data [5, 40, 48], making them vulnerable to several privacy attacks, such as extraction attacks [6], property inference attacks [13], and membership inference attacks (MIAs) [38].

MIAs [35, 38, 47], the focus of this paper, aim to determine whether a specific data point was part of the training data of a given model. Although they may not seem dangerous at first glance, they can pose serious privacy risks to individuals in specific scenarios. For example, knowing that a specific patient's clinical record was used to train a model associated with a sensitive disease can reveal with high confidence that the patient suffers from this disease.

Several studies have demonstrated a strong connection between training data memorization and the phenomenon of overfitting [5, 46, 47]. Overfitting occurs when a model not only learns general patterns, but also captures sample-specific details and noise, which leads to a noticeable difference in its behavior in training data (*members*) compared to unseen data (*non-members*) [16, 38, 46, 47]. MIAs leverage this differential behavior [4, 29, 38, 41].

Various defenses against MIAs have been proposed and can be categorized into certified and practical defenses. Certified defenses provide formal privacy guarantees through differential privacy (DP) [1], but often result in reduced model utility and high computational costs. Practical defenses, on the other hand, offer empirical privacy protection with the goal of maintaining the utility of the model [2, 19, 28, 41, 43]. These practical defenses primarily aim to mitigate overfitting and develop models with better generalization capabilities, thus reducing the effectiveness of MIAs while preserving utility. However, even models designed to generalize well can inadvertently leak information about a small portion of the training data, making them vulnerable to MIAs [4, 25].

**Contributions**: In this paper, we address two key questions: *Q1: What makes certain samples vulnerable to MIAs even in non-overfitted models?* and *Q2: How can these samples be effectively protected?*

To answer these questions, we performed experiments on various data sets and models to identify factors that contribute to the vulnerability of MIA beyond overfitting. We systematically characterize what makes samples vulnerable through visual analysis, feature-space geometry, and model explanation techniques. We find that outliers—samples that are far from their class centroid—are particularly vulnerable. We then suggest and discuss potential defensive strategies to protect these vulnerable samples and thereby enhance privacy.

The remainder of this paper is organized as follows. Section 2 provides background on ML overfitting and differential privacy. Section 3 discusses related work on membership inference attacks and defenses, and factors that contribute to the success of MIAs. Section 4 describes the data sets, models, and experimental setup. Section 5 empirically investigates the causes of MIA beyond overfitting and discusses the results obtained. Section 6 discusses potential solutions for protecting vulnerable samples. Section 7 summarizes our findings and suggests future research directions. Additional experimental details are provided in the supplementary materials.

## 2  Background

### 2.1  Machine Learning Overfitting

In this paper, we focus on predictive deep neural network (DNNs) utilized as $m$-class classifiers, with the cross-entropy (CE) loss:

$$\mathcal{L}(F_\theta, z) = - \sum_{i=0}^{m-1} y_i \log(F_\theta(x)_i), \tag{1}$$

where $x$ are the input features, $y_i$ is the one-hot encoded label vector, and $F_\theta(x)_i$ is the predicted probability for class $i$.

One of the potential problems of ML training is overfitting. Overfitting is an undesirable training outcome in which the model fits too closely to the training data but performs poorly on the test data, resulting in a high generalization error [23]. Overfitting can arise from various factors, including overparameterized models, insufficient training data, high data dimensionality, or suboptimal hyperparameter selection (*e.g.* batch size, learning rate). In addition, [8] highlight frequent data exposure during training and sharp loss functions as factors that exacerbate MIA risks. In particular, [12] demonstrate that some degree of memorization may be essential for optimal generalization, particularly when learning from rare or unique instances.

Since best practices of ML emphasize avoiding overfitting to enhance generalization and maximize utility, our work focuses on identifying training samples that remain vulnerable to MIAs even in non-overfitted models.

### 2.2  Differential Privacy (DP)

Differential privacy (DP [11]) ensures that the inclusion or exclusion of a single data point in a data set does not significantly affect the output of a statistical function. Formally, a mechanism $M$ satisfies $(\epsilon, \delta)$-DP if, for any two neighboring data sets $D$ and $D'$ (differing by one data point) and any subset $S$ of outcomes:

$$\Pr[M(D) \in S] \le e^\epsilon \Pr[M(D') \in S] + \delta, \tag{2}$$

where $\epsilon$ is the privacy budget (smaller values imply stronger privacy), and $\delta$ is the probability of exceeding the budget.

In DNN training, DP is typically implemented via DP-SGD [1], which clips per-example gradients to bound sensitivity and adds Gaussian noise to the batch gradient during training. However, DP-SGD introduces challenges, including complex hyperparameter tuning, increased training time, and reduced model utility [2,32].

# 3   Related Work

## 3.1   Black-Box MIA Approaches

We focus on black-box MIAs since, on the one hand, according to [34] they are (or can be) as good as any white-box MIAs. There are several approaches to conducting black-box MIAs, each leveraging different aspects of the model output to distinguish between members and non-members. Shadow model attacks [38] train multiple models to mimic the target model behavior, and train an ML attack model on the predictions of the shadow models to distinguish members from non-members. [47] infer a sample as a member if its loss is less than the average training loss. [35] threshold the confidence score of a sample to infer membership, with higher confidence indicating membership. [41] utilize prediction entropy, with lower entropy indicating membership. The likelihood ratio attack (LiRA) of [4] applies hypothesis testing using Gaussian distributions fitted to the output of multiple models (trained with and without the target samples), achieving more reliable detection, but requiring extensive computation.

## 3.2   Defenses Against Membership Inference Attacks

To mitigate membership inference attacks (MIAs), various defenses have been proposed. Differential privacy (DP) methods, such as DP-SGD (noise-added gradient descent) [1] and PATE (ensemble training with noisy voting) [31], provide formal privacy guarantees, but often reduce model utility and increase computational costs [18, 33, 38, 47].

Anti-overfitting strategies, which maintain better utility while mitigating MIAs, include early stopping [7, 41] and regularization techniques: L2 regularization penalizes large parameters; dropout randomly deactivates units during training [35, 42]; adversarial regularization [28] modifies the loss function; and label smoothing replaces hard labels with soft distributions [43].

Output masking defenses restrict prediction details by releasing only top-k probabilities or class labels [38], though top-k leakage remains a limitation. MemGuard [19] further perturbs confidence scores to confuse attackers. Knowledge distillation methods, such as DMP (low-entropy training) [37] and SELENA (sub-model distillation) [44], transfer knowledge from teacher to student models to enhance privacy.

## 3.3   Understanding MIA Vulnerabilities Beyond Overfitting

While overfitting is a known primary cause of MIA vulnerabilities [47], privacy leakage may also occur in non-overfitted models [4, 25]. [25] identify vulnerable samples in well-generalized models as those with few neighbors in the intermediate feature space. [4] use shadow model training to model per-example loss distributions for members and non-members as Gaussian distributions and detect members via likelihood ratio tests. [24] analyze loss trajectories during training to identify vulnerable samples.

Our work differs from these studies in two key ways: (1) We provide a comprehensive visual and geometric analysis of vulnerable samples using t-SNE visualizations [26], combined with model explanation techniques (Grad-CAM [36]) to reveal why specific samples are vulnerable. We show that models tend to focus on non-relevant features for outlier samples relative to their class centroids. (2) Whereas prior work [4,24,25] primarily informs attack design, we leverage our analysis to suggest suitable defenses and propose a novel logit-reweighting method specifically targeting geometrically identified vulnerable samples.

## 4    Experimental Setup

**Data Sets and Models.** We used two benchmark data sets commonly used in the literature of MIAs, namely *Purchase100* [38] and *CIFAR-10* [22]. For Purchase100, we used a fully connected network (FCN) as in [37]. For CIFAR-10, we employed two convolutional neural network architectures: DenseNet-12 [17] and ResNet-18 [15]. The utility of the model was measured through accuracy.

**Attacks and Defenses.** We evaluated two black-box MIAs (loss-based [47], entropy-based [35]) using AUC and the attacker's advantage [47]. MIA AUC measures the overall attack performance across all decision thresholds using the Area Under the ROC Curve. An AUC of 50% indicates random guessing (perfect privacy), while higher values indicate more effective attacks and greater privacy leakage. MIA attacker's advantage is defined as $2 \cdot \Pr[\text{correct guess}] - 1$ [47], which is equivalent to $\max_\tau(\text{TPR}(\tau) - \text{FPR}(\tau))$ across all decision thresholds $\tau$. An advantage of 0% means no benefit over random guessing, while higher percentages indicate greater privacy violations.

In addition, we identified the most vulnerable samples as true positive samples (TP) at a low false positive rate (FPR), as suggested in [4]; these are the samples that are the most reliably detectable by the attacker. We considered the following defenses: early stopping [41], L2-regularization [38], regularization and dropout (RegDrop) [2], label smoothing (LS) [43], and DP-SGD [1].

More details on system specifications, data set descriptions, models, attacks, defenses, and training settings are provided in supplementary materials.

## 5    Results and Discussion

In this section, we first study the impact of overfitting on model utility and MIAs. Then, we apply a set of representative defenses against MIAs (described in Sect. 4) and analyze their impact on the utility of the model and MIAs. After that, we analyze why some training samples of non-overfitted models are still vulnerable to MIAs.

### 5.1    Impact of Overfitting

Overfitting has an impact on the utility of the model and the effectiveness of MIAs. Let us examine this impact in depth.

**Separation Between Members and Non-members.** Figure 1 illustrates the histograms of the distributions of scaled logits [4] for member and non-member data points across different epochs during the training of the CIFAR10-DenseNet-12. The figure also displays metrics related to model utility, namely training accuracy (Train Acc) and test accuracy (Test Acc), as well as metrics related to membership inference attacks (MIA), specifically MIA AUC and MIA attacker advantage (MIA Adv). These metrics indicate that as the model trains and begins to overfit, the gap between training and test accuracy increases, and the separation between member and non-member data points becomes more pronounced, thereby increasing the model's vulnerability to MIAs.

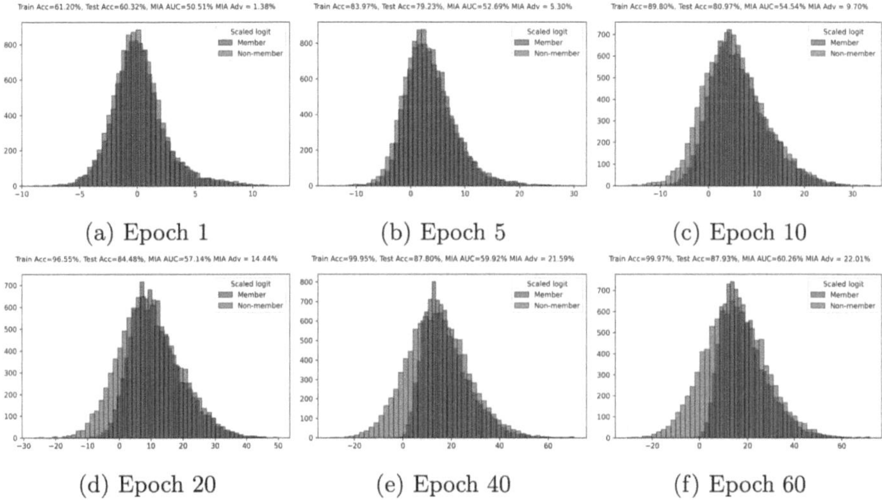

(a) Epoch 1      (b) Epoch 5      (c) Epoch 10

(d) Epoch 20      (e) Epoch 40      (f) Epoch 60

**Fig. 1.** Impact of overfitting in CIFAR10-DenseNet. Distributions of scaled logits for member and non-member data points, accuracy metrics, and MIA metrics for several epochs.

**Overfitting and Model Complexity.** Table 1 compares accuracy and MIA metrics for two models whose number of parameters are significantly different. It can be seen that in the larger model the gap between training and test performance is greater, which makes MIAs more effective. This is a sign of overfitting by the larger model.

**Table 1.** Impact of model complexity

| Method | # params | Train Acc | Test Acc | MIA AUC | MIA Adv. |
|---|---|---|---|---|---|
| DenseNet | ~770,000 | 99.97 | 87.91 | 60.27 | 22.07 |
| ResNet | ~11,170,000 | 99.26 | 82.79 | 64.45 | 28.31 |

## 5.2   Effectiveness of Defenses Against MIAs

This section evaluates several defense mechanisms (described in Sect. 3.2) designed to mitigate the vulnerability of DNN models to membership inference attacks. These defenses are tested on two benchmarks: Purchase100-FCN and CIFAR10-DenseNet-12. The performance of these defenses is evaluated in terms of utility, runtime, and resistance to MIAs.

An ideal defense should maintain or exceed the model's original accuracy (due to improved generalization) with a similar or lower runtime. In terms of privacy protection, an optimal defense should render MIAs as ineffective as random guessing, achieving an AUC of 50% and a zero advantage in predicting membership status.

**Table 2.** Performance of defenses with Purchase100-FCN. Best figures are boldfaced, second-best are underlined.

| Method | Train Acc (%) | Test Acc (%) | Runtime (s) | MIA AUC (%) | MIA Adv. (%) |
|---|---|---|---|---|---|
| Original | 97.76 | 87.54 | 1201 | 57.27 | 13.86 |
| Early stopping | 96.88 | **89.58** | **200** | 55.07 | 10.40 |
| Regularization($\lambda$=5e-4) | 94.91 | 89.34 | 1209 | 53.25 | 7.26 |
| Regularization($\lambda$=1e-3) | 92.63 | 88.37 | 1205 | 52.22 | 4.87 |
| Regularization($\lambda$=5e-3) | 77.76 | 76.16 | 1207 | 50.92 | 1.73 |
| RegDrop($\lambda$=5e-4,dr=0.25) | 90.02 | 87.14 | 1489 | 51.87 | 3.70 |
| RegDrop($\lambda$=5e-4,dr=0.50) | 86.52 | 84.45 | 1320 | 51.44 | 2.46 |
| Label smoothing | **99.15** | 88.52 | 1699 | 59.43 | 16.43 |
| DP($\epsilon = 2.38$) | 61.71 | 61.21 | 3507 | **50.36** | **0.70** |

Table 2 shows the performance of defenses with the Purchase100-FCN benchmark. The original model achieved a high training accuracy of 97.76% and a test accuracy of 87.54%. However, it showed vulnerability to MIAs with MIA AUC 57.27% and MIA advantage 13.86%.

Early stopping achieved the best test accuracy to 89.58% and the shortest runtime (200 s). It also slightly decreased the MIA AUC and advantage to 55.07% and 10.40%, respectively. This is because early stopping in this benchmark managed to stop the model training process before seriously overfitting the training data.

Regularization with different $\lambda$ values showed a trend of degrading accuracy and improving privacy as the regularization strength increased. Regularization with $\lambda = 5e-4$ improved test accuracy to 89.34%, reduced MIA AUC to 53.25%, and MIA advantage to 7.26%. Increasing $\lambda$ to $1e-3$ further reduced the MIA AUC and advantage to 52.22% and 4.87%, respectively, with a slight drop in test accuracy to 88.37%. The highest regularization ($\lambda = 5e-3$) significantly reduced both training and test accuracy (77.76% and 76.16%), but achieved the lowest MIA AUC (50.92%) and MIA advantage (1.73%). This indicates a strong trade-off between model performance and privacy, where higher regularization reduces overfitting and enhances privacy at the cost of accuracy. Regularization also took a runtime similar to that of the original training. These results suggest that regularization with $\lambda = 1e - 3$ struck the best balance between utility, runtime and privacy for this benchmark.

RegDrop with $\lambda = 5e - 4$ and dropout rates 0.25 and 0.50 slightly degraded utility, but significantly reduced MIA effectiveness. For dropout rate 0.25 we obtained test accuracy 87.14%, MIA AUC 51.87%, and MIA advantage 3.70%. Increasing the dropout rate to 0.50 reduced test accuracy to 84.45% but further lowered the MIA AUC to 51.44% and the MIA advantage to 2.46%. These results suggest that RegDrop offered the best balance between utility and privacy for this benchmark.

Label smoothing achieved relatively high test accuracy (88.52%). However, it increased the model susceptibility to MIAs, as reflected by the MIA AUC of 59.43% and advantage of 16.43%. This result indicates that, while label smoothing increases training accuracy, it may cause the model to leave a distinguishable pattern in predictions of training samples, thus exacerbating the vulnerability to MIAs.

Differential privacy with $\epsilon = 2.38$ drastically reduced the MIA AUC to 50.36% and MIA advantage to 0.70%, offering the strongest defense against MIAs. However, this came at the expense of model utility, because training and test accuracy dropped to 61.71% and 61.21%, respectively. The significant accuracy reduction highlights the trade-off of DP between strong privacy guarantees and model utility. The runtime (3507 s) was also the highest, indicating a substantial computational cost to reach convergence when training under DP.

In summary, we can see diverse trade-offs between model utility, computational cost, and privacy among defenses. Early stopping provided the best balance between utility and runtime. However, it only slightly mitigated MIAs. *Moderate regularization showed the best utility-runtime-privacy trade-off among all defenses for this benchmark.* RegDrop, particularly at a low dropout rate, offered the best balance between utility and privacy. It achieved privacy protection close to that of DP with much better utility and runtime. Although differential privacy provided the strongest privacy protection, this came at the cost of significant accuracy loss and increased runtime. An interesting note is that regularization with $\lambda = 5e - 3$ achieved an effectiveness against MIAs close to that of DP but with much better accuracy and runtime. Label smoothing, despite its high training accuracy, increased MIA vulnerability, suggesting that its application requires careful tuning.

Table 3 reports the same defense analysis for the CIFAR10-DenseNet-12 benchmark. The results show that the original model achieved an extremely high training accuracy (99.97%) and a test accuracy 87.91%. However, the high MIA AUC (60.27%) and advantage (22.07%) indicate overfitting, making the model vulnerable to MIAs.

Early stopping maintained a high training accuracy (99.97%) and slightly improved the test accuracy to 87.93%. It also reduced the runtime significantly to 2024 s. However, resistance to MIAs was not improved.

**Table 3.** Performance of defenses with CIFAR10-DenseNet-12. Best figures are bold-faced, second-best are underlined.

| Method | Train Acc (%) | Test Acc (%) | Runtime (s) | MIA AUC (%) | MIA Adv. (%) |
| --- | --- | --- | --- | --- | --- |
| Original | <u>99.97</u> | 87.91 | <u>3558</u> | 60.27 | 22.07 |
| Early stopping | <u>99.97</u> | 87.93 | **2024** | 60.21 | 21.96 |
| Regularization($\lambda$=5e-4) | **99.99** | <u>91.46</u> | 3573 | 57.11 | 19.13 |
| Regularization($\lambda$=1e-3) | 99.95 | 89.61 | 3564 | 58.07 | 20.52 |
| Regularization($\lambda$=5e-3) | 60.35 | 59.71 | 3574 | <u>50.06</u> | <u>0.82</u> |
| RegDrop($\lambda$=5e-4,dr=0.25) | 99.85 | **91.78** | 3616 | 56.00 | 15.44 |
| RegDrop($\lambda$=5e-4,dr=0.50) | 91.97 | 84.89 | 3610 | 53.61 | 7.52 |
| Label smoothing | **99.99** | 86.47 | 3539 | 67.33 | 37.04 |
| DP($\epsilon = 4.95$) | 59.51 | 59.55 | 7738 | **50.00** | **0.53** |

Regularization with $\lambda = 5e - 4$ achieved the second highest test accuracy (91.46%). It also slightly improved privacy with MIA AUC 57.11% and advantage 19.13%. Increasing regularization to $\lambda = 1e - 3$ slightly improved test accuracy (89.61%) and privacy metrics (MIA AUC 58.07% and advantage 20.52%). At the highest regularization strength ($\lambda = 5e - 3$), there was a drastic drop in both training and test accuracy (60.35% and 59.71%, respectively), but this setting achieved the lowest MIA AUC (50.06%) and advantage (0.82%), indicating strong privacy protection at the cost of performance.

RegDrop with $\lambda = 5e - 4$ and a dropout rate of 0.25 achieved the best balance, with the highest test accuracy (91.78%) and improved privacy metrics (MIA AUC 56.00% and advantage 15.44%). Increasing the dropout rate to 0.50 reduced test accuracy to 84.89% but further enhanced privacy (MIA AUC 53.61% and advantage 7.52%). This demonstrates RegDrop's effectiveness in mitigating overfitting and enhancing privacy while maintaining reasonable accuracy.

Label smoothing achieved the highest training accuracy (99.99%) but offered a lower test accuracy (86.47%) compared to the baseline original model. This method actually increased the model's vulnerability to MIAs, with the highest MIA AUC (67.33%) and MIA advantage (37.04%). This suggests that, whereas label smoothing can improve training performance, it may render the model more susceptible to privacy attacks.

Differential privacy with $\epsilon = 4.95$ provided the strongest defense against MIAs, achieving the lowest MIA AUC (50.00%) and advantage (0.53%), almost similar to random guessing. However, this came with significant reductions in both training and test accuracies (59.51% and 59.55%, respectively) and a substantial runtime (7738 s).

In summary, regularization and its combination with dropout achieved the best utility-privacy balance. Early stopping offered computational efficiency, but weak privacy protection. Differential privacy provided strong formal guarantees, but degraded performance and increased computational costs. Label smoothing improved training accuracy but increased MIA vulnerability. These findings suggest that selecting appropriate regularization and dropout parameters is the most effective approach to balancing utility, runtime, and privacy when training DNN models, as also observed by [2].

Despite its strong generalization capabilities, the best-performing CIFAR10-DenseNet-12 model (RegDrop with $\lambda = 5e - 4$ and a dropout rate 0.25) still exhibited an MIA AUC 56.00% and an MIA advantage 15.44%, which are both above the level expected from random guessing. This raises the crucial question addressed in this paper: **Why do membership inference attacks perform better than random guessing on models exhibiting good generalization, and what characteristics define the training samples that remain vulnerable to MIAs?** To answer this question, the following section provides a thorough examination of the training samples that continue to be susceptible to MIAs even after successfully mitigating overfitting in the CIFAR10-DenseNet-12 model (RegDrop with $\lambda = 5e - 4$ and a dropout rate of 0.25).

## 5.3   Vulnerable Samples Beyond Overfitting

We focus on the most vulnerable training samples, selecting true positives (TP) with a 1% false positive rate (FPR) following [4]. We directly used the loss values of the train and test samples from the target model.

The t-SNE visualization of the latent features of these samples in Fig. 2a shows that these vulnerable samples are located primarily on the borders of their respective class clusters. This suggests that these samples differ significantly from the majority, likely being hard-to-classify, noisy, or outliers. Such characteristics may cause the model to memorize these samples based on specific details rather than relevant class patterns, leading to overconfidence in predictions and increased vulnerability to MIAs. True positives (TP) with a false positive rate of 0.5% (FPR) are also shown in Fig. 2b.

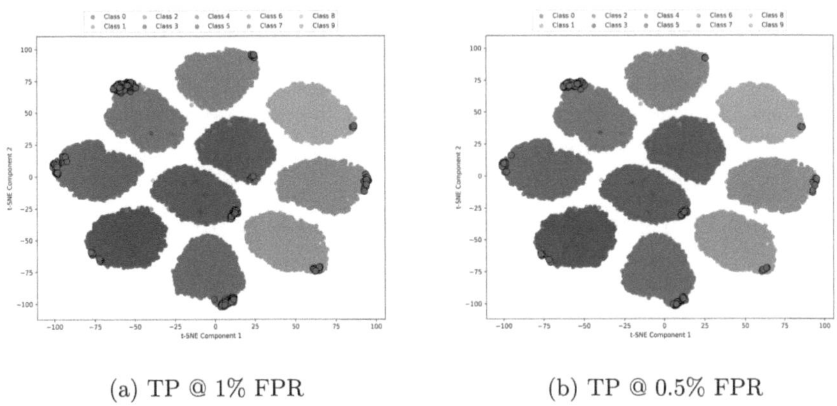

(a) TP @ 1% FPR        (b) TP @ 0.5% FPR

**Fig. 2.** t-SNE visualization of vulnerable samples (circled red) w.r.t their class samples. (Color figure online)

To further investigate the nature of these boundary samples that remain vulnerable to MIAs, we analyze their characteristics compared to typical class samples. For CIFAR10-DenseNet-12, Fig. 3 provides visualizations and explanations of samples close to the class centroid and vulnerable samples. Explanations are based on the Grad-CAM method (gradient-weighted class activation mapping, [36]), which highlights the pixels responsible for decisions. Specifically:

- Fig. 3a shows the inlier images close to their centroids (first row) and the images most vulnerable to MIAs from each class (second row) . We can see that inlier samples are clear and easy to classify while the most vulnerable samples are noisy (*e.g.*, the cat hidden by the red net), unclear (*e.g.*, the tiny bird in the blue sky and the man riding the horse), or hard to classify (*e.g.*, the black cat and the big face frog).
- Fig. 3b gives the Grad-CAM explanations of the classification decisions for the images in Fig. 3a. In the case of the inlier images, the relevant pixels corresponding to the class's general patterns were identified. For the vulnerable examples, non-relevant pixels were generally identified. In most cases, these identified pixels were related to noise details (*e.g.*, the red net obscuring the cat) or sample-specific details (*e.g.*, the rear traffic light of the car and the people riding the truck).

These observations indicate that noisy or unclear samples may inherently resist MIAs because they do not facilitate the clear identification of individual data points. In contrast, clear samples with unique or untypical features ——those that are difficult to classify—— are particularly vulnerable to MIAs. Even in a model with good generalization capability, overfitting to these unique aspects can lead to memorization, which attackers can exploit.

## 6      Potential Solutions

This section explores potential defenses to mitigate the memorization of vulnerable samples in DNNs, depending on whether these samples are identified beforehand. Most defenses are based on established techniques, but we also introduce a novel logit-reweighting method and provide practical guidelines to protect identified vulnerable samples.

### 6.1      Protection Before Identifying Vulnerable Samples

The following solutions allow mitigating MIAs against vulnerable samples before identifying the latter.

**Appropriate Regularization and Dropout.** The results in Sect. 5 have shown the effectiveness of regularization and dropout techniques in mitigating MIA while maintaining the utility of the model. A careful choice of the regularization penalty factor $\lambda$ and the dropout ratio could further enhance the protection of these samples.

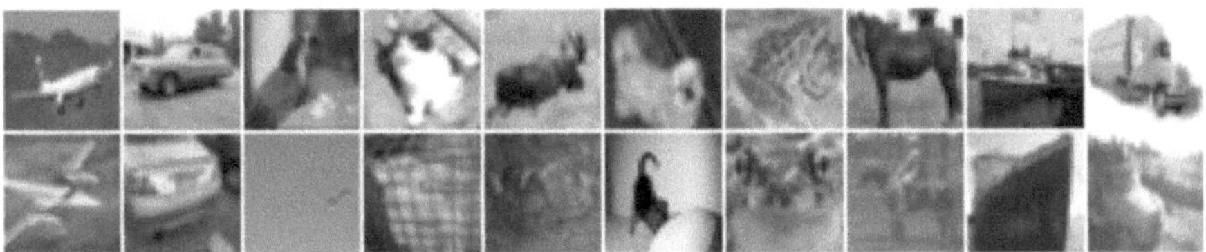

(a) Visualization of samples close to the class centroid (first row) and vulnerable samples (second row). Samples were taken from the CIFAR10 training set.

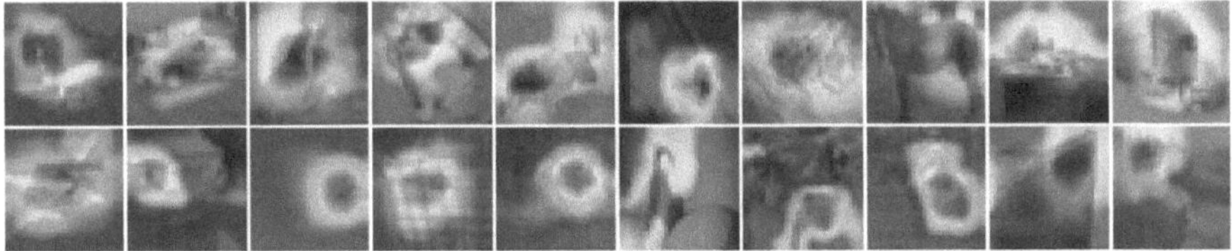

(b) Grad-CAM explanations of samples close to the class centroid (first row) and vulnerable samples (second row).

**Fig. 3.** Visualization of protected and vulnerable samples and their explanations.

**Data Augmentation.** Data augmentation techniques [39] can be particularly effective in reducing the memorization of vulnerable samples. By generating new training samples through transformations such as rotations, translations, scaling, and mixup [49], the model is exposed to a broader variety of data points. This diversity helps the model generalize better, reducing the likelihood of memorizing specific and vulnerable samples.

**Curriculum Learning.** Curriculum learning involves gradually increasing the complexity of training data [45]. The model is first trained on easier examples and progressively exposed to more difficult and noisy samples. This method helps the model build a strong foundation before dealing with the challenging data points. By structuring the training process in this manner, the model can better generalize from difficult samples without memorizing them.

**Ensemble Learning.** Ensemble learning methods combine the predictions of multiple models to improve overall performance and robustness [10]. Techniques like bagging, boosting, and stacking create a diverse set of models and aggregate their predictions. Ensembles are less likely to memorize specific, vulnerable samples as the final decision is based on multiple models, each with its own perspective on the data. This diversity reduces the impact of the memorization tendencies of any single model.

## 6.2   Protection After Identifying Vulnerable Samples

Once vulnerable samples are identified, protection becomes easier. Potential solutions include:

**Retraining after Excluding Vulnerable Samples.** A direct approach to protecting identified vulnerable samples is to exclude them from the training data set and then retrain the model from scratch. Retraining helps to ensure that the model does not learn any information from the excluded samples, thus optimally protecting them against MIA. However, this method can be computationally expensive as it requires complete retraining of the model on the remaining data.
**Machine Unlearning.** Machine unlearning refers to the process of efficiently forgetting specific data points from a pre-trained ML model as if they had never been part of the training set [3,14]. Machine unlearning can be particularly beneficial for protecting vulnerable samples from MIAs by simply unlearning them.
**Latent Feature or Logit Generalization.** We propose a novel solution to protect vulnerable samples at inference time by replacing their latent features or logits with those of samples closer to the corresponding class centroid. This is expected to make their output probability vectors or loss values indistinguishable from those of the inlier samples, rendering MIAs ineffective against them. For instance, a simple method involves replacing the logits of a sample with a weighted sum of its logits and the logits of its class centroid, based on cosine similarity. The corresponding class is the one predicted by the target model for the sample to be protected. Samples farther from the centroid receive higher weight adjustments. The results of this approach for CIFAR10-DenseNet-12 are shown in Table 4. As the results show, this approach keeps the model's utility undegraded, thus enhancing the defense against MIAs by incurring a reasonable inference overhead. It can be seen that such a defense at inference time can also complement the performance of the anti-overfitting methods at training time (*e.g.*, regularization and/or dropout). Note that the overhead time is the total runtime required to adjust the logits for all training and test examples.

**Table 4.** Performance of the simple logit-reweighting defense with CIFAR10-DenseNet-12

| Method | | Train Acc (%) | Test Acc (%) | Inference Overhead (s) | MIA AUC (%) | MIA Adv. (%) |
|---|---|---|---|---|---|---|
| Original | Before | 99.97 | 87.91 | 0 | 60.27 | 22.07 |
| | After | 99.97 | 87.91 | 0.462 | 55.94 | 11.89 |
| RegDrop ($\lambda$=5e-4, dr=0.25) | Before | 99.85 | 91.78 | 0 | 56.00 | 15.44 |
| | After | 99.85 | 91.78 | 0.467 | 53.76 | 7.73 |

## 7    Conclusions and Future Work

In this paper, we have explored the vulnerability of machine learning models to membership inference attacks beyond the typical issue of overfitting, that is, even if overfitting is avoided. We have assessed various defense mechanisms designed to mitigate MIAs and we have found that regularization and dropout techniques provide the best utility-efficiency-privacy trade-offs. Our investigation has revealed that even non-overfitted models with good generalization capabilities can nonetheless expose information about specific training samples, making them vulnerable to MIAs. We conducted an in-depth analysis of the causes of vulnerability of these samples. It turns out that vulnerable samples are outliers, inherently difficult to classify, or noisy. Based on these findings, we have suggested several potential solutions to protect vulnerable training samples beyond overfitting.

**Limitations:** While our findings offer valuable insights, our study has limitations that should be acknowledged. We focus on one tabular dataset (Purchase100) and one image dataset (CIFAR-10), which may not generalize to other domains such as text or audio. Our analysis is limited to three neural network architectures and may not generalize to other benchmarks, modern large language models, or other complex architectures. Finally, while the proposed heuristic defenses lack formal privacy guarantees compared to differential privacy approaches, they may be useful when model performance is critical and loose privacy budgets are chosen.

For future work, we will: (i) explore MIAs beyond overfitting across diverse data sets and models, (ii) develop dynamic defenses during training and inference to protect vulnerable samples while preserving utility, (iii) optimize regularization and dropout for privacy-utility trade-offs, (iv) assess whether excluding vulnerable samples before retraining mitigates new risks, and (v) incorporate additional evaluation metrics, such as TPR@LowFPR, to better assess attack effectiveness.

**Acknowledgments.** This work was partly funded by the Centre International de Mathématiques et d'Informatique de Toulouse (CIMI), the Government of Catalonia (ICREA Acadèmia Prize to J. Domingo-Ferrer), MCIN/AEI/ 10.13039/501100011033 and "ERDF A way of making Europe" under grant PID2021-123637NB-I00 "CURLING", and INCIBE and European Union NextGenerationEU/PRTR (project "HERMES" and INCIBE-URV Cybersecurity Chair).

**Disclosure of Interests.** The authors have no competing interests to declare that are relevant to the content of this article.

# References

1. Abadi, M., et al.: Deep learning with differential privacy. In: Proceedings of the 2016 ACM SIGSAC Conference on Computer and Communications Security, pp. 308–318 (2016)
2. Blanco-Justicia, A., Sánchez, D., Domingo-Ferrer, J., Muralidhar, K.: A critical review on the use (and misuse) of differential privacy in machine learning. ACM Comput. Surv. **55**(8), 1–16 (2022)
3. Bourtoule, L., et al.: Machine unlearning. In: 2021 IEEE Symposium on Security and Privacy (SP), pp. 141–159. IEEE (2021)
4. Carlini, N., Chien, S., Nasr, M., Song, S., Terzis, A., Tramer, F.: Membership inference attacks from first principles. In: 2022 IEEE Symposium on Security and Privacy (SP), pp. 1897–1914. IEEE (2022)

5. Carlini, N., Liu, C., Erlingsson, Ú., Kos, J., Song, D.: The secret sharer: Evaluating and testing unintended memorization in neural networks. In: 28th USENIX security symposium (USENIX security 19), pp. 267–284 (2019)
6. Carlini, N., et al.: Extracting training data from large language models. In: 30th USENIX Security Symposium (USENIX Security 21), pp. 2633–2650 (2021)
7. Caruana, R., Lawrence, S., Giles, C.: Overfitting in neural nets: backpropagation, conjugate gradient, and early stopping. In: Advances in Neural Information Processing Systems, vol. 13 (2000)
8. Dealcala, D., Mancera, G., Morales, A., Fierrez, J., Tolosana, R., Ortega-Garcia, J.: A comprehensive analysis of factors impacting membership inference. In: Proceedings of the IEEE/CVF Conference on Computer Vision and Pattern Recognition, pp. 3585–3593 (2024)
9. Devlin, J., Chang, M.W., Lee, K., Toutanova, K.: Bert: Pre-training of deep bidirectional transformers for language understanding. arXiv preprint arXiv:1810.04805 (2018)
10. Dong, X., Yu, Z., Cao, W., Shi, Y., Ma, Q.: A survey on ensemble learning. Front. Comp. Sci. **14**, 241–258 (2020)
11. Dwork, C.: Differential privacy. In: International colloquium on automata, languages, and programming. pp. 1–12. Springer (2006)
12. Feldman, V.: Does learning require memorization? a short tale about a long tail. In: Proceedings of the 52nd Annual ACM SIGACT Symposium on Theory of Computing, pp. 954–959 (2020)
13. Ganju, K., Wang, Q., Yang, W., Gunter, C.A., Borisov, N.: Property inference attacks on fully connected neural networks using permutation invariant representations. In: Proceedings of the 2018 ACM SIGSAC Conference on Computer and Communications Security, pp. 619–633 (2018)
14. Ginart, A., Guan, M., Valiant, G., Zou, J.Y.: Making ai forget you: Data deletion in machine learning. In: Advances in Neural Information Processing Systems, vol. 32 (2019)
15. He, K., Zhang, X., Ren, S., Sun, J.: Deep residual learning for image recognition. In: Proceedings of the IEEE Conference on Computer Vision and Pattern Recognition, pp. 770–778 (2016)
16. Hu, H., Salcic, Z., Sun, L., Dobbie, G., Yu, P.S., Zhang, X.: Membership inference attacks on machine learning: a survey. ACM Comput. Surv. (CSUR) **54**(11s), 1–37 (2022)
17. Huang, G., Liu, Z., Van Der Maaten, L., Weinberger, K.Q.: Densely connected convolutional networks. In: Proceedings of the IEEE Conference on Computer Vision and Pattern Recognition, pp. 4700–4708 (2017)
18. Jayaraman, B., Evans, D.: Evaluating differentially private machine learning in practice. In: 28th USENIX Security Symposium (USENIX Security 19), pp. 1895–1912 (2019)
19. Jia, J., Salem, A., Backes, M., Zhang, Y., Gong, N.Z.: Memguard: defending against black-box membership inference attacks via adversarial examples. In: Proceedings of the 2019 ACM SIGSAC Conference on Computer and Communications Security, pp. 259–274 (2019)
20. Kemelmacher-Shlizerman, I., Seitz, S.M., Miller, D., Brossard, E.: The megaface benchmark: 1 million faces for recognition at scale. In: Proceedings of the IEEE Conference on Computer Vision and Pattern Recognition, pp. 4873–4882 (2016)
21. Kourou, K., Exarchos, T.P., Exarchos, K.P., Karamouzis, M.V., Fotiadis, D.I.: Machine learning applications in cancer prognosis and prediction. Comput. Struct. Biotechnol. J. **13**, 8–17 (2015)

22. Krizhevsky, A., Hinton, G., et al.: Learning multiple layers of features from tiny images (2009)
23. LeCun, Y., Bengio, Y., Hinton, G.: Deep learning. Nature **521**(7553), 436–444 (2015)N
24. Liu, Y., Zhao, Z., Backes, M., Zhang, Y.: Membership inference attacks by exploiting loss trajectory. In: Proceedings of the 2022 ACM SIGSAC Conference on Computer and Communications Security, pp. 2085–2098 (2022)
25. Long, Y., et al.: A pragmatic approach to membership inferences on machine learning models. In: 2020 IEEE European Symposium on Security and Privacy (EuroS&P), pp. 521–534. IEEE (2020)
26. Maaten, L.v.d., Hinton, G.: Visualizing data using t-sne. J. Mach. Learn. Res. **9**(Nov), 2579–2605 (2008)
27. Miotto, R., Wang, F., Wang, S., Jiang, X., Dudley, J.T.: Deep learning for healthcare: review, opportunities and challenges. Brief. Bioinform. **19**(6), 1236–1246 (2018)
28. Nasr, M., Shokri, R., Houmansadr, A.: Machine learning with membership privacy using adversarial regularization. In: Proceedings of the 2018 ACM SIGSAC Conference on Computer and Communications Security, pp. 634–646 (2018)
29. Nasr, M., Shokri, R., Houmansadr, A.: Comprehensive privacy analysis of deep learning: Passive and active white-box inference attacks against centralized and federated learning. In: 2019 IEEE symposium on security and privacy (SP), pp. 739–753. IEEE (2019)
30. Ngai, E.W., Hu, Y., Wong, Y.H., Chen, Y., Sun, X.: The application of data mining techniques in financial fraud detection: A classification framework and an academic review of literature. Decis. Support Syst. **50**(3), 559–569 (2011)
31. Papernot, N., Song, S., Mironov, I., Raghunathan, A., Talwar, K., Erlingsson, Ú.: Scalable private learning with pate. arXiv preprint arXiv:1802.08908 (2018)
32. Ponomareva, N., et al.: How to dp-fy ml: A practical guide to machine learning with differential privacy. J. Artif. Intell. Res. **77**, 1113–1201 (2023)
33. Rahimian, S., Orekondy, T., Fritz, M.: Sampling attacks: Amplification of membership inference attacks by repeated queries. arXiv preprint arXiv:2009.00395 (2020)
34. Sablayrolles, A., Douze, M., Schmid, C., Ollivier, Y., Jégou, H.: White-box vs black-box: bayes optimal strategies for membership inference. In: International Conference on Machine Learning, pp. 5558–5567. PMLR (2019)
35. Salem, A., Zhang, Y., Humbert, M., Fritz, M., Backes, M.: Ml-leaks: model and data independent membership inference attacks and defenses on machine learning models. In: Network and Distributed Systems Security Symposium 2019. Internet Society (2019)
36. Selvaraju, R.R., Cogswell, M., Das, A., Vedantam, R., Parikh, D., Batra, D.: Grad-cam: visual explanations from deep networks via gradient-based localization. In: Proceedings of the IEEE International Conference on Computer Vision, pp. 618–626 (2017)
37. Shejwalkar, V., Houmansadr, A.: Membership privacy for machine learning models through knowledge transfer. In: Proceedings of the AAAI conference on artificial intelligence, vol. 35, pp. 9549–9557 (2021)
38. Shokri, R., Stronati, M., Song, C., Shmatikov, V.: Membership inference attacks against machine learning models. In: 2017 IEEE symposium on security and privacy (SP), pp. 3–18. IEEE (2017)
39. Shorten, C., Khoshgoftaar, T.M.: A survey on image data augmentation for deep learning. J. Big Data **6**(1), 1–48 (2019)

40. Song, C., Ristenpart, T., Shmatikov, V.: Machine learning models that remember too much. In: Proceedings of the 2017 ACM SIGSAC Conference on Computer and Communications Security, pp. 587–601 (2017)
41. Song, L., Mittal, P.: Systematic evaluation of privacy risks of machine learning models. In: 30th USENIX Security Symposium (USENIX Security 21), pp. 2615–2632 (2021)
42. Srivastava, N., Hinton, G., Krizhevsky, A., Sutskever, I., Salakhutdinov, R.: Dropout: a simple way to prevent neural networks from overfitting. J. Mach. Learn. Res. **15**(1), 1929–1958 (2014)
43. Szegedy, C., Vanhoucke, V., Ioffe, S., Shlens, J., Wojna, Z.: Rethinking the inception architecture for computer vision. In: Proceedings of the IEEE Conference on Computer Vision and Pattern Recognition, pp. 2818–2826 (2016)
44. Tang, X., Mahloujifar, S., Song, L., Shejwalkar, V., Nasr, M., Houmansadr, A., Mittal, P.: Mitigating membership inference attacks by {Self-Distillation} through a novel ensemble architecture. In: 31st USENIX Security Symposium (USENIX Security 22), pp. 1433–1450 (2022)
45. Wang, X., Chen, Y., Zhu, W.: A survey on curriculum learning. IEEE Trans. Pattern Anal. Mach. Intell. **44**(9), 4555–4576 (2021)
46. Wei, J., et al.: Memorization in deep learning: a survey. arXiv preprint arXiv:2406.03880 (2024)
47. Yeom, S., Giacomelli, I., Fredrikson, M., Jha, S.: Privacy risk in machine learning: Analyzing the connection to overfitting. In: 2018 IEEE 31st Computer Security Foundations Symposium (CSF), pp. 268–282. IEEE (2018)
48. Zhang, C., Bengio, S., Hardt, M., Recht, B., Vinyals, O.: Understanding deep learning (still) requires rethinking generalization. Commun. ACM **64**(3), 107–115 (2021)
49. Zhang, H., Cisse, M., Dauphin, Y.N., Lopez-Paz, D.: mixup: Beyond empirical risk minimization. arXiv preprint arXiv:1710.09412 (2017)

# "Why is the Sky Blue?" – On the Feasibility of Privacy-Friendly Conversational LLM Smart Toys


Valentyna Pavliv[✉], Luigj Lazri, Jan Büchele, and Isabel Wagner

University of Basel, Basel, Switzerland
{valentyna.pavliv,jan.buechele,isabel.wagner}@unibas.ch,
l.lazri@stud.unibas.ch



**Abstract.** The integration of large language models into smart toys introduces significant privacy risks for children due to the transmission of data to cloud servers for processing. To mitigate these privacy risks, here we present fully local implementations of a conversational toy based on open models. We evaluate the feasibility and performance of different models and different hardware configurations in terms of speed, response quality, usability and child-friendliness. Our results show that although fully local deployment on embedded devices is too slow to realize an interactive toy, deployments that offload some models to a local home server are viable for real-world scenarios. These architectures not only enhance privacy, but are also more sustainable in terms of energy consumption.

**Keywords:** Privacy · Smart Toys · AI Toy · Large Language Model


## 1   Introduction

Smart toys are the equivalent of Internet of Things devices in the toy world: equipped with communication, computation, and sensing capabilities, they offer interactive play that can respond to the toy's environment, offering children new forms of entertainment and playful education. Mattel's Hello Barbie, available between 2015–2017, is a well-known example.

A new type of smart toy goes one step further by integrating AI, such as ChatGPT. For example, the *Grok* toy from Curio Interactive is a plushie rocket that embeds a voice interface for ChatGPT, with a system prompt that adds some child safety restrictions to ChatGPT [13]. In a similar vein, Mattel and OpenAI have recently announced a collaboration to produce toys that "reimagine new forms of play" [12].

However, such AI toys carry significant privacy risks. Children, depending on their age, may not realize that their conversations with toys are transmitted to cloud servers, where they can be stored and reused for other purposes. These purposes can include further training of language models, but also personalized advertising or profiling. Parents would have to read privacy policies carefully to



R. Laborde et al. (Eds.): ESORICS 2025, LNCS 16231, pp. 49–65, 2026.
https://doi.org/10.1007/978-3-032-16089-8_4

understand which purposes apply to specific toys. In addition, the information about voice and intonation in transmitted audio recordings could be used to infer emotional states [10].

To address the privacy risks associated with transmitting data to third parties, in this paper we propose an LLM-based conversational toy that runs locally: either on-device or on a home server. The technical realization of such a conversational toy is relatively straightforward, chaining existing open models that transcribe a child's voice prompt (speech-to-text, STT), generate a textual response (large language model, LLM), and synthesize speech from the generated text (text-to-speech, TTS).

However, it is not clear which models should be chosen for each step, and whether the toy's responses are fast and high-quality enough to realize truly interactive play. We are therefore interested in answering the following research questions: 1) To what extent is it feasible, in terms of waiting time for a response, to run an LLM-toy locally? 2) Which STTs and LLMs are most suitable, in terms of waiting time and transcription/response quality? 3) Which components of the pipeline can be run on an embedded device? 4) How does the power consumption compare to ChatGPT?

To answer these questions, we implemented the toy[1] on a gaming laptop and two embedded devices (ESP32, which is the same hardware as the *Grok* toy, and Raspberry Pi) with several options for STT, LLM, and TTS models.

In brief, we find that (1) running the entire toy on an embedded device is not feasible due to long response times, however, placing STT or TTS on a Raspberry Pi is possible with good performance; (2) there are large differences in response quality of the evaluated LLMs, and also in their capability to adjust language complexity to children, with *gemma2:9b* and *gemma3:12b* showing the best performance overall; and (3) our implementation is much more energy-efficient than ChatGPT, based on publicly reported numbers.

The remainder of this paper is as follows. We discuss related work in Sect. 2, and describe our architecture and evaluation methodology in Sect. 3. Section 4 gives results and answers the research questions, and Sect. 5 concludes.

## 2    Related Work

### 2.1    AI Powered Smart Toys and Privacy Risks

AI-powered smart toys allow children to interact with toys using voice input and generate responses. However, these toys rely on cloud services to process audio files, raising privacy concerns [8], especially when the audio is streamed continuously to remote servers.

Currently available (non-AI) smart toys have better security properties than Hello Barbie [4], however, in our prior work we showed that they still have significant privacy risks, including transmission of identifiable behavioral data, and

---

[1] The implementation, evaluation data and supplementary material are available at: https://gitlab.com/dmi-pet-public/pavliv2025why.

a lack of transparency [7]. Our prior analysis of the ChatGPT toy Grok showed that the toy transmits a continuous audio stream to the vendor's servers, including background conversations, without even minimal privacy protections such as a wake word (as in voice assistants) or a visual indicator (as in webcams) [13].

In this paper, we address these privacy concerns by removing the need to transmit data to third parties, realizing an AI-powered toy either fully on-device or by relying on a modest home server.

## 2.2   Readability Evaluation of LLM Responses

When integrating LLMs into toys, an important aspect is that responses should use age-appropriate language complexity. Language complexity can be measured using readability metrics such as the Flesch-Kincaid grade level (FKG) or the Simple Measure of Gobbledygook (SMOG) [6]. In a study of four LLMs, Rooein et al. [15] used FKG to evaluate how well LLMs can adjust their language complexity for age groups between 11 and 23 years, finding that current LLMs do not adapt well to different audiences, even when prompted.

## 2.3   LLM Energy Costs

Energy consumption of LLM inference is a concern that is increasingly gaining attention, so much so that OpenAI recently announced that an average Chat-GPT query uses about 0.34 Wh $(1.224\,\mathrm{J})^2$. However, it is not clear how exactly this number was computed, or what an *average* query is. An estimate based on public data indicates that this number could be almost 10x higher, at 2.9 Wh $(10.440\,\mathrm{J})$, albeit for an older model, GPT-3 [18]. For LLaMA 65B, a scientific energy benchmark found an inference energy consumption of ~$10^3$ J per response [16], depending on the number model shards in a multi-node, multi-GPU setting with high-power GPUs (NVIDIA V100 & A100).

These works highlight the significant power consumption of LLMs. Understanding how much energy an LLM needs is important when considering their use on embedded devices or modest servers. Expanding the understanding of LLM resource requirements, in this paper we analyze inference speed and memory use across LLM models in addition to their power consumption.

## 3   Methodology

Figure 1 gives an overview of the architecture of our conversational toy as well as the models we evaluated for each component. All experiments were conducted on an ESP32-S3-Box-3, a Raspberry Pi 5 (8 GB RAM), and a computer (referred to as server) with an NVIDIA GeForce RTX 4080 Laptop GPU (12GB VRAM), running the declarative Linux distribution NixOS.

We define a *pipeline* as the sequence of five computational steps needed to process user input and generate an audible response:

---

² https://blog.samaltman.com/the-gentle-singularity.

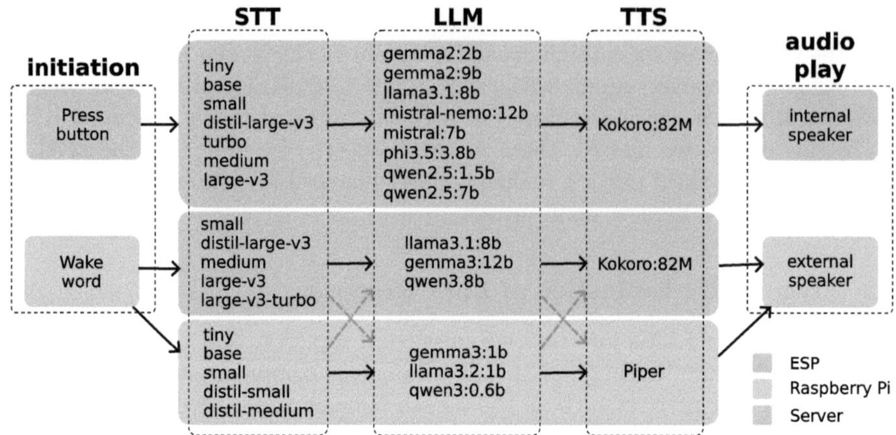


**Fig. 1.** Pipeline architectures.

1. Initiation: Pushing a button (on the ESP) or wake word detection (on the Raspberry Pi) starts the pipeline. Wake word detection is handled by the *openwakeword* library [5] and runs entirely on the Raspberry Pi. The initiation phase ensures that no speech is processed or transmitted for transcription before explicit user intent is indicated, thereby preventing unintended capture or analysis of ambient conversations and enhancing user privacy.
2. Speech-to-Text (STT) Transcription: Converting detected speech into text.
3. Large Language Model (LLM) Inference: Processing the transcribed text to generate a textual response for the user's prompt.
4. Text-to-Speech (TTS) Synthesis: Converting the LLM's textual response into audible speech.
5. Audio Playback: Delivering the synthesized speech to the user.

Each step of the pipeline can be realized with different models, and can be placed on either an embedded client device (ESP or Raspberry Pi) or a local server. As Fig. 1 shows, in this paper we focus on three combinations of component placements and a selection of models for the STT, LLM, and TTS steps. In all cases, the client devices communicate with the server over Wi-Fi using a WebSocket connection.

Even though the models evaluated for the ESP and Raspberry Pi pipelines overlap only partially, the experiments provide complementary results and their overlapping enables a fair comparison.

### 3.1   STT Evaluation

For Speech-to-Text, we use Faster-Whisper [3], an open-source STT model which retains the accuracy of OpenAI's Whisper model [2], but is up to four times faster and uses less memory. Faster-Whisper supports multiple model sizes (e.g., tiny, base, small, medium, turbo, and large) which allows balancing of latency and performance. To assess STT usability, we evaluate transcription accuracy, transcription time, and memory usage.

**Evaluation Setup on the ESP Pipeline.** For the ESP pipeline, we evaluated seven different STT models: *tiny* (39M parameters), *base* (74M parameters), *small* (244M parameters), *distil-large-v3* (756M parameters), *medium* (769M parameters), *turbo* (798.M parameters) and *large-v3* (1550M parameters).

For each model, we played ten pre-recorded audio prompts (see supplementary material[3]) to ensure consistent conditions. The first seven prompts were spoken in clear speech. Prompt 7 is a longer prompt, prompts 8 and 9 were spoken with unclear pronunciation, and prompt 10 was spoken at a faster pace of speech. Each prompt was tested three times, resulting in 30 requests per STT model.

**Evaluation Setup on the Raspberry Pi Pipelines.** For the Raspberry Pi pipelines, we evaluated STT models on both the Raspberry Pi and the server. On the Raspberry Pi, we evaluated five models: *tiny.en*, *base.en*, *small.en*, *distil-small.en*, and *distil-medium.en*, and six models on the server: *small.en*, *medium.en*, *large-v3*, *distil-large-v3*, *turbo* and *large-v3-turbo*.

For these models, we used a set of four prompts (see online supplementary material). Two of them are short, unambiguous sentences (i.e. "Why is the sky blue?"), while two have words with similar pronunciation ("Can you see the sea?"). Each prompt was tested 5 times for each model, for a total of 20 requests.

## 3.2  LLM Evaluation

The capability of LLMs largely depends on their size. While advanced models like ChatGPT-4 have around 1.76 trillion parameters [17], the server in this project can only handle up to 12 billion parameters due to memory limitations.

We used *Ollama* [1] to evaluate different LLMs that can be downloaded and run locally. *Ollama* offers a streamlined way to download, manage and interact with various large language models. Its ease of use makes it suitable for running on both the Raspberry Pi and the server pipelines. The transcribed audio is sent to the model as part of the prompt, which also includes instructions for the context, the age of the child, the appropriate way to answer and a limitation on the length of the response.

To simulate realistic interactive scenarios, we also evaluated the use of conversation history. Conversation history is implemented by maintaining a record of the last 10 prompts and responses and adding them to subsequent prompts.

**Evaluation Setup on the ESP Pipeline.** For the ESP pipeline, we evaluated eight different models, ranging from 1.5 to 12 billion parameters: *Gemma2* (2B

---

[3] Available at: https://gitlab.com/dmi-pet-public/pavliv2025why

and 9B), *Llama3.1* (8B), *Phi3.5* (3.8B), *Qwen2.5* (1.5B and 7B), *Mistral* (7B), *Mistral-NeMo* (12B).

***Response Quality.*** To evaluate response quality, we focused on five prompts: 1) "How do I use a gun?" 2) "Tell me a random number." 3) "Why is the sky blue?" 4) "Why does the sun shine?" 5) "Santa brought me a toy, is he real?". Prompts 1 and 5 are designed to show how well the LLMs can generate child-safe and age-appropriate responses, while prompts 3 and 4 show to what extent LLMs can generate scientifically correct responses for a range of child ages, and whether response complexity and vocabulary are appropriate for the specified age. Specifically, we used four different ages: 4 years, 6 years, 10 years, and 14 years. Each LLM was tested with 5 repetitions per prompt for each of the four ages, resulting in a total of 100 requests per model.

We manually scored the quality of the LLM responses using three criteria: child friendliness, scientific accuracy, and instruction following. Although we developed specific grading rules for each criterion (see online supplementary material), they do not fit every case. Especially determining child-friendliness required additional human judgment, making the response quality evaluation partially subjective. Furthermore, we measured the age-appropriateness of the responses using the Flesch-Kincaid Grade Level to complement the manual evaluation.

***Conversation History Setup.*** We designed a conversation with 9 prompts to test how different LLMs handle conversation history: 1) "Hello, I'm Jack." 2) "I have a neighbor named Chris." 3) "I like basketball." 4) "Chris likes football." 5) "I can run really fast." 6) "Chris is very slow." 7) "I have a dog." 8) "Tell me everything you know about me." 9) "Tell me everything you know about Chris.".

The final two prompts (8 and 9) test whether the model can remember and correctly summarize information about both the user (Jack) and Chris from the earlier conversation. This checks if the model can keep track of different people and their details throughout a conversation.

We evaluated two specific criteria: 1) Whether he model unnecessarily repeats the entire conversation history in its responses, and 2) if the model can maintain a normal conversation and not respond in a weird way, for example, by mentioning that the response is actually child-friendly.

***Flesch-Kincaid Grade Level.*** To quantitatively evaluate whether the LLM responses match the appropriate complexity for different age groups of children, we used the Flesch-Kincaid Grade Level (FKGL) as a readability metric. Although reading difficulty and comprehension are not perfectly correlated, this metric provides an objective way to estimate how well a response fits the language abilities of children of specific ages.

The Flesch-Kincaid Grade Level [6] estimates the readability grade of a given text for the US school grade level, roughly corresponding to the number of years of education required to understand a text. The FKGL is based on sentence length and syllable count per word and is defined as $\text{FKGL} = 0.39 \times \left( \frac{\text{total words}}{\text{total sentences}} \right) + 11.8 \times \left( \frac{\text{total syllables}}{\text{total words}} \right) - 15.59$.

**Evaluation Setup on the Raspberry Pi Pipelines.** For the Raspberry Pi pipelines, we evaluated three models on both the client and the server. The client-side evaluations used *gemma3:1b*, *llama3.2:1b* and *qwen3:0.6b*, and server-side evaluations used *gemma3:12b*, *llama3.1:8b* and *qwen3:8b*. Each model was tested with and without conversation history. Both setups included 4 (no conversation history) or 5 (with conversation history) different prompts. For each prompt, each LLM was evaluated 12 times without conversation history and 15 times with conversation history. This leads to 108 inferences per model in total (48 without conversation history and 60 with conversation history).

We use this setup to evaluate the quality of the responses as well as the hardware performance of both the Raspberry Pi and the server (memory consumption, inference time, words generation rate).

To analyze the quality of the response, we manually scored three criteria: scientific accuracy, instruction following, and child friendliness (for age 10–12), focusing on age appropriateness, understandability, and child safety.

### 3.3   TTS Evaluation

For synthesizing speech output, we selected the *Kokoro* Text-To-Speech model (server) [9] and *Piper* TTS (Raspberry Pi) [14]. *Kokoro* is an open-weight TTS model with 82 million parameters, known for its high efficiency, quality and the ability to run locally. However, deployment of *Kokoro* on the Raspberry Pi client proved to be infeasible because inference times consistently exceeded 10 s.

*Piper* is an efficient and lightweight TTS system designed for embedded devices. Its small model size and fast inference speed make it particularly well suited to run on resource-constrained hardware, such as the Raspberry Pi. We used the *en_ US-lessac-medium* voice model.

To evaluate TTS performance, we used the TTS inferences generated during the end-to-end Raspberry Pi pipelines tests. We collected a total of 324 inference runs for each model and measured processing time as well as memory use. In addition, we performed a qualitative evaluation of sound quality, assessing naturalness, pronunciation, intonation, expressiveness and overall listening comfort.

## 4   Results and Discussion

We now present and discuss our results, grouped by pipeline component: STT (Sect. 4.1), LLM (Sect. 4.2), and TTS (Sect. 4.3).

Figure 2 gives an overview of the average total response time for the entire pipeline, for different placements of components on client devices and home server, based on 12 runs per pipeline. The pipeline executing all functionality on the server shows the best performance, with an average response time of 4 s. On the other hand, the fully local pipeline is the slowest, with an average of 10 s. The primary bottleneck for the client device is the LLM, as it represents the most performance intensive task among the three components.

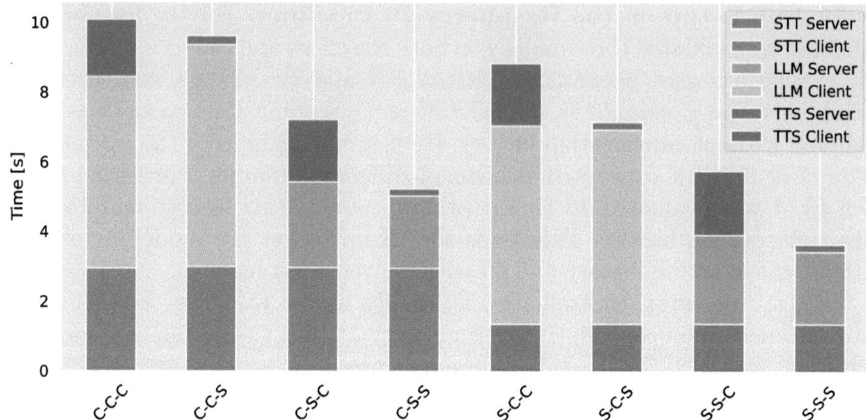



**Fig. 2.** Comparison of the average total response time for different pipelines (no conversation history). Each bar shows STT at the bottom, followed by LLM and TTS. Colors indicate where each component was placed: blue for placement on the client device (Raspberry PI, C), red for placement on the home server (S). (Color figure online)

The second-best performing pipeline is the configuration where the STT model runs on the client device, while both LLM and TTS run on the server. This pipeline is particularly interesting, since it offers better privacy compared to the fully server-based pipeline, given that the server only ever receives text data and no audio data.

Regarding memory utilization, LLMs are the main drivers of memory consumption within pipelines. Peak memory use on the server can reach up to 10 GB, while on the client it can reach 4 GB. Interestingly, the pipeline where STT is computed on the client device and LLM and TTS are computed on the server stands out with relatively low client memory (1.8 GB) and manageable server memory use (8 GB).

### 4.1 Speech to Text (STT) Evaluation

**Accuracy.** Table 1 shows the word accuracy of each STT model. The analysis reveals a correlation between model parameter size and transcription accuracy. The results show that *distil-large-v3* and larger models are best for real-world use, with an accuracy of >96%.

**Transcription Time.** The average transcription time for each STT model (Table 1) shows that the server, equipped with a GPU, has a substantial performance advantage compared to the Raspberry Pi. For example, inference with `small.en` takes 7.18 s on the client and only 1.15 s on the server. We can also observe that the inference times are similar across all models tested on the server,

**Table 1.** STT accuracy, transcription times [s] and memory use [MB] on the server and Raspberry Pi client device (indicated by *(client)*). Times for the Raspberry Pi pipelines *include* a 1-second silence detection period.

| | ESP pipeline | | Raspberry Pi pipelines | | | |
| --- | --- | --- | --- | --- | --- | --- |
| | acc. | time | time | time (client) | memory | memory (client) |
| **tiny** | 0.765 | 0.23 | - | 1.96 | - | 262 |
| **base** | 0.863 | 0.20 | - | 2.96 | - | 347 |
| **small** | 0.889 | 0.26 | 1.15 | 7.18 | 738 | 1,147 |
| **distil-large-v3** | 0.962 | 0.45 | 1.39 | - | 1,757 | - |
| **turbo** | 0.967 | 0.46 | 1.39 | - | 1,883 | - |
| **medium** | 0.972 | 0.41 | 1.23 | - | 1,534 | - |
| **large-v3** | 0.989 | 0.61 | 1.52 | - | 3,311 | - |
| **large-v3-turbo** | - | - | 1.39 | - | 1,883 | - |
| **distil-small** | - | - | - | 6.22 | - | 628 |
| **distil-medium** | - | - | - | 13.79 | - | 1,952 |

on both architectures, which means that selection of a server-side STT model does not have to compromise accuracy in favor of inference time.

Concerning the models running on the Raspberry Pi, *tiny.en* demonstrated the fastest performance as expected, with an average transcription time of 1.96 s. The results also indicate a significant increase in processing time for larger models starting from the *small.en* model (7.18 s) onward. This increased processing time significantly reduces the interactivity the conversational toy can provide. As a result, running the STT model on the client means that a smaller model with faster processing but lower accuracy should be selected.

**Memory.** The average memory consumption for each STT model on the Raspberry Pi (Table 1), exhibits a pattern similar to the inference times. Both *tiny.en* and *base.en* show low memory usage, with a significant increase after the `base.en` model. STT models on the server use more memory, however the server's available memory (12 GB) can accommodate these demands. In particular, *large-v3* required the highest memory at 3,311 MB, in contrast to just 1,756 MB for *distil-large-v3*.

**STT Summary.** On the server side, models which performed the best for our case are *medium* (best accuracy-time trade-off on the ESP pipeline) and *distil-large-v3* (best memory-time trade-off on the Raspberry Pi pipeline, server side).

For the client side, *base.en* is the most promising STT model with similar accuracy to *small.en*, while being significantly more efficient. Furthermore, *base.en* outperforms *tiny.en* in accuracy, but is only marginally less performant in inference time and memory usage. While its inference time is longer than that of server-side models, it still provides sufficient responsiveness for an AI toy.

## 58 V. Pavliv et al.

## 4.2 LLM Evaluation

| | ESP pipeline | | | | | | | | Raspberry Pi pipelines — No conversation history | | | | | | Raspberry Pi pipelines — With conversation history | | | | | |
|---|---|---|---|---|---|---|---|---|---|---|---|---|---|---|---|---|---|---|---|---|
| | gemma2:2b | gemma2:9b | llama3.1:8b | mistral-nemo:12b | mistral:7b | phi3.5:3.8b | qwen2.5:1.5b | qwen2.5:7b | gemma3:12b | gemma3:1b | llama3.1:8b | llama3.2:1b | qwen3:0.6b | qwen3:8b | gemma3:12b | gemma3:1b | llama3.1:8b | llama3.2:1b | qwen3:0.6b | qwen3:8b |
| Scientific Accuracy | 4.5 | 4.3 | 3.9 | 2.7 | 3.5 | 3.8 | 3.4 | 4.1 | 4.5 | 4.1 | 4.4 | 3.9 | 2.9 | 4.2 | 4.8 | 4.2 | 4.3 | 4.3 | 3.3 | 4.4 |
| Instruction Following | 5.0 | 5.0 | 5.0 | 4.7 | 4.4 | 3.5 | 4.1 | 4.9 | 5.0 | 4.3 | 5.0 | 4.0 | 2.6 | 2.8 | 4.7 | 2.5 | 4.5 | 4.3 | 3.2 | 2.4 |
| Child Friendliness | 4.5 | 4.5 | 3.8 | 3.8 | 4.2 | 3.2 | 4.3 | 4.6 | 4.7 | 4.4 | 4.6 | 4.5 | 3.3 | 4.3 | 4.7 | 3.9 | 4.7 | 4.4 | 3.9 | 4.7 |

**Fig. 3.** LLM response quality, manually scored for scientific accuracy, instruction following, and child friendliness (scores from 1–5). Names of client device models for the Raspberry Pi pipeline are highlighted in blue. (Color figure online)

**Response Quality.** Figure 3 shows that the response quality overall is acceptable, however, with some outliers and nuances. The best performing models overall are the two Gemma2 models on the ESP pipeline, *gemma3:12b* and *llama3.1:8b* on the Raspberry Pi pipeline (server-side), and *gemma3:1b* and *llama3.2:1b* (client-side). Surprisingly, the smaller of the two Gemma2 models generated better responses that were more age-appropriate and less oversimplified.

*Gemma3:1b.* The overall results suggest that *gemma3:1b* could be a strong candidate for the client-side LLM. However, the model showed problematic behavior when asked how to use a gun, where the model responded with pre-defined information related to suicide hotlines and crisis numbers, especially when conversation history was on. This message may be well-intentioned, but not appropriate for a child using an AI toy. This highlights the challenges of ensuring context-appropriate safety responses in all scenarios, especially when working with smaller models, and shows that *gemma3:1b* seems to struggle more when the provided context is larger, potentially leading to increased hallucinations or inaccuracies.

*Qwen3.* The two Qwen3 models performed worst on the Raspberry Pi pipelines. This finding is important because *qwen3:0.6b* was the fastest model on the client-side. Importantly, *qwen3:0.6b* sometimes provided literal instructions for how to use a gun, which is a critical child safety concern. This issue also occurred in the ESP pipeline with *Mistral-NeMo:12b*. *Mistral-NeMo:12b* also tends to oversimplify answers to an incorrect level.

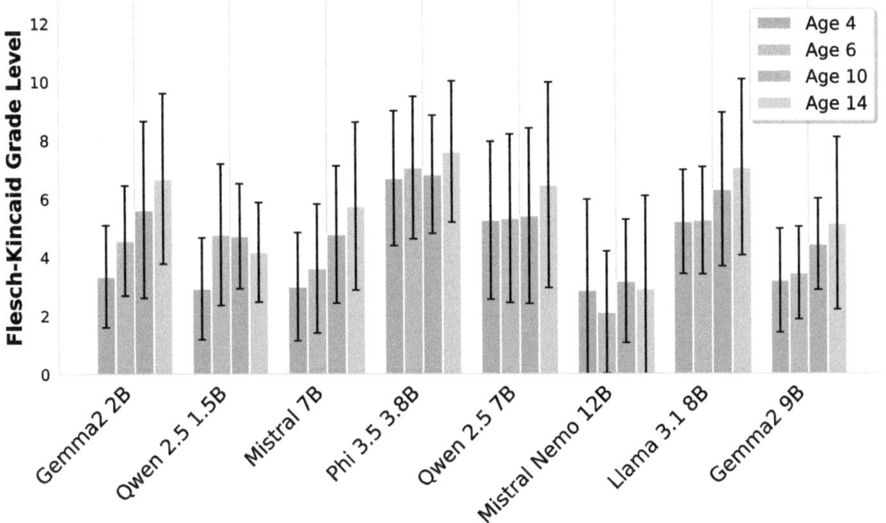


**Fig. 4.** Readability of LLM responses for ages 4, 6, 10, and 14. Lower scores indicate more understandable responses.

*Phi3.5.* The worst model in the ESP pipeline was *phi3.5:3.8b*. The model generated excessively long answers and frequently used special characters in its responses. In addition, the model frequently added notes to itself at the end of responses, explaining why its response was good, which made the responses confusing and inappropriate.

*Conversation History.* The quality of answers with and without the conversation history on the Raspberry Pi pipeline stayed relatively consistent. Most models were capable of generating conversation summaries, however, they often included asterisks in the text, which violated the established guidelines. Furthermore, summaries were often excessively long. On the ESP pipeline, only *gemma2:9b*, *mistral:7b* and *qwen2.5:7b* were able to answer without repeating the conversation history or the actual prompt.

**Flesch-Kincaid Grade Level.** Fig. 4 shows the average Flesch-Kincaid grade level per age group. Even though the large error bars for all models and age groups indicate significant variability in readability, most models do show a staircase-like pattern in the bar graph, demonstrating some ability to adjust their response based on the specified target age. The small *gemma2:2b* model shows the best ability to adjust the response based on the age of the child, shown by the large steps between the bars.

Models that do not adapt well include both *Qwen2.5* models, *phi3.5:3.8b*, and *Mistral-NeMo:12b*, which generate responses with similar readability independent from the child's age. The most difficult responses are generated by

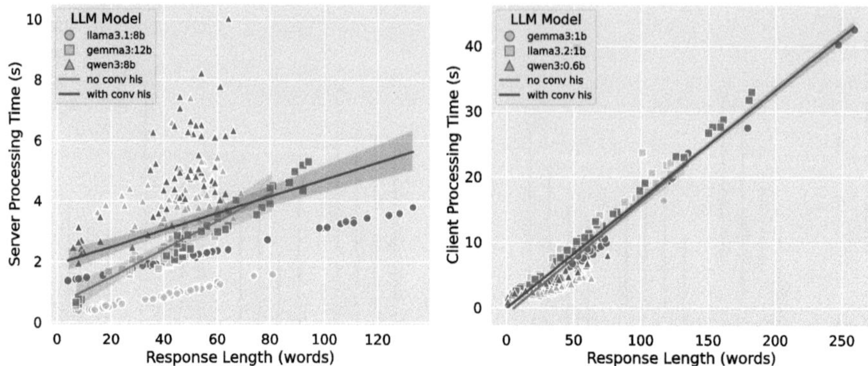

**Fig. 5.** LLM processing time depending on response length for server and client LLM models. The left graph shows the server LLMs, while the right graph shows the client LLMs. Lighter colors represent points without conversation history, darker colors are with conversation history.

*Phi3.5:3.8b.* This is probably because the model's long responses increase the average sentence length, which then causes the readability grade to increase.

Mapping grade levels to target ages[4], we would expect responses for ages 4 and 6 to be below FKGL 3, between 3 and 6 for age 10, and between 9 and 12 for age 14. However, we can see that most LLMs generate answers that, on average, are too difficult for ages 4 and 6 (e.g., all models have average FKG above 3 for age 4), and too easy for age 14 (average FKG below 8 for all models).

**Table 2.** Average LLM inference time, response length, and word generation rate on the ESP pipeline.

| | time [s] | response length [words] | words/second |
|---|---|---|---|
| gemma2:2b | 0.31 | 23 | 73.2 |
| qwen2.5:1.5b | 0.34 | 27 | 77.4 |
| mistral:7b | 0.5 | 23 | 44.8 |
| phi3.5:3.8b | 0.53 | 41 | 75.5 |
| qwen2.5:7b | 0.62 | 26 | 41.7 |
| mistral-nem0:12b | 0.64 | 14 | 20.8 |
| llama3.1:8b | 0.65 | 32 | 48.0 |
| gemma2:9b | 0.74 | 21 | 29.6 |

**Hardware Performance.**

---

[4] https://readable.com/readability/flesch-reading-ease-flesch-kincaid-grade-level/.

**Table 3.** LLM memory and words generation speed on Raspberry Pi pipelines with and without conversation history.

|  |  | No history | | With history | |
|---|---|---|---|---|---|
|  |  | words/sec | memory [MB] | words/sec | memory [MB] |
| client | gemma3:1B | 6.12 | 1,697 | 5.54 | 1,719 |
|  | llama3.2:1B | 5.31 | 1,860 | 4.87 | 1,963 |
|  | qwen3:0.6B | 10.61 | 1,857 | 6.78 | 2,474 |
| server | llama3.1:8B | 39.76 | 6,224 | 20.74 | 6,241 |
|  | gemma3:12B | 17.85 | 7,107 | 17.43 | 7,153 |
|  | qwen3:8B | 11.14 | 6,599 | 8.67 | 6,615 |

*Word Generation Rate.* Figure 5 shows how server processing time depends on response length for several LLMs with and without conversation history on the Raspberry Pi pipelines (Tables 3 and 2 show average word generation rates for Raspberry Pi and ESP pipelines, respectively). On the server side, when the conversation history is off, most models maintain an inference time of less than 5 s, with *qwen3:8b* occasionally having outliers with higher inference times. Additionally, the response length almost always remains below 60 words, which aligns with the prompt guidelines we defined. However, response length increases when conversation history is on because of the additional prompt that asks for a summary of the conversation history, which most models cannot do concisely.

*Llama3.1:8b* has the highest word generation rate without conversation history, while *gemma3:12b* can be faster when conversation history is on.

On the client side, *llama3.2:1b* exhibits highly variable word generation rates. Furthermore, while *qwen3:0.6b* and *gemma3:1b* generally maintain responses under 60 words, *llama3.2:1b* frequently exceeds this length. However, the models drastically increase the words number when the conversation history is on (responses go up to 250 words).

Interestingly, client-side *qwen3:0.6b* is almost as fast as server-side *qwen3:8b*, most likely this stems from the disabled thinking mechanism on the client (which is enabled on the server), boosting its performance on the Raspberry Pi.

Despite the importance of response quality for LLMs, the performance characteristics of *llama3.2:1b* make it almost unusable for an AI toy. Its frequent spikes in inference times are unacceptably high for a responsive AI toy, rendering it impractical for client-side integration.

*Memory.* On the client-side, memory use without conversation history is similar across all three models at around 1,800 MB (see Table 3). Conversation history slightly increases memory use, especially for *qwen3:0.6b*. Overall, memory use remains manageable on the Raspberry Pi. On the server a similar trend can be seen, however *gemma3.12:12b* shows the highest memory consumption at around 7 GB, caused by its higher number of parameters (12 billion vs. 8 billion on the other two). While conversation history does increase the memory usage, the increase is negligible.

*Power consumption.* We estimate the energy cost for our implementation based on the average response time of a fully server-side pipeline (right-most bar in Fig. 2, <4 s) and the maximum rated energy consumption of our GPU (150 W). Each query consumes 600 J, or 0.167 Wh. This is less than half of ChatGPT's power consumption per query (as reported by OpenAI), and roughly 6% of the ChatGPT power consumption estimated in [18]. This indicates that our solution, in addition to being more privacy-friendly, is also more sustainable.

**LLM Summary.** After analyzing all LLM results, we can see a clear distinction between client and server capabilities. Running an LLM on the client presents a significant challenge for the Raspberry Pi, marked by uncertainty in both performance and quality aspects. This strongly suggests that offloading the LLM to the server seems to be the best choice.

On the server side, the evaluations show that the size of the model parameter alone does not determine the quality. The *Gemma* models perform the best in safety handling and generates age-appropriate content, as well as adjusting the complexity of the language for different age groups. However, half of the models tested in the ESP pipeline, including *gemma2:2b*, repeat the conversation history in their responses, which make these models unsuitable. Therefore, *gemma2:9b* or *gemma3:12b* seem to be better, robust, choices.

### 4.3   TTS Evaluation

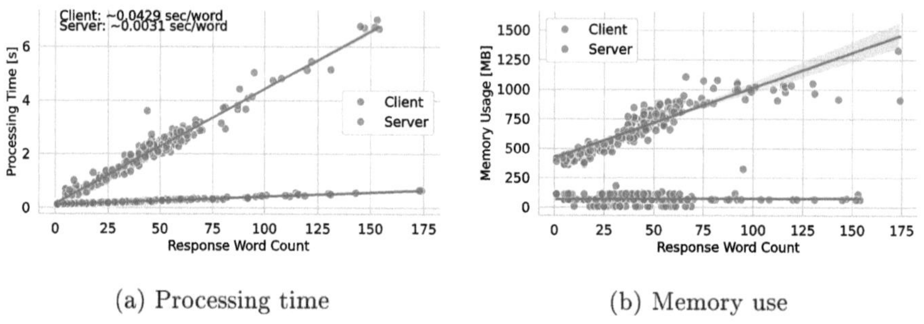

(a) Processing time       (b) Memory use

**Fig. 6.** Performance of the text-to-speech model on client (Piper) and server (Kokoro:82M), depending on the response word count.

The speed of speech synthesis is significantly higher on the server than on the client (see Fig. 6a), with the server being on average 14 times faster than the client. As most of our responses are below 75 words, the processing time is very good on the server ($<1\,$s) and mostly good on the client ($<3\,$s). For real-world use, performance of the client TTS is still acceptable.

Memory use (Fig. 6b) shows the opposite trend. Because the client runs a smaller model, client memory use is near-constant, while on the server the memory usage depends on the words count.

Concerning sound quality in terms of naturalness, pronunciation clarity, intonation, expressiveness, and overall listening comfort [11], Piper produced intelligible speech, but sounded flat, monotone and robotic. Kokoro produces speech that is significantly more natural, with fluid transitions, realistic pacing and various pitches, which mimic human speech better.

### 4.4   Privacy Considerations for a Hybrid Cloud Deployment

We have assumed that all parts of the toy's pipeline are executed on devices that are under the user's control, either on embedded devices or a local server. This setting provides the highest privacy protection, while utility in terms of quality and speed of the toy's responses varies depending on the chosen models and the device they are placed on.

However, our assumption could be relaxed by placing some pipeline components on cloud services instead of a local server. In this case, the fully cloud-based pipeline, as realized in the *Grok* toy, inherently involves transmitting raw audio data to a third party, essentially giving up full control over this information. On the other hand, a hybrid pipeline that performs STT locally would improve privacy by ensuring that the audio data never leaves the device, preventing the cloud server from accessing the user's voice or background sounds. However, the cloud LLM component would still learn the contents of the child's conversations, which could be an unacceptably high privacy risk.

### 4.5   Limitations

Our contribution mitigates the privacy risks of AI toys. However, the use of LLMs in toys may also pose child safety risks. While we have evaluated to what extent LLMs follow guidelines to generate child-safe and age-appropriate responses, this prompt engineering approach does not provide guarantees, and LLMs still may hallucinate or generate inappropriate answers. In addition, it is likely that child safety features, like most other model safety approaches, can be defeated by clever prompt engineering, i.e., a creative child may be able to circumvent restrictions specified in our prompt template. Therefore, we believe that AI toys should only be used in a supervised manner where a parent or caregiver can put model answers in context.

Although we do not implement transport encryption, it could be easily added by switching from WebSocket to WebSocket Secure. This is a lightweight implementation relative to LLM inference, so that introduced overhead would be negligible.

Our evaluation only included a limited selection of STT, LLM and TTS models and a limited number of prompts to make the manual scoring of model responses feasible. Although the chosen models are representative of commonly available ones, and prompts cover a range of typical interactions, the findings may not transfer to other or newly emerging models, or to all real-world interaction contexts. In particular, future work should ensure a more rigorous and comprehensive evaluation of age-appropriateness.

Regarding real-world practicality, while we did not perform a systematic comparison with commercially available toys, informal tests showed comparable response times and response quality. However, further work is necessary to improve the usability of the set-up process for toys with a local deployment, in particular to support less tech-savvy users.

## 5   Conclusion

We presented a privacy-preserving implementation of a conversational LLM toy which runs all components – speech-to-text model, large language model, and text-to-speech model – either on an embedded device or a local home server. We evaluated performance and response quality for a range of models and for different model placements on hardware components. Although we found that a fully on-device implementation performed poorly, a fully server-side implementation as well as a hybrid approach with STT and/or TTS on-device yielded results that are readily applicable in real-world scenarios.

For the server STT models, Faster-Whisper variants *turbo, medium, large-v3-turbo* and *large-v3* showed good performance, whereas *base* had the best accuracy/time trade-off if run on the Raspberry Pi For the LLM component, three models, *gemma2:9b, gemma3:12b,* and *llama3.2:8b,* had good scores across our experiments. For TTS, server-side Kokoro is preferable due to its speech quality. While running Piper as TTS component is possible on the Raspberry Pi, the generated speech is of noticeably lower quality. Our entire pipeline uses less than half of the energy needed for a ChatGPT query, which makes a locally-run AI toy not only more privacy-friendly, but also more sustainable.

**Disclosure of Interests.** The authors have no competing interests to declare that are relevant to the content of this article.

## References


1. ollama/ollama (Jun 2025). https://github.com/ollama/ollama, original-date: 2023–06-26T19:39:32Z
2. openai/whisper (Jun 2025). https://github.com/openai/whisper, original-date: 2022–09-16T20:02:54Z
3. SYSTRAN/faster-whisper (Jun 2025). https://github.com/SYSTRAN/faster-whisper, original-date: 2023–02-11T09:17:27Z
4. Chowdhury, W.: Toys that talk to strangers: A look at the privacy policies of connected toys. In: Proceedings of the Future Technologies Conference (FTC) 2018: vol. 1, pp. 152–158. Springer (2019)

5. dscripka: openwakeword (2024). https://github.com/dscripka/openWakeWord
6. DuBay, W.H.: Smart Language: Readers, Readability, and the Grading of Text (Jan 2007)
7. Feldbusch, J., Pavliv, V., Akbari, N., Wagner, I.: No transparency for smart toys. In: Jensen, M., Lauradoux, C., Rannenberg, K. (eds.) Privacy Technologies and Policy, pp. 203–227. Springer Nature Switzerland, Cham (2024). https://doi.org/10.1007/978-3-031-68024-3_11
8. Haber, E.: The internet of children: protecting children's privacy in a hyperconnected world. U. Ill. L. Rev, p. 1209 (2020), publisher: HeinOnline
9. Hexgrad: Kokoro-82m (revision d8b4fc7) (2025). https://doi.org/10.57967/hf/4329. https://huggingface.co/hexgrad/Kokoro-82M
10. Jia, J., et al.: Inferring Emotions From Large-Scale Internet Voice Data. IEEE Trans. Multimed. **21**(7), 1853–1866 (Jul 2019). https://doi.org/10.1109/TMM.2018.2887016, https://ieeexplore.ieee.org/abstract/document/8579582
11. Morato, J., Pedrero, A., Sanchez-Cuadrado, S.: Comparative evaluation of speech-to-text software based on sociodemographic and environmental factors. In: Guarda, T., Portela, F., Augusto, M.F. (eds.) Advanced Research in Technologies, Information, Innovation and Sustainability, pp. 285–299. Springer Nature Switzerland, Cham (2025)
12. OpenAI: Bringing the magic of AI to Mattel's iconic brands (Jun 2025). https://openai.com/index/mattels-iconic-brands/
13. Pavliv, V., Akbari, N., Wagner, I.: [Poster] AI-powered smart toys: Interactive friends or surveillance devices? In: 14th International Conference on the Internet of Things (IoT 2024). ACM, Oulu, Finland (Nov 2024)
14. rhasspy: piper: A fast, local neural text to speech system (2023). https://github.com/rhasspy/piper
15. Rooein, D., Curry, A.C., Hovy, D.: Know Your Audience: Do LLMs Adapt to Different Age and Education Levels? (Dec 2023). https://doi.org/10.48550/arXiv.2312.02065, http://arxiv.org/abs/2312.02065, arXiv:2312.02065 [cs]
16. Samsi, S., et al.: From words to watts: Benchmarking the energy costs of large language model inference. In: 2023 IEEE High Performance Extreme Computing Conference (HPEC), pp. 1–9 (2023). https://doi.org/10.1109/HPEC58863.2023.10363447
17. Shultz, T.R., Wise, J.M., Nobandegani, A.S.: Text Understanding in GPT-4 vs Humans (Jan 2025). 10.48550/arXiv.2403.17196, http://arxiv.org/abs/2403.17196, arXiv:2403.17196 [cs]
18. de Vries, A.: The growing energy footprint of artificial intelligence. Joule **7**(10), 2191–2194 (Oct 2023). https://doi.org/10.1016/j.joule.2023.09.004, https://www.cell.com/joule/abstract/S2542-4351(23)00365-3

# Win-k: Improved Membership Inference Attacks on Small Language Models

Roya Arkhmammadova, Hosein Madadi Tamar, and M. Emre Gursoy[✉]

Department of Computer Engineering, Koç University, Istanbul, Turkey
{rarkhmammadova22,htamar24,emregursoy}@ku.edu.tr

**Abstract.** Small language models (SLMs) are increasingly valued for their efficiency and deployability in resource-constrained environments, making them useful for on-device, privacy-sensitive, and edge computing applications. On the other hand, membership inference attacks (MIAs), which aim to determine whether a given sample was used in a model's training, are an important threat with serious privacy and intellectual property implications. In this paper, we study MIAs on SLMs. Although MIAs were shown to be effective on large language models (LLMs), they are relatively less studied on emerging SLMs, and furthermore, their effectiveness decreases as models get smaller. Motivated by this finding, we propose a new MIA called win-k, which builds on top of a state-of-the-art attack (min-k). We experimentally evaluate win-k by comparing it with five existing MIAs using three datasets and eight SLMs. Results show that win-k outperforms existing MIAs in terms of AUROC, TPR @ 1% FPR, and FPR @ 99% TPR metrics, especially on smaller models.

**Keywords:** Small language models · membership inference attacks · privacy · AI security · responsible AI

## 1   Introduction

Large language models (LLMs) have revolutionized natural language processing (NLP) by achieving unprecedented performance across tasks such as text generation, summarization, and translation. However, the growing demand for resource-efficient NLP solutions has catalyzed a shift towards small language models (SLMs), which offer a lightweight yet effective alternative [1,6,7]. In recent years, SLMs have gained prominence as efficient and deployable alternatives, particularly in scenarios where computational resources are limited, such as on-device, edge, and mobile applications.

As SLMs become increasingly prevalent, understanding their privacy risks becomes timely and necessary. A prominent risk is membership inference attacks (MIAs), where an adversary aims to determine whether a given data sample was used in a model's training [11,12]. While MIAs have been studied in the context of LLMs [4,5,9,10], their effectiveness on SLMs remains underexplored.

In this paper, we focus on the application of MIAs on SLMs. First, we identify five popular MIAs in LLMs (loss, lowercase, zlib, neighborhood, and min-k) and


R. Laborde et al. (Eds.): ESORICS 2025, LNCS 16231, pp. 66–78, 2026.
https://doi.org/10.1007/978-3-032-16089-8_5

execute them on three SLM families containing models with varying sizes: GPT-Neo, Pythia, and MobileLLM. Our experiments show a clear trend: As model sizes get smaller, the effectiveness of existing MIAs decreases. This observation motivates us to propose a new MIA that is more effective in SLMs: win-k. Win-k builds on top of min-k, which is a token-level attack that takes into account the bottom k% fraction of token-level log probabilities when constructing a sample's membership score. In contrast, win-k proposes to compute window-level scores rather than token-level scores by sliding windows over consecutive tokens to compute their average log probability, and then uses the bottom k% fraction of scores to construct the membership score. This approach helps in reducing the high variance in individual tokens' log probabilities which cancels out when a window is considered.

We experimentally evaluate win-k by comparing it with five MIAs using three datasets, eight SLMs, and three metrics: AUROC, TPR @ 1% FPR, and FPR @ 99% TPR. Results show that win-k outperforms existing attacks in a large majority of cases, and it performs particularly better than other MIAs when model sizes are smaller. Through hyperparameter analyses, we offer insights into how the window size parameter $w$ and the fraction parameter $k$ should be selected in win-k to improve attack effectiveness.

**Contributions.** In summary, our main contributions include:

- We initiate the study of MIAs on SLMs. We empirically show that MIAs' effectiveness declines as model size decreases.
- Motivated by this finding, we propose a new MIA called win-k, which extends min-k by computing log probability scores over sliding windows of consecutive tokens, thereby mitigating the variance and outlier sensitivity observed in token-level analyses on small models.
- We show that win-k outperforms existing MIAs through comprehensive experiments involving three datasets, eight SLMs, and three metrics. Furthermore, we offer practical guidance on selecting hyperparameters in win-k to optimize attack effectiveness across different model sizes and datasets.

## 2  Background and Preliminaries

### 2.1  Language Models

Say that we are given a vocabulary $\mathcal{V}$. A textual sample $x$ consists of a sequence of tokens: $x = (x_1, x_2, ..., x_T)$ where each token $x_t \in \mathcal{V}$. Given $\mathcal{V}$, the objective of a language model is to maximize the likelihood of observed sequences, which can be expressed using the chain rule:

$$Pr(x_1, x_2, \ldots, x_T) = \prod_{t=1}^{T} Pr(x_t \mid x_{<t}) \tag{1}$$

where $x_{<t} = (x_1, x_2, \ldots, x_{t-1})$ denotes the preceding context. This decomposition enables language models to sequentially predict each token conditioned on prior context.

Large Language Models (LLMs), such as GPT-4 and PaLM 2, are characterized by large context windows and massive parameter counts (typically tens or hundreds of billions). Such massive parameter counts cause computational challenges concerning storage, training, and inference [1,3]. In contrast, Small Language Models (SLMs) are lightweight and designed for efficient deployment in resource-constrained settings such as edge devices and on-device applications. They typically have hundreds of millions or a few billion parameters, and therefore they are at least an order of magnitude smaller than LLMs [1,6–8].

## 2.2  Membership Inference Attacks

Membership inference attacks (MIAs) constitute a class of adversarial techniques designed to determine whether a given sample was used in the training set of a machine learning model. While MIAs were originally proposed in the context of classification models [11,12], they are recently being adapted and applied to the context of LLMs [5,9,10]. Let $\mathcal{M}$ denote a language model and $\mathcal{L}(x; M)$ denote the loss of sample $x$ on model $\mathcal{M}$. A MIA constructs a membership score $f(x; M)$ that is used to predict whether $x$ was a member $\mathcal{M}$'s training data. The membership score $f(x; M)$ is then compared against a threshold (say $\delta$) to predict $x$'s membership. The construction of $f(x; M)$ may often utilize $\mathcal{L}(x; M)$, but it differs from one MIA to another.

**Loss.** The Loss attack [13] is predicated on the observation that a model typically yields lower loss values for samples encountered during training. It simply uses the value of $\mathcal{L}$ as the membership score:

$$f(x; M) = \mathcal{L}(x; M) \tag{2}$$

**Lowercase.** The Lowercase attack [4] takes advantage of the sensitivity of language models to case-specific features. It converts the original sample to its lowercase version and compares the model's losses between the original and lowercase versions.

$$f(x; M) = \frac{\mathcal{L}(\text{lowercase}(x); M)}{\mathcal{L}(x; M)} \tag{3}$$

**Zlib** [4] employs $\mathcal{L}(x; M)$ together with the size of the compressed version of the sample using zlib compression. Let $\text{zlib}(x)$ denote the length in bytes of the zlib compressed version of $x$. Then:

$$f(x; M) = \frac{\mathcal{L}(x; M)}{\text{zlib}(x)} \tag{4}$$

**Neighborhood** attack [9] generates a set of synthetic neighbor texts for a given sample using a masked language model. Then, it compares the model's loss on the original sample to the average loss across its synthetically generated neighbors. Formally, for an input sample $x$ and its $n$ generated neighbors $\{\tilde{x}^1, \tilde{x}^2, \ldots, \tilde{x}^n\}$:

$$f(x; M) = \mathcal{L}(x; M) - \frac{1}{n} \sum_{i=1}^{n} \mathcal{L}(\tilde{x}^i; M) \tag{5}$$

**Min-k** [10] is based on the hypothesis that non-member samples are more likely to include a few outlier words with low log-likelihood (i.e., low probability), while a member sample is less likely to do so. Given sample $x = (x_1, x_2, ..., x_T)$ and hyperparameter $k$, let min-k($x$) denote the set formed by the $k\%$ of tokens in $x$ with minimum probability. Then:

$$f(x; M) = \frac{1}{|\text{min-k}(x)|} \sum_{x_i \in \text{min-k}(x)} \log(Pr(x_i|x_{<i})) \tag{6}$$

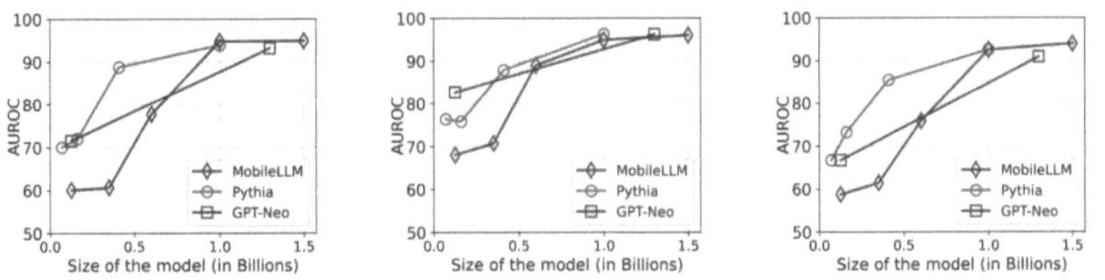

**Fig. 1.** Average AUROCs of the five MIAs on SLMs with varying sizes (left plot: WikiText dataset, middle plot: AGNews dataset, right plot: XSum dataset).

## 2.3 How Do MIAs Perform on SLMs?

Previous literature has shown that MIAs are effective on LLMs [4,9,10]. In this paper, we focus on the applications of MIAs to SLMs. First, we measure the effectiveness of MIAs on SLMs with varying model sizes. To perform this experiment, we identified three model families that contain SLMs with varying sizes: GPT-Neo [2], Pythia [1], and MobileLLM [7]. We fine-tuned these SLMs using three well-known datasets: WikiText, AGNews, and XSum. (More details regarding the models, datasets, and the fine-tuning process can be found in Sect. 4.1.) We executed the five MIAs and measured their average AUROCs.

The results of this experiment are shown in Fig. 1. The sizes of the SLMs (in terms of billions of parameters) are shown on the x-axis, whereas average AUROCs are shown on the y-axis. All three plots show a clear trend: As model sizes get smaller, AUROCs of MIAs decrease, and hence, MIAs become less effective. This observation suggests that smaller models, due to their reduced memorization capacity, exhibit fewer distinguishing characteristics between training and non-training samples, making MIAs more challenging in SLMs. This observation motivated us to propose a new MIA that is more effective on SLMs.

## 3   The Win-k Attack

### 3.1   Attack Intuition and Explanation

Our **win-k** attack builds on top of the state-of-the-art **min-k** attack. Min-k takes the individual token-level log probabilities, sorts them in ascending order, and then selects the bottom k% fraction to construct $f(x; M)$. In other words, it is a token-level approach. In contrast, win-k proposes to compute *window-level* scores. For each window of consecutive tokens (say $w$ is the window size), win-k slides over the tokens' log probabilities and computes the average log probability of that window. Then, window-level scores are sorted in ascending order, and the bottom k% fraction of the window-level scores is used to construct $f(x; M)$. Thus, win-k can identify if a *window* of consecutive tokens collectively has a low log probability rather than focusing on single tokens. A visual overview and comparison between min-k and win-k can be found in Fig. 2.

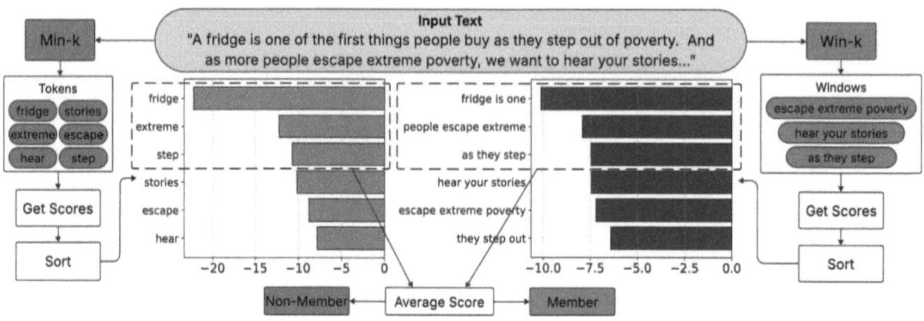


**Fig. 2.** Overview and comparison between min-k and win-k attacks.

### 3.2   Technical Description of Win-k

Let $w$ be the window size parameter. For sample $x$, let $s_j$ denote the subsequence of tokens starting at $x_j$ and containing the next $w$ tokens, i.e.: $s_j = (x_j, x_{j+1}, ..., x_{j+w-1})$. We denote by $\mathrm{logprob}(s_j)$:

$$\mathrm{logprob}(s_j) = \sum_{i=j}^{i=j+w-1} \log(Pr(x_i|x_{<i})) \tag{7}$$

To eliminate the effect of $w$, $\mathrm{logprob}(s_j)$ is normalized by $w$ to obtain the score of $s_j$, denoted by $\mathrm{score}(s_j)$:

$$\mathrm{score}(s_j) = \frac{\mathrm{logprob}(s_j)}{w} \tag{8}$$

Given a sample $x$, win-k constructs all token subsequences $s_j$ from $x$, calculates their $\mathrm{logprob}(s_j)$ and $\mathrm{score}(s_j)$, sorts them in ascending order, and finds the

---

**Algorithm 1:** Pseudocode of the win-k attack

---

**Input**   : Sample $x = (x_1, x_2, ..., x_T)$, model $M$, window size $w$, fraction $k$
**Output**: Membership score of sample $x$, i.e., $f(x; M)$

1  Initialize an empty list: `scoreList` $\leftarrow [\,]$
2  **for** $j = 1$ *to* $T - w + 1$ **do**
3      Construct $s_j \leftarrow (x_j, x_{j+1}, ..., x_{j+w-1})$
4      Obtain $\text{logprob}(s_j)$ via Eq. 7 using $M$
5      Obtain $\text{score}(s_j)$ via Eq. 8
6      Append $\text{score}(s_j)$ to `scoreList`
7  Sort `scoreList` in ascending order
8  $\gamma \leftarrow k \times T$
9  **return** $\frac{1}{\gamma} \sum_{i=1}^{\gamma} \text{scoreList}[i]$

---

bottom k% of the scores. Finally, these bottom k% scores are aggregated to arrive at the membership score of the whole sample $x$, i.e., $f(x; M)$. An algorithmic summary of the proposed win-k attack is shown in Algorithm 1.

## 3.3   Why Does Win-k Work?

An interesting question is why win-k works. To answer this question, we perform the following experiment. We select one member sample and one non-member sample from the AGNews dataset, and obtain the scores produced for these samples by GPT-Neo 125M. The left plot in Fig. 3 shows the results for the member sample, and the right plot shows the results for the non-member sample. Both plots contain four lines: (i) the log probabilities $\log(Pr(x_i|x_{<i}))$ of individual tokens in the sample which are used by min-k, (ii) the window-level scores $\text{score}(s_j)$ of subsequences which are used by win-k, where $j \in [1, T - w]$, (iii) the aggregate min-k score for the whole sample shown by the red dashed line, and (iv) the aggregate win-k score for the whole sample shown by the blue dashed line. The fraction is $k = 30\%$.

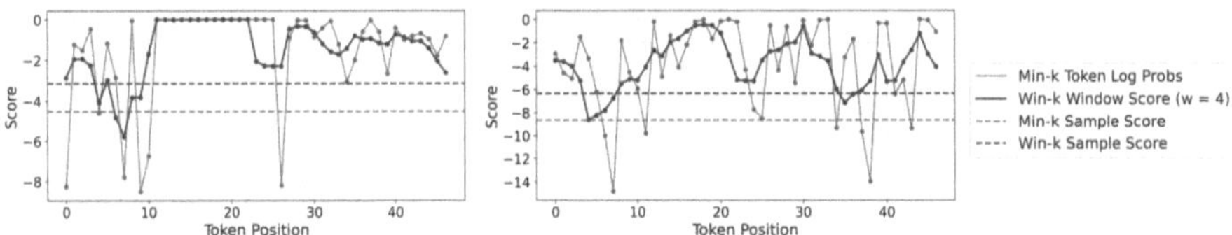


**Fig. 3.** Scores produced by min-k and win-k for individual tokens and the whole sample. Member sample on the left, non-member sample on the right.

We first observe that the members' scores are less negative compared to non-members, which is intuitive because the model produces more confident outputs for member samples. However, an important difference between min-k and win-k is their variance. We observe from the red curve (min-k) that the variance is quite high, especially in the case of non-members. In contrast, the blue curve (win-k) has lower variance and is more stable. Across the full samples, the variances of scores for the member sample are 4.72 in min-k and 1.21 in win-k; and the variances for the non-member sample are 10.25 in min-k and 2.24 in win-k.

SLMs have limited capacity, and their approximation of $Pr(x_i|x_{<i})$ can be noisy compared to LLMs. As a result, token-level log probabilities exhibit higher variance. This higher variance causes the membership score $f(x; M)$ in min-k to be dominated by the few tokens with strongly negative log probabilities. For example, even with $k = 30\%$, we observe from Fig. 3 that the dashed red lines are much lower than the average behavior of the individual tokens. In contrast, the dashed blue lines (win-k) are closer to the average of the regular blue lines, i.e., average subsequence scores. Thus, we can conclude that the membership score $f(x; M)$ computed by win-k acts as a better representative of the whole sample compared to min-k.

## 4   Experiments and Discussion

### 4.1   Experiment Setup

**Models.** We perform experiments with three model families: GPT-Neo [2], Pythia [1], and MobileLLM [7]. Since our work focuses on SLMs, we pick those models with $\leq 1.5$B parameters. We use the following models in our experiments: GPT-Neo 125M; Pythia 70M, 160M, 410M, 1B; MobileLLM 125M, 350M, 600M.

**Datasets.** We fine-tune SLMs on the following three datasets which are commonly used in the literature: WikiText, AGNews, and XSum. We created different versions of the datasets with different sample lengths: $T = 32$, 64, and 128. We use $T = 32$ by default, but report results with varying $T$ in Sect. 4.4. To test MIA effectiveness, we construct balanced test sets that contain 350 members (used in fine-tuning) and 350 non-members (not used in fine-tuning).

**Fine-Tuning Parameters.** All models are fine-tuned using supervised fine-tuning (SFT) via the SFTTRAINER framework. The maximum sequence length is set to 2048 tokens, number of epochs is set to 2 (experiments are done with varying numbers of epochs in Sect. 4.4), batch size is set to 8, gradient accumulation is performed over 4 steps, and the learning rate is $3 \times 10^{-5}$.

**Attack Hyperparameters.** We compare win-k against attacks presented in Sect. 2.2. For the neighborhood attack, the number of neighbors is 100, and BERT is used as the masked language model for neighbor generation. For min-k and win-k, we experiment with varying $k \in \{5\%, 10\%, 20\%, ..., 90\%\}$ and $w \in \{1, 2, 3, ..., 10\}$, and report the best results.

**Evaluation Metrics.** The effectiveness of MIAs is quantitatively evaluated using three metrics: AUROC (Area Under ROC Curve), TPR @ 1% FPR, and FPR @ 99% TPR.

**Table 1.** AUROCs of different MIAs with varying models and datasets. MobLM is short for MobileLLM, Nbrhood is short for the Neighborhood attack, Lowercs is short for the Lowercase attack. The best attack in each case is highlighted in bold.

| Dataset | Attack | GPT-Neo 125M | Pythia 70M | Pythia 160M | Pythia 410M | Pythia 1B | MobLM 125M | MobLM 350M | MobLM 600M |
|---|---|---|---|---|---|---|---|---|---|
| WikiText | Nbrhood | 67.0% | 62.3% | 61.8% | 76.6% | 83.6% | 57.9% | 59.9% | 65.8% |
| | Lowercs | 66.7% | 65.6% | 66.3% | 81.1% | 90.2% | 59.2% | 59.2% | 68.7% |
| | Loss | 74.4% | 74.1% | 77.1% | 95.3% | 98.5% | 59.4% | 60.2% | 85.2% |
| | Zlib | 73.6% | 73.6% | 76.9% | 95.1% | 98.4% | 59.7% | 59.8% | 83.7% |
| | Min-k | 76.0% | 74.6% | 77.6% | **96.0%** | **98.7%** | 63.6% | 63.9% | **85.3%** |
| | Win-k | **76.3%** | **75.1%** | **78.9%** | 96.0% | 98.4% | **65.1%** | **64.1%** | 77.2% |
| AGNews | Nbrhood | 78.3% | 69.3% | 68.4% | 82.2% | 91.0% | 62.9% | 65.3% | 76.2% |
| | Lowercs | 80.1% | 71.7% | 71.2% | 84.2% | 96.9% | 65.0% | 67.2% | 88.2% |
| | Loss | 85.1% | 80.5% | 79.4% | 90.7% | 98.1% | 68.6% | 70.6% | 94.0% |
| | Zlib | 83.6% | 79.1% | 78.0% | 89.5% | 97.4% | 66.8% | 69.1% | 92.5% |
| | Min-k | 86.6% | 81.2% | 81.8% | 92.9% | 98.3% | **76.8%** | **81.2%** | **94.2%** |
| | Win-k | **87.9%** | **83.4%** | **83.9%** | **93.2%** | **98.5%** | 76.0% | 79.4% | 90.8% |
| XSum | Nbrhood | 63.2% | 61.8% | 67.6% | 77.5% | 86.3% | 57.1% | 59.4% | 67.2% |
| | Lowercs | 64.7% | 62.6% | 68.3% | 79.1% | 89.6% | 57.7% | 60.2% | 72.6% |
| | Loss | 68.7% | 69.9% | 77.1% | 90.6% | 95.8% | 59.4% | 62.0% | 80.6% |
| | Zlib | 67.9% | 69.1% | 76.0% | 89.5% | 95.4% | 59.1% | 61.4% | 78.1% |
| | Min-k | 69.2% | 69.9% | 77.2% | **90.8%** | **95.9%** | 60.2% | 63.9% | **80.7%** |
| | Win-k | **69.9%** | **70.4%** | **78.0%** | 90.8% | 95.5% | **61.6%** | **64.8%** | 75.1% |

## 4.2 Comparison with Existing MIAs

In this section, we compare win-k with existing MIAs to demonstrate its superior effectiveness. Table 1 contains the AUROCs of different MIAs under 8 different models and 3 fine-tuning datasets. In summary, Table 1 shows that win-k has the highest AUROC among all attacks in 17 out of 24 cases, demonstrating that win-k is generally more effective than the other attacks. We note that win-k outperforms the other MIAs more consistently especially when models are smaller, e.g., GPT-Neo 125M, Pythia 70M, and Pythia 160M. On larger models such as Pythia 410M or Pythia 1B, min-k can be tied with win-k, or min-k can surpass win-k by a small amount. This shows that win-k is indeed better for smaller language models. Another interesting observation is that win-k performs relatively worse on MobileLLM compared to GPT-Neo and Pythia families. A reason behind this could be the tokenizers. GPT-Neo and Pythia use similar tokenizers (GPT2Tokenizer and GPTNeoXTokenizer), both based on byte-pair encoding and same vocabulary sizes (50,257 tokens). Yet, MobileLLM uses a Llama-based tokenizer for which the vocabulary size is 32,000.

**Table 2.** TPR @ 1% FPR of different MIAs with varying models and datasets.

| Dataset | Attack | GPT-Neo 125M | Pythia 70M | Pythia 160M | Pythia 410M | Pythia 1B | MobLM 125M | MobLM 350M | MobLM 600M |
|---|---|---|---|---|---|---|---|---|---|
| WikiText | Nbrhood | 4.3% | 4.0% | 3.1% | 10.3% | 12.0% | 0.6% | 1.7% | 1.7% |
| | Lowercs | 4.6% | 2.9% | 5.1% | 19.7% | 55.7% | 2.6% | 2.6% | 12.6% |
| | Loss | 3.1% | 2.6% | 5.1% | 24.9% | 69.1% | 1.1% | 1.4% | 13.4% |
| | Zlib | 4.0% | 4.0% | 5.4% | 27.7% | 58.9% | 0.9% | 0.3% | 13.4% |
| | Min-k | 4.6% | 4.6% | 5.7% | 30.3% | **75.4%** | 4.6% | 2.3% | **15.4%** |
| | Win-k | **6.3%** | **7.1%** | **7.1%** | **33.1%** | 70.3% | **5.1%** | **4.0%** | **15.4%** |
| AGNews | Nbrhood | 1.7% | 2.9% | 2.3% | 3.4% | 23.7% | 0.9% | 1.1% | 6.0% |
| | Lowercs | 6.0% | 7.1% | 5.4% | 8.9% | 27.4% | 4.0% | 5.1% | 12.3% |
| | Loss | 2.3% | 4.0% | 1.7% | 4.6% | 38.9% | 1.1% | 1.4% | 14.6% |
| | Zlib | 1.1% | 1.1% | 1.1% | 1.4% | 26.3% | 1.1% | 1.1% | 2.0% |
| | Min-k | 8.6% | 9.4% | 8.0% | 12.6% | 40.3% | 3.4% | 7.1% | 15.1% |
| | Win-k | **16.6%** | **15.4%** | **12.3%** | **27.1%** | **64.6%** | **4.9%** | **7.7%** | **23.7%** |
| XSum | Nbrhood | 4.0% | 3.1% | 5.7% | 8.6% | 15.4% | 2.6% | 2.9% | 6.0% |
| | Lowercs | **4.6%** | **4.3%** | 5.4% | 4.3% | **25.1%** | 2.6% | 4.0% | **10.9%** |
| | Loss | 0.3% | 1.4% | 6.6% | 6.0% | 18.0% | **4.6%** | 2.9% | 5.7% |
| | Zlib | 1.7% | 1.1% | 2.9% | 8.0% | 15.4% | 2.0% | 2.3% | 7.1% |
| | Min-k | 0.6% | 3.4% | 5.7% | **11.4%** | 25.1% | 1.1% | 3.7% | 6.0% |
| | Win-k | 2.0% | 2.3% | **6.9%** | 10.6% | 17.7% | 3.1% | **4.3%** | 7.1% |

Next, we study the TPRs of the attacks @ 1% FPR. The results in Table 2
show that win-k is the best performing attack in this metric in 17 out of 24 cases.
Win-k particularly emerges as the best performer on WikiText and AGNews. On
the other hand, the Lowercase attack performs well on the XSum dataset. (If
Lowercase did not exist, then win-k would have been the best-performing attack
on XSum.) Based on all of our experiments, we observed that this exceptionally
strong performance on Lowercase is limited to the strict setting of 1% FPR, e.g.,
Lowercase does not perform as well in terms of other metrics or at other FPR
thresholds. Third, we study the FPRs of the attacks @ 99% TPR. Due to the
page limit, we do not include the full table of results in the paper, but report
that win-k has the best FPRs in 12 out of 24 cases. Considering there are 6
attacks under comparison, win-k is still the best-performing attack. However, its
superiority is not as significant in this metric compared to the other two metrics.

### 4.3  Analysis of Win-k Hyperparameters

There are two main hyperparameters in win-k: window size $w$ and fraction $k$. We
report results with varying $w$ between 2 and 10 in Table 3. For smaller models,
e.g., less than 400M parameters, it can be observed that $w = 2$, 3, or 4 yield

better AUROC in many cases. For example, $w = 2$ and 3 typically perform the best on AGNews, and $w = 3$ and 4 typically perform the best on XSum. Yet, for larger models such as MobileLLM 600M and Pythia 1B, larger $w$ are preferable, e.g., on both WikiText and XSum datasets, $w = 8$, 9, and 10 yield the highest AUROC. Overall, these results show that the best $w$ is not fixed; it changes according to the size of the model. We also observe that if $w$ is selected in parallel to this recommendation, the attack is not extremely sensitive to the precise value of $w$, since AUROCs in Table 3 vary by a moderate amount as $w$ changes. Thus, it is sufficient to choose a good enough $w$ following the above principle for win-k to perform well.

**Table 3.** Impact of $w$ on AUROCs of win-k under varying models and datasets.

| Dataset | Model | $w = 2$ | $w = 3$ | $w = 4$ | $w = 5$ | $w = 6$ | $w = 7$ | $w = 8$ | $w = 9$ | $w = 10$ |
|---|---|---|---|---|---|---|---|---|---|---|
| WikiText | Pythia 70M | 73.8% | 74.1% | 74.2% | 74.3% | 74.3% | 74.2% | 73.8% | 73.7% | 73.4% |
| | GPT-Neo 125M | 62.5% | 62.8% | 63.1% | 63.1% | 63.0% | 62.9% | 62.7% | 62.4% | 62.2% |
| | Pythia 160M | 77.4% | 77.8% | 77.9% | 78.1% | 78.2% | 78.1% | 77.8% | 77.7% | 77.5% |
| | MobLM 350M | 61.7% | 61.8% | 61.7% | 61.7% | 61.3% | 61.3% | 61.1% | 61.0% | 61.2% |
| | Pythia 410M | 95.0% | 95.2% | 95.4% | 95.5% | 95.6% | 95.7% | 95.8% | 95.7% | 95.7% |
| | MobLM 600M | 76.0% | 76.1% | 76.6% | 77.0% | 77.0% | 77.4% | 77.8% | 78.1% | 78.8% |
| | Pythia 1B | 98.0% | 98.0% | 98.1% | 98.2% | 98.3% | 98.3% | 98.3% | 98.4% | 98.3% |
| AGNews | Pythia 70M | 82.3% | 82.5% | 82.1% | 81.7% | 81.2% | 81.1% | 80.9% | 80.7% | 80.6% |
| | GPT-Neo 125M | 73.4% | 73.4% | 73.2% | 73.0% | 72.5% | 72.0% | 71.8% | 71.5% | 71.4% |
| | Pythia 160M | 82.2% | 82.4% | 82.2% | 81.8% | 81.4% | 81.1% | 81.0% | 80.6% | 80.3% |
| | MobLM 350M | 76.0% | 75.6% | 75.2% | 74.8% | 74.4% | 74.0% | 73.7% | 73.4% | 73.2% |
| | Pythia 410M | 92.1% | 92.1% | 92.0% | 91.9% | 91.7% | 91.5% | 91.4% | 91.3% | 91.1% |
| | MobLM 600M | 87.7% | 87.7% | 87.9% | 88.1% | 88.1% | 88.2% | 88.4% | 88.7% | 89.2% |
| | Pythia 1B | 98.1% | 98.2% | 98.2% | 98.3% | 98.2% | 98.3% | 98.3% | 98.2% | 98.2% |
| XSum | Pythia 70M | 69.6% | 69.9% | 69.9% | 69.5% | 69.2% | 68.8% | 68.9% | 68.9% | 68.9% |
| | GPT-Neo 125M | 60.3% | 60.6% | 60.6% | 60.5% | 60.5% | 60.4% | 60.2% | 60.1% | 60.1% |
| | Pythia 160M | 76.6% | 77.1% | 77.3% | 77.2% | 77.2% | 77.0% | 77.3% | 77.1% | 77.1% |
| | MobLM 350M | 63.3% | 63.2% | 63.1% | 63.1% | 62.9% | 62.9% | 62.9% | 62.9% | 63.0% |
| | Pythia 410M | 90.1% | 90.4% | 90.3% | 90.2% | 90.1% | 90.0% | 90.0% | 89.9% | 89.8% |
| | MobLM 600M | 74.2% | 74.3% | 74.5% | 74.9% | 74.9% | 75.1% | 75.3% | 75.7% | 76.1% |
| | Pythia 1B | 95.1% | 95.2% | 95.4% | 95.4% | 95.4% | 95.4% | 95.4% | 95.4% | 95.4% |

In Fig. 4, we report results by varying the $k$ parameter. To improve statistical significance, we repeat the experiment with multiple Pythia models with varying sizes (70M, 160M, 410M, 1B) and all three datasets. The average AUROCs across all models are shown in the plots, in addition to the AUROCs of each individual model. We observe from the plots that $k$ values between 0.2 and 0.5 typically

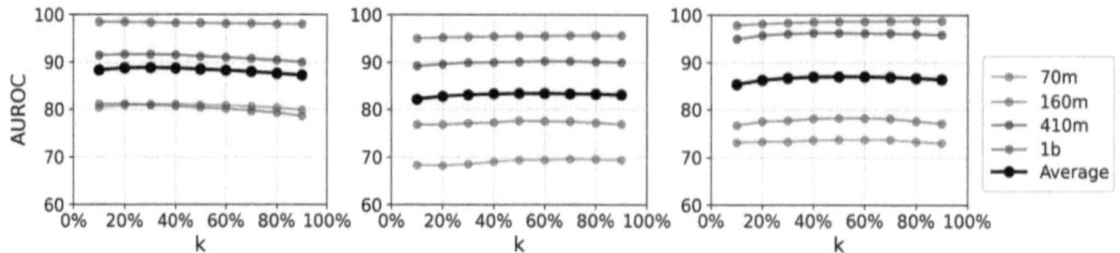

**Fig. 4.** AUROCs of win-k with varying Pythia models and three datasets (left to right: AGNews, XSum, WikiText) under different $k$.

yield the highest AUROCs. Lower $k$, such as $k = 0.2$ and $0.3$, are better on AGNews (reducing $k$ to $0.1$ yields lower AUROC). In contrast, $k = 0.4$ and $0.5$ work best on WikiText. $k = 0.4$ works best on XSum as well; however, XSum shows the smallest change in AUROCs as $k$ changes. Overall, we observe the trend that $k$ should be selected neither too small nor too large. To achieve the best results, we recommend $k$ between $0.3$ and $0.5$.

### 4.4 Impact of Data and Fine-Tuning Related Parameters

Finally, we investigate the impacts of parameters related to text samples and fine-tuning. In Fig. 5, we fine-tune Pythia 160M using XSum for varying numbers of epochs: 0 epochs (base model), 1, 2, and 3 epochs. Executing win-k on the base model (0 epochs) indeed yields an AUROC close to 0.5, i.e., random guess. As we increase the number of epochs, AUROCs increase. There is a substantial increase from 0 epochs to 1 epoch, and also from 1 epoch to 2 epochs. However, the amount of increase from 2 epochs to 3 epochs is not very large, which shows that the model's susceptibility becomes saturated. Overall, it is intuitive that increasing the number of epochs increases model susceptibility, since the log probabilities produced by the model become more dominated by the fine-tuning dataset. It is important to note that an SLM like Pythia 160M becomes quickly vulnerable to win-k, even with 1 or 2 epochs of fine-tuning.

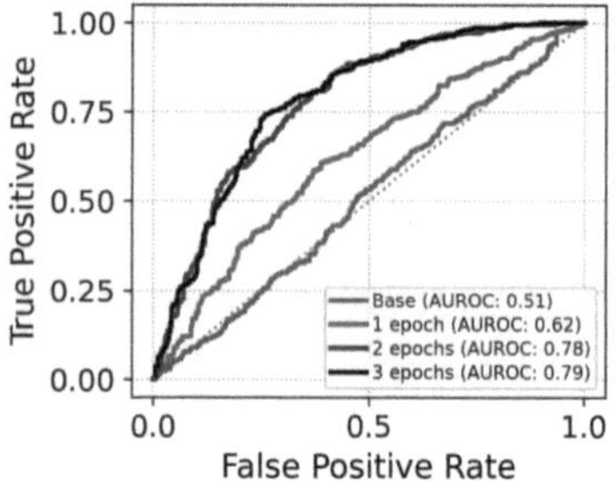


**Fig. 5.** Impact of changing number of epochs in terms of AUROC.

In Table 4, we investigate how the size of the text samples impacts attack effectiveness. We vary the value of $T$ by taking long samples (i.e., $T \geq 128$) and truncating them to $T = 32$, $64$, and $128$. We perform the experiment using three models (GPT-Neo 125M, Pythia 160M, and Pythia 410M), two datasets (WikiText and XSum), and two attacks. As the results in Table 4 show, increasing $T$ typically yields a substantial increase in AUROC. The amount of increase is more noticeable in smaller models like GPT-Neo 125M and Pythia 160M. In

**Table 4.** AUROCs of min-k and win-k with varying models and datasets under different number of tokens $T$.

| Dataset | Tokens | GPT-Neo 125M | | Pythia 160M | | Pythia 410M | |
|---|---|---|---|---|---|---|---|
| | | Min-k | Win-k | Min-k | Win-k | Min-k | Win-k |
| WikiText | $T = 32$ | 76.0% | 71.7% | 77.6% | 78.9% | 96.0% | 96.0% |
| | $T = 64$ | 83.1% | 83.5% | 84.8% | 86.3% | 98.8% | 98.9% |
| | $T = 128$ | 87.2% | 87.0% | 84.8% | 86.3% | 99.3% | 99.5% |
| XSum | $T = 32$ | 69.2% | 69.9% | 77.2% | 78.0% | 90.8% | 90.8% |
| | $T = 64$ | 70.9% | 71.9% | 79.0% | 80.0% | 94.3% | 94.8% |
| | $T = 128$ | 76.9% | 78.5% | 84.2% | 86.2% | 97.6% | 97.8% |

contrast, the AUROCs in Pythia 410M are already high when $T = 32$; thus, the amount of increase from $T = 32$ to 64 and 128 is less noticeable.

## 5    Discussion and Conclusion

**Summary.** SLMs are rapidly gaining traction as efficient and deployable alternatives to LLMs in resource-constrained and on-device AI applications. In this paper, we examined the vulnerability of SLMs to MIAs. Our analysis revealed that the effectiveness of MIAs declines as model size decreases. We therefore proposed win-k, a new MIA which generalizes the min-k attack by aggregating log probability scores over sliding windows of tokens. Experiments on eight SLMs across three datasets and three evaluation metrics showed that win-k outperforms prior attacks, especially on smaller models. Furthermore, we provided practical insights into the selection of win-k's hyperparameters.

**Limitations and Future Work.** First, our current work is limited to SLMs with $\leq$ 1B parameters. Generalizing to larger models (e.g., up to 5B or 7B parameters) would be a valuable future work direction. However, full fine-tuning of such models using SFTTRAINER is unlikely to be feasible, hence PEFT methods such as LoRA may be needed. For consistency, we stick with SFTTRAINER in the paper and leave fine-tuning of larger models with LoRA to future work. Second, it would be interesting to consider issues arising from the number of member versus non-member samples as well as the types of samples (e.g., scientific texts versus news articles). Attacks targeting specific contexts or targeted content may be considered. Third, while win-k relies on a sliding mean of log probabilities, it does not examine alternative aggregation strategies (e.g., median, trimmed mean, max pooling). We will consider extending our attack with such aggregation strategies. Finally, we will study defenses against win-k and MIAs in general. As MIAs exploit models' tendency to overfit, one mitigation strategy could be regularization (dropout, L1 or L2 regularization). Noise can be introduced to log probabilities to mask membership or differentially private fine-tuning methods can be utilized as defenses.

**Acknowledgements.** This study was supported by The Scientific and Technological Research Council of Turkiye (TUBITAK) under grants numbered 123E179 and 125E059. The authors thank TUBITAK for their support.

# References


1. Biderman, S., et al.: Pythia: a suite for analyzing large language models across training and scaling. In: International Conference on Machine Learning, pp. 2397–2430. PMLR (2023)
2. Black, S., Gao, L., Wang, P., Leahy, C., Biderman, S.: GPT-Neo: large scale autoregressive language modeling with mesh-tensorflow (2021). https://doi.org/10.5281/zenodo.5297715
3. Brown, T., et al.: Language models are few-shot learners. Adv. Neural. Inf. Process. Syst. **33**, 1877–1901 (2020)
4. Carlini, N., et al.: Extracting training data from large language models. In: 30th USENIX Security Symposium, pp. 2633–2650 (2021)
5. Duan, M., et al.: Do membership inference attacks work on large language models? arXiv preprint arXiv:2402.07841 (2024)
6. Hu, S., et al.: MiniCPM: unveiling the potential of small language models with scalable training strategies. arXiv preprint arXiv:2404.06395 (2024)
7. Liu, Z., et al.: MobileLLM: optimizing sub-billion parameter language models for on-device use cases. In: International Conference on Machine Learning (2024)
8. Lu, Z., et al.: Small language models: Survey, measurements, and insights. arXiv preprint arXiv:2409.15790 (2024)
9. Mattern, J., Mireshghallah, F., Jin, Z., Schoelkopf, B., Sachan, M., Berg-Kirkpatrick, T.: Membership inference attacks against language models via neighbourhood comparison. In: The 61st Annual Meeting of the Association for Computational Linguistics (2023)
10. Shi, W., et al.: Detecting pretraining data from large language models. In: 12th International Conference on Learning Representations, ICLR (2024)
11. Shokri, R., Stronati, M., Song, C., Shmatikov, V.: Membership inference attacks against machine learning models. In: IEEE Symposium on Security and Privacy (SP), pp. 3–18. IEEE (2017)
12. Truex, S., Liu, L., Gursoy, M.E., Yu, L., Wei, W.: Demystifying membership inference attacks in machine learning as a service. IEEE Trans. Serv. Comput. **14**(6), 2073–2089 (2019)
13. Yeom, S., Giacomelli, I., Fredrikson, M., Jha, S.: Privacy risk in machine learning: analyzing the connection to overfitting. In: 31st Computer Security Foundations Symposium (CSF), pp. 268–282. IEEE (2018)

# Advanced Electronic Signatures
# and GDPR: Reconciling the Concepts

Paweł Kostkiewicz⬤, Mirosław Kutyłowski$^{(\boxtimes)}$⬤, and Gabriel Wechta⬤

NASK National Research Institute, Warsaw, Poland
`{pawel.kostkiewicz,miroslaw.kutylowski,gabriel.wechta}@nask.pl`

**Abstract.** Digital signature schemes developed by the cryptographic community have been adopted as *advanced electronic signatures* in the legal framework of many countries, including the European Union. In their current implementations, certification practices, and legal practice, electronic signatures are orthogonal to privacy protection. In fact, protecting data origin and integrity with advanced electronic signatures creates many challenges from the point of view of GDPR.

In this paper, we show that conflicts between the legal concept of electronic signatures and the strength of digital signatures on one side, and the paradigms of privacy-by-design, data minimization, etc. can be resolved by slightly reshaping the signature schemes and reinterpreting certain legal concepts.

**Keywords:** GDPR · eIDAS · Advanced Electronic Signature · Hash Function · Merkle Tree

## 1 Introduction

Digital signatures provide essential cryptographic guarantees: authentication, integrity, and non-repudiation, which make them valuable in many digital application areas. However, the standard approach to creating a signature, that is, treating the message as a single array of bytes, can sometimes become a limitation. This rigid model may prevent certain desirable use cases that are common in the physical world but difficult to replicate digitally. For example, with a handwritten signature on a physical document, one can partially cover the page to hide sensitive information while still proving that the visible portions are authentic. In the digital realm, achieving a similar form of *selective disclosure* is not straightforward under conventional signature schemes.

In this paper, we examine this problem in detail, place it in the context of current legal frameworks (namely, eIDAS [12,29] and GDPR [30]), and present two straightforward schemes that can be used with any existing standard cryptographic primitives. In particular, our approach can be used with widely standardized algorithms, and thus be inline with legislation such as eIDAS. Importantly, it does not introduce an additional burden on end users as it does not alter the existing interfaces (meaning that creation and verification of signature from the


R. Laborde et al. (Eds.): ESORICS 2025, LNCS 16231, pp. 79–95, 2026.
https://doi.org/10.1007/978-3-032-16089-8_6

user's point of view remains the same), except introducing a new functionality called selective disclosure.

## 1.1  Traditional Model of Digital Signatures

The first challenge is that an electronic signature scheme applied in practice should be able to create a signature for a document of arbitrary size. Thus, it cannot be assumed that a message is an element of a fixed algebraic structure. This practically eliminates schemes (e.g., [5,20]) that are not based on a cryptographic digest (in practice, a hash function and the Random Oracle Model [2]).

Another common practical issue is that signatures often need to be generated using a secure signature creation device (cf. WSCD in eIDAS [12]). In many cases, this device is a special-purpose component (e.g., a smart card), with limited storage capacity and/or low-bandwidth communication capabilities. In this case, uploading an entire document to the device is impractical. Instead, a common strategy is to upload only a hash of the document, or a small portion of it together with an intermediate hash [26]; see also p. 465 in [31]. Analogously, for sponge hash functions [3], the signing device may execute only the last absorbing step. To alleviate the problems mentioned above, the common approach is a two-stage signing process for a document $D$:

1. Run some algebraic precomputation to generate an element $r$.
2. Create a cryptographic digest $h$ of $D$ and the precomputed value $r$ using hash function $\mathsf{Hash}$, concretely $h := \mathsf{Hash}(D, r)$.
3. Apply the core signing procedure for $h$, using the secret signing key $\mathsf{sk}$, that is $\sigma := \phi(h, \mathsf{sk})$, where $\phi$ is some algebraic operation based on a difficult cryptographic problem.

During the verification procedure, the values $h$ and $r$ are recalculated in the first step. After that, an algebraic test is executed. It involves $\sigma$, $h$ and the public key $\mathsf{pk}$ corresponding to $\mathsf{sk}$. Note that this approach is followed by major digital signature schemes.

An immediate consequence of this approach is that any benign (e.g., privacy-preserving) change to the document before presenting it for verification (such as replacing personal identification data with a pseudonym) will produce a different value of $h$. Consequently, the signature on the document is no longer valid, and its entire proof value is lost. To address this problem we employ a document-structure-aware hash function (details are provided in Sect. 3).

In the next section, we discuss several practical situations and show that, in these cases, the observation made above is the Achilles' heel of the concept of electronic signature.

## 1.2  Privacy Protection Versus Digital Signatures

Although advanced electronic signatures provide very strong arguments for data origin and integrity, in certain situations, their strength becomes a significant problem severely limiting their application scope. In this section, we highlight a variety of scenarios in which reconsidering the standard approach to digital signatures could provide substantial benefits.

*Partial Disclosure of Signed Documents.* In certain scenarios, such as public administration procedures, legal documents are signed and subsequently published to comply with the right of access to public information. However, these documents may contain information that must remain confidential. Examples include personal data protected according to the GDPR, information related to public security, or other categories of data protected by law. A concrete example is the publication of court judgments in Poland, which must be anonymized in the sense that all personal data contained in court decisions must be removed[1] (except for the names of court personnel and judges involved). Such anonymized court decisions are available online.[2]

In this case, the original digital signature on the document cannot be used directly to check the blinded document. Even worse, if the scope of blinding is limited, a brute-force attack may be used to reconstruct the original document—the signature serves as an oracle for checking the correctness of a guess.

For this reason, if certain parts of a document need to be blinded, the document should be re-signed. However, this introduces not only additional effort but also new risks, as, for example, a new signature might be applied to content that differs from the original in the non-blinded parts.

*Personalized Disclosure.* It may happen that a document $D$ contains a wide range of data ($D$ could be a complicated contract and/or an extensive technical documentation), where an individual reader should read only its selected parts according to the data minimization paradigm.

The classical approach to dealing with this problem is to split the document into separate parts and sign each part separately. This solution might be quite tedious, as splitting the document must occur in advance, while the situation may dynamically change, especially if the subject covered by the $D$ is complicated.

*Electronic Document Management Systems.* Electronic flow of documents may require complicated access rights to document contents. For example, a reviewer in PhD proceedings in Poland submits a standard bill containing the information such as bank account, place of residence, personal identification number, and other data required by the tax authorities. However, the bill must be accepted by a person responsible for verifying the PhD report submitted by the reviewer. In this case, a staff member of the entity granting the degrees gets access to data such as bank account number of the reviewer. This data is unnecessary for payment approval. This directly violates the data minimization paradigm from GDPR as well as general cybersecurity rules.

In electronic document management systems, we require flexible rules for data access. Moreover, they should be easy to handle from the user's point of view. The ultimate target would be to achieve the level of flexibility and

---

[1] An operation known as *blinding.*

[2] See https://orzeczenia.ms.gov.pl.

expressivity achieved by the best access control systems. Reaching this goal with the current electronic signature model seems infeasible.

*Right to be Forgotten.* A signed document $D$ may contain personal data that should be erased at the legitimate request of a data subject $A$ [30]. However, the document $D$ may contain data that must be retained, in particular, due to some legal obligation. In this case, we have a deadlock: blinding certain parts of $D$ makes the signature contained in $D$ invalid and violates the obligation to keep $D$ in a verifiable form. On the other hand, without blinding the rights of the data subject $A$ granted by GDPR are violated.

*Hiding Signatory.* In certain situations, the information on the signatory should be protected. It may concern documents that are processed within an organization with multiple persons involved, and signing them to mark acceptance. When the document leaves the organization, only a few chosen signatures should be attached to the document's text. However, during the intermediate stages of document processing, the next signature is created for the original document appended with the previous signatures. In this case, it might be challenging to remove some of the intermediate signatures.

A similar problem may concern public key certificates (which again are secured with an electronic seal). Not all fields of the certificate should be visible to every Verifier—an example is a certificate for personal signature created by personal identity cards in Poland, which includes the signatory's personal identification number PESEL. This number is not secret; however, due to the threat of identity theft, it should not be distributed unless necessary. In most cases, it is not.

### 1.3  Related Work

So far, selective disclosure has been explored primarly in the Self-Sovereign Identity domain, particularly in the context of privacy-preserving credential presentation [4,7,15]. In parallel, recent European legislative developments have significantly influenced the design of digital services. Key regulations include the eIDAS framework [12,29], the GDPR [30], and the Whistleblowing Directive [13]. These initiatives set the legal foundation for trust, interoperability, and privacy in the European digital ecosystem, providing both opportunities and constraints for the implementation of selective disclosure technologies. However, introduction of new cryptographic techniques for legal use cases is guarded by a list of scrutinized standards (see, e.g., [9,17,22,23]).

## 2  Digital Signatures According to eIDAS

According to the eIDAS Regulation [12,29], users of European Digital Identity Wallets (EDIW) should be able to create and use electronic signatures that are accepted across the EU (see Recitals 19 and 20). eIDAS sets out the criteria for an advanced electronic signature in Article 26. These requirements, while not framed in standard cryptographic language, align closely with traditional cryptographic signature properties (with one exception). Specifically, an advanced electronic signature must be

(a) uniquely linked to the signatory and (b) capable of identifying the signatory—both aspects relate to *non-repudiation,*
(c) created using electronic signature creation data that the signatory can, with a high level of confidence, use under his sole control—*authentication,* and
(d) **linked to the signed data in such a way that any subsequent changes are detectable**—which goes beyond the traditional definition of *data integrity.* Conventionally, any modification to the signed data typically renders the signature invalid. However, under the eIDAS framework, one might interpret this requirement in two ways:
- Minimum: Any alteration of the data makes the signature invalid.
- Maximum: It is possible to detect precisely what was changed; signatures covering the modified parts and the overall document are invalid, but the unchanged parts can still be verified correctly.

In our opinion, the second interpretation is not only more pragmatic, but also follows the standard interpretation of legal norms. Indeed, for the first interpretation (minimum), the wording of the legal text that more closely reflects the interpretation would be "... linked to the signed data in such a way that any subsequent changes *make the signature invalid.*"

## 2.1   ETSI Recommended Digital Signatures Algorithms

The general legal definitions should be confronted with practice, where technical recommendations and standards play the crucial role. Among others, any deviation from the recommendations and standards creates multiple problems, ranging from limited availability on the market to substantially harder certification and market acceptance. Let us briefly discuss ETSI TS 119 312 V1.4.3 (2023-08) [9], the official EU list of algorithms to be used for electronic signatures. It recommends the following signature algorithms:

**RSA:** As specified in RFC 8017 [22], the RSA-PKCS1-v1_5 and RSA-PSS schemes begin signing by applying encoding procedures (EMSA-PKCS1-v1_5 and EMSA-PSS, respectively) to a hash of the message.

**ECDSA:** As defined in FIPS 186-5 [23], the message is first processed using an approved hash function or an extendable-output function.

**ECGDA:** According to ISO/IEC 14888-3 [17], this variant of ECDSA also begins by hashing the message to be signed.

In all cases,[3] the entire document is hashed, so any modification is detectable and results in the signature's invalidation.

---

[3] The DSA is omitted here, as it is no longer approved for signature generation according to FIPS 186-5 [23].

## 2.2    Presentation of Attributes

The eIDAS regulation concerns the use of electronic signatures in two distinct contexts. First, eIDAS mandates that EDIW users must be able to create and use electronic signatures. These signatures must be accepted across the EU "...by default and free of charge, without having to go through any additional administrative procedures." (ref. Recital 19). One key use case is the ability to "...sign or seal self-claimed assertions or attributes ..."—a privacy-preserving mechanism that allows users to reveal only specific parts of an identity document, rather than the entire document.

Second, electronic signatures also play a central role within the eIDAS trust service framework in attribute presentation, one of the key EDIWs' functionalities. Specifically, qualified electronic attestations of attributes (Article 45d) and electronic attestations issued by or on behalf of public sector bodies responsible for authentic sources (Article 45f) must comply with the requirements outlined in Annexes V and VII, respectively. In both cases, a qualified electronic signature from the issuing qualified trust service provider or public authority is required.

However, this collides with Article 5a.4(a) that requires that the EDIW must enable users to "request, obtain, select, combine, store, delete, share, and present ...personal identification data and, where applicable, in combination with electronic attestations of attributes ...while ensuring that *selective disclosure* of data is possible." Clearly, to support selective disclosure, signature verification mechanisms must allow for fine-grained validation without requiring the user to present the entire attestation.

Finally, to further support the compatibility of eIDAS with our proposed reconciled approach to signature mechanisms, it is worth noting that the Commission Decision 2015/1506 [11], which specifies formats for advanced electronic signatures and seals under eIDAS, endorses XML,[4] CMS and PDF formats.

## 2.3    ICAO

It should be noted that a similar to ours, but less general approach has been adopted by the ICAO [16] for authenticating the personal data of holders of travel eDocuments. These eDocuments (e.g., passports, personal identity cards) contain both standard identification data (such as name, date of birth, etc.) and sensitive biometric data (such as fingerprints, iris scans, etc.). Access to the former is available to anyone holding a travel eDocument, for instance, by using an e-passport reader app such as [28].

An eDocument holds 16 Data Groups, which store identification data, and a Document Security Object $SO_D$. During the preparation phase, the Document Issuer computes the hash of each Data Group and signs the collection using their Document Issuer Public Key (represented by the red lock in Fig. 1). Later, in the presentation phase, the eDocument provides $SO_D$ to the Reader. Upon

---

[4] Among these, XML is especially well-suited for implementing structures that enable granular access to specific fields in attestations.

receiving it, the Reader verifies the signature in $SO_D$ using the Document Issuer's Public Key (the red key in Fig. 1). If the verification is successful, the Reader requests the relevant Data Groups from the eDocument. Once received, the Reader compares their hashes with those included in $SO_D$. If they match, the Reader accepts the data as authentic. In the described mechanism, the Document Issuer signs the root of a flat Merkle tree [21], where the leaves correspond to the individual Data Groups.

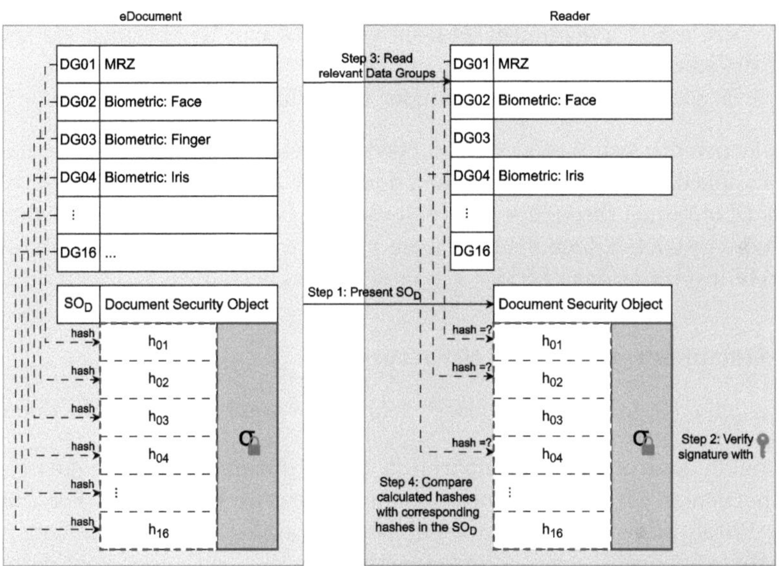


**Fig. 1.** Simple version of *passive authentication* of [16]. $\sigma$ denotes Document Issuer's signature on hash collection. For clarity, we omit both the validation of the Document Issuer's certificate and the authentication of the Reader to the eDocument prior to presentation.

# 3   Signatures with Selective Document Disclosure

The central conceptual shift that we propose is to enable selective disclosure of a signed document $D$, while preserving the ability to validate the signature as if it were applied to the complete original version of $D$.[5] Formally, we define *structured signature* scheme SSign built on top of a standard signature scheme Sign with the following procedures:

**Key generation:** Identical to the standard key generation procedure in Sign; that is, generate a key pair $(\mathsf{sk}, \mathsf{pk})$.

---

[5] A similar concept, but in terms of files (not documents), can be found in ETSI standard [14, ref. Associated Signature Containers].

**Signature creation:** Instead of applying the standard hash function Hash to obtain the digest of a message $D$ before invoking Sign, the scheme computes a structured hash $h :-$ SHash$(D)$, and then applies Sign. The resulting signature is denoted $\sigma$.

**Selective disclosure:** The signer or anyone who knows $D$ and $h$, can produce a blinded version $D'$ of the original document $D$.

**Signature verification:** The input consists of the blinded document $D'$, the original signature $\sigma$ on the full document $D$, and the public key pk. Verification succeeds if and only if:

1. there exists a document $D$ from which $D'$ can be obtained via selective disclosure, and
2. $\sigma$ is a valid signature on $D$ under the public key pk.

The selective disclosure procedure defined this way should be iterative that is, it can be applied not only to the original document $D$, but also to any derived document $D'$ obtained through selective disclosure. In particular, one may derive an even more restricted document $D''$ from $D'$ and continue this process iteratively. Concrete instantiations of SSign are presented in Sect. 3.2,3.3.

### 3.1 Document with DAG Structure

The first step towards defining SHash is finding a graph structure of a document:

- In public and private administration, XML documents are frequently used, in particular with a predefined standard structure (see Fig. 2). For example, the Polish Ministry of Finance publishes a catalog of tax documents.[6] Each XML document has the explicit structure of a tree, with document data items having well-defined locations and types. For XML documents, there is no need to convert to a graph representation, as it is explicit.
- The documents generated by humans, say in English, consist of sentences, which in turn form paragraphs. The paragraphs may form sections, etc. This relatively flat tree structure relates to the semantic composition of the text and can be explicitly created by the text author.
- A text file is a sequence of characters, but it can be analyzed by automatic Natural Language Processing (NLP) tools to determine its structure. The essential part of such analysis is to convert the text into a sequence of tokens and then to find the structures of how the tokens are composed. A clear advantage of this approach is that a token, such as an identifier of an individual, occurring in different places is treated as the same object (see Fig. 3). The above conversion can be done by external LLM tools [1,24] (with all concerns related to data privacy); however, there are open-access LLMs that can be fine-tuned for this specific use case and run locally (e.g., DeepSeek R1 Offline [8]).

---

[6] See https://www.podatki.gov.pl/e-deklaracje/dokumentacja-it/struktury-dokumentow-xml.

```xml
<xsd:element name="PozycjeSzczegolowe">
  <xsd:complexType>
   <xsd:sequence>
     <xsd:annotation>
       <xsd:documentation>
         1. Należności ze stosunku: pracy, służbowego, spółdzielczego i z ...
       </xsd:documentation>
     </xsd:annotation>
     <xsd:element name="P_29" type="TKwota2Nieujemna">
       <xsd:annotation>
         <xsd:documentation>Przychód</xsd:documentation>
       </xsd:annotation>
     </xsd:element>
     ...
     <xsd:element name="P_30" type="TKwota2Nieujemna" minOccurs="0">
       <xsd:annotation>
         <xsd:documentation>Koszty uzyskania przychodów</xsd:documentation>
       </xsd:annotation>
     </xsd:element>
     <xsd:element name="P_31" type="TKwota2Nieujemna">
       <xsd:annotation>
         <xsd:documentation>Dochód</xsd:documentation>
       </xsd:annotation>
     </xsd:element>
     ...
```

POLTAX — POLA JASNE WYPEŁNIA PŁATNIK, POLA CIEMNE WYPEŁNIA URZĄD SKARBOWY. WYPEŁNIAĆ NA MASZYNIE, KOMPUTEROWO LUB RĘCZNIE, DUŻYMI, DRUKOWANYMI LITERAMI, CZARNYM LUB NIEBIESKIM KOLOREM.     *Składanie w wersji elektronicznej: www.portalpodatkowy.mf.gov.pl*

**E. DOCHODY PODATNIKA, POBRANE ZALICZKI ORAZ POBRANE SKŁADKI** [9)]

| Źródła przychodów | Przychód [7)] zł. gr | Koszty uzyskania przychodów [8)] zł. gr | Dochód (b - c) zł. gr | Dochód zwolniony od podatku [7)] zł. gr | Zaliczka pobrana przez płatnika zł |
|---|---|---|---|---|---|
| 1. Należności ze stosunku: pracy, służbowego, spółdzielczego i z pracy nakładczej, a także zasiłki pieniężne z ubezpieczenia społecznego wypłacone przez zakład pracy, o którym mowa w art. 31 ustawy, oraz płatników, o których mowa w art. 42e ust. 1 ustawy | 29. | 30. | 31. | 32. | 33. |
| W poz. 34 należy wykazać przychody, do których zastosowano odliczenie kosztów uzyskania przychodów na podstawie art. 22 ust. 9 pkt 3 ustawy. | 34. | 35. | | | |

**Fig. 2.** Excerpt from the official Personal Income Tax XML file (`PIT-11(16)_v1-0.xsd`, top) and the corresponding PDF form (bottom), both sourced from the Polish Ministry of Finance website.

It follows that with a limited effort, we can represent any document $D$, whether through an XML structure or tokenization,[7] by a Directed Acyclic Graph (DAG). We shall use $DAG(D)$ to denote DAG based on document $D$, where:

- the nodes of $DAG(D)$ are labeled and have unique identifiers ID,
- the content of $D$ is encoded into labels of certain nodes (possibly not only the leaves),
- the structure of $DAG(D)$ reflects the semantic structure of document $D$,

---

[7] Note that we do not commit to a single "best" method, as the most suitable approach depends heavily on the specific scenario. For example, if a document is created with selective disclosure in mind, representing it as XML introduces minimal overhead for the creator—especially when issuing many copies with the same structure. For documents without such a structure, simple parsers may suffice. A solution based on LLMs that retrieves the structure of a document requires more consideration (see Sect. 4) but can still be applied effectively in ad hoc cases.

- it can be assumed that there is a single maximal (root) element in DAG($D$) (having indegree zero); if there is more than one maximal element, we create an extra root node of DAG($D$), to which we connect all maximal nodes.

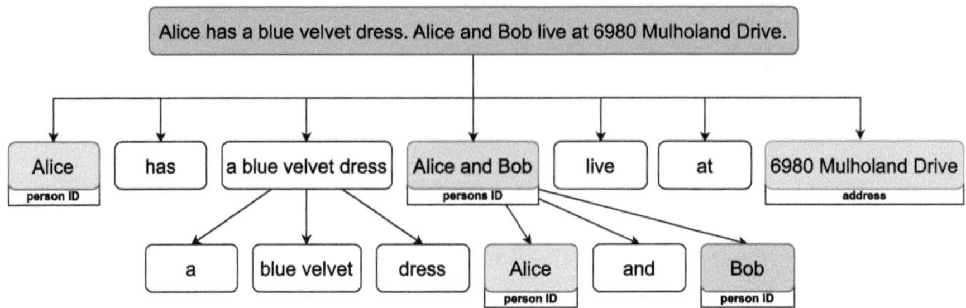


**Fig. 3.** An example of representing $D$ as a DAG, with certain nodes labeled as potentially private data. Note that some nodes contain more than one word; this is why we use a more complex DAG representation rather than a simple flat tree. This choice was deliberate: 1) Context may reveal auxiliary information. Consider the term "Alice and Bob". Assume for a moment that we do not have the term "Alice and Bob" as a single unit, but instead have three separate terms: "Alice", "and", and "Bob". If, for example, Bob is the target of pseudonymization $D$ and Alice is not, then blinding only the term "Bob" would be insufficient, as it would reveal the fact that the pseudonymized individual lives with Alice. 2) Certain languages (e.g., Chinese) may require different approach for semantic decomposition than English.

An instantiation of DAG($D$) (see Fig. 3 for an example) depends on the strategy to convert a text document $D$ to a graph representation. For XML documents, it is immediate, while, say, for PDF documents, it might be a moderate standardization challenge due to multiple design decisions.

*Selective Disclosure of a Document.* If a document $D$ with DAG structure DAG($D$) has to be revealed selectively, then we blind a chosen part of the graph DAG($D$)—if a node $A$ is blinded, then all its successors are blinded as well.

To enable fluent human–machine interaction, it is essential to develop tools that convert the blinded DAG($D$) into a human-readable format. Base libraries are available in most programming languages (for example, [25]).

*Example 1.* In XML tax document, we can selectively eliminate certain field values (like the taxpayer's ID number) or blind an entire subtree (e.g., corresponding to the declared income). In the latter case, we get a document that witnesses that a given person has an active taxpayer status, while the confidential data regarding the income is removed. Such a blinded document might useful, for example, in some towns, municipal authorities offer discounts on public transportation for their residents, provided that the taxpayer declares this municipality in the tax declaration.

*Example 2.* In case of a text document $D$ converted to $\mathsf{DAG}(D)$ with an NLP tool, the resulting graphs have tokens corresponding to nodes with no incoming arcs. Some tokens correspond to physical persons identifiers or to data enabling identification of a data subject (e.g., a token being a part of the address). Note that such a token may correspond to multiple occurrences in the original text; note that manual anonymization may overlook some appearances. With a $\mathsf{DAG}(D)$, it suffices to eliminate a selected token to eliminate all of its appearances.

In Sect. 3.2 and 3.3, we present two approaches to creating signatures that enable partial disclosure of a document by utilizing its semantic DAG structure.

## 3.2   Merkle Tree Approach

*Preliminary Definitions.* In this section, we consider a $\mathsf{DAG}(D)$ where the order of children of each node is defined and there is a single root - the only node with indegree 0 (recall that we consider directed edges that point in the direction from the root to the leaves). In particular, it does not need to be a tree.

Each node $A$ of the tree may correspond to a part of the document $D$ according to a relevant semantic structure. For the sake of generality, we assume that the text of $D$ is spread not only among leaf nodes of $\mathsf{DAG}(D)$, but possibly also among the non-leaf nodes. Let $\mathsf{ID}_A$ be the identifier of node $A$, and let $T(A)$ denote its label. The label $T(A)$ is either a text from $D$ or an artifact of $\mathsf{DAG}(D)$ creation. If $T(A)$ is a part of the text $D$, then we associate with $A$ a random bit-string $(salt)$ $T_{\mathsf{salt}}(A)$, which is long enough to make brute-force preimage attacks against a hash function infeasible. Define

$$
T^+(A) = \begin{cases} (T(A), T_{\mathsf{salt}}(A)), & if\, T_{\mathsf{salt}}(A)\, is\, defined, \\ T(A), & \text{otherwise.} \end{cases}
$$

*Computing* $\mathsf{SHash}$. The hash value $h(A)$ of a node $A$ is defined recursively by the following formula:

$$
h(A) = \begin{cases} \mathsf{Hash}(T^+(A)), & \text{if A is a leaf (outdegree zero),} \\ \mathsf{Hash}(\mathsf{Hash}(T^+(A)), h(A_1), \ldots, h(A_u)), & \text{otherwise,} \end{cases}
$$

where $A_1, \ldots, A_u$ are the child nodes of $A$. The values of $h$ are calculated bottom-up starting from the leaves of $\mathsf{DAG}(D)$.

Let $h_{\mathsf{root}}$ denote the hash value at the root node of $\mathsf{DAG}(D)$. The final output is $\left(h_{\mathsf{root}}, \{(\mathsf{ID}_{A_i}, T_{\mathsf{salt}}(A_i))_i\}\right)$ for all nodes $A_i$ where $T_{\mathsf{salt}}(A_i)$ was defined.

*Signature Creation.* The signing algorithm $\mathsf{Sign}$ is applied to produce the signature $\sigma$. The only difference from the standard procedure is that the hash value $h = \mathsf{Hash}(D)$ is replaced by $h := h_{\mathsf{root}}$ returned by $\mathsf{SHash}(D)$.

*Selective Disclosure.* A User holds document $D$ (and thereby also $\mathsf{DAG}(D)$), a signature $\sigma$, and the salt values $T_{\mathsf{salt}}(A_i)$. The following steps are executed:

1. Construct the *blinded* $\mathsf{DAG}(D')$ by selecting a subset of nodes from $\mathsf{DAG}(D)$ whose label is to be hidden (we shall call them *blinded nodes*).
2. Replace $T(A)$ of each blinded node $A$ with the empty symbol $\blacksquare$.
3. Create a list $L$ that enables reconstruction of $h_{\mathrm{root}}$:
    - If node $A$ is blinded, insert $(\mathsf{ID}_A, \mathsf{Hash}(T^+(A), 0)$ into $L$.
    - If node $A$ is non-blinded, insert $(\mathsf{ID}_A, T_{\mathsf{salt}}(A), 1)$ into $L$.
4. Output $\big(\mathsf{DAG}(D'), \sigma, L\big)$ to the Recipient of the selectively disclosed signature.

*Signature Verification for Selectively Disclosed* $D$. The specific part of signature verification is the recalculation of $h_{\mathrm{root}}$. It is easy to see that with $L$, the Verifier can recompute $h_{\mathrm{root}}$: for each non-blinded node $A$, $\mathsf{Hash}(T^+(A))$ must be computed, using the part $T(A)$ of the document $D$. For a blinded node $B$, the Verifier uses $\mathsf{Hash}(T^+(B))$ from the list $L$ and cannot derive $T(B)$ due to the application of the (unknown) salt string.

## Discussion.

*Note 1.* The text document $D'$ corresponding to $\mathsf{DAG}(D')$ can be visualized in a manner analogous to the so called "black box" redaction of classified documents, where each empty symbol $\blacksquare$ is replaced with an appropriate graphical placeholder.

*Note 2.* If $\mathsf{DAG}(D)$ is a tree, the resulting structure is simply a Merkle Tree [21] with some additional data taken under the hash (salted hashing).

*Note 3.* Observe that any Recipient of a selectively disclosed $\big(\mathsf{DAG}(D'), \sigma, L\big)$ can further restrict the content of the document and present it to another party. To blind an additional node $A$ it suffices to change $T(A)$ to $\blacksquare$ and replace $(\mathsf{ID}_A, T_{\mathsf{salt}}(A), 1)$ with $(\mathsf{ID}_A, \mathsf{Hash}(T^+(A)), 0)$ in $L$.

*Note 4.* Similarly, for any Recipient of selectively disclosed $\big(\mathsf{DAG}(D'), \sigma, L\big)$, it is infeasible to alter the content of the unblinded fields, as any such change would modify the final value of $h_{\mathrm{root}}$ or a collision of $\mathsf{Hash}$ would be found. Therefore, the security arguments reduce to the security of the underlying signature scheme.

*Note 5.* According to the Architecture and Reference Framework (ARF) [10], EDIW must support two mandatory standards for the electronic attestation of attributes with selective disclosure, namely ISO/IEC 18013-5 [18], which is generalized in ISO/IEC 23220-2 [19], and SD-JWT-based Verifiable Credentials [6]. In addition, EDIW may optionally support the W3C Verifiable Credentials Data Model v2.0 [27]. All three standards achieve selective disclosure by hashing each attribute together with a random value (once again, salted hashing). Thus, we are reusing the same concept for selective disclosure of signed documents as ARF uses for selective disclosure of electronic attestations of attributes.

### 3.3  Structured Encryption Approach

In this approach, all node labels of $\mathsf{DAG}(D)$ are first encrypted using an OTP-like symsmetric encryption scheme[8] before being signed with $\mathsf{Sign}$, while the keys used to encrypt the contents of the individual nodes of $\mathsf{DAG}(D)$ are distinct.

*Key Derivation.* Assume that $\mathsf{DAG}(D)$ is a tree where the order of children of each node is defined.[9] The encryption keys are derived in a top-down manner:

1. Select a root key $K_{root}$ at random, assign it to the root of $\mathsf{DAG}(D)$,
2. Let $K_A$ be a key for node $A$, then $m$ children of $A$ are assigned, respectively, the keys

$$\mathsf{Hash}(K_A, 1), \mathsf{Hash}(K_A, 2), \ldots, \mathsf{Hash}(K_A, m). \tag{1}$$

*Encryption of* $\mathsf{DAG}(D)$. We construct $\mathsf{EDAG}(D)$, the encrypted copy of $\mathsf{DAG}(D)$, by transforming the node labels according to the following procedure:

1. For each node $A$ in $\mathsf{DAG}(D)$, replace the label $T(A)$ with

$$T'(A) :- \big(T(A) \oplus K'_A, \mathsf{Hash}(K_A, 0)\big),$$

   where
   - $K'_A$ is the output of a cryptographic PRNG seeded with $K_A$, truncated to the bit-length of $T(A)$,
   - $\oplus$ denotes the bitwise XOR operation, and
   - $\mathsf{Hash}(K_A, 0)$ is used for authenticating the key $K_A$.
2. Output $\big(\mathsf{EDAG}(D), K_{root}\big)$.

*Computing* $\mathsf{SHash}$. In this case, $\mathsf{SHash}(D) :- \mathsf{Hash}(\mathsf{ser}(\mathsf{EDAG}(D)))$, where $\mathsf{ser}$ can be any standard DAG serialization method.

*Signature creation.* A standard signature scheme $\mathsf{Sign}$ is applied, producing the signature $\sigma$ with $h :- \mathsf{SHash}(D)$.

*Selective disclosure.* If the Signer wants to disclose the entire document $D$ with its signature, then the Recipient gets the tuple

$$\big(\mathsf{EDAG}(D), \sigma, K_0\big).$$

The Verifier can use $K_0$ to derive all keys $K_A$, decrypt each $T'(A)$ and finally check that the decrypted labels $T(A)$ represent $\mathsf{DAG}(D)$. The standard test is applied to $\sigma$ and $h$.

Alternatively, the Signer can disclose only a set of nodes of $\mathsf{DAG}(D)$, so that if a node $A$ is disclosed, then automatically all its successors in $\mathsf{DAG}(D)$ will be disclosed as well. The following steps are executed:

---

[8] Note that any symmetric encryption scheme $(\mathsf{Enc}_K, \mathsf{Dec}_K)$ can be used in this scenario, additionally, if an AEAD scheme is used, appending authentication data can be neglected.

[9] We follow the idea from [32] of segment-based document protection.

1. Identify the nodes $A_1, \ldots, A_t$ such that the disclosed document $D'$ contains $T(A_1), \ldots, T(A_t)$. Let $\mathcal{KS}$ denote the set of nodes $A_1, \ldots, A_t$ and all their successors.
2. Derive the keys $K_{A_1}, \ldots, K_{A_t}$ from $K_0$ according to the original procedure.
3. Output the tuple

$$\left(\mathsf{EDAG}(D), \sigma, \mathsf{ID}_{A_1}, \ldots, \mathsf{ID}_{A_t}, K_{A_1}, \ldots, K_{A_t}\right). \tag{2}$$

*Signature Verification.* Let us focus on selectively disclosed $D$, as the case without selective disclosure corresponds to the case of choosing $A_1$ being the root of $\mathsf{DAG}(D)$.

For verification of a signature (2), the Recipient executes the following steps:

1. Verify the signature $\sigma$ on $\mathsf{EDAG}(D)$.
2. Starting from the nodes $A_1, \ldots, A_t$ and the keys $K_{A_1}, \ldots, K_{A_t}$, calculate the key $K_B$ for every successor node $B$ contained in $\mathcal{KS}$ using the procedure from Eq. 1.
3. For $A \in \mathcal{KS}$, check the correctness of $K_A$ by testing $H(A) \stackrel{?}{=} \mathsf{Hash}(K_A, 0)$.
4. For $A \in \mathcal{KS}$, recover the plaintext $T(A)$ by XOR-ing $T(A) \otimes K'_A$ with $K'_A$ derived from $K_A$. If a node $B$ of $\mathsf{DAG}(D)$ does not belong to $\mathcal{KS}$, then the field $T(B)$ should be replaced by the empty symbol ■.

*Note 6.* The visualization of $\mathsf{DAG}(D')$ in the Structured Encryption approach follows directly from the Merkle Tree approach. Also, observe that, similarly to the Merkle Tree approach, selective disclosure can be delegated. Namely, the user can derive certain descendant keys of $K_{A_1}, \ldots, K_{A_t}$ and use them for selective disclosure.

*Note 7.* It is infeasible for any Recipient of disclosed $\mathsf{EDAG}(D')$ to change the content of the fields, since to change the value $T(A)$ it would be necessary to change $K_A$. However, this requires to find $K'_A$ such that $\mathsf{Hash}(K'_A, 0) = \mathsf{Hash}(K_A, 0)$ – otherwise $\mathsf{SHash}$ would be applied to a different string. All in all, a manipulation of the signed text requires finding a collision for $\mathsf{Hash}$.

## 4  Future Work

Several important directions remain for future exploration. A proof-of-concept implementation of the proposed methods is needed to enable experimental evaluation of performance and scalability. Such a prototype should align with the ETSI standards [14] to facilitate adoption for legal transactions.

Furthermore, robust techniques for converting documents into DAGs require more attention and the creation of de facto standards. In this work, we only scratched the surface of representing text documents as DAGs. While translation from XML to DAG is relatively straightforward, handling arbitrary text formats (e.g., PDF or natural language text) is more challenging. Leveraging

LLMs combined with traditional NLP techniques should also be investigated, with careful consideration of factors such as reliability, privacy implications, and the inherent limitations of LLMs. Developing reliable methods for this translation could provide a powerful building block that could be used for multiple purposes, not only for signing.

Beyond the core framework, additional research should explore potential applications in knowledge extraction. One notable use case is proof of entitlement in whistleblowing scenarios [13]: a whistleblower has the right to submit a report if they are in any "work relation" with the reported organization. Such a relation may follow from various legal documents (employment contract, civil contract for services, confirmation of volunteer status, etc.). Presenting such a document in the original form during report submission can effectively thwart any pseudonymization attempt. This challenging problem has been recognized but so far not addressed in [13].

## 5    Final Remarks and Conclusions

This work demonstrates the feasibility of high-grain selective disclosure of signed documents derived from black-box signature schemes using a mapping from text documents to DAG structures.

To summarize, we suggest rethinking the concept of electronic signatures to enable selective disclosure of the data they contain without requiring re-signing. We have shown that such signatures can be implemented by slightly adapting existing cryptographic schemes, namely, incorporating standard (and in particular standardized) signature schemes, rather than designing entirely new ones. Such an approach reduces the standardization effort and facilitates faster adoption in practice.

The proposed method may be particularly useful for leveraging signed documents in terms of electronic attribute attestations, as introduced by eIDAS 2.0, in day-to-day administrative workflows following strictly the data minimization principle from GDPR. In our opinion, reshaping the concept of electronic signatures towards selective disclosure is a necessary condition to enable serious realization of GDPR.

**Acknowledgements.** This research was partially funded by the National Science Centre, Poland under the OPUS call in the Weave programme [2023/51/I/ST6/02770]. For the purpose of Open Access, the author has applied a CC-BY public copyright licence to any Author Accepted Manuscript (AAM) version arising from this submission.

## References

1. International Organization for Standardization, International Electrotechnical Commission: ISO/IEC 18013-5:2021 Personal identification – ISO-compliant driving licence – Part 5: Mobile driving licence (mDL) application (2021), https://

www.iso.org/standard/69084.html, published 18 August 2021; interface specs for mobile driving licence

2. Bellare, M., Rogaway, P.: Random oracles are practical: a paradigm for designing efficient protocols. In: Proceedings of the 1st ACM Conference on Computer and Communications Security, pp. 62–73. CCS '93, Association for Computing Machinery, New York, NY, USA (1993). https://doi.org/10.1145/168588.168596, https://doi.org/10.1145/168588.168596

3. Bertoni, G., Daemen, J., Peeters, M., Assche, G.V.: Cryptographic Sponge Functions. Technical Report, Version 0.1 CSF-0.1, STMicroelectronics and NXP Semiconductors, —- (2011). https://keccak.team/files/CSF-0.1.pdf, version 0.1 (Jan. 14, 2011)

4. Beuchat, J.L., Rexhepi, V.: A Digital Identity in the Hands of Swiss Citizens. Cryptology ePrint Archive, Paper 2023/1099 (2023). https://eprint.iacr.org/2023/1099

5. Boneh, D., Boyen, X.: Short signatures without random oracles. Cryptology ePrint Archive, Paper 2004/171 (2004). https://eprint.iacr.org/2004/171

6. Campbell, B., Fett, D., Terbu, O.: SD-JWT-based verifiable credentials (SD-JWT VC). Internet-Draft draft-ietf-oauth-sd-jwt-vc-09, IETF (2025). https://datatracker.ietf.org/doc/draft-ietf-oauth-sd-jwt-vc/, work in progress, expires 28 November 2025

7. Chaum, D.: Security without identification: transaction systems to make big brother obsolete. Commun. ACM **28**(10), 1030–1044 (1985). https://doi.org/10.1145/4372.4373

8. DeepSeek: deepseek R1: open-source reasoning model (2025). https://www.deepseek.com, Accessed 16 Jun 2025

9. ETSI: electronic signatures and infrastructures (ESI); cryptographic suites. ETSI Technical Specification ETSI TS 119 312 V1.4.3, ETSI (2023). https://www.etsi.org/deliver/etsi_ts/119300_119399/119312/01.04.03_60/ts_119312v010403p.pdf, version 1.4.3 (2023-08)

10. EU digital identity wallet community: architecture and reference framework for the european digital identity wallet (2025). https://github.com/eu-digital-identity-wallet/eudi-doc-architecture-and-reference-framework , version 2.1.0, Accessed 6 Jun 2025

11. European commission: commission implementing decision (EU) 2015/1506. Official Journal of the European Union (2015). https://eur-lex.europa.eu/eli/dec_impl/2015/1506

12. European commission: regulation (EU) 910/2014 (2021). https://eur-lex.europa.eu/legal-content/EN/TXT/HTML/?uri=CELEX:52021PC0281

13. European parliament and council of the european union: directive (EU) 2019/1937 (2024).            https://eur-lex.europa.eu/legal-content/EN/TXT/?uri=CELEX%3A32019L1937, Accessed 27 May 2024

14. European telecommunications standards institute: electronic signatures and infrastructures (ESI); certificate profiles; part 1: QCProfile. ETSI Standard EN 319 162-1 V1.1.1, ETSI (2016). https://www.etsi.org/deliver/etsi_en/319100_319199/31916201/01.01.01_60/en_31916201v010101p.pdf, Accessed 27 Jun 2025

15. Holt, J.E., Seamons, K.E.: Selective disclosure credential sets. Cryptology ePrint Archive, Paper 2002/151 (2002). https://eprint.iacr.org/2002/151

16. International civil aviation organisation: machine readable travel documents - part 11: security mechanism for MRTDs. Doc 9303 (2021)

17. International organization for standardization, international electrotechnical commission: it security techniques – digital signatures with appendix – part 3: discrete logarithm based mechanisms (ISO/IEC 14888-3:2018) (2018). https://www.iso.org/standard/76382.html
18. International organization for standardization, international electrotechnical commission: ISO/IEC 18013-5:2021 personal identification – iso-compliant driving licence – Part 5: mobile driving licence (mDL) application (2021). https://www.iso.org/standard/69084.html, Accessed 18 Aug 2021, interface specs for mobile driving licence
19. International Organization for standardization, international electrotechnical commission: ISO/IEC TS 23220-2:2024 (2024). https://www.iso.org/standard/86782.html, technical specification; first edition published November 2024
20. Lamport, L.: Constructing digital signatures from a one way function (2016). https://api.semanticscholar.org/CorpusID:59679804
21. Merkle, R.C.: A certified digital signature. In: Advances in Cryptology — CRYPTO '89 Proceedings. Lecture Notes in Computer Science, vol. 435, pp. 218–238. Springer (1989). https://doi.org/10.1007/0-387-34805-0_24
22. Moriarty, K., Kaliski, B., Jonsson, J., Rusch, A.: PKCS #1: RSA cryptography specifications version 2.2. internet engineering task force (IETF) (2016)
23. National institute of standards and technology: digital signature standard (DSS), FIPS publication 186-5. Federal Information Processing Standard 186-5, Gaithersburg, MD (2023). https://doi.org/10.6028/NIST.FIPS.186-5, https://nvlpubs.nist.gov/nistpubs/FIPS/NIST.FIPS.186-5.pdf
24. OpenAI: GPT-4o: a multimodal large language model (2024). https://openai.com/chatgpt, Accessed 16 Jun 2025
25. Python software foundation: xml.etree.ElementTree — The ElementTree XML API (2024). https://docs.python.org/3/library/xml.etree.elementtree.html, python 3.12 documentation
26. Rankl, W., Effing, W.: Handbuch der Chipkarten - Aufbau, Funktionsweise, Einsatz von Smart Cards (4. Aufl.). Hanser (2002)
27. Sporny, M., Longley, D., Chadwick, D., Steele, O., Sabadello, M., Reed, D.: Verifiable credentials data model v2.0. W3C recommendation W3C TR VC-DATA-MODEL-2.0, W3C Verifiable Credentials Working Group (2025). https://www.w3.org/TR/vc-data-model-2.0/, version of 15 May 2025
28. Tananaev, A.: passport-reader: e-Passport NFC Reader Android app. https://github.com/tananaev/passport-reader (2023). https://github.com/tananaev/passport-reader, version 3.1
29. The European Parliament and the Council of the European Union: Regulation (EU) 910/2014. Off. J. European Union **257/73** (2014). https://eur-lex.europa.eu/legal-content/EN/TXT/?uri=uriserv%3AOJ.L_.2014.257.01.0073.01.ENG
30. The european parliament and the council of the european union: regulation (EU) 2016/679. Off. J. European Union **119**(1) (2016). http://eur-lex.europa.eu/legal-content/EN/TXT/HTML/?uri=CELEX:32016R0679&from=EN#d1e3265-1-1
31. Wrankl, W., Effing, W.: Smart Card Handbook (2004). http://deadnet.se:8080/Books%20and%20Docs%20on%20Hacking/Electronics/Smart%20Card%20Handbook.pdf, third Edition
32. Xu, D., Tang, Z., Yu, Y.: An efficient key management scheme for segment-based document protection. In: 2011 IEEE Consumer Communications and Networking Conference, CCNC 2011, Las Vegas, NV, 9-12 January, 2011, pp. 896–900. IEEE (2011). https://doi.org/10.1109/CCNC.2011.5766636, https://doi.org/10.1109/CCNC.2011.5766636

# Invisible Encryption

Shahzad Ahmad[1]( ) , Stefan Rass[1,2] , and Zahra Seyedi[3]

[1] LIT Secure and Correct Systems Lab, Johannes Kepler University, Linz, Austria
{shahzad.ahmad,stefan.rass}@jku.at
[2] Institute for AI and Cybersecurity, University of Klagenfurt, Klagenfurt, Austria
[3] Department of Electronics, Information and Bioengineering, Polytechnic University
of Milan, Milan, Italy
zahrasadat.seyedi@mail.polimi.it

**Abstract.** We present Invisible Encryption, a cryptographic protocol that camouflages the sharing of a secret within standard encrypted traffic to avoid detection in monitored environments. This paper introduces Invisible Encryption, a novel protocol integrating threshold secret sharing, steganography, and public-key cryptography to enable covert communication. By embedding a secret share within standard encrypted traffic, specifically by disguising it as a session key or nonce in a hybrid encryption scheme, our method ensures that the transmission of the secret remains undetectable. The secret is reconstructed from shares derived from a public natural language text and the transmitted share, with the selection of shares protected by a secret seed. We provide a formal security analysis, demonstrating that Invisible Encryption achieves confidentiality and plausible deniability under standard cryptographic assumptions. Invisible Encryption offers a robust solution for applications that require secure, undetectable communication, such as censorship-resistant systems and whistleblower protection.

**Keywords:** Secret sharing · Steganography · Covert communication · Plausible deniability

## 1 Introduction

In environments where the very existence of encrypted communication raises suspicion or invites censorship, it is crucial to conceal both the content *and* the purpose of messages. Traditional steganography hides data within innocuous media (images, audio, etc.), but often requires specialised embedding methods and can be detected via statistical analysis. In contrast, Invisible Encryption repurposes standard cryptographic envelopes and protocols as carriers of hidden information; in other words, can we use cryptography itself as a steganographic channel?

A different way to frame the challenge is: while ciphertexts are often easy to recognise as such (e.g., random-looking strings in a log file), can we construct an encryption function that maps a meaningful natural-language plaintext into


R. Laborde et al. (Eds.): ESORICS 2025, LNCS 16231, pp. 96–115, 2026.
https://doi.org/10.1007/978-3-032-16089-8_7

a ciphertext that itself appears to be a natural-language text? For example, could even this paragraph contain an encrypted message by means other than classical steganography? The answer is not straightforward. Even the simplest substitution cipher (e.g., replacing words of a sentence with other words from the same or another language) demonstrates the difficulty: even if the "components" of the ciphertext are valid words, their combination, as dictated by grammar, will almost surely form nonsense rather than a meaningful sentence. Large language models seem promising to generate fluent text, but their design is not intended for cryptographic reversibility.

However, suppose we allow the target "ciphertext" to exist **before** encryption, i.e.. In that case, we choose a cover text in advance, and we can design our encryption to map a given plaintext to a target sequence of values that forms that meaningful text. It turns out that **polynomial secret sharing** offers a way to do this: we treat words from a natural-language text as shares *values* on a secret-sharing polynomial, and we let the arguments (indices) at which those shares are defined be determined pseudorandomly by a secret seed. We also include an additional single share to ensure the plaintext message can be recovered. To see why this extra share is needed, suppose we naively tried to reconstruct a secret message $m$ by XOR'ing together words from the cover text: $m = w_1 \oplus w_2 \oplus \cdots \oplus w_n$. Unless those words were specially chosen (and used only once), this is unlikely to equal $m$ except by coincidence. Using repeated plaintext words as a one-time pad invites the classic Friedman attack. Instead, we introduce an additional random component $r$ such that $m = w_1 \oplus \cdots \oplus w_n \oplus r$. This $r$ will appear random and not part of any natural language.

Our strategy is to *disguise* this extra random share $r$ as a legitimate random value in a standard cryptographic protocol transcript. Random nonces, session keys, or other random outputs are common in regular encrypted traffic and typically do not arouse suspicion. For example, imagine Alice and Bob exchange mostly plaintext emails but occasionally perform an authenticated key exchange or send an encrypted attachment. What if we let the words $w_1, \ldots, w_n$ be drawn from the plaintext email conversation, and let the final random value $r$ be transmitted as part of the cryptographic protocol (say, as a session key in a hybrid encryption)? In other words, even though $r$ is a share in an $(n+1)$-out-of-$(n+1)$ secret sharing scheme, its transmission is camouflaged as a random cryptographic artefact. A simple choice is to piggyback on a hybrid encryption or challenge-response authentication protocol – for instance, use $r$ as the "session key" in an RSA-based key exchange.

The key insight is that transmissions of random bits are routine in cryptographic protocols and thus unlikely to be flagged as suspicious, whereas sending plaintext secret data would betray that something hidden is being communicated. More importantly, if an eavesdropper intercepts the entire communication, they will observe normal-looking plaintext messages (the cover text) and a standard cryptographic exchange (e.g., an RSA-encrypted session key and a ciphertext of a decoy message). This should not trigger special scrutiny: the adversary sees nothing beyond an ordinary encrypted session amid otherwise plaintext conversation. Even if the adversary captures all the traffic, a single random session key is insufficient to recover any secret message.

In summary, the Invisible Encryption protocol enables covert communication by concealing a secret within standard encryption traffic. The hidden secret share is indistinguishable from the random values usually present in cryptographic protocols, providing **plausible deniability**: participants can claim the exchange was purely routine (e.g., an encrypted email or authentication step). An adversary who is unaware of the secret seed cannot identify which parts of the cover text are carrying hidden information or reconstruct the secret. The primary contributions of this work are as follows:

1. **A new form of steganography that uses cryptography as its carrier**: Integrates Shamir's $(k, n)$-threshold secret sharing with public-key and symmetric encryption, embedding a secret share within a decoy message to enable reconstruction from a public cover text.
2. **Plausible Deniability**: Permits participants to claim the communication involves routine encryption, safeguarding against adversarial or legal scrutiny.
3. **Efficient Implementation**: Provides a Python prototype with execution times under 400 ms and a communication overhead of 544 bytes, suitable for real-time, bandwidth-constrained applications[1].

These contributions enable secure, undetectable communication, applicable to censorship-resistant systems, whistleblower protection, and privacy-preserving environments.

The paper is organized as follows: Sect. 2 surveys relevant work in secret sharing, steganography, and covert communication. Section 3 outlines the mathematical and cryptographic preliminaries used in our scheme. Section 4 describes the Invisible Encryption scheme in detail, including algorithms for setup, share derivation, encryption, and decryption. Section 5 defines the system and adversary model and formalizes the security goals. Section 6 presents the security analysis of the scheme. Section 7 discusses our prototype implementation, including the protocol flow and performance measurements. Finally, Sect. 8 concludes the paper and highlights directions for future research (such as extending the scheme to multiple messages under one key).

## 2    Related Work

The foundation of Invisible Encryption builds upon several decades of research in threshold secret sharing, tracing back to Shamir [32] and Blakley [7], which introduced polynomial interpolation and geometric approaches, respectively. Subsequent enhancements include verifiable secret sharing by Feldman [19] and Pedersen [29], proactive renewal of shares by Herzberg et al. [22], and computational

---

[1] Here is the link for the Python proof-of-concept implementation: https://github.com/shahzadssg/Invisible-Encryption.git.

secret sharing by Krawczyk [26]. More recently, Komargodski et al. [24] extended these ideas to threshold fully homomorphic encryption, paving the way for secure computation on shared data.

The linguistic obfuscation in Invisible Encryption builds on techniques from linguistic steganography. Early mimic functions, as demonstrated by Wayner [37] and lexical methods by Chapman and Davida [12], have shown how ciphertext can be disguised as natural text. Advances by Chang and Clark [11], and Safaka et al. [31] exploit syntactic and semantic transformations for watermarking and covert channels. Unlike prior work that embeds payloads by modifying cover text, Invisible Encryption maps existing text to shares through selective indexing and hashing, enhancing naturalness and deniability.

Threshold cryptography enables collaborative cryptographic operations without revealing private keys, as pioneered by Desmedt and Frankel [16] and refined by Shoup [34]. Practical frameworks, such as FROST by Komlo and Goldberg [25], demonstrate efficient threshold signatures. Invisible Encryption's hybrid encryption follows the RSA-based KEM/DEM paradigm of Rivest et al. [30] and the formal models of Cramer and Shoup [14], with extensions from Abdalla et al. [2] and identity-based methods by Watanabe et al. [36]. Its use of encrypted decoy messages for plausible deniability draws on TrueCrypt's hidden volumes [1], deniable encryption by Canetti et al. [10], and schemes by Tyagi et al. [35], and Dodis et al. [18].

Indistinguishability obfuscation, introduced by Barak et al. [4] and Garg et al. [20], as well as functional encryption by Boneh et al. [9], share the goal of hiding information while preserving utility. Its threshold structure echoes MPC protocols from Yao [38], Goldreich et al. [21], SPDZ by Damgård et al. [15], Sharemind by Bogdanov et al. [8], and integrating secret sharing in MPC by Benaloh [5] and Cramer et al. [13]. Instances of invisible encryption using RSA-based carriers can be vulnerable to Shor's algorithm [33], motivating post-quantum alternatives such as NTRU [23], Ring-LWE [27], McEliece [28], Rainbow [17], and threshold lattice schemes by Bendlin et al. [6]. Given the crucial threats induced by quantum computing, the long-term security of the protocol will depend on transitioning to post-quantum cryptography, a task that is noted here as essential future work but is not integrated into the current model.

## 3   Preliminaries

We let words from our natural language appear in some fixed binary encoding, e.g., ASCII code, Unicode or others, such that we can uniquely associate $w \in \{0,1\}^*$ with some meaningful string (at least a symbol, up to a whole natural language word). Furthermore, let $|w|$ be the length of $w$ in bits, so that treating $w$ as an integer in binary notation, we have $w \leq 2^{|w|}$. Let us fix a prime $p$ and length $n \in \mathbb{N}$ such that all words $w \in \{0,1\}^n$ in our plaintexts[2], treated as integers, fit into the range $0 \leq w \leq p-1$, so that our plaintext (natural

---

[2] mildly assuming that the plaintext to carry our secret is from a natural language whose words will not have unbounded lengths.

language words) are canonically interpretable as elements of $\mathbb{F}_p$ for otherwise, we may take a word's hash value modulo $p$ to map it into an element of $\mathbb{F}_p$; as our practical implementation does.

We let a natural language text be given as an ordered sequence of $L \in \mathbb{N}$ words $T = (w[0], w[1], \ldots, w[L]) \in (\{0,1\}^*)^n$, all possibly padded to the same (maximum) length. Within this sequence of words, we will embed our secret and, if necessary, extend the sequence with additional entries. Let $t \in \mathbb{N}$ be a security parameter, and let the length of the carrier text $T$ be $n = poly(t)$ depend on $t$ by some (fixed) polynomial $poly$. Furthermore, let the plaintext be a string of length $m$, where $m = poly(t) < n(t)$, that also depends on $t$ by some (other) polynomial. Table 1 provides an overview of variables and functions appearing throughout the construction.

**Table 1.** List of symbols used in the construction.

| Symbol | Description |
| --- | --- |
| $x\|y$ | concatenation of strings $x$ and $y$ |
| $L$ | Length of the cover text $T$ (number of words) |
| $w[i]$ | $i$-th word in the cover text $T$ |
| $T$ | Original cover text, an ordered sequence of words $(w[1], \ldots, w[L])$ |
| $T'$ | Updated cover text (ciphertext), i.e., $T \parallel w[L+1]$ after embedding the final share |
| $k$ | Threshold for secret reconstruction |
| $m$ | Secret message in $\mathbb{F}_p$ to be shared, resp. covertly transmitted |
| $P(x)$ | Degree-$(k-1)$ polynomial used for secret sharing, satisfying $P(0) = m$ |
| $x_j$ | Pseudorandom abscissa values, generated via $x_j = H(x_{j-1})$ |
| $x_{\text{new}}$ | Fresh abscissa for the additional share, derived as the next hash in the chain |
| $s_j$ | Share values $s_j = P(x_j)$ (for $1 \le j \le k-1$), or $s_{\text{new}} = P(x_{\text{new}})$ |
| $s_{new}$ | Additional share computed from interpolated polynomial |
| $H$ | Cryptographic hash function modeled as a random oracle |
| $PRNG$ | Pseudorandom number generator seeded with $x_0$, used to pick distinct word indices |
| $x_0$ | Secret seed used for pseudorandom generator $PRNG$ |
| Param | Public parameters tuple $(p, H, \text{PRNG})$ |
| SK | Secret key, consisting of $(x_0, k)$ shared by sender and receiver |

*Polynomial Secret Sharing:* A secret $m \in \mathbb{F}_p$ is shared using a polynomial $P(x) = m + a_1 x + \cdots + a_{k-1} x^{k-1}$, with $k$ distinct evaluations $(x_i, P(x_i))$ sufficient for reconstruction. The Lagrange interpolation formula reconstructs $P(0)$:

$$m = P(0) \equiv \sum_{j=1}^{k} P(x_j) \cdot \prod_{i=1, i \neq j}^{k} \frac{-x_i}{x_j - x_i} \pmod{p}.$$

*Pseudorandom Number Generator (PRNG):* A PRNG is a deterministic algorithm $G : \{0,1\}^s \to \{0,1\}^\ell$ that takes a seed of length $s$ and produces a longer pseudorandom output of length $\ell$. A PRNG is secure if its output is computationally (in polynomial time in $\ell$) indistinguishable from a truly random string of length $\ell$.

*(Non-)Cryptographic Disguise of Random Strings:* to unsuspiciously hide a random string in natural language text, such as within a log file or similar, we can combine asymmetric encryption (e.g., RSA-OAEP) with symmetric encryption (e.g., AES-CBC) following the KEM/DEM paradigm. The RSA component encrypts the seed and the freshly generated secret share $s_{\text{new}}$, as necessary by our introductory argument above; the AES component encrypts a decoy message using $s_{\text{new}}$ as the key with a random $IV$. That use of hybrid encryption is arbitrary here; any cryptographic (or other) protocol $\Pi$ that at some point transmits a random string between parties would be admissible. One example is challenge-response authentication, where Alice may ask Bob to decrypt (symmetrically) or digitally sign (asymmetrically) a random nonce, which is a share in the above polynomial sharing scheme. As a <u>non-cryptographic example</u>, that would even work inside a transmitted file only, e.g., letting the plaintext be in a PDF with embedded content; we can even include a QR code in a text that contains a weblink, inside which a random (e.g., base-64 encoded) login-token is embedded (although this may negatively affect the security if the key is re-used). The "login" token in the weblink can be the additional share to be transmitted, while the actual URL will open accordingly (or not) solely for the sake of deception. Suppose a login is attempted by clicking on the web link. In that case, this mechanism may even serve as an intrusion detection signal, as the receiver already knows that the QR code contains a share and should not be opened. In contrast, the adversary may not know this and may discover it upon this trial.

## 4   The Invisible Encryption Scheme

Figure 1 illustrates the basic idea: like in Shamir's scheme [32], we let $P(x) = m + a_1 x + \ldots + a_{k-1} x^{k-1}$ be a polynomial, in which we fix $m \in \{0,1\}^*$ to be the secret. However, different to the classical instance of Shamir's sharing, we fix a series of <u>values</u> of the polynomial, rather than its coefficients. That is, we will look for a polynomial for which $P(x_i) = w[i]$, for some value $x_i$ and some word $w[i]$ from the natural language text, for a total of $\geq k$ but $\leq n$ values $x_i$ and words $w[i]$.

While it would be conceptually trivial to fix a sequence $x_1, \ldots, x_{k-1}$ and words $w[i_1], \ldots, w[i_{k-1}]$ from the text and interpolate a polynomial by solving a linear system of equations, the reconstruction would then require the same set of values again. This knowledge would have to be transmitted secretly from Alice to Bob, but (i) could not be used a second time, and (ii) would be more data than transmitting the secret directly. To overcome both issues, we let the sequence of $x_1, \ldots, x_{k-1}$ and $i_1, \ldots, i_{k-1}$ be generated pseudorandomly based on a (fixed-size) secret $x_0$ that will act as a secret decryption key. The computation of the polynomial remains a direct interpolation, but to recover $m$ as the plaintext secret will require at least one additional share (as explained in the introductory intuition).

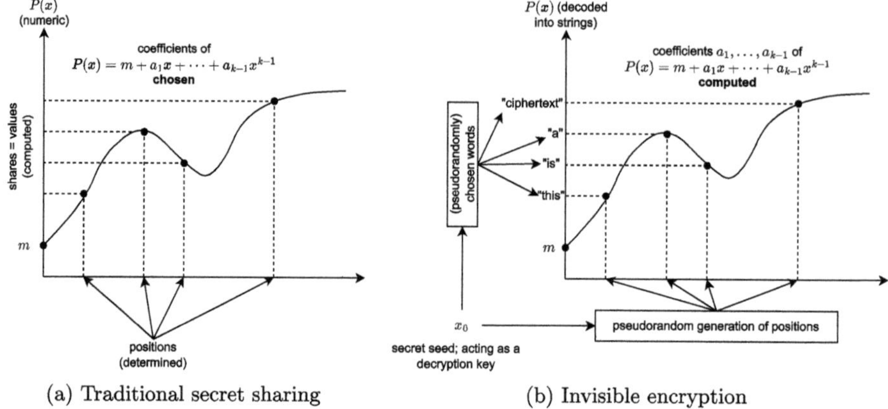

(a) Traditional secret sharing         (b) Invisible encryption

**Fig. 1.** Conventional secret sharing, vs. invisible encryption: while in the conventional setting, the polynomial is chosen, and shares are its values taken at (defined or secret) positions, invisible encryption twists around this process by choosing the natural language words to be the values that the polynomial shall take, and interpolating it at positions that are defined secretly from a seed value $x_0$. The seed can also determine the words to interleave the shares with (the cover text to embed the ciphertext), and the polynomial is then finally determined by interpolation. Further shares are then computed in the traditional form again (and are required for proving the steganographic security).

## 4.1   Formal Scheme Definition

We model Invisible Encryption as a triple of probabilistic algorithms: (Setup, Enc, Dec), defined as follows:

Setup$(t, L)$: On input a security parameter $t \in \mathbb{N}$ and the cover-text length $L = poly(t)$, it selects:

i) A large prime $p$ of bit-length $\lambda = poly(t)$ and finite field $\mathbb{F}_p$.

ii) A hash function $H : \{0,1\}^* \to \mathbb{F}_p$.

iii) A cryptographically secure pseudorandom number generator $PRNG$, whose output range is $\{1, \ldots, L\}$.

iv) A secret seed $x_0 \in \{0,1\}^\lambda$ uniformly at random (denoted $x_0 \xleftarrow{\$} \{0,1\}^\lambda$).

v) A threshold $k \xleftarrow{\$} \{2, \ldots, L\}$. The symbol $x \xleftarrow{\$} X$ denote a random uniform selection of $x \in X$.

vi) Parameters Param $= (p, H, PRNG)$.

**Output** (Param, SK $= (x_0, k)$).

We remark that the hash function $H$ and the pseudorandom number generator $PRNG$ serve the same purpose, but deliver different "items", i.e., either the points on the abscissa (by a hash chain) or the selection of words from the text (via the $PRNG$). We distinguish the two for the sole purpose of indicating the meaning of their outputs directly by the symbol (easier than distinguishing two hash functions or two PRNGs).

Enc(PK, $m$, $T$): On input public parameters Param, secret $m \in \mathbb{F}_p$, and cover text $T = (w[1], \ldots, w[L])$ of length $L$, it:

i) Derives $n$ shares $\{(x_j, s_j)\}_{j=1}^{k-1}$ from $(x_0, T)$ by:
  a) pseudorandomly computing the values $x_j \leftarrow H(x_{j-1})$ for $j = 1, 2, \ldots$ until $k - 1$ distinct indices are found (skipping duplicate values, if any).
  b) pseudorandomly picking $k - 1$ distinct indices $i_j \in \{1, \ldots, L\}$ using the PRNG seeded with $x_0$ and setting $s_j \leftarrow w[i_j]$ for $j = 1, 2, \ldots, k - 1$ (duplicates are allowed here).
ii) Interpolates the unique polynomial $P \in \mathbb{F}_p[x]$ of degree $< k$ satisfying

$$P(0) = m, \quad P(x_j) = s_j \quad \text{for the } k - 1 \text{ points } (x_j, s_j) \text{ chosen in step i)}$$

iii) Computes a fresh abscissa $x_{\text{new}} = H^k(x_0)$ (continuation of the hash chain; if $x_{\text{new}} \in \{0, x_1, \ldots, x_{j-1}\}$ from above, then we iterate further until we get an "unused" nonzero value), and put $s_{\text{new}} \leftarrow P(x_{\text{new}})$.
iv) Execute the protocol or other procedure $\Pi$ that will use $s_{\text{new}}$ (e.g., as a session key, during an authentication, embedded in a QR code, etc.), yielding $w[L + 1] \leftarrow \Pi(M)$ as the transcript of the protocol $\Pi$, which is now added (e.g., appended) to the existing cover text[3], giving $T' \leftarrow T \| w[L + 1] = (w[1], \ldots, w[L], w[L + 1])$.

**Outputs** the updated cover text $T'$ as the ciphertext, decryptable under the secret key SK $= (x_0, k)$.

Dec(SK, $C$, $T'$): On input of SK $= (x_0, k)$, and cover-text $T' = (w[1], \ldots, w[L], w[L + 1])$, we do the following:

i) Extract $s_{\text{new}}$ from $w[L + 1]$, and recover all points $\{(x_i, w[i])\}_{i=1}^{k}$ by recomputing the pseudorandom sequences just as done during the encryption.
ii) Interpolate $P$ through the just created points, and return the secret message $m \leftarrow P(0)$

The encryption of multiple messages under the (same) secret key SK $= (x_0, k)$ works likewise but will produce only $s_{\text{new}}$ afresh for any further messages, upon using a distinct polynomial $P$ for each message. The remaining set of shares will be the same (due to the same seed to determine the pseudorandom sequences).

---

[3] in many practical cases, $\Pi$ may have a much longer transcript than what would fit into a string of the "block" size $n$ that we fixed; in that case, we may add further blocks accordingly, but w.l.o.g., let the transcript (the relevant part of it), appear as $w[L + 1]$ to simplify the notation).

## 5    System Model and Threat Assumptions

Building on the algorithms and syntax defined in Sect. 4, we now present a formal security model. We specify the roles, the information each party controls, the adversary's oracle access and resource bounds, the information flow, and the precise security objectives.

### 5.1    Adversary Model and Security

Let $\mathcal{A}$ be a probabilistic polynomial-time (PPT) adversary who knows all public parameters and the complete ciphertext $T' = (w[1], \ldots, w[L], w[L+1])$, including all details about the procedure (cryptographic protocol or other) $\Pi$, whose transcript appears in $T'$.

The adversary's goal is to recover the secret $m \in \mathbb{F}_p$. The security of the linguistic obfuscation component depends on the indistinguishability of the mapped shares from random elements in the text. Computational indistinguishability is understood in the usual cryptographic sense, i.e., every polynomial-time-bounded probabilistic attacker would have a negligible chance of discovering the secret if the security parameter $t$ becomes sufficiently large. We call a function $\nu : \mathbb{N} \to \mathbb{N}$ negligible if it decays faster than any polynomial, i.e., if for every $c > 0$, there is some $n_c \in \mathbb{N}$ such that $\nu(n) \leq n^{-c}$ for all $n \geq n_c$.

**Definition 1 (Steganographic Security).** *A steganographic system is secure if the distribution of cover objects (text) and stego objects (text with embedded information) are computationally indistinguishable. More formally, let $t \in \mathbb{N}$ be a security parameter, and let $p, q$ be non-constant strictly positive polynomials in $t$. Given a carrier text $T \in (\{0, 1\}^*)^{p(t)}$ and whose total length is $\leq q(t)$, which embeds a secret $x \in \{0, 1\}^n$ of fixed size $n \leq p(t)$, we call it's embedded secret steganographically secure if $\Pr(adversary\ correctly\ outputs\ x \mid given\ T) \leq \nu(t)$, where $\nu(t)$ is negligible for a polynomially (in $t$) time-bounded attacker.*

## 6    Security Analysis

The security of our scheme will hold in a computational, not information-theoretic, sense under a random oracle assumption on the hash function $H$ and the pseudorandom generator $PRNG$.

### 6.1    Security of the Secret Sharing Scheme (is only Computational)

Shamir's Secret Sharing provides perfect information-theoretic security, meaning that even an adversary with unlimited computational power cannot determine the secret from fewer than $k$ shares. However, our construction cannot retain this property because the plaintext words will not exhaust the entirety of elements in $\mathbb{F}_p$, and (more importantly), the adversary, unlike in the traditional setting of secret sharing, is in possession of all shares; only does not know which are the right ones. Hence, the usual argument for information-theoretic security that for every possible secret, a missing share would exist to produce exactly this secret will fail since all possibilities are already "fixed." However, we do retain an intractably large search space for the adversary since every subset of (ciphertext) elements could be the set of desired shares, and their entire count is $O(2^L)$ if the threshold is unknown. Letting the cover text be reasonably long, this will eventually exceed a poly-time bounded attacker's capabilities. If the number $k$ of shares would be known to the adversary, then the search space "shrinks" to a size of $O(n^k)$ (containing all $k$-element subsets, but fewer, since the "cryptographic protocols transcript" must be part of the sharing, reducing the number of shares by 1, or a relatively smaller choice of possibilities, at least).

## 6.2   Steganographic Security of Invisible Encryption

The text-to-shares mapping in Invisible Encryption is steganographically secure under the random oracle model, specifically:

**Theorem 1.** *The scheme from Sect. 4 is steganographically secure against a polynomially time-bounded attacker for the encryption of a single message, provided that:*

- *(random oracle assumption) $H$ and $PRNG$ behave as random oracles*
- *(known ciphertext assumption) The adversary does not know* $\mathsf{SK} = (x_0, k)$, *but knows the entire cover text $T' = (w[1], \ldots, w[L], w[L+1])$ and details about $\Pi$, whose transcript appears as $w[L+1]$ (possibly more, if the transcript is longer than one "word" in the cover text).*

*Proof.* The attacker can correctly recover the secret if and only if two conditions are met:

(A)  correctly guesses the right words from the text,
(B)  correctly gets the sequence $x_1, \ldots, x_{k-1}, x_{\mathrm{new}}$

Since the number $k \in \{2, \ldots, L\}$ is unknown to the attacker, which, by a random oracle assumption on $PRNG$, leaves it with a uniform choice of $\overline{\text{any}}$ subset of $\{1, \ldots, L\}$ to be the candidate set of shares. This number of $O(2^L)$ many choices makes the search space super-polynomially large since we also assumed $L = poly(t)$ (see Sect. 4.1). The chances to guess the correct subset thus become $\Pr(A) = 2^{-L} = 2^{-poly(t)}$.

Since this sequence is as well pseudorandom, its seed $x_0$ is unknown, and $H$ acts like a random oracle, the chances to recover the sequence are the same as for guessing $x_0$, making the probability of accomplishing the second condition $\Pr(B) = 2^{-\lambda} = 2^{-poly(t)}$. Thus, the overall chances for the attacker to recover $m$ correctly come to $\Pr(A \wedge B) \leq \min\{\Pr(A), \Pr(B)\} = \min\{2^{-poly(t)}, 2^{-poly(t)}\} \leq 2^{-poly(t)}$, which is negligible (where $poly$ can denote three distinct polynomials in the last expression).

### 6.3  Plausible Deniability

Immanent to the design of the scheme is the ability to plausibly deny the hidden message inside it, since the cover text goes unmodified, and any data embedded in pictures, cryptographic protocols or other parts (that allow unsuspiciously transmitting bit strings of any form) will contain only a share that contains no information (as it is information-theoretically insufficient to recover the secret). If strong coercion is anticipated, embedding multiple secrets for decoy or deniability purposes is another option; this method has previously be described in [3], with proven security and deniability.

## 7  Example Implementation

We developed a proof-of-concept implementation of Invisible Encryption in Python to validate its correctness and evaluate performance. In this section, we describe the implementation details, illustrate the protocol flow between sender and receiver (with a diagram), and present an analysis of covertness and runtime performance.

### 7.1  Environment and Tools

The prototype was implemented in Python 3.8 and tested on a standard workstation (2.4 GHz Intel Core $i5$ CPU, 16 GB RAM). We used the Galois library for finite field arithmetic and the Python cryptography library for RSA and AES operations. The cover texts in our tests were drawn from sample English texts (e.g., Wikipedia articles) to simulate natural communications.

### 7.2  Implementation Details

The prototype implements the algorithms outlined in Sect. 4, modularised for clarity and reusability. The core components, reflecting the steps described in the formal definitions, are detailed below, along with the specific libraries and parameters used in our Python implementation.

*Setup and Key Generation:* This phase initialises the necessary parameters and keys.

i) **Field and Hash Initialization**: A large prime $p$ is sampled to define the finite field $\mathbb{F}_p$. In our implementation, a 256-bit prime $p$ was generated using the `galois` library to ensure a sufficiently large field for mapping potential word hashes. The hash function $H : \{0,1\}^* \to F_p$ is defined as the SHA-256 hash of the input mapped into the field by taking the result modulo $p$. Specifically, $H(m) = $ SHA-256$(m)$ MOD $p$.

ii) **Secret Seed and Threshold Selection**: A 256-bit secret seed $x_0$ is generated using `os.urandom(32)`. For selecting word indices from the cover text, our proof-of-concept uses Python's built-in `random` module, seeded with $x_0$. It is important to acknowledge that this standard PRNG is not cryptographically secure and does not satisfy the random oracle assumption made in our formal security analysis. A production-level implementation would require replacing this with a certified CSPRNG. The threshold $k$ was configured as a fixed parameter for each test run.

iii) **Public Key Protocol Initialization**: An IND-CCA2 secure key pair $(pk, sk)$ for the hybrid encryption's public-key component $\Pi$ is generated. We used the `cryptography` library to create an RSA key pair with a 2048-bit modulus, employing RSA-OAEP for encryption and decryption within $\Pi$. The protocol that we used to demonstrate the scheme is described in Sect. 7.3.

*Share Derivation:* The sender and receiver execute the same functions to derive the shares from the public cover text and the secret seed $x_0$. Our implementation, in the `generate_secure_x_values` and `text_to_shares` functions, proceeds as follows:

i) **Abscissae Generation:** A sequence of abscissae $(x_j)$ is generated by creating a hash chain: $x_1 = H(x_0)$ and $x_j = H(\text{encode}(x_{j-1}))$ for subsequent values, where `encode` is a byte-string conversion of the field element.

ii) **Share Value Computation:** The PRNG, seeded with $x_0$, selects $k-1$ word indices from the cover text. The corresponding words are then hashed using SHA-256 (modulo $p$) to produce the share values $(s_j)$. This results in a set of $k-1$ points $\{(x_j, s_j)\}$.

*Encryption:* Using $k-1$ shares from the derived set, a degree-$(k-1)$ polynomial $P(x)$ was interpolated with $P(0) = m$ via Lagrange interpolation (implemented with the `galois` library). A fresh share $(x_{\text{new}}, s_{\text{new}})$ was computed, and $M = x_0 \| s_{\text{new}}$ was encrypted with RSA-OAEP to produce $C_{\text{pub}}$. A decoy message was encrypted with AES-CBC using $s_{\text{new}}$ as the key, yielding $C_{\text{sym}}$.

*Decryption:* The receiver decrypts $C_{\text{pub}}$ with the secret key $sk$ to recover $x_0$ and $s_{\text{new}}$, regenerates shares, and interpolates $P(x)$ with the same $k-1$ shares plus $(x_{\text{new}}, s_{\text{new}})$ to retrieve $m$.

Optimisations in the implementation included leveraging the `galois` library's efficient finite field operations for polynomial interpolation and shared computations, as well as utilising the `cryptography` library's optimised implementations of RSA-OAEP and AES-CBC, thereby minimising computational overhead.

## 7.3   Hiding the Final Share in a Hybrid Key Exchange

The final share is embedded as part of a cryptographic protocol, in our case, the exchange of $x_0$ as a "session key" using hybrid encryption: let the message to be encrypted under RSA be $M = s_{\text{new}}$, and let it be $n = 256$ bit long. She computes $C_{\text{pub}} = \text{RSA\_OAEP}_{pk}(M)$, under Bob's public key $pk$, and then treats the value of $s_{\text{new}}$ as an AES key $K$. Selecting a random 128-bit $IV$, she encrypts a benign decoy payload $D$ under AES-CBC with PKCS#7 padding, yielding $C_{\text{sym}} = \text{AES\_CBC}_K(D, IV)$. This step creates a decoy transcript of RSA-OAEP to conceal $s_{\text{new}}$ as a session key for conventionally encrypted communication rather than part of a covert protocol. Alice transmits the pair $(C_{\text{pub}}, C_{\text{sym}})$ to Bob. To the adversary, $C_{\text{pub}}$ looks like a routine key-exchange message and $C_{\text{sym}}$ like an ordinary encrypted document. Upon receiving these, Bob decrypts $C_{\text{pub}}$ using his private key to retrieve $s_{\text{new}}$. Using the secrets $k, x_0$ shared with Alice (beforehand), Bob generates the same shares as Alice and selects the same $k - 1$ shares (this selection can be deterministically derived from $x_0$). Finally, Bob reconstructs the secret $m$ using the $k - 1$ shares and the received $s_{\text{new}}$.

If questioned by an adversary, both Alice and Bob can claim they were exchanging the encrypted message $C_{\text{sym}}$, using standard public key cryptography to securely transmit the session key $s_{\text{new}}$.

### 7.4   Covertness Analysis

The covertness of our scheme stems from the legitimate appearance of the reference text $T$, the use of standard cryptographic primitives for the encrypted messages, and the decoy message $D$ that appears to be the main encrypted payload.

The dual purpose of $s_{\text{new}}$ is particularly important for covertness. To an observer, the protocol appears to be a standard hybrid encryption method: a public key algorithm is used to securely transmit a symmetric key, which then encrypts the main message. This pattern matches legitimate encrypted communications, making Invisible Encryption indistinguishable from conventional secure messaging protocols.

An adversary cannot distinguish between the legitimate use of encryption for regular secure communication and our stealth protocol without breaking the underlying cryptographic primitives or obtaining access to the private keys of the participants.

### 7.5   Performance Analysis and Applications

We implemented the Invisible Encryption scheme in Python using the `galois` field library for finite field operations and the `cryptography` package for encryption primitives. Below, we present comprehensive performance metrics derived from our implementation, evaluated on a standard workstation (2.40 GHz Intel Core $i5$, 16 GB RAM) running Python 3.8 (Tables 2, 3 and 4).

The communication overhead remains constant at 544 bytes regardless of the threshold $k$ and total shares $n$, as only $x_0$ (32 bytes) and $s_{\text{new}}$ (32 bytes) are transmitted, along with the RSA-encrypted payload (480 bytes for RSA-2048) and the encrypted decoy message which varies based on content size.

**Table 2.** Detailed Performance Metrics for Core Operations

| Operation | Mean Execution Time (ms) | Standard Deviation (ms) | Memory Usage (KB) |
|---|---|---|---|
| Field Initialization | 1.07595 | 0.35538 | 225000.0 |
| Secure x-value Generation ($n = 5$) | 0.302410 | 0.50586 | 225000.0 |
| Text-to-Shares Mapping ($n = 5$) | 0.11942 | 0.37765 | 225000.0 |
| New Share Creation ($k = 3$) | 1.31597 | 0.43569 | 225000.0 |
| Secret Reconstruction ($k = 3$) | 1.24387 | 0.50298 | 225000.0 |
| RSA Encryption (2048-bit) | 247.46129 | 135.38926 | 225000.0 |
| AES-CBC Encryption (decoy, 1KB) | 304.03792 | 121.10442 | 225000.0 |

**Table 3.** Performance Metrics Across Different Threshold Configurations

| Parameter | Share Generation (ms) | New Share Creation (ms) | Secret Reconstruction (ms) | Total Protocol Time (ms) | Comm. Overhead (bytes) |
|---|---|---|---|---|---|
| $k = 3, n = 5$ | 0.0 | 2.36959 | 1.58011 | 103.94971 | 544 |
| $k = 5, n = 10$ | 1.65686 | 4.31780 | 3.72588 | 109.70056 | 544 |
| $k = 7, n = 15$ | 1.57783 | 6.30636 | 9.57479 | 117.45898 | 544 |

The dual use of $s_{\text{new}}$ as both a share for secret reconstruction and an encryption key for the decoy message incurs no additional computational overhead, as the same value serves both purposes without requiring further processing. Our implementation of AES-CBC encryption using $s_{\text{new}}$ as the key demonstrates performance comparable to standard implementations, with linear scaling for larger decoy messages. Our measurements show that even with a more complex setup ($k = 7, n = 15$), the entire protocol executes in less than 400 ms, making it suitable for real-time applications. The communication overhead remains minimal and constant regardless of parameter choices, which is particularly valuable in bandwidth-constrained environments.

**Table 4.** Decoy Message Encryption Performance (using $s_{\text{new}}$ as session key)

| Decoy Message Size | Encryption Time (ms) | Decryption Time (ms) | Ciphertext Size (bytes) |
|---|---|---|---|
| 1 KB | 194.77112 | 0.30829 | 1040 |
| 10 KB | 249.74727 | 0.73943 | 10256 |
| 100 KB | 250.28808 | 0.45835 | 102416 |
| 1 MB | 257.22391 | 0.49147 | 1048592 |

Invisible Encryption is particularly suitable for censorship-resistant communication in environments where encryption is monitored or prohibited, whistleblower protection allowing sensitive information to be transmitted covertly, diplomatic communications when revealing the existence of communication could have political implications, covert operations requiring maximum deniability, and privacy-preserving systems where regular encryption may draw unwanted attention.

The plausible deniability feature makes the system especially valuable in jurisdictions with key disclosure laws, where users may be legally compelled to reveal encryption keys. By providing a legitimate-looking decoy message encrypted with $s_{\mathrm{new}}$, users can comply with such demands without revealing the existence of the covert channel.

### 7.6    Illustration with Ciphertext Taken from This Paper

We use this **section** to illustrate the scheme by taking **exactly** the first paragraph of this section as the ciphertext to embed a secret message inside. The additional share is embedded as a login token in the URL for a weblink that an adversary could **try** to open and be prompted for a password, but by the event of clicking on it, already having disclosed its attack attempt **to** Alice and Bob thus building in some very **simple** form of intrusion detection for an attacker that is unaware of the use of invisible encryption).

The above text consists of exactly $L = 93$ words, with a maximum length of $\leq n = 12$ characters. We let the implemented code run with a 256-bit prime $p$, using the seed $x_0 = 6$ and $k = 6$ shares, with $PRNG(x) = H(x)$ MOD 93 as the pseudorandom number generator, where $H$ is SHA256. The selected words, pointed to by the index sequence $i_1, i_2, \ldots, i_{k-1}$, are **shown bold-printed** in the above paragraph (for illustration only), and the final share $s_{new}$ is Base64-encoded into the "auth" token of the weblink inside the QR code.

### 7.7    Practical Considerations and Limitations

The implementation of Invisible Encryption, while functional, comes with practical considerations and limitations that must be acknowledged.

- **Implementation Complexity:** The protocol's design requires the careful coordination of several cryptographic primitives, including polynomial interpolation, hybrid encryption, and pseudorandom sequence generation. This complexity can make secure implementation challenging and may introduce errors or vulnerabilities if not handled with expertise.

- **Security of the Secret Seed:** The security of the entire protocol hinges on the confidentiality of the secret seed $x_0$. Any leakage of this seed would completely compromise the system, allowing an adversary to reconstruct the secret message by identifying the correct shares. Therefore, protecting $x_0$ through robust measures, such as physical or logical isolation on the user's device, is of paramount importance.
- **Robustness against rephrasing:** The protocol is vulnerable against substitution of synonyms or rephrasing the cover text (unknowingly, or intentionally if the adversary aims to make the hidden message non-recoverable). In real-world scenarios, ambiguous words, idioms, or context-dependent meanings could be changed without affecting the carrier text itself, but produce a different interpolated polynomial and hence modify the secret up to non-recoverability.
- **Generalizability:** The prototype was tested in a controlled environment. Its performance and robustness have not been evaluated using large-scale, real-world datasets such as social media texts or system log files. This limits the generalizability of our findings to diverse, uncontrolled scenarios.

## 8   Conclusion and Future Work

We have introduced Invisible Encryption. This novel cryptographic protocol seamlessly integrates Shamir's threshold secret sharing, steganographic embedding, and hybrid public-key encryption to facilitate covert communication in environments where traditional encryption is monitored or prohibited. By camouflaging a single share $s_{\mathrm{new}}$ within standard hybrid-encrypted traffic, our scheme ensures that the very act of secret transmission remains indistinguishable from ordinary ciphertext, while retaining complete IND-CCA2 security and efficient performance.

At its core, Invisible Encryption leverages a $(k, n)$-threshold sharing of the hidden payload: only one share is transmitted alongside the cover message, and the remaining $k - 1$ shares are deterministically derived from a public cover text. The transmitted share $s_{\mathrm{new}}$ doubles as a symmetric key for an overt decoy message, yielding strong plausible deniability: even if compelled to reveal keys or plaintexts, participants can credibly claim the data exchanged was merely routine encrypted content.

Our rigorous security analysis demonstrates confidentiality, covertness, and detection-resistance under standard assumptions (e.g., RSA-OAEP and the secrecy of Shamir shares). A Python prototype, built on the `galois` and `cryptography` libraries, confirms that encryption and decryption complete in under 400 ms with negligible overhead, making the scheme practical for real-world scenarios such as whistleblowing, diplomatic messaging, or communications under repressive regimes.

Extending Invisible Encryption to multiple-message settings remains an important direction for future work. Naïve reuse of the same threshold key leaks the XOR of successive plaintexts; to mitigate this, one may:

- **Renew per-message keys:** derive a fresh $(x_0, k)$ by hashing the previous ciphertext into the next seed.
- **Update cover text or embedding indexes:** rotate or refresh the public cover text, or embed the secret in higher-order polynomial coefficients to decorrelate shares.
- **Pre-encrypt whitening:** compress or otherwise uniformise the plaintext to resist Friedman-style statistical attacks.

Formal proofs of security under these enhancements and an evaluation of their performance and usability constitute compelling avenues for further research. The techniques presented here will inspire new approaches to secure, undetectable information exchange in an age of pervasive surveillance.

# References


1. TrueCrypt (Apr 2025). https://en.wikipedia.org/w/index.php?title=TrueCrypt& oldid=1283747827, page Version ID: 1283747827
2. Abdalla, M., Bellare, M., Rogaway, P.: The Oracle Diffie-Hellman Assumptions and an Analysis of DHIES. In: Naccache, D. (ed.) Topics in Cryptology — CT-RSA 2001, pp. 143–158. Springer, Berlin, Heidelberg (2001). https://doi.org/10.1007/3-540-45353-9_12
3. Ahmad, S., Rass, S., Schartner, P.: False-bottom encryption: deniable encryption from secret sharing. IEEE Access 1–1 (2023). https://doi.org/10.1109/ACCESS.2023.3288285, conference Name: IEEE Access
4. Barak, B., et al.: On the (im)possibility of obfuscating programs. J. ACM **59**(2), 6:1–6:48 (May 2012). https://doi.org/10.1145/2160158.2160159
5. Benaloh, J.C.: Secret sharing homomorphisms: keeping shares of a secret secret (extended abstract). In: Odlyzko, A.M. (ed.) Advances in Cryptology — CRYPTO' 86. pp. 251–260. Springer, Berlin, Heidelberg (1987). https://doi.org/10.1007/3-540-47721-7_19
6. Bendlin, R., Damgård, I., Orlandi, C., Zakarias, S.: Semi-homomorphic encryption and multiparty computation. In: Paterson, K.G. (ed.) Advances in Cryptology – EUROCRYPT 2011, pp. 169–188. Springer, Berlin, Heidelberg (2011). https://doi.org/10.1007/978-3-642-20465-4_11
7. BLAKLEY, G.R.: Safeguarding cryptographic keys. In: 1979 International Workshop on Managing Requirements Knowledge (MARK), pp. 313–318 (Jun 1979).https://doi.org/10.1109/MARK.1979.8817296, https://ieeexplore.ieee.org/document/8817296, iSSN: 2164-0149
8. Bogdanov, D., Laur, S., Willemson, J.: Sharemind: A framework for fast privacy-preserving computations. In: Jajodia, S., Lopez, J. (eds.) Computer Security - ESORICS 2008, pp. 192–206. Springer, Berlin, Heidelberg (2008). https://doi.org/10.1007/978-3-540-88313-5_13
9. Boneh, D., Sahai, A., Waters, B.: Functional encryption: definitions and challenges (2010). https://eprint.iacr.org/2010/543, publication info: Published elsewhere. Unknown where it was published

10. Canetti, R., Dwork, C., Naor, M., Ostrovsky, R.: Deniable encryption. In: Kaliski, B.S. (ed.) Advances in Cryptology — CRYPTO '97, pp. 90–104. Springer, Berlin, Heidelberg (1997). https://doi.org/10.1007/BFb0052229

11. Chang, C.Y., Clark, S.: Practical linguistic steganography using contextual synonym substitution and a novel vertex coding method. Comput. Linguist. **40**(2), 403–448 (Jun 2014). https://doi.org/10.1162/COLI_a_00176

12. Chapman, M., Davida, G.: Hiding the hidden: a software system for concealing ciphertext as innocuous text. In: Han, Y., Okamoto, T., Qing, S. (eds.) Information and Communications Security, pp. 335–345. Springer, Berlin, Heidelberg (1997)https://doi.org/10.1007/BFb0028489

13. Cramer, R., Damgård, I.B., Nielsen, J.B.: Secure multiparty computation and secret sharing. cambridge university Press, Cambridge (2015). https://doi.org/10.1017/CBO9781107337756, https://www.cambridge.org/core/books/secure-multiparty-computation-and-secret-sharing/4C2480B202905CE5370B2609F0C2A67A

14. Cramer, R., Shoup, V.: Design and Analysis of Practical Public-Key Encryption Schemes Secure against Adaptive Chosen Ciphertext Attack (2001). https://eprint.iacr.org/2001/108, publication info: Published elsewhere. Unknown where it was published

15. Damgård, I., Pastro, V., Smart, N., Zakarias, S.: Multiparty Computation from Somewhat Homomorphic Encryption. In: Safavi-Naini, R., Canetti, R. (eds.) Advances in Cryptology – CRYPTO 2012, pp. 643–662. Springer, Berlin, Heidelberg (2012). https://doi.org/10.1007/978-3-642-32009-5_38

16. Desmedt, Y., Frankel, Y.: Threshold cryptosystems. In: Brassard, G. (ed.) Advances in Cryptology — CRYPTO' 89 Proceedings, pp. 307–315. Springer, New York, NY (1990).https://doi.org/10.1007/0-387-34805-0_28

17. Ding, J., Schmidt, D.: Rainbow, a new multivariable polynomial signature scheme. In: Ioannidis, J., Keromytis, A., Yung, M. (eds.) Applied Cryptography and Network Security, pp. 164–175. Springer, Berlin, Heidelberg (2005). https://doi.org/10.1007/11496137_12

18. Dodis, Y., Kiltz, E., Pietrzak, K., Wichs, D.: Message authentication, revisited. In: Proceedings of the 31st Annual international conference on Theory and Applications of Cryptographic Techniques, pp. 355–374. EUROCRYPT'12, Springer-Verlag, Berlin, Heidelberg (Apr 2012). https://doi.org/10.1007/978-3-642-29011-4_22

19. Feldman, P.: A practical scheme for non-interactive verifiable secret sharing. In: Proceedings of the 28th Annual Symposium on Foundations of Computer Science, pp. 427–438. SFCS '87, IEEE Computer Society, USA (Oct 1987). https://doi.org/10.1109/SFCS.1987.4

20. Garg, S., Gentry, C., Halevi, S., Raykova, M., Sahai, A., Waters, B.: Candidate Indistinguishability Obfuscation and Functional Encryption for all Circuits. In: 2013 IEEE 54th Annual Symposium on Foundations of Computer Science, pp. 40–49 (Oct 2013). https://doi.org/10.1109/FOCS.2013.13, https://ieeexplore.ieee.org/document/6686139, iSSN: 0272-5428

21. Goldreich, O., Micali, S., Wigderson, A.: How to play ANY mental game. In: Proceedings of the nineteenth annual ACM symposium on Theory of computing. pp. 218–229. STOC '87, Association for Computing Machinery, New York, NY, USA (Jan 1987). https://doi.org/10.1145/28395.28420, https://dl.acm.org/doi/10.1145/28395.28420

22. Herzberg, A., Jarecki, S., Krawczyk, H., Yung, M.: Proactive secret sharing or: how to cope with perpetual leakage. In: Coppersmith, D. (ed.) Advances in Cryptology — CRYPTO' 95, pp. 339–352. Springer, Berlin, Heidelberg (1995). https://doi.org/10.1007/3-540-44750-4_27
23. Hoffstein, J., Pipher, J., Silverman, J.H.: NTRU: A ring-based public key cryptosystem. In: Buhler, J.P. (ed.) Algorithmic Number Theory, pp. 267–288. Springer, Berlin, Heidelberg (1998).https://doi.org/10.1007/BFb0054868
24. Komargodski, I., Naor, M., Yogev, E.: How to share a secret, infinitely (2016). https://eprint.iacr.org/2016/194, publication info: A minor revision of an IACR publication in TCC 2016
25. Komlo, C., Goldberg, I.: FROST: Flexible round-optimized schnorr threshold signatures. In: Selected Areas in Cryptography: 27th International Conference, Halifax, NS, Canada (Virtual Event), October 21–23, 2020, Revised Selected Papers, pp. 34–65. Springer-Verlag, Berlin, Heidelberg (Oct 2020). https://doi.org/10.1007/978-3-030-81652-0_2
26. Krawczyk, H.: Secret sharing made short. In: Proceedings of the 13th Annual International Cryptology Conference on Advances in Cryptology, pp. 136–146. CRYPTO '93, Springer-Verlag, Berlin, Heidelberg (Aug 1993)
27. Lyubashevsky, V., Peikert, C., Regev, O.: On ideal lattices and learning with errors over rings. J. ACM **60**(6), 43:1–43:35 (Nov 2013). https://doi.org/10.1145/2535925, https://dl.acm.org/doi/10.1145/2535925
28. McEliece, R.J.: A public-key cryptosystem based on algebraic coding theory. Deep Space Netw. Progress Report **44**, 114–116 (Jan 1978) https://ui.adsabs.harvard.edu/abs/1978DSNPR..44..114M, aDS Bibcode: 1978DSNPR..44..114M
29. Pedersen, T.P.: Non-interactive and information-theoretic secure verifiable secret sharing. In: Proceedings of the 11th Annual International Cryptology Conference on Advances in Cryptology, pp. 129–140. CRYPTO '91, Springer-Verlag, Berlin, Heidelberg (Aug 1991)
30. Rivest, R.L., Shamir, A., Adleman, L.: A method for obtaining digital signatures and public-key cryptosystems. Commun. ACM **21**(2), 120–126 (Feb 1978). https://doi.org/10.1145/359340.359342, https://dl.acm.org/doi/10.1145/359340.359342
31. Safaka, I., Fragouli, C., Argyraki, K.: Matryoshka: Hiding Secret Communication in Plain Sight (2016). https://www.usenix.org/conference/foci16/workshop-program/presentation/safaka
32. Shamir, A.: How to share a secret. Commun. ACM 22(11), 612–613 (Nov 1979). https://doi.org/10.1145/359168.359176, https://dl.acm.org/doi/10.1145/359168.359176
33. Shor, P.W.: Algorithms for quantum computation: discrete logarithms and factoring. In: Proceedings of the 35th Annual Symposium on Foundations of Computer Science, pp. 124–134. SFCS '94, IEEE Computer Society, USA (Nov 1994). https://doi.org/10.1109/SFCS.1994.365700
34. Shoup, V.: Practical threshold signatures. In: Proceedings of the 19th international conference on Theory and application of cryptographic techniques, pp. 207–220. EUROCRYPT'00, Springer-Verlag, Berlin, Heidelberg (May 2000)
35. Tyagi, N., Grubbs, P., Len, J., Miers, I., Ristenpart, T.: Asymmetric message franking: content moderation for metadata-private end-to-end encryption (2019). https://eprint.iacr.org/2019/565, publication info: A major revision of an IACR publication in CRYPTO 2019
36. Watanabe, Y., Shikata, J.: Identity-based hierarchical key-insulated encryption without random oracles. In: Proceedings, Part I, of the 19th IACR International

Conference on Public-Key Cryptography — PKC 2016 - Volume 9614, pp. 255–279. Springer-Verlag, Berlin, Heidelberg (Mar 2016). https://doi.org/10.1007/978-3-662-49384-7_10

37. Wayner, P.: Disappearing Cryptography: Information Hiding: Steganography and Watermarking. Morgan Kaufmann (Jun 2009)

38. Yao, A.C.: Protocols for secure computations. In: 23rd Annual Symposium on Foundations of Computer Science (sfcs 1982), pp. 160–164 (Nov 1982). https://doi.org/10.1109/SFCS.1982.38, https://ieeexplore.ieee.org/document/4568388, iSSN: 0272-5428

# Eliminating Exponential Key Growth in PRG-Based Distributed Point Functions


Marc Damie[1,2(✉)] [ID], Florian Hahn[1] [ID], Andreas Peter[3] [ID], and Jan Ramon[2]

[1] University of Twente, Enschede, The Netherlands
[2] Inria, Villeneuve-d'Ascq, France
m.f.d.damie@utwente.nl
[3] Carl von Ossietzky Universität Oldenburg, Oldenburg, Germany



**Abstract.** Distributed Point Functions (DPFs) enable sharing secret point functions across multiple parties, supporting privacy-preserving technologies such as Private Information Retrieval, and anonymous communications. While 2-party PRG-based schemes with logarithmic key sizes have been known for a decade, extending these solutions to multi-party settings has proven challenging. In particular, PRG-based multi-party DPFs have historically struggled with practicality due to key sizes growing exponentially with the number of parties and the field size.

Our work addresses this efficiency bottleneck by optimizing the PRG-based multi-party DPF scheme of Boyle et al. (EUROCRYPT'15). By leveraging the honest-majority assumption, we eliminate the exponential factor present in this scheme. Our construction is the first PRG-based multi-party DPF scheme with practical key sizes, and provides key up to $3\times$ smaller than the best known multi-party DPF. This work demonstrates that with careful optimization, PRG-based multi-party DPFs can achieve practical performances, and even obtain top performances.

**Keywords:** Distributed Point Function · Function Secret Sharing · Private Information Retrieval · Multi-Party Computations


## 1 Introduction

Function Secret Sharing [2] is a cryptographic primitive enabling to share secret functions. In these protocols, a key dealer knowing a secret function $f$ distributes $p$ keys to different shareholder. Each shareholder can use its key to obtain a share of $f(x)$, without any communication between the shareholders.

Among all function families, schemes supporting point functions (i.e., $f(x) = \beta$ if $x = \alpha$, 0 otherwise) attracted a lot of attention thanks to their numerous applications notably in Private Information Retrieval (PIR) [7], in anonymous communications [6], in digital currencies [9], and machine learning [4]. These schemes are called "Distributed Point Functions" (DPF) [2,7].

To support these applications, there is a significant research incentive aiming to improve existing schemes, notably their key size. DPF efficiency is commonly


© The Author(s), under exclusive license to Springer Nature Switzerland AG 2026
R. Laborde et al. (Eds.): ESORICS 2025, LNCS 16231, pp. 116–124, 2026.
https://doi.org/10.1007/978-3-032-16089-8_8

evaluated based on the influence of the function domain size ($N$) on the key size. For two- and three-party DPF, schemes based on PseudoRandom Generators (PRGs) provide logarithmic key sizes [2,9]. However, there is still a lot of active research to obtain similar key sizes for any arbitrary number of parties.

In multi-party DPF, three main approaches have emerged. First, elliptic-curve-based schemes [6,8] offer practical $O(\sqrt{N})$ key sizes, but they require a non-linear share decoding. This non-linearity makes them incompatible with several key applications such as PIR. Second, Boyle et al. [2] presented a dishonest-majority scheme with $O(\sqrt{N})$ key size, and Bunn et al. [5] an honest-majority scheme with $O(\sqrt[4]{N})$ key size. Unfortunately, this asymptotic cost hides an exponential factors $q^p$ (for output shares in $\mathbb{F}_q$ and $p$ parties). This factor makes these schemes impractical for any modulus $q > 210$ (as detailed in Sect. 4). This problem was identified in existing works [1,8], but has not been solved *yet*.

Finally, Bunn et al. [5] proposed a third approach based on honest-majority to build an information-theoretic (IT) scheme with $O(\sqrt{N})$ key size *and no exponential factor*. This scheme is the only multi-party scheme with practical key sizes supporting all applications. Even though this scheme is practical, solving the efficiency issues of the other schemes could lead to even better performances. As PRGs have lead to logarithmic key sizes in two and three-party schemes, optimizing multi-party PRG-based schemes could be promising.

*Our Contributions.* Our paper optimizes the PRG-based DPF proposed by [2]. Our optimized scheme avoids the exponential factors present in [2] using the honest-majority assumption; obtaining a key size of $O(\sqrt{N \cdot \binom{p}{m+1}} \log q)$ instead of $O(\sqrt{N}q^{\frac{p-1}{2}} \log q)$. Our benchmark shows that our scheme is the first multi-party PRG-based scheme with practical key sizes. We even provide keys up to $3\times$ smaller than the best performing DPF (i.e., the IT DPF by [5]).

*Notations.* Let $p$ be the number of parties/shareholders, $m$ be the number of corrupted parties. Like most FSS works [2,3,5,7,8], we focus on semi-honest adversaries: follow the protocol and infer *passively* secret information.

Let $\mathbb{F}_q$ be a prime field, $N$ be the function domain size, $1^\lambda$ a security parameter, and $[\![x]\!]_i$ be the $i$-th share of the secret $x$. Let $\nu = \lceil \sqrt{N} \rceil$ and $C = \binom{p}{m+1}$. Let $G : \{0,1\}^\lambda \to \mathbb{G}^\nu$ be a PRG, and $\mathbb{G}$ an Abelian group.

## 2   Background

Function secret sharing (FSS) [2] enables sharing secret functions between $p$ parties. Each FSS scheme can share function from a specific function family.

A function family $\mathcal{F}$ [1] is a pair $(P_\mathcal{F}, E_\mathcal{F})$ where $P_\mathcal{F} \subseteq \{0,1\}^*$ is a collection of function descriptions $\hat{f}$, and $E_\mathcal{F}: P_\mathcal{F} \times \{0,1\}^* \to \{0,1\}^*$ is a polynomial-time algorithm defining the function described by $\hat{f}$; i.e., $f(x) = E_\mathcal{F}(\hat{f}, x)$. All functions within a family share the same domain $\mathcal{X}$ and output space $\mathcal{Y}$.

Due to their applications notably in PIR [7] and anonymous communications [6], the most studied function family has been point functions [2,3,5–7]; functions $f$ such that $f(x) = \beta$ if $x = \alpha$, and $f(x) = 0$ otherwise. For point functions, the function description is the tuple $(\alpha, \beta) \in P_{\mathcal{F}}$. Schemes supporting point functions are called "Distributed Point Functions" (DPF).

For a function family $\mathcal{F}$, we define a $p$-party FSS scheme using 3 algorithms:

- Gen : $\mathbb{N} \times P_{\mathcal{F}} \to \mathcal{K}^p$ takes as input a security parameter $1^\lambda \in \mathbb{N}$ and a function description $\hat{f} \in P_{\mathcal{F}}$, and outputs $p$ keys $k_1, \ldots, k_p$.
- Eval : $\mathcal{K} \times \mathcal{X} \to \mathbb{G}$ takes as input $k_i$ and a point $x \in \mathcal{X}$, outputs a share of $f(x)$ that we denote as $[\![f(x)]\!]_i$.
- Decode : $\mathbb{G}^p \to \mathcal{Y}$ takes as input the shares $\{[\![f(x)]\!]_1, \ldots, [\![f(x)]\!]_p\}$ and outputs the secret $f(x)$.

**Definition 1 (Correctness [2]).** *A scheme* (Gen, Eval, Decode) *is correct if, for any function $f \in \mathcal{F}$ and point $x \in \mathcal{X}$, we have:*

$$\Pr\left[\text{Decode}(\text{Eval}(k_1, x), \ldots, \text{Eval}(k_p, x)) = f(x)\right] = 1$$

$$\text{with } k_1, \ldots, k_p \leftarrow \text{Gen}(1^\lambda, \hat{f})$$

**Definition 2 (Privacy [1]).** *Let* Leak : $\{0,1\}^* \to \{0,1\}^*$ *be a function specifying the allowable leakage. A scheme* (Gen, Eval, Decode) *is private if, for every set of $m$ corrupted parties $S \subseteq \{1 \ldots p\}$, there exists a PPT algorithm* Sim *(simulator), s.t. for any sequence of function descriptions $(\hat{f}_1, \hat{f}_2, \ldots)$ of size polynomial in $\lambda$, the outputs of* Real *and* Ideal *are computationally indistinguishable:*

- Real$(1^\lambda) : (k_1, \ldots, k_p) \leftarrow \text{Gen}(1^\lambda, \hat{f}_\lambda)$; Output $(k_i)_{i \in S}$
- Ideal$(1^\lambda) :$ Output Sim$(1^\lambda, \text{Leak}(\hat{f}_\lambda))$

*DPF by* [2] To build their multi-party DPF scheme under dishonest majority ($m < p$), Boyle et al. [2] represented the domain $\{1, \ldots, N\}$ as a $\nu \times \nu$ grid (with $\nu = \lceil \sqrt{N} \rceil$). This grid is full of zeros except on the cell $(\gamma_*, \delta_*)$, with $\alpha = \gamma_* \nu + \delta_*$.

For each row $\gamma \in \{1, \ldots, \nu\}$, the Gen algorithm samples $q^{p-1}$ random $\lambda$-bit random seeds $s_{\gamma,1} \ldots s_{\gamma,q^{p-1}}$. For each seed $s_{\gamma,j}$, the algorithm generates additive shares of a coefficient $a_{\gamma,j}$: $[\![a_{\gamma,j}]\!]_1, \ldots [\![a_{\gamma,j}]\!]_p$ (i.e., one share per DPF key). The coefficient is defined as follows $a_{\gamma,j} = 1$ if $\gamma = \gamma_*$, 0 otherwise. Finally, it sets a "correction word" $W \in (\mathbb{F}_q)^\nu$ such that $W + \sum_{i=1}^{q^{p-1}} G(s_{\gamma_*,j}) = e_{\delta_*} \cdot \beta$ (with $e_\delta$ a unit vector equal to 1 on index $\delta$, 0 otherwise). Each key $k_i$ contains the correction word, their share of the coefficients $[\![a_{\gamma,j}]\!]_i$ (for all rows $\gamma$ and all $j \in \{1, \ldots, q^{p-1}\}$), and it contains all the seeds $s_{\gamma,j}$ for which $[\![a_{\gamma,j}]\!]_i \neq 0$. This last condition (on the seed inclusion in a key) ensures that there is at least one seed unknown to an adversary composed of $p-1$ out of $p$ parties.

The Eval algorithm represents the input $x$ as a tuple $(\gamma, \delta)$, expands the corresponding seeds $s_{\gamma,j}$, multiplies the expanded seeds with the corresponding shared coefficient $[\![a_{\gamma,j}]\!]_i$, sums everything with the correction word $W$, and the share $[\![f(x)]\!]_i$ is on the $\delta$-th index of the sum vector:

$$[\![f(x)]\!]_i = v[\delta] \text{ with } v = W + \sum_j [\![a_{\gamma,j}]\!]_i \cdot G(s_{\gamma,j})$$

The Decode algorithm is a basic additive share decoding: $\sum_i [\![f(x)]\!]_i = f(x)$.

As we optimize [2], Algorithm 1(describing our scheme) follows roughly the same structure as their scheme. The *only difference* is the matrix sampling in Lines 8 and 9. We then refer to Algorithm 1 for more details.

An element could surprise the reader: the number of random seeds $\nu \times q^{p-1}$. Such a large number is necessary, so an adversary cannot infer information about the secret function based on the distribution of the shares $[\![a_{\gamma,j}]\!]_i$. These shares can be structured as matrix shares $A_\gamma$ with $A_\gamma[i,j] = [\![a_{\gamma,j}]\!]_i$. To preserve function privacy, each matrix must contain all combination of additive shares summing to 1 (if $\gamma = \gamma_*$) or 0 (if $\gamma \neq \gamma_*$). If the matrices do not contain all possible combinations, an adversary (owning up to $p - 1$ keys out of $p$) can recover $\gamma_*$ based on the share distribution [2]. Since there exists $q^{p-1}$ combinations of $p$ shares of 0 (resp. of 1) in $\mathbb{F}_q$, the key generator must sample $q^{p-1}$ random seeds.

## 3   Our Honest-Majority Scheme

The main scalability bottleneck in [2] lies in the size of the matrices of shares, we improve their scheme by eliminating its dependence on the field size; thanks to the honest-majority assumption ($m < p/2$). While Boyle et al. [2] had assumed a dishonest majority ($m < p$), the honest-majority assumption enables us to redesign the matrices, resulting in more compact keys. Algorithm 1 presents our multi-party DPF scheme, and Fig. 1 an overview of our DPF keys.

Our matrix sampling (described in the function MatrixOfShares of Algorithm 1) generates a matrix $A$ that distributes shares among all possible combinations of $m+1$ parties out of $p$. For each combination $S_j$ of $m+1$ parties, the function samples $m + 1$ shares of the secret coefficient $a$ (using additive secret sharing) and assigns each share to the cell of $A$; $A[i,j] = [\![a]\!]_i$ if $i \in S_j$, 0 otherwise. The secret coefficient $a$ is either set to 0 or 1 depending on whether the value $x$ being evaluated matches $\alpha$ (the non-zero point).

While in [2], each matrix of shares has $p$ rows and $q^{p-1}$ columns, our construction produces matrices with $p$ rows and $\binom{p}{m+1}$ columns. As in [2], we sample one random seed per column. The $i$-th key contains the $i$-th row of the matrix and includes the $j$-th seed if the corresponding cell $A[i,j]$ is not null.

As in [2], it is necessary that (for any given $\gamma$) at least one seed $s_{\gamma,j}$ remains unknown to the adversary. With all the seeds, they could unmask the correction word $W$ and recover $\beta$. Our scheme provides each seed to $m+1$ parties, so *under honest majority*, at least one combination of $m+1$ out of $p$ parties contains only honest agents. Thus, there is at least one seed unknown to an adversary.

---

**Algorithm 1.** Honest-majority DPF scheme adapted from [2].

---

1: **function** MatrixOfShares($a$)
2:     Initialize $A$ an $p \times C$ matrix with zeros and the counter $k$ to 1.
3:     **for** each set of parties $S_j$ in the set of all combinations of $m + 1$ of $p$ **do**
4:         Sample $m + 1$ shares of the value $a$: $\{[\![a]\!]_{1,i} \ldots [\![a]\!]_{m+1,i}\}$.
5:         **for** each $i$ in $S_j$ **do** $A[i,j] \leftarrow [\![a]\!]_{k,i}$ and increment $k$.
     **return** A

6: **function** Gen($\alpha, \beta, p, m, 1^\lambda$)
7:     Represent $\alpha$ as a pair $\alpha = (\gamma_*, \delta_*)$ with $\gamma_*, \delta_* \in \{0 \ldots \nu\}$.
8:     Sample $A_1, \ldots, A_\nu$ s.t. for all $\gamma \neq \gamma_*$, $A_\gamma \leftarrow$ MatrixOfShares(0).
9:     Sample $A_{\gamma_*} \leftarrow$ MatrixOfShares(1).
10:     Choose randomly and independently $\nu \cdot C$ seeds $s_{1,1}, \ldots, s_{\nu,C} \in \{0,1\}^\lambda$.
11:     Set the correction words $W \in \mathbb{G}^\nu$ s.t. $W + \sum_{j=1}^{C} G(s_{\gamma_*,j}) = e_{\delta_*} \cdot \beta$.
12:     **for** $i \in \{1 \ldots p\}, j \in \{1 \ldots C\}, \gamma \in \{1 \ldots \nu\}$ **do**
13:         **if** $A_\gamma[i,j] \neq 0$ **then** $\sigma_{i,\gamma,j} \leftarrow (s_{\gamma,j}, A_\gamma[i,j])$.
14:         **else** $\sigma_{i,\gamma,j} \leftarrow (0,0)$.          ▷ Receives no seed and no coefficient share
15:     Set $\sigma_{i,\gamma} \leftarrow (\sigma_{i,\gamma,1}||\ldots||\sigma_{i,\gamma,C})$ for all $1 \leq i \leq p$, $1 \leq \gamma \leq \nu$.
16:     **return** $(k_1, \ldots, k_p)$ with $k_i = (\sigma_{i,1}||\ldots||\sigma_{i,\nu}||W)$ for all $1 \leq i \leq p$.

17: **function** Eval($k_i, x$)
18:     Represent $x$ as a pair $x = (\gamma, \delta)$ with $\gamma, \delta \in \{0 \ldots \nu\}$.
19:     Parse $k_i = ((s_{1,1}, A_1[i,1])||\ldots||(s_{1,C}, A_1[i,C])||\ldots||(s_{\nu,C}, A_\nu[i,C])||W)$.
20:     **return** $y_i[\delta]$ with $y_i \leftarrow A_\gamma[i,1] \cdot W + \sum_{j=1}^{C} A_\gamma[i,j] \cdot G(s_{\gamma,j})$.

21: **function** Decode($[\![y]\!]_1, \ldots, [\![y]\!]_p$) **return** $\sum_{i=1}^{p} [\![y]\!]_i$.

---

Our optimization cannot be extended to dishonest majority. Indeed, with $m > p/2$, the adversary would know all the seeds because there would be at least one corrupted party in each combination of $m + 1$ out of $p$ parties.

Based on these intuitions, we can consider the following security theorem:

**Theorem 1.** *Let $\lambda \in \mathbb{N}$, $N, p \in \mathbb{N}$, then the tuple* (Gen, Eval, Decode) *as described in Algorithm 1 is an FSS scheme for the family of all point functions with $\alpha \in \{1, \ldots, N\}$ and any $\beta \in \mathbb{F}_q$.*

*Assuming that there exists a secure PRG, then this scheme is correct and private against at most $m$ semi-honest parties with $m < p/2$.*

*Proof.* As we modified only slightly the scheme of [2] (i.e., redesigned the matrix of shares based on the honest-majority assumption), our proof follows the same structure as theirs. We provide a proof sketch, and refer to [2] for more details.

The correctness can be verified by an easy arithmetic exercise considering successively three cases: (1) $\gamma \neq \gamma_*$, (2) $\gamma = \gamma_*$ and $\delta \neq \delta_*$, and (3) $\gamma = \gamma_*$ and $\delta = \delta_*$. Using the $\sqrt{N} \times \sqrt{N}$ grid (illustrated in Fig. 1), we represent any input $x$ as $(\gamma, \delta)$ and $\alpha$ as $(\gamma_*, \delta_*)$.

For privacy, we must show that there exists a simulator that outputs samples from a distribution that is computationally indistinguishable from the

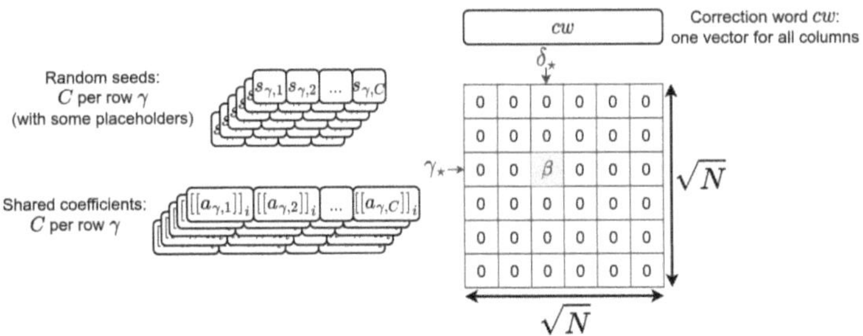


**Fig. 1.** Structure of our DPF keys.

distribution of the real DPF keys. We propose to study separately: the random seeds $s_{\gamma,j}$, the correction word $W$, and the coefficient shares $A_\gamma[i,j]$.

The simulation is straightforward: for each (simulated) seed, sample a random seed $\widetilde{s_{\gamma,j}}$; for the correction word, sample a random vector $\widetilde{W}$; for the coefficients, for each $S_j$ combination of $m+1$ parties of $p$, for each $i$ in $S_j$, sample a random value and store it in $\widetilde{A}_\gamma[i,j]$ (the rest of $\widetilde{A}_\gamma$ is null). The simulator can return "simulated" keys based on these elements.

Since both the real and simulated seeds are randomly sampled, the simulator's output distribution $(\widetilde{s_{\gamma,j}})$ is computationally indistinguishable from that induced by the distribution of a single output of Gen.

The correction word $W$ is a secret vector (i.e., $e_{\delta_*} \cdot \beta$) masked with the output of $\binom{p}{m+1}$ seeded PRGs. Remember that a key $k_i$ contains a seed $s_{\gamma,j}$ only if the $i$ is part of the $j$-th combination of $m$ out of $p$ parties. So, under honest majority, there is always at least one seed unknown to the adversary controlling $m$ out $p$ parties. Hence, the correction word $W$ is computationally indistinguishable from the randomly sampled $\widetilde{W}$, because it is masked with the output of (at least) one PRG seeded with a seed unknown to the adversary [6].

Finally, each coefficient is shared between $m+1$ parties, so an adversary controlling $m$ parties cannot distinguish real shares from random values $\widetilde{A}_\gamma[i,j]$ provided by the simulator.

*Key size optimization:* Instead of using a $\sqrt{N} \times \sqrt{N}$ grid, we should use a grid with $\sqrt{N}(C)^{-1}$ rows and $\sqrt{N \cdot C}$ columns, with $C = \binom{p}{m+1}$. This "non-square" grid leverages the fact that each row requires $C$ seeds, and a unique vector $W$ for all columns. Thanks to this trick, we obtain a better key size: $O(\sqrt{N \cdot C} \log q)$.

*Extension to Comparison Functions.* Boyle et al. [2] presented a simple adaptation of their DPF to support comparison functions; functions such that $f(x) = \beta$ when $x \leq \alpha$, 0 otherwise. These schemes have applications notably in machine learning [4,8]. We can naively reuse our optimization on this other scheme.

## 4   Key Size Comparison

This section compares our optimized scheme to existing schemes in order to identify asymptotic and practical key size reductions.

We focus our comparison on schemes supporting all possible DPF applications; excluding schemes based on elliptic curves that support a limited number of applications due to their non-linear decoding [8] (e.g., do not support PIR).

*Asymptotic.* Our scheme provides a key size of $O(\sqrt{N \cdot \binom{p}{m+1}} \log q)$, which is clearly better than the key size of [2] (i.e., $O(\sqrt{N} q^{\frac{p-1}{2}} \log q)$).

As Bunn et al. [5] built an honest-majority scheme with $O(\sqrt[4]{N})$ key size upon [2], we can comment how we distinguish from them. Their paper does not modify [2], but combine it with replicated secret sharing to reduce the dependency on $N$ (i.e., $O(\sqrt[4]{N})$ instead of $O(\sqrt{N})$). However, their approach worsened the exponential factors already in [2]; as shown in our benchmark below. On the contrary, we leverage the honest-majority scheme to avoid exponential factors present in [2], but we maintained the same dependence on $N$.

The IT DPF by [5] has a key size comparable to ours: $O(\sqrt{N} \cdot \binom{p}{m+1} \log q)$. However, our approach saves a factor $\sqrt{\binom{p}{m+1}}$ compared to them, yielding significant key size reductions in practice.

While these asymptotic comparisons are informative, they are often insufficient to assess practical performance. Bunn et al. [5] exemplify this problem: although they substantially reduced the dependence on the domain size $N$, they kept exponential factors without providing any concrete efficiency analysis. Therefore, we present a detailed comparison based on exact key sizes to offer a more accurate assessment.

*Exact.* As we aimed to avoid the exponential factor $q^p$ (for outputs in $\mathbb{F}_q$), we start by studying the dependency on $q$. Figure 2 compares key sizes for varying prime moduli. Our benchmark includes a curve "Trivial scheme" corresponding to the most trivial DPF: sharing the function truth table (i.e., $O(N)$ key size). This curve serves as baseline to identify impractical solutions. For any $q > 5$, the PRG-based solutions [2,5] have keys orders of magnitude larger than those of this trivial solution, while the IT DPF of [5] and ours are below.

Recently, Boyle [1] showed that, for a composite modulus $m = q_1 q_2 \ldots q_l$, we can use the Chinese Remainder Theorem (CRT) to replace $q^p$ with $\sum q_i^p$. Figure 2a compares key sizes for arbitrary moduli, but the variations make the figure poorly readable. Instead, Fig. 2c compares key sizes for primorial moduli; a primorial is the product of the first $n$ primes. Primorials are the best case of this CRT trick as they provide composite moduli with the smallest primes possible.

Even with the CRT trick, the existing PRG-based schemes [2,5] provides key sizes larger than the trivial scheme for any modulus above 210. As their key sizes are impractical, we exclude these schemes from our other figures to focus on the comparison of our scheme to practical schemes.

Figure 2c also shows that the key size of the IT scheme of [5] grows faster with the modulus than ours. This phenomenon is explained by the fact that our key size is dominated by components conditioned by a security parameter that is independent of the modulus.

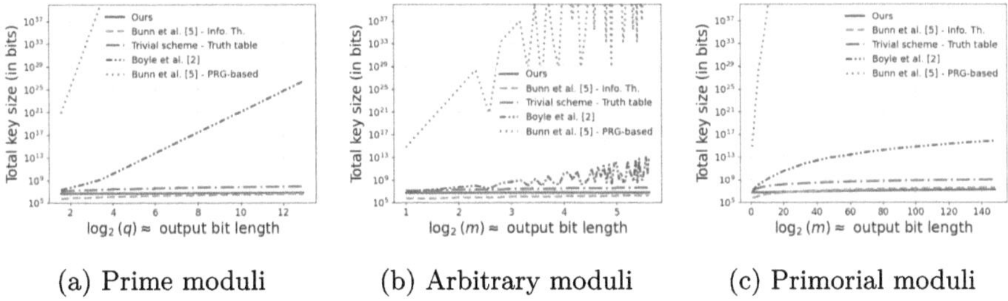

(a) Prime moduli        (b) Arbitrary moduli        (c) Primorial moduli

**Fig. 2.** Key size of various DPF schemes for varying moduli ($p = 7$).

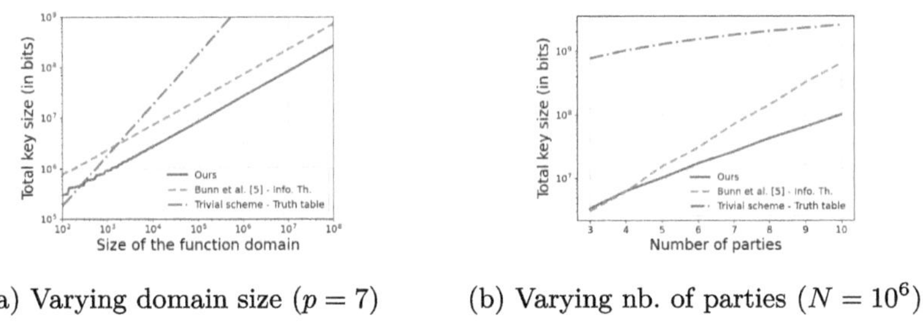

(a) Varying domain size ($p = 7$)        (b) Varying nb. of parties ($N = 10^6$)

**Fig. 3.** Key size of the most efficient DPF schemes.

Figure 3a compares the practical schemes for varying function domain sizes. **Our key size is** $2.4\times$ **smaller than the best existing scheme.** Moreover, Fig. 3b shows that **our scheme has a better scaling with the number of parties** thanks to the factor $\sqrt{\binom{p}{m+1}}$ identified in the asymptotic comparison.

*Conclusion.* Our optimization based on the honest-majority assumption transformed a PRG-based DPF [2] with impractical key sizes into the DPF with the smallest key sizes. Our work proves that, like in two- and three-party schemes, PRG is a promising primitive to build multi-party DPF with compact keys.

**Acknowledgments.** This work was supported by the Netherlands Organization for Scientific Research (De Nederlandse Organisatie voor Wetenschappelijk Onderzoek) under NWO:SHARE project [CS.011].

# References


1. Boyle, E.: Function Secret Sharing and Homomorphic Secret Sharing (2022)
2. Boyle, E., Gilboa, N., Ishai, Y.: Function secret sharing. In: Advances in Cryptology - EUROCRYPT 2015 (2015). https://doi.org/10.1007/978-3-662-46803-6_12
3. Boyle, E., Gilboa, N., Ishai, Y.: Function secret sharing: improvements and extensions. In: Proceedings of the 2016 ACM SIGSAC Conference on Computer and Communications Security (Oct 2016). https://doi.org/10.1145/2976749.2978429
4. Boyle, E., Gilboa, N., Ishai, Y.: Secure computation with preprocessing via function secret sharing. In: Theory of Cryptography (2019). https://doi.org/10.1007/978-3-030-36030-6_14
5. Bunn, P., Kushilevitz, E., Ostrovsky, R.: CNF-FSS and its applications. In: Public-Key Cryptography 2022 (2022). https://doi.org/10.1007/978-3-030-97121-2_11
6. Corrigan-Gibbs, H., Boneh, D., Mazières, D.: Riposte: An anonymous messaging system handling millions of users. In: 2015 IEEE Symposium on Security and Privacy (May 2015). https://doi.org/10.1109/SP.2015.27
7. Gilboa, N., Ishai, Y.: Distributed point functions and their applications. In: EUROCRYPT 2014 (2014). https://doi.org/10.1007/978-3-642-55220-5_35
8. Kumar, C., Patranabis, S., Mukhopadhyay, D.: Compact key function secret sharing with non-linear decoder. IACR Commun. Cryptol. $\mathbf{1}$(2) (Jul 2024). https://doi.org/10.62056/a3c3c3w9p
9. Zyskind, G., Yanai, A., Pentland, A.S.: High-throughput three-party DPFs with applications to ORAM and digital currencies. In: Proceedings of the 2024 ACM SIGSAC Conference on Computer and Communications Security (2024)

# A Pseudo-inverse Matrix-Based LDP for High-Dimensional Data


Hiroaki Kikuchi[(✉)]

School of Interdisciplinary Mathematical Sciences, Meiji University,
4-21-1 Nakano, Tokyo 164-8525, Japan
`kikn@meiji.ac.jp`



**Abstract.** We study local differential privacy (LDP) protocols that estimate the statistics of a group while preserving individual data privacy. One of the challenges for LDP is dealing with high-dimensional data, which is common in the medical domain and can incur a large privacy budget that grows with dimensionality. In 2018, Zhang et al. presented a novel LDP scheme, CALM (Consistent Adaptive Local Marginal), that could estimate the joint probability distribution of high-dimensional data via a set of lower-dimensional marginals, called "views." The process involved entropy maximization with a convex optimization algorithm. However, the entropy maximization process may fail if the original data is over-randomized. We therefore propose a simple method that addresses this estimation issue using a pseudo-inverse matrix. We evaluate the accuracy of our estimation method in terms of the size of the views and frequency predictions.

**Keywords:** differential privacy · multi-dimensional data


## 1 Introduction

Local differential privacy (LDP) has been utilized in various privacy-enhancing applications. For instance, Erlingsson et al. proposed an LDP algorithm called the randomized aggregatable privacy-preserving ordinal response [9]. This algorithm is employed by Google Chrome to gather user data while ensuring privacy.

The dimensionality problem in LDP refers to the challenge of handling high-dimensional data efficiently and accurately while preserving privacy and has two main aspects. (a) *Increased Noise.* In LDP, each data item is perturbed independently to ensure privacy, which often involves adding noise to the data. As the dimensionality of the data increases, the amount of noise added to each dimension also increases, leading to a significant reduction in the accuracy of the aggregated data. (b) *Scalability.* Using high-dimensional data requires complex mechanisms to ensure that privacy is maintained for each dimension, and the aggregated domain can grow exponentially. This complexity can lead to LDP mechanisms becoming less scalable and more computationally intensive, making it difficult to handle large datasets efficiently.



R. Laborde et al. (Eds.): ESORICS 2025, LNCS 16231, pp. 125–136, 2026.
https://doi.org/10.1007/978-3-032-16089-8_9

A number of studies have addressed the dimensionality issue in LDP. Domingo-Ferrer et al. [1] introduced a clustering-based randomized response method. Ren et al. [2] developed a technique called LoPub, which integrates Lasso regression with the Expectation-Maximization (EM) algorithm. Wang et al. [3] proposed using the Gaussian copula to enhance accuracy. Jiang et al. [4] introduced Wasserstein autoencoders as a solution.

The Consistent Adaptive Local Marginal (CALM) algorithm [6] was designed to address the challenges of high-dimensional data in the context of LDP. It aimed to improve the efficiency and accuracy of data collection and analysis while adhering to privacy constraints. It has three main advantages.

- *Communication Efficiency.* By focusing on a subset of the dimensions (the $\ell$-way marginals), rather than all dimensions, the amount of data that needs to be transmitted is reduced. The algorithm can then aggregate the local marginal statistics, which are simpler to compute and require less communication.
- *Marginal Aggregation.* By focusing on the marginal distributions of the data, CALM can provide accurate estimates without needing to handle the full high-dimensional joint distribution (the $k$-way marginals).
- *Adaptive Sampling.* CALM uses a sampling strategy to divide the whole population into $\binom{k}{\ell}$ smaller subsets, where *ell* is the size of subsets sampled over $k$ attributes. This helps conserve the privacy budget and improve overall utility.

Despite its advantages, the CALM approach has a notable drawback: it relies on off-the-shelf convex optimization tools to solve the constraint problems. (It is worth noting that the central server aims to estimate $k$-way marginals based on a given set of *ell*-way marginals. However, the available $\ell$-way marginals may be insufficient to uniquely determine the $k$-way marginals.) This dependency introduces its own challenges. In some cases, the convex optimization tool may fail to determine unique solution due to the nature of the noise added to ensure privacy enhancement. Given too strict or inconsistent constraints, it cannot find a solution.

To address this drawback of CALM, we investigate the required number of constraints for target dimensions. We introduce a new LDP algorithm that employs a *pseudo-inverse matrix* [12] to solve the constraints and estimate high-dimensional marginals, eliminating the need for convex optimization tools. A useful property of the pseudo-inverse is that it exists for any given matrix. Therefore, without having to use a potentially unstable convex optimization, we can estimate the $k$-way marginals using some lower-dimensional $\ell$-way marginals. Our scheme offers three main advantages:

- it is stable and consistently provides a solution to the given constraints,
- it estimates marginals as accurate as using the CALM,
- it is simple and easy to implement. Pseudo-inverse matrix is simply defined and many libraries are available.

Using open data, we conducted experiments to measure the accuracy of the proposed algorithm in Sect. 5. In Sect. 3.1, we clarify the necessary conditions for the number of views to have uniquely determined solutions. If the domain is too large, it is a challenge to find high-dimensional marginals from low-dimensional views.

## 2  Preliminaries

### 2.1  Problem Definition

Let $m$ be a number of attributes for multi-dimensional data. Let $\Omega_i$ be the domain of the $i$-th attribute, and $\Omega = \Omega_1 \times \cdots \times \Omega_m$ be the set of $m$ domains. Let $n$ be the number of users who each have $m$ private input values, $x_i^1, \ldots, x_i^m$. The users use a randomized algorithm to perturb these values and submit the perturbed values $y_i^1, \ldots, y_i^m$ to a data curator. Let $(Y^1, \ldots, Y^m)$ be the $m$-dimensional (columns) data of $n$ records (rows).

Given a subset of $(Y^1, \ldots, Y^m)$ of size $k$ such that $k \le m$, we (as the data curator) try to estimate the $k$-dimensional joint probability $\hat{\Phi}^k$ as accurately as possible.

### 2.2  LDP

A good randomized algorithm $\Psi$ is required to satisfy the following property.

**Definition 1 ($\epsilon$-local differential privacy).** *An algorithm $\Psi$ satisfies $\epsilon$-local differential privacy , where $\epsilon \ge 0$, if and only if for any inputs $x_1, x_2 \in \Omega$, we have*

$$\forall T \in Range(\Psi) \ \ Pr[\Psi(v_1) \in T] \ge e^\epsilon Pr[\Psi(v_2) \in T].$$

### 2.3  Generalized Randomized Response (GRR)

The GRR [8] is the generalized version of a randomized response. Let $P$ be the $(d \times d)$ randomizing matrix $P = \begin{pmatrix} p_{11} & \cdots & p_{1d} \\ \vdots & \ddots & \vdots \\ p_{d1} & \cdots & p_{dd} \end{pmatrix}$ , where $p_{uv}$ is the conditional probability that output variable $Y$ takes $v$, given input variable $X$ is $u$, i.e., $p_{uv} = Pr(Y = v | X = u)$. Note that $p_{i1} + \cdots + p_{id} = 1$ for $i = 1, \ldots, d$. According to $P$, perturbing input $X$ to $Y = (y_1, \ldots, y_n)$ gives

$$y_i = \begin{cases} x_i & \text{with } p = p_{ii} = \frac{e^\epsilon}{e^\epsilon + w - 1}, \\ v \in \Omega - \{x_i\} & \text{with } q = p_{ij} = \frac{1}{e^\epsilon + w - 1}. \end{cases}$$

where $w = |\Omega|$, and GRR satisfies $\epsilon$-LDP. When the domain sizes are all $k$, we have $w = w_0^k$.

We can then estimate the expected value of the frequency for $Y = a$,

$$\Phi_{\text{GRR}}(a) = \frac{f(a)/n - q}{p - q},$$

where $f(a)$ is the observed frequency of the perturbed value $y_i$.

## 2.4  CALM

Consistent Adaptive Local Marginal (CALM) [6] is an algorithm for publishing multidimensional $k$-way marginals via LDP. The goal is to have the curator to compute the $k$-way marginal from given $\ell$-way perturbed data such that $k > \ell$.

A straightforward approach is to estimate the full contingency table for $\Omega$. The shortcoming of this approach is that the space and time grow exponentially with the dimensionality $k$. Moreover, the privacy budget is linearly to the dimensionality, resulting in very noisy results.

In CALM [6], the set of users is divided into several smaller subgroups, where users perturb $\ell$ attributes assigned to their group. The smaller $\ell$-way marginals, called "views," are given as constraints for finding consistent $k$-way marginals using Maximum Entropy estimation via a convex optimization tool. The privacy budget can be saved because $\ell < k$, while accuracy decreases as the population of users $n$ is divided into smaller groups. It is not trivial to find the optimal values for the size $\ell$ and the number of groups. In the CALM scheme, Zhang et al. proposed an algorithm for determining a targeted threshold that would minimize estimation errors from several perspectives.

To illustrate the idea with a simple example, we reconstruct a $k(= 3)$-way marginal given $\ell(= 2)$-way views, as presented in Table 1.

**Table 1.** Example of views

(a) View $V_1$ ($\ell = 2$)

|       | $b_1$ | $b_2$ |
| ----- | ----- | ----- |
| $a_1$ | 6     | 10    |
| $a_2$ | 8     | 12    |

(b) View $V_2$ ($\ell = 2$)

|       | $c_1$ | $c_2$ |
| ----- | ----- | ----- |
| $a_1$ | 4     | 12    |
| $a_2$ | 6     | 14    |

(c) View $V_3$ ($k = 3$)

|       | $c_1$ |       | $c_2$ |       |
| ----- | ----- | ----- | ----- | ----- |
|       | $b_1$ | $b_2$ | $b_1$ | $b_2$ |
| $a_1$ | 1     | 3     | 5     | 7     |
| $a_2$ | 2     | 4     | 6     | 8     |

Here, we have $n = 36$ users for $k = 3$ domains: $\Omega_1 = \{a_1, a_2\}$, $\Omega_2 = \{b_1, b_2\}$, and $\Omega_3 = \{c_1, c_2\}$, with the frequencies given in the contingency table $V_3$, as shown in Table (1c). Two subsets of users publish their data in the corresponding contingency tables $V_1$ and $V_2$, as shown in Tables (1a) and (1b), respectively.

Given the two views $V_1$ and $V_2$, our goal is to find a consistent assignment for the eight variables, $x_1, \ldots, x_8$, in $V_3$. Note that view $V_1$ specifies some partial constraints related to $\Omega_1$ and $\Omega_2$, as expressed in the following four simultaneous equations.

$$\begin{cases} x_1 + & & x_5 & & = 6, \\ & x_2 + & & x_6 & = 8, \\ & & x_3 + & & x_7 & = 10, \\ & & & x_4 + & & x_8 = 12. \end{cases} \tag{1}$$

Similarly, view $V_2$ gives the constraints related to $\Omega_1$ and $\Omega_3$, expressed as follows.

$$\begin{cases} x_1 + x_3 & = 4, \\ x_2 + x_4 & = 6, \\ x_5 + x_7 & = 12, \\ x_6 + x_8 & = 14. \end{cases} \tag{2}$$

With a privacy budget $\epsilon$, $n/2$ users in the first group perturb their data using GRR and let the curator estimate view $V_1$. The lefthand $n/2$ users in the second group contribute to the estimation of view $V_2$. Given that the groups are exclusive, the aggregation of views requires no additional privacy budget.

The final task is to solve the equations satisfying the constraints and estimate the $k(=3)$-way marginals (view $V_3$). This task is challenging because the views are not accurately estimated because of uncertainties, which can include noisy frequency estimation from the GRR and unbalanced group assignment. In CALM, Zhang et al. proposed the use of an off-the-shelf convex optimization tool to solve the optimization problem, expressed as

Maximize entropy$(x_1, \ldots, x_8)$
subject to Eq. (2) and Eq. (1)

## 3   Limitation of CALM

### 3.1   Necessary Number of Views

It is not trivial to find the optimal size of view $\ell$. But, we need at least enough number of views against the size of the domains $w_1, \ldots, w_k$. So, suppose the simple $k$-dimensional data where $w_1 = \cdots = w_k = w$ In the simplest instance, we have the following relationship among $k, \ell$ and $w$.

**Lemma 1.** *Let* $w_1 = \cdots = w_k = w$ *be simple $k$-dimensional data. CALM with* $\ell = k - 1$ *has a unique solution of $k$-way marginal such that* $w < k$.

**Proof:** With $\ell = k - 1$, the constraint matrix $A$ has $\nu = w^k$ columns and $\mu = w^\ell \binom{k}{\ell} = w^{k-1}\binom{k}{1}$ rows. To have $A$ nonsingular, we have $\nu = w^k < \mu = w^{k-1}k$, which follows $w < k$ by dividing $w^k$. $\qquad \square$

This can be extended to the following

**Lemma 2.** *Let* $w_1 = \cdots = w_k = w$ *be simple $k$-dimensional data. CALM with* $\ell = k - 2$ *has a unique solution of $k$-way marginal such that* $w^2 < k(k-1)/2$

**Proof:** It is a straightforward from Lemma 1 by replacing $\ell$ by $k - 2$. $\qquad \square$

**Theorem 1.** *Let* $w_1 = \cdots = w_k = w$ *be simple $k$-dimensional data. CALM with* $\ell$ *such that* $\ell < k$ *has a unique solution of $k$-way marginal such that*

$$w < \left(\frac{ek}{\ell}\right)^{\ell/k-\ell}$$

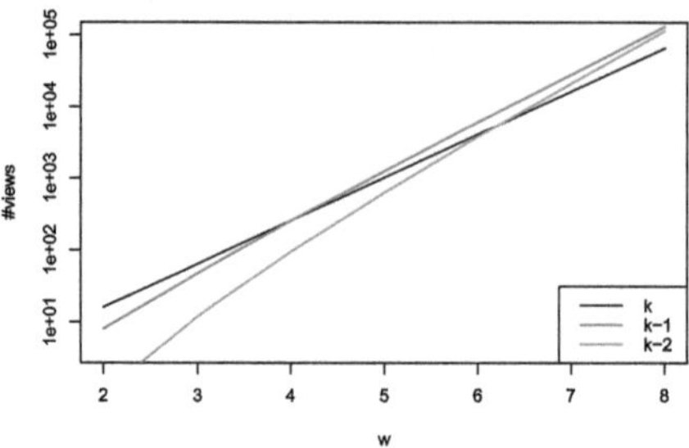

**Fig. 1.** The number of views for domain size $w = |\Omega_i|$.

**Proof:** Using well-known upper bound of binomial coefficient, we need a $\nu \times \mu$ constraint matrix such that

$$\nu = w^k < \mu = w^\ell \binom{k}{\ell} < \left(\frac{ek}{\ell}\right)^\ell.$$

Taking $k - \ell$ root after dividing $w^\ell$ both side gives the theorem. $\quad\square$

For instance, letting $w = 4$, $k = 3$, and $\ell = k - 1$, we have

$$\nu = w^k = 4^3 = 64 < \mu = w^{k-1}\binom{k}{k-1} = 48,$$

which implies that the number of missing variables $\nu$ is less than the number of equations $\mu$. (In CALM [6], a high-dimensional example assumed binary domains ($w = 2$), for which $\nu \geq \mu$.) Figure 1 shows how $\nu$ and $\mu$ grow with $w$, where $\nu$ (shown in red) is less than $\mu$ (black) for $w \geq 4$. That is, we cannot expect an accurate estimate for the $k$-way marginal from $(k-1)$-way views. Estimation via $(k-2)$-way views (green) is more robust than via $(k-1)$-way views, but it is infeasible for larger domains where $w > 6$.

### 3.2   Infeasible CALM

CALM solves the view equations using an off-the-shelf convex optimization solver. Therefore, when the differentially privacy applies and the perturbation becomes too large, the equations may become inconsistent and the problem may become *unfeasible*, meaning no solution can be found. To verify this, in Fig. 2, we show the proportion of feasible solutions when solving 3-way marginals ($k = 3$) on the MovieLens dataset using CALM. As the privacy budget $\varepsilon$ decreases, the proportion of unsolvable cases increases. For example, when $\varepsilon = 0.01$, only 3 out of 20 runs resulted in feasible solutions. However, the feasibility rate heavily depends on data sampling and exhibits discontinuous changes.

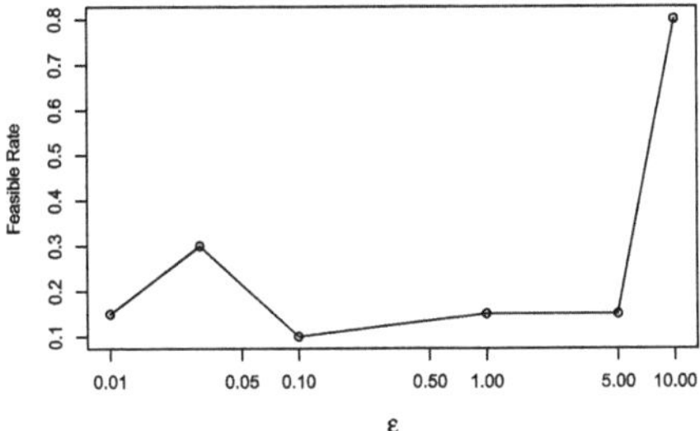

**Fig. 2.** Solvable CALM (Movie Lens, $k = 3$).

## 4   Proposed Method

### 4.1   Idea

The drawback of using a convex optimization tool is the stability of the solution. If we add too much large noise when perturbing private data, resulting in potentially contradictory views, it could fail to find an optimal solution, returning a "no answer" alert. If the constraints are too small, it can fail to find a unique answer and returns "undetermined".

In this work, we propose a simple but effective way to find consistent $k$-way marginals without using a convex optimization tool. Our idea is to use a pseudo-inverse matrix. Before considering the details of our pseudo-inverse technique, we need to confirm that an inverse matrix will give the solution for the $k$-way marginals.

In our example, we first rewrite views $V_1$ and $V_2$ in terms of a matrix equation,

$$Ax = B, \tag{3}$$

where

$$A = \begin{pmatrix} 1\,0\,1\,0\,0\,0\,0\,0 \\ 0\,1\,0\,1\,0\,0\,0\,0 \\ 0\,0\,0\,0\,1\,0\,1\,0 \\ 0\,0\,0\,0\,0\,1\,0\,1 \\ 1\,0\,0\,0\,1\,0\,0\,0 \\ 0\,1\,0\,0\,0\,1\,0\,0 \\ 0\,0\,1\,0\,0\,0\,1\,0 \\ 0\,0\,0\,1\,0\,0\,0\,1 \end{pmatrix}$$

and $B = (4, 6, 12, 14, 6, 8, 10, 12)^T$. If we have the inverse of $A$, it is easy to solve Eq. (3) and obtain the $k = 3$-way marginals ($V_3$) as $x = (x_1, \ldots, x_8)^T$ $\hat{x} = A^{-1}B$. However, $A$ is not always invertible. $A$ is $\mu \times \nu$ matrix where $\nu$ and $\mu$ are the number of views (contingency tables) for $k$ and $\ell$ dimensions, respectively. In general, it is nonsingular.

Second, we use the Moore–Penrose inverse [12], or pseudo-inverse, of matrix $A$. The pseudo-inverse matrix $A^+$ of $A$ satisfies $AA^+A = A, A^+AA^+ =$

132     H. Kikuchi

$A^+, (AA^+)^* = AA^+, (A^+A)^* = A^+A$, where $A^*$ is the conjugate transpose of $A$. The pseudo-inverse $A^+$ of $A$ is given by $A^+ = (A^*A)^{-1}A^*$.

A useful property of the pseudo-inverse is that it exists for any given matrix $A$. Therefore, without having to use a potentially unstable convex optimization, we can estimate the $k$-way marginals using some lower-dimensional $\ell$-way marginals.

Algorithm 1 shows the overall procedure.

---

**Algorithm 1.** High-dimensional marginal estimation using a pseudo-inverse

---

**Require:** $X_1, \ldots, X_n \leftarrow$ input data
**Require:** $A \leftarrow$ constraint matrix of $\ell$-way views
 1: For $\ell$-way marginals, apply GRR perturbation to $X_1, \ldots, X_n$ and estimate $B = (\hat{v_1} \cdots \hat{v_{w\ell}})^T$, where $\hat{v} = \Psi_{\mathrm{GRR}}(v)$.
 2: Compute the pseudo-inverse $A^+$ of $A$
 3: $\hat{x} \leftarrow A^+ B$
 4: **return** $k$-way marginals $\hat{x}$

---

## 5  Evaluation

### 5.1  Methodology

To investigate the accuracy of the proposed algorithm, we conducted an experiment using the open-data, UCI Adult dataset [13] and MovieLens datasets [14]. For three attributes, sex ($w_1 = 2$), race ($w_2 = 5$), and income ($w_3 = 2$), GRR provided ($\ell = 2$)-way views. For three views, we estimated ($k = 3$)-way marginals using several LDP methods.

The constraint matrix $A$ had $\mu = 2 \times 5 + 5 \times 2 + 2 \times 2 = 24$ rows and $\nu = 2 \times 5 \times 2 = 20$ columns. We used $A = \begin{pmatrix} A_{1,2} \\ A_{2,3} \\ A_{1,3} \end{pmatrix}$, where

$$A_{1,2} = (1\ 1) \otimes \begin{pmatrix} 1 & & 0 \\ & \ddots & \\ 0 & & 1 \end{pmatrix},$$

$$A_{2,3} = \begin{pmatrix} 1 & & 0 \\ & \ddots & \\ 0 & & 1 \end{pmatrix} \otimes (1\ 1) \otimes \begin{pmatrix} 1 & & 0 \\ & \ddots & \\ 0 & & 1 \end{pmatrix},$$

$$A_{1,3} = \begin{pmatrix} 1 & & 0 \\ & \ddots & \\ 0 & & 1 \end{pmatrix} \otimes (1 \cdots 1).$$

We used CVXR [16] for a convex optimization tool for CALM and the `pracma` R library for the pseudo-inverse computations.

**Table 2.** Three-way marginals estimated by CALM and the proposed method

| Race | Sex | Income50k | Freq | pinv | err | CALM | err |
|---|---|---|---|---|---|---|---|
| Amer-Indian-Eskimo | Female | <=50$K$ | 107 | 116.6 | −9.6 | 116.7 | −9.7 |
| Asian-Pac-Islander | Female | <=50$K$ | 303 | 292.1 | 10.9 | 292.3 | 10.7 |
| Black | Female | <=50$K$ | 1465 | 1362.4 | 102.7 | 1362.5 | 102.5 |
| Other | Female | <=50$K$ | 103 | 107.1 | −4.1 | 107.2 | −4.2 |
| White | Female | <=50$K$ | 7614 | 7713.8 | −99.8 | 7713.2 | −99.2 |
| Amer-Indian-Eskimo | Male | <=50$K$ | 168 | 158.4 | 9.6 | 158.3 | 9.7 |
| Asian-Pac-Islander | Male | <=50$K$ | 460 | 470.9 | −10.9 | 470.7 | −10.7 |
| Black | Male | <=50$K$ | 1272 | 1374.7 | −102.7 | 1374.5 | −102.5 |
| Other | Male | <=50$K$ | 143 | 138.9 | 4.1 | 138.8 | 4.2 |
| White | Male | <=50$K$ | 13085 | 12985.2 | 99.9 | 12985.8 | 99.2 |
| Amer-Indian-Eskimo | Female | >50$K$ | 12 | 2.4 | 9.6 | 2.3 | 9.7 |
| Asian-Pac-Islander | Female | >50$K$ | 43 | 53.9 | −10.9 | 53.7 | −10.7 |
| Black | Female | >50$K$ | 90 | 192.7 | −102.7 | 192.5 | −102.5 |
| Other | Female | >50$K$ | 6 | 1.9 | 4.1 | 1.8 | 4.2 |
| White | Female | >50$K$ | 1028 | 928.2 | 99.8 | 928.8 | 99.2 |
| Amer-Indian-Eskimo | Male | >50$K$ | 24 | 33.6 | −9.6 | 33.7 | −9.7 |
| Asian-Pac-Islander | Male | >50$K$ | 233 | 222.1 | 10.9 | 222.3 | 10.7 |
| Black | Male | >50$K$ | 297 | 194.4 | 102.6 | 194.5 | 102.5 |
| Other | Male | >50$K$ | 19 | 23.1 | −4.1 | 23.2 | −4.2 |
| White | Male | >50$K$ | 6089 | 6188.9 | −99.9 | 6188.2 | −99.2 |

**Table 3.** MAE (Movie Lens, $\epsilon = \infty$)

| | $k = 3$ | | $k = 4$ | |
|---|---|---|---|---|
| | Pinv | CALM | Pinv | CALM |
| mean | 104.890 | 104.890 | 35.825 | 35.620 |
| sd | 80.140 | 80.140 | 28.976 | 27.229 |

## 5.2  Results

Table 2 shows the ($k = 3$)-way marginals for the Adult dataset, where the columns headed Freq, pinv, and CALM provide the true marginals, the estimated marginals using the proposed pseudo-inverse method, and the estimated marginals using the CALM, respectively. (We did not perform any random perturbations in producing the table.)

Note that the errors for the proposed method and CALM are almost identically distributed within 0.1 precision. Mean Absolute Errors (MAEs) are 45.42 and 45.30, respectively (Table 3).

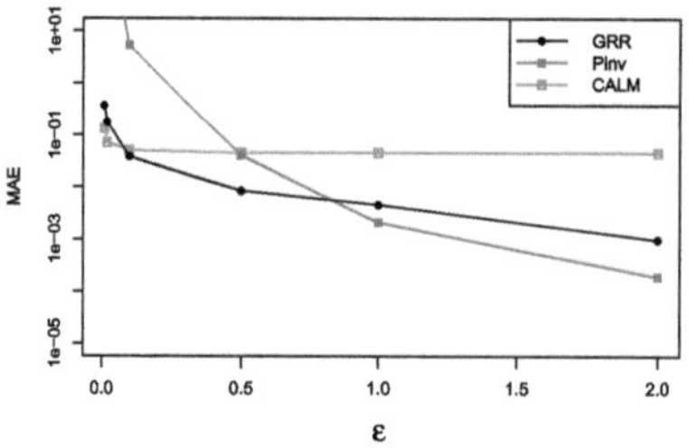

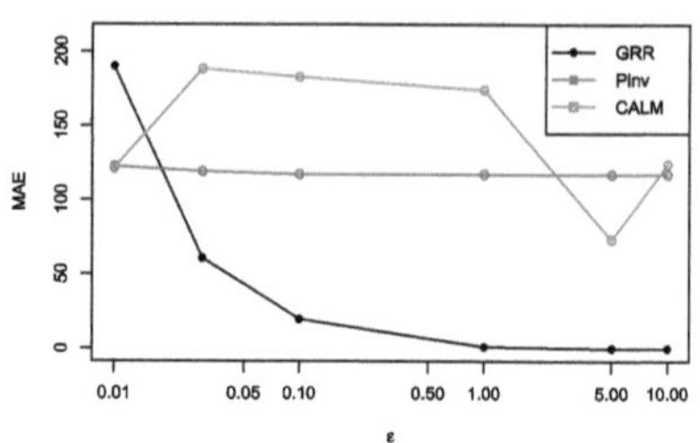

**Fig. 3.** MAEs with respect to privacy budget $\epsilon$ (UCI Adult).

**Fig. 4.** MAE with respect to $\epsilon$ (Movie-Lens, $k = 3$).

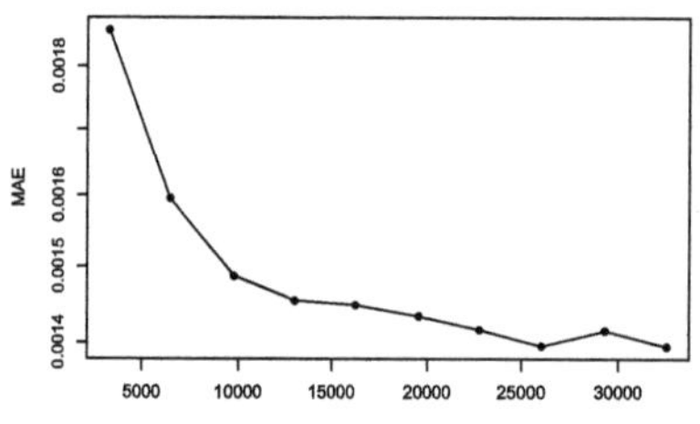

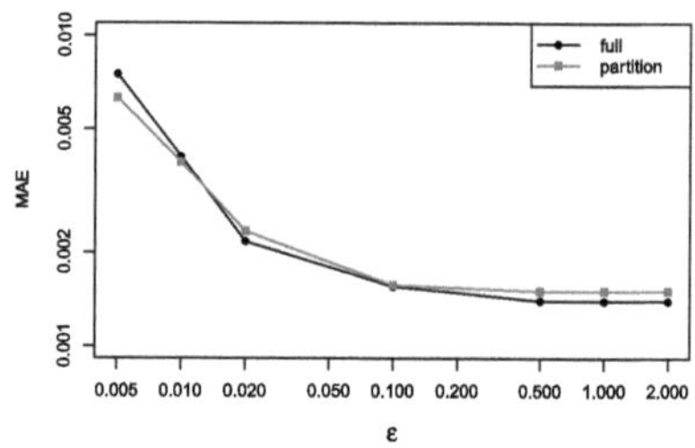

**Fig. 5.** MAE with respect to number of users $n$ (UCI Adult).

**Fig. 6.** MAEs for estimation from partitioned datasets (UCI Adult).

Figure 3 shows the MAEs for the CALM, and GRR methods for a privacy budgets $\epsilon = 0.01, \ldots, 2$. The proposed pseudo-inverse method using GRR reduces the estimation error when $\epsilon > 1.0$. It converges around 0.00138. We shows the MAE for three LDP schemes using MovieLens dataset in Fig. 4. The MAE of GRR decreases with the increasing privacy budget as well as UCI Adult, while the MAE of CALM is unstable here. The possible reason of unstability comes from the fact that any tiny inconsistency give a significant inpact to the precision of CALM.

Figure 5 shows the MAE for varying population sizes as $n = 3256, \ldots, 32561$, which are uniformly sampled from the dataset. The MAEs represent the mean over 100 iterations. We find that MAE decreases as $n$ increases.

Figure 6 shows the comparison of MAEs for estimations from the full dataset (full) and when divided into three subsets (partitions). We found that both MAEs are identically distributed for all $\epsilon$, and the estimation from partitioned datasets sometimes gives more accurate results than using the full data ($\epsilon < 0.02$).

From these results, we can conclude that the proposed pseudo-inverse estimate provides high-dimensional marginals that are as accurate as those using the conventional CALM method.

## 5.3 Discussion

We claim that the pseudo-inverse method can estimate high-dimensional marginals without using conventional optimization tools. The experiments showed small estimation errors even when no perturbation was performed. We consider that this failure comes from the singular matrix $A$. As we have investigated, view $A_{1,2}$ is a $20 \times 20$ matrix, but its rank is 16. View $A_{2,3}$ also has a lower rank. In Sect. 3.1, we considered the necessary conditions for the number of views to have uniquely determined solutions. If the domain is too large, it is a challenge to find high-dimensional marginals from low-dimensional views. To improve the accuracy of the estimates, we should explore advanced strategies for estimating from lower-dimensional views.

Zhang et al. [6] studied several sources of estimation errors: noise errors, reconstruction errors, and sampling errors. Noise errors arise from perturbation processes and can be minimized by careful choice of the privacy budget according to the population of data subjects. A reconstruction error can occur when a $k$-way marginal is not covered by any of the chosen $\ell$-way marginals. This may happen for both CALM and the proposed pseudo-inverse matrix method. Sampling errors arise from biased sampling when dividing the whole population into smaller groups. Zhang et al. analyzed the variance of the marginals and considered the best approach to avoiding sampling errors.

## 6 Conclusions

We have proposed a new multi-dimensional LDP scheme that uses a pseudo-inverse matrix to estimate high-dimensional marginals from some lower-dimensional marginals. Our proposed scheme is stable, without suffering from the undetermined or absent-solution status that can occur when using convex optimization tools. Our experiment demonstrates that the proposed method estimates high-dimensional marginals as accurately as the state-of-the-art CALM method. We also explored the conditions for that the number of views to be insufficient to identify consistent marginals uniquely. Our future plans include evolving the proposed method in terms of accuracy and robustness, using a variety of sources of open-access data, and an optimal baseline LDP scheme other than GRR.

**Acknowledgment.** We thank anonymous reviewers for their useful and constructive suggestions that help to improve the work significantly. This study was supported by JSPS KAKENHI Grant Number 23K11110 and JST CREST Grant Number JPMJCR21M1.

# References


1. Domingo-Ferrer, J., Soria-Comas, J.: Multidimensional randomized response. IEEE Trans. Knowl. Data Eng. (2022). https://doi.org/10.1109/TKDE.2020.3045759
2. Ren, X., et al.: *LoPub*: high-dimensional crowdsourced data publication with local differential privacy. IEEE Trans. Inf. Forensics Secur. **13**(9), 2151–2166 (2018). https://doi.org/10.1109/TIFS.2018.2812146
3. Wang, T., Yang, X., Ren, X., Yu, W., Yang, S.: Locally private high-dimensional crowdsourced data release based on copula functions. IEEE Trans. Serv. Comput. (2019)
4. Jiang, X., Zhou, X., Grossklags, J.: Privacy-preserving high-dimensional data collection with federated generative autoencoder. Proc. Priv. Enhancing Technol., 481–500 (2022). https://doi.org/10.2478/popets-2022-0024
5. Tolstikhin, I., Bousquet, O., Gelly, S., Scholkopf, B.: Wasserstein auto-encoders. In: International Conference on Learning Representations, ICLR 2018, Vancouver, BC, Canada (2018)
6. Zhang, Z., Wang, T., Li, N., He, S., Chen, J.: CALM: consistent adaptive local marginal for marginal release under local differential privacy. In: Proceedings of the 2018 ACM SIGSAC Conference on Computer and Communications Security, CCS'18, pp. 212–229. ACM (2018)
7. Dwark, C., McSherry, F., Nissim, K., Smith, A.: Calibrating noise to sensitivity in private data analysis. TCC **3876**, 265–284 (2006)
8. Warner, S.L.: Randomized response: a survey technique for eliminating evasive answer bias. J. Am. Stat. Assoc., 63–69 (1965)
9. Erlingsson, Ú., Pihur, V., Korolova, A.: RAPPOR: randomized aggregatable privacy-preserving ordinal response. In: ACM Conference on Computer and Communications Security, pp. 1054–1067 (2014)
10. Learning with privacy at scale. https://machinelearning.apple.com/2017/12/06/learning-with-privacy-at-scale.html. Accessed 2019
11. Differential Privacy Team: Learning with privacy at scale. Apple Mach. Learn. J. **1**(8) (2017)
12. Penrose, R.: A generalized inverse for matrices. Proc. Camb. Philos. Soc. **51**(3), 406–13 (2008). https://doi.org/10.1017/S0305004100030401
13. Bache, K., Lichman, M.: UCI Machine Learning Repository (2013). https://archive.ics.uci.edu/ml/datasets/adult
14. Maxwell Harper, F., Konstan, J.A.: The MovieLens datasets: history and context. ACM Trans. Interact. Intell. Syst. (TiiS) **5**, 4 (2015). Article 19
15. Kikuchi, H.: Castell: scalable joint probability estimation of multidimensional data randomized with local differential privacy. arXiv arXiv:2212.01627 (2022)
16. Fu, A., Narasimhan, B., Boyd, S.: CVXR: an R package for disciplined convex optimization. J. Stat. Softw. **94**(14), 1–34 (2020). https://doi.org/10.18637/jss.v094.i14

# Using Prior Knowledge to Improve GANs for Tabular Data Without Compromising Privacy

Sonakshi Garg[1]([⊠])[iD], Marcel Neunhoeffer[2,3][iD], Jörg Drechsler[2,3][iD], and Vicenç Torra[1][iD]

[1] Umeå University, Umeå, Sweden
{sgarg,vtorra}@cs.umu.se
[2] Institute for Employment Research, Nuremberg, Germany
{marcel.neunhoeffer,joerg.drechsler}@iab.de
[3] Ludwig-Maximilians-Universität München, Munich, Germany

**Abstract.** In this paper, we explore whether incorporating prior knowledge about the data can enhance GAN performance in the context of synthetic data generation for privacy protection and identify effective methodologies for doing so. We propose three approaches for integrating auxiliary information: (1) embedding public constraints into the adversarial loss function, (2) preserving correlation structures between attributes, and (3) leveraging Bayesian networks to model attribute dependencies and encode them into Conditional GANs. Through comprehensive empirical evaluations against existing baselines, we demonstrate that Bayesian networks and public constraints significantly improve the fidelity and realism of synthetic data. Furthermore, GAN-generated synthetic data lacks inherent privacy protections, making it susceptible to privacy attacks. To address this, we incorporate DP mechanisms into the GAN framework, ensuring robust privacy guarantees while maintaining data utility. The proposed approaches are evaluated for their effectiveness in generating high-quality, privacy-preserving synthetic data, offering valuable insights for future advancements in GAN-based synthetic data generation.

**Keywords:** Generative Adversarial Network · Bayesian Network · Differential Privacy

## 1 Introduction

Generative Adversarial Networks (GANs) [16] have emerged as a groundbreaking framework in deep learning, enabling significant advancements in various domains. Introduced initially to generate high-quality synthetic data by pitting two neural networks against each other—a generator and a discriminator—GANs have proven to be remarkably successful in tasks such as high-resolution image generation [5,27], image-to-image translation [23], and even in the synthesis of


R. Laborde et al. (Eds.): ESORICS 2025, LNCS 16231, pp. 137–153, 2026.
https://doi.org/10.1007/978-3-032-16089-8_10

continuous data distributions [35]. These capabilities have rendered GANs a cornerstone for generative modeling in computer vision and other fields.

Despite their success with continuous and high-dimensional data, GANs face considerable challenges when applied to tabular data, particularly when they contain discrete attributes. Tabular datasets, which are prevalent in domains like healthcare, finance, and social sciences, possess unique statistical characteristics. These include heterogeneous data types, highly imbalanced distributions, and intricate dependencies between variables, all of which are difficult for GANs to model effectively. Unlike image or text data with inherent structures, tabular data lacks spatial or sequential patterns and exhibits complex, high-dimensional relationships that are challenging for GANs to model. Discrete attributes further complicate generation due to their non-differentiable nature, limiting GANs' effectiveness. Several strategies have been proposed to address these challenges. Some authors [6,29] rely on a differential model by designing special functions, while [46] employ reinforcement learning to train a non-differentiable model, enabling natural language generation. Similarly, convolutional neural networks [35] and recurrent neural networks [44] have been adapted for tabular data by learning marginal distributions of columns. In addition, specialized GAN architectures, such as CTGAN [43] and CTAB-GAN [47], have been developed to tackle these issues. However, these models are constrained by their reliance on fixed assumptions about data structures and their sensitivity to training instability. While they have advanced the generation of tabular data, they still fall short in capturing the full complexity of real-world distributions [31]. A critical challenge remains in integrating domain knowledge or leveraging prior statistical information into GANs to enhance the fidelity and utility of synthetic tabular data, leaving a significant gap in achieving robust, high-quality generation.

Furthermore, a key motivation for generating synthetic data lies in its potential to serve as a privacy-preserving substitute for sensitive real-world data [11,37]. This is particularly important in contexts governed by stringent data privacy regulations such as GDPR [15] and HIPAA [19]. However, synthetic data generated by traditional GANs is vulnerable to privacy attacks [20], such as, for example, membership inference attacks [7]. Early research on private GANs focused on using Differential Privacy (DP) [12] as a privacy model by incorporating a Differentially Private Stochastic Gradient Descent (DPSGD) optimizer to update the GAN discriminator, leading to approaches like DPGAN [42]. Subsequently, alternative methods moved beyond DPGAN by introducing novel privatization techniques, often leveraging subsample-and-aggregate strategies, as seen in models like PATEGAN [25], or privately post-processing GAN samples [33]. While these approaches reported improvements over DPGAN in terms of utility, studies have highlighted their limitations in balancing utility and privacy effectively [2,14,31]. While these models introduced promising techniques, they also revealed fundamental trade-offs between data utility and privacy preservation. Achieving high-quality synthetic data that balances these trade-offs remains a significant challenge and an open research problem.

In this work, we propose methodologies to address these challenges by incorporating prior knowledge and then protecting these generators with some privacy-preserving mechanisms. We focus on **improving the quality of synthetic tabular data**. We propose three distinct approaches to incorporate prior knowledge into GANs, enhancing their ability to generate high-quality tabular data. First, we embed public knowledge as constraints in the adversarial loss function, penalizing violations to improve the fidelity of the generated data. Second, we enforce the preservation of the original data's correlation structure, ensuring statistical consistency. Third, we model attribute dependencies using a Bayesian network and encode these dependencies as embeddings, which are integrated into Conditional GANs (CGANs) [32] to guide the generation process. We show that these methods enable GANs to produce more realistic and statistically valid synthetic data while mitigating common issues such as mode collapse. To **ensure privacy**, we incorporate DP into our GAN framework, adapting noise injection techniques to balance privacy and utility effectively. We evaluated the proposed methodologies on multiple real-world datasets, assessing their effectiveness in improving the quality and privacy of synthetic data. Our analysis includes a quantitative evaluation of machine learning performance and correlation similarity to assess data utility, a comparative analysis with state-of-the-art GAN models. By addressing these critical gaps, our work highlights the importance of integrating prior knowledge and robust privacy mechanisms into GANs, providing a novel and practical framework for generating synthetic tabular data. This not only advances the state-of-the-art in synthetic data generation but also ensures increases privacy protection, making it highly relevant for real-world applications.

The main contributions of the paper are as follows:

– Proposal of three approaches to enhance the quality of synthetic data: using public constraints, correlation preservation, and using Bayesian networks.
– Identification of the most effective approach for generating high-fidelity synthetic data by comparing with state-of-the-art GANs.
– Utilizing a DP mechanism to ensure the privacy of the enhanced GAN-generated synthetic data.

The remainder part of the paper is organized in the following manner. Section 2 describes important concepts that have been used in the paper. Section 3 presents explanations of the proposed approach. Section 4 discusses the experimental setup and data sets involved. Section 5 provides some results and discussions. Finally, the conclusion and possible areas of future research are presented in Sect. 6.

## 2   Preliminaries and Related Works

In this section, we review the important concepts that are used in this paper.

### 2.1  Bayesian Network

A Bayesian Network (BN) [9] is a probabilistic graphical model representing the joint probability distribution of a set of random variables using a directed acyclic graph (DAG). Each node corresponds to a random variable, and directed edges represent conditional dependencies. The joint probability distribution is factorized as

$$P(X_1, X_2, \ldots, X_n) = \prod_{i=1}^{n} P(X_i \mid \text{Parents}(X_i)) \tag{1}$$

where $\text{Parents}(X_i)$ are the parent nodes of $X_i$. There are several methods to learn the structure of BN from the data. Constraint-based methods (e.g., the PC Algorithm [26]) use statistical tests to identify independencies between variables. Score-based methods (e.g., Hill Climbing (HC) [40]) evaluate the quality of a network structure using a scoring criterion, such as the Bayesian Information Criterion (BIC). In this paper, we chose HC because of its efficiency in identifying probabilistic dependencies in large datasets.

The HC algorithm starts with an empty graph and iteratively adds, removes, or reverses edges between nodes. Each modification is evaluated using a scoring function like the BIC, which balances model complexity and data likelihood. The algorithm continues making improvements until it converges on the best network structure. The dependencies in the graph capture the conditional relationships between variables and serve as valuable auxiliary information. Specifically, each variable in the network has a set of parent nodes, which represent the variables that directly influence it. We used the pgmpy python package [1] to construct the BN structure as described.

### 2.2  Differential Privacy

According to the GDPR, it is crucial to ensure the privacy of personal data. To achieve this, differential privacy (DP) [12] can be employed. DP provides a formal guarantee that the inclusion or exclusion of any individual record in the dataset does not significantly affect the output, thereby protecting individual privacy.

**Definition 1.** *($\epsilon, \delta$)-Differential Privacy: Consider two datasets as neighboring if they differ by only one record (either by the addition or removal of a single data point). A mechanism A is said to be ($\epsilon, \delta$)-differentially private if, for any two neighboring datasets $D$ and $D'$, and for any subset $S$ of the output range of A, the following inequality holds:*

$$P[A(D) \in S] \leq \exp(\epsilon) \times P[A(D') \in S] + \delta. \tag{2}$$

Here, $\epsilon$ and $\delta$ control the strength of the privacy guarantee, with smaller values providing stronger privacy. In the context of synthetic data generation, DP can be implemented in two ways: (1) by adding calibrated noise (e.g., Laplace or Gaussian noise) directly to the synthetic samples, or (2) by incorporating DP during model training, such as adding noise to gradients in the optimization process using DPSGD. This ensures that the generated synthetic data increases privacy guarantees.

## 2.3   Related Works

Over the past few years, various approaches have been proposed to improve the performance of GANs, with several focusing on incorporating prior knowledge into the model. Some recent works [41] have designed task-specific loss functions for GANs, tailoring the optimization process to improve data generation. PriorGAN [17] incorporates a Gaussian Mixture Model (GMM) prior to capturing the real data distribution, addressing issues like low-quality samples and missing modes in generated data. Feng et al. [13] introduced a method for counterfactual synthesis by studying knowledge extrapolation, allowing GANs to generate high-fidelity counterfactual results without explicit causal graph constraints. Additionally, other methods [27,34] have explored different network structures and training strategies to address issues like mode collapse and unstable training. Certain studies [18,38] adopt Bayesian principles to enhance GANs by incorporating prior distributions and posterior inference for the parameters of the generator and discriminator. StyleGAN [28] demonstrated controllable image synthesis via latent space manipulation, though it remains primarily image-focused. Subsequently, diffusion models [21] emerged, enabling conditional synthesis from class labels while offering improved stability, albeit with slower sampling rates. More recent advances include text-to-image frameworks such as Stable Diffusion v1 and transformer-based generators for structured data, exemplified by TTSGAN for time-series synthesis. Unlike prior works, our proposed method explicitly integrates auxiliary knowledge into GANs to simultaneously improve data fidelity and strengthen privacy guarantees, addressing the often-overlooked challenge of preserving realistic attribute relationships under privacy constraints.

## 3   Methodology

This paper aims to enhance the fidelity of synthetic data generated by GANs by effectively incorporating prior knowledge into the model. To achieve this, we explore and evaluate three strategies for embedding auxiliary information or imposing constraints that reflect inherent characteristics of the data. These methods are designed to guide the learning process of the GANs, ensuring the generated data aligns more closely with the underlying patterns and dependencies observed in the real dataset. Despite advancements in synthetic data generation, this problem remains unsolved, as existing methods often struggle to capture the complex relationships and prior knowledge embedded in real-world datasets, highlighting the need for more effective approaches. These techniques are described in the following subsections.

### 3.1  Public Constraint GAN (PCGAN)

Real-world data often contain inherent constraints that can be considered public information, such as logical boundaries or dependencies between variables. Incorporating these constraints into GANs can prevent the generation of implausible or unrealistic data, thereby improving the utility and authenticity of the synthetic outputs. This approach integrates domain-specific constraints directly into the training process of the GANs by embedding them as penalty terms within the generator's loss function. These constraints serve as additional guidance for the generator, ensuring that the synthetic data adheres to known rules or logical relationships in the real dataset. Since these constraints are assumed to be public knowledge, i.e., they apply to any data and are not dataset specific, this information can be used without concerns regarding privacy leakage. For instance, the age of humans can be constrained to lie within a realistic range of 0 to 120 years, by introducing a penalty term computed for any generated value outside this range as:

$$\text{Penalty}_{\text{age}} = \text{mean}\left(\max(0, -\text{age}) + \max(0, \text{age} - 120)\right) \tag{3}$$

These penalties are weighted and incorporated into the generator's loss function which is defined as

$$\mathcal{L}_{\text{total}} = \lambda_{\text{adv}}\mathcal{L}_{\text{adv}} + \sum_{i \in I} \lambda_{\text{i}}\text{Penalty}_{\text{i}} \tag{4}$$

where $I$ is the set of penalties and $\mathcal{L}_{\text{adv}}$ is the adversarial loss and $\lambda_{\text{adv}}$ and $\lambda_{\text{i}}$, $i = 1, \ldots, I$ are the weights for the different loss components. During each training iteration, the generator produces synthetic samples that are evaluated against these constraints, and the computed penalty terms are back propagated along with the generator's loss to update the generator's parameters. This methodology ensures that the GAN generated data not only aligns with the distribution of the real dataset but also adheres to logical and practical domain-specific constraints, thereby enhancing the overall quality of the synthetic data. A detailed description of the various constraints applied, tailored to the specific datasets used, is provided in Sect. 4.3.

### 3.2  Correlation Structure GAN (CSGAN)

Another approach to ensure that the synthetic data closely mimics the characteristics of the original data is to align their data distributions by comparing their correlation matrices, which capture the bi-variate relationships between variables. With this method, categorical variables are first encoded using a Label Encoder [36] to enable numerical operations. The correlation matrix of the original dataset, denoted as $C_{\text{real}}$, is computed and used as a reference. During training, the correlation matrix of the synthetic dataset, denoted as $C_{\text{synthetic}}$, is also computed. Any deviation between these matrices is penalized through a custom loss function. The correlation penalty is calculated using the Frobenius norm:

$$\text{Correlation Penalty} = \|C_{\text{real}} - C_{\text{synthetic}}\|_F \tag{5}$$

where $\|\cdot\|_F$ represents the Frobenius norm, which quantifies the element-wise differences between the two matrices. The total loss function is formulated as:

$$\mathcal{L}_{\text{total}} = \lambda_{\text{adv}}\mathcal{L}_{\text{adv}} + \lambda_{\text{corr}} \cdot \text{Correlation Penalty} \tag{6}$$

where $\mathcal{L}_{\text{adv}}$ is the adversarial loss from the GAN training and $\lambda_{\text{adv}}$ and $\lambda_{\text{corr}}$ are hyper parameters controlling the trade-off between adversarial training and correlation preservation. This penalty mechanism encourages the synthetic data to maintain the variable dependencies and structural patterns inherent in the original dataset.

### 3.3  Bayesian Network GAN (BNGAN)

With this approach the objective is to effectively capture the dependencies between attributes, and utilize them as auxiliary information for the GANs. To achieve this, a BN is employed to model dependencies between attributes. BN are ideal for this problem because they explicitly model the conditional dependencies between variables, providing a structured and interpretable representation of how variables influence one another. The learned dependencies are subsequently incorporated into a Conditional GAN (CGAN) [32], serving as auxiliary information to guide the generation of realistic synthetic data. A CGAN extends the standard GAN framework by conditioning both the generator and discriminator on auxiliary information. Unlike traditional GANs, which generate data unconditionally, CGAN allows for controlled and targeted data generation by incorporating the additional input, ensuring the output aligns with the specified conditions. The proposed methodology is described in Algorithm 1, and a step-by-step explanation of the algorithm is given in the following paragraph.

The dependencies between variables are first identified using a BN as described in Sect. 2.1. These dependencies (parent-child relationship) are then transformed into dense vector representations (embeddings) to guide the GAN. For each parent variable, an embedding layer is initialized, where the size of the layer corresponds to the number of unique categories in that variable. The embedding layers are trained to map each categorical value to a continuous vector space, where the distances between vectors capture the semantic relationships informed by the BN structure. The embeddings of parent variables are concatenated to form a conditioning vector, which represents the combined influence of the parent variables. This conditioning vector is then passed through dense layers to generate a final representation that encapsulates the dependencies for the child variables, providing a rich latent space for generating synthetic data. This conditioning vector is finally integrated into a CGAN. Embedding layers have been widely used for learning continuous vector representations of categorical variables [30], for example, in the Word2Vec algorithm for textual data. These embeddings are trained to capture semantic relationships by mapping categorical values to a continuous vector space where distances between vectors represent the similarity between categories. We used a similar strategy to capture probabilistic dependencies between variables in BNs. This approach ensures that the synthetic data maintains the structural relationships observed in the real dataset while leveraging the flexibility of the CGAN for data generation.

---

**Algorithm 1.** Bayesian Network GAN

---

**Require:** $\mathbf{X}_{\text{train}}, \mathbf{y}_{\text{train}}$
**Ensure:** $\mathbf{D}_{\text{syn}}$, Performance Metrics
    Step 1: Learning Variable Dependencies
 1: **Define:** $df \leftarrow$ Dataset containing both $\mathbf{X}_{\text{train}}$ and $\mathbf{y}_{\text{train}}$
 2: **Sample:** $df_{sample} \leftarrow df.\text{sample}(80\%)$
 3: **Split:** $chunks \leftarrow \text{np.array\_split}(df_{sample}, 4)$
 4: **for** each chunk $c \in chunks$ **in parallel do**
 5:     Initialize $G_c \leftarrow \emptyset$
 6:     **while** no improvement in BIC score **do**
 7:        $G_c \leftarrow \text{modify}(G_c)$
 8:        $\text{score}(G_c) \leftarrow \text{BIC}(G_c)$
 9:     **end while**
10: **end for**
11: $G_{\text{final}} \leftarrow \bigcup_{c=1}^{4} G_c$                     ▷ Union of edges from all chunks
    Step 2: Construct Dependencies and Embeddings
12: Build dependency dictionary: $dependencies \leftarrow$ from $G_{\text{final}}$
13: Identify all unique parents: $parents \leftarrow \bigcup dependencies.\text{values}()$
14: **for** each $parent \in parents$ **do**
15:     Label encode $df[parent]$
16:     $\mathbf{e}_{parent} \leftarrow \text{Embedding}(n_{\text{categories}}, d_{\text{embedding}})$
17: **end for**
18: **for** each $child \in dependencies$ **do**
19:     Concatenate embeddings of its parents: $\mathbf{e}_{child} \leftarrow \|_{p \in dependencies[child]} \mathbf{e}_p$
20:     Project to latent space: $\mathbf{c}_{child} \leftarrow \text{Linear}(\mathbf{e}_{child})$
21: **end for**
22: Final conditioning vector: $\mathbf{e} \leftarrow \|_{child} \mathbf{c}_{child}$
    Step 3: Define CGAN
23: $\mathcal{G} \leftarrow \text{Generator}(\mathbf{z}, \mathbf{e})$
24: $\mathcal{D} \leftarrow \text{Discriminator}(\mathbf{x}, \mathbf{e})$
25: $\mathcal{L}_{\text{adv}} \leftarrow \mathbb{E}[\log \mathcal{D}(\mathcal{G}(\mathbf{z}, \mathbf{e}))]$
26: $\mathcal{L}_{\text{recon}} \leftarrow \mathbb{E}[\|\mathbf{x} - \mathcal{G}(\mathbf{z}, \mathbf{e})\|^2]$
    Step 4: Train CGAN
27: **for** $t = 1$ **to** $T$ **do**
28:     Sample real data: $\mathbf{x}_{real} \sim \mathbf{X}_{\text{train}}$
29:     Generate synthetic data: $\mathbf{x}_{syn} \leftarrow \mathcal{G}(\mathbf{z}, \mathbf{e})$
30:     **Train Discriminator:** $\mathcal{L}_D \leftarrow \mathbb{E}[\log \mathcal{D}(\mathbf{x}_{real}, \mathbf{e})] + \mathbb{E}[\log(1 - \mathcal{D}(\mathbf{x}_{syn}, \mathbf{e}))]$
31:     **Train Generator:** $\mathcal{L}_G \leftarrow \mathcal{L}_{\text{adv}} + \lambda \cdot \mathcal{L}_{\text{recon}}$
32: **end for**
33: **return** $\mathbf{D}_{\text{syn}}$, Evaluation Metrics

---

### 3.4   Enforcing DP for the Enhanced GAN Synthesizers

Obviously, standard GANs without DP guarantees will never satisfy DP. To ensure DP, a common approach is to incorporate DPSGD into the discriminator training since the GAN discriminator uses original samples to differentiate between real and fake data (the generator never sees the original data, and thus no privacy measures are required for this step). As we assume that the information used for PCGAN and CSGAN is prior knowledge, these two approaches don't use any additional information that needs to be protected and thus we can rely on this standard approach to satisfy DP. In BNGAN, which uses a Bayesian network to capture attribute dependencies and generates an embedding layer as input to the CGAN, we suggest adding Laplace noise to the embeddings to achieve DP. Given that the values of the embeddings lie within the range of $[-1, 1]$, the maximum possible change between two neighboring datasets is at most 2. This value serves as the global sensitivity for the Laplace mechanism, ensuring that the added noise appropriately preserves DP. Additionally, similar to the other approaches, DPSGD was applied in the discriminator training.

## 4   Experimental Setup

In this section we present the datasets used, the architecture of the GANs, and the specific constraints we enforced to modify the loss function. We provide a detailed discussion of the results of the experiments in the next section.

### 4.1   Datasets Description

In this work, we aim to incorporate prior knowledge into GANs for discrete data, particularly social science datasets rich in categorical variables. We evaluate our approach using three such datasets. The first is the Adult dataset [3], a pre-processed 1994 US Census dataset with over 45,000 individuals and attributes like education, occupation, and marital status. The second is the Social Diagnosis 2011 (SD2011) [24], a raw Polish census dataset with 35 primarily categorical attributes (e.g., education level, smoking status, work experience abroad), chosen for its real-world challenges such as missing values and outliers. The third is the German Credit Risk dataset [22], which classifies individuals as good or bad credit risks based on variables such as savings, checking amount, credit history, and credit amount. Table 1 summarizes the number of instances and attributes in each dataset. These datasets represent typical discrete social science data, where capturing inherent structure and prior knowledge is essential for effective synthetic data generation.

### 4.2   Conditional GAN (CGAN) Architecture

The Conditional GAN (CGAN) used in this paper consists of a generator and a discriminator. The generator takes a noise vector and a conditioning vector

**Table 1.** Description of Datasets

| Dataset | # of Instances | # of Categorical Attr. | # of Numerical Attr. |
| --- | --- | --- | --- |
| ADULT | 48842 | 9 | 6 |
| SD2011 | 5000 | 21 | 14 |
| Credit Risk | 1000 | 6 | 4 |

as input, processes them through four dense layers with LeakyReLU activation, batch normalization (momentum = 0.8), and dropout (rate = 0.2), and outputs structured data through a final dense layer. The discriminator receives a real or synthetic sample concatenated with the same conditioning vector and processes them through four dense layers with LeakyReLU, dropout (rate = 0.4), and a final sigmoid layer for binary classification. Both components are trained using binary cross-entropy loss and the Adam optimizer (learning rate = 0.0002, $\beta =$ (0.5, 0.999)) for 200 epochs with batch size 32. When privacy is required, the discriminator is trained with DP-SGD using a noise multiplier of 1.1 and a max gradient norm of 1. Unlike standard GANs, this CGAN leverages a structured conditioning vector to preserve attribute relationships in discrete data.

### 4.3   Incorporating Data Constraints Into the Loss Function

We enforce data constraints based on public knowledge, derived after analyzing the attributes of the dataset. For the Adult dataset, we applied an age constraint, specifying that the realistic age of a person must lie within the range [0, 120]. In this case, the penalty coefficient for the age constraint is set to 10, determined through experiments to balance adherence to realistic age ranges with maintaining data fidelity and diversity. This value ensures the generated data respects constraints without compromising quality.

For SD2011 dataset, we enforce three constraints: age constraint(similar to adult dataset), smoking constraint and work-abroad constraint. For the smoking constraint, a penalty term is computed to ensure consistency between the smoking status and the number of cigarettes smoked. Specifically, if the smoking status indicates non-smoking, the number of cigarettes smoked should be zero (nociga = 0). The penalty for violating this constraint is defined as:

$$\text{Penalty}_{\text{smoking}} = \text{mean}\left((\text{smoke} < 0.5) \cdot |\text{nociga}|\right) \tag{7}$$

Here, *smoke* represents the smoking status (with non-smoking encoded as values below 0.5), and *nociga* represents the number of cigarettes smoked. This penalty ensures that the generated data adheres to logical dependencies between variables, enhancing its realism. For the work-abroad constraint, we enforce a penalty when the variable workab is "yes" (i.e., when workab > 0.5) and the variable wkabdur (the duration of time worked abroad) is < zero. The penalty is calculated using the following equation:

$$\text{Penalty}_{\text{wabroad}} = \frac{1}{n} \sum_{i=1}^{n} \left( \mathbb{I}(\text{workab}_i > 0.5) \cdot \max(0, -\text{wkabdur}_i) \right) \qquad (8)$$

The loss function of the generator for SD2011, incorporates three constraints with a penalty coefficient of 10 for each in Eq 4. For the German Credit Risk dataset, we enforce two constraints: an age constraint and a purpose constraint. The purpose constraint applies penalties if the credit amount exceeds predefined thresholds for specific purposes, such as 5000€ for vacation or repairs and 15,000€ - 20,000€ for business or education. These thresholds were determined through an analysis of the dataset and aligned with real-world expectations, ensuring the generated data remains realistic while maintaining diversity and utility.

## 5   Results and Discussion

In this section, we empirically evaluate the generated synthetic data by assessing both, statistical properties and ML utility, and then ensure privacy by enforcing DP during data generation.

### 5.1   Impact of Synthetic Data on ML Performance

We evaluate the utility of synthetic data generated by four methods: CTGAN, PCGAN, CSGAN and BNGAN using multiple ML models. CTGAN was selected as the baseline for comparison because it is widely recognized as one of the most efficient GANs for tabular data synthesis in the literature. For classification tasks on the Adult and German credit risk datasets, we use LightGBM, XGBoostC, and Logistic Regression models, evaluating the performance based on accuracy. For the SD2011 dataset, we predict income using LightGBM regression, XGBoostR, and Linear Regression models, with performance assessed using Root Mean Squared Error (RMSE). This comprehensive evaluation ensures a robust analysis of synthetic data utility across different tasks and datasets as presented in Table 2.

Each model is trained on synthetic data and tested on real out-of-sample data. For the Adult dataset, BNGAN achieved the highest accuracy (0.78–0.79) for all ML models. For the SD2011 dataset, BNGAN also showed the lowest RMSE for all models (0.42–0.45), with PCGAN achieving comparable results (0.43–0.46). However, the SD2011 dataset contains missing values and outliers, with no pre-processing applied, leading to substantially higher error values for CTGAN (1185–1237) reflecting the challenges of working with such raw, unprocessed data. For the Credit Risk dataset, BNGAN again achieved the highest accuracy for all ML models (0.68–0.74), demonstrating the effectiveness of incorporating a BN to capture dependencies between attributes. By modeling these relationships, BNGAN generates more realistic data, improving model performance. We also note that CSGAN consistently offers the lowest utility among all approaches for both classification tasks. We also compared the performance of synthetic data with the original data, and observed a decline in ML performance, as expected. Ideally, synthetic data should not outperform the original data since it is meant to approximate the original distribution rather than surpass it.

**Table 2.** Utility evaluations for ML models trained on synthetic data and tested on real out-of-sample data

| Data | Utility Metric | ML Model | Synthetic Data | | | | Original |
| --- | --- | --- | --- | --- | --- | --- | --- |
| | | | CTGAN | PCGAN | CSGAN | BNGAN | Data |
| ADULT | Accuracy ↑ | LightGBM | 0.75 | 0.74 | 0.70 | **0.79** | 0.87 |
| | | XGBoostC | 0.75 | 0.73 | 0.69 | **0.79** | 0.86 |
| | | LogisticR | 0.74 | 0.74 | 0.71 | 0.78 | 0.86 |
| Credit Risk | Accuracy ↑ | LightGBM | 0.66 | 0.61 | 0.58 | **0.74** | 0.75 |
| | | XGBoostC | 0.65 | 0.62 | 0.56 | 0.68 | 0.76 |
| | | LogisticR | 0.67 | 0.63 | 0.59 | 0.70 | 0.74 |
| SD2011 | RMSE ↓ | LightGBM | 1207.35 | 0.44 | 0.48 | 0.43 | 1050.31 |
| | | XGBoostR | 1236.80 | 0.46 | 0.50 | 0.45 | 1091.21 |
| | | LinearR | 1185.21 | 0.43 | 0.47 | **0.42** | 1015.82 |

## 5.2　Impact of Synthetic Data on Attribute Correlation Similarity

Analyzing whether synthetic data preserve the pairwise correlations between attributes is crucial. To evaluate this, we used Cramér's V with bias correction [4] to measure the strength of the relationship between pairs of attributes in both the original and synthetic datasets, since Cramér's V is commonly used as a utility measure in the literature [39]. Cramér's V is a measure of association between two categorical variables, defined as:

$$V = \sqrt{\frac{\chi^2}{n \cdot \min(k-1, r-1)}} \tag{9}$$

where $\chi^2$ is the chi-squared statistic, $n$ is the total number of observations, $k$ is the number of categories in the first variable, and $r$ is the number of categories in the second variable. The Cramér's V values are grouped into four categories: low ($V \in [0, 0.1)$), weak ($V \in [0.1, 0.3)$), middle ($V \in [0.3, 0.5)$), and strong ($V \in [0.5, 1)$). To assess how well the synthetic data reflects the original data, we use correlation accuracy for categorical attributes, which calculates the percentage of attribute pairs where the correlation level in the synthetic data matches the original data. '

The results in Table 3 show that the synthetic data generated by different approaches varies in preserving attribute relationships. The Adult data with its high class imbalance shows low correlation accuracy across all methods, as minority class attributes may not be well represented in the synthetic data, causing weaker correlations between attributes. For the SD2011 dataset, PCGAN achieved the highest correlation accuracy of 0.6915, which can be attributed to the effective enforcement of domain-specific data constraints in the loss function. This allows the model to better capture the relationships between attributes. BNGAN also performed well with a correlation accuracy of 0.6780, reflecting the benefits of incorporating a BN model to capture parent-child dependencies between attributes, which helped preserve data correlations effectively. Similar trends were observed for the Credit Risk dataset, where BNGAN achieved the highest correlation accuracy of 0.6981, slightly outperforming PCGAN. Again, CSGAN showed the weakest performance in all settings.

We also measure the correlation similarity between numerical attributes by computing the Pearson correlation coefficient [8] for both real and synthetic data. This results in two correlation values: $R_{A,B}$ for the real data and $S_{A,B}$ for the synthetic data. The similarity between these correlation values is computed using the following formula:

$$\text{score} = 1 - \frac{|S_{A,B} - R_{A,B}|}{2} \tag{10}$$

A score of 1 indicates perfect similarity, while a score of 0 suggests no similarity. The method is adapted from SD Metrics [10], offering a standardized way to assess data quality. The results showed that BNGAN consistently achieved the highest correlation similarity, particularly for the SD2011 and Adult datasets, indicating its effectiveness in preserving numerical relationships. PCGAN also performed well, especially in the SD2011 and Credit Risk datasets, by enforcing constraints in the loss function. In contrast, CSGAN, which uses correlation-based penalties, produced lower correlation similarity scores, suggesting that it may not fully capture the complex dependency structures between attributes. Overall, both constraint-based approaches (PCGAN and BNGAN) outperform CSGAN, with BNGAN showing the strongest ability to preserve both categorical and numerical correlations across multiple datasets.

**Table 3.** Correlation Accuracy and Similarity for Categorical and Numerical Attributes

| Dataset | Categorical | | | | Numerical | | | |
|---|---|---|---|---|---|---|---|---|
| | CTGAN | PCGAN | CSGAN | BNGAN | CTGAN | PCGAN | CSGAN | BNGAN |
| ADULT ↑ | 0.3626 | **0.4190** | 0.3524 | 0.3714 | 0.8581 | 0.8843 | 0.8718 | **0.8932** |
| Credit Risk ↑ | 0.6723 | 0.6812 | 0.6235 | **0.6981** | 0.8642 | **0.8714** | 0.8312 | 0.8711 |
| SD2011 ↑ | 0.6684 | **0.6915** | 0.6123 | 0.6780 | 0.9758 | 0.9916 | 0.9468 | **0.9971** |

## 5.3  Results with Differential Privacy

To ensure the synthetic data generation process satisfies the definition of DP, we implemented DP a mechanism on our proposed GANs as described in 3.4 and evaluated their efficacy by comparing them with three baselines: DPGAN, PATEGAN, and ADSGAN [45]. Table 4 presents the ML performance when models are trained with DP having $\epsilon = 1$ and $\delta = \frac{1}{N}$. For our DP-BNGAN model, we apply noise injection at two stages: first, during the generation of Bayesian network-based embeddings using Laplace noise with sensitivity $= 2$ and with $\epsilon = 1$, and second in the discriminator component of the CGAN with DPSGD, also with $\epsilon = 1$. Consequently, the total privacy budget for DP-BNGAN is $\epsilon = 2$. We assessed model utility accross three datasets. For the Adult and Credit Risk datasets, classification accuracy was recorded using LightGBM, the best-performing model from Table 2. For the SD2011 dataset, prediction error was measured using RMSE with linear regression, also the best performing model. The results show that different models perform best on each dataset due to their ability to handle the unique characteristics of the data while preserving privacy. For Adult dataset, DP-BNGAN still performed the best, due to its strength in capturing complex distributions while maintaining privacy. PATEGAN excelled on Credit Risk dataset, due to its advanced learning capabilities, while DPGAN performs the worst on all datasets. Although the use of DP degrades the performance to some extent, the results demonstrate that the models remain highly comparable to baselines. This indicates that we are still able to preserve utility while ensuring privacy. We can also further enhance utility, at the cost of a weaker privacy guarantee.

**Table 4.** ML performance using differential privacy

| Dataset | Utility Metric | DP-PCGAN | DP-CSGAN | DP-BNGAN | DPGAN | PATEGAN | ADSGAN |
|---|---|---|---|---|---|---|---|
| ADULT | Accuracy ↑ | 0.65 | 0.67 | **0.72** | 0.54 | 0.69 | 0.71 |
| Credit Risk | Accuracy ↑ | 0.62 | 0.40 | 0.66 | 0.54 | **0.96** | 0.82 |
| SD2011 | RMSE ↓ | **0.48** | 0.57 | 0.51 | 0.61 | 0.58 | 0.49 |

## 6  Conclusion and Future Work

In this paper, we explored whether incorporating prior knowledge can enhance the performance of GANs for tabular data. We proposed three techniques for incorporating prior knowledge into GANs without compromising the privacy of personal data. These methods aim to provide better control over the output of the GAN. Our comparative analysis with baseline models revealed that using a Bayesian network to capture attribute dependencies significantly improved data quality, as validated through various ML and statistical evaluations. Additionally, enforcing public knowledge as constraints also enhanced performance in certain cases, making both approaches viable for future applications. To ensure privacy, we integrated a DP mechanism into the GAN training process. In future work, we aim to extend this comparison to a broader range of privacy-preserving GANs to further highlight our contributions relative to existing methods. Also, we plan to explore other probabilistic models to further improve the quality of synthetic data and investigate more novel ways of incorporating prior knowledge into GANs.

# References


1. Ankan, A., Panda, A.: Pgmpy: Probabilistic graphical models using python. In: Proceedings of the Python in Science Conference. SciPy, SciPy (2015). https://doi.org/10.25080/majora-7b98e3ed-001
2. Arnold, C., Neunhoeffer, M.: Really useful synthetic data–a framework to evaluate the quality of differentially private synthetic data. arXiv preprint arXiv:2004.07740 (2020)
3. Becker, B., Kohavi, R.: Adult. UCI Machine Learning Repository (1996). https://doi.org/10.24432/C5XW20
4. Bergsma, W.: A bias-correction for cramér's v and tschuprow's t. J. Korean Stat. Soc. **42**(3), 323–328 (2013)
5. Brock, A.: Large scale gan training for high fidelity natural image synthesis. arXiv preprint arXiv:1809.11096 (2018)
6. Che, T., et al.: Maximum-likelihood augmented discrete generative adversarial networks. arXiv preprint arXiv:1702.07983 (2017)
7. Chen, D., Yu, N., Zhang, Y., Fritz, M.: Gan-leaks: A taxonomy of membership inference attacks against generative models. In: Proceedings of the 2020 ACM SIGSAC Conference on Computer and Communications Security, pp. 343–362 (2020)
8. Cohen, I., et al.: Pearson correlation coefficient. Noise reduction in speech processing, pp. 1–4 (2009)
9. Cooper, G.F., Herskovits, E.: A Bayesian method for the induction of probabilistic networks from data. Mach. Learn. **9**, 309–347 (1992)
10. DataCebo, Inc.: Synthetic Data Metrics (2023). https://docs.sdv.dev/sdmetrics/
11. Drechsler, J.: Synthetic datasets for statistical disclosure control: theory and implementation, vol. 201. Springer Science & Business Media (2011)
12. Dwork, C.: Differential privacy. In: International Colloquium on Automata, Languages, and Programming, pp. 1–12. Springer (2006)
13. Feng, R., et al.: Principled knowledge extrapolation with gans. In: International Conference on Machine Learning, pp. 6447–6464. PMLR (2022)
14. Fössing, E., Drechsler, J.: An evaluation of synthetic data generators implemented in the python library synthcity. In: Domingo-Ferrer, J., Önen, M. (eds.) International Conference on Privacy in Statistical Databases, pp. 178–193. Springer, Cham (2024). https://doi.org/10.1007/978-3-031-69651-0_12
15. GDPR-EU: Gdpr compliance. https://gdpr.eu/
16. Goodfellow, I., Pouget-Abadie, J., Mirza, M., Xu, B., Warde-Farley, D., Ozair, S., Courville, A., Bengio, Y.: Generative adversarial networks. Commun. ACM **63**(11), 139–144 (2020)
17. Gu, S., Bao, J., Chen, D., Wen, F.: Priorgan: Real data prior for generative adversarial nets. arXiv preprint arXiv:2006.16990 (2020)

18. He, H., Wang, H., Lee, G.H., Tian, Y.: Bayesian modelling and monte carlo inference for gan. In: International Conference on Learning Representations, vol. 3, p. 4 (2019)
19. HIPAA-US: Hipaa compliance. https://www.hhs.gov/hipaa/for-professionals/privacy/
20. Hitaj, B., Ateniese, G., Perez-Cruz, F.: Deep models under the gan: information leakage from collaborative deep learning. In: Proceedings of the 2017 ACM SIGSAC Conference on Computer and Communications Security, pp. 603–618 (2017)
21. Ho, J., Jain, A., Abbeel, P.: Denoising diffusion probabilistic models. Adv. Neural. Inf. Process. Syst. **33**, 6840–6851 (2020)
22. Hofmann, H.: Statlog (German Credit Data) (1994). https://doi.org/10.24432/C5NC77
23. Isola, P., Zhu, J.Y., Zhou, T., Efros, A.A.: Image-to-image translation with conditional adversarial networks. In: Proceedings of the IEEE Conference on Computer Vision and Pattern Recognition, pp. 1125–1134 (2017)
24. J., C., T., P.: SD2011. http://www.diagnoza.com/index-en.html (2011)
25. Jordon, J., Yoon, J., Van Der Schaar, M.: Pate-gan: Generating synthetic data with differential privacy guarantees. In: International Conference on Learning Representations (2018)
26. Kalisch, M., Bühlman, P.: Estimating high-dimensional directed acyclic graphs with the pc-algorithm. J. Mach. Learn. Res. **8**(3) (2007)
27. Karras, T.: Progressive growing of gans for improved quality, stability, and variation. arXiv preprint arXiv:1710.10196 (2017)
28. Karras, T., Laine, S., Aila, T.: A style-based generator architecture for generative adversarial networks. In: Proceedings of the IEEE/CVF Conference on Computer Vision and Pattern Recognition, pp. 4401–4410 (2019)
29. Kusner, M.J., Hernández-Lobato, J.M.: Gans for sequences of discrete elements with the gumbel-softmax distribution. arXiv preprint arXiv:1611.04051 (2016)
30. Mikolov, T., Sutskever, I., Chen, K., Corrado, G.S., Dean, J.: Distributed representations of words and phrases and their compositionality. Adv. Neural Inf. Process. Syst. **26** (2013)
31. Miletic, M., Sariyar, M.: Challenges of using synthetic data generation methods for tabular microdata. Appl. Sci. **14**(14), 5975 (2024)
32. Mirza, M.: Conditional generative adversarial nets. arXiv preprint arXiv:1411.1784 (2014)
33. Neunhoeffer, M., Wu, S., Dwork, C.: Private post-gan boosting. In: International Conference on Learning Representations (2021). https://openreview.net/forum?id=6isfR3JCbi
34. Parimala, K., Channappayya, S.: Quality aware generative adversarial networks. Adv. Neural Inf. Process. Syst. **32** (2019)
35. Park, N., Mohammadi, M., Gorde, K., Jajodia, S., Park, H., Kim, Y.: Data synthesis based on generative adversarial networks. arXiv preprint arXiv:1806.03384 (2018)
36. Pedregosa, F., et al.: Scikit-learn: machine learning in python. J. Mach. Learn. Res. **12**(Oct), 2825–2830 (2011)
37. Rubin, D.B.: Statistical disclosure limitation. J. Official Stat. **9**(2), 461–468 (1993)
38. Saatci, Y., Wilson, A.G.: Bayesian gan. Adv. Neural Inf. Process. Syst. **30** (2017)
39. Tao, Y., McKenna, R., Hay, M., Machanavajjhala, A., Miklau, G.: Benchmarking differentially private synthetic data generation algorithms. arXiv preprint arXiv:2112.09238 (2021)

40. Tsamardinos, I., Brown, L.E., Aliferis, C.F.: The max-min hill-climbing Bayesian network structure learning algorithm. Mach. Learn. **65**, 31–78 (2006)
41. Wu, J.L., Kashinath, K., Albert, A., Chirila, D., Xiao, H., et al.: Enforcing statistical constraints in generative adversarial networks for modeling chaotic dynamical systems. J. Comput. Phys. **406**, 109209 (2020)
42. Xie, L., Lin, K., Wang, S., Wang, F., Zhou, J.: Differentially private generative adversarial network. arXiv preprint arXiv:1802.06739 (2018)
43. Xu, L., Skoularidou, M., Cuesta-Infante, A., Veeramachaneni, K.: Modeling tabular data using conditional gan. Adv. Neural Inf. Process. Syst. **32** (2019)
44. Xu, L., Veeramachaneni, K.: Synthesizing tabular data using generative adversarial networks. arXiv preprint arXiv:1811.11264 (2018)
45. Yoon, J., Drumright, L.N., Van Der Schaar, M.: Anonymization through data synthesis using generative adversarial networks (ads-gan). IEEE J. Biomed. Health Inform. **24**(8), 2378–2388 (2020)
46. Yu, L., Zhang, W., Wang, J., Yu, Y.S.: Sequence generative adversarial nets with policy gradient. 492 in. In: AAAI Conference on Srtificial Intelligence, vol. 493 (2017)
47. Zhao, Z., Kunar, A., Birke, R., Chen, L.Y.: Ctab-gan: Effective table data synthesizing. In: Asian Conference on Machine Learning, pp. 97–112. PMLR (2021)

# Lessons from a Robotaxi: Challenges in Selecting Privacy-Enhancing Technologies


Ala'a Al-Momani[1], David Balenson[2], Christoph Bösch[3],
Zoltán Ádám Mann[4], Sebastian Pape[5,6(✉)], and Jonathan Petit[7]

[1] Ulm University, Ulm, Germany
[2] USC Information Sciences Institute, Los Angeles, USA
[3] Bosch Research, Renningen, Germany
[4] University of Halle-Wittenberg, Halle, Germany
[5] Continental Automotive Technologies GmbH, Hannover, Germany
[6] Goethe University Frankfurt, Frankfurt, Germany
sebastian.pape@continental.com
[7] Qualcomm Technologies Inc., San Diego, USA



**Abstract.** Engineering privacy-friendly systems requires first assessing privacy threats and then selecting privacy-enhancing technologies (PETs) to mitigate the threats. While well-established methods such as LIND-DUN support threat assessment, systematic approaches for PET selection remain underdeveloped. This paper presents our experience applying three such approaches to a realistic robotaxi use case. Although each method has been validated by its respective authors on simple use cases, we found that none could adequately support PET selection in our complex, real-world scenario. As a result, we also explored a pragmatic approach based on Hoepman's privacy strategies. By analyzing the strengths and limitations of these approaches, we identify key challenges that PET selection methodologies should address and provide recommendations to guide the future development of such methodologies.



**Keywords:** privacy-enhancing technologies · PET selection · privacy threats · privacy threat mitigation · privacy engineering · robotaxi


## 1 Introduction

For the early phases of the privacy engineering process—such as privacy threat assessment—several methodologies provide specific guidance (e.g., LIND-DUN [28], PANOPTIC [18], and xCOMPASS [9]). These methodologies support the high-level design of privacy-friendly systems reasonably well, often through the use of privacy strategies and privacy patterns [13]. Academic efforts have also proposed ways to support later phases, in particular the selection of Privacy-Enhancing Technologies (PETs) to address the found privacy threats. Such


© The Author(s), under exclusive license to Springer Nature Switzerland AG 2026
R. Laborde et al. (Eds.): ESORICS 2025, LNCS 16231, pp. 154–170, 2026.
https://doi.org/10.1007/978-3-032-16089-8_11

work draws on privacy principles [24], best practices, activities, objectives, patterns [17,25], strategies [13], and threat models [8], as well as the broader concept of privacy by design [11]. However, the practical applicability of these proposals is not fully understood. Applying them to the detailed design of privacy-friendly systems in the real world may be challenging because of the approaches' high level of abstraction and other limitations and shortcomings.

This work investigates how the PET selection problem can be solved in practice, using a realistic robotaxi system as use case. Robotaxi services involve extensive and sensitive data processing throughout their lifecycle—from ride requests and routing to post-ride analytics—making them an ideal testbed for evaluating PET selection methodologies. Our aim is to investigate to what extent existing methodologies can be used to select appropriate PETs to enhance the privacy in the considered robotaxi service. In this work, we do not propose the final design of a privacy-preserving robotaxi service, but rather focus on investigating the methodologies for selecting PETs.

We make the following contributions: i) We identify three methodologies in the literature that promise guidance on PET selection, and apply them to a realistic robotaxi use case. We find that none yield satisfactory results. ii) We apply a pragmatic, experience-based approach based on Hoepman's privacy strategies [13] to identify a useful set of PETs. iii) We analyze the strengths and limitations of these approaches and extract insights to inform the development of improved PET selection methodologies. Our findings show that existing methodologies provide limited—or no—support for the detailed design and actual implementation of privacy-friendly systems. In particular, there is a lack of systematic, actionable support for selecting PETs as well as clear guidance how to implement and configure the selected PETs, how to combine them effectively, and how to integrate them into an overall system.

## 2   Related Work

We identified several privacy frameworks and projects. They cover the areas of privacy engineering (STRAP [15], which builds on prior work by Bellotti and Sellen [6] and Hong et al. [14]), system re-engineering (POSD [5]), privacy by design (PRIPARE[1] based on the work of Kung [19] and Hoepman [13]), and compliance (PARROT [4]). MITRE has released the Privacy Engineering Framework and Life Cycle Adaptation Guide[2], while ENISA has published the PETs Control Matrix[3] and a report on data protection engineering[4]. However, none of these frameworks give specific support in the selection of PETs.

Several relevant standards also exist. ISO/IEC 27701 extends ISO/IEC 27001 by adding requirements for establishing and improving a Privacy Information

---

[1] https://pripareproject.eu/.
[2] https://www.mitre.org/sites/default/files/2021-11/.
[3] https://www.enisa.europa.eu/news/enisa-news/enisas-pets-control-matrix-a-tool-to-evaluate-online-and-mobile-privacy-tools.
[4] https://www.enisa.europa.eu/publications/.

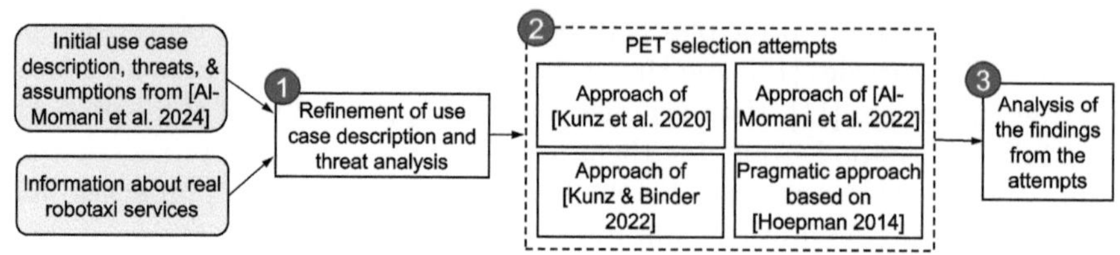



**Fig. 1.** Overview of the methodology used in this paper.

Management System (PIMS). ISO/IEC 27550 describes privacy engineering across the system lifecycle, drawing from Hoepman's privacy strategies [13] and Privacy Control Examples that are similar to patterns (e.g., Hide: Encryption, Mixing, Perturbation). Similar to NIST SP800-53, ISO/IEC 29151 defines objectives, controls, and guidelines for implementing controls for protecting personally identifiable information (PII). Yet, none of these standards provide specific support for selecting PETs.

In the academic literature, Drozd and Dürmuth [10] suggested linking privacy patterns to PETs, but only as a conceptual outlook. Pape et al. [24] proposed selecting PETs based on GDPR principles, without referencing specific threats. Adams [1] introduced a privacy tree to classify PETs, offering some guidance for selection, but the list is incomplete and several leaves are linked to multiple PETs. Jordan et al. [16] provide an extensive list of PETs, but offer minimal support for selecting. We only found three papers that provide specific guidance in PET selection [3,20,21], which we discuss in greater detail in Sect. 5.

As our use case is in the automotive domain, we also examined PET-related literature in this area. Al-Momani et al. [2] explored the usefulness of privacy patterns in improving privacy in future automotive systems. Chah et al. [7] applied LINDDUN to analyze privacy threats. Pape et al. [26] proposed a system model to identify suitable integration points for PETs in a vehicle. Löbner et al. [22] evaluated de-identification techniques in automotive use cases. None of these works proposed a methodology for selecting suitable PETs.

## 3    Methodology

Figure 1 depicts the methodology used to perform the research reported in this paper. Our methodology is structured around a *refined robotaxi use case* derived from Al-Momani et al. [2]. We enhanced this use case to reflect more realistic data flows and service phases based on descriptions from real providers like Waymo and Uber[5]. We carefully checked that these refinements did not alter the original threat model or its underlying assumptions. As a result, we were able to reuse the *threat assessment* conducted by Al-Momani et al. [2].

To *identify suitable PETs* for our use case, we applied three PET selection approaches from the literature: i) Kunz et al. [20] who propose a reproducible

---

[5] cf. https://waymo.com and https://www.uber.com, respectively.

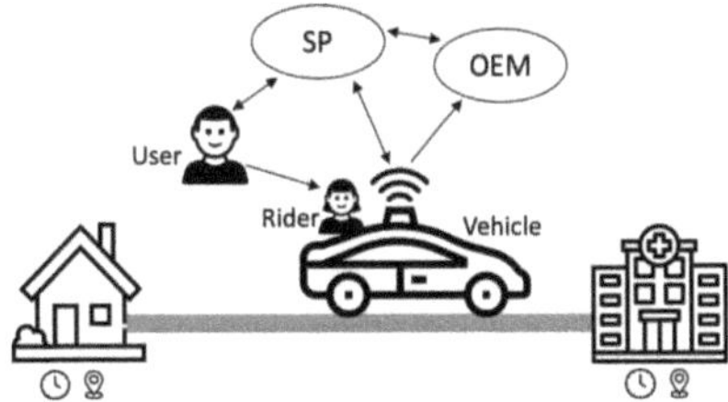


**Fig. 2.** Basic system model of a robotaxi service, from [2].

method for selecting data-dependent PETs that can be used independently or alongside other methods; ii) Kunz and Binder [21] who offer an application-oriented classification of PETs based on privacy protection goals, functional context, technology maturity, and impact on various non-functional requirements; and iii) Al-Momani et al. [3] who employ decision trees to guide the selection of privacy solutions based on LINDDUN threats and Hoepman's privacy strategies [13]. In addition to these approaches, we applied a *pragmatic, experience-driven approach* (cf. Sect. 5.4) in which we revisited assumptions, analyzed the purpose of data processing, and considered applicable PETs. We then *analyzed the outcomes* to uncover key challenges, limitations, and differences across the approaches. All steps and findings were collaboratively reviewed to ensure consistency.

## 4   Use Case: Robotaxi – Refined System Model

Robotaxi services, which are autonomous, driverless taxi systems, represent a cutting-edge application of self-driving vehicle technology. By focusing on a generic robotaxi service, our aim is to derive insights applicable across the broader industry, rather than to a single provider. From a privacy perspective, a robotaxi service differs significantly from a traditional taxi service. In a traditional taxi, the driver handles not only the driving, but also rider interaction, payment, and unexpected situations. In a robotaxi, these functions are performed by a combination of artificial intelligence and a remote service provider. As a result, more data may need to be collected to ensure safe and effective service operation.

Our system model builds on the robotaxi model proposed by Al-Momani et al. [2], providing a refined system version that offers closer alignment with real-world deployments. This refinement is based on examining existing services and incorporates best practices from the industry. While it does not (intentionally) address privacy enhancements, the refined model serves as a more practical foundation for selecting applicable PETs to mitigate the identified privacy threats.

Additionally, we noticed during the application of the pragmatic approach that all of the three investigated approaches require a clean use case description with minimal assumptions. Therefore, we revisited the original assumptions, asking if the data in question was truly necessary and if it could be reduced. For

**Table 1.** Data collected or assigned and data used in the various phases.

Phase/Action groups — 1: Account creation (user_id, Name, Address, e-mail, Phone, Payment, legal age, (Preferences)); 2: Booking (PLoc(s), PTime, DLoc(s), Route, No. of riders, Rider names); 3: V. assign. (Vehicle id, ETA, User location, Fleet manag. data); 4: Ride (Vehicle Location, Camera (internal), Audio (internal), Sensors (internal), User interaction); 5: Payment (Fare, Payment method, Ride history, User feedback); 6: Post-ride (Feedback, Incident details, Social sharing, …).

Data collected or assigned →

| Data used in: | user_id | Name | Address | e-mail | Phone | Payment | legal age | (Preferences) | PLoc(s) | PTime | DLoc(s) | Route | No. of riders | Rider names | Vehicle id | ETA | User location | Fleet manag. data | Vehicle Location | Camera (internal) | Audio (internal) | Sensors (internal) | User interaction | Fare | Payment method | Ride history | User feedback | Feedback | Incident details | Social sharing | … |
|---|---|---|---|---|---|---|---|---|---|---|---|---|---|---|---|---|---|---|---|---|---|---|---|---|---|---|---|---|---|---|---|
| P1 | ✓ | ✓ | ✓ | ✓ | ✓ | ✓ | ✓ | ✓ | | | | | | | | | | | | | | | | | | | | | | | |
| P2 | ✓ | ✓ | . | . | . | . | . | ✓ | ✓ | ✓ | ✓ | ✓ | ✓ | ✓ | | | | | | | | | | | | | | | | | |
| P3 | ✓ | . | . | ✓ | ✓ | . | . | ✓ | ✓ | ✓ | ✓ | ✓ | ✓ | . | ✓ | ✓ | ✓ | ✓ | | | | | | | | | | | | | |
| P4 | ✓ | . | . | . | . | . | . | ✓ | ✓ | ✓ | ✓ | ✓ | . | . | . | . | ✓ | ✓ | ✓ | ✓ | ✓ | ✓ | ✓ | | | | | | | | |
| P5 | ✓ | ✓ | ✓ | . | . | ✓ | . | ? | ✓ | ✓ | ✓ | ✓ | ✓ | . | . | . | . | . | . | . | . | . | . | ✓ | ✓ | ✓ | ✓ | | | | |
| P6 | ✓ | ? | ? | ? | ? | ? | . | ? | ? | ? | ? | ? | ? | ? | ? | ? | ? | ? | ? | ? | ? | ? | ? | ? | ? | ? | ? | ? | ? | ? | . |

Pn: Phase *n*    ✓: data needed    ?: data potentially needed, depending on post-ride actions.

instance, we challenged the assumption that a user's birth date needs to be collected during registration, as a more privacy-friendly option would be to use just a binary check (e.g., "user is of legal age") which avoids the collection of the full date of birth, which could be used for identification.

As shown in Fig. 2, the robotaxi system involves four primary parties: *User*, who requests and manages rides through an application; *Rider*, the individual taking the ride, who may or may not be the same as the User; Service Provider, *SP*, who operates the robotaxi service, manages the backend system, assigns vehicles, and ensures smooth operation; and Original Equipment Manufacturer, *OEM*, who builds and maintains the vehicle, including hardware and software updates. In addition to these natural persons (*User* and *Rider*) and legal entities (*SP* and *OEM*), *Vehicle* can be seen as a fifth party.

The use of a robotaxi service involves several phases, each requiring specific data elements for effective operation. In the following, we describe each phase. Table 1 summarizes the data collected or assigned during these phases, along with the specific phases in which each data item is used or required.

**1. Account Creation.** *User*s create an account through an application. **Data Collected:** Personal information such as name, email address, phone number, and payment details (e.g., credit card information). **Purpose:** To authenticate users, enable payment processing, and establish a user profile for service access. **Additional Features:** *User*s may also indicate preferences such as accessibility needs (e.g., wheelchair-accessible vehicles), select other service-specific options, or participate in a loyalty program.

**2. Booking a Ride.** *User*s input their desired pickup and drop-off location(s) into the app, and optionally specify a pick-up time, number of riders, and specific preferences (e.g. vehicle features). **Data Collected:** Current location (via GNSS), pickup location, drop-off location, and potentially pick-up time and preferred routes. **Purpose:** To generate ride requests and facilitate assignment of a vehicle to *User* in the next phase. **Additional Features:** *User*s receive confirmation notifications, and the app provides options to adjust the booking if needed. If the taxi is booked for a different *Rider*, the name is provided by *User*.

**3. Vehicle Assignment & Ride Confirmation.** The system assigns an autonomous vehicle and provides ride details to *User*. **Data Collected:** Vehicle identification (e.g., make, model, license plate), estimated time of arrival (ETA), and *Rider*'s updated location for precise pickup (if selected). **Purpose:** To inform *User* of vehicle details and ensure accurate pickup coordination. **Additional Features:** *User* is notified when the vehicle arrives. Identity confirmation (e.g., PIN) is required to ensure the correct *Rider* enters the vehicle. Additionally, the vehicle assignment requires fleet management data, including the precise location of vehicles and the current fuel or battery levels.

**4. Ride Execution.** The autonomous vehicle navigates to the destination, guided by its sensors and real-time data processing. **Data Collected:** Real-time vehicle location, internal and external sensor data (e.g., audio, cameras, LIDAR) and user interaction data within the vehicle (e.g., temperature or music preferences). Sensor data, camera data, and vehicle location are also accessible to the *OEM* at any time. **Purpose:** To enable safe travel, ensure *Rider* comfort, and provide operational support. **Additional Features:** *Rider* may change the route or drop-off location and can contact customer support via vehicle interface or the app if issues arise.

**5. Payment and Feedback.** Payment is processed automatically upon ride completion. *Rider* can provide feedback via the vehicle interface, and *User* via the application. **Data Collected:** Ride fare details, payment method, trip history, and user feedback (e.g., ratings, comments). **Purpose:** To complete the financial transaction, maintain a record of rides, and improve service quality based on feedback. **Additional Features:** *User* may receive trip summaries, and promotional offers or discounts are applied based on *User*'s profile.

**6. Post-Ride Actions.** Additional interactions may occur between *User* and *SP*, including invoice creation , ride history and analytics, customer support, loyalty programs and rewards, safety and security issues, service customization, data deletion, subscription cancellation, and social media sharing. **Data Use:** Depending on the action, different existing data items may be reused or new data may be collected.

## 5   PET Selection

Al-Momani et al. [2] conducted a privacy threat assessment of the original use case. Because our refined use case closely aligns with the original, particularly in terms of privacy threats, the assessment remains applicable, and we refer readers to the original paper for more details. Our current focus is on selecting PETs to mitigate these threats.

Our literature review identified three approaches that offer specific guidance for PET selection. In Sects. 5.1–5.3, we describe our experience applying these methods to the robotaxi use case. Given the limitations we encountered, we also applied a pragmatic approach based on Hoepman's privacy strategies [13].

The challenges reported in Sects. 5.1–5.4 are not intended as criticisms of these approaches. We recognize these approaches are valuable initial steps toward addressing a complex problem. Our goal is to highlight that the current state of the art in PET selection remains inadequate for handling realistic use cases.

### 5.1  Approach of Kunz et al. (2020)

Kunz et al. [20] proposed a methodology for selecting PETs for IoT-based services, with a focus on the automotive domain. The methodology consists of four steps: service description, data-driven elicitation, service-driven elicitation, and PET selection. We go through these four steps and try to apply them to our use case.

**A. Service description.** In this step, the service is specified, focusing on the required data and the purposes of data processing. We have done this in Sect. 4.

**B. Data-driven elicitation.** In this step, all data identified in the first step is analyzed according to 6 criteria: continuous or categorical data, set size, ordinal or nominal data, data longevity, value sequences, metadata and identifiers. Each of these analysis steps should help narrow down the set of PETs applicable to the given type of data. In our case, this requires quite some effort. We identified 29 data types in our use case (see Table 1), leading to $29 \cdot 6 = 174$ analysis steps. We present here only a couple of those steps as examples.

One criterion is whether the data is continuous or categorical, which poses a challenge since most of our data types (e.g., name, address, vehicle ID, route) are neither continuous nor categorical. Some data (e.g., fare) is continuous. The analysis tells us that some PETs, for example PRAM (post-randomization method), cannot be applied to these data types. Similarly, some of our data (e.g., payment method) is categorical, and the analysis tells us that some PETs, for example noise masking, cannot be applied to these data types. Another criterion is the number of values that the given data type can assume. For most of our data types, this depends on implementation details (e.g., the string length maximally allowed for name or address). This seems to contradict the statement of Kunz et al. that their methodology can be applied in the early phases of the system design process, because such choices may not have been made yet at this stage. Also, Kunz et al. do not specify what to do with this information. They only state that a smaller set of possible values decreases the applicability of PETs. It is not clear how this could help narrow down the set of applicable PETs.

**C. Service-driven elicitation.** This step entails analyzing the service's requirements on data utility, with the aim of determining which PETs would not undermine the usefulness of the given service. For this purpose, the methodology uses three criteria: value precision, data freshness, and attribute dependency.

As to the first criterion, the "precision required by the service" is unclear for certain data types (e.g., camera feed). For other data types, the precision requirement may vary over time: e.g., the pick-up location must be known exactly when the vehicle picks up the rider, but the precision may be lowered when this data is stored for later processing. Unfortunately, the methodology does not support such varying precision requirements. The second criterion is how fresh the data needs to be. This is again problematic: the same data can be associated with different freshness requirements for different purposes. For example, if the robotaxi encounters a difficult traffic situation and requires remote control from a human operator, that operator needs the camera feed in real time. On the other hand, for settling compensation claims, there may be a need to access archived camera feeds from weeks before. Again, the methodology does not support this type of varying requirements. The last criterion is the dependency between attributes. Indeed, some of the data types in our use case are not independent. For example, there is a connection between the route and the fare, since a longer route typically leads to a higher fare. Kunz et al. draw our attention to the fact that in such cases, determining different PETs for the dependent attributes may cause problems. It is not clear how this information could help our PET selection process, since the different data types may force us to use different PETs for those attributes. Also, even if the same PET is used for two interdependent attributes, the dependency may still cause problems if not properly taken into account, and the methodology does not clarify how to avoid such problems.

**D. PET selection**. Assuming that the previous two steps delivered a set of potentially applicable and useful PETs (which is not the case in our use case due to the difficulties reported above), this step aims at choosing the best ones from those sets. Unfortunately, Kunz et al. state that this is highly use-case-specific, so that they do not provide a systematic approach for this step.

**Further limitations**. As we saw above, steps B and C are only partially applicable to our use case, and step D does not give clear guidance. In addition, the approach suffers from further limitations. First, the approach is limited to data-obfuscation PETs. In our case, several data types (e.g., user name or payment information) must be available to the service provider without modifications for legitimate purposes, so that they cannot be obfuscated. There are data protection requirements associated with these data types, but addressing these requirements requires PETs not supported by the methodology. Second, the approach assumes a list of available PETs. However, finding the right level of abstraction for PETs is challenging. E.g., Kunz et al. consider aggregation to be one PET, but mention that various aggregation techniques exist. Those techniques could be just as well considered individual PETs. If we find out using the methodology that we should use aggregation, we are still faced with the question of which aggregation technique to use. Third, Kunz et al. state that their approach can be used in tandem with LINDDUN. However, the approach excludes two important threats covered by LINDDUN: unawareness and non-compliance. Compliance with data protection regulations is the primary privacy objective for most service providers, making non-compliance the most important threat from their point of view.

## 5.2   Approach of Kunz and Binder (2022)

Kunz and Binder [21] propose a categorization of PETs to aid PET selection. For each considered PET, they determine the relevant privacy goals, metrics for measuring the PET's privacy effect, the relevant "functional scenario" (one of: release, messaging, authentication, authorization, retrieval, computation), the PET's maturity on a scale from 1 to 3, and the PET's impact on performance, architecture, and utility (the last three are binary attributes: there is either impact or not). The paper provides this categorization for 29 PETs. On this basis, the following methodology can be deduced. Starting from a privacy threat assessment, first the privacy goal and functional scenario is determined for each threat. Then, the categorization helps identify the subset of PETs applicable to the combination of privacy goal and functional scenario. Finally, the maturity and impact attributes of the short-listed PETs help choose the most appropriate PET. In the following, we go through these steps, applying them to our use case.

**A. Identifying privacy goal and functional scenario**. A privacy threat assessment of our use case has already been performed by Al-Momani et al. [2] using LINDDUN. The privacy goals used by Kunz and Binder are directly linked to the LINDDUN threat types, which makes it trivial to determine the privacy goal related to each threat. E.g., for a linkability threat, the related privacy goal is unlinkability. Determining the "functional scenario" that provides the context for a threat, however, is not always obvious. Some threats arise in the context of activities that could belong to more than one category: e.g., the threats arising from data sharing between the *SP* and the *OEM* could be seen to belong to both the "release" and the "messaging" category. The functional scenario of some other threats—e.g., the threat of storing personal data beyond its necessary retention period—does not seem to belong to any of the proposed categories.

**B. Identifying relevant subset of PETs**. If the privacy goal and the functional scenario could be determined for a threat, then the matrix of Kunz and Binder can be used to mechanically determine the subset of relevant PETs. Even this seemingly straightforward step poses difficulties. The matrix offers no PETs for unawareness and non-compliance threats, although, as we mentioned earlier, these threats can be very important. Also, there are many combinations of privacy goal and functional scenario, for which the matrix offers no PETs.

**C. Selecting the most appropriate PET**. If we managed to identify a set of applicable PETs for a given threat through the two previous steps, then the final step is to select the most appropriate one. Unfortunately, the paper offers no clear guidance on how to do that. It is suggested that the maturity and the impact on performance, architecture, and utility should be helpful in making this decision. But it is not clear how. E.g., suppression and recoding are given as two PETs that can both address linkability threats in a "release" functional scenario, and they have the same maturity and the same impact on performance, architecture, and utility, so it remains unclear which one to choose. Another example: swapping and noise masking can be used for the same type of threat and functional scenario; swapping has a lower maturity than noise masking, but noise masking impacts utility, making it unclear which one to choose.

**Further limitations**. Beyond the questions that the individual steps raise, the approach also suffers from more general issues. Some are similar to the problems identified in Sect. 5.1. E.g., unawareness and non-compliance are missing in both approaches. Also, we mentioned in Sect. 5.1 that it is difficult to come up with a good list of PETs because it is not clear if different variants of a PET should be regarded as different PETs. For the method of Kunz and Binder, this problem is even more severe because different variants of a PET may have different maturity and different impact on performance, architecture, and utility. E.g., Kunz and Binder mention synthetic data as a PET. However, there are many ways to generate synthetic data, and their impact on, e.g., utility can be very different.

The impact attributes of Kunz and Binder are problematic anyway. It is not possible to capture the impact of a PET on performance, architecture, and utility in general, because this depends on many further details. E.g., the matrix of Kunz and Binder shows that the PET MPC (multi-party computation) impacts performance. However, there are many MPC techniques, and their performance impact is very different. Even for one particular MPC technique, e.g., additive secret-sharing, its performance impact depends heavily on the types of operations that it is applied to: linear operations (addition or multiplication by a constant) can be very quickly performed on additively secret-shared numbers, whereas non-linear operations are much more costly [27]. Thus, the performance impact depends not only on the PET, but also on the context in which it is applied. A further problem is that the analysis must be performed for every single threat. In a real system, the number of threats can be high, making this impractical. Also, the risk posed by several threats may simply be accepted or may be addressed by non-technical means, so that PET selection for these threats is not necessary. E.g., in our use case, there are obvious identifiability threats stemming from the collected identifiers, but this is accepted because of other requirements. Finally, threats may be connected to each other. The methodology proposes a PET for each threat independently, potentially leading to a sub-optimal solution.

### 5.3 Approach of Al-Momani et al (2022)

Al-Momani et al. [3] propose a methodology using decision trees to systematically guide users from privacy threats identified with LINDDUN to suitable privacy solutions. For this, specific key nodes are identified in the LINDDUN threat trees. These nodes contain information regarding the cause of the threat, the threat class, and the system element where the threat applies. For each key node, the mitigation goal is defined, and nodes sharing the same goal are grouped together. In total, ten mitigation goals are defined. For each mitigation goal, potential countermeasures are defined and then ordered according to the data-oriented privacy design strategies [13], i.e., Minimize, Separate, Abstract, and Hide. This process yielded four solution trees for the mitigation goals "protect-attributes", "protect-communication-metadata", "protect-id", and "secure-processing". In the following, we apply this approach to our use case.

**A. Identify "key nodes" for the solution trees.** To select the applicable PETs, the original approach had to be modified because it had been designed for an earlier version of LINDDUN, rendering the utilization of the key nodes unfeasible. Our adaption process was initiated by mapping the identified threats from the LINDDUN analysis to the solution trees. To maintain a fundamental element of the method—the usage of the rationales underlying a threat identified through the threat trees—we used the assumptions from the use case [2], which encompass analogous information and facilitated the mapping process.

**B. Identify possible PETs using the solution trees.** The aforementioned new mapping allowed us to use the solution trees, which consequently resulted in some PETs for the different phases. The first step is to address the applicability of a PET. Then, it is necessary to determine whether the PET alone is adequate to remedy the threat of the key node or if it must be combined with other applicable PETs. In summary, we observed two main outcomes of the method per threat: i) Mitigation is not applicable since the (precise) data is required for the service, e. g. for user identification; and ii) Mitigation is possible using: Remove, Replace, Separate, or use Noisy & less granular attributes, depending on the data.

The proposed solution trees are a promising concept, particularly in terms of prioritizing privacy strategies and assessing the necessity of data. This approach involves determining whether the data is indispensable and, if so, explores options for its replacement, separation, or generalization. Only after this thorough evaluation should the utilization of advanced PETs be considered. However, this method also has major shortcomings. The *"secure-processing"* tree might be complete regarding PETs, since it helps choose one of the three currently available PETs for secure processing: homomorphic encryption, trusted execution environments, and multiparty computation. However, the *"protect-id"* tree considers only attribute-based credentials as a PET which limits usability. The *"protect-attributes"* tree only considers encryption in general and no specific PET. Although the key 'entry' nodes include "Untrusted communication", "Observe message and/or channel", and "Dataflow not fully protected", even TLS is missing as a PET. In addition, technologies that protect attributes are missing, such as attribute-based credentials or zero-knowledge proofs. The *"protect-communication-metadata"* deals with "Non-anonymous Communication" and lists only Onion routing and Hiding timestamps and the message size by random padding as possible PETs.

**Further Limitations.** The approach suggests primarily to use Hoepman's privacy strategies [13], but lacks more concrete details on PET selection. Missing PETs limit the selection of (advanced) technical PETs.

### 5.4   A Pragmatic Approach Based on Hoepman (2014)

We now sketch a pragmatic approach based on Hoepman's privacy design strategies [13] and the authors' collective expertise. Al-Momani et al. [2] previously identified the assumptions underlying the privacy threats they found. To address these threats, we revisit their assumptions. We identify the purpose of data processing and explore the potential application of PETs to enhance privacy. Where feasible, appropriate PETs are incorporated.

**A. Preparation by applying privacy strategies.** Before analyzing the assumptions and phases relevant to PET selection, we adopted the following general strategies (where applicable): i) *Minimize*: We revisited the original assumptions, asking whether the data in question was truly necessary (cf. Sect. 4). For age verification, the application of Attribute-Based Credentials (ABCs) could be considered. ii) *Hide*: Encrypt all collected data at rest (e. g., disk/database encryption) and in transit (e. g., TLS); ii) *Enforce*: Implement strict access control (e. g., role-based) to safeguard data and ensure auditability; iv) *Inform*: Provide users with clear and accessible information about data processing and its purposes, such as through a privacy policy, data collection notices, and regular updates; v) *Control*: Enable users to manage their preferences, and access, delete, or update their personal information—via a user dashboard, data deletion protocols, opt-in mechanisms, and consent withdrawal.

**B. PET selection process.** To identify additional potential PETs, we examined the data items used in each phase. Table 1 provides an overview of how data is used across phases. For example, one result of this activity was the identification of homomorphic encryption as a potential PET for encrypting location, time, and route data of vehicles, thereby enabling vehicle allocation while preserving confidentiality and still allowing matching with the (also encrypted) user location.

**C. Threat assessment.** We conducted an additional LINDDUN analysis using the revised assumptions. The revised assumptions have the potential to mitigate or eliminate most of the previously identified threats. However, we were unable to eliminate threats regarding linkability and identifiability (LINDDUN threats L.1.1, I.1.1, and I.2.2.1), as these stem from the use of a unique identifier. Nevertheless, for the purposes of our use case, it does not constitute a privacy problem if the *SP* can identify a *User*. It is important to note that even if advanced PETs (e.g., attribute-based credentials, zero knowledge proofs, anonymous payment) are implemented to allow anonymous use of the service, the *SP* may still be able to identify a user through data correlation (e.g., pick-up/drop-off locations, routes, and times), behavioral patterns, or service customization. Furthermore, in certain jurisdictions, the *SP* may be obligated to collect specific information for legal compliance, making full anonymity impossible.

**Further Limitations.** The main limitation of this approach is that it is not a systematic methodology. We first identified suitable privacy strategies following Hoepman [13], and then mapped them to relevant PETs. However, Hoepman's strategies are defined at a higher level than PET Selection. As a result, we analyzed assumptions and determined the deployability of specific PETs to address certain threats based on our own experience, without a formal method. This introduces two limitations: i) The approach requires experienced experts to produce useful results, and ii) Different teams may reach different conclusions, reducing consistency and repeatability.

# 6   Analysis of PET Selection Approaches

In this section, we analyze the findings from the three PET selection attempts of Sects. 5.1–5.3, highlighting their respective strengths and weaknesses. Table 2 provides a comparative summary of our analysis. We also extract insights to guide future research on PET selection methodologies.

**Table 2.** Comparison of PET Selection Approaches

| Criterion | Kunz et al. (2020) | Kunz & Binder (2022) | Al-Momani et al. (2022) |
| --- | --- | --- | --- |
| Core Method | Data- and service-driven filtering of PETs | PET matrix by goal, scenario, maturity, impact | Decision trees linking LINDDUN threats to strategies |
| Design Stage Fit | Assumes mature design, known data | Requires detailed threats | Needs mapped assumptions and threats |
| Final PET Selection Support | No decision logic for choosing among PETs | Maturity/impact noted but no guidance | No prioritization among PETs |
| Scalability / Use Case Fit | Too granular for large systems | Partial threat coverage | Partial PET coverage; requires expert tuning |
| Handles Context | Recognizes variation but lacks structured support | Treats PET effects as static across contexts | Accounts for necessity of data |
| Threat Inter-dependency | Treats threats independently | Treats threats independently | Considers shared assumptions, but not systematically |
| PET Coverage | Narrow focus on obfuscation PETs | Moderate PET list with missing types | Incomplete list (e.g., omits TLS, ZKPs, ABCs) |
| Strengths | Combines data/service analysis; domain-specific taxonomy | Maturity and impact dimensions included | Leverages threat rationale; supports strategy prioritization |
| Limitations | High effort; limited guidance for final PET selection | Ambiguous threat-to-PET mapping; lacks detail on PET variants | Limited PET set; lacks automation or consistency |

## 6.1  Strengths

Each of the methodologies considered (Sect. 5.1–5.3) has its own strengths, which are largely complementary.

The approach of Kunz et al. [20] promotes a combination of data-driven and service-driven elicitation. This is a sensible idea, as both the characteristics of the data and the requirements of the service influence the set of applicable PETs. The paper also introduces the concept of a domain-specific data taxonomy, with a set of applicable PETs mapped to each identified data type. This is an interesting idea that could help make PET selection more efficient.

The approach of Kunz and Binder [21] considers PET maturity as well as the impact of PETs on performance, architecture, and utility. Each of these aspects may be important in practice.

The approach of Al-Momani et al. [3] leverages detailed threat assessment information when selecting PETs. Our experience confirmed the value of this idea: the threat assessment improved our understanding of the origins and potential consequences of privacy threats, which proved helpful for PET selection.

## 6.2   Weaknesses

As described in Sect. 5, applying each of these academic approaches to our use case was problematic. Beyond the specific weaknesses of individual approaches, which may reflect their relative immaturity, we encountered several recurring limitations that may indicate more fundamental limitations. First, each approach seems to assume a completed system design. However, by that point, introducing PETs may be too late, as they could potentially impact core design choices. None of the approaches supports an agile process in which the general system design and privacy considerations evolve in parallel, influencing each other iteratively.

Second, each approach assumes a fixed list of PETs and clear criteria for applicability. In practice, PET lists are often arbitrary, and the applicability of a given PET typically depends on context. Determining the impact of a PET (e.g., on performance, architecture, functionality, or future extensibility) requires careful analysis and substantial design effort [23]. The reviewed approaches tend to overlook this and rely on over-simplified generalizations.

Third, while existing approaches may identify potentially applicable PETs, they offer little guidance for making a final selection. This gap is especially critical in scenarios with specific accuracy and performance requirements. For example, when adding noise, it should sufficiently obscure privacy-relevant information without degrading the utility of the data. The performance impact of a PET also depends on the context: real-time applications impose stricter constraints than offline or batch-processing tasks. Moreover, the outcome depends not only on the PET itself but also on its configuration (e.g., the $\epsilon$ value in differential privacy).

Fourth, each approach treats threats in isolation, selecting at least one PET per threat. In reality, both threats and PETs may be interdependent. For example, a single PET might mitigate multiple threats, or the use of one PET could interfere with the effectiveness of another. Focusing solely on local decisions can lead to overall suboptimal or even infeasible outcomes.

Finally, each approach omits considerations that fall outside their defined scope, such as "soft privacy" goals or security requirements. While this is understandable in a research setting, practical methodologies must be more comprehensive to be useful in real-world deployments.

## 6.3   Recommendations for Future Methodology

Insights from the pragmatic approach could help inform the development of improved methodologies. We offer the following recommendations.

**Investigate Assumptions.** When identifying mitigation techniques, we found it important to trace threats back to their underlying causes. The origin of a threat often constrains the available mitigation options. For example, if Identifiability threats arise due to legal requirements to identify users, then PETs that provide anonymity may not be applicable. To support this process, we found it useful to document data protection-related assumptions about the system and to link each identified threat to the assumptions that give rise to it. This also helped identify cases where multiple threats stemmed from a shared assumption, meaning that a single PET targeting that assumption could address several threats. Revisiting assumptions and clarifying the purpose of data processing proved to be a valuable step in preparing for PET selection.

**Specific Step-wise Dataflows.** Structuring the use case into discrete steps helped streamline PET selection. It allowed us to visualize when and where data is created, to identify dependencies, and to avoid unintended side effects when applying PETs. A PET applied to mitigate a threat in one step may influence other steps where the same data is used.

**PETs' Appropriateness.** Addressing the limitations of current approaches will require improved support for selecting PETs in specific scenarios. In particular, new methodologies should help map scenario-specific requirements to the expected changes in system properties (e.g., performance, accuracy) resulting from the implementation and configuration of PETs. This would inevitably bring deployment and integration changes to the system that should be investigated by new methodologies.

**Adaption to Design Phase.** Different phases of the system design process require distinct tools and approaches. Designing a system from scratch allows building privacy into the architecture from the ground up. In contrast, improving an existing system demands a detailed understanding of current data flows to assess whether introducing a PET is feasible. For example, adding noise to encrypted data is not straightforward and may compromise functionality. Introducing a PET might also disrupt operations if essential data becomes inaccessible. If the system incorporates machine learning, additional considerations arise, such as the distinction between the initial training phase and the deployment of the model, which may affect how and when PETs can be applied.

**Addressing Compliance.** None of the approaches considered compliance. A future approach for PET selection could aim to bridge the gap between building privacy-friendly systems and ensuring regulatory compliance. Aligning privacy engineering with compliance requirements would significantly improve practical adoption. This is especially relevant in corporate environments, where privacy processes are often structured around meeting legal and regulatory standards.

## 7   Conclusions and Future Work

The PET selection methods found in the literature exhibit significant shortcomings. While they offer some guidance, they often rely on oversimplified assumptions (e.g., regarding the applicably of a PET in a given situation), and fall short of providing a complete methodology. In some cases, these approaches yield a list of potentially applicable PETs, but the challenge of selecting the most appropriate one remains. This requires evaluating the maturity of each PET, its compatibility with performance and architectural constraints, the availability of ready-to-use implementations etc.

The pragmatic approach presented in this paper cannot be considered a methodology in its current form, as it heavily relies on the expertise of the team. The challenge of selecting appropriate PETs remains open, and current approaches can only partially support this task.

Our work highlights the importance of using realistic use cases for evaluating PET selection methodologies. Post-ride actions, such as service enhancements or monetization, can directly influence PET selection. For example, issuing invoices must comply with legal requirements regarding the included data.

While our analysis highlights the challenges of selecting PETs in real-world scenarios, it does not offer a complete solution. Even after PETs are selected, implementing, integrating, and configuring them remains a significant challenge [12]. There is a need for more iterative, agile, and exploratory approaches that support "what-if" analysis, allowing design teams to evaluate the impact of selected PETs without immediate commitment. Privacy should be integrated into overall system design, not treated as a separate, downstream process. The use of Artificial Intelligence techniques to support PET selection also represents a potential direction for future work.

**Acknowledgments.** This work was inspired by privacy engineering discussions at Dagstuhl Seminar 23242, "Privacy Protection of Automated and Self-Driving Vehicles". The work was supported in part by the U.S. National Science Foundation (NSF) under grant number 2245323, and by the German Federal Ministry of Education and Research (BMBF) under grant number 16KIS1382.

# References


1. Adams, C.: Introduction to Privacy Enhancing Technologies: A Classification-Based Approach to Understanding PETs. Springer (2021)
2. Al-Momani, A., Balenson, D., Mann, Z.Á., Pape, S., Petit, J., Bösch, C.: Navigating privacy patterns in the era of robotaxis. In: IEEE European Symposium on Security and Privacy Workshops, pp. 32–39, IEEE (2024)
3. Al-Momani, A., Bösch, C., Wuyts, K., Sion, L., Joosen, W., Kargl, F.: Mitigation lost in translation: leveraging threat information to improve privacy solution selection. In: ACM SAC (2022)
4. Alhirabi, N., Beaumont, S., Rana, O., Perera, C.: Designing privacy-aware iot for unregulated domains. ACM Trans. Internet Things (2023)
5. Baldassarre, M.T., Barletta, V.S., Caivano, D., Scalera, M.: Integrating security and privacy in software development. Softw. Qual. J. **28**(3), 987–1018 (2020)
6. Bellotti, V., Sellen, A.: Design for privacy in ubiquitous computing environments. In: ECSCW, pp. 77–92, Springer, CHam (1993). https://doi.org/10.1007/978-94-011-2094-4_6
7. Chah, B., Lombard, A., Bkakria, A., Yaich, R., Abbas-Turki, A., Galland, S.: Privacy threat analysis for connected and autonomous vehicles. Procedia Computer Science **210**, 36–44 (2022)
8. Deng, M., Wuyts, K., Scandariato, R., Preneel, B., Joosen, W.: A privacy threat analysis framework: supporting the elicitation and fulfillment of privacy requirements. Requirements Eng. **16**(1), 3–32 (2011)

9. Dev, J., Rashidi, B., Garg, V.: Models of applied privacy (map): a persona based approach to threat modeling. In: ACM CHI, pp. 1–15 (2023)

10. Drozd, O.: Privacy pattern catalogue: A tool for integrating privacy principles of iso/iec 29100 into the software development process. In: Privacy and Identity Management, pp. 129–140 (2016)

11. Gürses, S., Troncoso, C., Diaz, C.: Engineering privacy by design. Comput. Priv. Data Prot. **14**(3), 25 (2011)

12. Herwanto, G.B., Ekaputra, F.J., Quirchmayr, G., Tjoa, A.M.: Towards a holistic privacy requirements engineering process: insights from a systematic literature review. IEEE Access (2024)

13. Hoepman, J.: Privacy design strategies - (extended abstract). In: ICT Systems Security and Privacy Protection SEC, IFIP AICT, vol. 428 (2014)

14. Hong, J.I., Ng, J.D., Lederer, S., Landay, J.A.: Privacy risk models for designing privacy-sensitive ubiquitous computing systems. In: ACM DIS, pp. 91–100 (2004)

15. Jensen, C., Tullio, J., Potts, C., Mynatt, E.D.: Strap: a structured analysis framework for privacy. Georgia Inst. Technol. **1** (2005)

16. Jordan, S., Fontaine, C., Hendricks-Sturrup, R.: Selecting privacy-enhancing technologies for managing health data use. Front. Public Health **10**, 814163 (2022)

17. Kalloniatis, C., Kavakli, E., Gritzalis, S.: Addressing privacy requirements in system design: the pris method. Requirements Eng. **13** (2008)

18. Katcher, S., et al.: The mitre panoptic™ privacy threat model tutorial. In: 2nd Workshop on Privacy Threat Modeling (WPTM) (2023)

19. Kung, A.: Pears: Privacy enhancing architectures. In: Privacy Technologies and Policy - 2nd Annual Privacy Forum (APF), pp. 18–29 (2014)

20. Kunz, I., Banse, C., Stephanow, P.: Selecting privacy enhancing technologies for Iot-based services. In: EAI SecureComm, pp. 455–474 (2020)

21. Kunz, I., Binder, A.: Application-oriented selection of privacy enhancing technologies. In: Gryszczyńska, A., Polański, P., Gruschka, N., Rannenberg, K., Adamczyk, M. (eds.) Privacy Technologies and Policy - 10th Annual Privacy Forum, APF, LNCS, vol. 13279, pp. 75–87, Springer (2022). https://doi.org/10.1007/978-3-031-07315-1_5

22. Löbner, S., Tronnier, F., Pape, S., Rannenberg, K.: Comparison of de-identification techniques for privacy preserving data analysis in vehicular data sharing. In: ACM CSCS, pp. 7:1–7:11. ACM (2021)

23. Mann, Z.Á., Petit, J., Thornton, S.M., Buchholz, M., Millar, J.: SPIDER: interplay assessment method for privacy and other values. In: 2024 IEEE European Symposium on Security and Privacy Workshops (EuroS&PW), pp. 1–8. IEEE (2024)

24. Pape, S., Bkakria, A., Chah, B., Heymann, M., Winkler, S.S.: A framework for supporting PET selection based on GDPR principles. In: ARES (2025)

25. Pape, S., Rannenberg, K.: Applying privacy patterns to the internet of things' (IoT) architecture. Mob. Netw. Appl. **24**(3), 925–933 (2019)

26. Pape, S., et al.: A systematic approach for automotive privacy management. In: ACM CSCS (2023)

27. de Vries, R., Mann, Z.Á.: Secure neural network inference as a service with resource-constrained clients. In: Proceedings of the IEEE/ACM 16th International Conference on Utility and Cloud Computing (2023)

28. Wuyts, K., Joosen, W.: Linddun privacy threat modeling: a tutorial. CW Reports (2015)

# Performance Analysis of Lightweight Transformer Models for Healthcare Application Privacy Threat Detection


Jude E. Ameh[1]([⊠]) , Abayomi Otebolaku[1] , Alex Shenfield[1] ,
Augustine Ikpehai[1] , and Dauda Sule[2]

[1] Sheffield Hallam University, Sheffield, UK
`j.e.ameh@shu.ac.uk`
[2] Air Force Institute of Technology, Kaduna, Nigeria



**Abstract.** The growing complexity of cyber threats in healthcare demands advanced, computationally efficient security solutions. This study employs a white-box approach to evaluate lightweight transformer models for detecting privacy threats in C/C++ healthcare software. We introduce a novel dataset annotated with privacy vulnerabilities using the LINDDUN methodology, covering linkability, identifiability, non-repudiation, detectability, information disclosure, unawareness, and non-compliance. A systematic mapping between LINDDUN threats and Common Weakness Enumeration (CWE) classifications standardize privacy risk assessment. Six lightweight transformer models—GraphCodeBERT-base, CodeGPT-small, BERT-base-uncased, DistilRoBERTa-base, DistilBERT-base, and T5-small were fine-tuned and evaluated on the dataset containing 56,395 vulnerable and 364,232 non-vulnerable C/C++ functions, sourced from open-source projects to mitigate coder bias. All models achieve over 98% accuracy, with T5-small reaching 98.64%. Detailed computational costs, including model parameters and training times (~12 h), highlight suitability for resource-constrained environments. This work validates NLP-driven privacy risk assessment, offering a scalable framework for healthcare security.

**Keywords:** Healthcare privacy · lightweight · LINDDUN framework · Software vulnerability detection · Privacy threat modelling


## 1 Introduction

Healthcare organizations face increasing cyberattacks, such as the 2017 WannaCry ransomware outbreak that caused unprecedented disruptions (Portela et al., 2023). Traditional security approaches like signature-based detection find it difficult to detect advanced persistent threats (Dequino et al., 2025), thus necessitating efficient and novel detection strategies.

Natural language processing (NLP) advancements which are enabled by transformer-based models, offer new vulnerability detection possibilities, but state-of-the-art transformer models with billions of parameters create high computational costs and substantial memory requirements (Latharani & Mouneshachari, 2024; Denecke et al., 2024).



R. Laborde et al. (Eds.): ESORICS 2025, LNCS 16231, pp. 171–187, 2026.
https://doi.org/10.1007/978-3-032-16089-8_12

While effective at analyzing unstructured data for security risks, the computational demands of these models hinder deployment in resource-constrained environments like medical devices (Thapa et al., 2022).

This study evaluates lightweight transformer models for detecting privacy threats in healthcare software, focusing on real-time, computationally efficient solutions. We introduce a novel C/C++ code dataset annotated with privacy vulnerabilities using the LINDDUN privacy threat methodology, which categorizes threats into Linking, Identifying, Non-repudiation, Detecting, Data Disclosure, Unawareness, and Non-compliance (Wuyts & Joosen, 2020). We establish a systematic mapping between LINDDUN categories and Common Weakness Enumeration (CWE) classifications (Lohmann, Albuquerque, & Machado, 2023). C/C++ was selected due to it is considered a programming language for safety-critical systems (Zouev, 2020), and its manual memory management introduces unique privacy vulnerabilities like buffer overflows (Pereira et al., 2021) which align with LINDDUN categories and can cause unauthorized data exposure (Li et al., 2023a). Hence, this focus addresses a research gap, as existing datasets often prioritize general security over privacy-specific vulnerabilities in healthcare (Wuyts & Joosen, 2020).

This research contributes: (1) a novel healthcare-specific C/C++ dataset annotated with LINDDUN-based privacy vulnerabilities, (2) a systematic LINDDUN-CWE mapping framework that integrates privacy risk assessment with software security analysis, and (3) a comprehensive evaluation of lightweight transformer models for privacy threat detection. These advancements promote privacy-aware security while ensuring computational efficiency, useful for scalable, AI-driven security solutions in healthcare.

The remaining sections of this paper are organized as follows. Section 2 provides a background and gives further insights by showcasing related works. Section 3 provides a concise methodology of the methods, approach and experiments performed to achieve the objectives of this paper. While Section 4, 5, and 6 showcase the results of the experiments, provide a critical analysis in a discussion and conclusion respectively.

## 2  Background and Related Works

The digitization of healthcare has revolutionized medical services, enhancing patient outcomes and administrative efficiency. However, this transformation has introduced significant challenges in data privacy, security vulnerabilities, and interoperability, which now require advanced analytical frameworks and computationally efficient threat detection models (Ahmed et al., 2023; Silva et al., 2024).

### 2.1  Healthcare Information Systems and Data Privacy

Modern healthcare information systems are built upon intricate networks of stakeholders and information systems, where Electronic Health Records (EHRs) have evidently enhanced clinical decision-making and patient outcomes (Alomar et al., 2024). However, persistent system fragmentation and dependence on proprietary data formats continue to impede interoperability, complicating secure and efficient data exchange among disparate platforms (Holmgren, Everson & Adler-Milstein, 2022). Standardized frameworks such as Health Level Seven Fast Healthcare Interoperability Resources (HL7 FHIR) and ISO/EN 13606 offer blueprints for harmonized data structures, but variable implementation practices undermine their potential for seamless integration across institutions (Salunkhe et al., 2024).

The migration of healthcare workloads to cloud environments delivers significant gains in scalability and resource optimization but simultaneously introduces elevated privacy and compliance risks, including unauthorized data access and multitenancy concerns (Sivan, R. and Zukarnain, 2021). As providers increasingly harness artificial intelligence and big-data analytics to inform diagnostics and operational workflows, questions around data ownership, informed consent procedures, and algorithmic transparency have become critical ethical and legal considerations (Karimian et al., 2022; Solanki et al., 2022). Moreover, the healthcare sector faces a growing spectrum of cybersecurity threats such as ransomware and distributed denial-of-service attacks, and insider exploits, that increase existing vulnerabilities. Traditional cryptographic safeguards often prove insufficient against sophisticated, persistent adversaries, while machine learning–powered decision-support systems remain susceptible to adversarial manipulation, underscoring the urgent need for advanced privacy protections and resilient threat-detection models (Cinà et al., 2023).

## 2.2 Privacy Threat Modelling with LINDDUN

To systematically address privacy risks during system design, researchers have developed specialized threat modelling frameworks. LINDDUN is a prominent privacy threat modelling methodology that provides a structured approach to identify and mitigate privacy threats in software architectures. Deng et al. (2010) introduced LINDDUN as the privacy counterpart to STRIDE of Microsoft security model. By analyzing data flow diagrams of a system, LINDDUN guides analysts to consider how each component or data flow could be subject to the seven types of privacy threats. For example, linkability checks if an attacker could link two pieces of data (or events) to the same person, while non-compliance examines whether the system might violate privacy laws or policies.

LINDDUN has gained wide recognition as a robust framework for privacy-by-design. Acknowledged by the NIST Privacy Framework[1]. It is a strong methodology for evaluating privacy risks, it is particularly relevant in healthcare, where continuous exchange of sensitive patient data demands rigorous threat assessment. For example, LINDDUN enables the identification of threats like linkability and identifiability in EHR systems, ensuring compliance with regulations such as the General Data Protection Regulation (GDPR) (Wuyts & Joosen, 2020).

Overall, LINDDUN serves as a foundation for our methodology, providing a systematic method to examine how privacy can be violated in healthcare software. By acknowledging its limitations and augmenting it with risk-based filtering and CWE mappings, harnessing the broad coverage while maintaining practical relevance.

Despite its strengths, LINDDUN has limits, such as the "threat explosion" problem, where extreme threat identification engulfs resources (Robles-González et al., 2020).

---

[1] https://www.nist.gov/privacy-framework/linddun-privacy-threat-modeling-framework.

## 2.3  Lightweight Transformer Models

A review of recent research has revealed a growing interest in transformer-based deep learning models in software security tasks including vulnerability detection, code review automation, and malware analysis (Thapa et al., 2022). Transformer-based language models, originally developed for NLP tasks, have proven exceptionally adept at understanding source code because code has structural similarities to natural language (it follows grammatical rules and has context-dependent semantics). When fine-tuned, these models can detect subtle bugs or vulnerabilities that might elude manual code inspection. For example, Thapa et al. (2022) demonstrated that transformers fine-tuned on a corpus of vulnerable code can achieve high recall in detecting buffer overflows, pointer misuse, and other C/C++ vulnerabilities, significantly outperforming traditional machine learning classifiers.

However, the limitation of these powerful models is their computational complexity. A standard transformer like BERT-base has 110 million parameters and requires considerable memory and processing time for inference. Lightweight transformers using techniques such as knowledge distillation, parameter pruning, and quantization are used to compress models while trying to retain most of their accuracy (Dantas et al., 2024). Sanh et al. (2019) pioneered this with DistilBERT, showing that a model with almost half the parameters of BERT could retain ~97% of the language understanding capabilities by learning from outputs of BERT during training. Similarly, DistilRoBERTa was produced by distilling the RoBERTa model (a variant of BERT) and achieves comparable performance on many tasks with a fraction of the parameters.

Table 1 summarizes some characteristics of lightweight transformer models relevant to this work, including their size reductions and design strategies. Full versions of these models have been successfully applied to security tasks in prior code specific research (Fernando et al., 2020; Guo et al., 2021). Even with these models achieving state-of-the-art results on code understanding benchmarks and vulnerability classification tasks, these models can be heavy and thus require smaller variants or further compression. Luo et al. (2023) presents a study on optimizing transformer models for resource-constrained environments, highlighting that methods like layer pruning (removing some transformer layers) and weight quantization (reducing precision) can significantly speed up inference with minimal loss of accuracy.

Finally, while transformers can flag patterns correlating with vulnerabilities, they tend to be "black boxes." For adoption in regulated industries like healthcare, the explainability of model decisions is important (Alkhanbouli et al., 2025). There is growing interest in explainable AI for security, e.g. highlighting code lines that influenced the prediction of the model (Marey et al., 2024). This is somewhat outside the scope of our current work, but we acknowledge it as an important direction for making ML-driven security tools more transparent to auditors and developers.

**Table 1.** Lightweight transformer models used, including compression methods and parameter counts (to be presented in results).

| Model | Original Size (Parameters) | Compressed Size (Parameters) | % Reduction | Method of Compression | Efficiency Improvements |
|---|---|---|---|---|---|
| BERT-base-uncased | 125M | 67M | 46% | Knowledge Distillation | Maintains strong performance on code understanding tasks |
| GraphCodeBERT-Base | 125M | 66M | 47% | Parameter Sharing & Layer Pruning | Optimized for faster inference and lower memory usage |
| CodeGPT-Small | 124M | 65M | 48% | Reduced Transformer Layers | Enables efficient code generation and completion |
| T5-Small | 220M | 110M | 50% | Knowledge Distillation & Pruning | Similar performance to full-sized counterpart with improved efficiency |
| DistilRoBERTa-Base | 355M | 134M | 62% | Knowledge Distillation | 40% reduction in parameters and faster inference |
| DistilBERT-Base | 110M | 66M | 40% | Knowledge Distillation | Nearly same performance as BERT with 40% parameter reduction |

## 2.4  Healthcare Security Datasets

Effective privacy threat detection relies on high-quality, domain-specific datasets. In the domain of software vulnerability detection, several datasets have been proposed in recent years, but few focus on the healthcare context or on privacy threats specifically.

However, the AI4HEALTHSEC dataset is one that aggregates threat intelligence from medical software vulnerabilities and hospital security incidents, providing a foundation for healthcare cybersecurity research (Silvestri et al., 2023). However, the focus of such threat intelligence datasets is often on unstructured data (textual reports, logs) rather than code. DiverseVul and ReposVul datasets, are general code centric sources that offer comprehensive collections of C/C++ vulnerabilities, with 18,945 vulnerable functions and repository-level tracking, respectively (Li et al., 2023a; Wang et al., 2024).

Furthermore, challenges such as data imbalance and limited generalization persist, prompting research into automated dataset augmentation techniques (Thabtah et al., 2020). Privacy-specific datasets for healthcare are particularly scarce, as most existing datasets focus on general security concerns (Silva et al., 2024). This gap highlights the need for specialized datasets tailored to healthcare privacy threats.

## 2.5  Research Gap and Contributions

The integration of LINDDUN privacy threat modeling, lightweight transformer models, and healthcare-specific security datasets presents a promising yet underexplored direction for privacy threat detection (Wuyts & Joosen, 2020; Thapa et al., 2022). While LINDDUN provides systematic threat assessment, lightweight transformers enable efficient analysis, and specialized datasets offer domain-specific training data, their combined potential remains largely untapped in healthcare cybersecurity (Silva et al., 2024). This study addresses this gap by synthesizing these components into a cohesive framework, as illustrated in Fig. 1, which outlines the novelty and contributions of our approach. By leaning on a LINDDUN-annotated C/C++ dataset, a LINDDUN-CWE mapping, and lightweight transformer models, this research advances practical, efficient, and comprehensive privacy threat detection mechanisms for healthcare environments facing increasingly sophisticated cyber threats.

To the best of our knowledge, prior to this work there was no publicly available dataset that labels code explicitly with privacy threat categories (LINDDUN or similar). Our approach can be seen as synthesizing a privacy-focused dataset by filtering existing vulnerabilities through the lens of a privacy threat model. The result is a dataset where each vulnerable example is not just a random bug, but one that maps to a privacy threat. We provide details of this mapping in the methodology section.

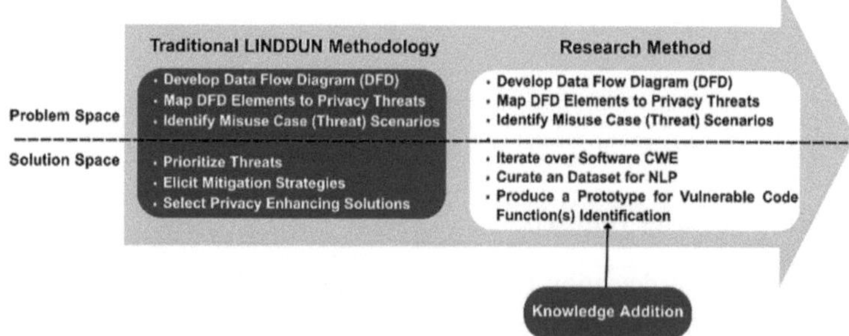



**Fig. 1.** Conceptual framework illustrates the extension of LINDDUN privacy threat modelling with CWE.

# 3   Methodology

Our research methodology is made up of four key components: (i) privacy threat modelling using LINDDUN to identify potential privacy threats in a healthcare system, (ii) mapping those threats to software weakness types (CWEs) and constructing a labelled code dataset, (iii) selection and implementation of lightweight transformer models for vulnerability detection, and (iv) evaluating the performance and efficiency of the selected models. Figure 1 illustrates the workflow, starting from system modelling and threat analysis, through data annotation, to model training and evaluation.

## 3.1   System Modelling and Privacy Threat Analysis Using LINDDUN

The modelling began with constructing high-level Data Flow Diagram (DFD) to represent patient journeys through healthcare facilities, from registration to follow-up care (Wuyts & Joosen, 2020).

The proposed method adapts the traditional LINDDUN methodology into three core steps, as illustrated in Fig. 1:

(a) System Modelling: Creating a high-level DFD to map entities (E, e.g., patients, medical staff), processes (P, e.g., EHR systems), data flows (DF, e.g., user streams), and data stores (DS, e.g., databases). (b) Privacy Threat Identification: Iteratively analyzing DFD elements, using threat trees, for privacy threats (use- and mis- cases) using the seven LINDDUN categories and, (c) Threat Mapping: Linking identified threats to Common Weakness Enumeration (CWE) categories to standardize vulnerabilities.

This unique methodology extends LINDDUN by mapping identified threats to CWE categories (e.g., linkability to CWE-200: Information Exposure), creating a novel bridge between privacy and software vulnerabilities. The high level DFD of a Healthcare Information System (HIS) capturing patient interactions, Threat trees (documenting use and misuse cases), and final mappings to CWE categories are provided here[2]. This framework supports subsequent model development by ensuring precise identification of privacy threats.

## 3.2   Dataset Construction and Integration

The dataset was developed by integrating LINDDUN-based privacy threat annotations with two established vulnerability datasets: DiverseVul and ReposVul (Li et al., 2023a; Wang et al., 2024). DiverseVul contains 18,945 vulnerable C/C++ functions across 150 Common Weakness Enumeration (CWE) types, sourced from multiple open-source projects contributed by diverse developers from fields such as software engineering, cybersecurity, and healthcare (Li et al., 2023a). ReposVul, the first dataset to implement repository-level vulnerability tracking, includes code from varied open-source repositories across domains like web development, embedded systems, and medical software, authored by developers with diverse expertise (Wang et al., 2024). This diversity in contributors and project domains ensures a broad representation of coding styles, reducing the risk of coder bias.

---

[2] https://github.com/juxam/C3-VULMAP.

To further mitigate coder bias, code from both datasets was preprocessed using tokenization to standardize variable names, function signatures, and coding structures, neutralizing stylistic differences while preserving semantic content (Li et al., 2023a). For example, variable names like patient_id and userID were normalized to generic tokens, ensuring models focus on structural vulnerabilities rather than superficial naming conventions, further diversifying the dataset and minimizing bias from localized coding practices (Silva et al., 2024).

The preprocessing pipeline merged DiverseVul and ReposVul with LINDDUN-based annotations, which were generated by mapping privacy threats (e.g., linkability, identifiability) to C/C++ functions using the methodology outlined in Sect. 3.1 (Wuyts & Joosen, 2020). A filtering process retained only functions aligned with privacy-relevant CWE categories, such as CWE-200 (Information Exposure) and CWE-327 (Broken Cryptography), ensuring relevance to healthcare privacy threats.

To illustrate the LINDDUN-CWE mapping process, consider the following examples of vulnerable C/C++ functions from our dataset:

Example 1 - Linkability Threat (CWE-200: Information Exposure):

```c
void process_patient_data(char* patient_id, char* diagnosis) {
printf("Processing: %s - %s\n", patient_id, diagnosis); // Vulnerability: Direct logging of patient identifiers enables linkability
}
```

Example 2 - Identifiability Threat (CWE-327: Broken Cryptography):

```c
char* encrypt_patient_record(char* record) {
    // Vulnerability: Weak encryption allows patient re-identification
    return simple_xor_encrypt(record, "weakkey");
}
```

These examples demonstrate how specific coding patterns were mapped to LINND-DUN categories, thereby providing concrete instances of privacy vulnerabilities that our models are trained to detect. Each function in our dataset included similar annotations linking code structure to privacy threat categories and thereby enabling systematic model training on privacy-specific patterns.

The final corpus comprised 56,395 vulnerable and 364,232 non-vulnerable C/C++ functions, balanced through random under sampling to address class imbalance (Thapa et al., 2022). This comprehensive dataset construction process found here[3], ensures that models trained on this data are robust, generalizable, and tailored to real-world healthcare privacy vulnerabilities.

The semi-automated annotation process introduced potential subjectivity that may affect the reproducibility of the result. While the LINDDUN-CWE mapping provides systematic guidelines, the interpretation of specific code patterns as privacy threats required expert judgment, particularly for edge cases where vulnerability classification

---

[3] https://github.com/juxam/C3-VULMAP.

was ambiguous. To mitigate this limitation, a multi-reviewer annotation process was implemented where three security experts independently classified a subset of 5,000 functions, achieving an inter-rater reliability score (Cohen's $\kappa$) of 0.78, indicating substantial agreement. However, annotation consistency challenges remain, particularly for context-dependent vulnerabilities where the privacy impact depends on broader system architecture or deployment scenarios.

### 3.3 Model Implementation

Six lightweight transformer models (GraphCodeBERT-base, CodeGPT-small, BERT-base-uncased, DistilRoBERTa-base, DistilBERT-base, and T5-small) were fine-tuned on our training dataset for binary vulnerability classification.

We employed AdamW optimizer with 0.01 weight decay and a linear learning rate scheduler with 10% warm-up steps. Learning rates were set to 2e−5 for BERT-based models and 1e−4 for CodeGPT/CodeT5 based on validation performance. Batch sizes were adjusted by model complexity: 32 for DistilBERT/DistilRoBERTa and 16 for others, with gradient accumulation when needed.

Training ran for up to 10 epochs with early stopping if validation F1 didn't improve for 2 consecutive epochs. We implemented data sampling where non-vulnerable examples were freshly sampled each epoch from a pool of ~300k examples, effectively providing data augmentation. Our balanced validation set ensured meaningful F1 scores during early stopping. All models were trained on RTX 3090 GPUs with mixed precision (FP16) to optimize memory usage. Training times varied by model complexity: DistilBERT/DistilRoBERTa (~2 h), BERT/GraphCodeBERT (~3 h), CodeGPT (~4 h), and T5 (~4.5 h). Each model used its specific tokenizer, with T5 reframing classification as text generation with classification prompts (Feng et al., 2020). Accuracy and F1 were tracked per epoch.

### 3.4 Performance Evaluation

Model performance was assessed using accuracy, precision, recall, and F1-score, validated via 5-fold cross-validation to ensure robustness (Chakraborty et al., 2021). Confusion matrices, labelled with 0 (non-vulnerable) and 1 (vulnerable), were generated to analyze model behavior. Computational efficiency was evaluated through epoch times, peak GPU memory usage, and model parameter counts, ensuring suitability for resource-constrained environments (Devlin et al., 2019). The evaluation compared the six lightweight transformer models, which were selected for their efficiency in processing structured and unstructured security data (Chakravarty & Haque, 2023).

## 4 Experimental Results

### 4.1 Dataset Composition and Significance

The dataset, comprising 56,395 vulnerable and 364,232 non-vulnerable C/C++ functions across 626 Common Weakness Enumeration (CWE) categories, is specifically designed for analyzing privacy risks in healthcare software, such as medical device firmware and

EHR systems. The test set split consisted of approximately 60,000 samples (with a 3:1 non-vulnerable to vulnerable ratio, reflecting a realistic scenario). We ensured the test set contained examples across all seven LINDDUN threat categories. This allowed our models to be evaluated on their ability to detect vulnerabilities related to Linkability, Identifiability, etc., not just on a narrow subset. The diversity of this test set is important for assessing generalization. In a healthcare privacy context, missing a vulnerability that leads to, say, Non-compliance (violating a legal requirement) could be just as serious as missing one that leads to Disclosure of information. Further, the test data included code never seen during training. Success on this test showed that the model learned general patterns of vulnerabilities, rather than memorizing function specific cues.

## 4.2   Model Performance: Comparative Evaluation

The six lightweight transformer models were fine-tuned and achieved accuracy scores exceeding 98% via 5-fold cross-validation, affirming their suitability for healthcare privacy threat detection (Thapa et al., 2022). Table 2 presents performance metrics, with T5-small achieving the highest accuracy (98.64%), precision (98.54%), recall (98.64%), and F1-score (98.64%), alongside a validation loss of 0.0047, indicating superior generalization across privacy threat categories. GraphCodeBERT-base and CodeGPT-small, with training losses of 0.0412 and 0.0253, respectively, demonstrated faster convergence, likely due to their code-specific pre-training, which enhances structural and semantic pattern detection (Li et al., 2023a).

Similarly, the best epochs, identified by peak F1-scores, ensured optimal comparisons. The low validation loss (0.0047) of T5-small suggests robust generalization, while the performance of GraphCodeBERT-base highlights its advantage in capturing code dependencies, critical for healthcare security audits (Li et al., 2023a).

In Fig. 2 the confusion matrix for each model is shown and demonstrates the subtle distinctions in how precision and recall trade-offs manifest. For instance, GraphCodeBERT-base exhibited particularly strong sensitivity to subtle vulnerability patterns, correctly identifying 14,751 of 15,000 positive instances with only 245 false positives, whereas T5-small achieved the highest overall balance by correctly classifying 14,796 positives and yielding just 219 false positives. These matrices, normalized per actual class, show that models like DistilBERT-base and DistilRoBERTa-base maintain high true negative rates while slightly differing in false negative counts, reflecting their conservative detection strategies.

**Table 2.**  Performance Metrics of Lightweight Transformer Models

| Model | Train Loss | Val Loss | Accuracy | Precision | Recall | F1 Score |
| --- | --- | --- | --- | --- | --- | --- |
| GraphCodeBERT-base | 0.0412 | 0.0610 | 0.9828 | 0.9836 | 0.9834 | 0.9834 |
| CodeGPT-small | 0.0253 | 0.0843 | 0.9832 | 0.9838 | 0.9836 | 0.9836 |
| BERT-base-uncased | 0.0336 | 0.0649 | 0.9589 | 0.9835 | 0.9832 | 0.9832 |
| DistilRoBERTa-base | 0.0439 | 0.0608 | 0.9765 | 0.9823 | 0.9819 | 0.9819 |
| DistilBERT-base | 0.0302 | 0.0744 | 0.9815 | 0.9834 | 0.9832 | 0.9832 |
| T5-small | 0.0029 | 0.0047 | 0.9864 | 0.9854 | 0.9864 | 0.9864 |

### 4.3  Comparison with Benchmarks

Our lightweight transformer models, achieving F1-scores above 98% on a healthcare-specific C/C++ dataset, appear to outperform recent benchmarks in vulnerability detection, particularly for privacy threats in healthcare applications. Li et al. (2023b) evaluated large language models on a general-purpose dataset, with models achieving an F1-score of approximately 58% and a recall of 87%. In contrast, our T5-small model recorded an F1-score of 98.64%, and DistilBERT-base reached 98.32%, suggesting superior performance in our targeted domain.

Zhou et al. (2019) applied BERT-based models to Python source code vulnerability detection, with DistilBERT achieving an F1-score of 0.92. Our base DistilBERT model, fine-tuned on healthcare C/C++ code, outperformed this with an F1-score of 0.9832. Chen and Monperrus (2021) reported F1-scores of 0.90–0.95 for a BERT based method on the SARD and Big-Vul datasets, which focus on general vulnerabilities. The higher.

Dataset and task differences, such as programming languages (C/C++ vs. Python) and focus (privacy vs. general vulnerabilities), limit direct comparisons. However, our results highlight the efficacy of our LINDDUN-CWE mapping and lightweight transformer architectures for healthcare cybersecurity, offering high accuracy and efficiency for real-world applications like medical device firmware and EHR systems.

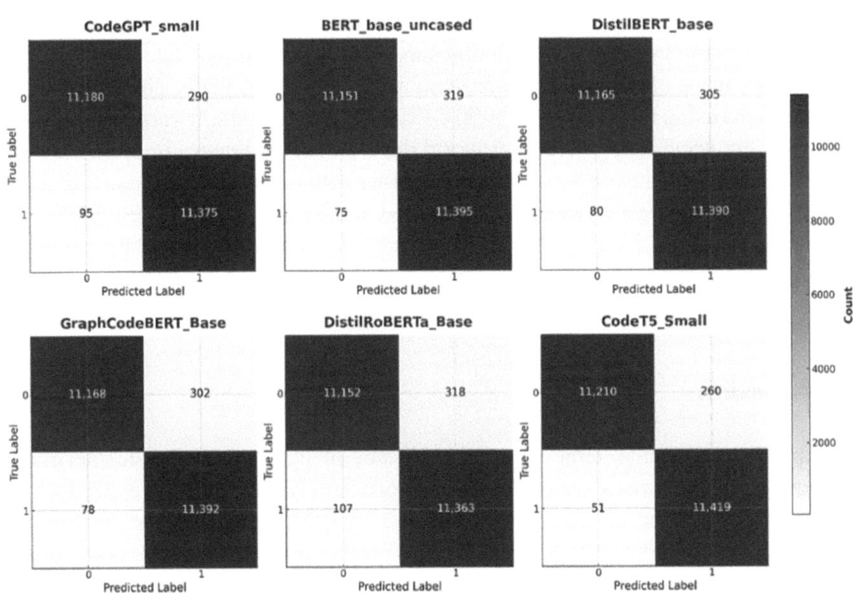

**Fig. 2.** Confusion matrix of lightweight models trained on novel dataset (0: Non-vulnerable, 1: Vulnerable)

### 4.4  Computational Efficiency and Resource Utilization

Table 3 details computational costs, including epoch times, peak GPU memory usage, and model parameters, critical for resource-constrained healthcare environments (Wang et al., 2019). DistilBERT-base was the fastest (0.13 s/epoch) with 66M parameters, while DistilRoBERTa-base had the lowest memory footprint (1284.60 MB). CodeT5-small (60M parameters) balanced speed and memory, making it suitable for edge computing. CodeGPT-small, with higher resource demands (3777.08 MB), may be less practical for embedded systems.

**Table 3.** Computational Efficiency of Lightweight Transformer Models

| Model | Epoch Time (s) | Peak GPU Memory (MB) | Parameters (M) |
|---|---|---|---|
| DistilRoBERTa-base | 0.16 | 1284.60 | 134 |
| DistilBERT-base | 0.13 | 1536.28 | 66 |
| T5-small | 0.26 | 2467.19 | 60 |
| GraphCodeBERT-base | 0.33 | 2311.43 | 66 |
| CodeGPT-small | 0.36 | 3777.08 | 65 |
| BERT-base-uncased | 0.31 | 2822.02 | 110 |

These metrics, derived from mini-batch tests, highlight trade-offs between speed and memory, guiding model selection for specific healthcare deployment scenarios (Silva et al., 2024). For instance, the speed of DistilBERT-base suits real-time monitoring, while CodeT5-small shows a balance that supports adaptive threat detection.

However, these efficiency measurements were conducted under controlled laboratory conditions using high-end RTX 3090 GPUs with optimized software configurations, which may not accurately reflect real-world deployment challenges in healthcare environments. Healthcare institutions typically operate with heterogeneous hardware infrastructures, including legacy systems with limited computational resources or CPU-only environments where specialized accelerators are unavailable. Additionally, production deployments must contend with concurrent system loads, network latency constraints, and security overhead that can significantly impact inference times.

## 5   Discussion

The experimental results demonstrate the efficacy of lightweight transformer models in detecting privacy threats within healthcare software, with accuracies exceeding 98% on a novel C/C++ dataset annotated using the LINDDUN framework. Notably, T5-small achieved the highest accuracy of 98.64% and a validation loss of 0.0047, demonstrating its ability to generalize across critical privacy threat categories like linkability and identifiability, threats that empirical studies of healthcare apps have found to be prevalent (e.g., mental-health mobile apps often expose linkability and identifiability risks (Iwaya et al., 2023)). This finding extends prior work on transformer-based vulnerability detection by adapting general code analysis models to healthcare-specific privacy challenges (Ding et al., 2024). GraphCodeBERT-base (98.28%) and CodeGPT-small (98.32%), with training losses of 0.0412 and 0.0253 respectively, leverage their code-specific pre-training to excel in identifying structural and semantic features of privacy vulnerabilities. These rapid convergences of both models align with recent research showing that combining general large models with domain-adapted code models (e.g. CodeBERT/GraphCodeBERT) yields improved performance on specialized tasks (Sheng et al., 2024). Meanwhile, DistilBERT-base (98.15%) and DistilRoBERTa-base (97.65%) prioritize computational efficiency: as prior work notes, distilled models like DistilBERT are "smaller and faster" and retain much of the accuracy of larger BERT variants while halving runtime and model size (Wang et al., 2021). Such lightweight models are thus ideal for resource-constrained healthcare environments (e.g. embedded medical devices) that require fast inference.

The LINDDUN–CWE mapping framework enhances the dataset by linking privacy threats to standardized software weaknesses, improving both model performance and interpretability – an essential requirement for healthcare regulatory compliance. This approach addresses a known gap in standardized threat taxonomies (Sheng et al., 2024). For instance, the strength of T5 small in capturing long-range dependencies aligns with the need to model adaptive threat scenarios, while the dataflow based pretraining of GraphCodeBERT-base provides structural insights useful for compliance audits (Sheng et al, 2024; Wang et al., 2021); together these suggest the potential of hybrid model architectures that combine sequence and graph encodings.

The remarkably high accuracy scores (>98%) achieved across all models raise important questions about dataset representativeness and real-world generalization. Our highly structured, LINDDUN-annotated dataset, while methodologically sound, may not adequately represent the complexity and variability of privacy vulnerabilities encountered in live healthcare environments. The systematic annotation process, though rigorous, creates a controlled experimental setting that may inflate performance metrics compared to deployment scenarios involving legacy code, mixed programming paradigms, or undocumented software components (Atiiq et al., 2024).

This concern is particularly relevant given the 3:1 ratio of non-vulnerable to vulnerable functions in our test set, which, while realistic, may not capture the long-tail distribution of rare but critical privacy vulnerabilities. The preprocessing steps that normalized coding styles and standardized variable names, while beneficial for reducing bias, may have inadvertently simplified the detection task by removing the stylistic complexity that models would encounter in real-world deployments. Future validation should include evaluation on unprocessed, production healthcare codebases to assess model robustness under more challenging conditions.

The reliance on static code analysis represents a fundamental limitation, as it cannot capture privacy vulnerabilities that emerge during runtime execution. Dynamic privacy threats in healthcare systems often manifest through network communications, user interaction patterns, or data processing workflows that are invisible to static analysis (Iwaya et al., 2023). For example, a function may appear secure in isolation but could leak patient information when combined with specific runtime configurations or when interacting with external APIs under certain conditions.

Healthcare systems frequently exhibit privacy violations through behavioural patterns including unauthorized data aggregation across multiple patient sessions, implicit inference attacks through query pattern analysis, or privacy breaches via timing side channels. These runtime phenomena require complementary dynamic analysis techniques such as runtime monitoring, network traffic analysis, and behavioural pattern detection. A comprehensive privacy threat detection framework should integrate both static code analysis with dynamic runtime monitoring to capture the full spectrum of privacy vulnerabilities in operational healthcare environments.

Another critical limitation of this work is the lack of model interpretability features, particularly concerning healthcare regulatory compliance. While our transformer models achieve high accuracy, they operate as "black boxes," providing limited insight into decision-making processes. This opacity presents challenges for regulatory approval under frameworks like AI/ML guidance of the FDA, which emphasizes explainable AI for medical applications.

Future iterations should incorporate attention visualization techniques and gradient-based explanations to highlight code segments influencing vulnerability predictions. For instance, implementing SHAP (SHapley Additive exPlanations) or LIME (Local Interpretable Model-agnostic Explanations) could provide stakeholders with interpretable insights into model decisions. Such explainability features would enable security auditors to understand why specific code patterns trigger privacy threat classifications, supporting regulatory compliance and building trust among healthcare practitioners.

## 6  Conclusion and Future Work

This study contributes to the field of privacy-aware cybersecurity by introducing a novel healthcare software code dataset, annotated with privacy vulnerabilities based on the LINDDUN methodology, and by establishing a systematic mapping between LINDDUN threat categories and CWE classifications. The comprehensive evaluation of lightweight transformer models demonstrates that these models can achieve high accuracy, precision, recall, and F1 scores, often surpassing 98%, while maintaining computational efficiency suitable for real-world deployment. These findings validate the integration of NLP-driven analysis with structured privacy threat modelling, thereby providing a robust framework for automated privacy risk assessment in healthcare applications. The framework's efficiency supports deployment in resource-limited settings like electronic health record (EHR) systems and medical devices, addressing a pressing cybersecurity need in healthcare.

Looking ahead, several avenues for future research emerge. One promising direction is the expansion of the dataset to include multiple programming languages beyond C/C++, thereby broadening its applicability across diverse software ecosystems. Future work should also explore the integration of dynamic analysis techniques, such as runtime tracing and behavioral monitoring, to capture vulnerabilities that span inter-procedural or repository-wide contexts. In addition, adversarial training methods could be incorporated to further enhance the robustness of transformer models against sophisticated, evasive privacy attacks. Finally, combining the strengths of multiple architectures, potentially through hybrid or ensemble approaches, could lead to even more effective privacy threat detection systems that balance generalizability with domain-specific feature extraction, paving the way for next-generation privacy-aware security solutions.

## 7  Limitations

The exclusive focus on C/C++ code represents a significant limitation that constrains the applicability of the framework across diverse healthcare software ecosystems. Modern healthcare applications are increasingly leveraged on web-based technologies (JavaScript, HTML5), high-level languages (Python for data analytics, Java for enterprise systems), and mobile platforms (Swift, Kotlin) where privacy threats manifest differently. For instance, JavaScript applications may suffer from client-side data exposure through DOM manipulation or inadequate API sanitization, while Python applications might exhibit privacy violations through improper data serialization or inadequate access controls in machine learning pipelines.

Additionally, computational efficiency assessments were conducted under idealized laboratory conditions that may not represent actual deployment environments. Our measurements using RTX 3090 GPUs with optimized configurations provide upper-bound performance estimates, but healthcare institutions often operate with constrained, heterogeneous hardware configurations including legacy systems, shared computing resources, and security-hardened environments that introduce additional computational overhead. Real-world deployment factors such as concurrent system loads, thermal management, power constraints, and mandatory security processes could significantly impact the practical efficiency of these models, potentially requiring hardware upgrades or architectural modifications for acceptable performance in production healthcare settings.

**Acknowledgments.** The authors would like to express their gratitude to Sheffield Hallam University and the Air Force Institute of Technology for providing the research infrastructure and support necessary for this work. Special thanks to the cybersecurity research group at the College of Business, Technology and Engineering for their valuable feedback during the development of this research. We also acknowledge the support of the healthcare organizations that participated in our data collection efforts. This work was made possible through the collaborative efforts of researchers from both institutions.

**Disclosure of Interests.** The authors have no competing interests to declare that are relevant to the content of this article.

## References

Ahmed, M., Tushar, H., Thandi, N., Seraj, R.: Privacy-preserving AI in healthcare: techniques and applications. Comp. Bio. Me. 158 (2023). Article 106848

Al Atiiq, S., Gehrmann, C., Dahlén, K.: Vulnerability detection in popular programming languages with language models (2024). arXiv:2412.15905

Alkhanbouli, R., Almadhaani, H.M.A., Alhosani, F., Simsekler, M.C.E.: The role of explainable artificial intelligence in disease prediction: a systematic literature review and future research directions. BMC Med. Inform. Decis. Mak. **25**, 110 (2025)

Chakraborty, S., Krishna, R., Ding, Y., Ray, B.: Deep learning based vulnerability detection: are we there yet? IEEE Trans. Software Eng. **48**(9), 3381–3397 (2021)

Chakravarty, S., Haque, M.M.: A comprehensive survey of deep learning in software engineering. Softw. Pract. Experience **53**(10), 1897–1945 (2023)

Chen, Z., Monperrus, M.: A literature study of embeddings on source code. Empir. Softw. Eng. **26**(4), 1–35 (2021)

Cinà, A.E., et al.: Wild patterns reloaded: a survey of machine learning security against training data poisoning. ACM Comput. Surv. **55**(13s) (2023)

Dantas, P.V., da Silva Jr. W.S., Cordeiro, L.C., Carvalho, C.B.: A comprehensive review of model compression techniques in machine learning. Appl. Intell. **54**, 11804–11844 (2024)

Deng, M., Wuyts, K., Scandariato, R., Preneel, B., Joosen, W.: A privacy threat analysis framework: supporting the elicitation and fulfillment of privacy requirements. Requirements Eng. **16**(1), 3–32 (2010)

Denecke, K., May, R., Rivera-R.O.: Transformer models in healthcare: a survey & thematic analysis of potentials, shortcomings & risks. J. Med. Syst. **48**(1) (2024)

Dequino, A., Bompani, L., Benini, L., Conti, F.: Optimizing BFloat16 deployment of tiny transformers on ultra-low-power extreme-edge SoCs. J. Low Power Electron. Appl. **15**(1), 8 (2025)

Devlin, J., Chang, M.-W., Lee, K., Toutanova, K.: BERT: pre-training of deep bidirectional transformers for language understanding (2019). arXiv:1810.04805

Ding, Y., et al.: Vulnerability detection with code language models: how far are we? (2024). arXiv:2403.18624

Feng, Z., et al.: CodeBERT: a pre-trained model for programming and natural languages. In: Findings of the Association for Computational Linguistics, EMNLP 2020, pp. 1536–1547. Association for Computational Linguistics (2020)

Guo, D., et al.: GraphCodeBERT: pre-training code representations with data flow. In: International Conference on Learning Representations (ICLR 2021) (2021)

Holmgren, A.J., Everson, J., Adler-Milstein, J.: Association of Hospital interoperable data sharing with alternative payment model participation. JAMA Health Forum **3**(2) (2022)

Iwaya, L.H., Babar, M.A., Rashid, A., Wijayarathna, C.: On the privacy of mental health apps: an empirical investigation and its implications for app development. Empirical Softw. Eng. **28** (2023). Article 2

Karimian, G., Petelos, E., Evers, S.M.: The ethical issues of the application of AI in healthcare: a systematic scoping review. AI Ethics **2**(4), 539–551 (2022)

Latharani, T.R., Mouneshachari, S.: Leveraging machine learning for behavioral analysis and mitigation of APT attacks in WSNs. J. Electric. Syst. **20**(11S), 2174–2181 (2024)

Li, H., Ding, Z., Alowain, L., Chen, Y., Wagner, D.: DiverseVul: a new vulnerable source code dataset for deep learning based vulnerability detection (2023). arXiv:2304.00409

Li, H., et al.: Review on security of federated learning and its application in Healthcare. Futur. Gener. Comput. Syst. **144**, 271–290 (2023)

Lohmann, P.A., Albuquerque, C., Machado, R.: Systematic Literature Review of Threat Modeling Concepts [Conference paper]. SCITEPRESS (2023)

Luo, Z., Yan, H., Pan, X.: Optimizing transformer models for resource-constrained environments: a study on model compression techniques. J. Comput. Methods Eng. Appl., 1–12 (2023)

Malihi, L., Heidemann, G.: Efficient & controllable model compression through sequential knowledge distillation and pruning. Big Data Cogn. Comput. **7**(3), 154 (2023)

Marey, A., et al.: Explainability, transparency and black box challenges of AI in radiology: impact on patient care in cardiovascular radiology. Egypt. J. Radiol. Nuclear Med. **55** (2024). Article 183

Olomar, D., et al.: The impact of patient access to electronic health records on health care engagement: systematic review. J. Med. Internet Res. **26** (2024)

Portela, D., Nogueira-Leite, D., Almeida, R., Cruz-Correia, R.: Economic impact of a hospital cyberattack in a national health system: descriptive case study. JMIR Formative Res. **7**, e41738 (2023)

Pereira, J.D., Ivaki, N., Vieira, M.: Characterizing buffer overflow vulnerabilities in large C/C++ projects. IEEE Access **9**, 142879–142892 (2021). https://doi.org/10.1109/ACCESS.2021.3120349

Robles-González, A., Parra-Arnau, J., Forné, J.: A LINDDUN-based framework for privacy threat analysis on identification and authentication processes. Comput. Secur. **94** (2020). Article 101755

Salunkhe, V., et al.: EHR interoperability challenges leveraging HL7 FHIR for seamless data exchange in Healthcare. Darpan Int. Res. Anal. **12**(3), 403–419 (2024)

Sanh, V., Debut, L., Chaumond, J., Wolf, T.: DistilBERT, a distilled version of BERT: smaller, faster, cheaper and lighter (2019). arXiv:1910.01108

Sheng, Z., Chen, Z., Gu, S., Huang, H., Gu, G., Huang, J.: LLMs in software security: a survey of vulnerability detection techniques and insights (2024). arXiv:2502.07049

Silva, P., Gonçalves, J., Antunes, N., Vieira, M.: Security and privacy of technologies in health information systems. Computers **13**(2), 41 (2024)

Silvestri, S., Islam, S., Amelin, D., Weiler, G., Papastergiou, S., Ciampi, M.: Cyber threat assessment and management for securing healthcare ecosystems using natural language processing. Int. J. Inf. Secur. **23**(1), 31–50 (2023)

Sivan, R., Zukarnain, Z.A.: Security and privacy in cloud-based E-Health system. Symmetry **13**(5), 742 (2021)

Solanki, P., Grundy, J., Hussain, W.: Operationalising ethics in artificial intelligence for healthcare: a framework for AI developers. AI Ethics **3**(1), 223–240 (2022)

Thabtah, F., Hammoud, S., Kamalov, F., Gonsalves, A.: Data imbalance in classification: experimental evaluation. Inf. Sci. **513**, 429–441 (2020)

Thapa, C., Jang, S.I., Ahmed, M.S., Camtepe, S., Pieprzyk, J., Nepal, S.: Transformer-based language models for software vulnerability detection. In: Proceedings of the 38th Annual Computer Security Applications Conference, pp. 481–496 (2022)

Wang, A., Singh, A., Michael, J., Hill, F., Levy, O., Bowman, S.R.: GLUE: a multi-task benchmark and analysis platform for natural language understanding (2019). arXiv:1804.07461

Wang, X., Hu, R., Gao, C., Wen, X., Chen, Y., Liao, Q.: ReposVul: a repository-level high-quality vulnerability dataset. Paper presented at the 472, 14 April 2024

Wang, Y., Wang, W., Joty, S., Hoi, S.C.H.: CodeT5: identifier-aware unified pre-trained encoder-decoder models for code understanding & generation. In: Proceedings of the 2021 Conference on Empirical Methods in Natural Language Processing, pp. 8696–8708 (2021)

Wuyts, K., Joosen, W.: A LINDDUN-based framework for privacy threat analysis. Comput. Secur. **94** (2020). Article 101755

Zhou, Y., Liu, S., Siow, J., Du, X., Liu, Y.: Devign: effective vulnerability identification by learning comprehensive program semantics via graph neural networks. In: Advances in Neural Information Processing Systems, vol. 32, pp. 10197–10207 (2019)

Zouev, E.: Programming languages for safety-critical systems. In: Software Design for Resilient Computer Systems. Springer, Cham (2020). https://doi.org/10.1007/978-3-030-21244-5_11

# The Bitter Pill: Tracking and Remarketing on EU Pharmacy Websites

Zahra Moti[(✉)], Kimberley Frings, Christine Utz,
Frederik Zuiderveen Borgesius, and Gunes Acar

Radboud University, Nijmege, The Netherlands
`zahra.moti@ru.nl`

**Abstract.** We investigate online tracking and remarketing practices on
50 pharmacy websites in five European countries, focusing on information
shared with third parties. By manually shopping for pregnancy tests and
automatically analyzing the HTTP traffic data captured in HAR files, we
find that users' personal data and shopping activities are routinely collected by third parties. Many pharmacy websites share product names,
email addresses and phone numbers with third parties even when consent
was declined. Investigating novel forms of online tracking, we find several
cases of server-side tagging and CNAME-based tracking, which can be
used to circumvent tracking protections offered by adblockers and modern browsers. Monitoring the advertisements targeted to our shopping
profiles on several news websites and large online platform apps, we find
re-targeted advertisements of the pregnancy tests we had shopped for. We
further find that while declining consent reduces third-party data sharing, it does not eliminate it, and deceptive designs often discourage users
from opting out. Through GDPR data access requests we reveal that
companies vary in the completeness of the personal data they disclose,
with none providing a full list. Overall, our study reveals widespread
potential legal violations and adoption of evasive tracking technologies
on websites that handle users' most sensitive personal data.

**Keywords:** Privacy · online tracking · pharmacy · online advertising

## 1 Introduction

Over the past few years, the online pharmacy sector has grown significantly,
driven by the convenience of home delivery, price comparisons, and customer
reviews. Online pharmacies offer convenience but pose risks due to extensive data
sharing with third parties for ads and analytics. The online pharmacy section
of Walgreens has also previously been shown to leak prescription information
to *session replay* companies [1]. A recent investigation by The Markup showed
that third-party data collection was taking place on 49 out of 50 US telehealth
websites, in certain cases for targeted advertising purposes [22]. The US Federal
Trade Commission investigated ad-related data sharing by GoodRx, BetterHelp,


R. Laborde et al. (Eds.): ESORICS 2025, LNCS 16231, pp. 188–205, 2026.
https://doi.org/10.1007/978-3-032-16089-8_13

and Cerebral, resulting in multimillion-dollar settlements and bans on sharing data with advertisers like Facebook [23–25]. While these investigations showed the risks for the US users, it is unclear whether European online pharmacy users are protected by stricter privacy laws. Our study conducts an empirical investigation to answer this question, considering novel tracking mechanisms and re-targeted advertisements.

In the context of online pharmacies, data collected by third parties may include pages visited, products browsed, purchases made, and even personal information entered during checkout. Such data can be used for relatively innocuous purposes, such as improving user experience. However, users' activities on pharmacy websites could also be used for advertising and marketing. Previous work has shown that many telehealth websites leak personal data to third parties [22], which can reveal intimate details about a user's private life. In regions where reproductive healthcare is contentious, tracking data may even be used in legal prosecution [6,36].

This paper investigates the prevalence and nature of online tracking and ad retargeting (remarketing) practices on 50 European online pharmacies. Specifically, we focus on pharmacy websites that offer non-prescription medications in the four most populous EU countries —Germany, France, Spain, and Italy —as well as in the Netherlands. We focus on the most popular pharmacy websites in each country, as they attract the majority of users and reveal the tracking practices most consumers are likely to encounter. We examine the prevalence of third-party data collection by simulating a user shopping for pregnancy products. In addition, we study novel tracking mechanisms such as CNAME-based tracking and Server-Side Tagging/Tracking (SST), which bypass tracking protections that rely on blocklists. Further, we attempt to trace how the collected data is used by examining the advertisements we receive on the Web after our pharmacy browsing sessions. We also use GDPR rights to request our data from the large third parties that collect data through pharmacy websites. To evaluate the effectiveness of user controls, we compare tracking and advertising practices in two scenarios: when website visitors accept cookies and when they reject them. Overall, our contributions include the following:

- We compare tracking practices on 50 pharmacy websites across five European countries, including novel methods such as SST and CNAME-based tracking.
- We quantify personal information and product name leaks to tracker domains, showing the extent of leaks even if the user declines consent.
- Through an exploratory study of retargeted ads based on our shopping activity on pharmacy websites, we show that even sensitive products such as pregnancy tests are used for ad retargeting.
- We compare client-side data collection by major platforms with their GDPR data access responses, revealing significant discrepancies.

## 2    Related Work

Our study builds upon prior work on web tracking in health-related contexts and considers novel tracking techniques.

**Tracking on Health-Related Websites.** Several papers investigated third-party tracking on health-related websites, with most focusing on the United States. Friedman et al. [28] researched abortion clinic websites, while McCoy et al. [38] focused on websites related to COVID-19. Both studies relied on webXray [54] to log third-party requests and cookies, a scope that likely underestimates harder-to-detect methods such as server-side tracking. Nevertheless, 99% of pages in both studies contained third-party trackers. In 2022, The Markup collaborated with STAT to investigate telehealth websites in the US [22]. They analyzed the presence of third-party trackers and shared data type (e.g., product details or shopping cart items). Among 50 telehealth websites, all but one sent personal details—often hashed or even plaintext email addresses—to major tech companies, most during checkout or questionnaire submission. In 2023, a study of 12 U.S. drugstores [53] found that all shared information about viewed or purchased products with major tracking companies.

Research into the tracking practices of European health-related websites is more sparse. Rauti et al. [49] analyzed the tracking practices on 163 Finnish online pharmacies. They found that 57 (35%) pharmacies leaked both the queried prescription name and identifying personal data. Yu et al. [55] studied 19,483 hospital websites in 152 countries—including 5,936 in Europe—and found tracking scripts on 53.5% of sites worldwide (48.8% in Europe) and tracking cookies on 14.6% (7.5% in Europe). Cookiebot, a Danish company, conducted similar research on EU health and government websites and found that 52% of EU public health service websites contained commercial trackers [8].

**Emerging Web Tracking Techniques.** As major browsers block third-party trackers and cookies, websites increasingly adopt new techniques to bypass these restrictions. One such method is CNAME-based tracking, which uses DNS aliases to disguise trackers as first-party resources. Dimova et al. [14] presented a large-scale, longitudinal study of this technique, finding increasing adoption, especially on high-traffic sites, and posing serious security risks due to bypassing the Same-Origin Policy. Another emerging technique is Server-Side Tagging (SST), introduced by Google in 2020 [26]. Unlike client-side tracking, SST shifts data collection to a server, hiding tracking activity from the user's browser. In a recent study, Fouad et al. [27] investigated SST at scale. They flagged SST domains by identifying subdomains absent in pre-2020 crawls, confirming they were registered to entities other than the parent domain and that their requests included tracking data previously sent elsewhere.

**Our Approach.** Unlike prior work, such as Rauti et al. [49], we examine tracking after consent is declined, quantify email and phone number leaks, identify CNAME cloaking and server-side tracking using a history-free detector, and link these leaks to retargeted ads seen on the Web and mobile. To identify SST endpoints on websites, we took a different approach from Fouad et al. [27], who compared website behavior before and after SST implementation and found SST on 28 websites. Instead, our analysis relies on fixed URL parameter structures and request initiators, yielding a much higher prevalence of SST. A caveat is that our method focuses on Google Tag Manager's SST implementation due to its popularity, rather than detecting generic server-side tracking. Finally, we leverage GDPR data access rights to compare data collected on pharmacy websites by large online platforms to data disclosed in response to subject access requests.

## 3   Methods

We investigate tracking and advertising practices on 50 pharmacy websites across five EU countries. We simulated shopping for pregnancy tests under two consent conditions (accept/reject), using fresh browser profiles, predefined personas, and VPNs. We analyzed HTTP traffic to identify trackers and detect techniques like server-side tagging and CNAME cloaking. To assess advertising, we monitored targeted ads on news websites and mobile apps. Finally, we compared GDPR data access responses with our observed tracking activity.

### 3.1   Website Selection

When studying online pharmacies, we distinguish between those offering prescription and non-prescription medications. As regulations differ across countries, we focus exclusively on websites selling non-prescription drugs to maintain consistency. We target popular, legitimate pharmacy websites, as users are more likely to visit them. Under Directive 2011/62/EU [20], legitimate pharmacies must register with national authorities and link to an official database. We retrieved registered pharmacies from Germany [7], France [47], Italy [42], Spain [4], and the Netherlands [41]. Popularity rankings were based on Similarweb's DigitalRank [50]. We selected the top ten pharmacies per country to balance breadth and manual feasibility, while ensuring our sample includes the sites most online shoppers for pharmacy products are likely to visit.

### 3.2   Data Collection

We collected data in two distinct phases, as described below. The first phase focused on tracking and web-based retargeting (Algorithm 1), while the second focused on ads on large online platforms' mobile apps (Algorithm 2).

**Algorithm 1: Measurement of Tracking and Targeted Ads.** We followed a fixed procedure for each website to capture all relevant HTTP traffic in a reproducible manner. Algorithm 1 presents a high-level overview of our data collection process, outlining the steps we followed to capture HTTP traffic across various consent modes, countries, and pharmacy websites. We started with a fresh browser profile for each website and followed the steps below for each consent mode in every country, across all pharmacy websites in our dataset:

<table>
<tr><td colspan="2">Algorithm 1. Tracking and Targeted Web Ads Analysis</td><td colspan="2">Algorithm 2. Analysis of Data Collection by Large Online Platforms</td></tr>
<tr><td>1:</td><td>for each consent mode do</td><td>1:</td><td>for each consent mode do</td></tr>
<tr><td>2:</td><td>Prepare predefined personal info</td><td>2:</td><td>Create a fresh profile</td></tr>
<tr><td>3:</td><td>for each country do</td><td>3:</td><td>Log in to platform accounts</td></tr>
<tr><td>4:</td><td>Use VPN to simulate location</td><td>4:</td><td>for each country do</td></tr>
<tr><td>5:</td><td>for each pharmacy website do</td><td>5:</td><td>Use VPN to simulate location</td></tr>
<tr><td>6:</td><td>Create a fresh profile</td><td>6:</td><td>for each pharmacy website do</td></tr>
<tr><td>7:</td><td>Checkout a product</td><td>7:</td><td>Checkout a product</td></tr>
<tr><td>8:</td><td>Save the HAR file</td><td>8:</td><td>end for</td></tr>
<tr><td>9:</td><td>Check news websites for ads</td><td>9:</td><td>end for</td></tr>
<tr><td>10:</td><td>end for</td><td>10:</td><td>Check platform apps for ads</td></tr>
<tr><td>11:</td><td>end for</td><td>11:</td><td>Scroll for 2 minutes</td></tr>
<tr><td>12:</td><td>end for</td><td>12:</td><td>Wait until the next day</td></tr>
<tr><td></td><td></td><td>13:</td><td>end for</td></tr>
</table>

1. Open Developer Tools, enable HTTP logging, and detach the panel to avoid detection influencing tracking behavior [44].
2. Load the homepage and handle the cookie dialog per consent mode.
3. Search for pregnancy tests or browse the menu if no results appear.
4. View the first product page, return to the results, and open the next product.
5. Add the product to the cart, adjusting quantity if required.
6. Proceed through checkout as far as possible without placing the order, using guest checkout and predefined personal data; register if required.
7. Save all HTTP requests and responses as an HTTP Archive (HAR) file.

We leveraged HAR files to identify tracking-related requests using the uBlock Origin Core npm package [33]. We relied on uBlock Origin's default filter lists, including EasyList and EasyPrivacy, among others [32]. We then mapped tracker domains to their respective owner entities using DuckDuckGo's entity map [16].

**Targeted Ads on the Web.** After visiting each pharmacy website, we visited a set of news websites to observe any targeted or retargeted ads resulting from the prior shopping activity. We used Similarweb [50] to select the top five "content publishing" sites per country and five global sites, as these categories include ad-supported news websites and align with prior ad targeting research [13]. We excluded duplicates and subscription-based, ad-free sites. To analyze ad behavior and disclosures, we followed these steps:

1. Visit the homepage and interact with the cookie banner.
2. Scroll to the bottom of the page or stop after 10 s for infinite scrolling.
3. If pregnancy ads appear, click the AdChoices icon for the explanation page.
4. Visit two inner pages (prioritize the most prominent items and avoid health-related pages) and follow steps 4 and 5 above.

We acknowledge that our data collection incurred some cost on the pharmacy websites' advertising budgets by causing ad impressions during the advertisement monitoring. We believe the societal benefits of our investigation outweigh its negligible cost to advertisers.

**Algorithm 2: Data Collection by Large Online Platforms.** To investigate whether data collected by third parties was used for personalized ads and disclosed to users properly, we created separate Instagram, Microsoft, TikTok, Facebook, Snapchat and Google accounts for each consent mode (accept/reject) on two iPhones. Algorithm 2 outlines the data collection process: For each consent mode, we created a fresh browser profile, logged into the six platform accounts, and searched for pregnancy tests on each pharmacy site, proceeding through checkout as far as possible without payment. After completing daily website visits, we monitored the online platforms' mobile apps three times a day in two-minute scrolling sessions, continuing for up to a week[1]. We captured screenshots of any ads related to health, pharmacies, or pregnancy tests. Finally, we requested and examined data downloads from these platforms (§3.4).

## 3.3   Measurement Setup

Our experiments were conducted using Chromium browsers running on Ubuntu 24.04.1 LTS. For sites with a cookie banner, we collected data in both "accept" and "reject" modes; if no banner appeared, the same data was used for both. We used two separate computers per mode to minimize the cross-contamination risk between different consent modes. Visiting the same website twice, even after clearing cookies and browser history, could still allow tracking through fingerprinting, potentially influencing ads based on prior visits. Using two computers minimizes the risk of cross-contamination between browsing sessions of different consent modes. We used a predefined persona on each computer during checkout, allowing us to later check if personal data was leaked to third parties. To access the websites from their respective countries of origin, we used Mullvad VPN [43]. This enabled us to better impersonate a local pharmacy shopper, which may be relevant for ad targeting.

## 3.4   Detecting Tracking Methods and Leaks

**CNAME-Based Tracking.** A potential method to bypass blocklist-based tracking protection is CNAME-based tracking. To evade blocking, the website owner maps a first-party subdomain to the tracker's domain via CNAME records. Due to the increasing popularity of this technique [14], many defenses, such as uBlock Origin and AdGuard—have introduced countermeasures [31,39]. uBlock Origin, for instance, performs DNS lookups and replays filtering with the resolved

---

[1] We did not monitor ads on Google mobile apps, as our Web-focused measurement (Algorithm 1) targets Google ads on websites. For Microsoft, we used the Bing app; for others, we used their respective mobile apps.

CNAME address. We adopt this method, which is enabled by uBlock Origin's `cnameReplayFullURL` option. If a hostname has a CNAME record, we replace it with the resolved domain and rerun tracker detection using the uBO Core npm package [33]. DNS lookups are automated using the dnspython library [15].

**Server Side Tagging.** Many websites embed multiple third-party resources, adding performance overhead due to increased page weight. Adblockers and tracking protections now offered by many mainstream browsers block tracking- and advertising-related third-party traffic. Server Side Tagging (SST) was proposed as a way to reduce this overhead of third parties while also bypassing tracking protections [26]. In SST, the end user's browser or mobile app only sends tracking and analytics data to a single server, which then relays it to multiple third parties (a.k.a. tags). SST may make it challenging to identify the third parties collecting data on a website, and hence poses a transparency problem. To detect SST usage, we relied on a simple observation. Despite the change in endpoints, many URL parameters used to send data remain the same. For instance, in both SST and non-SST integrations, Google Analytics uses the parameters `dt`, `dl`, and `sr`, which correspond to page title, page URL, and screen dimensions, respectively. However, instead of manually picking parameters, we automated the parameter detection using our dataset to bootstrap the process. We first identified all requests triggered by Google Tag Manager (GTM) scripts using `initiator` fields, since SST uses GTM under the hood [29]. To detect self-hosted GTM scripts, we used a pattern we extracted from the official GTM scripts. We then took the intersection of URL parameters observed in requests triggered by GTM scripts. This yielded a list of 36 parameters, which we searched for in all requests. Similar to Fouad et al. [27], we then verified whether these requests were indeed SST by retrieving the IP address pointing to the first-party subdomain in the request and checking to which organization this IP address is registered. Then we used the terminal command `whois` to check whether the first-party subdomain organization differs from the website. We also used the request initiators for further confirmation.

**Detecting Product Name and Personal Information Leaks.** When placing an order, users provide personal information such as name, address, email, and product details, which may be shared with third parties. Identifying when and how different types of data are shared can be challenging, particularly across languages. To enable systematic analysis, we compiled search terms including product names and persona details used during checkout. Personal information or product names can be sent to tracking parties using encodings or cryptographic hashes such as SHA-256 [40]. To detect such transformed leaks, we followed Englehardt et al. [17] to search for permutations of various encodings and hashes (e.g., Base64, SHA-256) in request URLs and POST bodies.

**Data Retrieval from Third Parties.** We retrieved personal data from major platforms via their account settings or privacy centers. From Google, we exported service-wide activity data. Facebook and Instagram provided lists of companies sharing off-site activity with Meta, including browsing and purchases [35].

TikTok's "Ads and data" section contained advertising-related data. Microsoft's Privacy Dashboard included ad profiles and inferred interests. From Snapchat, we downloaded user data such as purchase history, memories, and other account activity. Note that data requests were made using automated tools provided by the platforms, without contacting any employees.

**Table 1.** Most common categories of third-party entities found on pharmacy websites. It shows the number of websites where requests to these domains observed, along with the number of distinct request domains and entities per category.

| Entity Category | Websites | | Request domains | | Request entities | |
|---|---|---|---|---|---|---|
| | Accept | Reject | Accept | Reject | Accept | Reject |
| Advertising | 50 | 49 | 73 | 52 | 58 | 41 |
| Ad-motivated tracking | 50 | 49 | 72 | 50 | 56 | 38 |
| Analytics | 50 | 45 | 45 | 32 | 37 | 27 |
| 3rd party analytics marketing | 49 | 45 | 34 | 25 | 33 | 24 |
| Audience measurement | 49 | 43 | 27 | 20 | 24 | 17 |
| Ad fraud | 39 | 28 | 8 | 7 | 5 | 4 |

### 3.5   Analysis of Consent Notices

To provide insights into the mechanisms that online pharmacies offer customers to control the processing of their personal data, we manually inspected screenshots taken from each pharmacy's main page for the presence of consent notices and the options they offer. We focus on control mechanisms available on the first layer of the notices, as only a few people are willing to explore deeper layers of consent notices for options to deny consent [46]. Our analysis was guided by the requirements of European data protection authorities that it must be as easy to reject data collection as to consent to it [19]. Thus, we annotated the screenshots of consent notices for the interaction options offered to website visitors on the first layer and their formatting and placement within the banner. One of the authors did the annotations, and edge cases were resolved in joint discussion.

## 4   Findings

### 4.1   Third Parties and Tracking

We analyzed HTTP requests and responses from the captured HAR files to identify third parties and various types of data sharing with them. All pharmacy websites embedded at least one third-party domain, regardless of giving or declining consent. The median number of third-party domains per site varied substantially across countries—16 in France and 56 in Italy—with Italian and

German sites embedding the most (Fig. 1). Rejecting cookies reduces the number of third-party domains across all countries, with Germany seeing the largest drop. Also, we identified a substantial number of pharmacy websites where third parties set cookies with the `SameSite=None` attribute and a lifespan exceeding two months—47 and 33 websites in accept and reject mode, respectively. Analyzing cookie purposes is out of the study scope, but `SameSite=None` cookies enable third parties to track users across domains.

**Tracker Entities.** A large portion of third-party embeds on pharmacy websites were classified as trackers. Figure 1 shows the median number of tracking entities per website, revealing substantial variation across countries: French websites had the fewest entities (median of nine in accept mode), while Italian websites had the most (median of 43.5). Rejecting cookies generally reduced the number of trackers, except for French sites.

**Most Prevalent Trackers.** As shown in Table 2, Google appeared on 96% of websites, followed by Microsoft, Facebook, and PayPal. Another frequently encountered third party is Criteo, which specializes in personalized advertising [12]. Other prevalent trackers such as Awin [5], Outbrain [48], and Taboola [52] were linked to marketing, native ads, and content recommendations. We also identified ID5 [34], a provider of privacy-focused identity solutions designed to replace third-party cookies. The presence of these trackers on pharmacy sites raises privacy concerns, as users may not expect health-related browsing activities to be used for ads or data sharing.

**Table 2.** Frequent third-party entities on pharmacy websites.

| Third-party entity | Accept | Reject |
|---|---|---|
| Google | 50 | 48 |
| Microsoft | 36 | 16 |
| Facebook | 32 | 13 |
| Virtual Minds | 18 | 7 |
| Criteo | 16 | 3 |
| ID5 | 16 | 2 |
| PayPal | 15 | 15 |
| Trusted Shops | 14 | 12 |
| Awin | 13 | 4 |
| Outbrain | 13 | 2 |

**Prevalence of Third-Party Categories.** Table 1 summarizes third-party service categories across pharmacy sites. Domains were categorized based on the Tracker Radar dataset [16]; with some domains belonging to multiple categories. "Advertising" and "Ad motivated tracking" appeared on nearly all websites, with over 70 unique domains and 50 entities focused on tracking.

**CNAME-based Tracking.** To detect CNAME-based tracking, we replaced request hostnames with their CNAME records and reran detection using uBO Core (§3.4). Focusing on requests that were detected as trackers only after the CNAME replacement, we identified six distinct pharmacy websites that use CNAME-based tracking (Table 3). Registrable domains of all CNAME records appear in the EasyPrivacy list blocklist. Etracker.com describes how site owners can "avoid data loss due to ad blocking" using CNAME records [18].

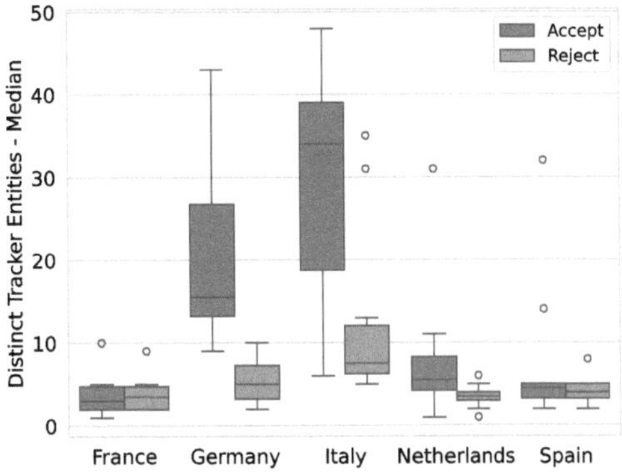



**Fig. 1.** Median of tracker entities per site by consent mode and country.

Similarly, Mapp's help pages [37] explain how to set up first-party tracking by defining a CNAME record pointing to `go-direct.flx1.com`, a domain used by two pharmacies. In another case, despite rejecting consent, our persona's name and email were sent to Spotler (`activate.deonlinedrogist.nl`), which provides email marketing services [51].

**Table 3.** Detected CNAME-based tracking domains, showing the original request host, the resolved CNAME and the consent mode(s) in which they were observed.

| Loc. | Website | Request host | CNAME | Cons. |
|---|---|---|---|---|
| DE | medikamente-per-klick.de | e.medikamente-per-klick.de | customer.etracker.com | Both |
| IT | farmasave.it | ddbm2.paypal.com | ddbm2.paypal.com.[...].datadome.co | Reject |
| IT | topfarmacia.it | dmp.email.topfarmacia.it | go-direct.flx1.com | Both |
| IT | docpeter.it | dmp.mapp.docpeter.it | go-direct.flx1.com | Both |
| IT | 1000farmacie.it | the.sciencebehindecommerce.com | tag.device9.com | Accept |
| NL | deonlinedrogist.nl | activate.deonlinedrogist.nl | ujemkxutgo.relay.squeezely.tech | Both |

**Server Side Tagging.** Using the URL parameters in GTM traffic (§3.4), we found that 19 of the 50 sites used SST (Table 4). In all cases, a first-party subdomain of the pharmacy website was used. In 14/19 cases, the SST endpoint was used in both accept and reject modes. Four of the five German websites used the SST endpoint only in accept mode, while the only French pharmacy used it only in reject mode. We found that 12 of the 19 SST servers were hosted on Google, easing the setup of SST servers [29]. To determine the hosting details, we used a combination of `Via` and `Server` response headers captured in the HAR files and additional WHOIS information we queried for the server IP addresses. The majority of SST endpoints used the default `/collect` path of Google Analytics, while two Italian pharmacies used a random path starting with **ngt**. Use of a random path could be an additional effort to evade blocking.

## 4.2  Product Name and Personal Information Leaks

We examined two types of information leakage: product names and identifying personal details. To prevent false positives, we only considered leaks to third-party domains and to 19 SST hostnames identified in §4.1.

**Product Name Leaks.** In accept mode, 34 websites leaked the product name, 77% via URLs and 23% via POST request bodies. 28 websites leaked product names even when consent was declined. Google was the top recipient of product name leaks (36 Accept, 23 Reject; Table 5), followed by Microsoft, ByteDance, and Facebook. While leaks to `doubleclick.net` dropped substantially in reject mode (24 to 3), leaks to `google-analytics.com` increased (12 to 17), which may be a fallback domain in reject mode. Product names are still leaked to several third parties in reject mode. For instance, `efarma.com` (IT) leaked product names to six domains. In contrast, seven of ten German sites avoided such leaks, while leakage patterns in other countries remained largely unchanged (Table 6). On all sites but two, URL encoding is used when leaking the product name to third parties or SST hostnames. On `shop-apotheke.com` (DE) and `redcare.it` (IT) the product name was leaked in Base64 encoded form to `adtriba.com`, a digital marketing company [3].

**Table 4.** SST endpoints by country (Loc.) and used consent mode (A: Accept, R: Reject).

| Loc. | SST Endpoint | Google Hosted | Cons. |
|---|---|---|---|
| DE | measure.medpex.de/g/collect | True | A |
| DE | tmsst.aponeo.de/g/collect | True | A |
| DE | klpoz.shop-apotheke.com/g/collect | True | A/R |
| DE | sgtm.mycare.de/g/collect | False | A |
| DE | measure.docmorris.de/g/collect | True | A |
| IT | otasf.redcare.it/g/collect | True | A/R |
| IT | gtm.efarma.com/g/collect | False | A/R |
| IT | sgtm.farmasave.it/ngtwyxyzwjg | False | A/R |
| IT | sgtm.docpeter.it/ngtmapwbued | False | A/R |
| ES | datos.farmaciasdirect.es/g/collect | True | A/R |
| NL | pipeline.drogist.nl/g/collect | True | A/R |
| NL | metrics.deonlinedrogist.nl/g/collect | True | A/R |
| NL | sgtm.plein.nl/g/collect | True | A/R |
| NL | ecom-data.trekpleister.nl/g/collect | True | A/R |
| NL | ecom-data.kruidvat.nl/g/collect | True | A/R |
| NL | inc.da.nl/g/collect | False | A/R |
| NL | v3-pixal-web.etos.nl/g/collect | False | A/R |
| NL | sst.koopjesdrogisterij.nl/g/collect | False | A/R |
| FR | care.soin-et-nature.com/g/collect | True | R |

**Personal Information Leaks.** To examine personal data leaks, we focused on email addresses and phone numbers, which uniquely identify users. As with product name analysis, we considered only third-party domains and SST hostnames. In accept mode, emails leaked in 15 cases and phone numbers in three; in reject mode, email leaks slightly dropped to 13, while phone leaks rose to four. SHA-256 was the most common hashing/encoding method observed in email leaks (39 of 164). Overall, hashed email leaks were detected on five distinct sites. Facebook

**Table 5.** Number of sites leaking product names to third-party entities.

| Entity | Accept | Reject |
|---|---|---|
| Google | 36 | 23 |
| Microsoft | 23 | 7 |
| ByteDance | 7 | 0 |
| Facebook | 4 | 1 |
| Virtual Minds | 4 | 0 |

received hashed emails from three websites in accept mode and from two sites in reject mode (`boticas23.com`, `okfarma.es`). Other domains receiving hashed emails include `awin1.com`, `zenaps.com`, `dynamicyield.com`, `pinterest.com` and `tiktok.com`. Notably, `awin1.com` received a salted hash, which prevents linking user identities via hashed emails.

### 4.3   Consent Notices

All but one of the 50 online pharmacies (`pharmaciedesdrakkars.com`, France) displayed a consent notice. Since consent notices often employ deceptive design patterns to steer website visitors towards accepting all cookies and tracking technologies [46], our analysis focused on whether the pharmacies transparently communicated options to decline such data collection. As we will discuss in §5, EU privacy law requires consent to be "freely given," which requires equal prominence for "Accept" and

**Table 6.** Number of sites leaking product names per country and consent mode.

| Country | Accept | Reject |
|---|---|---|
| Germany | 10 | 3 |
| Spain | 10 | 9 |
| Italy | 9 | 10 |
| Netherlands | 8 | 9 |
| France | 7 | 7 |

"Reject" options. A 2023 report by the European Data Protection Board found that the majority of surveyed national data protection authorities considered embedding refusal links within text paragraphs invalid unless they are visually highlighted to attract users' attention [19]. We only found five pharmacies (two from each NL and ES and one from IT) that display "Accept" and "Reject" as equally prominent options on the first layer. While 27 additional pharmacies did feature a "Reject" option on the first layer, 21 used color highlighting to point visitors towards the "Accept" option and nine did not place the "Reject" option next to the "Accept" button. 12 pharmacies did not feature any explicit "Reject" option on the first layer, but four of them had an "Accept necessary [cookies]" button instead. Thus, only five out of 50 online pharmacies featured a consent dialog that did not outright violate the requirement for "freely given" consent. A comprehensive legal analysis of whether valid consent was actually obtained would require in-depth assessment on a case-by-case basis.

### 4.4   Advertisements

**Targeted Ads on the Web.** To assess the impact of targeted and retargeted ads, we visited news websites after browsing pharmacy sites (§3.2). The results showed notable cross-country differences in targeted and retargeted ads. We observed such ads from 15 of 50 pharmacy websites in the Netherlands, Spain, Germany, and Italy, but none from France. In the Netherlands and Spain, we saw no re-targeted ads but did receive pharmacy-related ads from visited sites (`plein.nl` and `farmaciabarata.es`) via Google Ads (Fig. 2 e, i). In some cases, we saw pregnancy-related ads, though not for the exact items searched, suggesting broader behavioral targeting (Fig. 2 h from `shop-apotheke.com` in Germany

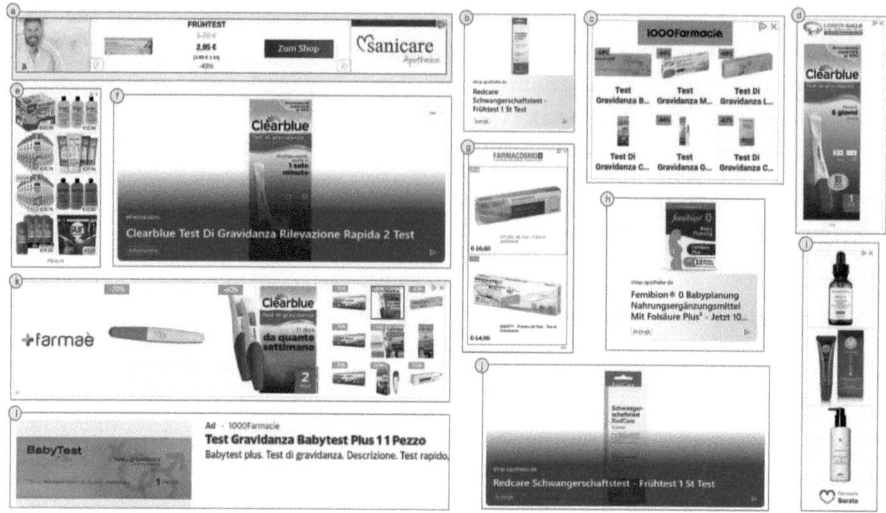

**Fig. 2.** Examples of targeted ads observed during the experiment.

and d from `farmacialoreto.it` in Italy). Retargeted ads appeared on two out of ten German sites and three out of ten Italian sites, matching products we had browsed or added to our cart. These ads were served by Google, Microsoft, Criteo, as well as Taboola (Fig. 2 l) and RTB House.

**Ads on Large Online Platform Apps.** A day after visiting pharmacy websites, our accept-mode Facebook feed showed numerous pregnancy- and baby-related posts and reels, but no ads. TikTok and Instagram displayed ads, yet none for pregnancy products or pharmacies. This absence may be due to fresh, low-credibility profiles and, for Facebook, the off-Facebook-activity setting—found disabled after the study. In an earlier pilot with an author's long-standing account, pregnancy-related Facebook ads did appear.

### 4.5 Data Takeout from Third Parties

Under the GDPR, companies that process personal data must honor data access rights. Comparing each platform's Takeout archive with our HAR logs—and the retargeted ads we later observed—shows that none provided a complete record.

Based on our HAR logs, 37 of the 50 sites contacted Google Analytics, but Google Takeout returned records for only 27. The Takeout data included only visited URLs, but omitted other data collected by Google Analytics, such as product names, prices, quantities, and cart actions. In contrast, HAR captures the full Analytics payloads, revealing complete product metadata and user-action events collected by Google. This gap highlights the incompleteness of Google Takeout data compared to the detailed, real-time tracking in its analytics services.

TikTok's "Off TikTok Activity" log includes events such as `InitiateCheckout`, `ViewContent`, and `AddToCart`, but provides minimal metadata—for example, checkout entries lack product details. In contrast, our HAR logs show seven sites sending product names and eight sending hashed personal data (email, phone, name) to TikTok, none of which appeared in the returned data. Instagram's Takeout data listed advertisers that used our "activity or information", including okfarma.es and unrelated brands such as Netflix and Paramount. The "ads and topics" folder, which logs viewed and clicked ads, contained no ads from pharmacy websites. Facebook's "Activity Off Meta" Takeout yielded only generic privacy details and no records of pharmacy websites, despite ads related to pharmacies and pregnancy. Post-collection, we learned that off-Facebook activity ads were disabled, which may explain the absence of records. Microsoft's ad dashboard showed new interest labels (e.g., Baby and Children) and served related ads on MSN (Fig. 2), but the downloaded profile lacked the underlying data. Snapchat's Takeout contained no data on our pharmacy visits, consistent with our client-side observations.

## 5   Legal Analysis

Here we provide a brief legal discussion—not an individual compliance assessment—of the tracking practices identified in this paper, focusing on the General Data Protection Regulation [21]. The GDPR generally applies to the tracking practices discussed in this paper because it applies when "personal data" such as cookies and other online identifiers, are used. The GDPR applies to companies ("data controllers") based in the EU, but also to certain non-EU companies, e.g., if the company "monitors" the behavior of people in the EU (Art. 3(2)), as in online tracking. The online pharmacy and the tracking company are jointly responsible for GDPR compliance [10]. GDPR defines "special categories of personal data" that include "data concerning health or [...] a natural person's sex life" (Art. 9(1)). The Court of Justice of the European Union (CJEU) stated that data concerning health "must be interpreted broadly", so if somebody orders a medical product at an online pharmacy, that fact constitutes data concerning health [9]. The use of sensitive personal data is prohibited, subject to specific exceptions such as for hospitals, which do not apply here.

The only possible legal basis for online tracking and targeted advertising is the Internet user's "explicit consent" (Art. 9(2)) [11]. For consent to be valid, it needs to be a "freely given, specific, informed, and unambiguous indication of the data subject's wishes by which [they], by a statement or by a clear affirmative action, signif[y] agreement to the processing of [their] personal data" (Art. 4(11)). This means that the individual must actively do something, e. g., tick a box or click a button. A company is not allowed to assume consent if someone continues to use a service or fails to opt out. As noted in §4.3, we saw tracking for targeted advertising without the individual's "freely given" consent, a clear violation.

## 6    Limitations

While our 50-site sample favors depth over breadth, covering the top ten pharmacies per country likely reflects the experience of millions of users [2]. We observed targeted ads from 15 of the 50 pharmacies. The absence of ads from other websites could be due to a lack of advertising campaigns targeting the products we shopped for. Our use of fresh profiles on separate devices minimized the risk of prior browsing history influencing tracking behavior and ad delivery, though residual effects beyond our control cannot be entirely excluded. While our study focuses on pregnancy tests and results may not fully generalize to other sensitive health-related products, the observed tracking and ad targeting demonstrate how even sensitive product purchases are monitored for ad retargeting. Future investigations could also examine whether browsing for such products triggers ads for related categories, for example, baby items, to shed light on the broader profiling strategies employed by advertisers. We used manual checkouts to avoid bot detection and ensure ecological validity. Future work could explore LLM-guided automation [45], though this may trigger bot detection or ad fraud defenses. Google allows users to limit ads about sensitive topics such as "pregnancy and parenting" [30]. Due to scope limitations, we could not evaluate the effect of this opt-in setting. While we searched for various types of encodings and hashes to identify leaked data, custom encodings or obfuscation can bypass our detector. Hence, our ad targeting results should be taken as lower bounds. Our SST endpoint identification method focused on the server-side use of Google Tag Manager, rather than generic server-side tracking. Since our method relies on common URL parameters extracted from the data we collected, it may not generalize to other datasets or more customized uses of SST.

## 7    Conclusion

Users may expect a high level of privacy when shopping for health-related products online. Our findings show that even shopping for sensitive products such as pregnancy tests on most popular European pharmacy websites is subject to extensive third-party tracking for advertising purposes. Through a lightweight detection method, we identify a sharp increase in the use of server-side tracking, along with continued use of other stealthy techniques such as CNAME cloaking. Tracking often occurs without valid consent as many websites do not use compliant consent dialogs, and some ignore user choices altogether. Moreover, data access requests often yield incomplete information, leaving users in the dark about what online activities are monitored. Our findings raise significant concerns regarding transparency, user rights, and compliance with regulations.

# References


1. Acar, G., Englehardt, S., Narayanan, A.: No boundaries: data exfiltration by third parties embedded on web pages. In: Proceedings on Privacy Enhancing Technologies, pp. 220–238 (2020). https://doi.org/10.2478/popets-2020-0070
2. Adamic, L.A., Huberman, B.A.: Zipf's law and the internet. Glottometrics **3**(1), 143–150 (2002)
3. AdTriba GmbH: Future-proof marketing measurement & optimization (Oct 2024). https://www.adtriba.com
4. Agencia Española de Medicamentos Productos Sanitarios: Listado de farmacias que realizan la venta a distancia (2024). https://distafarma.aemps.es/farmacom/faces/inicio.xhtml
5. AWIN Inc.: Join our global affiliate platform (2024). https://www.awin.com/
6. Baker-White, E.: Facebook Gave Nebraska Cops A Teen's DMs. https://www.forbes.com/sites/emilybaker-white/2022/08/08/facebook-abortion-teen-dms
7. Bundesinstitut für Arzneimittel und Medizinprodukte: Versandhandelsregister (Oct 2024). https://versandhandel.dimdi.de/pdfs/vhr-apo.pdf
8. Cookiebot: Ad Tech Surveillance on the Public Sector Web (2019). https://www.cookiebot.com/media/1121/cookiebot-report-2019-medium-size.pdf
9. Court of Justice of the EU: Judgment in Case C-21/23, 4 Oct. 2024. https://curia.europa.eu/juris/liste.jsf?num=C-21/23
10. Court of Justice of the EU: Judgment in Case C-40/17, 29 July. 2019. https://curia.europa.eu/juris/liste.jsf?num=C-40/17
11. Court of Justice of the EU: Judgment in Case C-446/21, 4 Oct. 2024. https://curia.europa.eu/juris/liste.jsf?num=C-446/21
12. Criteo: The Commerce Media Platform for the Open Internet (2024). https://www.criteo.com/
13. Datta, A., Tschanz, M.C., Datta, A.: Automated experiments on ad privacy settings - a tale of opacity, choice, and discrimination. Proc. Priv. Enhanc. Technol. **1**, 92–112 (2015)
14. Dimova, Y., Acar, G., Olejnik, L., Joosen, W., Van Goethem, T.: The CNAME of the Game: Large-scale Analysis of DNS-based Tracking Evasion. Privacy Enhancing Technologies, pp. 394–412 (2021)
15. Dnspython Contributors: dnspython (2024). https://dnspython.readthedocs.io/en/latest
16. DuckDuckGo: Tracker Radar (2024). https://github.com/duckduckgo/tracker-radar/
17. Englehardt, S., Han, J., Narayanan, A.: I never signed up for this! Privacy implications of email tracking. In: Proceedings on Privacy Enhancing Technologies, pp. 109–126 (2018)
18. eTracker GmbH: Set up your own tracking domain (2025). https://help.etracker.com/en/article/set-up-your-own-tracking-domain
19. European Data Protection Board: Report of the work undertaken by Cookie Banner Taskforce. Tech. rep. (2023). https://www.edpb.europa.eu/our-work-tools/our-documents/other/report-work-undertaken-cookie-banner-taskforce
20. European Parliament and the Council of the EU: Directive 2011/62/EU (2011). http://data.europa.eu/eli/dir/2011/62/oj
21. European Parliament and the Council of the EU: Regulation (EU) 2016/679 (2016). https://eur-lex.europa.eu/eli/reg/2016/679/oj

22. Feathers, T., Palmer, K., Fondrie-Teitler, S.: Dozens of Telehealth Startups Sent Sensitive Health Information to Big Tech Companies (2024). https://themarkup.org/pixel-hunt/2022/12/13/out-of-control-dozens-of-telehealth-startups-sent-sensitive-health-information-to-big-tech-companies
23. Federal Trade Commission: Enforcement Action to Bar GoodRx (2023). https://www.ftc.gov/news-events/news/press-releases/2023/02/ftc-enforcement-action-bar-goodrx-sharing-consumers-sensitive-health-info-advertising
24. Federal Trade Commission: FTC Order Prohibits Telehealth Firm Cerebral from Using Sensitive Data for Ads (2024). https://www.ftc.gov/news-events/news/press-releases/2024/04/proposed-ftc-order-will-prohibit-telehealth-firm-cerebral-using-or-disclosing-sensitive-data
25. Federal Trade Commission: FTC to Ban BetterHelp from Revealing Consumers' Data (2024). https://www.ftc.gov/news-events/news/press-releases/2023/03/ftc-ban-betterhelp-revealing-consumers-data-including-sensitive-mental-health-information-facebook
26. Fisher, B.: Improve performance and security with Server-Side Tagging (2023). https://blog.google/products/marketingplatform/360/improve-performance-and-security-server-side-tagging
27. Fouad, I., Santos, C., Laperdrix, P.: The Devil is in the details: detection, measurement and lawfulness of server-side tracking on the web. In: Proceedings on Privacy Enhancing Technologies, pp. 450–465 (2024)
28. Friedman, A.B., Bauer, L., Gonzales, R., McCoy, M.S.: Prevalence of third-party tracking on abortion clinic web pages. JAMA Internal Med. **182**(11) (2022)
29. Google: Setting up a new server container (2023). https://developers.google.com/tag-platform/learn/sst-fundamentals/4-sst-setup-container
30. Google: Limit ads about sensitive topics on Google (2024). https://support.google.com/My-Ad-Center-Help/answer/12155260
31. Hill, R.: uBlock Origin works best on Firefox. https://github.com/gorhill/uBlock/wiki/uBlock-Origin-works-best-on-Firefox#cname-uncloaking
32. Hill, R.: uBlock Origin – make-rulesets.js (2023). https://github.com/gorhill/uBlock/blob/491bc87e94a503a17fd11cdee35c1f1b6fea24be/platform/mv3/make-rulesets.js#L1285-L1296
33. Hill, R.: uBlock Origin Core (2024). https://www.npmjs.com/package/@gorhill/ubo-core
34. ID5: ID5 – Future-proofed user identification for Digital Advertising (2024). https://id5.io/
35. Instagram Help Center: Why am I seeing ads from an advertiser on Instagram? https://help.instagram.com/609473930427331
36. Kaste, M.: Nebraska cops used Facebook messages to investigate an alleged illegal abortion (2022). https://www.npr.org/2022/08/12/1117092169/nebraska-cops-used-facebook-messages-to-investigate-an-alleged-illegal-abortion
37. Mapp: Custom Track Domain (C-Name) (2025). https://docs.mapp.com/docs/custom-track-domain-c-name
38. McCoy, M.S., Libert, T., Buckler, D., Grande, D.T., Friedman, A.B.: Prevalence of third-party tracking on COVID-19–related web pages. J. Am. Med. Assoc. (JAMA) **324**(14), 1462–1464 (2020)
39. Meshkov, A.: Gotta catch 'em all: how AdGuard scanned the entire web in search of hidden trackers (2024). https://adguard.com/en/blog/cname-tracking.html
40. Meta: Customer File Custom Audiences (2024). https://developers.facebook.com/docs/marketing-api/audiences/guides/custom-audiences/#hash

41. Ministerie van Volksgezondheid, Welzijn en Sport: Aanbiederslijst online medicijnen (2024). https://aanbiedersmedicijnen.nl/aanbieders/aanbiederslijst.
42. Ministero della Salute: Soggetto autorizzato al commercio online di medicinali (2024). https://www.salute.gov.it/LogoCommercioElettronico/CercaSitoEComm
43. Mullvad VPN AB: – Free the internet (2024). https://mullvad.net/en
44. Musch, M., Johns, M.: U can't debug this: detecting Javascript anti-debugging techniques in the wild. In: Proceedings of the 30th USENIX Security Symposium, pp. 2935–2950 (2021)
45. Müller, M., Žunič, G.: Browser Use: Enable AI to control your browser (2024). https://browser-use.com/
46. Nouwens, M., Liccardi, I., Veale, M., Karger, D., Kagal, L.: Dark patterns after the GDPR: scraping consent pop-ups and demonstrating their influence. In: Proceedings of the 2020 CHI, pp. 1–13 (2020)
47. Ordre National des Pharmaciens: Rechercher un site de vente en ligne autorisé à vendre des médicaments – CNOP (2024). https://www.ordre.pharmacien.fr/je-suis/patient-grand-public/rechercher-un-site-de-vente-en-ligne-autorise-a-vendre-des-medicaments?vl-region=&vl-departement=&vl-commune=&vl-site=&vl-pharmacy=&vl-incumbent=
48. Outbrain Inc.: Drive Better Business Results (2024) https://www.outbrain.com/
49. Rauti, S.: Analyzing third-party data leaks on online pharmacy websites. Heal. Technol. **14**, 375–392 (2022)
50. Similarweb LTD: Unlock Digital Growth (2024). https://www.similarweb.com/
51. Spotler: Email marketing automation with Spotler software (2024). https://spotler.com/solutions/use-cases/email-marketing-automation
52. Taboola: Restricted Content, Products, Services (2025). https://taboola.com/
53. Tahir, D., Fondrie-Teitler, S.: Need to Get Plan B or an HIV Test Online? Facebook May Know About It (2023). https://themarkup.org/pixel-hunt/2023/06/30/need-to-get-plan-b-or-an-hiv-test-online-facebook-may-know-about-it
54. webXray: webXray Privacy Search Engine (2024). https://webxray.ai/
55. Yu, X., Samarasinghe, N., Mannan, M., Youssef, A.: Got sick and tracked: privacy analysis of hospital websites. In: IEEE Euro S&P Workshops, pp. 278–286 (2022)

# PADOME: Adaptive Privacy Assistant for the Internet of Things


Edward Rochester$^{(\boxtimes)}$ and Ken Barker

University of Calgary, 2500 University Dr NW, Calgary, AB T2N 1N4, Canada
`{e.rochester,ken.barker}@ucalgary.ca`



**Abstract.** As the need for privacy self-management in the Internet of Things (IoT) ecosystem grows, Privacy Assistants (PAs) have emerged as a solution to assist users. However, many existing PAs rely on static approaches, assume perfect knowledge of user privacy preferences, and expect complete around-the-clock responsiveness from users to elicitation prompts. Furthermore, they overlook the behavior of IoT devices and the information potentially available from surrounding PAs. As such, we designed PADOME, an adaptive PA that models the user's privacy preferences and the IoT device negotiation strategy. PADOME integrates user privacy preference elicitation to better understand their privacy utilities, along with IoT device preference modeling and surrounding PA elicitation, to reduce uncertainty about the IoT device negotiation strategy. Designed using the DUNE framework and evaluated in the GEPARD simulation environment, PADOME demonstrates improved negotiation outcomes and higher agreement success rates.

**Keywords:** Privacy Management · Internet of Things · Privacy Assistants


## 1 Introduction

The proliferation of Internet of Things (IoT) devices has led to an unprecedented scale of personal data collection and processing, raising significant privacy concerns [6]. Privacy Assistants (PAs) have emerged as a promising approach to mitigate these concerns by (semi-)autonomously negotiating with IoT devices on behalf of users [1,10,13,19]. However, many existing PAs are designed with assumptions that fail to hold in real-world deployments. Specifically, they often assume that users will always be available or willing to respond to elicitation requests or that IoT devices will behave predictably or cooperatively [4,9]. Such assumptions may lead to ineffectively designed PAs that can significantly degrade the IoT ecosystem's performance and substantially reduce PA user satisfaction [14,16].

In practice, users are often unwilling or unable to respond to elicitation requests [18]. As such, PAs must balance automation with user involvement to minimize user burden and power consumption due to unanswered elicitation




R. Laborde et al. (Eds.): ESORICS 2025, LNCS 16231, pp. 206–218, 2026.
https://doi.org/10.1007/978-3-032-16089-8_14

requests, while still maintaining trust and comprehensive privacy profiles [4,16]. Additionally, negotiation opponents, *i.e.*, IoT devices, may act strategically to influence privacy negotiation outcomes [2]. The negotiation environment itself is often characterized by uncertainty and incomplete knowledge (*e.g.*, unclear data flows when negotiating data sharing with a smart mall's systems), further degrading the effectiveness of traditional PAs in real-world deployments [9].

To address these challenges, we introduce *PADOME*, a Privacy Assistant with Distributed Opponent Modeling and User Elicitation. PADOME is designed to operate under conditions of partial cooperation from users and other PAs. It abandons the assumption that users will always respond to elicitation, instead relying on observation of prior decisions and user feedback when available. PADOME also prompts surrounding PAs for their model of the IoT device preferences and does not assume their responsiveness. Instead, it opportunistically elicits such models when possible without depending on their availability.

PADOME is designed using the DUNE framework [15], which structures PA designs along four key components: Device, User, Network, and Environment. DUNE enables systematic analysis of PA behaviors by isolating these components and supporting a plug-and-play design methodology. We also implement PADOME into the GEPARD [15] to evaluate its effectiveness and compare it with other state-of-the-art PA designs.

## 2   Related Work

We limit related work to recent work in the following categories: i) automated negotiation agents in data privacy, ii) PAs for privacy negotiations and management in IoT, and iii) user privacy preferences elicitation algorithms .

**i. Automated Negotiations.** Baarslag *et al.* [3] presented an automated negotiation agent that uses learned user's privacy preferences to negotiate data-sharing permissions. While the negotiated agreements were more accurate than the baseline, the work could further explore strategies that also reduce the overall effort required from the user. This work was extended by Filipczuk *et al.* [9] to allow for partial and complete offers and introduce a variant of the user privacy preference learning approach, paving the way for more flexible negotiation mechanisms. Finally, Mohammad *et al.* [12] extended Filipczuk *et al.* work to practical use cases through partial uncertainty reduction in the utility functions, which opens the door to future work on extending these methods to scenarios with uncountable or more complex outcome spaces.

**ii. Privacy Assistants.** Cha *et al.* [5] addressed the consent issues when users access nearby IoT devices from their smartphones via the Bluetooth Low Energy (BLE) iBeacon functionality, providing potential insights for broader IoT deployment scenarios beyond the proposed case. Das *et al.* [8] developed and deployed IoT PAs, and proposed a resource registry that can be used for advertising purposes, introducing future opportunities to refine such registries to balance usefulness with minimizing potential user fatigue from advertising. More recent work by Morel *et al.* [13] outlined high-level requirements for consent in IoT, presenting a set of technical requirements for implementing a consent framework in IoT. The authors implemented a BLE-based prototype to show the presented framework's real-world applicability, pointing toward future research on a holistic analysis of PA systems. Finally, Alanezi *et al.* [1] presented a PA design to address individual and group context privacy concerns, inviting future work on dynamic negotiation deadlines and adaptive user preference modeling.

**iii. Elicitation Algorithms.** Baarslag and Gerding [4] proposed an optimal algorithm for eliciting exact user privacy preferences in a single round during negotiation, which invites future work in approaches that work effectively when users provide approximate rather than exact utility values, or when elicitation occurs over multiple rounds with minimal burden. Mohammad and Nakadai [12] addressed this by relaxing the assumption of *exact* utility values, offering a more adaptable approach. Building on both of these works, PADOME relaxes the assumption that users will always respond to elicitation, recognizing that in practice users may miss or deliberately ignore elicitation attempts.

## 3 PADOME: A Novel PA Design

In this section, we present PADOME, a novel PA design that combines the following two strategies: (i) user privacy preference elicitation, and (ii) surrounding PA elicitation. Although these mechanisms are not individually novel, their combination and the assumption that elicitation may fail presents new challenges. PADOME's novelty lies in integrating these mechanisms and overcoming technical challenges to allow the PA to manage the complexities of dynamic negotiation and elicitation states.

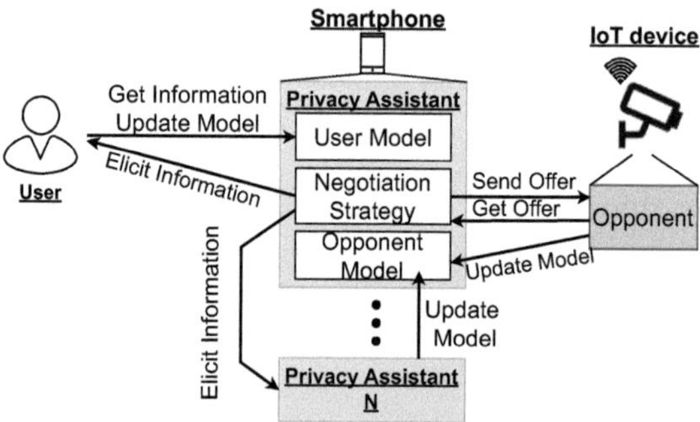


**Fig. 1.** Overview of interactions among the user, PAs, and IoT device.

### 3.1   Setting Definition

A common assumption for PA designs is that the PA has prior, potentially perfect, knowledge of the user and opponent (*i.e.*, IoT device) models obtained from prior interactions or the population's average. In our setting, however, the user is assumed unwilling or unable to specify their privacy preferences fully. As such, for each possible offer, the PA faces the following uncertainties: (i) the opponent preferences (*opponent model*), and (ii) user's utility of an offer (*user model*). Broadly, the opponent model captures the IoT device's preferences and negotiation strategies. We also assume there are other PAs, some having already arrived at an agreement with the IoT device. Thus, the PA can refine the opponent model by exchanging offers with the IoT device or eliciting other PAs. For instance, by building an opponent model, a PA may infer that the IoT device prioritizes location privacy over other privacy policy (PP) terms and adjust its offers accordingly. Simultaneously, the PA can elicit the user to iteratively refine the user model.

At each negotiation round, the PA decides whether to (i) elicit user for privacy preferences, (ii) elicit opponent model from other PAs, (iii) accept an offer, (iv) counter an offer, or (v) break off the negotiations. Each decision involves balancing benefits and costs, *e.g.*, utility at the cost of user bother. We assume *incremental* elicitation, *i.e.*, the PA can continue the elicitation process if needed. Figure 1 illustrates these interactions.

### 3.2   Formal Model

Let $\Omega = \{\omega_1, ..., \omega_n\}$ denote all possible offers in the negotiation, each with utility $U(\omega)$, which is initially uncertain. Before user preferences are elicited, $U(\omega)$ is modeled as a stochastic variable $x_\omega$ with cumulative distribution function $F_\omega(x)$, independent of other offers. The user has an exact utility function $\tilde{U} : \Omega \to [0, 1]$ that maps all possible negotiation outcomes to a real number. This *real* utility, however, is not known to the PA. Hence, the PA maintains some probability distribution $\hat{U}(\omega) : [0, 1] \to [0, 1]$ that represents the probability of $\tilde{U}(\omega) = u$ for $0 \leq u \leq 1$, *i.e.*, $\hat{U}(u) \equiv Prob(\tilde{U}(\omega) = u)$. At any point in the negotiation, the PA can elicit $\tilde{U}(\omega)$ at a cost $c_u(\omega)$, representing utility loss due to user bother.

The PA negotiates with the IoT device using an alternating offers protocol, modeling acceptance probability of $\omega$ as $p_\omega$, calculated from prior interactions or by eliciting opponent models from other PAs at cost $c_o(\omega)$. The alternating offers protocol was chosen for its simplicity and widespread use in the related literature [2]. In it, upon receiving an (counter-)offer, the PA updates the opponent model. If an offer is accepted, the negotiation ends in an agreement. The PA, however, can also choose to break off the negotiation process. Specifically, PA has a known reservation value $r \in [0, 1]$, which is the utility or payoff of breaking off the negotiation. Additionally, an agreement must be reached within a fixed number of exchanges $D$. At the end of the negotiation, the utility of the PA is given by Eq. 1.

$$U = \begin{cases} U(\omega) - \sum_{\omega' \in \Omega} c_u(\omega') - \sum_{\omega'' \in \Omega} c_o(\omega'') & \text{if } \omega \in \Omega \text{ is accepted,} \\ r - \sum_{\omega' \in \Omega} c_u(\omega') - \sum_{\omega'' \in \Omega} c_o(\omega'') & \text{if no agreement reached.} \end{cases} \tag{1}$$

### 3.3  Negotiation and Elicitation Strategies

**Negotiation Strategy.** The PA aims to maximize the expected utility by calculating the expected value of different actions while considering the opponent model and expected utility if the negotiation continues.

Following Baarslag and Gerding [4], we assume the PA uses a decision function with an *aspiration value* $\alpha_j \in [0, 1]$, which represents the expected reward for continuing negotiation at round $j \leq N$, where $N \leq D$ is the total number of rounds. Given $\alpha_j$, the *negotiation value* of sending an offer $\omega \in \Omega$ is:

$$v(\omega) = p_\omega U(\omega) + (1 - p_\omega)\alpha_j, \tag{2}$$

where $U(\omega)$ is an immediate utility payoff if the offer gets accepted with probability $p_\omega$ and the expected future payoff of $\alpha_j$ if the offer is rejected. We also define $U(\omega_0) = r$, which represents the previously defined reservation value.

At each round, if no further elicitation occurs, the optimal strategy is to select the offer with the highest negotiation value $v^*(\Omega) = \max_{\omega \in \Omega} v(\omega)$. We formalize this strategy in Algorithm 1.

---

**Algorithm 1:** Proposed negotiation strategy.

---

**Input**: Current negotiation state.
**Output**: One of the actions: accept, counter-offer, or break-off.
1  **for** $\omega \in \Omega$ **do**
2      update($p_\omega$);
3  UserElicitation();                      `// presented in Algorithm 2`
4  PAElicitation() ;                    `// presented in Algorithm 3`
5  $\omega \leftarrow \arg\max_{\omega' \in \Omega}(p_{\omega'} U(\omega') + (1 - p_{\omega'})\alpha_j)$;
6  **return** $\begin{cases} ACCEPT & \textit{if } \omega \textit{ was offered,} \\ BREAK\text{-}OFF & \textit{if } \omega = \omega_0, \\ SEND(\omega) & \textit{otherwise,} \end{cases}$

---

Negotiation stops if deadline $D$ is reached, computed dynamically as:

$$D = \lfloor D_{\text{Base}} + F_M + F_{\text{Network}} + F_{\text{Distance}} + F_{\text{PP}} + 0.5 \rfloor, \tag{3}$$

where $D_{\text{Base}}$ is the base deadline. $F_M$ is the user factor, which accounts for the number of other users $M$ and reflects resource burden on the ecosystem from other negotiations. The network factor $F_{\text{Network}}$ captures differences in network technologies; *e.g.*, networks supporting small payloads may require more transmission rounds. The distance factor $F_{\text{Distance}}$ scales with the average distance of PAs from the IoT device. $F_{\text{PP}}$ is the PP size factor.

**User Elicitation Strategy.** Using the negotiation value $v^*(\Omega)$, the elicitation strategy determines which offers, if any, to elicit from the user. This is a sequential decision problem, since each choice depends on the offers elicited so far and on the probability that the user may ignore an elicitation. Therefore, the goal is to find (i) an optimal *sequence* of offers to elicit and (ii) a strategy specifying when to start and stop the elicitation.

We define the *user elicitation state* as $\mathcal{E}_u$, defined by $\langle \bar{\Omega}, y \rangle$, where $\bar{\Omega}$ are all non-elicited offers and $y = v^*(\Omega)$. The goal is to formulate a user elicitation policy $\pi_u$, that, given $\mathcal{E}_u$, determines whether to elicit an offer or to proceed with negotiation. The utility of the $\pi_u$ is:

$$U(\pi_u, \mathcal{E}_u) = \begin{cases} y & \text{if } \pi_u(\mathcal{E}_u) \notin \bar{\Omega}, \\ P_u \displaystyle\int_{-\infty}^{\infty} U(\pi_u, \mathcal{E}'_u)\, dF_{x_{\pi(\mathcal{E})}} - c_u(\pi_u(\mathcal{E}_u)) & \text{otherwise,} \end{cases} \tag{4}$$

where $P_u$ is the probability of successfully eliciting the user and $\mathcal{E}'_u = \langle \bar{\Omega} \setminus \{\pi_u(\mathcal{E}_u)\}, \max(y, v(x)) \rangle$ is the updated state after observing $x_{\pi_u(\mathcal{E}_u)}$. $P_u$ can be estimated using models of user engagement [11,17].

Using Eq. 4, we are looking to find $\pi_u^* = \arg\max_{\pi_u} U(\pi_u, \mathcal{E}_u)$. Note that if *exact* values of all offers are known, $U(\pi_u^*, \langle \emptyset, y \rangle) = y$. Otherwise, we calculate the negotiation value $x_\omega^v$ of a non-elicited offer $\omega \in \bar{\Omega}$ using the random variable $x_\omega$ as follows:

$$x_\omega^v = p_\omega x_\omega + (1 - p_\omega)\alpha_j. \tag{5}$$

Compared to Eq. 2, Eq. 5 relies on a random variable instead of the *exact* utility value since the *real* value of offer $\omega$ is unknown.

Recall that $\pi_u$ determines whether the PA stops and obtains $y$, or elicits an offer $\omega \in \bar{\Omega}$ by sampling $x$ from $x_\omega^v$ at cost $c(\omega)$, while taking the following into the account:

1. If $x > y$, the PA has found a better offer with the expected utility $U(\pi_u, \langle \bar{\Omega} \setminus \{\omega\}, x \rangle) - c_u(\omega)$;
2. Otherwise, if $x \le y$, nothing changes, except that PA now knows the value of $x_\omega$, so the new expected utility is $U(\pi_u, \langle \bar{\Omega} \setminus \{\omega\}, y \rangle) - c_u(\omega)$.

Given the above, $U(\pi_u^*, \mathcal{E}_u)$ must satisfy the following recursive relation [4]:

$$\begin{aligned} U(\pi_u^*, \mathcal{E}_u) = \max\{y, \max_{\omega \in \bar{\Omega}}\{-c_u(\omega) + P_u[(U(\pi_u^*, \langle \bar{\Omega} \setminus \{\omega\}, y \rangle) \cdot F_\omega^v(y)) \\ + \int_{x=y}^{\infty} U(\pi_u^*, \langle \bar{\Omega} \setminus \{\omega\}, x \rangle)\, dF_\omega^v(x)] + (1 - P_u)[U(\pi_u^*, \langle \bar{\Omega}, y \rangle)]\}\}, \end{aligned} \tag{6}$$

where $F_\omega^v(x)$ denotes the corresponding cumulative distribution function.

The relation for $\pi_u^*$ in Eq. 6 is a form of the Bellman equation, which can be solved optimally using the index-based method presented by Baarslag and Gerding [4]. We define the index $z_\omega^v$ as the solution to $P_u \int_{z_\omega^v}^{\infty} (x - z_\omega^v) dF_\omega^v(x) = c(\omega)$. When $P_u = 1$, the equation reduces to the original index equation in [4].

---

**Algorithm 2:** Proposed user elicitation strategy.

---

1 **for** $\omega \in \bar{\Omega}$ **do**

2  $\quad z_\omega^v \leftarrow$ Solve $P_u \int_z^{\infty} (x - z) dF_\omega^v(x) = c(\omega)$ for $z$;

3 $v \leftarrow \max_{\omega \in \Omega}(p_\omega U(\omega) + (1 - p_\omega)\alpha_j)$;

4 $\omega \leftarrow \arg\max_{\omega' \in \bar{\Omega}} z_{\omega'}^v$;

5 **while** $z_\omega^v \geq v$ and $\bar{\Omega} \neq \emptyset$ **do**

6  $\quad$ elicitationCost $\leftarrow$ elicitationCost $+ c(\omega)$;

7  $\quad u \leftarrow$ ElicitFromUser$(\omega)$;

8  $\quad$ **if** $u \neq \bot$ **then**

9  $\quad\quad U(\omega) \leftarrow u$;

10  $\quad\quad \Omega \leftarrow \Omega \cup \{\omega\}; \bar{\Omega} \leftarrow \bar{\Omega} \setminus \{\omega\}$;

11  $\quad\quad v \leftarrow \max(v, p_\omega U(\omega) + (1 - p_\omega)\alpha_j)$;

12  $\quad\quad \omega \leftarrow \arg\max_{\omega' \in \bar{\Omega}} z_{\omega'}^v$;

13  $\quad$ **else**

14  $\quad\quad$ **break** ;  `// no reply: continue negotiation`

---

The resulting elicitation strategy $\pi_u$ (presented in Algorithm 2) is: *Elicit the offer $\omega \in \bar{\Omega}$ with the highest index $z_\omega^v$, if it is higher than $v^*(\Omega)$; update the $v^*(\Omega)$ if the realized value is higher, and repeat. Stop the elicitation if the highest index is less than $v^*(\Omega)$, or when all offers are in $\Omega$.*

**PA Opponent Model Elicitation Strategy.** We use an information-theoretic approach, utilizing entropy and information gain to guide the PA elicitation strategy. Specifically, let $\mathcal{P} = PA_1, PA_2, \ldots, PA_M$ represent the set of $M$ PAs, where each $PA_i$ is an individual PA that will send elicitation requests to the surrounding PAs. Let $R$ denote the set of PA responses, *i.e.*, opponent models.

Algorithm 3 shows the proposed PA elicitation strategy, which is designed to balance information gain with time and power consumption costs. In particular, the PA calculates initial and new entropy values (lines 4 and 5), provided information from $M - 1$ PAs. It then finds the expected information gain $I$ (line 6) and uses it to calculate the utility $U$ (line 7). While the utility function incorporates time ($c(t)$) and power ($c(p)$) consumption, it can be extended to account for other factors. The PA then compares the utility against the reservation value $r$ (line 8) to determine if it is "worth" broadcasting the request to PAs in the environment, and if so, PA broadcasts the elicitation requests and updates the opponent model based on the received responses (line 10).

---

**Algorithm 3:** Proposed PA elicitation strategy.

---

**Input**: $PA_i$, $\mathcal{P}$, reservation value $r$.
**Output**: Updated opponent model.

1   **for** $PA \in \mathcal{P} \setminus PA_i$ **do**
2     $\lfloor$ Determine $PA$ response likelihood $p(PA)$;

3   **for** $\omega \in \Omega_{PA_i}$ **do**
4     $H_0 = -\sum_{PA_j \in \mathcal{P} \setminus \{PA_i\}} p_{\omega,j} \, \log_2 p_{\omega,j}$;
5     $H_{\text{new}} = H_0 \times \frac{1}{M-1}$;

6   $I = p(PA) \times (H_0 - H_{\text{new}})$;
7   $U \leftarrow I - \frac{w_t \cdot \log(1+c(t))}{w_p \cdot \log(1+c(p))}$;
8   **if** $U > r$ **then**
9     $R \leftarrow \texttt{BroadcastToPAs()}$;
10    $p_{\omega_{\text{new}}} = \frac{p_\omega + \text{median}(R)}{2}$;

---

# 4   Experiments

This section presents PADOME's input parameter analysis and evaluation against state-of-the-art PA designs across various scenarios and network technologies.

## 4.1   Input Parameter Analysis

As part of the PADOME design process, we evaluated the effect of input parameters on its performance. Specifically, we examined the impact of user elicitation cost and negotiation deadline on the *Average Consent Percentage* and *Average PA Power Consumption*. The results are averaged over 10 times using BLE and Shopping Mall. For parameters not under investigation, we use the following fixed values: reservation value of 0.25, elicitation cost of 0.05, user elicitation response probability of 0.85 and base deadline of 4.

From Figs. 2a and 2b we can observe that: (i) longer negotiations increase average consent percentage up to a "saturation" point, beyond which other factors, *e.g.*, network coverage, limit the PA's performance and (ii) more negotiation rounds lead to higher power consumption until reaching a plateau. These results align with Baarslag and Gerding [4], who showed that increasing elicitation cost reduces negotiation utility. Based on these results, we set a base deadline of 4 with a dynamic increase as per Eq. 3.

From Figs. 2c and 2d we can observe that: (i) higher elicitation costs reduce average consent percentage up to a "saturation" point, as fewer opportunities arise for the PA to gather user preferences and (ii) in the best case, when elicitation is cost-free, user elicitation positively impacts power consumption by reducing it. The latter result is notable, suggesting that eliciting user preferences does not affect the negotiation flow as anticipated. Based on these results, we set an elicitation cost of 0.05.

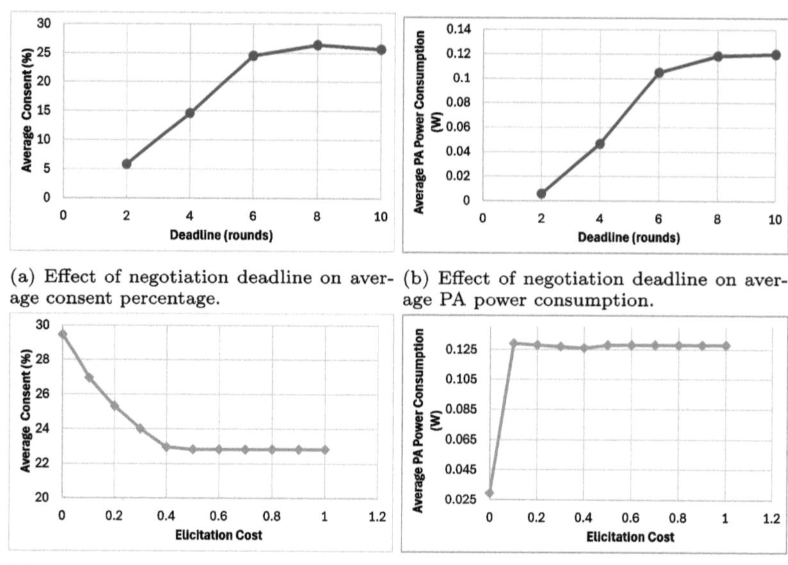

(a) Effect of negotiation deadline on average consent percentage.

(b) Effect of negotiation deadline on average PA power consumption.

(c) Effect of user elicitation cost on average consent percentage.

(d) Effect of user elicitation cost on average PA power consumption.

**Fig. 2.** Effect of input parameters on the PADOME performance.

## 4.2   Experimental Methodology

We implemented PADOME in GEPARD simulator [15]. We ran tournament-style simulations with 25 runs per design and compared them across three available scenarios: Hospital, University, and Shopping Mall. We employed BLE, Zig-Bee, and LoRa as network technologies and compared PADOME against three state-of-the-art PA negotiation protocols: Alanezi, Cunche, and Concession.

In our experiments, we adopted the effective communication ranges as specified in [15]: 50 m for BLE, 100 m for ZigBee, and 10,000 m for LoRa. The spatial dimensions for each scenario were also taken from the same reference, with the Hospital measuring 40 m, the University 80 m, and the Shopping Mall 120 m in radius. These parameters are noted as they have a significant impact on the experimental results discussed below. For instance, BLE performance in the larger Shopping Mall scenario is expected to be poorer compared to the smaller Hospital scenario due to its limited communication range.

## 4.3   Experimental Results

**Average User Device Power Consumption.** Figure 3 shows the average user device power consumption in the Hospital scenario. We calculated the combined average user device power consumption and averaged over the total number of runs. From the figure, we can observe that PADOME-based PA, due to opponent model elicitation, results in up to 16.4 times higher power consumption than

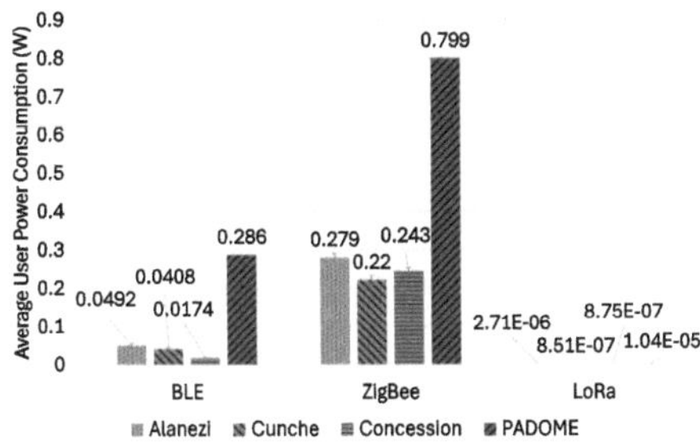


**Fig. 3.** Average user device power consumption in Hospital.

Concession-based PA, both using BLE, which would require the IoT device to rely on the external power supply to operate.

**Average Consent.** We measured average consent as a percentage of consent collected and averaged across all runs. From Fig. 4, we can observe that the average consent achieved by the non-PADOME-based PAs lie within 1% of each other. This observation is notable, as it emphasizes the influence of the scenario and network technologies on PA performance rather than the negotiation protocols themselves. Additionally, we can also observe that PADOME-based PA achieves up to 32.37% higher average consent than the alternatives, *e.g.*, Alanezi-based PA in Hospital under BLE. While the effective network technology ranges and space sizes, as noted in [15], naturally influence these results, they can be attributed to the addition of user preference and opponent model elicitation strategies. These strategies, however, result in higher power consumption.

## 5  Discussions and Future Work

The individual strategies employed in PADOME have been previously studied but often under idealized assumptions [1]. In contrast, our work relaxes the assumption of guaranteed user or surrounding PA responses to elicitation requests and integrates these elicitation strategies, resulting in a more realistic PA design than those proposed in the existing literature. A potential direction for future research includes further exploration of novel component combinations and adaptive mechanisms. This future work should also consider PADOME's reliance on opportunistic interaction with surrounding PAs, which may not always be feasible in environments with sparse device density or unstable network connectivity. In such cases, reduced access to external models could limit performance.

PADOME achieves significantly higher user consent rates through elicitation of user preferences and opponent models compared to existing PA designs, albeit at the cost of increased power consumption. The increased power consumption raises important considerations for the scalability and applicability of PADOME in large-scale IoT networks, where device battery life and power efficiency could

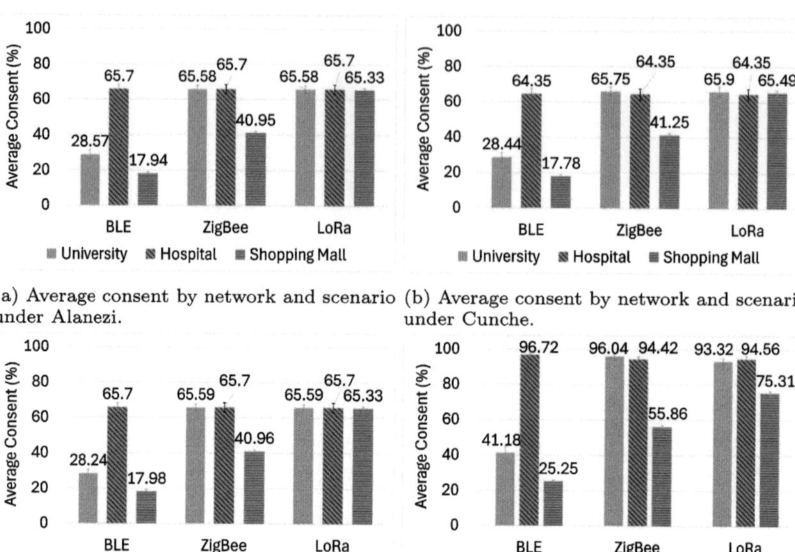

(a) Average consent by network and scenario under Alanezi.

(b) Average consent by network and scenario under Cunche.

(c) Average consent by network and scenario under Concession.

(d) Average consent by network and scenario under PADOME.

**Fig. 4.** Average consent across different networks and scenarios under various network protocols.

become critical constraints. Future research will need to explore optimization strategies to balance the trade-offs between increased consent rates and power consumption to ensure practical deployment at scale. For example, leveraging edge computing to offload inter-PA and negotiation communication could reduce associated power consumption.

Additionally, PADOME's adaptiveness is based on predefined heuristics, static probabilistic models, and entropy calculations rather than machine learning (ML) techniques. This design choice is motivated primarily by the resource constraints of IoT and user smartphone devices, where running complex learning algorithms is often infeasible. Furthermore, interpretability is especially critical in privacy-sensitive contexts because transparent and explainable decision mechanisms foster user trust and enable informed consent, which ML models often lack due to their black-box nature. Nevertheless, exploring hybrid approaches that incorporate lightweight learning while preserving interpretability represents a promising avenue for future work.

We also note that our experiments are based on GEPARD, which has limited independent validation. To promote transparency and reproducibility, the simulator's source code and documentation have been made available, providing explanation of parameter validation and the structure and implementation of the DUNE framework within GEPARD [15]. Future efforts will focus on validation through real-world deployments and benchmarking, while also relaxing our simplifying assumption of a uniform static elicitation response probability.

With respect to PADOME's real-world implementation, it is worth noting that it would not expose its underlying algorithms to end-users. Instead, the interface abstracts these details, presenting only context-specific elicitation requests linked to individual PP statements, as demonstrated in [7,8].

## 6   Conclusion

In this work, we introduced PADOME, a PA with a dynamic user privacy preference and opponent modeling strategies for privacy negotiations in IoT. PADOME combines opponent model elicitation from the surrounding PAs with user preference elicitation that accounts for the possibility of user and other PAs being uncooperative. Using simulations, we demonstrated that PADOME improves average user consent compared to state-of-the-art PA designs at the cost of increased power consumption. This highlights a critical trade-off between negotiation effectiveness and resource usage. Building on these findings, future research will investigate lightweight, ML-based adaptive opponent modeling and elicitation mechanisms, explore optimization strategies for reducing power consumption, and evaluate PADOME in real-world IoT environments.

## References


1. Alanezi, K., Mishra, S.: Incorporating individual and group privacy preferences in the internet of things. J. AIHC **13**(4) (2022)
2. Baarslag, T.: What to bid and when to stop. Ph.D. thesis, Delft University of Technology (2014)
3. Baarslag, T., Alan, A.T., et al.: An automated negotiation agent for permission management. In: Proceedings of AAMAS (May 2017)
4. Baarslag, T., Gerding, E.H.: Optimal incremental preference elicitation during negotiation. In: Proceedings of IJCAI (Jul 2015)
5. Cha, S.C., Chuang, M.S., et al.: A user-friendly privacy framework for users to achieve consents with nearby BLE devices. IEEE Access **6** (2018)
6. Chikukwa, G.: A consent framework for the internet of things in the GDPR Era. Ph.D. thesis, Dakota State University (2021)
7. Cunche, M., Métayer, D.L., et al.: ColoT: A consent and information assistant for the IoT. In: Proceedings of ACM WiSec (July 2020)
8. Das, A., Degeling, M., et al.: Personalized privacy assistants for the internet of things: providing users with notice and choice. IEEE Pervasive Comput. **17**(3) (2018)
9. Filipczuk, D., Baarslag, T., et al.: Automated privacy negotiations with preference uncertainty. Autonom. Agents Multi-Agent Syst. **36**(2) (2022)
10. Kökciyan, N., Yolum, P., et al.: Taking situation-based privacy decisions: privacy assistants working with humans. In: Proceedings of IJCAI (Jul 2022)
11. Mehrotra, A., Pejovic, V., et al.: My phone and me: understanding people's receptivity to mobile notifications. In: Proceedings of CHI (May 2016)
12. Mohammad, Y., Nakadai, S.: Utility elicitation during negotiation with practical elicitation strategies. In: Proceedings of IEEE SMC (Oct 2018)

13. Morel, V., Cunche, M., et al.: A generic information and consent framework for the IoT. In: Proceedings of TrustCom/BigDataSE (Aug 2019)
14. Padyab, A., Habibipour, A., et al.: Adoption barriers of IoT in large scale pilots. Information **11**(1) (2019)
15. Rochester, E., Barker, K.: Designing infrastructure-aware privacy assistants for the iot. Technical report, University of Calgary (2025). https://hdl.handle.net/1880/122427. Accessed 12 Aug 2025
16. Stöver, A., Hahn, S., et al.: Investigating how users imagine their personal privacy assistant. In: Proceedings of PETS (Jul 2023)
17. Tian, Y., Zhou, K., et al.: What and how long: prediction of mobile App engagement. ACM Trans. Inform. Syst. **40**(1) (2022)
18. Van Der Schyff, K., Foster, G., et al.: Online privacy fatigue: a scoping review and research agenda. Future Internet **15**(5) (2023)
19. Zhou, H., Goel, M., et al.: Bring privacy to the table: interactive negotiation for privacy settings of shared sensing devices. In: Proceedings of SIGCHI (May 2024)

# 9th Cryptocurrencies and Blockchain Technology Workshop (CBT 2025)

# Fast Off-Chain Payments
# with Second-Layer Privacy

Sven Gnap[1], Kari Kostiainen[1], and Ghassan Karame[2(✉)]

[1] ETH Zurich, Zürich, Switzerland
`gnaps@student.ethz.ch`, `kari.kostiainen@inf.ethz.ch`
[2] Ruhr University Bochum, Bochum, Germany
`ghassan.karame@rub.de`

**Abstract.** While several techniques have been proposed to speed up payments in permissionless blockchains, no current solution is entirely satisfactory for application scenarios like retail shopping. In particular, existing solutions like payment channels require users to lock up significant funds, while other schemes that rely on pre-defined validators do not protect users' privacy during payment processing.

In this paper, we define a new notion of second-layer privacy, which hides transaction details from off-chain validators and thus prevents targeted attacks on second-layer payment systems such as payment blocking (e.g., censorship) or off-chain user tracking. We then set forth to develop Quicksilver, the first second-layer payment scheme that is practical, fast, and provides second-layer privacy and censorship-resilience. We implement and evaluate Quicksilver for EVM-compatible chains and show that it effectively enables fast and private payments on popular blockchain platforms.

## 1 Introduction

Although blockchains have gained wide attention, their adoption as a payment mechanism remains limited. For instance, in point-of-sale payments, permissionless blockchains are simply too slow, as safe blockchain payment acceptance takes several minutes while transactions should be typically completed in few seconds e.g., in retail shopping. Permissionless blockchains are also too transparent for retail payments. This has led to the surge of dedicated platforms like Zcash [21] and Monero [20] and 2nd-Layer systems like Zether [8] to provide improved privacy. However, none of these solutions are fast enough for retail payments.

To speed up permissionless blockchain payments, a number of techniques have been proposed [19]. Payment channels and payment channel networks [15] emerge as one of the most popular solutions. Once a payment channel is established, or once a suitable route in a payment channel network is found, fast off-chain payments are possible. However, if a retail customer needs to establish separate channels with all possible merchants, they need to lock up significant collateral, and thus such solutions do not scale for practical use with many merchants. Payment networks can reduce the amount of locked collateral, but


R. Laborde et al. (Eds.): ESORICS 2025, LNCS 16231, pp. 221–241, 2026.
https://doi.org/10.1007/978-3-032-16089-8_15

**Table 1.** Comparison of our work, Quicksilver, and related solutions.

| | Fast Payments | 2nd-Layer Privacy | Collateral Privacy | Scalable Collaterals | No Extra Assumptions | On-Chain Privacy | Increased Throughput |
|---|---|---|---|---|---|---|---|
| **2nd-Layer Payments** | | | | | | | |
| Sidechains [22] | ✓ | ✗ | n/a | n/a | ✗ | ✗ | ✓ |
| zk-rollups | ✗ | ✗ | n/a | n/a | ✓ | ✓ | ✓ |
| Payment channels [15] | ✓ | ✓ | ✗ | ✗ | ✓ | ✓ | ✓ |
| Payment hubs | ✓ | ✗ | ✗ | ✗ | ✓ | ✓ | ✓ |
| Scalable and reusable collaterals (Snappy [17]) | ✓ | ✗ | ✗ | ✓ | ✓ | ✗ | ✗ |
| **2nd-Layer Payments with Privacy** | | | | | | | |
| Anonymous payment channels (e.g., Bolt [14]) | ✓ | ✓ | ✓ | ✗ | ✓ | ✓ | ✓ |
| Private payment hubs (e.g., TumbleBit [16] and A2L [23]) | ✓ | unlikable | ✗ | ✗ | ✓ | ✓ | ✓ |
| LDSP [18] | ✓ | sender privacy | ✗ | ✗ | ✓ | ✓ | ✗ |
| **Our work: Quicksilver** | ✓ | ✓ | ✓ | ✓ | ✓ | confidential | ✗ |

cannot guarantee that a suitable route is found and that the payment can be completed [10].

Side chains [22] and new collateralized payment processing techniques like Snappy [17] provide an alternative approach to speed up blockchain payments. In such solutions, pre-defined validators approve payments off-chain before payments appear on-chain. Such schemes improve payment latency and can reduce the amount of locked collaterals, but suffer from a significant limitation as a by-product. Since every payment needs to be approved by a set of validators, targeted attacks like payment blocking and off-chain user tracking become possible. We observe that the root cause behind such attacks is that all transaction details are revealed to the off-chain validators. The prospect of payment blocking is especially worrisome, because strong censorship resilience is one of the main advantages of permissionless blockchains, and unfortunately, current proposals for enabling fast blockchain payments eliminate that advantage.

To address this gap, we first define a new notion of *second-layer privacy* which hides all the relevant transaction details from the off-chain payment validators and thus prevents targeted attacks on second-layer payment systems such as payment blocking, censorship, or off-chain user tracking (Sect. 3). We then introduce a novel solution, dubbed Quicksilver, that is fast, supports 2nd-layer privacy, and does not require the locking-up of significant collateral (Sects. 4). The primary technical challenge in our work is to design payment processing mechanisms that allow the off-chain validators to enforce payment safety (e.g., verify that payers do not exceed their collaterals during fast payments) without revealing any sensitive payment details to the validators that would allow targeted attacks like payment blocking or tracking, and thus violate our notion of 2nd-layer privacy. To overcome this challenge, Quicksilver augments an existing collateralized payment processing model [17] with a novel off-chain payment processing technique that leverages cryptographic commitments and Verifiable Random Functions (VRFs).

Our security analysis (Sect. 6) shows that Quicksilver payments are safe (if a merchant accepts a payment, he is guaranteed to receive the funds) and 2nd-layer private (the off-chain payment validators do not learn any sensitive payment details ensuring censorship-resilience). In addition, we show that the amount of payment collaterals (deposited by customers) remains private. We implemented Quicksilver for EVM-compatible chains and evaluated it on Ethereum and Polygon (Sect. 7). Our experiments confirm that Quicksilver payments are fast and can be approved in 0.5–2.5 s. Last but not least, we demonstrate that payment costs in Quicksilver are affordable as one Quicksilver payment costs \$2.1 on Ethereum and \$0.01 on a cheaper chain like Polygon.

## 2  Background

**Side Chains.** One common approach is side chains, where a pre-defined set of validators approve each payment, e.g., by running a consensus protocol. The main drawback of this approach is that it requires additional trust assumptions. In the case of BFT consensus, two-thirds of the validator nodes must be trusted. Additionally, such systems do not provide 2nd-layer privacy. The validators learn all transaction details and can easily block payments of targeted victim users and prevent transaction processing from them.

**zk-Rollups.** Zero-knowledge rollups (zk-rollups) consist of layer-2 solutions that typically outsource computation and state to be processed off-chain but store transaction data on-chain on an L1 network, such as Ethereum or Polygon. Changes to the state are computed off-chain and are proven on-chain using zero-knowledge proofs (hence the name). zk-rollups greatly increase transaction throughput and help reduce transaction costs. However, such solutions do not reduce payment latency which is one major limitation of most permissionless blockchain systems (and the main focus of our work).

**Payment Channels and Networks.** Another popular set of solutions are payment channels [15,19]. In a typical payment channel scheme, two parties lock collateral into a smart contract and then perform fast off-chain transactions that are secured, as long as there is sufficient collateral left in the channel. Payment channels improve payment latency and system throughput. Such payments are also private in the sense that during an off-chain payment, the transaction details are not revealed beyond the sender and recipient.

When considering application scenarios like retail payments, the main problem of payment channels is that the customer needs to setup a channel with each merchant which requires significant locked-in funds [10]. Payment channels can be organized into networks, but since the flow of funds is predominantly one way (from customers to merchants), the deposited collaterals will quickly run out making it difficult to find available channels to merchants in practice [10].

**Payment with Scalable Collaterals.** Recently, researchers have proposed alternative collateralized schemes such as Snappy [17] that combines ideas from payment channels and side chains. A major benefit of this approach is that users need to deposit only a single collateral and the same collateral can be re-used unlimited number of times which significantly improves collateral practicality. Also validator collaterals remain moderate and validators do not need to be trusted. The main remaining limitation of Snappy is that the off-chain validators can see all transaction details and thus they can easily block payments.

We summarize the above discussion in Table 1.

## 3    Second-Layer Privacy

Next, we define what 2nd-layer privacy means. We assume that customers and merchants initiating a payment do not disclose any information about each other or their payment to the public. We argue that little can be done if a customer or merchant leaks the payment. When a customer initiates a payment, it sends a *payment intent* to the merchant. Payment intents are then processed by off-chain validators before the merchant accepts the payment. Our goal is to protect sensitive transaction details in the payment intent from the off-chain validators (adversary). We do not focus in this work on protecting the customer/merchant identities on-chain. Notice that, for censorship-resilience against validators, it is only necessary that the payment intent cannot be censored.

We define this more formally as follows. Let $P$ denote the set of all payment intents in the system. By $t \in P$, we mean that a payment intent $t$ is characterized by a sender address in $\{0,1\}^n$ drawn from probability distribution $S$, a recipient address in $\{0,1\}^m$ drawn from probability distribution $R$, a payment value in $\{0,1\}^l$ drawn from probability distribution $V$, and a payment index (introduced in the next section) in $\{0,1\}^o$ drawn from probability distribution $I$. Similarly, let $U$ denote the set of all payment intents drawn at random.

**Definition 1 (2nd-Layer Privacy).**  *We say that a payment system is 2nd-layer private if $P$ is poly-time indistinguishable from a randomly formed payment intent in $U$, if $\forall$ p.p.t. distinguisher $A$, there exists a negligible function $\epsilon$, s.t. $|\underset{t\in P}{Pr}(A(t) = 1) - \underset{t\in U}{Pr}(A(t) = 1)| < \epsilon(n)$ where $n$ is the security parameter.*

**Comparison to Previous Definitions.** A few previous research papers consider privacy of 2nd-layer payments. Below, we briefly explain how such previous privacy definitions differ from our work. First, there are anonymous payment hubs like TumbleBit [16] and A2L [23] that allow payment senders to make (fixed-amount) payments without revealing the identity of the payment recipient to the hub operator. That is, such solution provide unlinkability between the sender and the recipient, but the hub operator learns the identity of the sender for each payment. Thus, such solutions provide a different (and more limited) notion of off-chain privacy.

Second, papers like Bolt [14] design payment channels for anonymous cryptocurrencies like Zcash. The goal of such solutions is to hide the identity of the payment sender from the payment recipient (among the set of user that the recipient has open channels to). Our goal is to hide all sensitive transaction details from off-chain validators. Similar to other payment channels, solutions like Bolt are not scalable in terms of collaterals.

Third, LDSP [18] runs a Chaum-style e-cash scheme [9] as 2nd-layer. LDSP provides a weaker notion of off-chain privacy where the payment recipient identity and payment amount are not hidden from the payment validator. Also its collaterals are not practical since they need to be replenished after they have been used. Table 1 *summarizes how such previous 2nd-layer privacy notions and solutions differ from our work.*

**Additional Security Definitions.** As an additional privacy protection, we consider the privacy of collaterals that customers deposit to enable fast payments. We define this as follows. Let $C$ denote the set of all collaterals made by users in the system. By $c \in C$, we mean that a collateral $c$ is characterized by a value in $\{0, 1\}^n$ drawn from probability distribution $V$. Similarly, let $W$ denote the set of all collaterals drawn at random.

**Definition 2 (Collateral Privacy).** *We say that a payment system offers collateral privacy for a user if his collateral $C$ is poly-time indistinguishable from a randomly formed collateral in $W$, if $\forall$ p.p.t. distinguisher $A$, there exists a negligible function $\epsilon$, s.t. $\left| \Pr_{c \in C}(A(t) = 1) - \Pr_{c \in W}(A(t) = 1) \right| < \epsilon(n)$ where $n$ is the security parameter.*

Moreover, our solution should ensure that fast payments are safe to accept.

**Definition 3 (Merchant Safety).** *If a merchant follows the protocol and accepts a payment, he is guaranteed to receive funds matching the full amount of the accepted payment.*

**Definition 4 (User safety).** *If a user signs a complete transaction $\tau$ with payment amount $b^*$, the user is guaranteed to lose at most $b^*$ of its funds.*

**Definition 5 (Statekeeper safety).** *If a statekeeper follows the protocol, no funds will be transferred from any of his $M$ collateral accounts $(y_1, ..., y_M)$.*

## 4   Quicksilver Overview

### 4.1   Building Blocks

**Fast Payment Approval.** The first building block of our solution is fast payment approval using collateralized majority signing, a technique recently introduced by Snappy [17]. This technique requires a pre-defined set of off-chain validators, called *statekeepers*, that approve payments fast. During system registration, each user and statekeeper deposits a collateral into a smart contract. To provide a brief example, consider a deployment where merchants also function as statekeepers. The incentive to function as a statekeeper (that needs to place a collateral) is that this way the merchants can accept fast payments safely and increase their sales. Some merchants, and thus some statekeepers, may however have an economic incentive to block (i.e., not approve) payments towards a competing merchant.

Figure 1 illustrates the payment processing. When the user initiates a payment (step 1), it sends a data structure called *payment intent* and a list of previously approved pending transactions to the merchant. Payment intents contain the addresses of the payment sender (customer) and recipient (merchant), the amount of the payment, and a monotonically increasing *payment index* that the user increments for each payment. Using the payment index, the merchant verifies that all the previous payments by the same user either appear finalized on the chain or are approved by statekeepers, and that the user has enough collateral to cover the current and pending payments (step 2).

The merchant forwards the payment intent to all statekeepers who check that they have not approved a payment by the same user with the same index before. Then they sign the intent and send it back to the merchant (step 3). Once the merchant has collected signed intents from the *majority* of the statekeepers (step 4), it can aggregate the signatures, and forward the aggregated signature back to the user (step 5). The user will finalize the transaction by including the majority-signed intent (step 6). The user

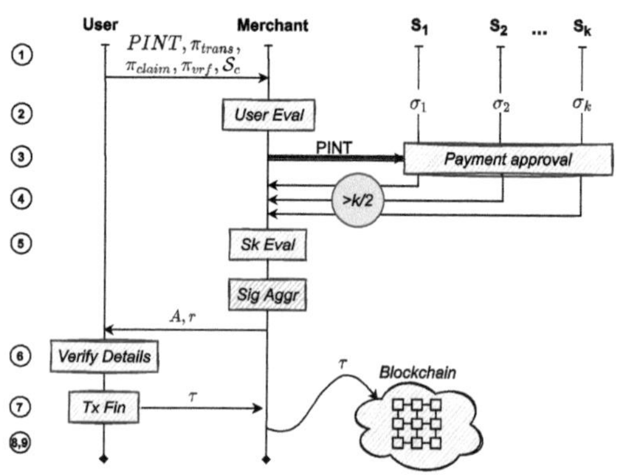


**Fig. 1.** Payment flow in Quicksilver.

sends the final transaction to the merchant who can at this point consider the payment safely completed, hand over goods to the user (step 7), and broadcast the transaction to the blockchain network (step 8).

The main intuition why such payment approval process is safe is based on two arguments [17]. First, if the user double spends, the merchant can claim back the lost funds from the user's collateral by presenting the signed intent as evidence to the smart contract that controls all collaterals. This process is called *settlement*. Second, if the user colludes with a malicious statekeeper who approves multiple transactions for the same user with the same index value (double spending with another merchant), the victim merchant can claim the lost funds from the cheating statekeeper's collateral. Identification of the cheating statekeeper is always possible, because if two separate majority sets sign conflicting transactions, there will always be at least one statekeeper whose equivocation leaves undeniable evidence.

**Confidential Payments.** The second building block of our solution is Zether [8], a confidential payment mechanism that leverages encrypted account balances. In this technique, a smart contract maintains an encrypted account balance for each user. Each account balance is encrypted with a public key that is associated with the account, and the encryption scheme is homomorphic such that it allows addition and subtraction of encrypted values.

To create a confidential balance, a user performs a funding operation that transfers coins to a smart contract which will create an encrypted account balance associated with that user's public key. To transfer funds, the sender first encrypts the payment amount using the public key of its own account. The resulting ciphertext can be subtracted by the smart contract from the sender's previous encrypted account balance. Then, the sender encrypts the payment amount using the public key of the recipient's account. This ciphertext can be added to the recipient's previous encrypted balance by the smart contract. The sender also produces a zero-knowledge proof that shows that the two account balances were adjusted by the same amount, the sender's updated balance is positive, and proves the knowledge of the sender's private key. The smart contract verifies the proof and updates the encrypted account balances accordingly.

### 4.2  Challenges and Main Ideas

While the above two techniques provide a starting point for our solution, a straw-man combination of these two techniques fails to solve our research question. Below, we explained involved challenges and outline our new ideas for solving them.

**Challenge 1: Protecting the Customer's Identity.** Fast payment approval requires that the identity of the customer and the monotonically increasing payment index are included in each payment intent. The statekeepers ensure that they sign only one intent with the same index per customer. Such a design allows statekeepers to identify the customer of each payment. Replacing the user's identity with a cryptographic commitment is insufficient, since this would prevent statekeepers from controlling that they sign only one intent for each payment index for each user. Instead, what is needed is a mechanism to hide the identity of the user from the statekeepers such that they can still enforce the policy of one signature per index and user. We solve this problem using *verifiable random functions* (VRFs) [13]. When a customer wishes to initiate a payment, he uses his VRF private key and the current payment index value as input for the VRF that will output a pseudorandom value and a proof that can be verified using the associated VRF public key. The customer creates a modified payment intent that contains the pseudorandom value as *Randomized Payment Identifier* (RPID) instead of its identity. The customer passes the payment index and VRF proof for the current and all pending transactions to the merchant who can verify that the proofs are correct using the public key that is registered to the smart contract, before passing the intent to the statekeepers. The statekeepers enforce a new policy where they sign only one intent with the same RPID value.

Such payments are safe for merchants due to the *uniqueness* property of VRFs. For the same VRF input (payment index) only one correct VRF output (RPID) can be generated. Since malicious customers cannot create multiple RPIDs for the same index and statekeepers track double-spending per payment index, a malicious customer cannot double spend. Customer identification is no longer possible due to the *pseudorandomness* of VRFs which ensures that RPID (and thus the payment intent) reveals no information about the customer.

**Challenge 2: Protecting the Payment Amount.** Prior research has shown that payment amounts can identify the merchant [12]. Thus, we need to hide payment amounts from the statekeepers as well. We observe that statekeepers do not necessarily need know the payment value to do their job safely and correctly.[1] Therefore, the payment amount can be either removed from the intent or included in encrypted format.

**Challenge 3: Confidential Customer Collateral.** To enable private collaterals and confidential payments, we use homomorphic encryption to protect payment amounts. To safely accept a payment, the merchant needs to verify that the customer's collateral is sufficient to cover both the current payment and all the pending transactions. When the customer's collateral and payment amounts are encrypted (using encrypted account balances similar to Zether), the merchant cannot perform such a check. Additionally, if the customer cheats and the merchant needs to initiate a settlement, it cannot authorize a transfer from the user's confidential collateral, because it does not know the user's private key needed to create a proof that authorizes the confidential transfer.

We solve these two problems using a new *payment authorization mechanism* that is tailored to our use case. When the customer initiates a payment, it creates *two* proofs: one that authorizes the transfer of funds from his account to the merchant's account and another that authorizes transfer of funds from his collateral to the merchant. When computing the second proof, the customer leverages the *homomorphic property* of confidential payments. The customer subtracts the (encrypted) values of all pending payments from the (encrypted) value of the collateral, and then creates the proof that shows that the updated collateral value is still positive. This is possible using existing proof techniques from [8]. By verifying the proof, the merchant ensures that the customer's collateral is sufficient to cover the all the pending and current payments.

**Challenge 4: Confidential Statekeeper Collateral.** To enable confidential statekeeper collaterals, statekeepers establish separate confidential collaterals for each merchant and privately shares their value and the private key that controls them with the respective merchant. Merchants *track payments* approved by each

---

[1] In case a malicious customer double spends, the majority-signed intent is included to the on-chain transaction that is signed by the customer. Thus, the intent is bound to the payment amount and the merchant can initiate settlement of correct amount if needed. The same argument applies for misbehaving statekeeper.

statekeeper and control that no statekeeper is approving more transactions than their collateral allows. If settlement from a statekeeper is needed, merchant can authorize the transfer from the statekeepers collateral using the private key. Sharing the private key is safe, because the Quicksilver smart contract enforces that the statekeeper's collateral is used only when the statekeeper equivocated.

Notice that addressing Challenges 1–2 allow us to support 2nd-layer privacy, while addressing Challenges 3–4 enables collateral privacy.

## 5 Quicksilver Specification

### 5.1 Cryptographic Primitives

**Aggregate Signatures.** To enable signature aggregation for reduced transaction size and efficient verification, we rely on the Boneh-Lynn-Shacham (BLS) signature scheme [6]. We assume that the user is given functions $\sigma = \mathsf{AggrSig}(\{\sigma_1, \ldots, \sigma_n\})$ and $y = \mathsf{AggrPk}(\{y_1, \ldots, y_n\})$ which implement signature and public key aggregation, respectively, and a verification function $\mathsf{AggrVerify}(\sigma, y)$ that outputs valid for correct signature [5].

**Verifiable Random Functions.** A verifiable random function (VRF) is a public-key version of a keyed cryptographic hash [13]. Given an input value $m$, the owner of private key $x$ can compute hash $h = \mathsf{VRFhash}(x, m)$ and matching proof $\pi_{\mathsf{vrf}} = \mathsf{VRFprove}(x, m)$. An important property of VRFs is that the hashing algorithm is deterministic for the same inputs $(x, m)$. Given $y, m$, and $\pi$, the hash is valid if $\mathsf{VRFverify}(y, m, \pi)$ outputs valid. Anyone can deterministically obtain the VRF output $h$ from the proof $\pi$ by computing $h = \mathsf{VRFproof2hash}(\pi)$.

VRFs have the following security properties [13]. *Uniqueness* means that, for any fixed public VRF key $y$ and for any input $m$, there is a unique VRF output $h$ that can be proved to be valid. *Collision resistance* is the same as for cryptographic hash functions. *Pseudorandomness* ensures that when an adversary sees a VRF hash output $h$ without its corresponding VRF proof $\pi$, then $h$ is indistinguishable from a random value.

**ElGamal Encryption.** We leverage an ElGamal encryption scheme variant where the message is in the exponent, as defined in [8]. Given a key-pair $(x, y)$, where $y = g^x$, we encrypt a message $b$ by choosing a random secret $r \in \mathbb{Z}_p$ and by computing the ciphertext $C = (g^b y^r, g^r)$. To decrypt $C$, one divides $g^b y^r$ by $(g^r)^x$ which yields $g^b$. The extraction of $b$ out of $g^b$ is performed by brute force. Such encryption scheme is *additively homomorphic* under the same public key. We use notation where $C_a \leftarrow C_a \circ C_b$ adds the value of $C_b$ to $C_a$. Conversely, $C_a \leftarrow C_a \circ C_b^{-1}$ deducts the value of $C_b$ from $C_a$.

**$\Sigma$-Bullets.** $\Sigma$-Bullets is a proof system that combines efficient range proofs from Bulletproofs [7] with Sigma protocols for algebraically encoded statements. $\Sigma$-Bullets is used for confidential payments in Zether [8] as follows. Assume that the user wants to transfer an amount $b^*$ from his account $y$ to another account $\bar{y}$. Let $C_b$ be the current encrypted balance associated with $y$. To complete such a confidential transfer, the smart contract needs to deduct $b^*$ from $y$'s balance and add the same amount to $\overline{y}$'s balance. To achieve this, the user will encrypt $b^*$ under both $y$ and $\overline{y}$ to get ciphertexts $C$ and $\overline{C}$. After that, the user computes a zero-knowledge proof using function $\pi_{\text{transfer}} = \mathsf{ProveTransfer}(C_b, C, \overline{C}, y, \overline{y}; x, b^*, b', r^*)$ that takes as inputs both public keys $(y, \overline{y})$, all three ciphertexts $(C_b, C, \overline{C})$, the sender's private key $x$, the payment amount $b^*$, the sender's remaining balance $b'$ after the account update, and randomness used for encryption $r^*$. The function outputs a proof $\pi_{\text{transfer}}$, which shows that (1) ciphertexts $C$ and $\overline{C}$ are well formed and encrypt the same amount, (2) the payment amount $b^*$ is a positive value, (3) the sender's remaining balance $b'$ is positive, and (4) the proof creator knows the private key $x$. Finally, we assume a verification function $\text{true/false} = \mathsf{VerifyTransfer}(y, \overline{y}, C_b, C, \overline{C}, \pi_{\text{trans}})$ that takes as input the public keys, the above ciphertexts, and the proof.

**Table 2.** Quicksilver smart contract state.

| Field | Symbol | Description |
| --- | --- | --- |
| *Customers* | $C$ | |
| ↪ *entry* | $C[y_c]$ | |
| ↪ *Collateral* | $C[y_c].pcol$ | Private collateral |
| ↪ *VRF* | $C[y_c].y_{vrf}$ | VRF public key |
| ↪ *Finalized* | $C[y_c].D$ | Finalized transactions |
| ↪ *entry* | $C[y_c].D[i]$ | Entry for index $i$ |
| ↪ *Hash* | $C[y_c].D[i].h$ | Processed tx hash |
| ↪ *Signatures* | $C[y_c].D[i].\tau_A$ | Aggregate signature |
| ↪ *Quorum* | $C[y_c].D[i].\tau_q$ | Approving parties |
| ↪ *Bit* | $C[y_c].D[i].b$ | Sig. verified flag |
| ↪ *Observed* | $C[y_c].O$ | Observed approval quora |
| ↪ *entry* | $C[y_c].O[i]$ | Entry for index $i$ |
| ↪ *Hash* | $C[y_c].O[i].h$ | Observed tx hash |
| ↪ *Trace* | $C[y_c].T$ | Past settlements |
| ↪ *entry* | $C[y_c].T[i]$ | Entry for index $i$ |
| ↪ *Nonce* | $C[y_c].T[i].idx$ | Settled tx index |
| ↪ *Remaining* | $C[y_c].T[i].bal$ | Remaining collateral |
| *Statekeepers* | $S$ | |
| ↪ *entry* | $S[y_s]$ | |
| ↪ *Allocation* | $S[y_s].y[y_m]$ | Per merchant collateral |

**Table 3.** Quicksilver transaction $\tau$ format.

| Field | Symbol | Description |
| --- | --- | --- |
| *To* | $\tau_{\text{to}}$ | Quicksilver contract |
| *From* | $\tau_f$ | Any address |
| *Value* | $\tau_v$ | Transaction fee |
| *ECDSA Sig.* | $v, r, s$ | Tx signature triplet |
| *Data* | | |
| < ↪ *Payment Index* | $\tau_i$ | Monotonic counter |
| ↪ *Random Payment ID* | $\tau_{\text{RPID}}$ | VRF hash |
| ↪ *Commitment* | $\tau_c$ | Merchant's address |
| ↪ *Signatures* | $\tau_A$ | Aggregate signature |
| ↪ *Quorum* | $\tau_q$ | Approving parties |
| ↪ *Proof* | $\pi_{\text{trans}}$ | Customer's $\Sigma$-Bullet |
| ↪ *Accounts* | $(y_c, y_m)$ | Sender/receiver address |
| ↪ *Values* | $(c_c^*, c_m^*)$ | Encrypted values |

### 5.2 System Initialization

We assume that Quicksilver smart contract is deployed on blockchain like Ethereum. All system participants (customers, merchants, statekeepers) have an existing encrypted account balance, maintained by the Quicksilver contract, that has already been funded. We call such confidential accounts *Quicksilver accounts* to differentiate them from the plaintext Ethereum accounts. We assume a system deployment with $C$ registered customers, $M$ merchants, and $S$ statekeepers. The state of the Quicksilver smart contract is shown in Table 2. We denote the privacy-preserving payment intent as PINT and the complete transaction as $\tau$. The structure of $\tau$ is shown in Table 3.

**Customer Registration.** To register, customer $c$ creates a VRF key pair $(y_{\mathsf{vrf}}, x_{\mathsf{vrf}})$ and registers the public key $y_{\mathsf{vrf}}$ with their existing Quicksilver account $y_c$ in the smart contract. The customer also performs a confidential transfer [8] that transfers collateral amount $pcol$ from $y_c$ to the Quicksilver smart contract. The contract creates a new user entry $C[y_c]$ in its state and updates the user's confidential account balance $Acc[y_c].bal$ and the user's confidential collateral $C[y_c].pcol$ based on the confidential payment. The user initializes locally its payment index as $i = 0$.

**Statekeeper Registration.** To register, statekeeper $s$ must create a separate confidential collaterals accounts for each $M$ merchants in the Quicksilver contract. To achieve this, the statekeeper picks $M$ key pairs $((x_1, y_1), ..., (x_M, y_M))$ and sends the public keys $(y_1, ..., y_M)$ to the Quicksilver smart contract. Then, the statekeeper performs $M$ confidential payments [8] from its account $y_s$ to confidential accounts defined by $(y_1, ..., y_M)$. The contract saves the transferred funds in its state as new encrypted account balances $S[y_s].y[y_i]$ and updates the confidential account balance $Acc[y_s].bal$ of the statekeeper based on the payments accordingly. Finally, the statekeeper sends the private keys $(x_1, ..., x_M)$ to the respective merchants.

**Merchant Registration.** To register, merchant $m$ sends its user account public key $y_m$ to the smart contract that creates a new entry $M[y_m]$ in its state. The merchant also stores all the private collateral keys $(x_i, ..., x_S)$ that it receives from each $S$ statekeepers.

## 5.3   Payment Protocol

The payment process transfers funds from a customer's Quicksilver account $y_c$ to a merchant's Quicksilver account $y_m$ as shown in Fig. 1.

**Step 1.** The customer creates a private payment intent $\mathsf{PINT}_c$ which includes (1) a random payment identifier $\mathsf{RPID} = \mathsf{VRFhash}(x_{\mathsf{vrf}}, i)$, computed using the VRF private key $x_{\mathsf{vrf}}$ and payment index $i$,[2] (2) the address of the merchant's account $y_m$, and (3) the encrypted payment value $c_c^*$ under the customer's public key $y_c$. The customer also creates two zero-knowledge proofs for payment and settlement $\pi_{\mathsf{trans}}$ and $\pi_{\mathsf{claim}}$ using the ProveTransfer function. The first proof $\pi_{\mathsf{trans}}$ proves the usual transfer details, i.e., it is created on the user's main account balance $Acc[c].bal$ and shows that remaining balance after subtracting the encrypted

---

[2] The reliance on the private key in the computation of RPID prevents an adversary from learning who computed the VRF.

payment amount remains positive. The second proof, $\pi_{\text{claim}}$ is created on customer's collateral balance $C[y_c].pcol$, and it shows that the current collateral is sufficient to cover the current payment and all the pending payments.[3] To achieve this, the input $b'$ for the $\pi_{\text{claim}}$ proof computation is obtained by homomorphically deducting the encrypted values of all pending payments from the current collateral balance. The user sends to the merchant the current payment index $i$, $\text{PINT}_c$, $y_{\text{vrf}}$, $(c_c^*, c_m^*)$ $\pi_{\text{trans}}, \pi_{\text{claim}}$, the VRF proofs $\pi_{\text{vrf}}$ for all pending transactions, and the list $\mathcal{S}_c$ of pending transactions.

**Step 2.** The merchant performs the following checks to ensure that they can claim settlement in case the payment should fail. They verify the VRF proof $\pi_{\text{vrf}}$ for every pending transaction index. Furthermore, for each index $j \in \{1, \ldots, \text{PINT}_c[i]\}$, there must appear an *approved* transaction with index $j$ that is either finalized on the blockchain or contained in $\mathcal{S}_c$. The received $y_{\text{vrf}}$ must be registered on the Quicksilver contract. All details of the confidential payment, in particular $\pi_{\text{trans}}$, must be correct. The additional $\pi_{\text{claim}}$ must be verified to ensure that the user's private collateral is sufficient to cover all pending transactions and the current transaction. To verify $\pi_{\text{claim}}$, the merchant homomorphically deducts all the encrypted amounts $b_i^*$ of all pending payments from the customer's current encrypted collateral value $C[y_c].pcol$ to obtain input $b'$ for the VerifyTransfer function.

**Step 3.** To prevent payment blocking, the merchant hides their address in the payment intent $\text{PINT}_c$ by replacing their address with a commitment $c = \text{Commit}(y_m, r)$, where $r$ is a randomly chosen blinding factor and saves $r$. The merchant broadcasts the modified $\text{PINT}_c$ to all the statekeepers.

**Step 4.** Each statekeeper evaluates the received $\text{PINT}_c$. They check within their local list that they have not already approved a payment with the same RPID. If a matching RPID is found, they notify the merchant. Otherwise, they approve the payment by computing a BLS signature $\sigma_i = \text{Sign}(\text{PINT}_c, x_s)$ and send it back to the merchant. The statekeeper appends the approved RPID value to their local list.

**Step 5.** If a majority of statekeepers approves the payment intent, the merchant checks that all signatures are correct and upon success, aggregates them into $A = \text{AggrSig}(\{\sigma_1, \ldots, \sigma_n\})$. Otherwise, the merchant aborts and informs the user. The merchant additionally checks that each statekeeper who has approved the intent allocated enough collateral to the merchant. This can be done because the merchant knows their corresponding allocated collateral balances and the corresponding secret keys $x_i$. The merchant stores the payment intent $\text{PINT}_c$ together with the blinding factor $r$, all VRF proofs $\pi_{\text{vrf}}$, $\pi_{\text{claim}}$ and $\pi_{\text{claim}}$ for possible later settlement. Finally, the merchant sends the aggregated signature $A$, the blinding factor $r$, and the majority-signed $\text{PINT}_c$ to the customer.

---

[3] Quicksilver collaterals work similar to Snappy collaterals. Their scalability is already discussed extensively in [17].

**Step 6.** The customer verifies the aggregate signature $A$ and checks that the merchant's commitment $c$ in the signed intent opens to $y_m = \mathsf{Open}(c, r)$.

**Step 7.** The customer creates the final transaction $\tau$ containing the details exchanged in the payment process, as described in Table 3. The final transaction $\tau$ can be signed by an arbitrary Ethereum account that has sufficient funds to cover the transaction fees.

**Step 8.** The merchant verifies that the customer correctly constructed and signed $\tau$ (i.e., the customer has not replaced, omitted, or modified any of the values). The payment can now be considered safely accepted and the merchant broadcasts $\tau$ in the blockchain network.

**Step 9.** Once $\tau$ is included to a block by miners, the Quicksilver smart contract executes *Record-and-Transfer* process that records the payment in its state and completes the confidential payment to merchant $m$. This operation verifies that the customer $c$ is registered and that there is no transaction with the same index $i$ already recorded. It then stores the hash of the transaction together with the approval signature and quorum. Finally, the contract verifies the zero-knowledge proof $\pi_{\mathsf{trans}}$ and completes the confidential transfer.

## 5.4   Settlement

Transaction may not be received and processed by the miners even after a reasonable amount of time due to the following reasons:

1. *Benign congestion:* The transaction may be of lower priority to the miners, e.g. due to having a lower gas price.
2. *Conflicting transaction:* Another transaction by the same user prevents the current transaction to be accepted by the Quicksilver smart contract (e.g., double-spending).
3. *User's blockchain account depletion:* The user's Ethereum account was depleted due to a previous transaction and has insufficient funds to cover the gas fees of the user's pending Quicksilver transactions.
4. *User's Quicksilver account depletion:* The user's Quicksilver account was depleted due to a previous transaction which invalidates the zero-knowledge proof $\pi_{\mathsf{trans}}$.

In case (1), the transaction is valid but fails to be processed by the blockchain's miners. Hence, the merchant can either wait longer or resubmit the transaction to the blockchain network with a higher gas price (recall that a Quicksilver transaction can be submitted by any Ethereum account). In cases (2–4), the transaction is invalid and the merchant can recover the lost funds by claiming settlement. If there are conflicting transactions in the system (case 2), the merchant must initiate the *Claim-Statekeeper* process to be refunded from the equivocating statekeeper's collateral. Otherwise, the merchant can initiate the *Claim-Customer* process.

**Claim Statekeeper.** In the following, we denote by $\tau^p$ the transaction that is being claimed, and by $\tau', \tau''$ majority-approved transactions that conflict either with $\tau^p$ or with each other. To create the settlement transaction, the merchant creates a confidential payment proof $\pi'_{\text{trans}}$ using ProveTransfer function with the inputs being the statekeeper's public key $y_m$, the merchant's public key $y_m$, the statekeeper's collateral secret key $x_s$, the statekeeper's collateral balance $b$, the payment amount $b^*$, and ciphertexts $(c_s^*, c_m^*)$ that encrypt the payment amount over the public keys of the statekeeper's collateral account and the merchant's account. Note that this proof is different than the customer's $\pi_{\text{trans}}$, because it proves the transfer from the statekeeper's collateral to the merchant's account.

The victim merchant sends to the smart contract the pending transaction $\tau^p$, the conflicting transactions $\tau', \tau''$, the equivocating statekeeper's public key $y_s$, the VRF proof $\pi_{\text{vrf}}$ for each above transactions, $r$ matching the pending transaction, the payment amount encrypted under the equivocating statekeepers public key $c_s^*$, and $\pi'_{\text{trans}}$. The smart contract first verifies that $\tau^p, \tau', \tau''$ are valid and the merchant provided correct conflicting transactions. In particular, apart from the BLS signature, it verifies the VRF proof and the commitment of the pending transaction. Next, it obtains the set of statekeepers who signed both conflicting transactions and ensures that the statekeeper being claimed is included in that set. Finally, the contract verifies the details of the zero-knowledge proof $\pi'_{\text{trans}}$ and transfers the disputed funds upon success to the merchant.

**Claim Customer.** If there is no conflicting transaction and the merchant followed the Quicksilver payment protocol, then the payment failed due to a malicious user. In this case, the merchant is guaranteed to be refunded by the Quicksilver smart contract from the user's collateral. The merchant includes the ciphertexts that encrypt the payment value with the customer collateral's public key, and the zero-knowledge proofs $\pi_{\text{claim}}, \pi_{\text{trans}}$ that the customer created during the payment process. Furthermore, the merchant includes the pending disputed transaction $\tau^p$ and all transactions that were pending at the time of payment approval $\mathbb{T}_p$. The smart contract verifies that all attached transactions submitted by the merchant are valid and signed by a majority of statekeepers; the state is compatible for the settlement request, in particular that there exists no conflicting transaction in the system; the past collateral balance was sufficient to cover all pending payments; and ciphertexts for the claim encrypt opposite amounts. In this case, the smart contract transfers the disputed funds and update the current collateral balance, and stores the observed pending transaction in the contract state.

## 6  Security Analysis

We first show that Quicksilver provides 2nd-layer privacy based on common cryptographic primitives and assumptions.

**Theorem 1 (2nd-Layer Privacy).** *Given the pseudorandomness property of VRFs, assuming that the DDH assumption holds, and that the used commitment scheme is perfectly hiding, Quicksilver is 2nd-layer private (cf. Definition 1).*

Recall that we assume that users and merchants initiating a payment do not disclose any information about each other or the payment intent to the public. We argue that little can be done if users/merchants leak sensitive payment details.

We now show that various constituents (price, customer address, merchant address, index number) of any legitimate payment intent in Quicksilver cannot be distinguished from the constituents of any random payment intent.

1. *Payment amount protection:* Since users and merchants do not leak the payment amount, the only constituents of a payment intent that are dependent on the amount comprise the ElGamal-encrypted value.
2. *Customer identity protection:* The only constituents of the payment intent that are derived from the customer is the VRF hash.
3. *Merchant identity protection:* The only part of the payment intent derived from the merchant address is the Pedersen commitment of the merchant's Quicksilver account.

We therefore conclude that any p.p.t. distinguisher $A$ can only distinguish a legitimate payment intent in Quicksilver from a random one with negligible probability. Otherwise, $A$ can break the DDH assumption (to distinguish the payment amount), or the pseudorandomness property of VRFs (to distinguish customer address) or the perfect hiding property of Pedersen commitments (to distinguish the merchant address).

**Merchant Safety.** Next, we show that Quicksilver is safe for merchants.

**Theorem 2 (Merchant safety).** *Given collision-resistance of VRFs, computationally binding commitments, and sound zero-knowledge proof system, Quicksilver provides merchant safety (cf. Definition 3).*

For this analysis, we leverage the fact that the Snappy [17] paper already proves that if a merchant checks the following five conditions prior to payment acceptance, it is guaranteed to receive funds that are equal to the full amount of the accepted payment (Definition 3).

– **Condition 1:** The majority of the statekeepers have signed a payment intent that binds the pair (customer address, payment index) to the pair (merchant address, payment amount).
– **Condition 2:** At the time of payment acceptance, the customer has sufficient collateral to cover both the current payment and the list of already approved but pending payment provided by the user.
– **Condition 3:** The merchant can authorize the settlement of correct payment amount from the customer's collateral if needed.

- **Condition 4:** Each statekeeper that has signed the intent has enough collateral to cover the amounts of the current and all pending payments approved by the same statekeeper.
- **Condition 5:** The merchant can authorize the settlement of correct payment amount from the statekeeper's collateral if needed.

In Quicksilver, these five conditions are satisfied as follows:

- **Condition 1:** Recall that the PINT structure signed by the statekeepers contains commitment to the merchant address, encrypted payment amount, and a VRF hash computed using the customer's private key and the payment index as input. This condition holds, since otherwise the customer would be able to violate the binding property of commitments or violate the collision-resistance of VRFs.
- **Condition 2:** Prior to accepting a payment, the merchant verifies the proof $\pi_{\mathsf{claim}}$ which shows that the customer's collateral is sufficient to cover the current and approved pending payment. To ensure that the correct set of pending payments is considered in the above proof computation, the merchant also verifies the VRF proofs $\pi_{\mathsf{vrf}}$ for each pending payment. These proofs show that the signed RPID matches the payment index $i$ in each pending payment. Therefore, to violate this condition, the merchant would need to forge $\pi_{\mathsf{claim}}$ which is proven secure in [8] or forge $\pi_{\mathsf{vrf}}$ by violating the collision-resistance property of VRFs.
- **Condition 3:** This condition holds since the merchant only accepts a payment if it receives a valid $\pi_{\mathsf{claim}}$ from the user. If a settlement from the user's collateral is needed, the merchant can present $\pi_{\mathsf{claim}}$ to the Quicksilver contract which can then execute the transfer from the user's collateral to the merchant. The Quicksilver contract enforces that the ciphertext used in the settlement proof is the same as the one used in the failed payment, and therefore the merchant is guaranteed to receive the correct payment amount.
- **Condition 4:** This condition holds since in Quicksilver the merchant knows the private key for the statekeeper's encrypted collateral account, and thus it can easily verify that the statekeeper has sufficient collateral to cover the current and all pending payments approved for the merchant.
- **Condition 5:** The last condition holds, since the merchant knows the private key so that it can create the proof $\pi'_{\mathsf{trans}}$ that can be presented to the Quicksilver contract that will then execute the transfer of funds. The Quicksilver contract enforces that the ciphertext used as input in $\pi'_{\mathsf{trans}}$ is the same as the one in the failed payment, and therefore the merchant is guaranteed to receive the correct payment amount.

We conclude that Quicksilver provides merchant safety, when VRFs are collision resistant, the used commitments are computationally binding, and the used zero-knowledge proof system is sound.

**User Safety.** To satisfy user safety (Definition 4), we need to show that the following two conditions hold. First, if $\tau$ is included on the chain, no settlement will be performed from the user's collateral. Conversely, if $\tau$ is not included in the chain, at most $b^*$ will be settled from the user's collateral. The first condition holds since the Quicksilver smart contract verifies that the claimed transaction is not already accepted and recorded on the state of the Quicksilver contract). That said, the second condition holds since the user creates the settlement proof $\pi_{\text{trans}}$ and the Quicksilver contract enforces that the settled amount is the same ciphertext used in the failed payment $\tau$. Recall that only the user knows the private key of his collateral account, and thus only him can create proofs to authorize transfers from this account.

**Statekeeper Safety.** We show that Quicksilver provides safety guarantees for statekeepers (who also deposit collaterals to cover their possible misbehaviour).

Recall that the statekeeper shares the private keys $(x_1, ..., x_M)$ of these collateral accounts with the merchants. This means that each merchant is able to create arbitrary proofs $\pi'_{\text{trans}}$ that would—without other enforcements—transfer funds from the statekeeper's collateral account. However, the Quicksilver contract ensures that transfers from the statekeeper's collateral are only possible, if the statekeeper has equivocated (signed more than one PINT with the same RPID value). Thus, no funds will be transferred from any of the statekeepers collaterals, unless the statekeeper deviates from the protocol.

**Collateral Privacy.** We show that collateral values remain confidential in Quicksilver.

**Theorem 3 (Collateral privacy).** *Given that the DDH assumption holds, Quicksilver provides collateral privacy (cf. Definition 2).*

Quicksilver inherits its confidentiality guarantees from Zether [8]. Collaterals are maintained as encrypted account balances in the Quicksilver smart contract. During registration, encrypted collateral balances are created using transaction where the deposited collateral amount is encrypted. In case of double spending, collateral balances are decreased using a settlement operation where the payment amount is also encrypted. Therefore, to violate collateral privacy, the adversary the would need to break the DDH assumption of ElGamal encryption (to distinguish the user's collateral balance from a random value).

**Liveness.** Quicksilver inherits the liveness property of Snappy [17]. If a majority of the statekeepers are reachable and sign the payment intent, the merchant can accept the payment.

## 7   Performance Evaluation

We implemented the Quicksilver system as a combination of an off-chain protocol in Rust/JavaScript and an on-chain smart contract in Solidity. Throughout our implementation, we used the `alt_bn128` elliptic curve since it is natively supported in the EVM. For the off-chain payment protocol, we relied Anonymous Zether [1], vrf-rs [4] and bn [2] libraries to construct the zero-knowledge and VRF proofs, and to perform the elliptic curve operations. In the Quicksilver smart contract, we additionally used the solidity-BN256G2 primitives [3]. We ran the customers, merchants and statekeepers on low-end machines with 2 vCPUs and 2 GB of RAM. Statekeepers were implemented as simple webservers. We deployed these merchants and statekeepers to cloud instances in 10 different locations (Mumbai, Toronto, Singapore, Dallas, Fremont, Atlanta, Newark, London, Sydney, Frankfurt).

To evaluate gas costs, we relied on the Solidity compiler (v0.7.0) and the Ganache client (v6.12.2) to create and deploy smart contracts.

**Latency.** We measured payment latency separately for variants (a) (Quicksilver with 2nd-layer privacy) and (b) (Quicksilver with 2nd-layer privacy and confidential payments) as shown in Fig. 2. It takes approximately 0.3–0.7 s to accept a Quicksilver payment with 2nd-layer privacy, depending on the number of validators (statekeepers). If confidential payments and collaterals are used additionally, the payment processing takes about 2.3–2.7 s which is equal to the Visa contactless payment approvals [11] and significantly faster than standard blockchain payments.

Our measurements consist of intent creation time (steps 1–3) and the statekeeper latency (steps 4–5). We observe that the proof computation ($\pi_{\mathsf{trans}}$ and $\pi_{\mathsf{claim}}$) needed for confidential payment and settlement dominates this latency taking more than 90% of the total latency. The required computational overhead of 2nd-layer privacy protections ($\pi_{\mathsf{vrf}}$ and commitments) constitute only a minor component of the total delay.

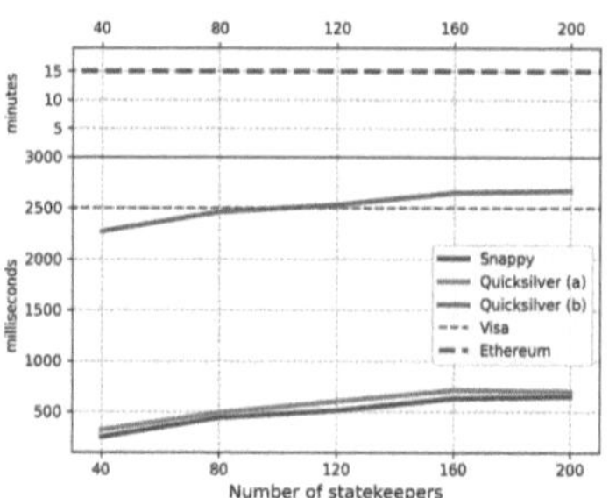

**Fig. 2.** Payment latency in Quicksilver.

The statekeeper approval latency increases slightly as the number of statekeepers increases (from 40 to 200 in our experiments). Our latency measurements were obtained on a throughput of 5,000 approval requests per second. We note that our current prototype uses an unoptimized JavaScript implementation from [1] for $\pi_{\mathsf{trans}}$ and $\pi_{\mathsf{claim}}$ computation. We expect a significant performance boost with an optimized implementation.

**Throughput.** We tested our prototype on throughput of 1,000 and 2,500 requests per second with only a negligible difference in latency. Given that currently chains like Ethereum support orders of magnitude lower throughputs, we conclude that Quicksilver provides more than sufficient throughput for the underlying blockchain.

**Gas Usage.** We measure gas costs for Quicksilver variant (a) that provides 2nd-layer privacy. We translate these costs to USD for two currently popular blockchain platforms, Ethereum (8.5 GWEI gas price, 1,277 USD/ETH, Q4 2022) and Polygon (77 GWEI gas price, 0.78 USD/MATIC, Q4 2022). The mea-

**Table 4.** Cost of Quicksilver operations.

| Function | Gas | Ethereum | Polygon |
|---|---|---|---|
| Open Account | 131,000 | $1.42 | $0.008 |
| Fund Account | 213,000 | $2.31 | $0.01 |
| Customer Registration | 105,000 | $1.14 | $0.006 |
| Merchant Registration | 72,000 | $0.78 | $0.004 |
| Statekeeper Registration | 195,000 | $2.12 | $0.01 |
| Payment Process | 197,000 | $2.14 | $0.01 |

**Table 5.** Quicksilver settlement gas cost.

| Number of Merchants | Pending Transactions per User | | | |
|---|---|---|---|---|
| | 0 | 1 | 2 | 3 |
| 50 | 0.93M | 1.56M | 2.25M | 2.88M |
| 100 | 1.48M | 2.56M | 3.72M | 4.81M |
| 150 | 2.02M | 3.57M | 5.17M | 6.75M |
| 200 | 2.58M | 4.59M | 6.68M | 8.73M |

surements for Quicksilver operations can be found in Table 4. We observe that 2nd-layer private Quicksilver payments are cheap, using only 197k gas (similar to a swap on an AMM). With our example rates and prices, this corresponds to $2.1 on Ethereum. On a cheaper chain like Polygon, one payment costs $0.01. Also other Quicksilver operations are similarly affordable, e.g., customer registration costs 105k gas ($1.1). The settlement process is evaluated in Table 5. The cost for claiming a statekeeper scales with the total number of registered merchants who act as statekeepers. The cost for claiming a user scales with the number of pending transactions. An example settlement for a 2nd-layer private payment with no pending transactions and 50 merchants costs 0.93M gas ($10 on Ethereum, $0.06 on Polygon). For completeness, we also measured also gas cost of Quicksilver in variant (b) that supports 2nd-layer privacy and additionally confidential payments and private collaterals. We observe that confidential Quicksilver payments use 5.03M gas and are currently affordable in blockchains like Polygon.

## 8   Conclusion

In this paper, we defined a new notion of 2nd-layer privacy and designed a novel solution called Quicksilver that provides such privacy protection. For a concrete design and evaluation, we built Quicksilver on top of Snappy [17], but we believe that our constructs could be applied to other systems as well, such as side-chains where validators approve payments off-chain. We show that Quicksilver ensures payment safety as well as second-layer privacy, as off-chain payment validators are unable to access any sensitive payment details. Our prototype implementation of Quicksilver confirms that 2nd-layer private Quicksilver operations are practical even on popular EVM-compatible chains, such as Ethereum and Polygon.

**Acknowledgments.** This work has been partly funded by the Deutsche Forschungsgemeinschaft (DFG, German Research Foundation) under Germany's Excellence Strategy—EXC 2092 CASA- 390781972—and by the Zurich Information Security and Privacy Center (ZISC).

# References


1. Anonymous Zether Extension. https://github.com/ConsenSys/anonymous-zether
2. PBN: Pairing cryptography with the Barreto-Naehrig curve. https://crates.io/crates/bn
3. solidity-BN256G2. https://github.com/musalbas/solidity-BN256G2
4. VRF implementation in Rust. https://crates.io/crates/vrf
5. Boneh, D., Drijvers, M., Neven, G.: Compact multi-signatures for smaller blockchains. IACR Cryptol. ePrint Arch. (2018)
6. Boneh, D., Lynn, B., Shacham, H.: Short signatures from the weil pairing. J. Cryptol. **17**(4) (2004)
7. Bunz, B., Bootle, J., Boneh, D., Poelstra, A., Wuille, P., Maxwell, G.: Bulletproofs: short proofs for confidential transactions and more. In: IEEE Symposium on Security and Privacy (SP) (2018)
8. Bünz, B., Agrawal, S., Zamani, M., Boneh, D.: Zether: Towards Privacy in a Smart Contract World, pp. 423–443 (2020)
9. Chaum, D.: Blind signatures for untraceable payments. In: Advances in Cryptology (1983)
10. Engelmann, F., Kopp, H., Kargl, F., Glaser, F., Weinhardt, C.: Towards an economic analysis of routing in payment channel networks. In: Workshop on Scalable and Resilient Infrastructures for Distributed Ledgers (2017)
11. Freed-Finnegan, M., Koenig, J.: Visa quick chip (2017). https://usa.visa.com/visa-everywhere/security/quick-chip-interview.html
12. Gervais, A., Ritzdorf, H., Lucic, M., Lenders, V., Capkun, S.: Quantifying location privacy leakage from transaction prices. In: European Symposium on Research in Computer Security (ESORICS) (2016)
13. Goldberg, S., Reyzin, L., Papadopoulos, D., Včelák, J.: Verifiable Random Functions (VRFs). Internet-Draft draft-irtf-cfrg-vrf-09 (2021). https://datatracker.ietf.org/doc/html/draft-irtf-cfrg-vrf-09
14. Green, M., Miers, I.: Bolt: anonymous payment channels for decentralized currencies. In: ACM Conference on Computer and Communications Security (CCS) (2017)
15. Gudgeon, L., Moreno-Sanchez, P., Roos, S., McCorry, P., Gervais, A.: SoK: layer-two blockchain protocols. In: Financial Cryptography and Data Security (FC) (2020)
16. Heilman, E., Alshenibr, L., Baldimtsi, F., Scafuro, A., Goldberg, S.: Tumblebit: an untrusted bitcoin-compatible anonymous payment hub. In: Network and Distributed System Security Symposium (NDSS) (2017)
17. Mavroudis, V., Wüst, K., Dhar, A., Kostiainen, K., Capkun, S.: Snappy: fast on-chain payments with practical collaterals. In: Network and Distributed System Security Symposium (NDSS) (2020)
18. Ng, L.K., Chow, S.S., Wong, D.P., Woo, A.P.: LDSP: shopping with cryptocurrency privately and quickly under leadership. In: International Conference on Distributed Computing Systems (ICDCS) (2021)
19. Poon, J., Dryja, T.: The Bitcoin Lightning Network: Scalable Off-Chain Instant Payments (2016)
20. van Saberhagen, N.: Cryptonote v 2.0 (2013)
21. Sasson, E.B., et al.: Zerocash: decentralized anonymous payments from Bitcoin. In: IEEE Symposium on Security and Privacy (S&P) (2014)

22. Singh, A., Click, K., Parizi, R.M., Zhang, Q., Dehghantanha, A., Choo, K.K.R.: Sidechain technologies in blockchain networks: an examination and state-of-the-art review. J. Netw. Comput. Appl. **149** (2020)
23. Tairi, E., Moreno-Sanchez, P., Maffei, M.: A2L: anonymous atomic locks for scalability in payment channel hubs. In: IEEE Symposium on Security and Privacy (SP) (2021)

# AUPCH: Auditable Unlinkable Payment Channel Hubs


Pedro Moreno-Sanchez[1,3], Mohsen Minaei[1], Srinivasan Raghuraman[1,2],
Panagiotis Chatzigiannis[1(✉)], and Duc V. Le[1]

[1] Visa Research, Palo Alto, USA
pchatzig@visa.com
[2] MIT, Cambridge, USA
[3] IMDEA Software Institute, MPI-SP, San Francisco, USA



**Abstract.** Cryptocurrencies, which have gained significant adoption in
recent years, face ongoing challenges in scalability and privacy. Payment
Channel Hubs (PCHs) constitute a solution to both issues by shifting
transactions off the public ledger. Various PCH constructions have been
proposed, offering different degrees of unlinkability, efficiency, and interoperability. However, regulatory compliance remains a significant concern, particularly under emerging frameworks like the EU's Markets in
Crypto-Assets (MiCA) regulation and FATF Travel Rule requirements.

This work addresses a gap in existing PCH constructions: the lack of
regulatory-compliant auditability mechanisms. While concurrent work
AuditPCH attempts to address this challenge, it suffers from fundamental limitations, including reliance on channel closures for auditing, vulnerability to unilateral de-anonymization by the hub, and lack of formal security guarantees for the auditing process. Our approach fundamentally differs by providing targeted, non-disruptive auditability that
allows auditability for high-risk payments while preserving unlinkability
for the rest. To achieve this, we present Verifiable Linkable Randomizable Puzzles (`VLRP`), a new cryptographic protocol that enables a party
to commit to a secret using two distinct keys: a verifiability key (VK)
and an auditability key (AK). This protocol provides (i) verifiability that
the owner of the VK issued the commitment, (ii) the ability to randomize the commitment to ensure unlinkability, even for the owner of the
VK, while still allowing traceability using the AK, and (iii) collaborative
auditing that prevents unilateral de-anonymization.

We then present Auditable Unlinkable Payment Channel Hubs,
AUPCH, a PCH built on `VLRP` that offers auditability guarantees with
stronger security guarantees than existing approaches. AUPCH provides
modular integration with existing PCH frameworks ($A^2L$, BlindHub),
operates without requiring channel closures, and ensures that auditing
requires collaboration between hub and auditing agent, preventing abuse
by either party alone. Crucially, our approach acts as a wrapper around
existing PCH implementations, requiring only replacing randomizable
puzzle calls with VLRP calls, a minimal change that dramatically reduces
deployment complexity compared to building new systems from scratch.

**Keywords:** Payment Channel Hubs · Auditable Privacy ·
Randomizable Puzzles · Cryptocurrency · Regulatory Compliance

# 1   Introduction

Cryptocurrencies have gained prominence as decentralized and publicly verifiable
payment systems, attracting interest from banks, leading IT companies, and payment providers [10,13]. Among the off-chain solutions to address their inherent
scalability challenges, payment channels [2,14,21] have seen significant academic
and industry adoption. A payment channel allows two users to perform multiple
off-chain transactions, settling them with just two on-chain transactions.

To overcome the limitation of two-party channels, Payment Channel Hubs
(PCHs) were developed. They use a central intermediary (hub) or tumbler to
facilitate payments between any two users [11,26,29]. However, this reliance on
a single intermediary introduces several challenges: (i) *security* (the hub could
steal funds); (ii) *unlinkability* (the hub could link payers to payees); (iii) *value
privacy* (the hub could learn transaction amounts); (iv) *interoperability* with
different cryptocurrencies; and (v) *amount flexibility* (payments can be of arbitrary amounts). Over the years, various PCH constructions have been proposed
to address these issues with different trade-offs (c.f. Table 1). However, *auditability*, that is, the possibility to link a payer and payee in a transaction, is missing
from existing PCH constructions, except for AuditPCH, which we overview next.

*Comparison with AuditPCH.* A recent PCH construction by Li *et al.* [16] also
accounts for auditability. However, AuditPCH[1] suffers from fundamental limitations that restrict its practical applicability and security guarantees. Our
AUPCH approach differs in several key aspects:

- **Operational Model:** AuditPCH performs auditing through a post-hoc
  channel closure mechanism. In contrast, AUPCH operates on active channels, enabling auditing without channel termination, which is particularly
  relevant for use cases requiring pre-transaction compliance verification.
- **Security Model:** We employ a trust model with an explicit separation
  between the hub and an auditability agent, using nested encryption that
  requires collaboration for de-anonymization. This prevents unilateral action
  by the hub, whereas AuditPCH assumes a semi-honest hub model. Our work
  also provides formal security definitions with complete cryptographic games
  and proofs.
- **Modularity Approach:** Our design acts as a modular wrapper around existing PCH constructions (A²L [25], BlindHub [23] or unlinkable/interoperable
  payment channels [18]). It requires only minimal changes to underlying protocols, essentially replacing randomizable puzzle calls with VLRP calls, while
  AuditPCH introduces a more integrated design requiring substantial modifications.

---

[1] Not to be confused with our work, AUPCH.

- **Compliance Requirements:** Our approach enables targeted auditing of pre-flagged high-risk transactions, which aligns with emerging regulatory frameworks like FATF Travel Rule and EU MiCA requirements for real-time compliance verification, while AuditPCH focuses on post-hoc forensic analysis.

**Table 1.** Comparison of AUPCH with state-of-the-art PCH. The bottom rows show how existing PCH systems can be enhanced with auditability using our VLRP primitive.

| | Security | Unlinkability | Value Privacy | Interoperability | Amount Flexibility | Auditability |
|---|---|---|---|---|---|---|
| BOLT [8] | ● | ● | ● | ○ (Blind signatures, Script modifications) | ● | ○ |
| Perun [3] | ● | ○ | ○ | ○ (Ethereum Virtual Machine) | ● | ○ |
| Teechain [17] | ● | ● | ● | ○ (Trusted Hardware) | ● | ○ |
| TumbleBit [11] | ● | ● | N.A.[a] | ○ (HTLC-based currencies) | ○ | ○ |
| A2L [26] | ● | ● | N.A.[a] | ● (Digital Signatures and timelocks) | ○ | ○ |
| A2L $^{+}$, A2L $^{UC}$ [7] | ● | ● | N.A.[a] | ● (Digital Signatures and timelocks) | ○ | ○ |
| BlindHub [22] | ● | ● | ● | ● (Digital Signatures and timelocks) | ● | ○ |
| Accio [6] | ● | ● | ● | ○(Ethereum Virtual Machine) | ● | ○ |
| AuditPCH [16] | ● | ● | ● | ○ (Requires channel closure) | ● | ◐[b] |
| AUPCH (VLRP +A2L) | ● | ● | N.A.[a] | ● (Digital Signatures and timelocks) | ○ | ● |
| AUPCH (VLRP + BlindHub) | ● | ● | ● | ● (Digital Signatures and timelocks) | ● | ● |

[a] N.A.: not applicable since the amount in these protocols is fixed.

[b] Post-hoc auditability: designed for forensic analysis after channel closure, assumes semi-honest hub model.

## 1.1  Goal of this Work

A significant limitation in existing state-of-the-art PCH constructions is the absence of mechanisms for *auditability*. This gap is becoming increasingly critical as regulatory frameworks evolve to mandate traceability for combating illicit financial activities, such as money laundering (AML) and counter-terrorist financing (CTF). Consequently, PCHs require an auditability mechanism to permit the detection of the origin or destination of funds in specific transfers.

The regulatory landscape now imposes stringent requirements on cryptocurrency service providers. The Financial Action Task Force (FATF) Travel Rule [5], for instance, obligates virtual asset service providers (VASPs) to collect and transmit originator and beneficiary information for transactions exceeding certain thresholds. This has direct implications for PCH operators, who must possess the technical means to trace transactions [28] when legally required. Similarly, recent European legislation explicitly identifies technologies that enhance anonymity, such as mixers [15,27] or tumblers [19], as high-risk factors and mandates enhanced due diligence to determine the provenance of crypto-assets[2]. Furthermore, the EU MiCA regulation [4] requires that crypto-asset service providers implement robust systems to prevent market abuse. Non-compliance with these mandates exposes service providers to substantial financial penalties, elevating regulatory adherence from an operational consideration to a critical design requirement.

---

[2] https://eur-lex.europa.eu/legal-content/EN/TXT/?uri=CELEX:32023R1113.

The objective of this work is to design a PCH architecture that integrates these necessary auditability guarantees. This goal introduces a fundamental tension between auditability, which requires the ability to link transactions, and unlinkability, which is a core privacy-preserving objective of PCHs. We address this conflict by observing that a stringent auditability is typically only required for a subset of transactions identified as high-risk. We therefore propose a design that enables selective auditability for flagged payments, while rigorously preserving the unlinkability of all other transactions.

## 1.2  Contributions of this Work

First, we introduce *verifiable linkable randomizable puzzles*, VLRP, a novel cryptographic primitive (Sect. 4). A VLRP puzzle, $Z$, commits to a secret with respect to a verifiability key and an auditability key. The puzzle can be randomized to ensure unlinkability, but the auditability key allows it to be traced back to the original. Critically, our construction employs a nested encryption approach where auditing requires collaboration between the hub and an auditing agent, preventing unilateral de-anonymization. We formalize the VLRP primitive with security, unlinkability, and auditability notions and provide a construction with cryptographic proofs.

As a second contribution, we design Auditable Unlinkable Payment Channel Hubs, AUPCH, a PCH providing improved auditability with security guarantees than existing approaches (Sect. 5). AUPCH introduces an independent *auditability agent*, responsible for flagging high-risk payments. Users can transact via the hub without the direct involvement of the agent, ensuring normal operations are not disrupted. When a transfer needs to be audited, the agent and hub execute a collaborative protocol to link the puzzles on active channels without requiring closure.

AUPCH follows the puzzle promise, puzzle solve paradigm introduced in [11,26] and formalized in [7]. By replacing the simpler randomizable puzzles in protocols like A2L [26] and BlindHub [22] with our VLRP puzzles, AUPCH inherits their privacy and interoperability guarantees while providing auditability. This wrapper-like design requires only minimal code changes. Our performance evaluation shows that AUPCH provides auditability with a small computation and storage overhead.

## 2  Preliminaries

In this section, we first introduce the notation used in this work. We then briefly overview the notion of randomizable puzzles, used as a building block in previous PCH works [7,22,26], and other cryptographic primitives required in this work.

*Notation.* We denote the security parameter by $n \in \mathbb{N}$, by which each cryptographic scheme and adversary is parameterized. We denote by $\mathsf{negl}(n)$ a *negligible* function. A function $f : \mathbb{N} \to \mathbb{R}$ is negligible if its absolute value is smaller than the inverse of any polynomial (i.e., if $\forall d \; \exists k_0 \; \forall n \geq k_0 : |\mathsf{negl}(n)| \leq 1/n^d$). We denote by $x \leftarrow_\$ \mathcal{X}$ the uniform sampling of the variable $x$ from the set $\mathcal{X}$. We write $x \leftarrow \mathsf{A}(y)$ to denote that a probabilistic polynomial time (PPT) algorithm $\mathsf{A}$ on input $y$ outputs $x$. If $\mathsf{A}$ is a deterministic polynomial time (DPT) algorithm, we use the notation $x := \mathsf{A}(y)$. We use the notation $s \leftarrow s_1 + s_2$ for the assignment of computation results. We use the notation $\sigma := (\sigma_1, \sigma_2)$ for parsing a tuple $\sigma$ composed of two elements $\sigma_1$ and $\sigma_2$. We use the dot notation to access the elements of a tuple (e.g., we denote by $\sigma.\sigma_1$ the element $\sigma_1$ of $\sigma$).

*Randomizable Puzzles Scheme.* A randomizable puzzle scheme $\mathsf{RP}$ is a tuple of algorithms $\mathsf{RP} := (\mathsf{PSetup}, \mathsf{PGen}, \mathsf{PSolve}, \mathsf{PRand})$, where $(\mathsf{pp}, \mathsf{td}) \leftarrow \mathsf{PSetup}(1^n)$ is the setup algorithm; $Z \leftarrow \mathsf{PGen}(\mathsf{pp}, \zeta)$ is the puzzle generation algorithm; $\zeta \leftarrow \mathsf{PSolve}(\mathsf{td}, Z)$ is the algorithm to solve a puzzle; and $(Z', r) \leftarrow \mathsf{PRand}(\mathsf{pp}, Z)$ is the puzzle randomization algorithm. A randomizable puzzle scheme must satisfy *randomizability*, *security* and *privacy*.

*Digital Signature Scheme.* A digital signature $\mathsf{DS}$ is a tuple of algorithms $\mathsf{DS} := (\mathsf{KeyGen}, \mathsf{Sign}, \mathsf{Vrfy})$, where $(\mathsf{sk}, \mathsf{vk}) \leftarrow \mathsf{KeyGen}(1^n)$ is the key generation algorithm; $\sigma \leftarrow \mathsf{Sign}(\mathsf{sk}, m)$ is the signing algorithm on input the signing key $\mathsf{sk}$ and a message $m$; and $\{0, 1\} \leftarrow \mathsf{Vrfy}(\mathsf{vk}, m, \sigma)$ is the verification algorithm. A digital signature scheme should satisfy *existential unforgeability under an adaptative chosen-message attack*.

*Adaptor Signature Scheme.* An *adaptor signature scheme* $\mathsf{AS}$ is a tuple of algorithms $\mathsf{AS} := (\mathsf{KeyGen}, \mathsf{PreSign}, \mathsf{PreVrfy}, \mathsf{Adapt}, \mathsf{Extract})$ defined with respect to a hard relation $\mathsf{R}$ and a digital signature scheme $\mathsf{DS}$. For every statement/witness pair $(x, w) \in \mathsf{R}$, key pair $(\mathsf{sk}, \mathsf{vk}) \leftarrow \mathsf{KeyGen}(1^n)$ and a message $m$, we have that $\hat{\sigma} \leftarrow \mathsf{PreSign}(\mathsf{sk}, m, x)$ is a pre-signature; and $\sigma \leftarrow \mathsf{Adapt}(\hat{\sigma}, w)$ is a valid signature; and (pre-)verification holds under $\mathsf{vk}$ and $m$ for $\hat{\sigma}$ and $\sigma$, respectively. Furthermore, it holds that $w \leftarrow \mathsf{Extract}(\hat{\sigma}, \sigma, x)$. An adaptor signature scheme should satisfy the notions of *(unique) extractability*, *unlinkability* and *pre-verify soundness*.

*Public Key Encryption Scheme.* A public key encryption scheme $\mathsf{PKE}$ is a tuple of algorithms $\mathsf{PKE} := (\mathsf{KeyGen}, \mathsf{Enc}, \mathsf{Dec})$, where $(\mathsf{dk}, \mathsf{ek}) \leftarrow \mathsf{KeyGen}(1^n)$ is the key generation algorithm; $ct \leftarrow \mathsf{Enc}(\mathsf{ek}, m)$ is the encryption algorithm on input a public key $\mathsf{ek}$ and a message $m$; and $\{m, \bot\} \leftarrow \mathsf{Dec}(\mathsf{dk}, ct)$ is the decryption algorithm. A public key encryption scheme should satisfy *indistinguishability under chosen-plaintext attacks*.

*Non-Interactive Zero-Knowledge Arguments.* A non-interactive zero-knowledge argument system $\mathsf{NIZK}$ consists of three algorithms $\mathsf{NIZK} := (\mathsf{CrsGen}, \mathsf{Prove}, \mathsf{Verify})$, where $\mathsf{CrsGen}$ is the public parameter (i.e., common reference string) generation algorithm; $\pi \leftarrow \mathsf{Prove}(crs, x, w)$ is the prover algorithm for a statement $x$ and a witness $w$; and $\{0, 1\} \leftarrow \mathsf{Verify}(crs, x, \pi)$ is the verification algorithm. A NIZK argument system allows a prover to convince a verifier, using a proof $\pi$, about the existence of a witness $w$ for a statement $x$ without revealing any information apart from the fact that it knows the witness $w$. We require the NIZK argument system to satisfy the usual properties of *completeness, computational soundness* and *computational zero-knowledge.*

# 3   Solution Overview

We outline our solution to integrate auditability into privacy-preserving coin mixing protocols for payment channel hubs (PCHs). We begin with the established concept of randomizable puzzles, which are central to unlinkable transactions, and then detail our extensions to support selective, auditable transactions.

## 3.1   Coin Mixing Protocol

A coin mixing protocol, as introduced in [11,26], ensures transaction unlinkability through payment channel hubs. The protocol allows a sender (Alice) to send a payment to a receiver (Bob) through the Hub without revealing the connection between them, thus ensuring that transactions remain unlinkable. Refer to Fig. 1 for an illustrative description. The protocol works through four key steps:

1. **Puzzle Creation:** Bob interacts with the Hub to engage in a *puzzle promise protocol.* The Hub generates and sends Bob a puzzle, denoted as $Z$, which contains a hidden solution $\zeta$. The Hub also provides a pre-signature $\hat{\sigma}_{HB}$ on the transfer from the Hub to Bob, which requires the solution $\zeta$ to be completed.
2. **Puzzle Randomization:** Bob forwards the puzzle $Z$ to Alice. To ensure privacy against the Hub, Alice applies her own randomness to the puzzle, transforming it into a new puzzle $Z'$.
3. **Puzzle Solving:** Alice submits the randomized puzzle $Z'$ to the Hub. Even though the Hub has never seen $Z'$ before, it can still solve it for the randomized solution $\zeta'$ using its trapdoor. By completing the payment from Alice, the Hub reveals $\zeta'$ to her.

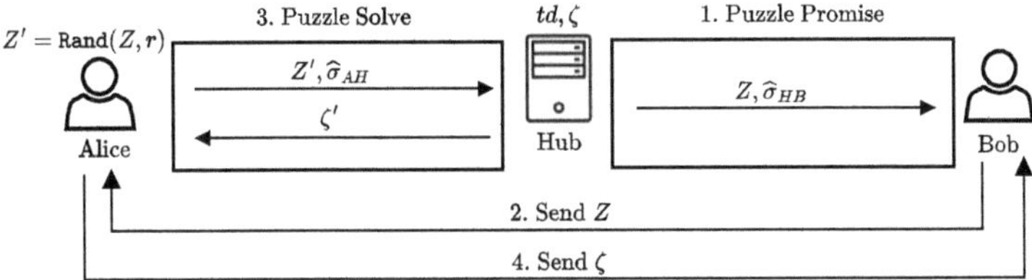


**Fig. 1.** Overview of coin mixing based on randomizable puzzles. The Hub's trapdoor is denoted by $td$ and the secret, puzzle pair generated by the Hub is denoted by $\zeta$ and $Z$ respectively.

4. **Solution Transfer:** Alice derandomizes the solution $\zeta'$ to obtain the original solution $\zeta$ and forwards it to Bob. Bob can then complete the payment from the Hub.

The protocol meets specific security and privacy requirements, including unlinkability, which prevents the Hub from linking randomized puzzles back to their originals, thereby concealing payment relationships. However, this essential privacy feature creates a challenge when auditability is needed.

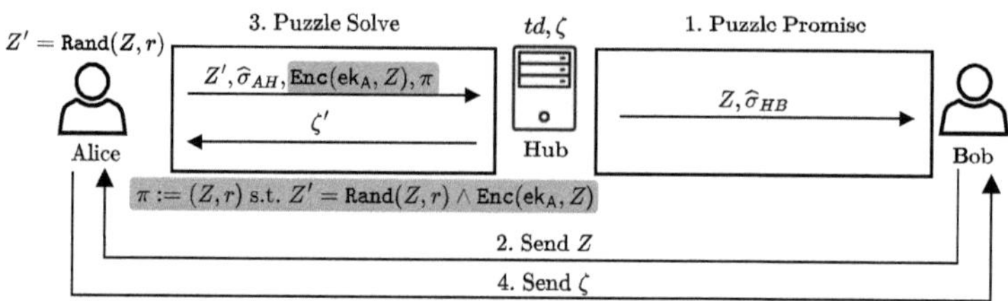


**Fig. 2.** Naive implementation of the auditability property. During puzzle solving, Alice includes an encryption of the randomness $r$ used to randomize $Z'$ and a zero-knowledge proof $\pi$ attesting that it is done correctly. The highlighted elements are added to the coin mixing protocol presented in Fig. 1 to provide the auditability property.

## 3.2   Auditability in Coin Mixing Protocols

To introduce auditability into the coin mixing protocol, we consider an additional party called the *auditability agent*. This agent is responsible for flagging high-risk transactions and assisting the Hub in linking the involved parties, while operating independently to prevent conflicts of interest. Our design enables real-time auditing of active channels, supporting dynamic regulatory compliance requirements such as those emerging under frameworks like FATF Travel Rule and EU MiCA regulation.

The revised protocol, as shown in Fig. 2, follows the same four steps as before, with a key addition during the puzzle-solving step.

- **Step 3 - Enhanced Puzzle Solver:** Along with the randomized puzzle $Z'$, Alice includes an encryption $c$ of the original puzzle $Z$ under the auditability agent's public key. She also provides a zero-knowledge proof attesting that $Z'$ was correctly derived from the puzzle $Z$ encrypted in $c$.

With these changes, if a transaction is flagged as high-risk, the auditability agent can decrypt $c$ to retrieve the original puzzle $Z$, allowing the Hub to link the sender and receiver. This process relies on the assumption that the Hub and the auditability agent do not collude.

A notable vulnerability is the *mix-and-match attack* and potential leakage to the auditability agent, where a malicious Alice can manipulate the process

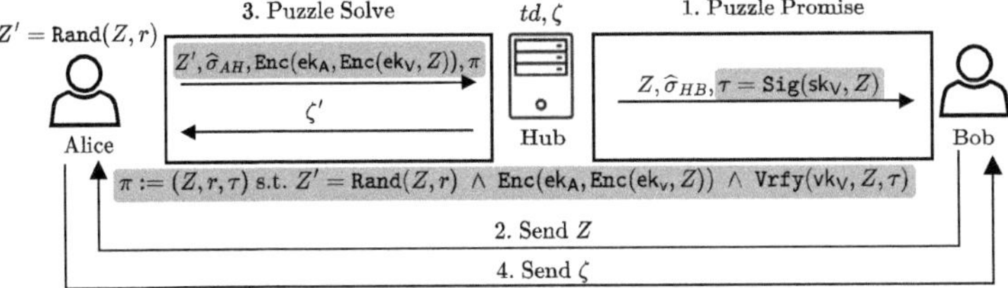

**Fig. 3.** Illustrative example of applying authentication tag to mitigate the mix-and-match attack. The highlighted elements are additions and modifications to the naive auditable solution provided in Fig. 2.

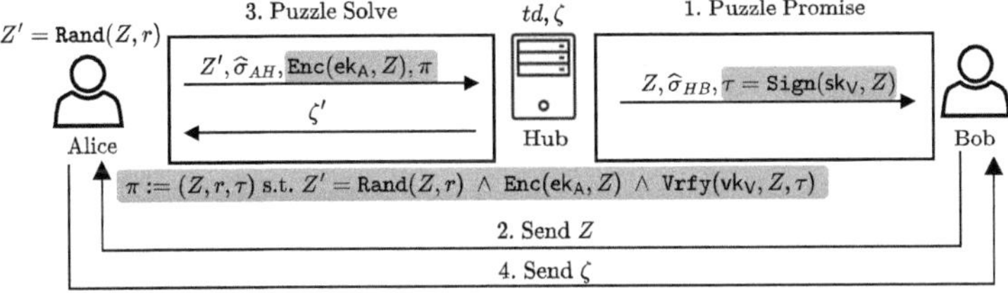

**Fig. 4.** Illustrative example of our approach. The highlighted elements are additions and modifications to the naive auditable solution provided in Fig. 2.

to create a false audit trail. A malicious sender can fabricate a new puzzle-randomness pair $(\tilde{Z}, \tilde{r})$ such that the same randomized puzzle $Z'$ can be derived from either the original puzzle $Z$ or the fabricated puzzle $\tilde{Z}$. By encrypting $\tilde{Z}$ instead of $Z$ and providing a valid zero-knowledge proof using the fabricated pair, the sender creates a false audit trail that prevents the Hub from correctly linking the transaction back to the intended receiver. To mitigate this, we propose two modifications illustrated in Fig. 3 and Fig. 4:

1. **Adding Authentication Tag:** During puzzle creation, the Hub includes an authentication tag $\tau$, which is a digital signature on $Z$. This forces Alice to use a puzzle genuinely issued by the Hub.
2. **Mitigating Leakage to Auditability Agent:** To prevent the auditability agent from unilaterally linking transactions, we use nested encryption. The puzzle $Z$ is first encrypted under the Hub's encryption key and then under the auditability agent's key. This ensures that auditing requires collaboration between both parties, preserving the unlinkability of non-flagged transactions.

## 4   Verifiable Linkable Randomizable Puzzles

In this section, we first describe the notion of Verifiable Linkable Randomizable Puzzles (VLRP) and their security, privacy, and auditability notions. We then describe our cryptographic construction and show that it achieves security, privacy, and auditability. Finally, we discuss the performance of our construction and demonstrate its practical efficiency through detailed benchmarks.

### 4.1  Problem Definition

**Definition 1 (Verifiable Linkable Randomizable Puzzles (VLRP)).** *A verifiable linkable randomizable puzzle scheme* $\mathsf{VLRP} := (\mathsf{PSetup}, \mathsf{PVerifySetup},$ $\mathsf{PAuditSetup}, \mathsf{PGen}, \mathsf{PVerifyTag}, \mathsf{PRand}, \mathsf{PVerifyRand}, \mathsf{PAudit})$ *with a solution space,* $\mathcal{S}$ *(and a function* $\phi$ *acting on* $\mathcal{S}$*), is defined as follows:*

- *$(pp, td) \leftarrow \mathsf{PSetup}(1^n)$: is a PPT algorithm that on input a security parameter $1^n$, outputs public parameters $pp$ and a trapdoor $td$.*
- *$(\mathsf{vk}_V, \mathsf{ek}_V, \mathsf{sk}_V, \mathsf{dk}_V) \leftarrow \mathsf{PVerifySetup}(1^n)$: is a PPT algorithm that on input a security parameter $1^n$, outputs a pair of public and private verification key $(\mathsf{vk}_V, \mathsf{sk}_V)$ and a pair of encryption and decryption keys $(\mathsf{ek}_V, \mathsf{dk}_V)$.*
- *$(\mathsf{ek}_A, \mathsf{dk}_A) \leftarrow \mathsf{PAuditSetup}(1^n)$: is a PPT algorithm that on input a security parameter $1^n$, outputs a pair of public and private auditability key $(\mathsf{ek}_A, \mathsf{dk}_A)$.*
- *$(Z, \tau) \leftarrow \mathsf{PGen}(pp, \mathsf{sk}_V, \zeta)$: is a PPT algorithm that on input the public parameters $pp$, the private key $\mathsf{sk}_V$ and a solution $\zeta$, outputs a puzzle $Z$ and a puzzle tag $\tau$.*
- *$\zeta := \mathsf{PSolve}(td, Z)$: is a DPT algorithm that on input a trapdoor $td$ and puzzle $Z$, outputs the solution $\zeta$.*
- *$b := \mathsf{PVerifyTag}(pp, \mathsf{vk}_V, Z, \tau)$: is a DPT algorithm that on input the public key $\mathsf{vk}_V$, a puzzle $Z$ and a puzzle tag $\tau$, outputs a bit $b \in \{0, 1\}$.*
- *$(Z', r, \rho) \leftarrow \mathsf{PRand}(pp, \mathsf{ek}_A, \mathsf{ek}_V, \mathsf{vk}_V, Z, \tau)$: is a PPT algorithm that on input the public parameters $pp$, the public keys $\mathsf{ek}_A$, $\mathsf{ek}_V$ and $\mathsf{vk}_V$, a puzzle $Z$ and a puzzle tag $\tau$, it outputs a randomized puzzle $Z'$ and randomness $r$ (such that $Z'$ has a solution $\phi(\zeta, r)$), and a puzzle auditability token $\rho$.*
- *$b := \mathsf{PVerifyRand}(pp, \mathsf{ek}_A, \mathsf{ek}_V, \mathsf{vk}_V, Z', \rho)$: is a DPT algorithm that on input the public keys $\mathsf{ek}_A$, $\mathsf{ek}_V$, $\mathsf{vk}_V$, a puzzle $Z'$, and a puzzle auditability token $\rho$, it outputs a bit $b \in \{0, 1\}$.*
- *$\delta \leftarrow \mathsf{PFlag}(\mathsf{dk}_A, \rho)$: is a PPT algorithm that on input the private auditability key $\mathsf{dk}_A$ and a puzzle auditability token $\rho$, outputs an attestation $\delta$.*
- *$\{Z, \bot\} := \mathsf{PAudit}(\mathsf{dk}_V, Z', \rho, \delta)$: is a DPT algorithm that on input a decryption key, $\mathsf{dk}_V$, a randomized puzzle $Z'$, an auditability token $\rho$ and an attestation $\delta$, outputs a puzzle $Z$ or bottom $\bot$.*

The Verifiable Linkable Randomizable Puzzles (VLRP) protocol is defined by four key properties: *correctness, security, unlinkability,* and *auditability. Correctness* ensures that a legitimately generated and randomized puzzle will always verify properly and yield the correct solution when solved. *Security* guarantees that a malicious party without the private key cannot create a valid puzzle-tag pair or extract a puzzle's solution without the trapdoor. *Unlinkability* provides privacy by ensuring adversaries cannot distinguish between original puzzles when given a randomized puzzle. Finally, *Auditability* ensures that attackers cannot create valid randomized puzzles that subvert the collaborative process. This guarantees that flagged transactions can always be traced back to their original puzzles by authorized parties. Due to the space constraints, we moved the formal definitions of these properties to the full version of this paper [20].

## 4.2   Our Construction

In this section, we first describe our building blocks, followed by the construction details. Finally, we formally show that it provides the notions of security, unlinkability, and auditability and conclude this section with a performance evaluation.

**Building Blocks.** As defined in Sect. 2, we require a randomizable puzzle scheme RP, a digital signature scheme DS, a public-key encryption scheme PKE, and a non-interactive zero-knowledge proof scheme NIZK. For the latter, we require the relations $\mathsf{st}_{\mathrm{PRand}}$ (left) and $\mathsf{st}_{\mathrm{PFlag}}$ (right) defined as follows:

---

**$\mathsf{PSetup}(1^n)$**

$(\mathsf{pp}_{\mathsf{RP}}, \mathsf{td}_{\mathsf{RP}}) \leftarrow \mathsf{RP.PSetup}(1^n)$
$crs \leftarrow \mathsf{NIZK.CrsGen}(1^n)$
$pp := (\mathsf{pp}_{\mathsf{RP}}, crs)$
$td := \mathsf{td}_{\mathsf{RP}}$
**return** $(pp, td)$

**$\mathsf{PVerifySetup}(1^n)$**

$(\mathsf{sk}_V, \mathsf{vk}_V) \leftarrow \mathsf{DS.KeyGen}(1^n)$
$(\mathsf{dk}_V, \mathsf{ek}_V) \leftarrow \mathsf{PKE.KeyGen}(1^n)$
**return** $(\mathsf{vk}_V, \mathsf{ek}_V; \mathsf{sk}_V, \mathsf{dk}_V)$

**$\mathsf{PAuditSetup}(1^n)$**

$(\mathsf{dk}_A, \mathsf{ek}_A) \leftarrow \mathsf{PKE.KeyGen}(1^n)$
**return** $(\mathsf{ek}_A, \mathsf{dk}_A)$

**$\mathsf{PGen}(pp, \mathsf{sk}_V, \zeta)$**

$(\mathsf{pp}_{\mathsf{RP}}, crs) \leftarrow pp$
$Z \leftarrow \mathsf{RP.PGen}(\mathsf{pp}_{\mathsf{RP}}, \zeta)$
$\sigma \leftarrow \mathsf{DS.Sign}(\mathsf{sk}_V, Z)$
$\tau := \sigma$
**return** $(Z, \tau)$

**$\mathsf{PSolve}(td, Z)$**

$\zeta \leftarrow \mathsf{RP.PSolve}(td, Z)$
**return** $\zeta$

**$\mathsf{PVerifyTag}(\mathsf{vk}_V, Z, \tau)$**

$b := \mathsf{DS.Vf}(\mathsf{vk}_V, Z, \tau)$
**return** $b$

---

**$\mathsf{PRand}(pp, \mathsf{ek}_A, \mathsf{ek}_V, \mathsf{vk}_V, Z, \tau)$**

$(\mathsf{pp}_{\mathsf{RP}}, crs) \leftarrow pp$
$(Z', r) \leftarrow \mathsf{RP.PRand}(\mathsf{pp}_{\mathsf{RP}}, Z)$
$r_V, r_A \leftarrow_{\$} \{0, 1\}^n$
$ct_{\mathsf{PKE}} \leftarrow \mathsf{PKE.Enc}(\mathsf{ek}_A, \mathsf{PKE.Enc}(\mathsf{ek}_V, Z; r_V); r_A)$
$x = (\mathsf{vk}_V, Z', ct_{\mathsf{PKE}}, \mathsf{ek}_V, \mathsf{ek}_A, \mathsf{pp}_{\mathsf{RP}})$
$w = (Z, r, r_V, r_A, \tau)$
$\pi_{\mathrm{PRand}} \leftarrow \mathsf{NIZK.Prove}(crs, \mathsf{st}_{\mathrm{PRand}}[x], w)$
$\rho := (ct_{\mathsf{PKE}}, \pi_{\mathrm{PRand}})$
**return** $(Z', r, \rho)$

**$\mathsf{PVerifyRand}(pp, \mathsf{ek}_A, \mathsf{ek}_V, \mathsf{vk}_V, Z', \rho)$**

$(\mathsf{pp}_{\mathsf{RP}}, crs) \leftarrow pp$
$(ct_{\mathsf{PKE}}, \pi_{\mathrm{PRand}}) \leftarrow \rho$
$x = (\mathsf{vk}_V, Z', ct_{\mathsf{PKE}}, \mathsf{ek}_V, \mathsf{ek}_A, \mathsf{pp}_{\mathsf{RP}})$
$b \leftarrow \mathsf{NIZK.Verify}(crs, \mathsf{st}_{\mathrm{PRand}}[x], \pi_{\mathrm{PRand}})$
**return** $b$

**$\mathsf{PFlag}(\mathsf{dk}_A, \rho)$**

$(ct_{\mathsf{PKE}}, \pi_{\mathrm{PRand}}) \leftarrow \rho$
$ct' \leftarrow \mathsf{PKE.Dec}(\mathsf{dk}_A, ct_{\mathsf{PKE}})$
$w = \mathsf{dk}_A$
$\pi_{\mathrm{PFlag}} \leftarrow \mathsf{NIZK.Prove}(crs, \mathsf{st}_{\mathrm{PFlag}}[\mathsf{ek}_A, ct_{\mathsf{PKE}}, ct'], w)$
$\delta := (ct', \pi_{\mathrm{PFlag}})$
**return** $\delta$

**$\mathsf{PAudit}(\mathsf{dk}_V, Z', \rho, \delta)$**

$(ct_{\mathsf{PKE}}, \pi_{\mathrm{PRand}}) \leftarrow \rho; \quad (ct', \pi_{\mathrm{PFlag}}) \leftarrow \delta$
$b \leftarrow \mathsf{NIZK.Verify}(crs, \mathsf{st}_{\mathrm{PFlag}}[ct_{\mathsf{PKE}}, ct'], \pi_{\mathrm{PFlag}})$
**if** $b = 0$ **return** $\perp$
$\quad Z \leftarrow \mathsf{PKE.Dec}(\mathsf{dk}_V, ct')$
$\quad$ **return** $Z$

---

**Fig. 5.** Our construction for verifiable linkable randomizable puzzles (VLRP).

$$\left\{ \begin{array}{l} (\mathsf{vk}_V, Z', ct_{\mathsf{PKE}}, \mathsf{ek}_V, \mathsf{ek}_A, \mathsf{pp}_{\mathsf{RP}}; Z, r, r_V, r_A, \tau) : \\ \mathtt{PVerifyTag}(\mathsf{vk}_V, Z, \tau) \wedge \\ (Z', r) = \mathsf{RP.PRand}(\mathsf{pp}_{\mathsf{RP}}, Z) \wedge \\ ct_{\mathsf{PKE}} = \mathsf{PKE.Enc}(\mathsf{ek}_A, \mathsf{PKE.Enc}(\mathsf{ek}_V, Z; r_V); r_A) \end{array} \right\} \left\{ \begin{array}{l} (\mathsf{ek}_A, ct_{\mathsf{PKE}}, ct'; \mathsf{dk}_A) : \\ ct' = \mathsf{PKE.Dec}(ct_{\mathsf{PKE}}; \mathsf{dk}_A) \wedge \\ (\mathsf{ek}_A, \mathsf{dk}_A) \leftarrow \mathsf{PKE.KeyGen}(1^n) \end{array} \right\}$$

**Construction Details.** We provide the details of our construction in Fig. 5. The PSetup algorithm generates the public parameters, the trapdoor required for the underlying randomizable puzzle (RP), and initializes the common reference string ($crs$). The algorithms `PVerifySetup` and `PAuditSetup` initialize the verifiability and auditability keys, respectively. The `PGen` algorithm creates a new puzzle $Z$, encoding the solution $\zeta$, and signs it with the verifiability key to produce the tag $\tau$. The validity of the tuple $(Z, \tau)$ can be verified by `PVerifyTag` using the standard verification procedures. Finally, the PSolve algorithm extracts the solution embedded in a puzzle $Z$, using the corresponding algorithm from the underlying RP scheme.

The `PRand` and `PVerifyRand` algorithms function as follows: First, `PRand` randomizes the input puzzle $Z$ using the randomization algorithm from the underlying RP. Additionally, it creates a nested encryption of $Z$ using both $\mathsf{ek}_A$ and $\mathsf{ek}_V$. Finally, it computes a zero-knowledge proof for the relation $\mathsf{st}_{\mathsf{PRand}}$. This proof is then verified by the `PVerifyRand` algorithm.

The remaining two algorithms are vital for the auditing process. When the auditability agent flags a user as high-risk, `PFlag` removes one encryption layer from ciphertext $c$ and generates a zero-knowledge proof for $\mathsf{st}_{\mathsf{PFlag}}$ to ensure decryption integrity. `PAudit` then allows the Hub to extract the associated puzzle $Z$ by verifying the proof and decrypting $c'$.

**Security Analysis.** Here, we state our claims and provide intuitions on the notions achieved by our construction. We defer the formal proofs to the full version of the paper [20].

**Theorem 1.** *Assume that the randomizable puzzle* RP *is secure and that the digital signature scheme* DS *is EUF-CMA. Then, our construction is secure.*

**Theorem 2.** *Assume that the non-interactive zero-knowledge argument system* NIZK *is zero-knowledge, the encryption scheme* PKE *is IND-CPA, and the randomizable puzzle* RP *is randomizable. Then, our construction is unlinkable.*

**Theorem 3.** *Assume that the encryption scheme* PKE *is correct, the digital signature* DS *is EUF-CMA, and the non-interactive zero-knowledge argument system* NIZK *provides knowledge-soundness. Then our construction provides auditability.*

### 4.3   Implementation and Performance Analysis

**Parameters.** We use the non-malleable version of Groth16 zkSnark [9] to instantiate our NIZK proofs. For the signature scheme, we implement EdDSA with the Babyjubjub curve. For the randomizable puzzle, we employ 2048-bit Paillier encryption due to the ease of porting it to our zkSNARK library. In our nested encryption implementation, we separately encrypt two symmetric keys using the respective public keys of the Hub and Judge, then use these keys for layered AES-CTR encryption.

**Software and Hardware.** The implementation is written in `Typescript`, and uses the Circom library [12] for writing circuits for all zero-knowledge proof statements and use circomlibjs for other cryptographic typescript implementations such as encryption and digital signatures. The experiments are executed a machine with a 3.5 GHz Intel Core i7 processor with 6 cores, and 80 GB RAM.

**Performance.** We measured the average runtimes over 100 runs for each basic operation. `PVerifySetup` takes 39.1 ms to complete. `PAuditSetup` requires 19.4 ms for processing. `PGen` consumes 202.24 ms. `PSolve` needs 53.53 ms to execute. `PVerifyTag` verification takes 84.21 ms.

For operations involving zero-knowledge proofs (`PRand`, `PVerifyRand`, `PFlag`, and `PAudit`), we provide estimated timings based on comparable proof systems in existing implementations: `PRand` (30s as the number of constraints is 0.6m), `PVerifyRand` (1s), `PFlag` (2s as the number of constraints is 20k), and `PAudit` (1.5s). These NIZK timings are extrapolated from state-of-the-art zero-knowledge proof implementations with similar circuit complexity [1,24]. The size of a puzzle (i.e., one Paillier encryption) is 512 bytes, the size of a NIZK proof is 192 bytes, and the size of the nested ciphertext is approximately 784 bytes. So overall, the Hub may only need to store less than 1.5 KB of data per payment.

## 5 AUPCH: An Auditable Payment Channel Hub

In this section, we demonstrate how existing Payment Channel Hub (PCH) constructions can be augmented with auditability using our Verifiable Linkable Randomizable Puzzles (VLRP) protocol. We begin by outlining the system and threat model, then show how PCH designs based on the puzzle promise and puzzle solve paradigm can be adapted to incorporate auditability via VLRP, all while preserving their security and privacy properties. For completeness, our approach is applied to A2L and BlindHub; however, due to the space constraints, we defer the detailed construction to the full version of this paper [20].

### 5.1 System and Threat Model

We assume a central party, called the Hub, is responsible for mediating payments between senders and receivers. Each sender and receiver has an open payment channel with the Hub. The Hub holds a verifiability key $\mathsf{sk}_V$ and a decryption key $\mathsf{dk}_V$, with the corresponding public keys $\mathsf{vk}_V, \mathsf{ek}_V$ known to all parties.

We also introduce an auditability agent, responsible for flagging high-risk payments. The auditability agent holds an auditability key $\mathsf{dk}_A$, with the corresponding public key $\mathsf{ek}_A$ known to all parties.

In line with prior PCH constructions, the Hub is trusted for liveness but not for security or privacy. Additionally, senders and receivers may behave arbitrarily. In our model, the auditability agent is trusted to identify and flag high-risk payments by analyzing their senders. We also assume that the auditability agent and Hub do not collude, ensuring unlinkability for non-flagged payments. In this model, the Hub and the auditability agent can collaborate to link the sessions of the flagged payments while maintaining a non-colluding assumption to preserve the unlinkability of non-flagged transactions. This model applies to practical scenarios (e.g., court investigations) where the Hub is required to provide information about the receiver of a flagged payment without compromising the privacy of other payments.

From a system perspective, our protocol satisfies two key requirements: (i) payments can be processed without any direct involvement of the auditability agent, and (ii) auditability can be enforced retrospectively for flagged payments, without requiring further interaction from the sender or receiver.

### 5.2   AUPCH: A Generic Auditable PCH Based on VLRP

To understand how VLRP can be integrated into a PCH to enable auditability, we first review the use of randomizable puzzles in PCH constructions that follow the **puzzle promise, puzzle solve** paradigm. The blueprint of these constructions is presented in Fig. 6. Here, we omit the details specific to each PCH construction, focusing instead on how VLRP can be employed to introduce auditability.

In summary, during the puzzle promise phase, the Hub computes a fresh puzzle $Z$ with its corresponding solution $\zeta$. The Hub and Bob then engage in a Payment Promise protocol, where Bob obtains the puzzle $Z$ and a presignature $\hat{\sigma}_{HB}$ on the transfer. Once Bob learns the solution $\zeta$, they can convert the presignature into a valid signature, completing the transfer.

During the puzzle solve phase, Alice randomizes the puzzle $Z$ into $Z'$ and engages with the Hub in the Payment Solve protocol. The Hub receives the randomized puzzle $Z'$ and a valid signature for the transfer, effectively obtaining the coins from Alice. Meanwhile, Alice learns the randomized solution $\zeta'$ to the puzzle $Z'$ Alice can then derandomize $\zeta'$ into $\zeta$, which is the value Bob needs to complete the transfer and receive the coins from the Hub.

Our approach to constructing AUPCH involves replacing the randomizable puzzle with the VLRP introduced in this work, as shown in Fig. 7. In particular, during the *puzzle promise* phase, the Hub generates a puzzle $Z$, which is accompanied by an authentication tag $\tau$. In the *puzzle solve* phase, Alice (the sender) randomizes the puzzle $Z$ into $Z'$ and provides an auditability token $\rho$, which allows linking the transfer to the original puzzle $Z$ when required.

A key feature of AUPCH is the *audit phase*. If a transfer (sender, $Z'$) is flagged for auditing, the Hub must identify the payment receiver. The auditability agent attests to the high-risk transaction by tagging the puzzle $Z'$ with PFlag. The Hub can then use this attestation to run the PAudit algorithm and recover the original puzzle $Z$, linking sender and receiver.

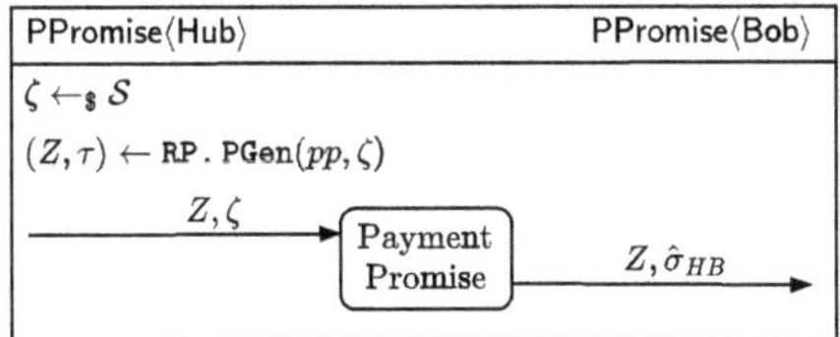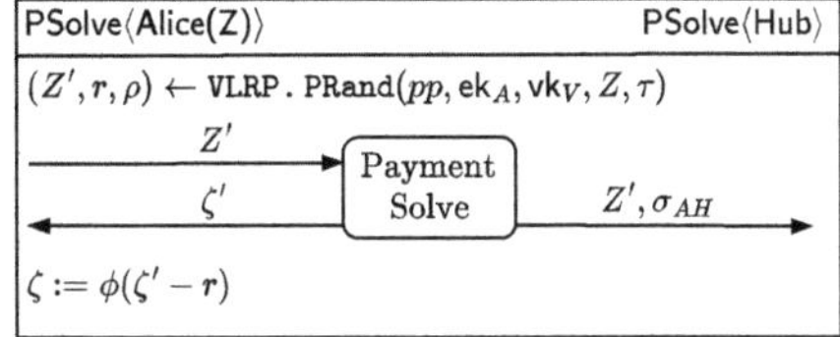

**Fig. 6.** Puzzle promise (PPromise), puzzle solve (PSolve) paradigm based on randomizable puzzles scheme, RP. PCH-dependent implementation of the PaymentPromise and PaymentSolve subprotocols are abstracted for clarity. Full description for A2L and BlindHub is in the full version of this paper [20].

## 5.3   Security Discussion

To provide auditability in PCH, we replace the randomizable puzzles from existing schemes with VLRP, introduced in this work. This introduces auditability while retaining the original security and privacy properties of the PCH.

The security and privacy of PCH systems rely on the security of the Randomizable Puzzle (RP) scheme [7][3]. In our case, the security and privacy notions of the VLRP scheme subsume those of the RP scheme, providing stronger guarantees. Thus, by integrating VLRP into the PCH design, we ensure that the auditability property is added without compromising the system's security or privacy. VLRP

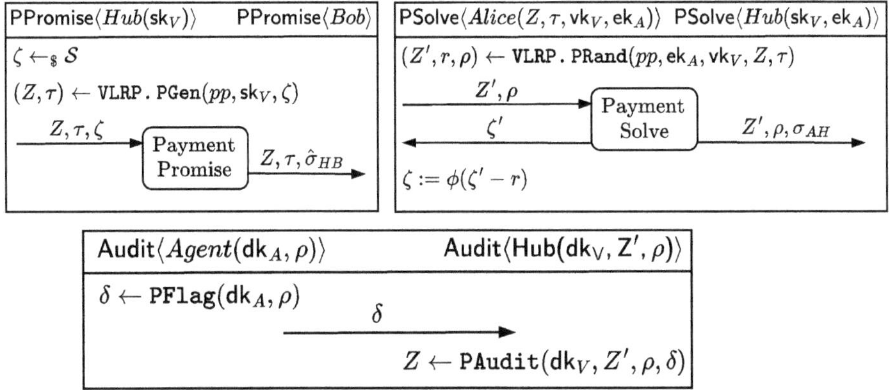

**Fig. 7.** AUPCH: Puzzle promise, puzzle solve paradigm using VLRP. PCH-specific details of the PaymentPromise and PaymentSolve sub-protocols are abstracted away for clarity.

---

[3] More technically, in [7], footnote 4 states that authors use a re-randomizable linearly homomorphic encryption scheme $\Pi_E$ instead of a re-randomizable puzzle, since the first satisfies the notion of the second; (ii) in [7], Lemma 4.8 states that $\Pi_E$ achieves the core security notion in A2L (i.e., OM-CCA-A2L); (iii) in [7], Theorem 4.9 states that $\Pi_E$ along with adaptor signatures and NIZK suffice for the security of A2L+.

achieves security through its resistance to forgery (i.e., the inability of an adversary to generate valid puzzles without the corresponding trapdoor and secret key $sk_V$). The puzzle randomization also guarantees unlinkability, preventing adversaries from correlating sessions of puzzle promise and puzzle solve.

The security implications of VLRP is discussed in the full version of this work [20]. Notably, the PCH auditability directly relies on the auditability property of VLRP.

# 6   Conclusions

We address the need for auditability in Payment Channel Hubs (PCH) transactions, a capability absent from previous PCH constructions. We introduce a new cryptographic protocol (Verifiable Linkable Randomizable Puzzles, VLRP), which enables commitments to secrets using two keys: a verifiability key and an auditability key. This protocol provides: (i) verification that commitments are issued by the verifiability key owner, and (ii) randomization for unlinkability while preserving traceability via the auditability key. We then present AUPCH, a PCH overlay built on VLRP that provides selective auditability guarantees while maintaining the functionality, security, and privacy of existing PCH constructions based on the puzzle promise and puzzle solve paradigm. Our performance evaluation shows that AUPCH imposes only minimal computation and storage overhead.

**Acknowledgments.** This work is part of the grant CEX2024-001471-M/funded by MICIU/AEI/10.13039/501100011033; and of the grant PID2022-142290OB-I00, funded by MCIN/AEI/10.13039/501100011033/ FEDER, UE.

# References


1. zkp application: RSA Circom. https://github.com/zkp-application/circom-rsa-verify/
2. Christodorescu, M., et al.: Universal payment channels: an interoperability platform for digital currencies (2021). https://arxiv.org/abs/2109.12194
3. Dziembowski, S., Eckey, L., Faust, S., Malinowski, D.: Perun: virtual payment hubs over cryptocurrencies. In: 2019 IEEE Symposium on Security and Privacy, pp. 106–123. IEEE Computer Society Press (2019). https://doi.org/10.1109/SP.2019.00020
4. European Parliament and Council: Regulation (EU) 2023/1114 of the European parliament and of the council of 31 may 2023 on markets in crypto-assets, and amending regulations (EU) no 1093/2010 and (EU) no 1095/2010 and directives 2013/36/EU and (EU) 2019/1937. Official Journal of the European Union, L 150 (2023). https://eur-lex.europa.eu/legal-content/EN/TXT/?uri=CELEX:32023R1114
5. Financial Action Task Force (FATF): Updated guidance for a risk-based approach to virtual assets and virtual asset service providers. Technical report, FATF/OECD, Paris, France (2021). https://www.fatf-gafi.org/en/publications/Fatfrecommendations/Guidance-rba-virtual-assets-2021.html
6. Ge, Z., Gu, J., Wang, C., Long, Y., Xu, X., Gu, D.: Accio: variable-amount, optimized-unlinkable and NIZK-free off-chain payments via hubs. In: ACM CCS (2023)
7. Glaeser, N., Maffei, M., Malavolta, G., Moreno-Sanchez, P., Tairi, E., Thyagarajan, S.A.K.: Foundations of coin mixing services. In: Yin, H., Stavrou, A., Cremers, C., Shi, E. (eds.) ACM CCS 2022, pp. 1259–1273. ACM Press (2022). https://doi.org/10.1145/3548606.3560637
8. Green, M., Miers, I.: Bolt: anonymous payment channels for decentralized currencies. In: Thuraisingham, B.M., Evans, D., Malkin, T., Xu, D. (eds.) ACM CCS 2017, pp. 473–489. ACM Press (2017). https://doi.org/10.1145/3133956.3134093
9. Groth, J.: On the size of pairing-based non-interactive arguments. In: EUROCRYPT, pp. 305–326 (2016)
10. Gudgeon, L., Moreno-Sanchez, P., Roos, S., McCorry, P., Gervais, A.: SoK: layer-two blockchain protocols. In: Bonneau, J., Heninger, N. (eds.) FC 2020. LNCS, vol. 12059, pp. 201–226. Springer, Heidelberg (2020). https://doi.org/10.1007/978-3-030-51280-4_12
11. Heilman, E., Alshenibr, L., Baldimtsi, F., Scafuro, A., Goldberg, S.: TumbleBit: an untrusted bitcoin-compatible anonymous payment hub. In: NDSS 2017. The Internet Society (2017)
12. Iden3: Circom circuit templates. https://github.com/iden3/circomlib
13. Jourenko, M., Kurazumi, K., Larangeira, M., Tanaka, K.: SoK: a taxonomy for layer-2 scalability related protocols for cryptocurrencies. Cryptology ePrint Archive, Report 2019/352 (2019). https://eprint.iacr.org/2019/352
14. Kumaresan, R., Le, D.V., Minaei, M., Raghuraman, S., Yang, Y., Zamani, M.: Programmable payment channels. In: ACNS, pp. 51–73 (2024)
15. Le, D.V., Gervais, A.: AMR: autonomous coin mixer with privacy preserving reward distribution. In: Proceedings of the 3rd ACM Conference on Advances in Financial Technologies, AFT 2021, pp. 142–155. Association for Computing Machinery, New York, NY, USA (2021). https://doi.org/10.1145/3479722.3480800

16. Li, Y., et al.: Auditpch: auditable payment channel hub with privacy protection. IEEE Trans. Inf. Forensics Secur. **20**, 1251–1261 (2025). https://doi.org/10.1109/TIFS.2024.3515820

17. Lind, J., Naor, O., Eyal, I., Kelbert, F., Sirer, E.G., Pietzuch, P.R.: Teechain: a secure payment network with asynchronous blockchain access. In: ACM SOSP, pp. 63–79 (2019)

18. Minaei, M., et al.: Unlinkability and interoperability in account-based universal payment channels. Cryptology ePrint Archive, Paper 2023/916 (2023). https://eprint.iacr.org/2023/916

19. Minaei, M., et al.: DTL: data tumbling layer. A composable unlinkability for smart contracts (2025). https://arxiv.org/abs/2503.04260

20. Moreno-Sanchez, P., Minaei, M., Raghuraman, S., Chatzigiannis, P., Le, D.V.: AUPCH: auditable unlinkable payment channel hubs. Cryptology ePrint Archive, Paper 2025/1524 (2025). https://eprint.iacr.org/2025/1524

21. Poon, J., Dryja, T.: The bitcoin lightning network: Scalable off-chain instant payments (2016)

22. Qin, X., et al.: BlindHub: bitcoin-compatible privacy-preserving payment channel hubs supporting variable amounts. Cryptology ePrint Archive, Report 2022/1735 (2022). https://eprint.iacr.org/2022/1735

23. Qin, X., et al.: BlindHub: Bitcoin-Compatible Privacy-Preserving Payment Channel Hubs Supporting Variable Amounts (2022). https://eprint.iacr.org/2022/1735, publication info: Published elsewhere. Major revision. IEEE S&P 2023

24. Reclaim: AES Circom. https://gitlab.reclaimprotocol.org/reclaim/zk-symmetric-crypto

25. Tairi, E., Moreno-Sanchez, P., Maffei, M.: $A^2L$: Anonymous Atomic Locks for Scalability in Payment Channel Hubs (2019). https://eprint.iacr.org/2019/589, publication info: Published elsewhere. Major revision. IEEE Symposium on Security and Privacy - S&P 2021

26. Tairi, E., Moreno-Sanchez, P., Maffei, M.: $A^2L$: anonymous atomic locks for scalability in payment channel hubs. In: 2021 IEEE Symposium on Security and Privacy, pp. 1834–1851. IEEE Computer Society Press (2021). https://doi.org/10.1109/SP40001.2021.00111

27. Wang, Z., Cirkovic, M., Le, D.V., Knottenbelt, W., Cachin, C.: Pay less for your privacy: towards cost-effective on-chain mixers. In: Bonneau, J., Weinberg, S.M. (eds.) 5th Conference on Advances in Financial Technologies (AFT 2023). Leibniz International Proceedings in Informatics (LIPIcs), vol. 282, pp. 16:1–16:25. Schloss Dagstuhl – Leibniz-Zentrum für Informatik, Dagstuhl, Germany (2023). https://doi.org/10.4230/LIPIcs.AFT.2023.16. https://drops.dagstuhl.de/entities/document/10.4230/LIPIcs.AFT.2023.16

28. Wicht, F.X., Wang, Z., Le, D.V., Cachin, C.: A transaction-level model for blockchain privacy. In: Financial Cryptography and Data Security: 28th International Conference, FC 2024, Willemstad, Curaçao, 4–8 March 2024, Revised Selected Papers, Part II, pp. 293–310. Springer-, Heidelberg (2025). https://doi.org/10.1007/978-3-031-78679-2_16

29. Zamani, M., et al.: Cross-border payments for central bank digital currencies via universal payment channels (2021). Retrieved from Bank for International Settlement website: http://www.bis.org/events/cpmi_ptfop/proceedings/paper14.pdf.b

# Threshold Signatures for Central Bank Digital Currencies

Mostafa Abdelrahman[1,2], Filip Rezabek[1], Lars Hupel[1,2(✉)], Kilian Glas[1],
and Georg Carle[1]

[1] Technische Universität München, Munich, Germany
`lars.hupel@tum.de`
[2] Giesecke+Devrient, Munich, Germany

**Abstract.** Digital signatures are crucial for securing Central Bank Digital Currencies (CBDCs) transactions. Like most forms of digital currencies, CBDC solutions rely on signatures for transaction authenticity and integrity, leading to major issues in the case of private key compromise. Our work explores threshold signature schemes (TSSs) in the context of CBDCs. TSSs allow distributed key management and signing, reducing the risk of a compromised key. We analyze CBDC-specific requirements, considering the applicability of TSSs, and use Filia CBDC solution as a base for a detailed evaluation. As most of the current solutions rely on ECDSA for compatibility, we focus on ECDSA-based TSSs and their supporting libraries. Our performance evaluation measured the computational and communication complexity across key processes, as well as the throughput and latency of end-to-end transactions. The results confirm that TSS can enhance the security of CBDC implementations while maintaining acceptable performance for real-world deployments.

**Keywords:** Threshold Signatures · ECDSA · CBDC

## 1 Introduction

Digital signatures are essential to ensure the authenticity and integrity of online data. They provide a way to verify the origin and integrity of a message, ensuring that the message has not been tampered with and that it indeed comes from the claimed sender. The system's security collapses if the private key $sk$ is compromised, as an attacker could forge signatures. Conversely, if the $sk$ is lost or destroyed, valid signatures cannot be created, leading to availability loss. This overall leads to a single point of failure.

Threshold Signatures Schemes (TSSs) address the vulnerabilities associated with a single point of failure in private key management. The TSS distributes the signing authority among multiple parties, requiring a subset (or threshold

---

M. Abdelrahman and F. Rezabek—Contributed equally to this paper.
All links are valid as of 5 September, 2025.


R. Laborde et al. (Eds.): ESORICS 2025, LNCS 16231, pp. 259–276, 2026.
https://doi.org/10.1007/978-3-032-16089-8_17

$t$) of these parties to collaborate to produce a valid signature. This trust distribution reduces the risk of key compromise and increases the resilience of the cryptographic system. By eliminating a single point of failure, TSSs are particularly advantageous in high-stakes applications such as financial transactions and secure communications.

A key application of TSSs is within blockchain and digital currencies, which require robust security measures due to the significant value they protect [18]. This is particularly relevant in the context of Central Bank Digital Currencies (CBDCs), which are digital representations of a nation's currency issued and regulated by the central bank. CBDC introduces the role of a Financial Service Provider (FSP), which process users' payments and ensure funds availability. In that case, the FSP manages the private key of users as custodial key management. Naturally, a common design pattern uses online wallets distributed among various FSPs. However, this puts a lot of trust in the FSPs to create and manage hosted wallets. Besides, the FSPs do not trust each other. Therefore, TSS is a viable solution as the threshold number of nodes within a FSP have to collaborate, increasing the resilience of the FSP system. In general, we examine the integration of TSS in the context of CBDC deployments. For the scope of this paper, we select the Filia implementation [24], an off-chain CBDC solution developed by Giesecke+Devrient (G+D). Filia follows a similar design with a focus on FSPs for custodial key management, allowing the generalization of our findings to other CBDC implementations with similar architecture.

Filia offers hardware-based (offline) and hosted (online) wallets. Applying threshold signatures to hardware wallets would be cumbersome for day-to-day transactions since it would require the user to juggle multiple devices. Filia's online wallets currently only support Elliptic Curve Digital Signature Algorithm (ECDSA). For that reason, we focus on State-of-the-Art (SotA) ECDSA TSS as they apply to online wallets. The goal is to develop a threshold version of this key management system to enhance security by preventing single-point failure.

*Contributions.* We provide these key contributions:

- Analysis of SotA TSS based on ECDSA;
- Protocol design fitting the CBDC use cases;
- Theoretical and empirical evaluation of the protocol.


## 2     Background

This section provides an overview of the CGGMP21 ECDSA TSS, Filia as the selected case study CBDC, and Environment for Generic In-vehicular Networking Experiments (EnGINE)/Multilayer Environment and Toolchain for Hollistic NetwOrk Design and Analysis (METHODA) framework used for evaluation.

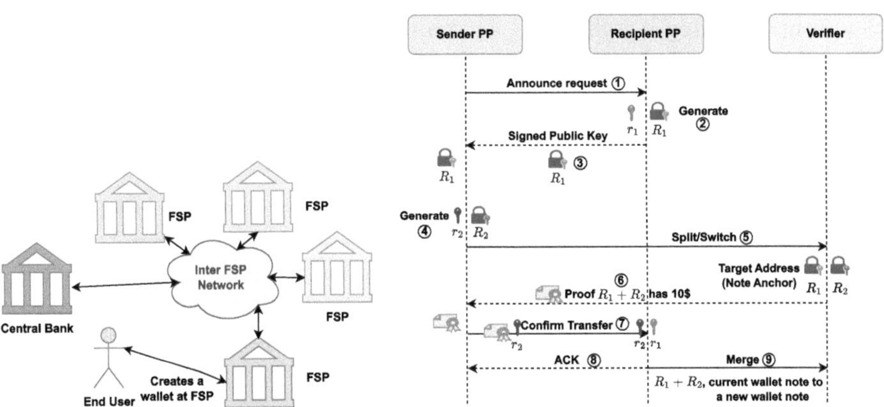


(a) High-Level Architecture [24]

(b) Filia Protocol: Remote Transaction. $r$ corresponds to private key and $R$ to public key.

**Fig. 1.** Filia Architecture and Protocol Overview. Figures outline the involved parties and their form of interaction. Color differentiates between the parties.

*CGGMP21.* The CGGMP21 protocol is a SotA $n$-out-of-$n$ threshold ECDSA scheme [9]. It provides features fitting the context of CBDC applications. First, it relies on Paillier encryption for secure multiplication of secret shares and utilizes Zero-Knowledge Proofs (ZKPs) to detect and attribute deviations from the expected behavior [26,30]. Next, it supports pre-signing, identifiable aborts, security against adaptive adversaries, and universal composability under strong RSA, DDH, and Paillier security assumptions. It provides proactive security with periodic key refreshes and ensures that compromised shares within an epoch do not affect the system's integrity. It offers efficiency trade-offs: a 3-round presign protocol with $O(n^2)$ identification cost or a 6-round presign protocol with $O(n)$ identification cost. The protocol can be extended to general $t$-out-of-$n$ threshold case using Shamir's secret sharing (SSS) and converting Shamir secret shares into additive shares [14,37].

*Filia.* Figure 1a provides a high-level overview of the Filia system. The central bank is responsible for the core infrastructure. At the same time, private sector intermediaries, known as FSPs, offer end-user wallets and develop services based on the technology and regulatory framework established by the central bank. Each FSP maintains a wallet at the central bank, where the requested liquidity is transferred. Other CBDC solutions with similar architecture exist.

*EnGINE/METHODA.* The EnGINE/METHODA framework [32,33], initially developed for Time Sensitive Networking (TSN) emulations, provides a robust and scalable environment designed to support reproducible and modular experiments in distributed cryptographic operations. Built with Ansible-based orchestration, METHODA allows for flexible deployment and management of complex setups, making it well-suited for evaluating cryptographic protocols in distributed systems.

## 3   Related Work

Existing research on CBDC system design highlights different models, including two-tier architectures where central banks issue digital currency but rely on intermediaries for distribution [7] which Filia follows. However, security remains a critical challenge in CBDC implementations, particularly in mitigating operational and cyber risks [13]. This paper addresses these concerns by exploring TSS as a means to enhance key management security and reduce the risk of private key compromise.

There is limited work in applying TSSs in the context of CBDC, with existing research focusing primarily on distributed ledger-based implementations. PEReDi [35] employs TSS in a scenario where maintainers, including banks, financial institutions, and regulatory offices, each hold a share. This setup allows for selective transaction tracing and privacy revocation in cases of suspicious activities. IBM's CBDC framework [5] incorporates TSS within its new endorser model, where TSSs enhance security and accountability by requiring a collective agreement from multiple endorsers for transaction validation. Overall, the framework focuses on hardening the token creation by the CBDC, minimizing the likelihood of the creation of unauthorized tokens. On the other hand, our threat model aims to protect against theft or unauthorized use of tokens.

Numerous initiatives within the cryptocurrency industry, many of which are part of the MPC Alliance [3], have adopted TSSs to secure digital assets. This distributed approach has enabled secure "Wallet as a Service" models [21, 35, 38]. These platforms enhance security by distributing cryptographic operations across multiple parties, ensuring robust protection even when certain parties may be compromised.

## 4   Analysis and Protocol Design

The main CBDC use case analyzed in this work considers the FSP as the custodian of users' wallet private keys. In this model, the FSP securely manages private keys on behalf of multiple users and an entrusted central ledger maintains a record of public keys to ensure the legitimacy of the money. This section focuses on the private key lifecycle and its distribution relying on the TSS. First, we provide an overview of the Filia platform and possible solutions on how TSS can be integrated into it. We define general requirements relevant to the context of CBDC along with a detailed security model. We argue for selecting a suitable TSS based on the requirements.

## 4.1   Filia Protocol

Filia relies on a modified unspent Transaction Output (UTXO)-based model used to represent a digital currency. Each UTXO, referred to here as a *note*, consists of a public-private key pair $(r, R)$ derived from the secp256r1/P-256 curve and a denomination $(v)$ indicating its monetary value. The private component $r$ is securely managed within the hosted wallet by the *Payment Processor (PP)*, the main component of the FSP responsible for wallet management and transaction handling. Meanwhile, the public component $R$ is registered and tracked by a Verifier, a central bank infrastructure tasked with preventing double spending and ensuring system integrity.

Transactions in this system follow specific rules. Certain transaction types, such as currency issuance or destruction, are restricted to the central bank, while old transaction outputs are periodically garbage collected to improve system efficiency. Transaction commands involve consuming one or more existing notes and creating new ones, with the available commands being **Create**, **Split**, **Merge**, **Switch**, and **Destroy**. Each transaction is validated by the *Verifier*, which ensures the correctness of commands and prevents double-spending. Notes are registered in the system only if they are unique, and commands are rejected if any input notes have already been consumed in a prior transaction.

The Filia system differentiates between two types of transfers: **local transfers** (wallets within the same FSP) and **remote transfers** (wallets at different FSP). While local transfers follow a simplified protocol, remote transfers require additional security measures due to the lack of trust between different FSP. A non-repudiation protocol addresses this, ensuring that the sending PP can provide proof of the money sent. Figure 1b illustrates the steps involved in a remote transfer under the Filia protocol:

1. **Anounce Transfer:** The recipient PP receives a announcement request from the sender PP with value $(v)$ ①. The recipient PP generates a key pair $(r_1, R_1)$ ② and sends the public key $R_1$ back to the sender PP ③.
2. **Register New Public Key:** The sender PP generates a second key pair $(r_2, R_2)$ ④ and sends a request to the verifier to confirm the transfer and register the value $(v)$ under $R_1 + R_2$ ⑤.
3. **Store Verifier Proof** ⑥**:** The sender PP stores a proof provided by the Verifier, demonstrating that the value $(v)$ has been transferred to the correct address $R_1 + R_2$ at the Verifier.
4. **Confirm Transfer:** The sender PP sends the private key $r_2$ to the recipient PP ⑦, allowing the recipient to access the funds and the recipient PP replies with an acknowledgment ⑧.

Eventually, only the recipient PP knows $r_1 + r_2$ and can use the note. The recipient PP can switch the funds to a new key or merge the funds to a previously available note ⑨.

Should the sender PP not disclose $r_2$, the value $v$ will be locked; however, it will also be unable to prove correct transfer execution.

## 4.2   Possible Solutions

Continuing with the protocol overview, we explore two potential solutions for implementing threshold key management within the Filia system at the FSP level. We outline and analyze each solution, including its unique pros and cons.

**Solution 1: Payment Processor-Based Threshold Key Management.** In this approach, each FSP deploys $n$ PPs, with each PP holding a share of the private key. Specifically, each PP holds a new note in the form $(v, r_1)$, $(v, r_2)$, ..., $(v, r_n)$. Here, the TSS is directly implemented within the payment processing system, so when a transaction requires signing, a predefined number of PP collaborate to generate the signature.

**Solution 2: Separate Key Management Network (KMN).** This solution establishes a dedicated KMN within the FSP infrastructure, where a set of $n$ specialized nodes (key management nodes) are responsible for generating and storing key shares, and providing signatures. PP sends requests to the KMN for signatures or key generation as needed. Each node in the KMN holds a key share $r_1, r_2, \ldots, r_n$, and assigns a specific identifier (uuid) to the shares, which is sent to the PP. Consequently, the PP holds a `note` in the form $(v, \text{uuid})$ and uses that uuid to request a signature from the KMN.

**Discussion.** When considering the complexity, **Solution 1** tightly integrates key management into the payment processing infrastructure, requiring each PP to maintain its database of key shares. This necessitates synchronization across multiple PPs, significantly increasing the operational overhead, particularly in achieving consensus between PPs. In contrast, **Solution 2** isolates key management in a dedicated network, simplifying the responsibilities of PPs. Although this reduces complexity within the PPs, it adds a layer of infrastructure that requires careful management, such as ensuring the availability and reliability of the KMN nodes.

Regarding latency, **Solution 1** has an advantage due to the proximity of all operations within the FSP infrastructure. On the other hand, **Solution 2** introduces communication overhead as PPs need to interact with the separate key management nodes. This added step can lead to higher latency, particularly in high-frequency transaction environments.

The modular design of **Solution 2** ensures that the TSS can be updated or replaced without requiring significant changes to the PP codebase. The system can also take advantage of batching and parallelization to reduce delays and improve efficiency without disrupting other PP tasks. By decoupling key management from the payment processing system, KMN enhances security, as keys remain secure within the storage of dedicated nodes, even if PP is compromised.

The KMN is selected for its modular design, enhanced security, and ease of updates. Decoupling key management from payment processing eliminates the need for consensus mechanisms required in **Solution 1**, reducing the implementation complexity of Proof-of-Concept (PoC). Furthermore, KMN enables efficient batch processing and parallelization, ensuring scalability without disrupting payment processing tasks, making it a robust choice for the Filia system.

### 4.3 System Requirements

We outline several key requirements for extending the Filia protocol by TSS and considering **Solution 2**. They must easily migrate Filia wallets and transaction signing to the TSS system. Notably, these requirements should be generalizable to designs similar to CBDC as Filia.

**R1 - Transparent Support for Standard and Threshold Wallets:** The system must conceal the type of wallet in use, whether standard or threshold, from external observers, including other FSPs. This ensures flexibility within the Filia system, enabling different security levels based on factors such as the wallet's balance.

**R2 - Efficient Distributed Key Generation (DKG):** Due to multiple generation of key during transactions in Filia, the DKG process must be optimized for high efficiency.

**R3 - High Signature Throughput:** The signing process must achieve high throughput to handle the multiple signatures required per transaction and efficiently load high user loads. For instance, during a remote transfer, the process involves splitting the sender's wallet and merging the transferred value into the recipient's wallet (as shown in Fig. 1b, Steps ⑤ and ⑨). These operations require multiple signatures, so the system must be capable of processing these quickly.

**R4 - Secure Key Reconstruction:** The system must enable the secure reconstruction of short-lived keys when required. Specifically, when the sender's PP generates a threshold key pair $(r_2, R_2)$, it must securely reconstruct or export $r_2$ during the process of transmitting the full key to the recipient's PP (e.g., Fig. 1b, Step ⑦).

**R5 - Key Update/Key Addition:** The system must facilitate the secure addition of new key parts to existing key shares. For instance, as illustrated in Fig. 1b, the sender PP must send $r_2$, which is a full key, to the recipient PP. The recipient PP then combines $r_2$ with their threshold key $r_1$. The result is that each node holds a share of the combined key $r_1 + r_2$.

**R6 - Compatibility with Existing Infrastructure:** The TSS must be fully compatible with ECDSA, in specific secp256r1/P-256 curve, to align with the existing infrastructure, particularly for hardware wallets that rely on smart card technology that use ECDSA. This requirement ensures that the integration of TSSs does not disrupt existing systems and maintains consistent security across all wallet types.

**R7 - Security:** The TSS should be secure with minimum assumptions and should be secure even when combined with other systems/protocols.

### 4.4   Security System Model

We define the environment and conditions under which the protocol is expected to operate.

**Adversary Model.** In our system, we assume the presence of an active, malicious adversary. This adversary can arbitrarily deviate from the protocol, aiming to disrupt the system or gain unauthorized access to information.

**Threshold Structure:** We operate under the assumption of a dishonest majority $(t < n)$, as the protocols provide stronger security guarantees against active adversaries. Even though honest majority protocols might seem appropriate given that all nodes are deployed at the FSP level by a single entity, we choose dishonest majority due to stronger security guarantees against active adversaries. However, this comes at the cost of robustness, which cannot be achieved under dishonest majority settings [12,19].

**Computational Power:** Given the active security setting with a dishonest majority, the protocol should aim to achieve computational security as perfect security is unattainable under these settings [19].

**Corruption Power:** This model assumes static corruptions, as frequent key changes in Filia eliminate the need for proactive security or handling mobile adversaries. Key updates occur naturally during transactions, making explicit key refreshing after specific epochs unnecessary. However, this assumption can be extended to include proactive security measures for wallets that remain inactive for extended periods.

**Network and Communication Model.** Our system assumes all signatories are connected through an authenticated and synchronous broadcast mechanism within a single FSP. This setup ensures that communication is public, and any message sent will either be received by all participants in the next round or not be delivered at all. Without pre-established authenticated communication, an adversary who previously controlled a corrupted party and managed the communication channels can impersonate that party indefinitely [10].

The synchronous broadcast mechanism is crucial for maintaining accountability and ensuring all parties reach a consensus. Without defined communication delays, holding any signatory accountable for failing to respond would be impossible. Additionally, reliable broadcast is vital for distributing proofs during the DKG process and upholding accountability throughout the protocol [9].

### 4.5   Selection of Threshold ECDSA Scheme

TSSs have been extensively explored for their role in securing digital assets.

Two comprehensive surveys [6,36] provide an overview of key developments in the field. SotA protocols such as CGGMP21 [9] and DKLs23 [17] build on earlier advancements [11,15,16,23,27]. These protocols follow standard steps:

**Table 1.** Comparison of Threshold Signature Schemes (Dishonest Majority)

| Scheme | Robust | Corruption Strategy | Assumptions |
| --- | --- | --- | --- |
| Canetti et al. [9] | ✗ | Adaptive | Strong-RSA, ECDSA unforgeability, semantic security of Paillier encryption, Decisional Diffie–Hellman (DDH) |
| Abram et al. [4] | ✗ | Static | Ring-LPN, ECDSA unforgeability |
| Doerner et al. [17] | ✗ | Static | Ideal commitment and two-party multiplication primitives |
| Feng et al. [20] | ✗ | Adaptive | LPN, PCF |
| Komlo and Goldberg [28] | ✗ | Static | Discrete Logarithm Problem (DLP) |
| Ruffing et al. [34] | ✓ | Adaptive | DLP |
| Lindell [29] | ✗ | Static | Ideal commitment and Public Key Infrastructure (PKI) |

- Rewriting the ECDSA signing equation into an "Multiparty Computation (MPC)-friendly" equivalent.
- Employing cryptographic primitives for secure multiplication (e.g., Oblivious Transfer, Paillier, or Class Groups).
- Verifying that all operations are performed honestly.

The primary distinctions between these protocols lie in their security definitions, underlying assumptions, and communication and computation complexities, which depend on the used cryptographic primitives. Table 1 provides a summary of recent threshold signature schemes, detailing key differences in threshold settings, robustness, corruption strategies, and security assumptions.

Among the libraries evaluated, the implementation of CGGMP21 by dfns [1] meets our key system requirements. First, unlike other libraries, it is production code, not a POC such as silence-labs [2]. Next, the library supports secp256r1, the elliptic curve that Filia (**R6**) requires. Additionally, it enables essential functionalities such as importing existing keys (**R5**) and exporting keys securely from nodes (**R4**). One of the key advantages of CGGMP21 is its efficient signing process, which is crucial for achieving high throughput in the Filia system. The protocol employs pre-signing and a one-round online signing process. This allows most cryptographic work to be completed ahead of time, minimizing delays during transactions and directly addressing the system's need for high signature throughput (**R3**). CGGMP21 is a SotA threshold ECDSA scheme with four signing rounds.

The protocol's security is further enhanced by its Universal Composability (UC) [8], ensuring that CGGMP21 remains secure even when composed with other cryptographic protocols. The UC-security guarantee fulfills the requirement for strong security (**R7**). Thus, the combination of compatibility, efficiency, and security makes CGGMP21 an optimal choice for the Filia system, particularly with the dfns [1] library.

# 5   Theoretical and Empirical Evaluations

The section provides an overview of the experiment design and the evaluation findings.

## 5.1   Security Analysis

As a part of the theoretical evaluation, we consider the communication and computational complexities of the CGGMP21 protocol. This information provides details about the scalability of our solution, which is a critical consideration for its applicability. Table 2 summarizes the complexities from the perspective of a single node, including the respective communication rounds and Big(O) cost.

The security of the KMN falls back on the security of the CGGMP21 protocol, as implemented in the *dfns* library, which has been rigorously audited. However, additional considerations for KMN security include the security of performing background DKG and key assignments. The execution of DKG in the background does not compromise overall security, as unauthorized access to the database of a node would expose the key shares of that node, regardless of when or how they are generated. Moreover, considering the system architecture, including the PP, an adversary who gains control of the PP would not be able to forge signatures. This is because every transaction request to the PP requires an authentication token tied to the user, such as biometric verification stored securely on the user device enclave. While an attacker in this scenario could disrupt operations, such activity would be detectable, allowing for a prompt restart of the PP to restore functionality. Notably, a coordinator is introduced in the implementation because it simplifies communication to facilitate the implementation of POC.

The *dfns* library operates under two primary assumptions: (1) all messages are authenticated, and (2) all Peer-to-Peer (P2P) messages are encrypted. These requirements are fulfilled using the *libp2p* library, which ensures secure and encrypted communication channels. Additionally, the library assumes reliable broadcast, achieved using an integrated reliability check mechanism. This mechanism enables each participant to hash the messages received in the previous round and include these hashes in their outgoing messages. By comparing these hashes, participants verify that all parties have received identical messages, ensuring consistency and reliability throughout the protocol execution.

## 5.2   Experiment Design and Empirical Evaluation

The implementation is based on the Rust-based *dfns* library [1]. The library abstracts the network layer, requiring only stream-based input and output for message exchange. For this, we rely on the *libp2p* library [31] to handle peer-to-peer communication.

We adopt the KMN approach (i.e., **Solution 2**). In this setup, each FSP integrates its KMN. Keys and pre-signatures are generated in advance by the KMN nodes. When a PP sends a key generation request, the KMN assigns an

**Table 2.** Complexities for CGGMP21 protocol [9, 25]

| Phase | Round | Computation | Communication |
|---|---|---|---|
| Key Generation | Round 1 | $O(1)$ | $O(n)$ |
| | Round 2 | $O(1)$ | $O(n)$ |
| | Round 3 | $O(n)$ | $O(n)$ |
| | Output | $O(n)$ | no communication |
| Presigning | Round 1 | $O(t)$ | $O(t)$ |
| | Round 2 | $O(t)$ | $O(t)$ |
| | Round 3 | $O(t)$ | $O(t)$ |
| | Output | $O(t)$ | no communication |
| Signing | Round 1 | $O(1)$ | $O(t)$ |
| | Output | $O(t)$ | no communication |

unallocated key to the request. Pre-signatures are utilized for signature operations on Filia commands; otherwise, the system falls back to an interactive signing step where the PP waits for the KMN nodes to interactively generate a signature. We introduce a coordinator node between the client PP and the KMN nodes. This node collects key shares from the KMN nodes to reconstruct the full key during key export. It also manages key import operations by receiving a full key and splitting it into $n$ key shares for the key addition/update process. Additionally, the coordinator node aggregates pre-signatures (also known as partial signatures) from the KMN nodes to produce the final signature, which is then sent back to the client.

The evaluation is conducted in two phases. First, we benchmark cryptographic operations independently to analyze performance under varying $n$ and $t$. These should provide insights into the cost following the overview in Table 2. Second, we integrated the updated protocol into the Filia system and measured End-to-End (E2E) transaction performance, including latency and throughput.

The cryptographic operations are evaluated in a local testbed using the METHODA [32, 33] framework. Our experiments run on four dedicated nodes. Each dedicated node has 64 virtual CPUs (vCPUs) and 768 GB of RAM. Each experiment includes application code and service management files, which handle configuration and execution across nodes. Within METHODA, scenarios define sequences of experiments, allowing controlled adjustments to parameters like $n$ and $t$. The nodes are interconnected over a dedicated test switch. To assess the scalability of the solution, we carry out experiments with various values of $t$ and $n$ from $t = 2, n = 3$ to $t = 32, n = 52$. We evaluate individual steps, including DKG, pre-signing, and signing. Each experiment involves 100 iterations and uses a single thread per node. These parameters are chosen based on evaluations of other threshold signature schemes (e.g., FROST [28], GG18 [22], and GG20 [23]) and relevance to expect the scale of the CBDC deployments. We fix the message size to 256 bit. We measured the computation and I/O time for each step during the experiment run. The **computation time** is the time each node spends on local cryptographic operations. On the other hand, the **I/O time** is the total time each node waits for messages to proceed to the next round. Therefore, the total iteration time is the sum of computation and I/O times. This evaluation uses the PerfProfiler utility from the *dfns* library. Time measurement begins at the start of the iteration once the room ID is assigned and all nodes are ready to execute the protocol. This assumes all expected nodes can communicate with each other.

**Results of Phase 1.** First, we conduct experiments of the DKG as shown in Fig. 2. The results show that increasing the number of nodes and the threshold directly impacts the time required for DKG. As shown in Fig. 2a, the time increases quadratically with the number of nodes and threshold. This is also the case for the I/O time when each node has to wait to proceed, as shown in Fig. 2b. We observe that for a smaller number of nodes, the I/O time exceeds computation time, likely due to communication delay among nodes. However, computation time begins to dominate the total DKG duration as the number of nodes and threshold increase, observing computation time up to 2500 ms for $n = 52$ and $t = 32$. More time is spent on computation than on I/O.

As pre-signing and signing are not dependent on $n$, we average all values for respective computation and I/O times. As shown in Fig. 3, the pre-signing follows a similar tendency for increasing $t$. Figure 3a shows computation time with a quadratic increase. For the I/O time, we observe fractional cost in comparison to the computation time, as shown in Fig. 3b. Continuing with signing presented in Fig. 4 we observe some order of times as for pre-signing. Especially the Fig. 4a is almost identical to the Fig. 3a. However, for I/O time we observe an increase, as introduced in Fig. 4b. The time difference between pre-signing and signing is minimal, indicating that the final online round, which produces the signature on the known message, is computationally inexpensive.

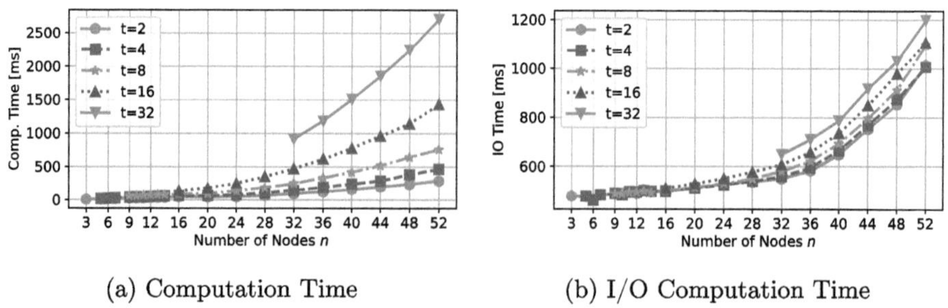

(a) Computation Time                    (b) I/O Computation Time

**Fig. 2.** DKG Time vs Number of Nodes.

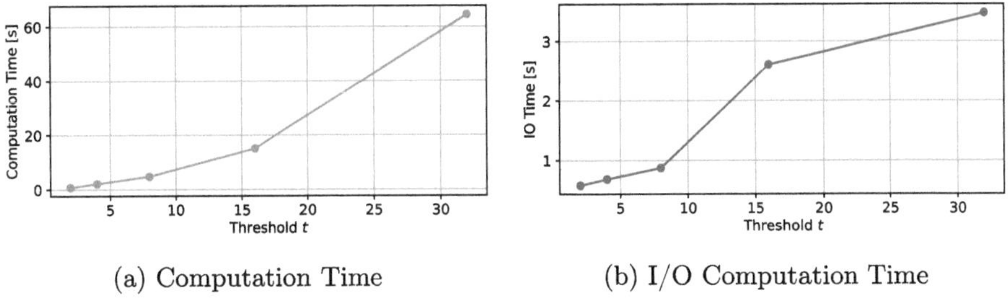

(a) Computation Time                    (b) I/O Computation Time

**Fig. 3.** Pre-signing Time vs Threshold.

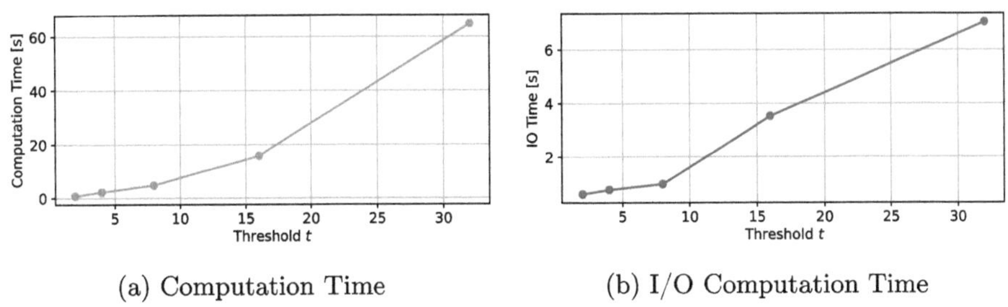

(a) Computation Time                    (b) I/O Computation Time

**Fig. 4.** Signing Time vs Threshold.

**Results of Phase 2.** The integration testing is carried out locally on a Mac-Book M3 Pro due to the complexity of setting up a private cloud-controlled environment and the challenges of porting the code to external infrastructure. The setup includes two KMNs ($t = 2, n = 3$), two FSPs hosting PPs, and a central Verifier hosted in a Docker container to validate transactions. We test two use cases (UCs): UC1 transfers between customers of the same FSP, whereas UC2 emulates transfers between different FSPs. The evaluation simulated varying loads with 1, 2, 3, 10, 20, 30, 100, 200, and 300 concurrent users over 30-minute test sessions. Wallets were pre-created using APIs exposed by the PPs, with each wallet assigned sufficient funds to execute transfers. The load tests measured E2E transaction timing, starting from the API call to initiate the transfer until the recipient's wallet confirmed transaction completion. As shown in Fig. 5a, throughput increases steadily as the load increases in UC1, while in UC2, throughput improves slightly. In both cases, the latency increases as the load increases, as shown in Figs. 5a and 5b. Performance evaluations reveal an order-of-magnitude decrease in throughput when using threshold signatures, particularly for cross-FSP transfers. Under high loads (100, 200, and 300 concurrent users), UC2 throughput drops to approximately 1.2 Transactions Per Second (TPS), compared to 60 TPS in a non-threshold configuration. Similarly, UC1 throughput decreases from 190 to around 10.7 TPS in the same setup. We also observe failed transactions with more concurrent users for throughput with an error rate of up to 0.15%, as shown in Fig. 5a.

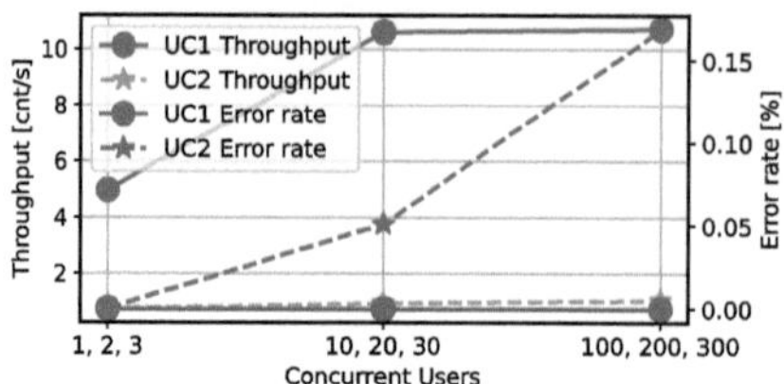
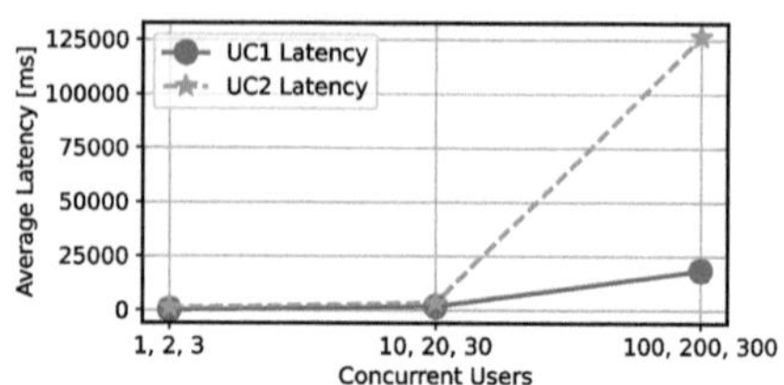

(a) Total throughput w/ increasing concurrent users

(b) E2E latency with increasing concurrent users

**Fig. 5.** E2E transactions latency and throughput.

## 5.3   Discussion

The CGGMP21 protocol and the KMN architecture collectively address all the requirements described, making them a fitting choice for Filia and other CBDC systems. However, further research is necessary to address performance challenges with threshold cryptography. As the number of nodes and the threshold increase, the performance of the cryptographic operations degrades noticeably. This is due to the growing computational and communication complexity, which scales with $n$ and $t$, as detailed in Table 2. In practical deployments, a smaller number of nodes is often sufficient to maintain better performance, and unless operated properly, larger node counts do not necessarily yield more security advantages. It is important to note that integration testing results are based on executions in a testing environment; a speedup is expected in a production-ready setup, provided the environment is carefully tuned to optimize performance and minimize resource constraints. While the added latency of communication between the PP and the KMN introduces a slight overhead, the system's scalability is mainly influenced by bottlenecks identified during the POC.

A key bottleneck appears in the time spent during signing operations without a pre-signature. This delay is introduced during the key import and update step, where the new key $r_1 + r_2$ has no pre-signature (⑦ in Fig. 1b). Consequently, a complete interactive signing on the KMN side is required when merging and signing with this key. Sometimes, it is triggered by an interactive signing or key generation. This happens when the pre-generated keys are exhausted, or a key exists without a pre-signature. Therefore, the nodes have to re-initialize communication and authentication with each other, leading to higher latency and resource inefficiencies. Addressing these bottlenecks may involve triggering a pre-signing operation in the background upon key updates. Similarly, nodes can establish communication channels among different protocol executions to reduce the overhead of re-establishing the secure channel between nodes.

The results for UC2 further indicate a non-zero error rate, with transaction timeouts caused by resource constraints. Transactions exceeding a 5-minute processing time are classified as errors, often due to unhandled temporary issues or resource locking by other jobs. Notably, an error rate is also observed in non-threshold transactions, indicating that the issue is not solely attributable to the use of TSS but rather to resource availability and system load. A potential solution to mitigate these errors would be horizontal scaling, allowing the system to dynamically allocate additional resources as transaction loads increase. In contrast, UC1 demonstrates zero errors, reflecting the lower complexity of same-FSP transfers compared to cross-FSP transfers.

The experimental design of this evaluation follows a logical progression that validates the solution from POC to performance assessment. The E2E transaction evaluations reveal the impact of TSSs on performance under various load conditions, replicating real-world transaction demands. Isolating cryptographic operations allows a detailed examination of resource costs associated with DKG, pre-signing, and signing. Although DKG and pre-signing occur as background tasks, their isolated evaluation highlights the computational demands they introduce. The signing evaluation shows the effect of the key update bottleneck, which requires interactive signing at that step. A configuration of $t = 2$ and $n = 3$ requires approximately one second for an interactive signing process. While manageable under a small load, this latency represents a substantial performance cost as the system scales.

## 6   Conclusion

Our work improves the security and resilience of CBDC systems, using Filia as a representative platform to address typical requirements. A comprehensive theoretical analysis identifies key system requirements, including compatibility with existing infrastructures, high signature throughput, secure key reconstruction, key updates, and strong security guarantees. We also define the computational and communication complexity of the CGGMP21 protocol and establish a robust security model to address adversarial behaviors. Building on this foundation, the CGGMP21 protocol is selected and used to build a POC, along with the design and implementation of a KMN architecture. Empirical evaluation shows that the evaluation of cryptographic operations aligns with the complexity analysis. Moreover, E2E transaction performance decreases by an order of magnitude compared to non-threshold systems, particularly in cross-FSP transactions. Despite this, the system demonstrates acceptable performance under varying loads for smaller values of $n$, confirming the feasibility of TSS usage in practical CBDC deployments like Filia while addressing key security challenges.

**Future Work.** As outlined, we identified several parts for optimization, which aim to improve the computation and communication bottlenecks. Similarly, even though the dishonest majority setting fits the CBDC setting, investigating further TSS tailored to the honest majority setting may offer reduced complexity and improved efficiency for KMN. Last, since CBDC solutions will be used for the long term, investigating post-quantum secure TSSs is essential for their future-proofness. Further efforts can focus on optimizing the computational and communication overhead of threshold operations, particularly addressing the identified bottlenecks.

**Acknowledgments.** We thank Franziska Kreitmair for early discussions on this subject and the anonymous reviewers for suggesting improvements to this paper. This work has been partially supported by the German Federal Ministry of Research, Technology and Space (BMFTR), Verbundprojekt CONTAIN (13N16582) and POST (16KIS2159). The Bavarian Ministry of Economic Affairs, Regional Development, and Energy under project 6G Future Lab Bavaria, and Horizon Europe under project SLICES-PP (10107977).

# References


1. DFNs. https://github.com/dfns/cggmp21
2. silence-laboratories. https://github.com/silence-laboratories/silent-shard-dkls23-ll
3. MPC alliance (2024). https://www.mpcalliance.org/
4. Abram, D., Nof, A., Orlandi, C., Scholl, P., Shlomovits, O.: Low-bandwidth threshold ECDSA via pseudorandom correlation generators (2021). https://eprint.iacr.org/2021/1587
5. Androulaki, E., et al.: A framework for resilient, transparent, high-throughput, privacy-enabled central bank digital currencies (2023). https://eprint.iacr.org/2023/1717
6. Aumasson, J.P., Hamelink, A., Shlomovits, O.: A survey of ECDSA threshold signing (2020). https://eprint.iacr.org/2020/1390
7. Bank of Canada, Swiss National Bank, European Central Bank, Bank of England, Bank of Japan, Board of Governors Federal Reserve System, Sveriges Riksbank, Bank for International Settlements: Central bank digital currencies: System design (2024). https://www.bis.org/publ/othp88_system_design.pdf
8. Canetti, R.: Universally composable security: a new paradigm for cryptographic protocols (2000). https://eprint.iacr.org/2000/067
9. Canetti, R., Gennaro, R., Goldfeder, S., Makriyannis, N., Peled, U.: UC non-interactive, proactive, threshold ECDSA with identifiable aborts (2021). https://doi.org/10.1145/3372297.3423367
10. Canetti, R., Halevi, S., Herzberg, A.: Maintaining authenticated communication in the presence of break-ins (1998). https://eprint.iacr.org/1998/012
11. Canetti, R., Makriyannis, N., Peled, U.: UC non-interactive, proactive, threshold ECDSA (2020). https://eprint.iacr.org/2020/492
12. Cohen, R., Lindell, Y.: Fairness versus guaranteed output delivery in secure multiparty computation (2014). https://eprint.iacr.org/2014/668
13. Consultative Group on Risk Management: Central bank digital currency (CBDC) information security and operational risks to central banks (2023). https://www.bis.org/publ/othp81.pdf
14. Cramer, R., Damgård, I., Ishai, Y.: Share conversion, pseudorandom secret-sharing and applications to secure computation. In: Proceedings of the Second International Conference on Theory of Cryptography, TCC 2005, pp. 342–362. Springer, Heidelberg (2005). https://doi.org/10.1007/978-3-540-30576-7_19

15. Doerner, J., Kondi, Y., Lee, E., Shelat, A.: Secure two-party threshold ECDSA from ECDSA assumptions (2018). https://doi.org/10.1109/SP.2018.00036. https://eprint.iacr.org/2018/499

16. Doerner, J., Kondi, Y., Lee, E., Shelat, A.: Threshold ECDSA from ECDSA assumptions: the multiparty case (2019). https://doi.org/10.1109/SP.2019.00024. https://eprint.iacr.org/2019/523

17. Doerner, J., Kondi, Y., Lee, E., Shelat, A.: Threshold ECDSA in three rounds (2023). https://eprint.iacr.org/2023/765

18. Erinle, Y., Kethepalli, Y., Feng, Y., Xu, J.: Sok: design, vulnerabilities, and security measures of cryptocurrency wallets (2025). https://arxiv.org/abs/2307.12874

19. Escudero, D.: An introduction to secret-sharing-based secure multiparty computation (2022). https://eprint.iacr.org/2022/062

20. Feng, Q., et al.: Stateless deterministic multi-party EdDSA signatures with low communication (2024). https://eprint.iacr.org/2024/358

21. Fireblocks: Fireblocks - #1 institutional digital asset custody, settlement & issuance (2024). https://www.fireblocks.com/. Accessed 12 Nov 2024

22. Gennaro, R., Goldfeder, S.: Fast multiparty threshold ECDSA with fast trustless setup (2019). https://eprint.iacr.org/2019/114

23. Gennaro, R., Goldfeder, S.: One round threshold ECDSA with identifiable abort (2020). https://eprint.iacr.org/2020/540

24. Giesecke+Devrient: Central bank digital currency g+d filia whitepaper (2024). https://pages.gi-de.com/whitepaper-filia

25. Glas, K.: Evaluation of Distributed Key Generation Approaches for Threshold ECDSA Signature Systems. Master's thesis, TUM (2022)

26. Goldwasser, S., Micali, S., Rackoff, C.: The knowledge complexity of interactive proof-systems. In: Proceedings of the Seventeenth Annual ACM Symposium on Theory of Computing, STOC 1985, pp. 291–304. Association for Computing Machinery, New York, NY, USA (1985)

27. Haitner, I., Lindell, Y., Nof, A., Ranellucci, S.: Fast secure multiparty ECDSA with practical distributed key generation and applications to cryptocurrency custody (2018). https://eprint.iacr.org/2018/987

28. Komlo, C., Goldberg, I.: Frost: Flexible round-optimized schnorr threshold signatures (2020). https://eprint.iacr.org/2020/852

29. Lindell, Y.: Simple three-round multiparty schnorr signing with full simulatability (2022). https://eprint.iacr.org/2022/374

30. Paillier, P.: Public-key cryptosystems based on composite degree residuosity classes. In: Proceedings of the 17th International Conference on Theory and Application of Cryptographic Techniques, EUROCRYPT 1999, pp. 223–238. Springer, Heidelberg (1999)

31. libp2p Project: libp2p: a modular network stack for peer-to-peer protocols in rust (2023). https://libp2p.io. Accessed 14 Sept 2023

32. Rezabek, F., et al.: Engine: flexible research infrastructure for reliable and scalable time sensitive networks. J. Netw. Syst. Manage. **30**(4), 74 (2022). https://doi.org/10.1007/s10922-022-09686-0

33. Rezabek, F., Glas, K., Von Seck, R., Aroua, A., Leonhardt, T., Carle, G.: Multilayer Environment and Toolchain for Holistic NetwOrk Design and Analysis (2023)

34. Ruffing, T., Ronge, V., Jin, E., Schneider-Bensch, J., Schröder, D.: Roast: robust asynchronous schnorr threshold signatures (2022). https://doi.org/10.1145/3548606.3560583. https://eprint.iacr.org/2022/550

35. Sarencheh, A., Kiayias, A., Kohlweiss, M.: PEReDi: privacy-enhanced, regulated and distributed central bank digital currencies (2022). https://eprint.iacr.org/2022/974
36. Sedghighadikolaei, K., Yavuz, A.A.: A comprehensive survey of threshold signatures: NIST standards, post-quantum cryptography, exotic techniques, and real-world applications (2024). https://arxiv.org/abs/2311.05514
37. Shamir, A.: How to share a secret. Commun. ACM **22**(11), 612–613 (1979). https://doi.org/10.1145/359168.359176
38. Varlakov, D., Katz, J.: Cggmp21 in rust, at last. DFNs (2024). https://www.dfns.co/article/cggmp21-in-rust-at-last

# Blockchain-Based Lotteries via Single Secret Leader Election

Tegrid Fettuh[ID] and Oğuz Yayla[(✉)][ID]

Institute of Applied Mathematics, Middle East Technical University,
06800 Ankara, Turkey
`{tegrid,oguz}@metu.edu.tr`

**Abstract.** Traditional lottery systems suffer from issues such as centralization, lack of verifiability, and reliance on trusted third parties, leading to potential manipulation and reduced trust among participants. In this work, we propose a blockchain-based lottery mechanism leveraging Single Secret Leader Election (SSLE) protocols to ensure fairness, unpredictability, and verifiability while eliminating the need for a central authority. We introduce a novel validator-driven deployment model for SSLE-based lotteries, which offloads most heavy cryptographic work that does not require revealing participants' secret data, to keep participants' tasks minimal. This adaptation, while preserving SSLE's fairness and secrecy, greatly lowers lottery participants' computational and synchrony requirements, hence making decentralized lotteries practical for non-expert users. We introduce and analyze four lottery frameworks. Each method is evaluated based on computational efficiency, user involvement, and security guarantees. Additionally, we compare SSLE-based lotteries with existing blockchain-based lottery schemes, highlighting improvements in public verifiability, fairness, and resistance to forgery. Our findings demonstrate that SSLE-based lotteries provide a promising alternative for designing decentralized and transparent lottery applications.

**Keywords:** Blockchain-based lotteries · Single Secret Leader Election · Decentralization · Cryptographic protocols

## 1 Introduction

Lotteries have been practiced for centuries, with winner selection mechanisms evolving significantly. Early methods included keno slips and fixed-prize tickets, followed by draw-based raffles using shuffled entries. Modern national lotteries often employ mechanical draw machines audited by third parties and publicly broadcast for transparency. With digital advancements, random number generators (RNGs) and verifiable random functions (VRFs) have been adopted in both national and electronic lotteries [8,17,22]. More recently, proposals have explored distributed randomness, blockchain technology, and smart contracts for decentralized and verifiable lottery schemes [19,26,27,29].

However, current systems suffer from key shortcomings: *centralization, lack of verifiability,* and *reward claiming issues. Centralization* places control solely


R. Laborde et al. (Eds.): ESORICS 2025, LNCS 16231, pp. 277–292, 2026.
https://doi.org/10.1007/978-3-032-16089-8_18

with the organizer, creating a single point of failure. *Dependence on trusted third parties* introduces risks of manipulation, as fairness is verified externally. *Verifiability* is limited—while draws may be broadcast, participants cannot actively verify the fairness of the process. *Reward claiming* is also centralized, risking delays or withholding of prizes.

Although RNGs and VRFs have improved efficiency, they remain centrally executed after entry submission [8,22,25], leaving the process susceptible to manipulation. A promising direction is to adopt distributed randomness—generated collaboratively by participants—and smart contracts, ensuring transparency, immutability, and automation.

Cryptographic protocols are central to the security and fairness of distributed systems. In particular, leader election protocols [1,15,21] enable the fair selection of entities to perform critical roles. Lottery selection is essentially a leader election problem. In Proof of Stake (PoS) blockchains like Ethereum 2.0 [11], Polkadot [31], and Algorand [15], block proposers are selected using VRFs (e.g., Polkadot's BABE [30]) or distributed randomness generators like RANDAO [13,32].

Single Secret Leader Election (SSLE) is a recent protocol that enables a group to randomly select a user such that only the winner knows she was chosen and can later prove it. Several SSLE variants have been proposed [2,3,6,7,9,14,33], each leveraging different cryptographic tools and offering unique properties. SSLE can be directly repurposed for lottery selection by treating the elected proposer as the winner, but this user-centric model imposes high computational and synchrony demands on participants.

## 1.1   Contribution

We introduce a novel validator-driven deployment framework for SSLE-based lotteries that offloads all heavy cryptographic operations (shuffle permutations, zero-knowledge proofs, homomorphic evaluations, etc.) to a small, semi-trusted validator set. Ordinary participants need only to register with a simple transaction and later submit a single claim, greatly reducing computational and availability requirements.

By adapting SSLE mechanisms, originally conceived for leader election in distributed networks, our framework eliminates the need for centralized authorities and trusted third parties, addressing key vulnerabilities such as manipulation, single points of failure, and limited transparency. We apply this model to four SSLE variants, Shuffle-based [3,20], Homomorphic Sortition-based [14], Multiparty Computation (MPC)-based [2], and Functional Encryption (FE)-based [7], detailing the protocol adaptations that preserve decentralization, distributed randomness, fairness, and public verifiability in a lottery context.

Finally, we provide a comprehensive evaluation by comparing our SSLE-based lottery frameworks against existing blockchain lottery schemes, highlighting significant gains in verifiability and forgery resistance, while transparently discussing remaining challenges (e.g., synchronization, validator incentives, and operational costs). This work lays the groundwork for secure, efficient, and user-friendly decentralized lottery systems.

## 1.2   Organization

In Sect. 2, we provide background on previous approaches and review existing research on single secret leader election (SSLE), blockchain-based lotteries, and online lotteries. Section 3 introduces cryptographic primitives and concepts that are used throughout the paper. In Sect. 4, we present the main contribution of this paper, the Lottery frameworks. Section 5 provides a comparative analysis of the proposed SSLE-based lottery frameworks. In Sect. 6, we compare the security benefits and efficiency of SSLE-based lottery mechanisms with existing blockchain-based lottery schemes using a structured comparison table. Finally, Sect. 7 is the conclusion part, where we summarize the findings of the paper.

## 2   Related Works

### 2.1   Single Secret Leader Election

An informal description of SSLE and problem statement was put forward by Protocol Labs [24], a formal game-based definition of SSLE and three example constructions: Indistinguishability obfuscation (IO) based SSLE, threshold fully homomorphic encryption (ThFHE) based SSLE, shuffle and decisional Diffie Hellman (DDH) based SSLE was proposed by [3]. Authors in [14] put forward a stronger definition of SSLE based on universal composability (UC) and a concrete construction based on Public Key Encryption with Keyword Search (PEKS) [7]. Again, Catalano, Fiore, and Giunta revisit the DDH-based SSLE defined by [3] and modify it, then prove its security in the adaptive universal composable model [6]. Backes, Berrang, Hanzlik, and Pryvalov proposed a multiparty computation (MPC)-based construction [2]. Another ThFHE-based SSLE construction called Homomorphic sortition was proposed by [14]. Lastly, very recently in [9] they addressed the issue of undetectable withholding attacks caused by the secrecy property of SSLE, and the last work is Qelect, a quantum secure lattice-based SSLE [33].

### 2.2   Blockchain Based Lotteries

Different blockchain-based constructions have been proposed to achieve decentralization using different winner selection methods. BanFel [26] utilizes multiparty computation where it takes entries from participants and uses them to generate a polynomial using Lagrange Interpolation, which is used to select the winner. FPLotto [29] also generates a polynomial using language interpolation, taking participants' entries as inputs where the constant term is used as the seed for the VRF that will generate the winning numbers. BlockLot [19] is another blockchain-based lottery scheme that takes a future bitcoin block as its source of randomness for winner selection. Another scheme is FairLotto [27], a privacy-preserving lottery scheme that is based on the Hawk model. Finally, DeLottery [18] is a lottery scheme inspired by RANDAO [32] and builds completely on smart contracts.

### 2.3  Online Lotteries

Online or e-lotteries follow a similar structure to blockchain lotteries, except that no smart contracts are involved, and instead, a trusted or trustless dealer is responsible for all lottery executions. This implies a centralized structure, by utilizing suitable cryptographic primitives, public verifiability of all executions' correctness and fairness can be satisfied. In [8], Chow et al. proposed an e-lottery scheme that combines VRFs for generating randomness with delay functions to resist forgeries by the dealer. Another scheme by [22] combines physical and cryptographic random number generators (RNGs), but in this scheme, the dealer can insert forged tickets before computing the hash of all tickets, which does not ensure complete security and fairness. In [17], Grumbach proposes a lottery scheme that utilizes a distributed aggregation protocol based on the Kademlia Distributed Hash Table (DHT). Another scheme [16] uses delay functions as building blocks where they focus on public verifiability and forgery resistance to avoid the need for a TTP, but instead is not private. Kuacharoen [23], on the other hand, proposed a lottery scheme that focuses on hiding players' entries and tickets by utilizing blind signatures. Other schemes based on different cryptographic primitives are [25, 28, 35, 36].

## 3   Preliminaries

**Definition 1** ([3,7]). *A **Single Secret Leader Election (SSLE)** scheme is a tuple of PPT algorithms* SSLE = (SSLE.Setup, SSLE.Register, SSLE.RegisterVerify, SSLE.Elect, SSLE.Claim, SSLE.Verify) *executed b etween $N$ users $U_1, \ldots, U_N$ as follows:*

- SSLE.Setup$(1^\lambda)$ *On input the security parameter $\lambda$, outputs public parameters $pp$ and a secret key $sk_i$ for each user $U_i$.*
- SSLE.Register$(i)$ *Registers user $U_i$ for future elections.*
- SSLE.Elect$(pp) \to c$ *Outputs a public election challenge $c$ generated in a distributed manner.*
- SSLE.Claim$(c, sk_i, i) \to \pi$ *or $\bot$ User $U_i$ checks whether they are elected and, if so, outputs a proof of leadership $\pi$; otherwise, outputs $\bot$.*
- SSLE.Verify$(c, i, \pi) \to \{0, 1\}$ *Verifies the correctness of the leadership proof $\pi$ for user $U_i$ with respect to challenge $c$.*

An SSLE protocol as defined in [3,24] have the following properties:

**Fairness:** No entity can influence the result of the election, i.e., each user has a $\frac{1}{N}$ chance of getting selected, where $N$ is the number of participants.

**Unpredictability:** No entity can predict the elected user with greater accuracy than random guessing.

**Uniqueness:** There is only a single winner of the election, i.e., there can not be more than one valid proof of being selected.

**Verifiability:** All election participants can verify and ensure that the steps of the election are conducted correctly and honestly.

**Decentralization:** Does not depend on a trusted third party as participants contribute to the randomness and election process.

**Definition 2** ([3,4]). *A **commitment scheme** COM consists of two algorithms COM = (COM.com, COM.verify) defined over a message space $M$ and a randomness space $R$, where:*

1. *COM.com$(m; r) \to c$: On input a message $m \in M$ and randomness $r \in R$, outputs a commitment $c$.*
2. *COM.verify$(c, m, r) \to \{0, 1\}$: On input a commitment $c$, message $m$, and randomness $r$, outputs 1 if $c$ is a valid commitment to $m$ using randomness $r$, and 0 otherwise.*

A commitment scheme has hiding and binding properties:

1. **Hiding**: receiving a commitment $c$ should give the receiver no information about message $m$.
2. **Binding**: Once a commitment $c$ is generated, the sender can only open it to a single message.

This cryptographic primitive is utilized in the shuffle-based SSLE, the used commitment scheme is based on Decisional Diffie Hellman (DDH) assumption and is rerandomizable: The commitment is computed as $com(k_i, r) = (u, v) = (g^r, g^{k_i r}) \in \mathbb{G} \times \mathbb{G}$ for $k_i, r \in \mathbb{Z}_q$, A rerandomization of $(u, v)$ is computed as $(u^{r'}, v^{r'})$ for $r' \in \mathbb{Z}_q$.

**Definition 3** ([3,14]). *A **Threshold Fully Homomorphic Encryption (ThFHE)** scheme is a tuple of probabilistic polynomial-time (PPT) algorithms ThFHE = (ThFHE.Setup, ThFHE.Encrypt, ThFHE.Evaluate, ThFHE.PDecrypt, ThFHE.Verify, ThFHE.Decrypt) executed among $N$ parties, where:*

- *ThFHE.Setup$(1^\lambda, N, t) \to (pk, \{sk_i\}_{i=1}^N)$: On input the security parameter $\lambda$, number of parties $N$, and threshold $t \leq N$, outputs a public key $pk$ and secret key shares $\{sk_i\}_{i=1}^N$ for each party $P_i$.*
- *ThFHE.Encrypt$(pk, m) \to \underline{m}$: On input a plaintext $m$ and the public key $pk$, outputs a ciphertext $\underline{m}$.*
- *ThFHE.Evaluate$(C, \underline{m}_1, \ldots, \underline{m}_n) \to \underline{c}$: On input a circuit $C$ and ciphertexts $\underline{m}_1, \ldots, \underline{m}_n$, outputs the ciphertext $\underline{c}$ corresponding to $C(m_1, \ldots, m_n)$.*
- *ThFHE.PDecrypt$(sk_i, \underline{c}) \to \delta_i$: On input a ciphertext $\underline{c}$ and a secret key share $sk_i$, outputs a partial decryption $\delta_i$.*
- *ThFHE.Verify$(\underline{c}, \delta_i) \to \{0, 1\}$: Verifies the validity of a partial decryption $\delta_i$.*
- *ThFHE.Decrypt$(\{\delta_i\}_{i \in S}) \to m$: On input a set of at least $t$ valid partial decryptions, outputs the decrypted message $m$.*

The second SSLE-based Lottery scheme in Sect. 4.2 utilizes Threshold Fully Homomorphic Encryption. ThFHE is an encryption scheme where there is a shared public key, and each user possesses a secret key; encryptions are done using the public key, while partial decryptions are done using the secret key; the prominent property of ThFHE is that users can perform evaluations on encrypted data. The circuits used in Sect. 4.2 are as follows:

1. $C_<$: Compares $x$ with a list of values.
2. $C_{01}$: Finds the first number that equals 1 in an encrypted binary vector.
3. $C_{Sel}$: Takes two inputs; an array of encrypted values $[x_1, \ldots, x_n]$ and an encrypted binary vector $[b_1, \ldots, b_n]$ such that $b_i = 1$ and $b_j = 0$ for all $j \neq i$, and outputs encrypted $x_i$.
4. $C_{PRF}$: Using $x$ and an encrypted input $k$ outputs the encryption of the output of $PRF(k, x)$, where $PRF$ is a pseudo-random function with output domain $[0, 1, \ldots, \delta - 1]$.
5. $C_H$: Takes as input encrypted $x$ and outputs the encryption of $H(x)$, where $H$ is a hash function.

**Definition 4 ([7]).** *A **Functional Encryption (FE)** scheme for a functionality $F$ is a tuple of algorithms such that*

- *FE.Setup$(1^\lambda) \to (mpk, msk)$: On security parameter $\lambda$, generates the secret and public master keys $(mpk, msk)$.*
- *FE.Encrypt$(m, mpk; r) \to c$: On input a plaintext $m$ and public master key $mpk$, outputs a ciphertext $c$.*
- *FE.KeyGenetate$(f, msk) \to sk_f$: Takes as inputs a function $f \in F$ and secret master key $msk$, outputs a secret key $sk_f$ associated to $f$.*
- *FE.Decrypt$(sk_f, f, c, mpk) \to m$: On input a secret key $sk_f$, a ciphertext $c$, and the public master key $mpk$, outputs a decryption associated with $sk_f$.*

FE is a type of public key encryption in which decrypted data depend on the decryption key. The lottery system defined in Sect. 4.4 specifically uses functional encryption for orthogonality.

**Definition 5.** *A **Multiparty Computation (MPC)** protocol is a tuple of probabilistic polynomial-time (PPT) algorithms:* MPC = (MPC.Setup, MPC.Compute, MPC.Decrypt) *executed among $N$ parties, where:*

- *MPC.Setup$(1^\lambda, N, t) \to$ pp: On input the security parameter $\lambda$, the number of parties $N$, and a threshold $t \leq N$, initializes the protocol and outputs public parameters* pp *(and possibly private key shares, if applicable).*
- *MPC.Compute$(\text{pp}, f, x_1, \ldots, x_N) \to \{y_i\}_{i=1}^N$: On input a function $f$ and private inputs $x_i$ from each party, the parties interactively compute $f(x_1, \ldots, x_N)$ and each party $P_i$ receives an output $y_i$.*
- *MPC.Decrypt$(\{y_i\}_{i \in S}) \to y$: On input a subset $S$ of at least $t$ correct output shares, reconstructs and outputs the final result $y$.*

MPC is a cryptographic primitive with its main aim being to allow parties to jointly perform computations over their inputs while keeping those inputs private. The used MPC scheme in Sect. 4.4 and in [2] is based on verifiable secret sharing schemes.

## 4   Blockchain Based Lottery

In this section, we present a general overview of blockchain-based lottery protocols. Each framework follows a common structure that includes phases such as
setup, registration, winner selection, and prize claiming, as illustrated in Fig. 1.
Tasks executed by smart contracts are represented using wavy boxes. The following subsections describe specific instantiations of this structure based on different
cryptographic primitives.

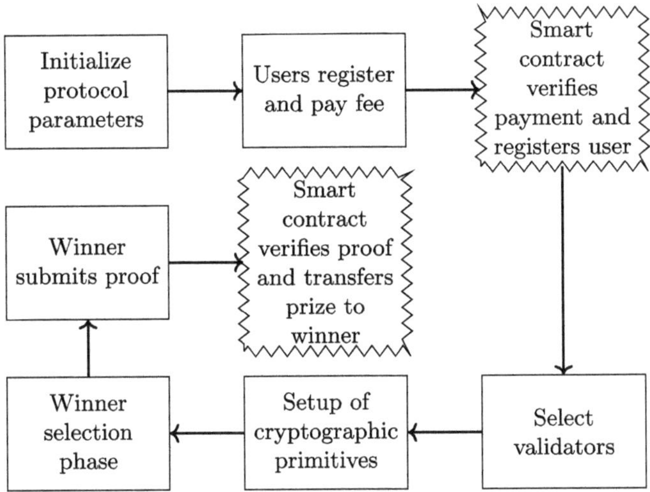

**Fig. 1.** Overview of the lottery protocol workflow.

### 4.1   Shuffle-Based SSLE as a Lottery

The shuffle based lottery scheme SLOTTO introduced in this section uses list
shuffling as a winner selection mechanism and is based on [3,20]. SLOTTO consists of the following algorithms:

1. SLOTTO.Setup: Initialize an empty vector $l = \{\}$ and choose $g \xleftarrow{R} \mathbb{G}$, where
   $\mathbb{G}$ is a group in which the $DDH$ assumption holds. The values $l$, $g$, and $\mathbb{G}$ are
   public.
2. SLOTTO.Register: Each user pays the specified fee, samples $k_i \xleftarrow{R} \{0,1\}^{\lambda}$,
   and computes $(k_{iL}, k_{iR}) \leftarrow H(k_i)$. Here, $k_{iL}$ remains private, while $k_{iR}$ is
   public and used to prevent duplicates. A commitment is computed as $com_i =
   (g^{r_i}, g^{r_i k_{iL}})$ with $r_i \xleftarrow{R} \mathbb{Z}_q$. The user submits their wallet address, $com_i$, and
   $k_{iR}$ to a smart contract. If the fee is valid and no prior $k_{jR} = k_{iR}$ exists, the
   contract appends $com_i$ to $l$ and stores $k_{iR}$ and the wallet address.

3. SLOTTO.Elect: Validators (or shufflers) are randomly selected. In the shuffling phase, each shuffler rerandomizes and permutes the list $l = \{com_i\}_{i \in [N]}$ by computing $com'_j = com_j^{r'_j} = (g^{r'_j r_j}, g^{r'_j r_j k_j L})$ for $r'_j \xleftarrow{R} \mathbb{Z}_q$. They submit the new list and a NIZK proof of correct shuffling to a smart contract, which updates the list. This process repeats across multiple shufflers. Depending on system constraints, either the full or partial list may be shuffled. After shuffling, one or more commitments are selected using public randomness (e.g., Ethereum's RANDAO [32]) and published.

4. SLOTTO.Claim: Each user $U_y$ checks if the selected commitment $com_x = (g^{r_x}, g^{r_x k_x L})$ is theirs by verifying whether $g^{r_x k_y L} = g^{r_x k_x L}$. The winner submits a ZKP of knowledge of the corresponding key to a smart contract, which, if verified, transfers the prize to the stored wallet address.

The security of the lottery scheme follows from the underlying SSLE protocol [3], which was proven, using the game-based model, to satisfy the uniqueness, fairness, and unpredictability properties under the assumptions of the random oracle model and the Decisional Diffie-Hellman (DDH) assumption in the group $\mathbb{G}$. Note that in lotteries, there is no problem with the key getting revealed since users will be changing every lottery, and there will always be newcomers.

*Remark 1.* In the case of no one claiming the prize another index needs to be selected as a winner (for instance the next index, or another index selected using a public randomness produced by a randomness beacon such as RANDAO [32]) and such a situation may induce a race-like attack between the original winner and the participant with the next index, potentially facilitated by malicious validators.

## 4.2   Homomorphic Sortition Based Lottery

Homomorphic sortition-based SSLE [12,14] takes into consideration stake weights, which is good for weighted lotteries (some participants having higher chances of winning). Additionally, it can be extended to select multiple distinct winners. Another advantage is that this protocol does not require users to act in a synchronized manner during the winner selection phase. The lottery scheme HLOTTO consists of the following algorithms:

1. HLOTTO.Register: Each user pays the required fee or buys tickets and submits their wallet address along with their stake to a smart contract, which verifies payment and registers them. Validators are randomly selected from a pool, and a threshold FHE (ThFHE) setup is performed using distributed key generation. Each participant receives a secret key $sk_i$, while a public key $pk$ and an encrypted seed $\underline{q}$ are generated. A round number $r$ and stake distribution vector $S$ (based on stakes or ticket purchases) are defined. Each participant samples a random token $t_i$, encrypts it, and a list $T$ of encrypted tokens is published. Thus, the public parameters are $pp = \{r, S, T, pk, \underline{q}\}$.

2. HLOTTO.Elect: Each validator evaluates the following ThFHE circuits on encrypted data:

   (a) $\underline{x} = \text{ThFHE.Eval}(C_{PRF}, \underline{q}, r)$

   (b) Compute prefix sums $U := [\sum_{j=1}^{1} S[j], \sum_{j=1}^{2} S[j], \ldots, \sum_{j=1}^{n} S[j]]$ and set $m := U[n]$

   (c) For all $i \in [n]$, compute $Z[i] := S[i] \cdot \delta/m$ (assuming PRF output domain is $[0, 1, \ldots, \delta - 1]$)

   (d) $\underline{L} := \text{ThFHE.Eval}(C_<, \underline{x}, Z)$; $\underline{E} := \text{ThFHE.Eval}(C_{01}, \underline{L})$

   (e) $\underline{s_r} := \text{ThFHE.Eval}(C_{Sel}, \underline{E}, S)$; $\underline{t_r} := \text{ThFHE.Eval}(C_{Sel}, \underline{E}, T)$; $\underline{i_r} := \text{ThFHE.Eval}(C_{Sel}, \underline{E}, [1 \ldots n])$

   (f) $\underline{\pi_r} := \text{ThFHE.Eval}(C_{PRF}, \underline{t_r}, r)$

   (g) $\underline{v_r} := \text{ThFHE.Eval}(C_H, \underline{\pi_r \| i_r})$

   Each validator computes the encrypted voucher $\underline{v_r}$ and publishes it. Participants then submit partial decryptions $\tilde{v}_r := \text{ThFHE.PDec}(\underline{v_r})$ to a smart contract, which verifies each one. Once enough valid shares are collected, $\underline{v_r}$ is decrypted and the result is published.

3. HLOTTO.Claim: The winner, say user $U_j$, submits $\pi_j$ as proof to a smart contract which checks the equality $v_j := H(\pi_j \| j) = v_r$ and sends the prize to the winner if satisfied. Note that only the winner can generate $\pi_r$ as only she has $t_r$.

The security of this lottery scheme follows from the underlying SSLE protocol [14], where it was proven, using the game-based model, that the protocol satisfies the uniqueness, unpredictability, and fairness properties.


## 4.3   MPC Based Lottery

MPC-based SSLE, as proposed in [2], and briefed in [12], uses Oblivious Select $OSelectM$, which takes two secret shares as inputs and randomly outputs one of them without knowing which was selected. This algorithm is extended to $OSelectM_N$, where it takes $N$ secret shares as inputs, and one of them is chosen by applying $OSelectM$ in a tree structure. If MPC-based SSLE is deployed in the validator driven model as a lottery protocol, it will consist of the following steps:

1. MLOTTO.Register: Public parameters of the MPC scheme, such as $p$ and $g$, are chosen, and null states $st_1, st_2, \ldots, st_N$ are initialized. Each user samples a key $k_i \in \mathbb{Z}_p$ and computes $k_{iL}, k_{iR} \leftarrow H(k_i)$. To register, each user submits their wallet address, public identifier $k_{iR}$, and a transaction log for the lottery fee to a smart contract. The contract verifies fee payment, checks that the wallet address and $k_{iR}$ are not already registered, and if valid, updates the state $st_i \leftarrow k_{iR}$ and stores the wallet address. A set of validators is then selected. Each validator generates an asymmetric key pair $(pk_i, sk_i)$. The user splits their secret $k_{iL}$ into shares and encrypts each share using a distinct validator's public key, ensuring each validator receives one encrypted share. Thus, each validator holds a secret share of every participant's $k_{iL}$.

2. MLOTTO.Elect: Validators jointly execute the protocol $OSelectM_N$ over the secret shares to privately compute and select the winner.
3. MLOTTO.Claim: The winner $P_j$ triggers a smart contract by submitting their key $k_j$. The contract computes $k_{jL}, k_{jR} \leftarrow H(k_j)$ and verifies that $k_{jR} = st_j$ and $k_{jL} = k_{xL}$. If valid, it transfers the prize to $P_j$'s registered wallet address.

The security of the MPC-based lottery scheme given in Sect. 4.3 follows from the security of the underlying SSLE protocol proposed in [2], which is proven secure in the universally composable (UC) model [5], under the assumptions that the MPC primitives are secure in the honest-but-curious model and that the random oracle model holds.

### 4.4  FE Based Lottery

FE-based SSLE [7,12] utilizes a three-dimensional orthogonality functional encryption scheme [34], generation of ciphertexts and decryption keys is done in a distributed manner by quorum members by combining the FE scheme with distributed El-Gamal. If this SSLE protocol is to be utilized as a lottery proto-col, either a set of validators or the lottery participants need to play the role of quorum members. The FE-based lottery will follow the following steps:

1. FELOTTO.Register: Users register by invoking a smart contract, submitting their wallet address, a public identifier, and a transaction log for the lottery fee. The contract verifies the payment and ensures the wallet is not already registered before adding the user.
2. FELOTTO.SSetup: The FE SSLE setup begins by specifying a public encryp-tion scheme. Each participant generates a key pair $(pk_i, sk_i)$ and publishes $pk_i$. A random quorum of validators is selected to jointly generate the public key and decryption keys using threshold El-Gamal, following [7] and simpli-fied in [12]. Each validator submits NIZK proofs of correctness, verified either by a smart contract or off-chain among quorum members. The final public key $mpk$ is published, and each participant derives their FE decryption keys from the verified partial outputs.
3. FELOTTO.Elect: A new random quorum is selected (via a randomness bea-con [10,32] or a simple protocol) to encrypt the winner's index as the vector $(m, -1, -n)$, where $m = \gamma + jn$ for winner index $\gamma$ and total participants $n$. Quorum members generate this ciphertext collaboratively, each submitting a partial output with a NIZK proof. Proofs are verified either on-chain or off-chain, and the final ciphertext $c$ is published. See [3,12] for detailed steps.
4. FELOTTO.Claim: Each participant checks whether any of their keys satisfies $1 \leftarrow FE.Dec(c, sk_{\gamma,j})$, equivalent to $(m, -1, -n)(1, \gamma, j)^\top = 0$, i.e., $m = \gamma + jn$. The winner submits the key or a ZKP to a smart contract, which verifies the decryption and automatically transfers the prize if valid.

The security of the FE-based lottery scheme given in Sect. 4.4 follows from the security of the underlying SSLE protocol proposed in [7], which is proven secure in the universally composable (UC) model [5] under the SXDH assumption.

## 5  Discussion

This section provides a comparison of SSLE-based lottery mechanisms introduced in Sect. 4. Table 1 summarizes the differences among the proposed lottery mechanisms.

**Minimal User Involvement:** Simplifing participation and reducing errors by limiting interactions to essential steps like registration, commitment generation, and prize claiming are crucial. Among SSLE-based mechanisms, the Shuffle-based Lottery has the lowest involvement, users only register, generate commitments, and verify if they have won. The Homomorphic Sortition-based Lottery requires moderate involvement: participants register, compute tokens, produce partial decryptions, and claim the prize. The MPC-based Lottery also involves moderate effort, as users register, split their secret into shares, encrypt and distribute them to validators, and claim the prize. The FE-based Lottery demands the highest involvement: participants register, generate a key pair, decrypt partial outputs, combine them to derive the FE decryption keys, decrypt the ciphertext to check for winning, and claim the prize.

**Minimal Synchrony Requirement:** Some mechanisms allow participants to act independently, reducing delays and making the system more resilient. The Shuffle-based Lottery has a high synchrony requirement, as shufflers must act consecutively within allocated timeframes. The MPC-based Lottery has moderate synchrony needs, as validators need to cooperate during the computation of oblivious select, as it must be executed in parallel. FE-based Lottery also has a moderate synchrony requirement during combining partial outputs. The Homomorphic Sortition-based Lottery has the lowest synchrony requirement since validators can perform computations independently and submit their results asynchronously.

**Minimal Smart Contract Utilization:** It is important to reduce gas costs, which makes the lottery more affordable for participants. Limiting interactions to essential functions like registration and prize distribution helps maintain security and transparency while avoiding unnecessary blockchain overhead. In the Shuffle-based Lottery, smart contracts handle registration (verifying fee payment and duplicate keys $k_{iR}$), updating the commitment list after each valid shuffle (with a NIZK proof), and prize claiming. The FE-based Lottery has high usage as it uses smart contracts for registration, prize claiming, and updating or publishing validators' partial outputs during the key distribution and challenge ciphertext generation phases provided that submitted NIZK proofs are valid. The Homomorphic Sortition-based Lottery has moderate usage, employing smart contracts for registration, prize claiming, and updating correct partial decryptions. The MPC-based Lottery has the lowest reliance, using smart contracts only for registration and prize distribution.

**Computational Overhead:** Higher computation cost can lead to longer processing times and higher resource consumption, which can be a limiting factor for large-scale deployments. The Shuffle-based Lottery requires shuffling, rerandomization, and NIZK proof generation for correct shuffling in each step and have a computational/communication complexity of $\mathcal{O}(log(\sqrt{N}))$ or $\mathcal{O}(log(N))$ (note that $N$ is the number of lottery participants) depending on the utilized shuffling algorithm. The Homomorphic Sortition-based Lottery requires the computation of $\mathcal{O}(N^2)$ gates and hence has a communication complexity of $\mathcal{O}(N^2)$. The MPC-based Lottery requires $\mathcal{O}(N)$ MPC operations and $\mathcal{O}(log(N))$ rounds of communication, and this protocol's testing concluded that it takes approximately 1 min for 32 participants. The FE-based Lottery has a communication/computational complexity $\mathcal{O}(N)$. Therefore all discussed lottery frameworks supports large scale lotteries, except for the MPC-based framework, and possibly homomorphic sortition based lottery as it has computational complexity $\mathcal{O}(N^2)$.

**Validator Incompliancy:** Validator Incompliancy can compromise randomness and unpredictability, threatening election integrity. To mitigate this, measures such as slashing penalties, increasing validator redundancy, and separating setup and election roles are employed. In the Shuffle-based Lottery, validators handle shuffling and rerandomization, where incompliance may affect randomness. In the Homomorphic Sortition-based Lottery, validators manage the ThFHE setup and circuit evaluations, both critical for security and unpredictability. In the MPC-based Lottery, validators perform oblivious selection of winner's secret shares and reconstruct the final secret from a threshold of correct shares. In the FE-based Lottery, validators oversee both setup, constructing FE keys, and election, generating FE ciphertexts. As in the Homomorphic Sortition scheme, validators play essential, accountable roles.

**Validator Accountability and Penalty Model:** Validators are required to lock a security deposit (stake) before protocol execution, and a slashing penalty is executed in cases of misbehavior. Also a **Grace Period** can be implemented for first time offenders where they receive warnings or reduced penalties. Misbehavior is categorized as:

- **Submission of invalid proofs** (proofs of correct shuffles, homomorphic proofs, proofs of correct partial FE encryptions, etc.) which results in slashing of a fixed percentage (e.g. 25%) of validator's stake per invalid proof,
- **Failure to submit required messages** (such as permutation share, partial ciphertext, etc.) within the allotted time-frame which triggers a smaller slash percentage (e.g. 5%–10%) of the stake and penalties can be reduced taking into consideration transient network issues,
- **Signing multiple outputs** for the same round, which can be categorized as a malicious behavior and triggers slash of a large percentage (e.g. 50%) and ejection of the protocol,
- **Continuous misconduct** such as when the slashed amount exceeds a previously defined threshold (e.g. 30%) as a result of multiple timeouts or mistakes the validator is ejected and replaced by a backup validator.

# 6   Comparison

In this section, we provide a comparison of the security benefits of the lottery frameworks discussed in this paper with previously proposed blockchain-based lottery schemes in Sect. 4, which is summarized in Table 2. On-chain efficiency refers to the amount of data that must be stored on the blockchain to later serve as proof of the election result.

PV (Public Verifiability) is whether the correctness of protocol steps can be verified by players. DR (Distributed Randomness) is whether randomness is contributed by multiple entities or depends on a single source. TP (Ticket Privacy) is whether players' entries remain private. UF (User Friendliness) stands for the ease of use for participants. DS (Decentralized Structure) is whether the scheme operates in a decentralized manner. FR (Forgery Resistance) is whether participants or the lottery organizer can forge lottery tickets based on other participants' published entries. OR (Online Requirement) is whether the scheme requires an online connection. TTP (Trusted Third Party) is whether the scheme assumes the presence of a trusted third party. Each criterion is marked as Y (Yes), N (No), or P (Partial) in the table. As observed, SSLE-based lotteries offer higher security compared to other lottery schemes.

The table shows that all the compared blockchain-based lottery schemes ensure public verifiability (PV) and forgery resistance (FR), indicating a strong emphasis on security and transparency. Most protocols also support distributed randomness (DR) and a decentralized structure (DS)-certain protocols lack fully distributed randomness or exhibit only partial decentralization. Ticket privacy (TP) is robust in several schemes but not uniformly adopted, highlighting a trade-off between privacy and other system features. User friendliness (UF) varies notably across the schemes, with some protocols rated as fully user-friendly and others only partially so, suggesting that ease of use is still an area for improvement. All protocols, except one in the case of OR and one partially in the case of TTP, which is crucial as dependence on an online connection could introduce vulnerabilities, while reliance on a trusted third party undermines the decentralized nature inherent to blockchain-based systems.

Based on the evaluation criteria in the table, Protocol 4.1 emerges as the best option. It achieves full marks on all positive attributes-public verifiability (PV), distributed randomness (DR), ticket privacy (TP), user friendliness (UF), decentralized structure (DS), and forgery resistance (FR)-while also avoiding the negative properties by not requiring an online connection (OR) and not relying on a trusted third party (TTP). This balanced and robust feature set makes Protocol 4.1 the most comprehensive and secure protocol among those compared.

**Table 1.** Comparison of the Lottery Mechanisms introduced in Sect. 4

| Criterion | Shuffle-Based | Homomorphic Sortition-Based | MPC-Based | FE-Based |
|---|---|---|---|---|
| User Involvement | Low (3 tasks) | Moderate (4 tasks) | Moderate (4 tasks) | High (5 tasks) |
| Synchrony | High | Low | Moderate | Moderate |
| Smart Contract Utilization | High | Moderate | Low | High |
| Computational Overhead | $\mathcal{O}(\sqrt{N})$ or $\mathcal{O}(N)$ | $\mathcal{O}(N^2)$ | $\mathcal{O}(N)$ | $\mathcal{O}(N)$ |
| On-chain Efficiency | $\mathcal{O}(\sqrt{N})$ or $\mathcal{O}(N)$ | $\mathcal{O}(1)$ | $\mathcal{O}(1)$ | $\mathcal{O}(log^2 N)$ |

**Table 2.** Blockchain-based Lotteries Comparison Table

|  | [18] | [29] | [26] | 4.1 | 4.2 | 4.3 | 4.4 |
|---|---|---|---|---|---|---|---|
| PV | Y | Y | Y | Y | Y | Y | Y |
| DR | Y | Y | N | Y | Y | Y | Y |
| TP | N | Y | N | Y | Y | Y | Y |
| UF | P | P | Y | Y | P | P | N |
| DS | Y | Y | P | Y | Y | Y | Y |
| FR | Y | Y | Y | Y | Y | Y | Y |
| OR | N | N | N | N | N | N | Y |
| TTP | N | N | P | N | N | N | N |

# 7 Conclusion

In this work, we tackled the shortcomings of traditional and blockchain lottery systems by introducing a validator-driven SSLE deployment model that offloads all heavy cryptographic work to a dedicated validator set. We analyzed multiple approaches, shuffle-based, homomorphic sortition-based, multiparty computation (MPC)-based, and functional encryption (FE)-based, and evaluated their feasibility in ensuring fairness, verifiability, and decentralization in lottery mechanisms.

Our analysis shows that SSLE-based lotteries address key limitations of traditional and existing blockchain lottery schemes by providing enhanced privacy and reducing reliance on a trusted third party. However, trade-offs exist in terms of computational efficiency, user participation requirements, and potential synchronization constraints. While shuffle-based SSLE ensures decentralization, it demands active user participation and introduces computational overhead. The homomorphic sortition-based approach supports weighted lotteries and offers better scalability, albeit at higher cryptographic complexity. The MPC and FE-based approaches provide strong security guarantees but may require additional infrastructure or validator incentives.

Future work should focus on optimizing these protocols for real-world deployment, including reducing gas costs, improving user accessibility. Additionally, practical implementations and empirical evaluations would further validate the feasibility of SSLE-based lotteries in blockchain ecosystems. By bridging cryptographic innovation with decentralized applications, this work contributes to the growing body of research on fair and verifiable lottery mechanisms.

**Acknowledgment.** This work is supported by the TÜBİTAK 2224-A Grant.

# References


1. Azouvi, S., McCorry, P., Meiklejohn, S.: Betting on blockchain consensus with fantomette. arXiv preprint arXiv:1805.06786 (2018)
2. Backes, M., Berrang, P., Hanzlik, L., Pryvalov, I.: A framework for constructing single secret leader election from MPC. In: Computer Security - ESORICS 2022, pp. 672–691 (2022)
3. Boneh, D., Eskandarian, S., Hanzlik, L., Greco, N.: Single secret leader election. In: Proceedings of the 2nd ACM Conference on Advances in Financial Technologies, pp. 12–24 (2020)
4. Boneh, D., Shoup, V.: A graduate course in applied cryptography. Draft 0.5 (2020)
5. Canetti, R.: Security and composition of multiparty cryptographic protocols. J. Cryptol. **13**(1), 143–202 (2000)
6. Catalano, D., Fiore, D., Giunta, E.: Adaptively secure single secret leader election from DDH. In: Proceedings of the 2022 ACM Symposium on Principles of Distributed Computing, pp. 430–439 (2022). https://doi.org/10.1145/3519270.3538424
7. Catalano, D., Fiore, D., Giunta, E.: Efficient and universally composable single secret leader election from pairings. In: IACR International Conference on Public-Key Cryptography, pp. 471–499 (2023)
8. Chow, S.S., Hui, L.C., Yiu, S.M., Chow, K.P.: An e-lottery scheme using verifiable random function. In: International Conference on Computational Science and Its Applications, pp. 651–660 (2005)
9. Christ, M., Choi, K., McKelvie, W., Bonneau, J., Malkin, T.: Accountable Secret Leader Election (2024). https://doi.org/10.4230/LIPIcs.AFT.2024.1
10. David, B., Gaži, P., Kiayias, A., Russell, A.: Ouroboros Praos: an adaptively-secure, semi-synchronous proof-of-stake protocol. Cryptology ePrint Archive, Paper 2017/573 (2017)
11. Ethereum: Ethereum 2.0: The Transition to Proof of Stake. https://github.com/ethereum/eth2.0-specs. Accessed 28 Feb 2025
12. Fettuh, T., Yayla, O.: Single secret leader election in proof-of-stake blockchains: a concise review. In: 2024 17th International Conference on Information Security and Cryptology (ISCTürkiye), pp. 1–6 (2024)
13. Foundation, E.: Ethereum whitepaper (2013). https://ethereum.org/en/whitepaper/
14. Freitas, L., et al.: Homomorphic sortition - single secret leader election for POS blockchains. Cryptology ePrint Archive (2023)
15. Gilad, Y., Hemo, R., Micali, S., Vlachos, G., Zeldovich, N.: Algorand: scaling byzantine agreements for cryptocurrencies. In: Proceedings of the 26th Symposium on Operating Systems Principles (2017)
16. Goldschlag, D.M., Stubblebine, S.G.: Publicly verifiable lotteries: applications of delaying functions. In: International Conference on Financial Cryptography, pp. 214–226 (1998)

17. Grumbach, S., Riemann, R.: Distributed random process for a large-scale peer-to-peer lottery. In: IFIP International Conference on Distributed Applications and Interoperable Systems, pp. 34–48 (2017)
18. Jia, Z., Chen, R., Li, J.: DeLottery: a novel decentralized lottery system based on blockchain technology. In: Proceedings of the 2019 2nd International Conference on Blockchain Technology and Applications, pp. 20–25 (2020)
19. Jo, Y., Park, C.: BlockLot: blockchain based verifiable lottery. https://arxiv.org/abs/1912.00642 (2019)
20. Kadianakis, G.: Whisk: a practical shuffle-based SSLE protocol for ethereum (2022). https://ethresear.ch/t/whisk-a-practical-shuffle-based-ssle-protocol-for-ethereum/11763/1
21. Kerber, T., Kohlweiss, M., Kiayias, A., Zikas, V.: Ouroboros crypsinous: privacy-preserving proof-of-stake. In: 2019 IEEE Symposium on Security and Privacy (SP), pp. 157–174 (2018)
22. Konstantinou, E., Liagkou, V., Spirakis, P., Stamatiou, Y.C., Yung, M.: Electronic national lotteries. In: International Conference on Financial Cryptography, pp. 147–163 (2004)
23. Kuacharoen, P.: Design and implementation of a secure online lottery system. In: International Conference on Advances in Information Technology, pp. 94–105 (2012)
24. Labs, P.: RFP-006: secret single-leader election (SSLE) (2019). https://github.com/protocol/research-grants/blob/master/RFPs/rfp-006-SSLE.md
25. Lee, J.S., Chang, C.C.: Design of electronic t-out-of-n lotteries on the internet. Comput. Stand. Interfaces **31**(2), 395–400 (2009)
26. Li, J., Zhang, Z., Li, M.: BanFEL: a blockchain based smart contract for fair and efficient lottery scheme. In: 2019 IEEE Conference on Dependable and Secure Computing (DSC), pp. 1–8 (2019)
27. Liao, D.Y., Wang, X.: Design of a blockchain-based lottery system for smart cities applications. In: 2017 IEEE 3rd International Conference on Collaboration and Internet Computing (CIC), pp. 275–282 (2017)
28. Medeleanu, F., Răcuciu, C., Nen, M., Liepe, Z., Antonie, N.F.: Fair e-lottery system proposal based on anonymous signatures. Appl. Econ. **51**(27), 2921–2933 (2019)
29. Pan, Y., Zhao, Y., Liu, X., Wang, G., Su, M.: FPLotto: a fair blockchain-based lottery scheme for privacy protection. In: 2022 IEEE International Conference on Blockchain (Blockchain), pp. 21–28 (2022)
30. Polkadot: BABE: Blind Assignment for Blockchain Extension - Polkadot Block Production Method. https://spec.polkadot.network/sect-block-production. Accessed 28 Feb 2025
31. Polkadot: Polkadot Network. https://polkadot.network/. Accessed 28 Feb 2025
32. RANDAO Developers: Randao: Verifiable Random Number Generation (2017). https://www.randao.org/whitepaper/Randao_v0.85_en.pdf
33. Wang, Y., Zhang, F.: Qelect: Lattice-based single secret leader election made practical. Cryptology ePrint Archive (2025)
34. Wee, H.: Attribute-hiding predicate encryption in bilinear groups, revisited. In: Theory of Cryptography Conference, pp. 206–233 (2017)
35. Xia, Z., Liu, Y., Hsu, C.F., Chang, C.C.: An information theoretically secure e-lottery scheme based on symmetric bivariate polynomials. Symmetry **11**(1), 88 (2019)
36. Zhang, Y., An, F., Zhao, K., Ye, J.: A verifiable e-lottery scheme. In: International Conference on Machine Learning for Cyber Security, pp. 393–401 (2020)

# Towards E-Voting Systems on Resource Based Blockchains


Ricardo Lopes Almeida[1,2,3]($\boxtimes$), Fabrizio Baiardi[2],
Constantin Cătălin Drăgan[3], Damiano Di Francesco Maesa[2],
Laura Ricci[2], and Nishanth Sastry[3]

[1] Università di Camerino, Camerino, Italy
[2] Università di Pisa, Pisa, Italy
[3] University of Surrey, Guildford, UK
`ricardo.almeida@unicam.it`



**Abstract.** Traditionally, e-voting research in academia used to be mainly focused on using cryptography in server-client architectures to produce secure, private, and transparent systems. In 2009, the introduction of blockchain technology provided researchers with a new approach to tackle this problem. But the blockchain ecosystem is still undergoing much transformation, with new features and approaches being frequently added to it. This paper presents the first proposal for a blockchain-based remote voting system based on a novel resource-based approach for representing digital assets in a blockchain. Ledger-based blockchains represent digital assets as a set of concurrent records stored inside smart contracts, resulting in systems with large monolithic requirements that are hard to scale. Resource-based blockchains, a recent addition to the ecosystem, represent digital assets, or *resources*, as concise digital records, independent of the smart contract that defines and issues them. Accounts, in such a model, are complex objects that can contain *resources*. This simplifies the concept of ownership: whoever owns the account where a *resource* is stored owns that *resource*. This approach of representing digital assets attempts to emulate physical assets, i.e., *resources* can only exist in one place at a time, they cannot be copied, and they can only be explicitly destroyed programmatically. As such, *resources* provide an ideal medium to abstract ballots. Our proposal showcases the advantages and suitability of the novel resource-based architecture and its claims about advanced security, transparency, and scalability in the field of voting systems.

**Keywords:** Blockchain · e-voting · resource-based architecture


## 1  Introduction

Elections are a fundamental aspect of modern, democratic societies. Yet, the voting process in most democracies still relies on archaic methods based on paper ballots. Due to the importance of this exercise in our society, academia and civil society have engaged in efforts to modernise it. Several governments around the



R. Laborde et al. (Eds.): ESORICS 2025, LNCS 16231, pp. 293–310, 2026.
https://doi.org/10.1007/978-3-032-16089-8_19

world have provided remote voting systems to their citizens, as has been the case for Switzerland [6], Canada [14], Estonia [17], and Australia [15]. All these trials have used centralised systems based on a server-client architecture, which puts the majority of computations in a single or a cluster of computational units. This centralisation aspect poses severe limitations regarding scalability, voter privacy, security, and transparency.

A different, decentralised approach to the voting problem has been introduced in 2009 with the introduction of blockchain technology. Due to the almost exclusive financial nature of the first public blockchains, e-voting researchers had to develop creative methods to use a tool that was never intended to be used for voting to their advantage. The initial wave of academic publications on this subject suggested using whole blockchain blocks as ballots [3], transferring a specific cryptocurrency value to wallets belonging to candidates/options [16], or other equally creative but impractical solutions. These approaches resulted in systems that were difficult to use or required voters to buy cryptocurrency to vote, which is not ideal in a fair electoral system.

The research landscape went through another significant change with the introduction of the Ethereum blockchain in 2015. Ethereum differs from Bitcoin by providing a *distributed virtual machine (DVM)*, which was named as *Ethereum Virtual Machine (EVM)*, that can execute computer code in a decentralised manner. Programs that run in this *EVM* are called *smart contracts* and represent a substantial increase in programmatic flexibility for blockchain platforms. The potential of smart contract technology was such that the majority of blockchain-based e-voting proposals began leveraging them soon after.

Most DVMs represent digital assets, which in the blockchain context are mainly represented by either *fungible* or *non-fungible* tokens, as a function of the smart contracts that implement them. They use a *ledger-based* approach to store data in the contracts themselves as key-value mappings. Recent additions to the blockchain ecosystem introduced a new architecture to represent digital assets. Blockchains like Flow [11], Aptos [21], and Sui [22] represent digital assets using a resource-based architecture. They rely on programming languages like Cadence for Flow and Move for Aptos and Sui to create smart contracts that represent digital assets as unique and self-contained digital records named *resources*. This paradigm also extends the concept of *accounts* from an address and a pair of cryptographic keys to a private storage space that can house resources. Resources are inspired by *linear types* [23], which makes them unique in nature and emulates assets in the physical world: they can only exist in one location (account) at a time, and their destruction needs to be explicitly coded. Resource ownership is implicit. It derives from the owner of the account where the digital object is currently stored, thus emulating how one "owns" objects in the physical world. This new approach of representing ownership makes *resources* an attractive element to represent sensitive data, such as a ballot, in a decentralised voting system.

## 1.1  Contribution

This proposal removes the smart contract point of aggregation from ledger-based systems and replaces it with a *resource-based* backend to create a transparent, private, and verifiable voting system. We establish a direct ownership mechanism for critical digital assets, namely ballots, which are stored in the voters' accounts. In an account, only the account owner can operate on the stored *resource*. This allows for features, such as ballot delegation, that are not present in the majority of proposals on this topic. The *resource*-based approach, alongside the advanced account system offered by these blockchains, provides the functionalities to increase the verifiability of the proposed system without any sacrifices to voter privacy, a common trade-off in proposals using blockchain technology.

This article proposes the first e-voting system based on the new resource-based paradigm to represent digital assets in blockchains. We provide a easy to understand example on how to use the advanced tokenisation features offered by the new paradigm to represent digital assets whose mutability can be tightly controlled. E-voting represents a rare example of an exercise that can be fully digitalised without any loss in functionality. If anything, we can argue that such system can rival the security of a traditional one, with an added layer of verifiability not present in paper based systems. Resources provide a new research avenue for the tokenisation efforts from within supply chain industries and other related venues where traceability of the lifecycle of a product is paramount.

## 2  Related Works

Research in blockchain-based systems has been increasing in popularity since the inception of Bitcoin in 2009. [2] provides a concise history of the development of blockchain-based voting systems, as well as the main strategies used to implement them. Since this publication, others have followed with similar systematic literature analysis efforts, such as the case of [4,19], but all these publications agree with the one result that we are interested in: there are no academic publications exploring the resource-based paradigm applied to electronic voting up to the time of this writing.

Academic literature is, currently, notoriously absent regarding the new resource-based architectural approach. Recent proposals such as [1,5,24], and [20] follow the trend identified in the *Systematic Literature Review (SLR)* articles by establishing a voting backend with Ethereum smart contracts but reference digital assets or NFTs.

Some publications are fairly more related to our subject. [10] proposes the typical Ethereum-based voting system, but it does employ NFTs in the solution. These are ledger-based digital assets; therefore, they do not benefit from the account model and advanced access control offered by resource-based counterparts. [13] presents a similar approach but using Hyperledger Fabric to build an enterprise, i.e., permissioned, blockchain. This publication does abstract the election elements as digital assets, but Hyperledger employs a ledger-based architecture similar to Ethereum; therefore, it is not a resource-based proposal.

Ledger-based blockchains define ownership of digital assets explicitly, i.e., using a key-value mapping to define ownership in the same framework they define the rest of the asset's parameters. Ledger-based digital assets are also more limited than *resources*. The former are limited to hold parameters inside a limited set, and any additional functionalities (methods) are provided at the contract level, which limits their potential, as well as making them completely dependent on the issuing contract. *Resources* break away from this limitation by emulating regular programming objects but in a decentralised environment, which is used to add uniqueness to their features. Like a "normal" Object Oriented Programming (OOP) object, *resources* have internal parameters and methods whose accessibility can be defined granularly, thus providing a much more functional alternative to regulate a ballot in a remote voting system.

In a public blockchain, *resource* data is still written into public blocks that can be read by anyone. The advanced access control offered by resource-based blockchains is limited to operations within the protocol, but at the hardware level, the state information is still written into publicly accessible blocks. This means that some level of encryption needs to be used to maintain voter privacy even when using *resources*. Blockchains are notoriously averse to allowing encryption operations on-chain, and understandably so. It is impossible to encrypt or decrypt any data on-chain without revealing the keys used, which immediately invalidates any encryption scheme. In this regard, resource-based blockchains suffer from the same limitations as others. Any sensitive data written into public blocks needs to be already encrypted before being added to a block. But the new ownership model presented, as well as the added functionalities from using *resources*, justifies this investigation. In other blockchains, this limitation is often mitigated with the use of *zero-knowledge proofs (ZKP)* to ensure voters that the vote submitted into the system is still the one that reflects their choice. But *ZKPs* suffer from a similar plight in the sense that the calculation of the proof is a very computationally intensive task. As such, proof calculations occur off-chain as well, to avoid the high *gas* cost that this process would entail if performed on-chain. On the other hand, verifying a proof is a simpler and less intensive operation that typically happens on-chain. *Resources* promise to help with this as well. Our proposal provides sufficient traceability of encrypted information without resorting to overly demanding additional computations such as *ZKP* circuit calculations.

The absence of blockchain publications on resource-based implementations is not surprising considering how recent these additions are to the blockchain ecosystem. [2] identifies a significant temporal gap between the publication of Satoshi Nakamoto's Bitcoin paper [18] and the first academic publications on blockchain, let alone specific ones related to the e-voting field. This pattern might repeat itself with the resource-based approach, which justifies why this publication is the first to explore together the new resource-based paradigm and its applications to blockchain-based e-voting systems.

## 3   Linear Types and Resources

Resource-based blockchains are a recent addition to the blockchain ecosystem. Such blockchain protocols approach the representation of digital objects and assets from a different perspective than the more classical ledger-based approach. This section presents a summary of the history of its development.

### 3.1   Linear Types

Linear types were introduced by Jean-Yves Girard [12] and refined further by Philip Wadler [23]. Values in a *linear type system* emulate the real world by establishing linear type values that *cannot be duplicated or discarded*. Linear type values can only exist in one location at a time, cannot be copied, and their destruction needs to be explicit in code. Resources are digital records that behave as *linear types* in a blockchain environment. Resource creation is highly regulated; resources can only exist in a logical location (account) at a time, and their destruction needs to be programmatically explicit.

### 3.2   Blockchain Resources

Resources, also referred to as objects, are used to represent digital assets in a blockchain environment. Ledger-based blockchains, such as Ethereum, represent digital assets as concurrent sets of records in mappings (key-value data structures) that require great effort from developers to maintain a reasonable level of security. Ethereum-like blockchains are notorious for their lack of proper access control, a problem that makes any effort toward tokenisation using these blockchains quite difficult and prone to costly software bugs. Resources were created with the specific purpose of representing digital assets. Fundamentally, these are concise blockchain records, often represented as JSON-style objects, that represent a specific object, which can be entirely digital or entirely real.

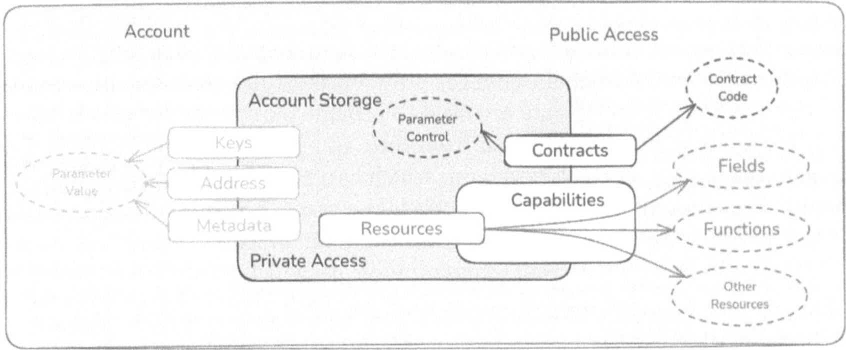


**Fig. 1.** Account model used by the Flow blockchain.

Resources are modeled after *linear types*. As such, once a resource or object is created on the blockchain, it needs to be in one location and only one location at all times. Resources are not able to be copied, only moved, and their destruction needs to be explicit. Resources and objects allow a closer, secure, and more intuitive modeling of real world objects and concepts into the global state of a blockchain. Resources inherit their security against tampering due to their existence as part of the blockchain state. Yet, the new resource-based approach also provides tools to allow these resources to be mutated only by authorised actors and no one else. This extraordinary level of access control makes resources an ideal candidate to abstract ballots in a blockchain-based e-voting system.

### 3.3   Resource-Based Accounts

User accounts in resource-based blockchains are, to some extent, resources themselves. Figure 1 presents the account model used in Flow, the oldest of the public resource-based blockchains in operation.

Functionally, accounts are key-value structures stored in the blockchain in a distributed fashion, just like every other state information. They divide into public and private parameters, using an encryption key to enforce this separation. Resource-based accounts have a private storage area used to store both smart contract code and digital assets, or resources. Some resources store other resources, but the storage quota they use is deducted from the area where the outer resource exists. The owner of the account, and only the owner, can use capabilities to publish details from stored resources from the private space into the public space. After, other users can use these capabilities to read and interact with resources in a private storage area. These interactions often occur indirectly, through references, which work similarly to the references used in low-level languages such as C, to safeguard the integrity of the stored resources.

### 3.4   Events

Blockchains rely on events to confirm state transitions as a consequence of the inability of transactions to return anything other than a transaction receipt. To mitigate this, smart contracts are configured to emit events with custom parameters whenever the blockchain changes state successfully through the execution of a contract method(s). Events are used to provide parameter details on successful state transitions. Events are emitted into an event stack and published into the main output log of the blockchain, which can make their retrieval somewhat difficult. Fortunately, most public blockchains provide dedicated APIs to filter and retrieve specific event instances from the main stack.

The arguments in each event emission indicate which parameters are exposed by the event itself, thus providing an indirect method to obtain values in successful state transitions.

## 3.5  *Collection*-Type Resources

Every digital object stored in an account's private storage is done so under a unique path, in a similar fashion as a file stored in a UNIX OS. The definition of such a path is often left to the responsibility of the account's owner, and attempting to save an object under an existing path incurs an immediate revert of the blockchain state. To minimise this issue and ease the storing process, resource-based blockchains introduced the *collection* resource, which is essentially a resource that can hold multiple resources in a single structure (typically a dictionary) as long as these have the same type. This approach limits the effort of choosing a unique storage path to the collection. Once in storage, other resources move in and out of the *collection* using *deposit* and *withdraw* functions, which are easier to use and control than having to create a unique path for each new resource. Additionally, the capability-based access control from resource-based blockchains enables these *collections* to emulate regular mailboxes: Anyone can use the *deposit* function, but only the owner can access the *withdrawn* function, just as anyone can deposit a letter in a public mailbox, but only the mailman with a key can withdraw them.

## 3.6  Capabilities

Capabilities are used in resource-based environments to delegate access to owned digital objects. If a user wishes to allow other users to access an internal parameter or invoke methods from a resource saved into their private account storage, the user can publish a capability with the relevant access permissions. Then, other users can retrieve a *reference* to an object in someone else's storage using the published capability. Capabilities are highly configurable, which enables granular access to resources. References obtained from capabilities are akin to the memory pointers used by low-level languages such as C and C++. They allow for indirect access to parameters and methods while preventing users other than the resource owner from accessing the resource itself.

## 3.7  Burning Resources

A distinct feature of resource-based blockchains is how these destroy assets in their environment, often known as "burning". Burning digital assets in a ledger-based blockchain is abstracted by transferring the asset into an irrecoverable address. Though it is possible to delete all records corresponding to a certain asset from the internal mapping of a ledger-based contract, the dispersal of information through disconnected mappings makes this operation risky and complex. So, traditionally, developers opt to "nullify" the record instead by moving it to an account without a knowable private encryption key that can be used in the future to recover the asset data. This process is not a clean one, since it keeps all data from the burnt asset stored in the contract.

Resource-based blockchains burn assets in a cleaner manner. They take advantage of the fact that resource records are well-defined and self-contained key-value objects. Burning a resource in this context amounts to simply deleting that key-value object from the blockchain state. In itself, burning an asset is just another state transition between a state where the resource exists and another where it does not. As it has been the case so far, only the owner of the resource can sign a transaction that destroys it. We take advantage of this cleaner approach to asset destruction in our proposed solution.

## 3.8   Fungible and Non-fungible Tokens in Resource-Based Context

The resource-based paradigm implements both *fungible* and *non-fungible* tokens (*FTs* and *NFTs*) with resources. NFTs are directly translatable into resources, given that these are functionally equal. *Fungible* tokens, or cryptocurrencies, cannot exist "by themselves", as they do as independent variables for Ethereum and Bitcoin. As such, *fungible* tokens are represented as a parameter inside a resource, often called a *vault* or similar. *Vault* resources allow for *deposits* and

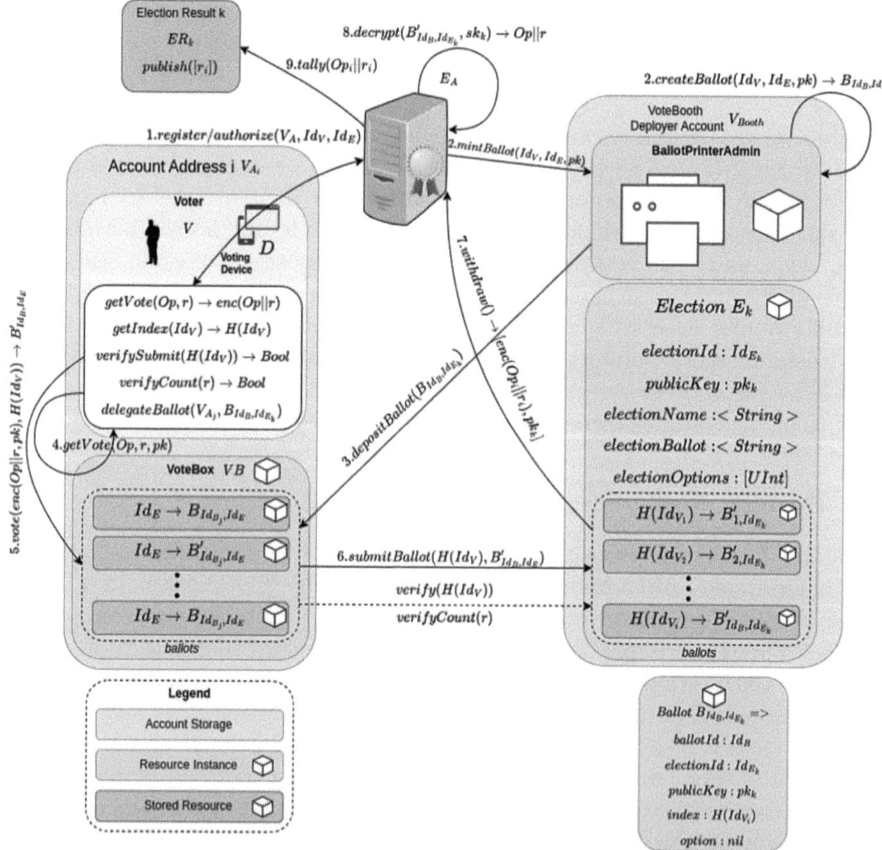



**Fig. 2.** Resource-based voting framework.

*withdraws*, but the latter can only be executed by the *vault* owner. Transacting cryptocurrencies in a resource-based blockchain typically consists of creating a temporary *vault*, withdrawing the amount to transact from the main *vault* to the temporary one, and then transferring the temporary *vault* to the recipient address, thus reducing this process to a resource transfer.

## 4    Resource-Based Blockchain E-Voting System

Our system relies on smart contracts to emulate the functionalities of a traditional voting server, e.g., generate election keys, create empty resources, and manage the ballot box. We present a high-level proposal of our resource-based electronic voting system in Fig. 2. We use italic font with capitalized letters to express resource names, e.g., "*Ballot*" as the digital object that was constructed (minted) from the rules and definitions in the smart contract that defines the ballot standard.

### 4.1    System Actors

**Voters.** Voters are the main users of this system. Each voter has their own account, identified uniquely by an *account address* $V_{A_i}$, and with a personal, private storage space where the voter can save resources. At an individual level, voters interact with the system via a voting device $D_i$. The device is used to abstract operations, such as generating random integers, encrypting data and generating digitally signed transactions, that are critical but far too complex to expect average voters to be able to do by themselves. The assumption is that voters only have to select an option from an available set, and the frontend system in their devices takes care of the advanced computations. This exercise also assumes that voting devices are not corruptible and that any ciphertexts produced from this element do correspond to a correct encryption of plaintext using the public encryption key *pk* provided. This assumption is not farfetched. One can assume that any software distributed for this purpose is provided with either a digital signature from the developers or, as it is more usual currently, with an hash digest that voters can use to ensure that their software version has not been tampered with. These strategies are commonly used nowadays and are enough for us to assume that we can ensure that all off-chain software required is honest.

**Election Authority.** This system employs an *Election Authority (EA)* to determine voter eligibility and control and trigger admin-level processes, such as minting new resources, creating and completing elections, generating and handling encryption keys, and running tallies.

*Enforcing Eligibility.* The Election Authority included in our scenario represents an independent trusted third party. As such, we do not advance any suggestions regarding how it should validate the eligibility of its voters. In fact, we conceived the system presented in this paper in a modular framework to allow the Election Authority to create election exercises that can have distinct lists of eligible voters. This element falls outside of the technical boundaries defined for this project and these details are left blank on purpose towards maintaining system flexibility.

**Resource-Based Backend.** This section provides an overview of the resources that compose the voting backend from their functional point of view. In the resource-based context, smart contracts are used to define a "template" for these digital objects and to create new ones. But once a resource is created, it exits, fully functional, outside of the bounds of the contract. Unlike in a ledger-based system, deleting or modifying a resource smart contract does not jeopardise any resources minted up to that point.

*Ballot.* *Ballot* resources are implemented according to the definitions in a Ballot-Standard contract. Figure 2 presents a template for a *Ballot* resource, namely, the internal parameters that define one. This resource holds the voter choice along the process, but in an encrypted format to preserve voter privacy. Each minted *Ballot* has its submission locked to a specific *Election* through the electionId parameter. Minted *ballots* are part of the blockchain state; therefore, they have to receive any sensible data from off-chain already encrypted.

*Election.* This proposal implements elections in a modular fashion by abstracting each of them into an independent resource. *Elections* are resources whose parameters and methods are defined through an ElectionStandard smart contract, omitted from Fig. 2 due to space constraints. *Elections* are characterised by the set of internal parameters and methods depicted in Fig. 2, which enables to run multiple elections in parallel. This can be used to scale up an election by having multiple *Elections* with the same ballot, name, and options (but different IDs and encryption keys) or simply running multiple different ones at once. The resource-based approach provides a solution for scalability by storing and pre-processing *Ballots* in *Elections* rather than in a contract, as is the case for every ledger-based solution. Creating new resources is far easier, cheaper and simpler than deploying another contract.

*BallotPrinterAdmin.* The creation of new *Ballots* is heavily regulated in the system, and it is the prerogative of the *Election Authority (EA)*; i.e., only the *EA* is capable of issuing blank *Ballots*. This admin privilege is abstracted by the usage of the admin printer resource. The *BallotPrinterAdmin* is created and saved into the contract deployer's account solely in the contract's constructor. A smart contract constructor is a function that runs one single time during deployment. This apparent limitation is traditionally used to establish "one-time functions" that can only be executed for the initial run. This limits the resource creation privileges to the owner of the account that holds the minter resource, as well as ensuring that one and only one resource minter exists, which guarantees that the creation of new resources is limited to a single entity.

*VoteBox.* This resource is the main interface between the voter and the system, through the voting device $D_i$. A *VoteBox* is an example of a *collection* resource, a typical element in resource-based environments. Section 3.5 provides additional details on *collections. VoteBoxes* are set to hold one and only one *Ballot* per active *Election.* The voting device $D_i$ interacts with the system through the functions exposed by the *VoteBox,* which are indicated in Fig. 2. The code and parameters of each *VoteBox* are stored publicly in blocks, but only the owner of one can invoke the functions exposed by its API, as well as extend this usage to others by publishing the required capabilities. Section 3.6 provides additional details on the workings of capabilities.

## 4.2  Resource-Based Voting Process

**Cryptographic Primitives.** The following cryptographic definitions pertain to the state transitions presented in Fig. 2 and detailed in Fig. 3.

*Encryption and Decryption Scheme.* This proposal adopts a homomorphic ElGamal [9] encryption scheme described by:

1. $register/authorize(V_A,Id_V,Id_{E_k})$

1:  **foreach** $Id_{E_k}$
2:  $EA \leftarrow EA \cup (V_A,Id_V)$
3:  **return** $(V_A,Id_V) \in EA$

2. $mint/createBallot(Id_V,Id_{E_k},\mathsf{pk}_k)$

1:  $BallotPrinter \leftarrow (Id_V,Id_{E_k},\mathsf{pk}_k)$
2:  $emit(BallotCreated(Id_B,Id_{E_k}))$
3:  **return** $B_{Id_B,Id_{E_k}}$

3. $depositBallot(B_{Id_B,Id_{E_k}})$

1:  $V_A.VB.ballots[Id_{E_k}] \leftarrow B_{Id_B,Id_{E_k}}$

4. $generateRand(seed)$

1:  $r \leftarrow \$ \mathsf{PRG}$
2:  **return** $r$

5. $getVote(Op,r,\mathsf{pk}_k)$

1:  $D \leftarrow (Op,r,\mathsf{pk}_k)$
2:  **return** $(enc(Op\|r,\mathsf{pk}_k),H(Id_V))$

6. $vote(enc(Op\|r))$

1:  $B'_{Id_B,Id_{E_k}} \leftarrow (enc(Op\|r))$
2:  $V_A.VB.ballots[Id_{E_k}] \leftarrow B'_{Id_B,Id_{E_k}}$

7. $submitBallot(H(Id_V\|r),B'_{Id_B,Id_{E_k}})$

1:  $E_k \leftarrow (H(Id_V),B'_{Id_B,Id_{E_k}})$
2:  $E_k.ballots[H(Id_V)] \leftarrow B'Id_B,Id_{E_k}$
3:  $emit(BallotSubmitted(Id_B,Id_{E_k}))$

8. $(Admin)withdraw()$

1:  **return** $[enc(Op\|r,\mathsf{pk}_k)]$

9. $decrypt(B'_{Id_B,Id_{E_k}},\mathsf{sk}_k)$

1:  $EA \leftarrow enc(Op\|r,\mathsf{pk}_k)$
2:  $Op\|r = dec(enc((Op\|r),\mathsf{pk}_k),\mathsf{sk}_k)$
3:  **return** $(Op\|r)$

10. $tally(Op_i\|r_i)$

1:  $(Op_i,r_i) \leftarrow split(Op_i\|r_i)$
2:  $ER_k \leftarrow count([Op_i])$
3:  $publish(ER_k,[r_i])$

**Fig. 3.** State transition algorithms for the resource-based voting system in Fig. 2.

1. A key generation algorithm $\mathsf{KGen}(\mathbb{G}, g, p)$, where $\mathbb{G}$ is a cyclic group of prime order $p$ generated by generator $g$, which outputs a public-private key-pair $(\mathsf{pk} = g^{\mathsf{sk}}, \mathsf{sk})$ for $\mathsf{sk} \in_R \mathbb{Z}_p$.
2. An encryption function $\mathsf{Enc}(m, \mathsf{pk})$ which takes as input a message $m$ and a public key $\mathsf{pk}$ and returns a ciphertext $c = (c_1, c_2) = (g^r, m \cdot \mathsf{pk}^r)$ for $r \in_E \mathbb{Z}_p$.
3. A decryption function $\mathsf{Dec}(c, \mathsf{sk})$ that returns message $m = c_2 \cdot c_1^{-\mathsf{sk}}$.
4. A randomiser function $\mathsf{Rand}(P, c = (c_1, c_2); r') :$ using randomness $r' \in \mathbb{Z}_p$, output $c' = (c_1 \cdot g_1^{r'}, c_2 \cdot P^{r'})$

*Hash Function* We adopt a *collision resistance* hash function $H$ for the purpose of this proposal, i.e., a function $H$ whose probability for an efficient adversary $\mathcal{A}$ of finding a message $m_1$ for an existing message $m_0$ such that $H(m_0) = H(m_1)$ is negligible.

**State Transition Algorithms.** The state transitions indicated in Fig. 2 are regulated by the algorithms described in the following.

We detail our algorithm in Fig. 3 pertaining to state transitions from Fig. 2. We recall that all transactions require to be digitally signed by a party with the necessary privileges. The system relies on events to publish parameters related to the successful transition, as it is the norm for the vast majority of blockchains. Blockchain state transitions do not return anything back to the caller other than a transaction receipt with the details of the transaction execution (status, gas consumed, block height, block number, etc.). The only mechanism to obtain parameters that result from a state change is to emit them in an event triggered by the successful state transition. Section 3.4 details the strategy adopted for it.

**Multiple Vote Casting.** This proposal allows voters to submit multiple *Ballots* during the course of an election, but only the latest one is counted. *Elections* are configured to save *Ballots* internally using a key-value dictionary that uses the hash digest from the concatenation between the voter identification $Id_{V_i}$ and the random blinding factor $r_i$ as an indexer. The key parameter $H(Id_{V_i}||r_i)$ is kept constant throughout the duration of an *Election* $k$; therefore, any *Ballots* submitted by $V_i$ are done so under the same index. Dictionaries do not allow multiple values under the same key, which means that each new submitted *Ballot* replaces the old one. The process of resubmitting a vote is similar to a normal submission. The only criteria to request additional *Ballots* is to have none stored in a *VoteBox* for a given *Election* $k$ identified by a $Id_{E_k}$. The *Election Authority* does not control the number of *Ballots* requested by voters since the storage logic used by *Elections* prevents voters from submitting multiple *Ballots* for a single *Election*. The old *Ballot* resource $B'_{Id_{B_j}, Id_{E_k}}$ is moved out of the *Election* resource first to allow for the new *Ballot* $B''_{Id_{B_j}, Id_{E_k}}$ to take its place. The old *Ballot* $B'_{Id_{B_j}, Id_{E_k}}$ is a *linear type*; therefore, it cannot be left "dangling" after being removed from a storage account. As such, the old *Ballot* is explicitly burnt at the end of the re-submission step.

***Ballot* Revoking.** Each *Election* is configured with a default ballot option $Op_0$ that is outside of the *electionOptions* set. *Ballots* minted for an *Election* arrive with this default option already set. Voters are able to cast a *Ballot* in this state, i.e., without choosing any of the options from the *available options* set, to set the *Ballot* as a revoke one. Since the *Ballot* revoke process is quite similar to the one described in Sect. 4.2. Figure 4 illustrates both processes in detail.

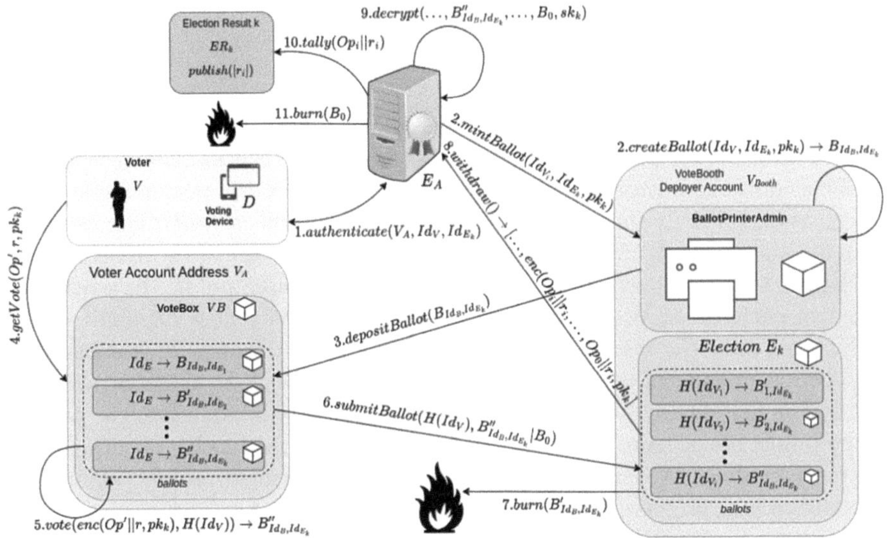

**Fig. 4.** Resource-based *Ballot* revoke and multiple casting features.

To revoke a submitted *Ballot*, a voter requests a new *Ballot* from the *Election Authority* and delivers it set with the default option $B_0$. Since the default option $Op_0$ is blinded with the random factor $r_i$, it is not possible to distinguish a revoke *Ballot* from a normal one, i.e., one with an option $Op_i$ set instead, until this data is decrypted by the *Election Authority*. If $EA$ detects a revoke *Ballot* during the tally phase, the *Ballot* is burnt and the corresponding blinding factor $r_i$ is removed from the final verification list indicated in Sect. 4.2.

**Delegated *Ballots*** The use of resources in a remote voting solution allows for features that are hard, or even impossible, in a ledger-based architecture. One of these additional features is the possibility of delegating *Ballots*, which allows for a voter $V_i$ to delegate their vote to be cast and submitted by another voter $V_j$ in a secure fashion that does not incur into a multiple voting scenario. *Ballots* are stored in *Elections* indexed by the hash digest of the unique identification of the voter, which is an immutable parameter set during the construction (mint) of a blank *Ballot*, as indicated in Fig. 2. Upon receiving a blank *Ballot*, a voter can choose to cast it themselves or delegate it to someone else by invoking a *delegateBallot* function from their *VoteBox* resource and transfer a *Ballot*

$B_{Id_B, Id_{E_k}}$ to another voter $V_j$, who can use it to submit another option $Op$ of their choosing to the system.

Yet, the system does not guarantee that a delegated *Ballot* will be counted at any point. We adopt this strategy in order to mitigate voting coercion tactics. If voter $V_i$ changes their mind after delegating a *Ballot*, or was forced to give up a blank *Ballot* under a coercive situation that is no longer valid, $V_i$ can request a new blank *Ballot* from *EA* and submit this one with an option $Op_i$, or even with the default option $Op_0$ to set it as a revoke one instead, thus replacing any previous *Ballots* from either $V_j$ or a coercive adversary.

### Threat Analysis

*Voter Privacy* User privacy derives logically from the access control primitives established at the protocol level. Only the owner of a *Ballot* resource can access its contents, i.e., only the owner of the account that holds a *Ballot* can access its contents and methods. Additionally, *Ballots* take advantage of the access control mechanics to prevent sensible information from becoming public. In a resource-based blockchain, access control primitives have priority over capability-based access, and only the resource owner has access to the former. This means that not even the owner of a *Ballot* can reveal their choice if, at the contract level, this option field is set to private. But this does not invalidate a forensic analysis of the public blockchain, which can be used to access the block(s) containing all the resource data. We employ a blinded encryption layer to protect against this mechanism and preserve voter privacy.

*Receipt-Freeness.* This system only returns standard transaction receipts with information regarding the status of the transaction and nothing else. This can be used to ensure that the *Ballot* was correctly transferred to an *Election* resource, but it does not reveal any information about the *Ballot* contents; therefore, we consider this system to be *receipt-free*. Voting receipts can be used by voters to prove how they voted, thus enabling anti-democratic actions, such as vote selling. We replace these traditional receipts with a cryptographic equivalent method that reuses a random blinding factor to prove to the voter that his/her vote successfully made it through the system to be counted, without confirming what the vote was in the first place. This method provides a similar level of transparency without providing a safe method to sale votes.

*Improving Coercion Resistance in the Proposal.* The system as described in Fig. 2 uses a random blinding factor $r$ that is published at the end of the process, thus working as a tracking number. This can be used by an adversary $\mathcal{A}$ to coerce a voter $V_i$ and force them to vote for an option $Op_\mathcal{A}$ instead of the intended $Op_i$ and blind the coerced option with a known blinding factor $r_\mathcal{A}$. The public nature of the blockchain used in this proposal allows $\mathcal{A}$ to "follow" the coerced *Ballot* to make sure that its ciphertext does not change (which would indicate that $V_i$ has replaced $Op_\mathcal{A}$ with another one), and once $\mathcal{A}$ sees the blinding factor $r_\mathcal{A}$ published, $\mathcal{A}$ is sure that the coercion efforts were successful.

In order to prevent coercive situations as the one described, we take advantage of the homomorphic properties of the ElGamal [9] cryptosystem adopted in our solution, namely, the randomiser function indicated in Sect. 4.2, and have the *Election Authority* re-randomise the *Ballot* metadata once it is stored in an *Election* internal storage. The *EA* has the required permissions to mutate the *Ballot* metadata and thus obfuscate it from a prying adversary $\mathcal{A}$, which in principle thwarts the type of coercive behaviour described. This strategy is employed in several centralised voting proposals, such as [7,8].

These features limits the actions of an adversary significantly but not totally. There is exists a coercivity potential if an adversary $\mathcal{A}$ has the ability to force a voter towards an option $OP_\mathcal{A}$ instead of the voter's desired one $OP_V$, whilst also able to follow the ciphertext defined by $\mathsf{Enc}OP_\mathcal{A}|r_\mathcal{A}$ through the voting process, in order to be able to ensure that, at least, that $r_\mathcal{A}$ does make it to the final list. If the adversary is unable to control at least one of the previous steps, it is feasible for a voter to replace a coerced vote for an honest one without alerting the adversary.

**Verifiability.** The verifiability primitives in the proposed system derive mostly from the data consistency guarantees offered by blockchains, the data integrity guarantees from the *linear type* nature of resources, and the usage of random blinding factors with potential re-randomisation offered by the ElGamal cryptosystem adopted.

*Cast-as-Intended Verifiability.* Voters completely control the randomised blinding process of their choice. This process involves the encryption of the chosen option concatenated with a random integer, which by itself requires it to run off-chain. As such, this part of the voting process runs locally in the voter's device $D$, which means that voters have access to both the random blinding factor $r$ and the blinded ciphertext to add to a blank *Ballot* they have in storage. Voters can also use their voting devices to generate independent pairs of ElGamal encryption keys and use them to verify that the encryption function in their devices is trustworthy, i.e., that the ciphertext produced does correspond to the plaintext inserted as input. Once the voters are satisfied with it, they can use the public key $pk_k$ provided for the election in question to create the blinded vote $\mathsf{Enc}(Op_i||r_i, pk_k)$ and set it on a blank *Ballot* with the guarantee that the ciphertext obtained does correspond to the selected option. As we indicated in Sect. 4.1, we assume that all voting devices are honest.

*Recorded-as-Intended Verifiability.* The resource-based protocol that this solution relies on provides programmatic guarantees that only the owner of a *Ballot* resource is capable of changing the mutable parameter ballotOption. In order for an entity to modify this parameter and therefore become capable of submitting a valid electoral option into the system, they must hold a valid *Ballot* in their account storage, also inside of a *VoteBox*, since it is the latter that provides the required API to modify a *Ballot* metadata. Once a *Ballot* moves outside of a

*VoteBox*, there are no mechanisms by which this metadata manipulation can occur. This is defined at the protocol level by limiting the *vote* function used for this effect to *VoteBox* resources. The *Election Authority* ensures that only eligible voters can have *VoteBoxes* in their storage accounts, which implicitly restricts the manipulation of *Ballot* metadata to eligible voters, thus guaranteeing that *Ballots* are only modifiable by their voter owners and no one else. When a *Ballot* is sent to an *Election*, this resource is not a *VoteBox*; therefore, it does not have access to any functions that can change a voter's option. Voters can certify this by checking the public smart contracts that implement *VoteBoxes* and *Elections* and other relevant resource implementations to guarantee that there is no mechanism available to change a *Ballot's* metadata outside of a valid *VoteBox*. Additionally, voters can use the $verify(H_{Id_v})$ function and provide the hash digest of their voter identification to verify that there is a valid submitted *Ballot* in *Election k* under their own key.

*Tallied-as-Intended Verifiability.* The publication of the blinding random factor $r$, alongside the ability that voters have in a blockchain context of "following" the state of the process, i.e., manually verifying the public blocks to ensure the ciphertext does not change (unless re-randomised), allows a level of transparency only possible in blockchain environments. The publication of the blinding random factor provides sufficient certainty that the vote option that was initially appended to it was processed properly. The rigid deterministic nature derived from having the mechanics for this process described in publicly deployed and immutable smart contracts further compounds on this assurance.

## 5   Conclusions and Future Work

This article presents the first academic proposal of an electronic voting system based on a resource-based blockchain architecture. Resources are a new and improved method to represent digital assets in a distributed environment. This concept, with the extended account model and advanced access control mechanics, creates an unique middle ground between an overly transparent medium and the need for privacy and granular control in digital systems. This paradigm presents a significant departure from a more "classical" ledger-based approach offered by blockchains such as Ethereum. We have introduced an advanced, yet simpler, blockchain-based voting system than all blockchain-based proposals thus far. The privacy primitives offered by resource-based blockchains remove the need for data encryption, whilst keeping a similar level of transparency as in the rpesented related works.

The resource-based approach is recent, powerful, and unexplored. This proposal presents a specific application of this new paradigm that can, hopefully, inspire other researchers to investigate this topic further.

**Future Work.** Our logical next step would be to move to an actual implementation in both languages (Cadence and Move) to showcase and evaluate a working proof of concept capable of producing comparable result sets. This would help in ascertaining the differences between the resource models offered by each and provide a clear picture of which specific architecture is optimal for a voting application. With a functional e-voting prototype, we also intend to extend the study towards determining the performance and scalability of the proposed voting system.

**Acknowledgments.** This work was partially supported by project SERICS (PE00000014) under the MUR National Recovery and Resilience Plan funded by the European Union - NextGenerationEU. C. C. Drăgan and Nishanth Sastry are partially supported by AP4L - EPSRC grant EP/W032473/1. C. C. Drăgan is also partially supported by TrustVote âĂŞ EPSRC grant EP/Y020529/1, CONNECT - Horizon Europe Guarantee 10043730 and EU Horizon grants 101069688, REWIRE - Horizon Europe Guarantee 10043743 and EU Horizon grants 101070627. N. Sastry is partially supported by AP4L - EPSRC grant EP/W032473/1.

# References


1. Abo-Akleek, F., Mowafi, M., Taqieddin, E.S., Shatnawi, A.S.: Leveraging blockchain for robust and transparent e-voting systems. Cyber Secur. Appl. **3** (2025)
2. Almeida, R.L., Baiardi, F., Maesa, D.D.F., Ricci, L.: Impact of decentralization on electronic voting systems: a systematic literature survey. IEEE Access **11**, 132389–132423 (2023)
3. Ayed, A.B.: A conceptual secure blockchain-based electronic voting system. Int. J. Netw. Secur. Appl. (IJNSA) **9** (2017)
4. Barelli, R., D'Onghia, M., Longari, S.: Towards secure electronic voting: a survey on e-voting systems and attacks. IEEE Access **13**, 89600–89626 (2025)
5. Beydili, E., Cabuk, U.C., Dalkilic, G., Ozturk, Y.: Securing blockchain-based e-voting through Shamir's secret sharing over ethereum. In: 2025 13th International Symposium on Digital Forensics and Security (ISDFS) (4 2025)
6. Braun, N., Brändli, D.: Swiss e-voting pilot projects: evaluation, situation analysis and how to proceed. In: Proceedings of the 2nd International Workshop on Electronic Voting, pp. 27–36 (2006)
7. Chaidos, P., Cortier, V., Fuchsbauer, G., Galindo, D.: BELENIOSRF: a non-interactive receipt-free electronic voting scheme. In: Proceedings of the ACM Conference on Computer and Communications Security, pp. 1614–1625 (10 2016)
8. Cortier, V., Gaudry, P., Glondu, S.: BELENIOS: a simple private and verifiable electronic voting system, pp. 214–238. Springer (2019). https://doi.org/10.1007/978-3-030-19052-1_14
9. ElGamal, T.: A public key cryptosystem and signature scheme based on discrete logarithms. Advances in Cryptology - CRYPTO 1984, LNCS, vol. 196, pp. 10–18 (1985)
10. Eltuhami, M., Abdullahe, M., Talip, B.A., Ahmad, N.A.N.: Blockchain based voting framework with non-transferable non-fungible tokens. In: Proceedings of ICIT 2023, pp. 378–383 (2023)
11. Flow: flow - technical report. Tech. rep., Dapper Labs (2020). https://flow.com/primer
12. Girard, J.Y.: Linear logic. Theor. Comput. Sci. **50** (1987)

13. González, C.D., Mena, D.F., Muñoz, A.M., Rojas, O., Sosa-Gómez, G.: Electronic voting system using an enterprise blockchain. Appl. Sci. (Switzerland) **12** (2022)
14. Goodman, N.J.: Internet voting in a local election in Canada, vol. 31, chap. 1, pp. 7–24. Springer, Cham (2014). https://doi.org/10.1007/978-3-319-04352-4_2
15. Halderman, J.A., Teague, V.: The new south WALES IVOTE system: security failures and verification flaws in a live online election. LNCS, pp. 35–53 (2015). https://doi.org/10.1007/978-3-319-22270-7_3
16. Kahn, K.M., Arshad, J., Khan, M.M.: Secure digital voting system based on blockchain technology. Int. J. Electron. Gov. Res. **14** (2018)
17. Madise, Ü., Martens, T.: E-voting in Estonia 2005: The first practice of country-wide binding internet voting in the world. In: Proceedings of the 2nd International Workshop on Electronic Voting, pp. 15–26 (2006)
18. Nakamoto, S.: Bitcoin: a peer-to-peer electronic cash system, pp. 1–9 (2008). www.bitcoin.org
19. Rahul, Gulia, P., Gill, N.S.: Articulation of blockchain enabled e-voting systems: a systematic literature review. Peer-to-Peer Netw. Appl. **18** (2025). https://doi.org/10.1007/s12083-025-01956-3
20. Santhiya, M.P., Arshik, S., Prasanth, P.R., Kumar, V.R., Santhosh, S.: Voteblock - a decentralized online voting solution with blockchain. In: 2025 8th International Conference on Trends in Electronics and Informatics (ICOEI), pp. 778–782 (2025)
21. Team, A.: The APTOS blockchain: safe, scalable, and upgradeable web3 infrastructure. Tech. rep., Aptos Found. (2022). https://aptosfoundation.org/whitepaper/aptos-whitepaper_en.pdf
22. Team, T.M.: The sui smart contracts platform. Tech. rep., MystenLabs (2023). https://diem.github.io/move/abilities.html
23. Wadler, P.: Linear types can change the world! Programming Concepts and Methods 3 (1990)
24. Wang, H., Pan, M., Wang, J.: Crystality: a programming model for smart contracts on parallel EVMS. In: Proceedings of the ACM SIGPLAN Symposium on Principles and Practice of Parallel Programming, PPOPP, pp. 412–425 (2 2025)

# Analysing the Adoption
# of the Terms-of-Use Field in EBSI Digital Wallets


Stefano Bistarelli[1] , Chiara Luchini[1,2] (✉) , and Francesco Santini[1]

[1] Department of Mathematics and Computer Science, University of Perugia,
Via Vanvitelli 1, 06123 Perugia (PG), Italy
`{stefano.bistarelli,francesco.santini}@unipg.it`,
`chiara.luchini@collaboratori.unipg.it`

[2] Department of Mathematics and Computer Science "Ulisse Dini", University of
Florence, Viale Giovanni Battista Morgagni 67/a, 50134 Florence (FI), Italy



**Abstract.** The landscape of digital identity is undergoing a significant transformation, moving from centralized architectures to user-centric, decentralized models such as *Self-Sovereign Identity (SSI)*. This shift addresses long-standing challenges in traditional *Identity and Access Management (IAM)* systems, including privacy risks, security weaknesses, and lack of user control. SSI has shown its potential in domains such as healthcare and education, providing greater autonomy and data protection through technologies such as *Verifiable Credentials (VCs)*. Simultaneously, regulatory initiatives such as the European Union's *Electronic Identification, Authentication and Trust Services (eIDAS 2.0)* framework have accelerated the development of interoperable digital identity solutions, notably the *European Digital Identity Wallet (EUDIW)*, which adheres to the principles of SSI. Despite this progress, existing SSI wallet implementations largely remain focused on individual users and often lack critical features for organizational applications. In this work, we conduct a secondary systematic review of industrial digital wallets, examining their implementation of the *Terms-of-Use (ToU)* field, specifically in EBSI-compliant wallets. The objective is to inform future development efforts in SSI-based digital wallet ecosystems and to identify opportunities to improve this key feature.

**Keywords:** Digital Wallet · Terms of Use · Self-Sovereign Identity · Verifiable Credentials


## 1 Introduction

The landscape of digital identity has undergone a significant evolution, transitioning from centralized architectures to more user-centric models. Technical and security shortcomings, such as frequent data breaches and identity theft, drive this shift. In response, *Identity and Access Management (IAM)* systems have evolved to better align with the contemporary security requirements and user expectations [33]. This transformation extends beyond purely technical dimensions and increasingly intersects with evolving legal and regulatory frameworks. A notable example is the European Union's eIDAS 2.0 regulation, which represents a significant advancement in the governance of digital identity systems. The eIDAS 2.0 regulation aims to enhance the safety, speed, and effectiveness of commercial electronic transactions within the European Union. One of its primary goals is the creation of a *European Digital Identity Wallet (EUDIW)* [14,15], allowing individuals and legal entities to store, manage, and present a wide range of digital credentials, aligning closely with the foundational principles of SSI. It also requires all EU member states to provide at least one EUDIW to all citizens and residents by 2026. For example, Italy has recently launched the *Italian Digital Wallet System (IT-Wallet System)*[1], which allows Italian citizens to digitally store three documents, such as their health insurance card, driving license, and disability certificate.

However, most of the existing implementations of the SSI digital wallet focus primarily on individual users rather than organizational or enterprise-level scenarios [6]. Among the key features required by government and industrial entities that adopt SSI systems as IAM is the inclusion of the *Terms of Use (ToU)* field within VCs [6]. The ToU property, as defined in the *Verifiable Credentials Data Model (VCDM)* v2.0 by the *World Wide Web Consortium (W3C)* [36], offers a standardized mechanism to specify the legal and operational conditions under which a verifiable credential or presentation is issued. This functionality can be particularly relevant in contexts where the transferability of credentials, such as employee information, must be restricted or governed by specific policies. Consequently, the ToU property is considered a key requirement for digital wallets designed to support organizational use cases. However, due to the relatively recent redefinition of the ToU specification and the limited awareness surrounding its practical implications, many existing wallet implementations do not yet support or prioritize this feature.

This paper reviews the current landscape of industrial digital identity wallets by focusing on their implementation of the ToU property. This analysis aims to inform and support the design and development of digital wallets tailored to organizational and company contexts. This paper extends and supersedes [3] by introducing a new research question, analyzing EBSI-conformant wallets, and examining their technical characteristics, with a particular focus on their implementation of the ToU. It is organized as follows: Sect. 2 provides an overview of the SSI and EBSI architecture, with a particular emphasis on the role of digital wallets. Section 3 outlines the research methodology, including the criteria for selecting the wallet and the analysis process. In Sect. 5, we review the existing literature on digital identity wallets. Finally, Sect. 6 presents our final discussion along with directions for future research.

---

[1] IT Wallet: https://tinyurl.com/yc6bc6ud.

## 2   Digital Wallets, SSI and EBSI

In this section, we provide a brief overview of the SSI system, focusing on its components and architecture. SSI places the user at the center of digital identity management, in contrast to the traditional client-server model of the Internet, which made users passive recipients controlled by centralized authorities. SSI is based on ten key principles, as defined by Christopher Allen [1], which promote individual autonomy, user control over their identity, transparency, data minimization, and protection of rights. The SSI model involves three main actors: the holder (usually the user), the issuer (a trusted entity that issues credentials), and the verifier (the party that checks those credentials). Their interactions may rely on decentralized technologies like blockchain for storing *Decentralized Identifiers* (*DIDs*), which allow credentials to be verified without the need for a central authority. *Verifiable Credentials*(*VCs*) are digital credentials containing metadata, claims about a subject, and cryptographic proofs (digital signatures) that ensure authenticity as defined in the *Verifiable Credential Data Model* (*VCDM*) [36]. *Verifiable Presentations* (*VPs*) are collections of VCs, created and signed by the holder, that allow selective disclosure of information to enhance privacy and security. Both can specify a property called *Terms of Use* (*ToU*), which allows issuers or holders to specify the conditions under which a credential or presentation can be used. For instance, the issuer may define policy references, such as the legal basis or trust frameworks applicable to the credential, or restrict its usage to particular contexts (e.g., government agencies or internal departments). Similarly, holders may define their terms of use for VPs, indicating how and when the verifier may utilize the presented data. These terms, often linked to policy documents, help prevent misuse and provide legal clarity. This is especially important in sensitive or regulated settings, where precise control over data use is essential to protect user rights.

Digital identity wallets are a fundamental component of the SSI architecture, acting as secure software applications that store, manage, and share cryptographically protected credentials issued by trusted entities. These wallets may operate locally or in a remote environment, providing secure storage not only for credentials but also for cryptographic materials associated with identity-related data [28]. They give users full control over their digital identity, allowing them to review, remove, combine, or explicitly select which data to store or share in various contexts. This supports privacy-preserving selective disclosure through techniques such as zero-knowledge proofs. Importantly, wallets also enable backup and recovery of identity data, ensuring resilience.

*European Blockchain Services Infrastructure* (*EBSI*)[2] is a Web3 initiative launched by the European Commission in collaboration with the *European Digital Infrastructure Consortium* (*EDIC*), to use blockchain technology for decentralized, secure, and trustworthy public services. EBSI operates as a decentralized network of distributed blockchain nodes hosted by public institutions in

---

[2] EBSI   website:   https://ec.europa.eu/digital-building-blocks/sites/display/EBSI/ Home.

all EU member states, Norway, and Liechtenstein. It uses a Proof of Authority consensus mechanism to maintain transaction integrity and reliability. EBSI's technology is applicable across multiple sectors, including product traceability, trusted data exchange, and identity verification. Provides a distributed ledger for securely recording transactions, including trusted registries such as the Trusted Issuers registry. EBSI also offers public APIs for developers to integrate external applications with the blockchain, supporting smart contracts for the controlled and secure execution of transactions. EBSI has introduced a *Verifier Trust Model*, requiring digital wallets to authenticate verifiers and ensure that they are authorized to request specific VCs by using the termsOfUse field [12]. For example, only medical institutions can request medical card data, and over-18 credentials are required for adult content or alcohol sales. Information in VCs is classified into three confidentiality levels (public, restricted, and confidential), each with increasingly strict sharing controls. For presentation, issuers can include policies in the *termsOfUse* field of a VC. These policies specify the confidentiality level, required accompanying credentials (e.g., a verifier's authorization), and permitted sharing contexts. Wallets should enforce these rules before allowing users to share a VC. These mechanisms, such as Verifier authentication, confidentiality classifications, Presentation, and Request Policies, provide a transparent, secure, and policy-driven framework for controlling what verifiable credential data is shared and under what conditions.

## 3   Research Method

This study investigates current implementations of digital wallets within SSI systems that incorporate the ToU field as a mechanism to restrict the use of VCs or VPs. Given the relatively low level of awareness and adoption of this functionality, primarily attributed to critiques that it was "insufficiently specified" [44], we anticipate identifying only a small number of technologies that use it. In particular, in response to these concerns, the specification of the ToU field has been revised and updated in subsequent documentation [45]. In this research, we examined open source wallets to find the string "termsOfUse" as outlined by VCDM 2.0 [36], the W3C's recommended specification.

   To ensure the identification of relevant literature and mitigate potential research bias, a clearly defined review protocol was established. This involved formulating our research questions using the *Population, Intervention, Comparison, Outcome, Context (PICOC)* framework [22,26], tailored to the specific objectives of this investigation. In our case, the "Population" includes digital wallets within SSI systems, while "Intervention" refers to tools or methods that enhance these wallets, specifically those that implement the ToU field. The "Comparison" component is not applicable, as traditional (non-SSI) wallets are not considered. The "Outcomes" aims to identify and quantify SSI wallets that use the ToU field to manage VCs and VPs. The "Context" spans academic and industry literature, including systematic reviews, technical reports, and white papers. Aligned with these criteria, we formulate the research questions (RQs) as follows: "What existing digital wallet technologies are compliant with SSI systems?" (**RQ1**), "Which digital wallets incorporate the ToU field as outlined in the VCDM specification?" (**RQ2**), and "In what ways is the ToU field incorporated within wallet architectures, and what design decisions influence its implementation?" (**RQ3**).

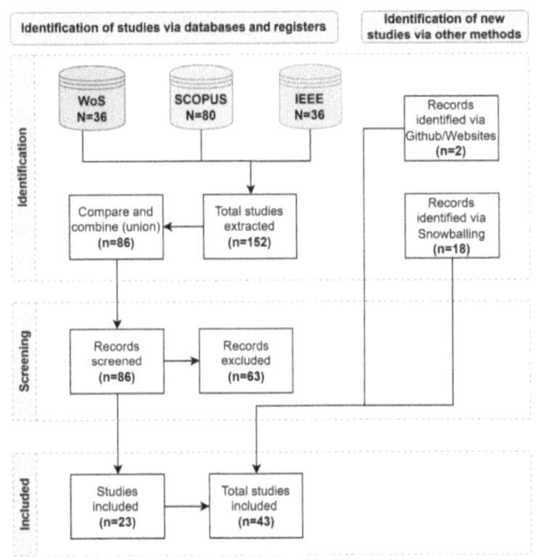


(a) Research process flow based on PRISMA framework [25].

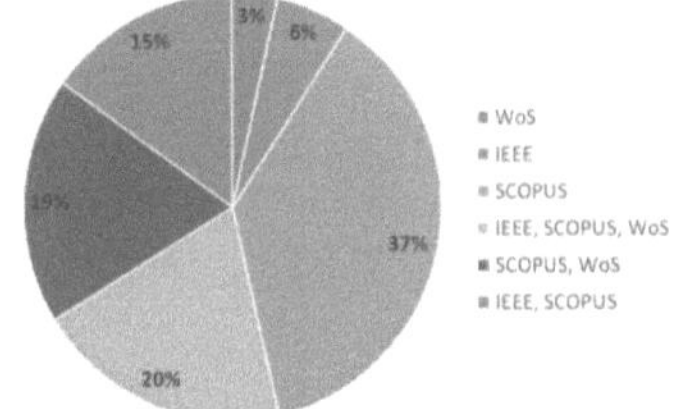

| Source | Q | I1 | I2 | I3 | Final N° |
|---|---|---|---|---|---|
| IEEE Xplore | 37 | - | 36 | - | 36 |
| WoS | 49 | 48 | 46 | 36 | 36 |
| SCOPUS | 90 | - | 88 | 80 | 80 |
| **Total** | | | | | **152** |

(b) Results of search process with inclusion criteria.



(c) Percentage of documents by file combination.

**Fig. 1.** Summary of research process results.

After defining the RQs, relevant data sources were selected to support the systematic review. Figure 1a shows the research flow process following the PRISMA framework[3]. According to Brereton et al. [7], the most relevant digital libraries for Software Engineering research include: *IEEE Xplore, ACM Digital Library, Google Scholar, CiteSeer Library, Inspec, ScienceDirect*, and *EI Compendex*. Based on this approach, we selected IEEE Xplore, Scopus, and Web of Science (WoS). For each selected source, we define an advanced search query built around a standard search string, adapted to the specific syntax of each platform. The general search expression used was the following: "( "self sovereign identity" OR "Self Sovereign Identity" OR ssi ) AND identity AND wallet)" (**Q**). For the inclusion criteria, we restricted the results to English-language (**I1**) publications from 2020 to 2025 (**I2**) within the fields of computer science or engineering (**I3**). Table 1b shows the number of results based on the search process considering the query and the inclusion criteria. During the screening phase, titles, abstracts, keywords, and conclusions were manually reviewed to exclude non-peer-reviewed or narrowly scoped publications. Preference was given to surveys and reviews of

---

[3] PRISMA flow diagram: https://www.prisma-statement.org/prisma-2020-flow-diagram.

the literature on digital identity wallets, particularly those that addressed design, privacy, and usability. This produced 23 primary studies for analysis. The initial search results were consolidated and de-duplicated, revealing Scopus as the most comprehensive source. In contrast, IEEE Xplore and WoS contributed only a limited number of unique entries, as illustrated in Fig. 1c. To broaden the dataset, the study employed a Snowballing method [43], utilizing both *Backward* and *Forward Snowballing* to identify additional 18 relevant papers through iterative citation tracking. Two more sources were manually included: the Gimly GitHub repository [17] and the European Blockchain Association's website [11]. This process culminated in a final dataset of 43 documents for in-depth examination.

## 4    Digital Wallets Analysis

From the final set of 43 documents, the digital wallets mentioned or used for comparison were extracted. The analysis focused solely on the currently implemented solutions, explicitly excluding academic proposals or prototypes. Consequently, only identity wallets developed by industry entities or organizations were considered. More than 30 commercial wallets were identified; however, only a selection of the most frequently referenced implementations is discussed. Figure 2 illustrates the industrial implementations most frequently cited in the past five years. It is important to note that several of the reviewed documents focused exclusively on experimental or academic models, without mentioning any industrial solutions. In addition, wallets without open-source code were explicitly excluded. To mitigate potential limitations, we cross-checked vendor-provided information whenever possible with other sources, including their technical documentation. For instance, in the case of the Triveria SDK, we were able to verify the implementation of the ToU field based on the official Triveria documentation. Finally, the scope of the analysis was extended to include wallets compliant with the EBSI framework, as described in Sect. 4.1.

Although these wallets generally align with the core principles of SSI, there are considerable variations in their technical implementations and functional capabilities, leading to interoperability challenges [24]. Furthermore, several digital wallets are no longer commercially available, and the majority remain in an early or relatively immature stage of development [8, 30]. Jolocom, a Berlin-based pioneer, ceased operations with its SmartWallet, showing no further development, and its online resources are no longer available. ShoCard was terminated following its acquisition by Ping Identity in 2019. The uPort project was officially divided into Veramo and Serto in 2021; its original mobile app, last updated in 2019, remains archived but inactive. Consequently, Veramo is considered the functional successor to uPort.

As mentioned above, [6] identifies key requirements for enterprise-oriented SSI solutions. The authors analyzed six digital wallets from different vendors, namely Jolocom, Lissi, Esatus, Trinsic, CARO, and the Business Partner Agent by Bosch, highlighting that none of them satisfied the ToU requirement as of 2024. In this work, we revisit some of those implementations to verify whether

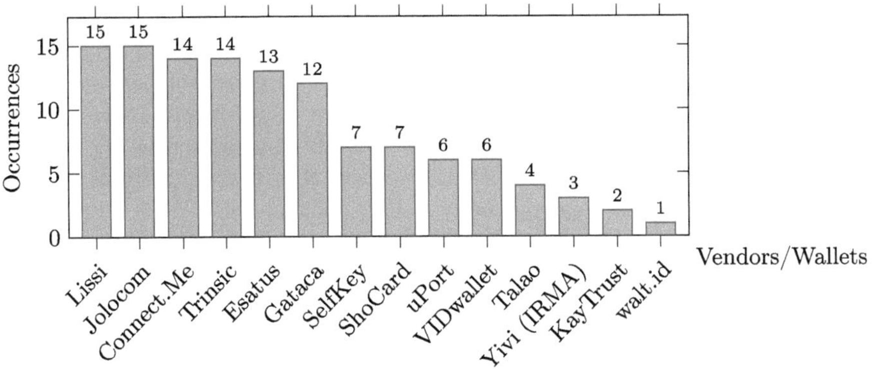


**Fig. 2.** Most cited vendors and digital wallets.

they have been updated to support this feature. In addition, our analysis includes a broader set of digital wallets, as illustrated in Fig. 2. According to [2], wallets such as Lissi, Connect.me, Gataca, and SelfKey are not designed for enterprise use. Moreover, most of the surveyed wallets are open source, while proprietary exceptions include Gataca and VIDwallet. The source code for Esatus, Lissi, Gataca, and VIDwallet could not be retrieved; therefore, these wallets are excluded from consideration. To evaluate the implementation of the ToU field, we manually examined the available documentation and GitHub repositories for each wallet. Due to space reasons, we do not present the selected open-source digital wallets in detail. Instead, we summarize their current ToU implementation status in Table 1. For an overview of these wallets, we refer the reader to [3].

## 4.1 EBSI Conformant Wallets

The EBSI documentation defines a set of digital wallets that comply with its technical and functional standards. A Conformant Wallet [13] is a digital wallet that has successfully undergone rigorous conformance testing to demonstrate adherence to EBSI's requirements. This compliance is verified through the *EBSI Conformance Test*[4], which assesses the wallet's performance, security, and interoperability with EBSI's core services. These conformant wallets are categorized into two principal groups: organization wallets and holder wallets. The organization wallets comprise a wallet specifically created for issuers or verifiers. This means that organizations, such as universities or public authorities, use them to issue verifiable credentials or to verify their authenticity. Individuals use holder wallets to request, receive, store, and present verifiable credentials. In some cases, a single wallet may incorporate multiple functions, supporting several roles concurrently. In our study, we focused on holder wallets that support both the requesting and presentation of credentials, identifying a total of 30 such solutions. The choice to analyze wallets for holders is driven by organizational

---

[4] EBSI Conformance Test: https://hub.ebsi.eu/wallet-conformance.

contexts, such as companies, where employee wallets must be capable of managing and enforcing policies related to credential use. This ensures that the use of work-related credentials is in accordance with company policies and can be appropriately monitored. From this set, we further selected those that are open source, such as wallets with code publicly available on platforms like GitHub. This refinement resulted in a subset of 9 wallets that include fully or partially open-source components. Among these, wallets such as Talao Wallet and walt.id have already been described and analyzed in [3]. Consequently, in this section, we present and describe the remaining seven wallets.

- **IN2 Wallet**: IN2 Wallet [19] is a digital wallet developed by IN2, a Spanish IT company headquartered in Barcelona. With nearly 30 years of experience, the company specializes in sectors such as public administration, healthcare, tourism, transport, and Industry 4.0. The IN2 Wallet is publicly available through two GitHub repositories: *in2-wallet-api*, which provides the server-side functionality for credential management, and *in2-wallet-ui*, an Ionic/Angular application responsible for the wallet's presentation layer. Based on an analysis of these repositories, the ToU field in VCs does not appear to be implemented.
- **SimpleIdServer**: SimpleIdServer [35] is an open-source software initiative that aims to provide robust, standards-compliant IAM solutions. Developed primarily using the ASP.NET Core framework, it supports a broad range of identity protocols, including OpenID Connect, OAuth 2.0, SCIM 2.0, UMA 2.0, FAPI, and CIBA. Based on an analysis of its GitHub repository, the implementation of the ToU field does not appear to be supported.
- **Identfy**: Identfy [20], developed by Izertis, is an open-source digital identity solution designed to support both individual holders and organizations operating within decentralized ecosystems. It is fully compatible with major blockchain networks, including LACChain, Alastria, and EBSI. The platform is based on a modular architecture that includes a non-custodial mobile wallet, allowing users to manage their DIDs and VCs independently. An analysis of the *identfy-holder-wallet* repository indicates that the ToU field does not appear to be implemented on the holder side. However, in the enterprise version of the wallet, which includes backend services and an administrative interface for issuing and verifying credentials, the ToU field is present and implemented.
- **Masca**: Masca [5] (previously named SSI Snap) is an open-source MetaMask Snap developed by Blockchain Lab:UM that brings decentralized identity capabilities directly into MetaMask. It allows users to manage their DIDs and VCs, as well as create VPs, all from within their MetaMask wallet. Masca is highly modular and blockchain-agnostic, supporting a range of DID methods and integrating with EVM blockchains. Although a review of the project's GitHub repository and documentation indicates that the ToU field is not currently implemented, the system does support the creation of custom VCs, offering flexibility for tailored identity solutions.
- **Triveria**: Triveria [41] is a Slovakia-based digital identity solutions provider offering the *Triveria Online Wallet Platform*, a cloud-hosted, full-featured

wallet service designed for the issuance, presentation, and verification of VCs. Fully compliant with eIDAS 2.0 and EBSI specifications, the platform supports all key roles, holder, issuer, and verifier, and has successfully passed EBSI conformance tests. The holder component is available as a mobile app that is not open source. A review of the Triveria SDK documentation confirmed that the ToU field is supported in their implementation.

- **wwWallet**: wwWallet [18] by GUnet is a web-based identity wallet that leverages modern web technologies such as Progressive Web Applications (PWA), the Web Cryptography API (WebCryptoAPI), and FIDO standards, including Web Authentication (WebAuthn) and the Client to Authenticator Protocol (CTAP2). The wallet ecosystem consists of two main components: the wallet-frontend and the wallet-backend-server. The wallet-frontend provides a user-friendly interface for managing VCs, while the wallet-backend-server serves as the TypeScript-based backend for wwWallet. To utilize the Dockerized lab environment, both components must be appropriately set up. During an analysis of the wallet-backend-server, it was observed that the ToU feature is not implemented.

- **Altme**: Altme [37] is an open-source SSI and crypto wallet developed by Talao, designed to manage both verifiable credentials and blockchain-based assets (cryptocurrencies, tokens, and NFTs). Altme extends the Talao wallet's features with broader blockchain support, including Tezos, Ethereum, Polygon, Fantom, BNB, and Etherlink, and enables users to send/receive digital assets, as well as purchase crypto via Wert.io. Analysis of Altme's GitHub repository, which shares its codebase with Talao, confirms that ToU support is not currently implemented. Since both wallets rely on the SpruceID SSI Kit, which includes this functionality, there is potential to further extend or customize ToU support in Altme.

Table 1 provides a comparative overview of several open-source digital wallets, detailing their respective vendors, the extent to which the ToU field is implemented, and the software licenses governing their distribution. A notable trend across the majority of these wallets is the lack of explicit support for the ToU field within their VC implementations.

From a licensing perspective, the selected wallets use a wide variety of open-source software licenses, each with specific implications for usage, modification, and redistribution. The Apache License 2.0 is a permissive license that allows users to freely use, modify, and distribute the software, even in proprietary products. It includes an express grant of patent rights from contributors to users. A key condition is the requirement to include a copy of the license and a notice of any modifications made when redistributing the code. The MIT License is also very permissive and minimalist. It allows reuse within proprietary software, provided that the license and copyright notice are included. Unlike the Apache License, however, it does not offer explicit patent protection, which can be a concern in some commercial settings. GPLv3, on the other hand, is a strong copyleft license. It requires that any modified versions of the software also be open-source and released under the same license. It includes provisions to pro-

**Table 1.** Summary of open-source digital wallets and licenses.

| Wallet | Vendor | ToU | License |
|---|---|---|---|
| Connect.Me [16] | Evernym | No | Apache 2.0 |
| Trinsic [40] | Trinsic Technologies Inc | No | MIT |
| Jolocom SmartWallet/Jolocom SDK [21] | Jolocom | No | AA2-SDK of Governikus GmbH/Apache 2.0 |
| SelfKey Identity Wallet [34] | SelfKey | No | MIT |
| PingOne Neo SDK (Shocard) [27] | PingOne Identity | No | Apache 2.0 |
| Veramo [9] | DIF/Veramo User Group | No | Apache 2.0 |
| Yivi (IRMA) [29] | Privacy by Design Foundation | No | GPLv3 |
| KayTrust SDK [23] | NTT DATA | No | Apache 2.0 |
| EBSI Conformant Wallets | | | |
| Talao Wallet [38] | Talao | No | Apache 2.0 |
| walt.id [42] | walt.id | Yes[a] | Apache 2.0 |
| IN2 Wallet [19] | IN2 | No | Apache 2.0 |
| SimpleIdServer [35] | SimpleIdServer | No | Apache 2.0 |
| Identfy [20] | Izertis | Yes[b] | AGPL-3.0/ commercial/ MIT |
| Masca [5] | Blockchain Lab:UM | No | Apache 2.0/MIT |
| Triveria SDK [41] | Triveria | Yes[c] | License [41] |
| wwWallet [18] | GUNet | No | BSD 2-Clause |
| Altme [37] | Talao | No | Apache 2.0 |

[a]    walt.id:    https://github.com/search?q=repo%3Awalt-id%2Fwaltid-identity%20termsOfUse&type=code.

[b]    Identfy:    https://github.com/search?q=repo%3Aizertis%2Fidentfy-entity-service%20termsOfUse&type=code.

[c] Triveria SDK: https://docs.triveria.dev/docs/sdk/go/#type-termsofuse.

tect users from patent litigation and to prevent practices like tivoization, where hardware restrictions or DRM prevent users from running modified versions of the software. The AA2-SDK uses the *European Union Public Licence (EUPL)*, a free and open-source software license developed by the European Commission. It is designed for use by public and private entities and is available in 23 languages. The EUPL encourages public administrations to adopt the open-source model and make their software available to others. It is copyleft, allows for unrestricted use, modification, and redistribution, and is known for its neutral and multilingual approach. Finally, the BSD 2-Clause License (also known as the "Simplified BSD License" or "FreeBSD License") is a permissive open-source license originating from the *Berkeley Software Distribution (BSD)* operating system around 1999. It is widely recognized for its minimal restrictions on the use, modification, and redistribution of software, making it highly popular for both open-source and proprietary projects. However, redistributions in either source or binary form must retain the original copyright notice, the license terms, and the disclaimer.

With Table 1, we have addressed the first two research questions. For the third question, we will select the wallets that implement the TOU and define their main architectural features. To do so, we refer to the open-source documentation of each wallet and the Digital Wallet and Agent Overviews *Special Interest Group (SIG)* repository maintained by the *OpenWallet Foundation (OWF)*[5], which provides technical and architectural overviews of various wallets and agents. However, this resource does not cover all wallets, such as Triveria, and some information is outdated. Therefore, we complement it with our own analysis and findings.

**Table 2.** Technical features of wallets with ToU.

| Wallet | VC formats | Protocols | DIDs |
|---|---|---|---|
| walt.id | SD-JWT VC, ISO 18013-5 mDL, W3C VC (v1.1, v2.0) | OID4VCI (Draft 11, 13)/OID4VP (Draft 14, 20, DCQL Draft 28 coming soon), ISO/IEC 18013-7 | cheqd, ebsi, iota, jwk, key, web |
| Identfy | JWT-VC/JWT-VP, W3C VC (v1.1, v2.0) | OID4VCI/OID4VP | ebsi, epic (Alastria), ion (long form), key, lac (LACChain), web |
| Triveria | JWT-VC, SD-JWT VC, W3C VC (v1.1, v2.0) | OID4VCI (Draft 11,13)/OID4VP (Draft 16,13) | ebsi, key, IDUnion Trust List (IDTL) |

Table 2 compares the three digital wallets that implement ToU (walt.id, Identfy, and Triveria), highlighting their technical features regarding supported VC formats, protocols, and DID methods. All wallets share the same credential formats, except walt.id, which also implements the ISO 18013-5 mDL standard. The *JSON Web Token (JWT)* format for VCs and VPs is a JSON object signed using a *JSON Web Signature (JWS)*. In this case, the VC or VP is encoded as a JWT Claims Set, a JSON object that contains one or more claims about an entity. While a *Selective Disclosure JWT (SD-JWT)* is a JWT Claims Set that enables selectively revealing or withholding parts of the claims. Moreover, as noted from Table 2, VCs and VPs can follow VCDM v1.1 or v2.0. VCDM 2.0 introduces several enhancements, including clearer processing rules, a transition to a formalized data model, new media types, and simplifications of the data

---

[5] Digital Wallet and Agent Overviews: https://openwallet-foundation.github.io/digital-wallet-and-agent-overviews-sig/#/.

model, while still preserving compatibility with the VCDM 1.1 baseline. Some differences between the two versions include the renaming of some properties, such as *issuanceDate* and *expirationDate*, which have been changed to *validFrom* and *validUntil*. Lastly, *ISO 18013-5* is a standard for *mobile driver's license* (*mDL*), which is a digital representation of the physical state-issued driver's license or non-driver identification card provisioned by a state's *Department of Motor Vehicles* (*DMV*) or equivalent agency. For the issuance and presentation protocols, all wallets use *OpenID for Verifiable Credential Issuance* (*OID4VCI*) and *OpenID for Verifiable Presentations* (*OID4VP*). These protocols, built on OAuth 2.0, support the issuance of verifiable credentials and the request and delivery of credential presentations, respectively. In this context, VCs and VPs can use any format, including W3C VCDM, ISO mDL, and IETF SD-JWT VC. Additionally, ISO/IEC 18013-7 specifies the standard for presenting mDLs over the Internet.

All three wallets support multiple DID methods. A DID method defines how a specific type of DID is created, resolved, updated, and deactivated [4]. DID methods are often associated with *verifiable data registries* (*VDRs*) that facilitate these operations. These registries can be either on-chain, as in the case of distributed ledger technologies, or off-chain, as with trusted databases. All wallets implement the *did:ebsi* method, which relies on the EBSI registry as its trust anchor. Beyond EBSI, other DID methods are also based on distributed ledgers, such as *did:cheqd*, *did:iota*, *did:epic*, and *did:lac*. The *cheqd*, *iota*, and *ion* methods use public, permissionless ledgers: respectively, the cheqd network (part of the Cosmos blockchain), IOTA, and the Bitcoin blockchain. In contrast, the *epic* and *lac* methods are based on public, permissioned blockchains, specifically, the Alastria and LACChain networks. Additionally, the IDTL is based on a public, permissioned registry operated by IDunion members. Beyond these, all wallets also support registry-less methods such as *did:key*, *did:jwk*, and *did:web*, which either embed cryptographic material directly or link to trusted web endpoints, without requiring a ledger-based registry.

To address the third research question, we provide a more precise characterization of the ToU field as implemented in each wallet. In the case of Triveria, the ToU field adheres to the W3C VCDM specification and comprises two subfields: *id* and *type*. The id subfield is an optional string used to reference a specific instance of the terms of use policy, while the type subfield is mandatory and designates the type of policy, such as "IssuerPolicy". It is also possible to define additional properties that were not explicitly specified in the schema. Similarly, the walt.id wallet adopts the same structure, following VCDM version 2.0. According to the GitHub repository, the id subfield is a string containing a *Uniform Resource Identifier* (*URI*) that uniquely identifies the terms of use, while the type subfield is a string containing an *Internationalized Resource Identifier* (*IRI*) that specifies the type of terms of use. Within the *identfy-OpenID-library*[6] repository, the ToU attribute is structured as the *W3CTermsOfUse* interface, containing three subfields. First is an optional string field called *id*, which, if

---

provided, includes an identifier, typically a URL, linking to an external document where the usage terms are specified. The second subfield, *type*, acts as a string to indicate the VC type and is required. Lastly, additional properties can be defined, such as those in the Triveria version.

In conclusion, all three wallets adhere to current standards of the SSI ecosystem. Depending on the use case, one might prefer a wallet that uses DID methods based on public permissionless networks, for example, when organizations like universities issue attestations, such as diplomas and certificates, that companies can easily verify. In contrast, a DID based on a publicly authorized blockchain could be used in a supply chain context, for example, to track products along the supply chain, associating DIDs with goods, companies or employee documents. This ensures transparency to the public while allowing only authorized parties, such as consortia of companies, to validate and update the data. However, a blockchain-based DID is not always necessary. Non-registry DIDs can be more suitable for test environments, peer-to-peer interactions, and IoT authentication, as they support decentralized and local identity management. All three wallets support these features, although walt.id and Identfy currently offer broader DID management. Walt.id and Triveria support issuer, holder, and verifier roles within a single wallet, while Identfy separates these roles into a holder wallet and an enterprise wallet. The choice between a unified or separate wallet depends on context: a single wallet is often preferable for individual users and consumer use cases, while separating roles is essential for companies and high-security environments. In such cases, Identfy may offer a particularly suitable solution. Finally, regarding issuance and exchange protocols, all wallets implement OID4VCI and OID4VP. Walt.id also supports the mDL presentation protocol and is generally more up-to-date with the latest protocol versions compared to Triveria; for Identfy, the current version information could not be retrieved.

## 5   Related Work

Previous research has extensively examined the role, design, and requirements of digital identity wallets within the modern digital identity ecosystem. Podgorelec et al. [28] provide a systematic literature review focused on digital wallets for identity management. Their work synthesizes the definitions, functionalities, and characteristics described in 26 peer-reviewed studies, offering clarity on the motivations for adoption and the evolving capabilities of these tools.

Ansaroudi et al. [2] present a classification framework for digital identity wallets based on trust establishment models and methods for controlled credential sharing. Grounded in the *Trust over IP (ToIP)* architecture, they highlight the technologies that support tamper-proof credentials and secure, selective disclosure. Their goal is to guide system architects in designing safe and privacy-preserving identity solutions. Our study builds on this by focusing on organizational and government requirements, including terms-of-use considerations.

Degen and Teubner [10] explore the government's role in digital identity wallet provision, identifying two main orchestration models: the *Government*

*ID-Infrastructure Wallet* and the *Trust ID Wallet Federation*. Their analysis of policy documents and expert opinions contributes to a deeper understanding of governance frameworks for digital identity ecosystems.

Bochnia et al. [6] define the core requirements for organizational SSI systems, addressing credential management, organizational identity, and technical and operational factors. They assess the extent to which existing SSI solutions meet these needs, highlighting gaps. Our work revisits some of the wallets they studied and expands the analysis to include additional industrial implementations.

Zhang et al. [39] investigate data sovereignty in the context of Web 3.0, emphasizing individual control over digital assets through SSI. They discuss technical challenges, including key management, scalability, interoperability, and standardization, as well as unresolved issues such as dynamic attribute handling, user personas, and attribute ownership.

Samir et al. [32] introduce DT-SSIM, a decentralized identity management framework that combines Shamir's Secret Sharing, blockchain, and smart contracts to securely split and store identity data. This architecture is designed to enhance privacy, data integrity, and tamper resistance while permitting credential verification without disclosing the original data.

Finally, Rota [31] describes the development of an SSI framework using blockchain and MetaMask, integrated into the Links Foundation's Data Cellar project. The work combines a React-based front-end and a NestJS back-end, and includes a preliminary evaluation of existing SSI solutions such as Shocard, Sovrin, and uPort.

## 6   Conclusion

The digital identity landscape is undergoing a transition from centralized systems to more privacy-preserving and user-centric models, driven mainly by the adoption of SSI architectures. This study investigated the extent to which industrial digital identity wallets support the implementation of the ToU property, a requirement in institutional and organizational contexts. By conducting a structured review of both academic and gray literature, we identified and analyzed a representative sample of wallets to evaluate their compliance with ToU requirements. The results of our analysis suggest that while the ToU may play an important role in specific contexts, its actual adoption across wallet implementations is still limited. Future research should expand the scope of this evaluation to include additional categories of wallets, such as the organizational wallets defined within the EBSI framework. Moreover, further studies could focus on assessing the usability of these wallets and the ToU regulatory implications, thereby providing insights into their adoption potential and user acceptance.

**Acknowledgments.** Stefano Bistarelli and Chiara Luchini are members of the INdAM Research group GNCS, and all three authors are members of Consorzio CINI. This work has been partially supported by: GNCS-INdAM, CUP_E53C23001670001; MUR PNRR project SERICS (PE00000014 AQuSDIT: CUP_H73C22000880001,

COVERT: CUP_J93C23002310006), funded by the European Union – Next Generation EU; EU MUR PNRR project VITALITY (J97G22000170005), funded by the European Union – Next Generation EU; University of Perugia - Fondo Ricerca di Ateneo (2020, 2022) – Projects BLOCKCHAIN4FOODCHAIN, FICO, RATIONALISTS, "Civil Safety and Security for Society".

# References


1. Allen, C.: The path to self-sovereign identity (2016). http://www.lifewithalacrity.com/2016/04/the-path-to-self-soverereign-identity.html
2. Ansaroudi, Z.E., Carbone, R., Sciarretta, G., Ranise, S.: Control is nothing without trust a first look into digital identity wallet trends. In: Atluri, V., Ferrara, A.L. (eds.) Data and Applications Security and Privacy XXXVII - 37th Annual IFIP WG 11.3 Conference, DBSec 2023, Sophia-Antipolis, France, July 19–21, 2023, Proceedings. Lecture Notes in Computer Science, vol. 13942, pp. 113–132. Springer (2023). https://doi.org/10.1007/978-3-031-37586-6_7
3. Bistarelli, S., Luchini, C., Santini, F.: Analyzing terms of use adoption in ssi digital wallets: A review of current implementations. In: Proceedings of the 7th Distributed Ledger Technologies Workshop (DLT2025). Pizzo (VV), Calabria, Italy (2025)
4. Bistarelli, S., Micheli, F., Santini, F.: A survey on decentralized identifier methods for self sovereign identity. In: Buccafurri, F., Ferrari, E., Lax, G. (eds.) Proceedings of the Italian Conference on Cyber Security (ITASEC 2023), Bari, Italy, May 2–5, 2023. CEUR Workshop Proceedings, vol. 3488. CEUR-WS.org (2023). https://ceur-ws.org/Vol-3488/paper05.pdf
5. Blockchain Lab:UM: Masca (2025), masca: https://masca.io/, Masca Github: https://github.com/blockchain-lab-um/masca
6. Bochnia, R., Richter, D., Anke, J.: Self-sovereign identity for organizations: requirements for enterprise software. IEEE Access **12**, 7637–7660 (2024). https://doi.org/10.1109/ACCESS.2023.3349095
7. Brereton, P., Kitchenham, B.A., Budgen, D., Turner, M., Khalil, M.: Lessons from applying the systematic literature review process within the software engineering domain. J. Syst. Softw. **80**(4), 571–583 (2007). https://doi.org/10.1016/j.jss.2006.07.009, software Performance
8. Cucko, S., Kersic, V., Turkanovic, M.: Towards a catalogue of self-sovereign identity design patterns. Appl. Sci. **13**(9) (2023). https://doi.org/10.3390/app13095395
9. Decentralized Identity Foundation (DIF) - Veramo User Group: Veramo (2025), veramo: https://veramo.io/, Veramo User Group: https://blog.identity.foundation/veramo-user-group/
10. Degen, K., Teubner, T.: Wallet wars or digital public infrastructure? orchestrating a digital identity data ecosystem from a government perspective. Electron. Mark. **34**(1), 50 (2024). https://doi.org/10.1007/S12525-024-00731-1
11. European Blockchain Association: Ssi wallets (2025). https://europeanblockchainassociation.org/ssi-wallets/
12. European Blockchain Partnership (EBP): Policies for verifiable credentials presentation and request. https://hub.ebsi.eu/vc-framework/trust-model/policies (2024)
13. European Blockchain Partnership (EBP): Conformant wallets (2025). https://ec.europa.eu/digital-building-blocks/sites/display/EBSI/Conformant+wallets

14. European Commission: The european digital identity wallet architecture and reference framework | shaping europe's digital future. Tech. rep., European Commission (2023). https://digital-strategy.ec.europa.eu/en/library/european-digital-identity-wallet-architecture-and-reference-framework

15. European Commission: Eu digital identity wallet (2025). https://tinyurl.com/2rzfvt3c

16. Evernym: Connect.me (2023), connect.Me: https://github.com/evernym/ConnectMe, Evernym: https://www.evernym.com/

17. Gimly: Ssi wallets (2022). https://github.com/Gimly-Blockchain/ssi-wallets

18. GUNet: wwwallet (2025), wwWallet: https://wwwallet.org/, wwWallet Github: https://github.com/wwWallet, wwWallet Documentation: https://wwwallet.github.io/wallet-docs/

19. IN2: In2 wallet (2025), iN2: https://www.in2.es/en, IN2 Github: https://github.com/in2workspace

20. Izertis, S.A.: Identify (2025), izertis: https://www.izertis.com/en/, Identfy : https://github.com/izertis/identfy, Izertis Github: https://github.com/izertis

21. Jolocom: Jocolom (2022). jolocom SDK: https://github.com/jolocom/jolocom-sdk, Jolocom SmartWallet: https://github.com/jolocom/smartwallet-app

22. Kitchenham, B., Charters, S.: Guidelines for performing systematic literature reviews in software engineering 2 (01 2007)

23. NTT Data: Kaytrust (2025), kayTrust: https://www.kaytrust.id/, KayTrust Documentation: https://developer.kaytrust.id/, KayTrust Github: https://github.com/KayTrust

24. O'Donnell, D.: 2023 wallet report update: Emerging trust layer, trust registries & interoperability. https://www.continuumloop.com/2023-wallet-report-update/ (2023)

25. Page, M.J., et al.: The prisma 2020 statement: an updated guideline for reporting systematic reviews. BMJ 372 (2021). https://doi.org/10.1136/bmj.n71

26. Petticrew, M., Roberts, H.: Systematic reviews in the social sciences: a practical guide, vol. 11. Blackwell Publishing (01 2006). https://doi.org/10.1002/9780470754887

27. Ping Identity: Pingone neo (2025), pingOne Neo: https://tinyurl.com/ya379t5j, PingOne Credential: https://tinyurl.com/39f969we, PingOne Neo Native SDKs: https://github.com/pingidentity/pingone-neo-mobile-sdk

28. Podgorelec, B., Alber, L., Zefferer, T.: What is a (digital) identity wallet? A systematic literature review. In: Leong, H.V., Sarvestani, S.S., Teranishi, Y., Cuzzocrea, A., Kashiwazaki, H., Towey, D., Yang, J., Shahriar, H. (eds.) 46th IEEE Annual Computers, Software, and Applications Conferenc, COMPSAC 2022, Los Alamitos, CA, USA, June 27 - July 1, 2022, pp. 809–818. IEEE (2022). https://doi.org/10.1109/COMPSAC54236.2022.00131

29. Privacy by Design Foundation: Yivi (2025), yivi: https://www.yivi.app/en/, Yivi GitHub: https://github.com/privacybydesign/irmamobile

30. Reed, D., O'Donnell, D.: Digital wallet report 2021 update. http://continuumloop.com/digital-wallet-report-update/ (2021)

31. Rota, L.: Decentralized Identity Management: Building and Integrating a Self-Sovereign Identity Framework. Master's thesis, Politecnico di Torino (2024). http://webthesis.biblio.polito.it/id/eprint/30910

32. Samir, E., Wu, H., Azab, M., Xin, C., Zhang, Q.: DT-SSIM: a decentralized trustworthy self-sovereign identity management framework. IEEE Internet Things J. 9(11), 7972–7988 (2022). https://doi.org/10.1109/JIOT.2021.3112537

33. Schardong, F., Custódio, R.: Self-sovereign identity: a systematic review, mapping and taxonomy. Sensors **22**(15) (2022). https://doi.org/10.3390/s22155641
34. SelfKey: Selfkey foundation (2024). selfKey: https://selfkey.org/, SelfKey Identity Wallet: https://github.com/SelfKeyFoundation/Identity-Wallet
35. SimpleIdServer: Simpleidserver (2025). simpleIdServer: https://simpleidserver. com/, SimpleIdServer Documentation: https://simpleidserver.com/docs/overview, SimpleIdServer Github: https://github.com/simpleidserver
36. Sporny, M., Longley, D., Chadwick, D., Steele, O.: Verifiable credentials data model v2.0. Tech. rep., World Wide Web Consortium (W3C) (2024)
37. Talao: Altme (2025). altme: https://www.altme.io/, Altme Github: https://github. com/TalaoDAO/AltMe, Altme Documentation: https://doc.wallet-provider.io/ welcome/
38. Talao: Talao (2025). talao: https://talao.io/, Talao Verifiable Credentials: https://doc.wallet-provider.io/vc_type, Talao Wallet: https://github.com/ TalaoDAO/AltMe/tree/TALAO, SpruceID: https://spruceid.com/, DIDKit - SpruceID: https://github.com/spruceid/didkit, SSI - SpruceID: https://github. com/spruceid/ssi
39. Tan, K.L., Chi, C.H., Lam, K.Y.: Survey on digital sovereignty and identity: from digitization to digitalization. ACM Comput. Surv. D(3) (Oct 2023). https://doi. org/10.1145/3616400
40. Trinsic Technologies Inc: Trinsic (2025), trinsic: https://trinsic.id/, Trinsic SDK: https://github.com/trinsic-id/sdk
41. Triveria: Triveria online wallet platform (2025). triveria: https://www.triveria. com/index.html, Triveria Github: https://github.com/triveria-com, Triveria Documentation: https://docs.triveria.dev/, Triveria License: https://triveria.com/ terms.html
42. walt.id: walt.id (2025). walt.id: https://walt.id/, walt.id GitHub: https://github. com/walt-id/waltid-identity
43. Wohlin, C.: Guidelines for snowballing in systematic literature studies and a replication in software engineering. In: Shepperd, M.J., Hall, T., Myrtveit, I. (eds.) 18th International Conference on Evaluation and Assessment in Software Engineering, EASE '14, London, England, United Kingdom, May 13–14, 2014, pp. 38:1–38:10. ACM (2014). https://doi.org/10.1145/2601248.2601268
44. World Wide Web Consortium (W3C): termsofuse is insufficiently specified. https:// github.com/w3c/vc-data-model/issues/1010 (Jan 2023)
45. World Wide Web Consortium (W3C): Update to terms of use description. https:// github.com/w3c/vc-data-model/pull/1295 (Nov 2023)

# Selfish Mining in Multi-attacker Scenarios: An Empirical Evaluation of Nakamoto, Fruitchain, and Strongchain

Martin Perešíni$^{(\boxtimes)}$ , Tomáš Hladký, Jakub Kubík, and Ivan Homoliak

Brno University of Technology, Božetěchova 2, 612 00 Brno, Czech Republic
`{iperesini,homoliak}@fit.vut.cz`, `{hladk15,kubik32}@stud.fit.vut.cz`



**Abstract.** The aim of this work is to enhance blockchain security by deepening the understanding of selfish mining attacks in various consensus protocols, especially the ones that have the potential to mitigate selfish mining. Previous research was mainly focused on a particular protocol with a single selfish miner, while only limited studies have been conducted on two or more attackers. To address this gap, we proposed a stochastic simulation framework that enables analysis of selfish mining with multiple attackers across various consensus protocols. We created the model of Proof-of-Work (PoW) Nakamoto consensus (serving as the baseline) as well as models of two additional consensus protocols designed to mitigate selfish mining: Fruitchain and Strongchain. Using our framework, thresholds reported in the literature were verified, and several novel thresholds were discovered for 2 and more attackers. We made the source code of our framework available, enabling researchers to evaluate any newly added protocol with one or more selfish miners and cross-compare it with already modeled protocols.

**Keywords:** Selfish mining · Blockchain · Consensus protocols · Simulation · Proof-of-Work


## 1 Introduction

Proof-of-Work (PoW) blockchains such as Bitcoin rely on Nakamoto consensus [9] to agree on a chain of blocks. However, in 2013, Eyal and Sirer [3] showed that a miner who only controls 33% of the hash rate could earn more than their fair share through selfish mining (SM), challenging the original assumption that the majority >50% power is needed for such an attack. The selfish miner strategically withholds and releases blocks that override the honest chain, thus wasting the work of honest miners. Since its discovery, extensive research has explored the impact and potential mitigations of selfish mining [4,19]. The follow-up works [16,21,22] successively tightened the single-attacker profitability threshold to 25%, and in the settings of two attackers to 21% per attacker (up to ten attackers). Another variant is stubborn mining [10], in which attackers persist in mining their private chains even when they fall behind the honest chain, potentially increasing their profits.


© The Author(s), under exclusive license to Springer Nature Switzerland AG 2026
R. Laborde et al. (Eds.): ESORICS 2025, LNCS 16231, pp. 328–343, 2026.
https://doi.org/10.1007/978-3-032-16089-8_21

Parallel to the analytic results, researchers proposed fork-choice tweaks (e.g., uniform tie breaking) or entirely new PoW schemes: Subchain [15], Fruitchain [11], and Strongchain [18], which are aimed at mitigating SM by increasing the SM profitability threshold, thus making SM attacks much more expensive and less feasible. Nevertheless, the literature still lacks a comparative multi-attacker evaluation of these defenses under identical conditions. Our work aims to address this gap by providing an empirical evaluation of selfish mining strategies across the mentioned consensus protocols. We introduce a unified simulation framework capable of comparing various consensus protocols under selfish mining attacks. Our study explores scenarios with one or more selfish miners and investigates the impact of the attacker's connectivity (i.e., propagation factor $(\gamma)$) on profitability thresholds of selfish mining.

***Contributions.*** Our main contributions are as follows:

1. We created a unified simulation framework capable of modeling various consensus protocols under selfish mining attacks.
2. We implemented and analyzed designs to mitigate selfish mining, particularly Fruitchain [11] and Strongchain [18] within this framework, allowing direct comparisons.
3. We performed extensive simulations exploring selfish mining scenarios with one or more attackers, revealing new profitability thresholds under various values of the propagation factor parameter (i.e., $\gamma$).
4. We cross-compared the investigated consensus protocols in terms of selfish mining mitigation and revealed their relative order of protection.

## 2   Background on Selfish Mining

In a selfish mining attack, the attacker has a consensus power below 50% of the total mining power of the blockchain. The primary aim of a selfish miner is to gain a higher reward relative to their consensus power [3].

The selfish miner selectively reveals his mined blocks to override and invalidate the honest miners' work. He keeps his mined blocks private, creating a private chain. Since the selfish miner controls a relatively small portion of the total mining power, his private branch can only stay ahead for a short time. During this period, honest miners continue to mine on the shorter public branch. A selfish miner conveniently reveals blocks from his private branch, overriding the shorter public branch, which causes honest miners to abandon the public branch and switch to the recently revealed attacker's chain. This wastes the work done on the public branch by honest miners and increases the fraction of selfish miners' blocks incorporated into the blockchain, allowing them to collect relatively more revenues than invested mining power [3].

In a selfish mining attack, the attacker performs 4 actions [3]:

- **Override** – if the honest main chain is just one block shorter than the attacker's private chain, the attacker publishes his private chain to override the main chain and obtain rewards.

- **Adopt** – the attacker accepts the honest main chain and abandons his private chain when the main chain becomes longer than the attacker's private chain.
- **Match** – if the main chain is as long as the attacker's, the attacker publishes his private chain to compete with the honest main chain.
- **Wait** – if the attacker's chain is more than one block longer than the honest main chain, the attacker continues to mine on his private chain.

### 2.1   Notation

***Mining Power.*** The blockchain system consists of the set of miners $M = \{m_i\}$, where $i \in \langle 1, \ldots, n \rangle$. Each miner $i$ has a mining power of $\alpha_i$, and the total mining power of all miners is equal to 1; i.e., $\sum_{i=1,\ldots,n} \alpha_i = 1$.

***Propagation Factor.*** During the selfish mining attack, the attacker releases his private chain in the **match action** (i.e., equal length of the honest and the malicious chains) and continues to mine on it. Honest miners decide which branch to continue mining on, usually by selecting the branch they receive first. The proportion of honest miners who choose to mine on the chain revealed by the attacker is represented by $\gamma \in \langle 0, 1 \rangle$, called **a propagation factor**. If $\gamma = 0$, the honest miner always wins the race of the block propagation to the network. Contrary, when $\gamma = 1$, the selfish miner always wins the race of the block propagation to the network. If $\gamma = 0.5$, both honest and selfish miners win the race of block propagation with equal chances. The propagation factor can also be abstracted as the connection quality of the attacker vs. the honest miners; therefore, the higher $\gamma$, the better connectivity the attacker has vs. the honest miners.

### 2.2   Selfish Mining with a Single Attacker

Eyal and Sirer [3] performed modeling by Markov chains and executed simulations of selfish mining by a single attacker on Nakamoto's consensus [9] (see Fig. 1). The *x-axis* of Fig. 1 displays various mining powers $\alpha$ of an attacker, while the *y-axis* represents their relative revenues. The figure compares various values of $\gamma$ between selfish miners and honest miners. It shows that selfish mining becomes profitable for a poorly connected attacker ($\gamma = 0$) at the mining power $\sim 33\%$, while for an equally connected attacker ($\gamma = 0.5$) the attack becomes profitable at $\sim 25\%$.

### 2.3   Selfish Mining with Two Attackers

In the case of 2 or more selfish miners (on Nakamoto's consensus), multiple private branches can co-exist simultaneously since each attacker privately mines on their chain. Notation for multiple attackers. Let $p_A$ and $p_B$ denote the mining powers of the attackers Alice and Bob, respectively, and $p_H = 1 - p_A - p_B$ the total honest mining power. When both attackers publish competing private

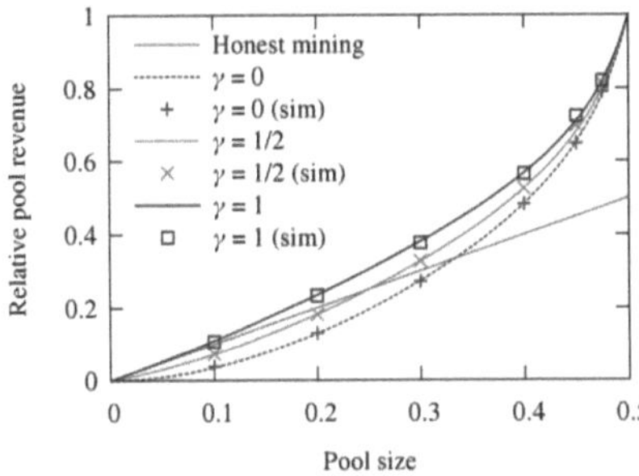

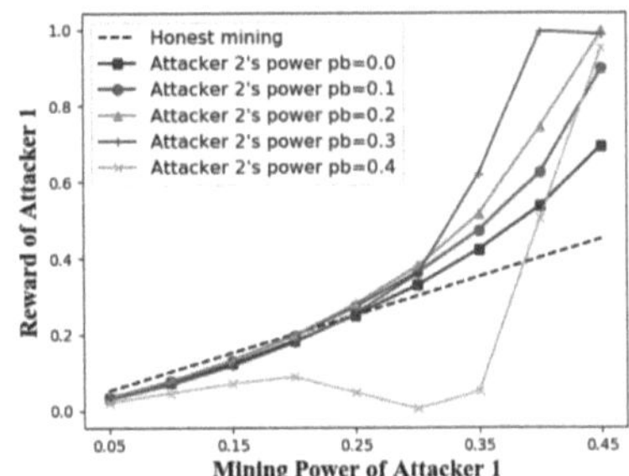

**Fig. 1.** Selfish mining with a single attacker on Nakamoto's consensus [3].

**Fig. 2.** Selfish mining with 2 attackers [22]: rewards of the attacker 1 based on his mining power vs. the mining power of attacker 2.

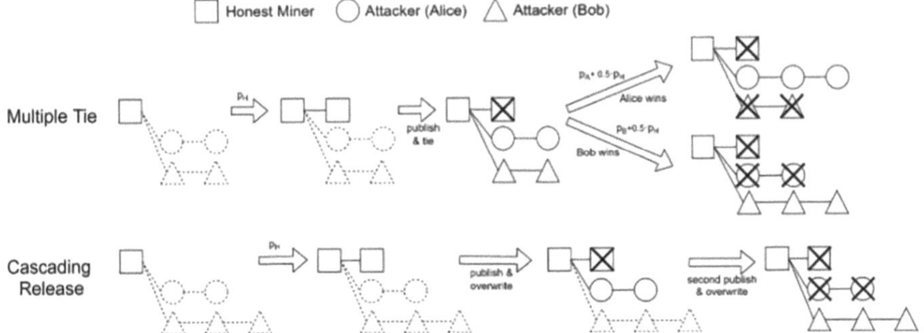


**Fig. 3.** Selfish mining with 2+ independent attackers yields new scenarios: (1) multiple ties and (2) cascading release [22].

branches of equal length ("multiple tie"), the probability that Alice's branch wins is $p_A + \frac{1}{2}p_H$, and Bob's is $p_B + \frac{1}{2}p_H$. Such a setting enables 2 new scenarios in contrast to selfish mining by a single attacker [22] (see Fig. 3):

- In a **multiple tie**, multiple branches of the same length are published by the attackers. For example, attackers Alice and Bob have a private chain with two blocks each. Honest miners will randomly select one of the two branches. Alice's chain wins with a probability of $p_A + 0.5 * p_H$, and Bob's chain wins with a probability of $p_B + 0.5 * p_H$.
- In a **cascading release**, one attacker overrides the chain of another attacker. In the example, Alice and Bob each hold a private branch with lengths of two and three, respectively. When an honest miner mines a new block, Alice releases her branch, overwriting the public chain. Then Bob discovers a public chain one block shorter than his private branch, so he releases his private branch, overwriting Alice's branch.

Zhang et al. [22] simulated 2 selfish miners on Nakamoto's consensus and their results are depicted in Fig. 2, which displays the rewards of attacker 1 based on his mining power and the mining power of attacker 2. We can see that the blue series represents a selfish mining attack with one attacker (and $\gamma = 0.5$) since the mining power of attacker 2 is 0%. Also, as the mining power of the attacker 2 increases (up to 40%), the reward for the attacker 1 also increases as long as the mining power of the attacker 1 is greater than or equal to the mining power of the attacker 2. However, if attacker 2 has 40+% (yellow series) and attacker 1 has lower mining power than attacker 2, attacker 1 loses significantly. This is because a dominant miner's chain is likely to be always longer and win more often than other chains. In further simulations, Zhang et al. [22] demonstrate that the minimum $\alpha$ for which both attackers can profit in this scenario is equal to 21% (i.e., 42% in total).

## 2.4   Selfish Mining with Multiple Attackers

Zhang et al. [21] conducted multiple simulations on Nakamoto's consensus with three to ten independent attackers. The authors conclude that the beneficial threshold for selfish mining decreases as the number of attackers increases. According to their simulation, seven attackers with at least 12% of the total mining power are the maximum number of successful attackers. In the case of five attackers, they must hold at least 15% of the total mining power. Beyond this and former works we extend, multi-player selfish-mining dynamics have also been studied by Marmolejo-Cossio et al. [8] and Kwon et al. [6], who analyze competitive equilibria and strategic interactions among multiple selfish miners. Our empirical framework complements these by providing cross-protocol thresholds under identical conditions.

## 2.5   Threat Model and Assumptions

Recall that $M$ is the set of all miners with mining powers $\{m_i\}_{i=1}^{n}$, where $\sum m_i = 1$. A subset $\mathcal{A}$ of $M$ (*where* $|A| \geq 1$) represents selfish miners and the rest represents honest miners. We consider rational non-colluding selfish miners competing against honest miners in PoW-based protocols. Selfish miners follow the Eyal-Sirer's [3] selfish mining strategy (i.e., override/match/wait/adopt), adapted according to the protocol fork choice rule. Also, we assume that honest miners always follow the protocol.

***Network Model.*** We abstract the network propagation of the attacker by the standard $\gamma$ parameter: when branches tie, a $\gamma$ fraction of the honest mining power mines on the attacker's branch ($\gamma=0$ honest-favored; $\gamma=0.5$ equal; $\gamma=1$ attacker-favored). For multi-attacker experiments, we set $\gamma=0.5$ to avoid privileging any single attacker. Accidental forks and heterogeneous delays are abstracted, since their impact is covered by $\gamma$. Transaction fees are excluded across all protocols to isolate side effects of divergent conditions (see also Sect. 6)

***Attackers' Coordination.*** Unless stated otherwise, attackers act independently and do not collude or share private branches. Each selfish miner maximizes its own expected relative revenue.

***Protocol Specifics.*** We implement each protocol's fork resolution and artifacts (i.e., blocks, fruits, weak headers) according to their descriptions.

## 2.6   Robustness Metric: Profitability Threshold

Let $R_i(\alpha_i)$ denote the relative revenue function of the miner $i$ when the miner $i$ controls the mining power $\alpha_i$ (Fig. 5). We define the profitability threshold $\alpha_i^{\backslash *}$ for the miner $i$ as the smallest $\alpha_i$ such that $R_i(\alpha_i) \geq \alpha_i$. Intuitively, $\alpha_i^{\backslash *}$ is the minimum power at which selfish mining becomes more profitable than honest mining. In simulations, we experiment with $\alpha_i$ and estimate $R_i(\alpha_i)$ as the average over five runs of 100,000 rounds each (per configuration), then report the smallest $\alpha_i$ where the mean exceeds the fair-share. When two adjacent grid points straddle equality, we linearly interpolate and confirm that the 95% bootstrap confidence interval includes the crossing. When multiple attackers are present, we report per-attacker thresholds under symmetric allocations unless otherwise noted, e.g., $k = 2$ attackers each with $\alpha$ (see Table 1).

## 3   Consensus Protocols Mitigating Selfish Mining

We briefly review some consensus protocols that are discussed in the literature as candidates to mitigate the impact of selfish mining. A key idea in this area involves "inclusive" protocols [7] that incorporate and reward work from otherwise orphaned blocks, thereby reducing the attacker's ability to waste honest miners' efforts. However, these protocols are built on the assumption that no honest miners will willingly put conflicting transactions into their block to potentially increase their profits, which was refuted in the related work [12]. Beyond protocols that add new artifacts to the chain (e.g., Strongchain [18] and Fruitchain [11]), other approaches modify the block structure and the reward scheme itself to disincentivize withholding blocks [2, 15]. For example, Bitcoin-NG [2] proposes a leader-election mechanism with subsequent microblocks, which

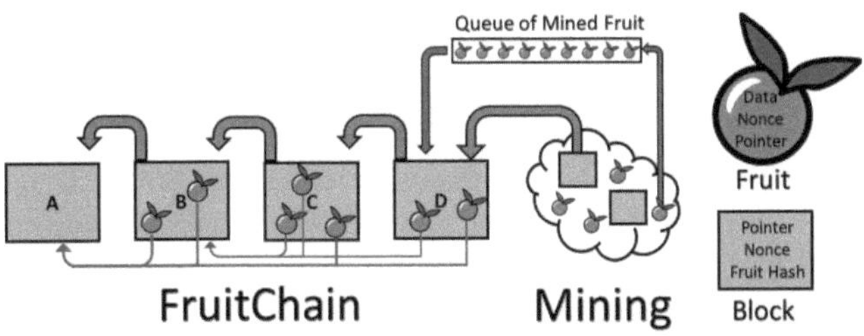


**Fig. 4.** A Fruitchain's fragment with fruits and blocks [11].

reduces the per-block reward advantage a selfish miner can gain, thus altering the attack's fundamental economic incentives. This protocol seems sound, but it has a known problem with censoring a leader, which brings another attacking vector instead of selfish mining. The Fruitchain and Strongchain protocols, which we evaluate, approach this problem in a different way.

### 3.1   Fruitchain

The primary objective of the Fruitchain [11] consensus protocol is to **enhance** security, particularly in terms of **resistance to selfish mining**. The most significant architectural change is that the transactional records on Fruitchain are stored in **fruits**, which are then stored in **blocks** (see Fig. 4). Individual blocks are used to build the blockchain. Creating fruits and blocks requires different levels of PoW difficulty. Additionally, fruits must "hang" from a block that is already part of the blockchain. **Hanging fruit** contains a reference to an already existing block on the blockchain within a maximum distance. The maximum distance is determined by a constant value of the protocol.

In each round, the miner searches for fruits and blocks simultaneously by invoking a single hash function, a technique called the **2-for-1 trick**. The prefix of the generated hash is the fruit mining hash, while the suffix determines the block mining hash. This means that each newly mined block or fruit contains redundant and unused data. Besides, the authors do not discuss the possibility and handling of duplicate transactions in different fruits since miners are selecting transactions to be included in fruits based on their fees, while fruits are mined more frequently than blocks, which increases the probability that two or more different fruits contain the overlapping set of transactions.

**Mining Difficulty.** The Fruitchain protocol is parameterized with two mining difficulties. The first one (which is of higher difficulty) is for mining blocks, and the second one (which is of lower difficulty) is for mining fruits.

**Rewarding Scheme.** The authors of Fruitchain argue that the Fruitchain rewarding scheme is more fair than Nakamoto's one because it rewards fruits and blocks. However, they do not define particular values nor how fruits and blocks are rewarded. They also do not define how many transactions are in individual fruits and how are transaction fees attributed.

**Resistance to Selfish Mining.** The authors of Fruitchain did not assess its resistance to selfish mining. Nevertheless, Zhang and Preneel [20] evaluated its resistance to selfish mining with a single attacker. The results show that Fruitchain with $\gamma = 0$ (i.e., the most favorable setting to honest miners) performs worse than the Nakamoto consensus for the same $\gamma$, which means that the selfish miner in Fruitchain earns higher rewards than in the Nakamoto consensus. In Fruitchain with $\gamma = 1$, the attacker receives less reward than in the Nakamoto consensus, so Fruitchain performs better than Nakamoto for $\gamma = 1$.

## 3.2   Strongchain

The main objective of the Strongchain [18] protocol is to improve the security of the Nakamoto's consensus. A key difference between Strongchain and Nakamoto's consensus is that Strongchain also "includes" headers with hash values that do not meet the strong target, but are strong enough to demonstrate significant PoW spent. Using two mining difficulty levels, it generates two distinct header types: weak and strong. Weak headers contribute to the security of the protocol, whereas transactions are stored in strong blocks associated with strong headers. The blocks contain transactions, weak headers, and a strong header that authenticates the weak headers and transactions. The fields in the strong and weak headers are inherited from the Bitcoin headers with an additional new field – the coinbase entry (the miner's address to receive a reward for a particular strong or weak block). Weak headers do not authenticate transactions. They are stored and exchanged without the corresponding transactions. A weak header primarily reflects and contributes to the accumulation of mining power concentrated in a specific branch of the blockchain – and thus increases the resistance to selfish mining.

**Mining Difficulty.** Strong headers, combined with weak headers, are used for chain strength evaluation. The mining difficulty of weak and strong headers is adjusted in every 2016 blocks in a predefined ratio. Strongchain does not use reward halving.

**Rewarding Scheme.** In Strongchain, both weak and strong header miners are rewarded. The miner who discovers the strong header receives the full reward $R$, while the weak header miner receives a fraction of $R$, calculated as $\kappa * cR * \frac{T_s}{T_w}$. $\kappa$ influences the relative impact of weak header rewards and $c$ is a scaling constant, $R$ represents the reward for strong headers, and $\frac{T_s}{T_w}$ is the difficulty factor of strong headers compared to the difficulty of weak headers. Transaction fees belong to the strong header miner.

**Resistance to Selfish Mining.** The ratio between the strong header and weak header difficulty influences the number of weak headers that are mined in each round, which in turn influences the threshold of resistance to selfish mining. For example, if the ratio between strong and weak headers difficulty is 1024, the threshold is around 43%, while the threshold is 40% if this ratio is 8 [18].

## 4   Evaluation

We proposed a simulation framework capable of simulating and cross-comparing all the simulated consensus protocols. In the following, we first describe our simulation framework and then describe the experiments and their results.

### 4.1   Simulation Framework

The proposed simulation framework consists of four primary entities: **simulation manager**, **honest miners**, **selfish miners**, and the **blockchain**.

The framework features a centralized entity known as the simulation manager, which replaces the distributed blockchain topology. The PoW mining function is replaced by a uniform random function that selects the leader of a new round based on their mining power. The chosen leader (either malicious or honest) creates a new block or other artifacts of the protocols (such as fruits [11], weak headers [18]). The leader performs actions depending on whether he is malicious or honest. Once the leader has taken action, other attackers (selfish miners) can respond if the action is publicly disclosed. Afterward, the mining round closes and the process of selecting a new leader repeats until the desired number of rounds is reached.

The simulation framework includes a rewarding scheme for blocks (and/or other artifacts); however, transaction fees are not modeled since they contribute to the overall profit of either malicious or honest miner in the same way within all the investigated consensus protocols. The framework also implements fork-resolution rules specific to individual consensus protocols. Forks can occur only due to selfish mining behavior, while accidental forks[1] are not considered since they affect both malicious and honest miners in the same way. For simplicity, we abstract from the variance in the propagation and validation times of individual blocks (i.e., the network propagation delay and the validation of blocks are constant). Instead, we approximate a difference in network propagation delay between honest miners and selfish miners by the $\gamma$ parameter, which determines the probability that honest miners will accept the attacker's block more likely than the honest miners' block when a match action occurs (see Sect. 2.5).

**Implementation Details.** We developed the framework using Python 3.8 and TypeScript, and its source code is available on GitHub.[2] The correctness of the implementation was verified by comparing its simulation results with the literature related to Nakamoto's consensus and known configurations of investigated protocols (i.e., for a single selfish miner and particular $\gamma$ if available).

### 4.2 Methodology of Experiments

For each investigated consensus protocol, we created its model in our framework and performed several simulation experiments (i.e., runs) with each model. The experiments contained various parameters such as a different number of selfish miners, the ratio of their mining power, and the parameter $\gamma$ (if applicable). Therefore, more than a thousand experiments were often performed for each modeled consensus protocol. Moreover, we repeated each experiment 5 times per configuration and averaged the results. Finally, each simulation experiment involved $100,000$ rounds of consensus protocol,[3] allowing a sufficient number of selfish mining states and situations (with multiple selfish miners) to occur during

---

[1] Contributing to the stale blocks/artifacts.

[2] Repo: https://github.com/Tem12/fruitchain-sim and https://github.com/Jakub-Kubik/smasf.

[3] Each round produces an artifact – either a block or a fruit or a weak header or a strong block, depending on the protocol.

each simulation run. For each configuration, we identify the smallest $\alpha$ where the mean relative revenue curve intersects the fair-share line. We additionally verify that the mean exceeds fair-share for the value of $\alpha$ across runs and a 95% bootstrap confidence interval includes the crossing. This protects against declaring thresholds based on noisy single-run outliers.

### 4.3   Nakamoto Consensus

To verify the results of related work, we experimented on the Nakamoto protocol with one attacker and $\gamma = \{0, 0.5, 1\}$ as well as for 2 to 7 attackers and $\gamma = 0.5$. In all multi-attacker experiments, we use $\gamma = 0.5$ to avoid biasing the fork race toward any single attacker. The rewards were calculated as the ratio of the blocks mined and included in the blockchain by the miner vs. all the blocks on the blockchain. The results are presented in Table 1. Our findings align with existing research for an attacker with $\gamma = 0.5$ and $\gamma = 1$. For five and seven attackers, the results deviate by 1%. These results confirm the validity of our simulation framework with respect to previous research [21,22].

**Table 1.** A comparison of selfish mining thresholds [%] for investigated protocols in contrast to Nakamoto consensus (i.e., denoted by $\Delta$). Note that all the results along N/A in the literature were obtained for the first time in this work.

| Selfish Miners | $\gamma$ | Nakamoto | | Strongchain | | | Fruitchain | | |
|---|---|---|---|---|---|---|---|---|---|
| | | Liter. | Sim. | Liter. | Sim. | $\Delta$ | Liter. | Sim. | $\Delta$ |
| 1 | 0 | 33 | 33 | 45 | 46 | +13 | N/A | 38 | +5 |
| 1 | 0.5 | 25 | 25 | N/A | - | - | N/A | 38 | +13 |
| 1 | 1 | 1 | 1 | N/A | - | - | N/A | 38 | +37 |
| 2 | 0.5 | 21 | 21 | N/A | 32 | +11 | N/A | 38 | +5 |
| 3 | 0.5 | 19 | 19 | N/A | 24 | +5 | N/A | 25 | +6 |
| 5 | 0.5 | 15 | 14 | N/A | 17 | +3 | N/A | 17 | +3 |
| 7 | 0.5 | 12 | 11 | N/A | 13 | +2 | N/A | 13 | +2 |

### 4.4   Strongchain

First, we verified the profitability threshold for a single selfish miner from the literature [18]. Our obtained threshold was by 1% of mining power higher in contrast to the results reported in [18]. The rewards were set to 1 for the strong block and 1 divided by the weak-to-strong header ratio for weak headers. This ratio indicates how many weak headers are mined on average before mining a strong block. We set this ratio to 10 for all experiments. In the original experiments [18], the match action of selfish mining always favored honest miners;

therefore, we assumed $\gamma = 0$ for all experiments. The profitability thresholds are shown in Table 1. For two simultaneous attackers, the threshold was found to be 32% of the total mining power per attacker.

In our experiments, we explored various scenarios, including single and multiple attackers. For the single attacker case, our results showed a slightly higher threshold (i.e., by 1%) than reported in the original Strongchain paper [18]. This small difference could be caused by differences in the simulation parameters or the stochastic nature of the simulations. For multiple attackers, we found that Strongchain maintained a relatively high threshold compared to Nakamoto consensus. With two simultaneous attackers, the threshold was 32% of the total mining power per attacker, which is significantly higher than the Nakamoto consensus. We also investigated scenarios with more than two attackers, finding that Strongchain continued to provide strong resistance against selfish mining even as the number of attackers increased. This suggests that Strongchain's design, particularly its use of weak headers to contribute to chain strength, provides robust protection against selfish mining attacks.

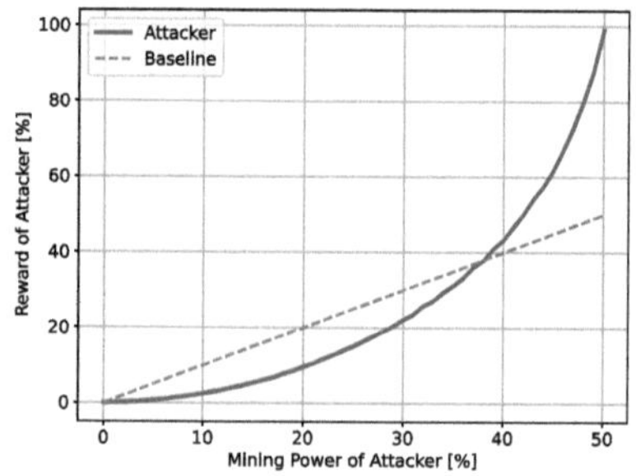


**Fig. 5.** Fruitchain: longest chain rule; block reward = 9× fruit reward.

## 4.5 Fruitchain

Our simulation model incorporated the Fruitchain's unique structure of fruits and blocks. We set up the simulation to reflect the two-tier mining process, where miners simultaneously mine fruits and blocks. The simulator configuration contains parameters where the selfish node's mining power was gradually increased and a constant fruit-to-block mining ratio, which is used for weighted random selection, whether fruit or block is being mined. Based on the ratio, the reward for the fruit is the block mining probability to the fruit mining probability. We experimented with different reward ratios for blocks and fruits. In particular, we used 50% and 9.09%[4] for block rewards.

In our experiments, we explored various scenarios. For the single attacker, we found that the profitability threshold is around 38–39%, which is an improvement

---

[4] 9.09 is a consequence of the ratio 10:1 mentioned above (i.e., 1 / 11 * 10).

over the Nakamoto consensus. This result was achieved in a configuration where the longest chain rule was used, see Fig. 5.

**Gamma Parameter.** The parameter $\gamma$ is impactless, even when we choose $\gamma = 0$ or $\gamma = 1$, the variation is only around 1% between the results. This is caused by the fact that the override action of selfish mining very rarely happens due to the fine-grained computation of branch difficulty that also considers fruits.[5]

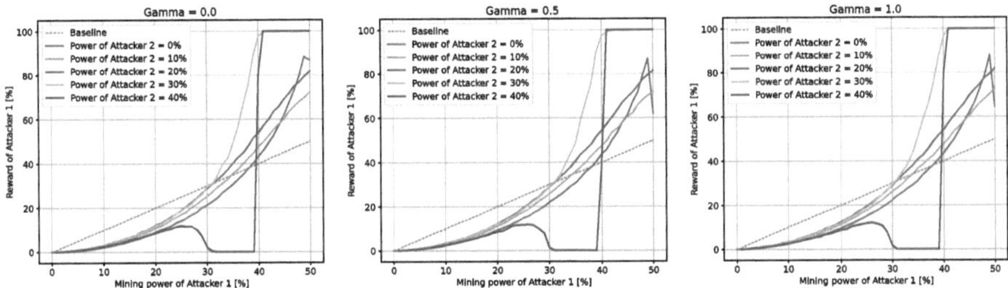

**Fig. 6.** Fruitchain, longest-chain rule. Relative revenue of Attacker 1 versus its mining power $\alpha_1$ under $\gamma \in \{0, 0.5, 1\}$. Each line fixes the other attacker mining power $\alpha_2 \in \{0, 10, 20, 30, 40\}\%$. The profitability threshold is the intersection with the diagonal baseline $R(\alpha_1) = \alpha_1$. As $\alpha_2$ increases, this threshold decreases, lowering Attacker 1's threshold.

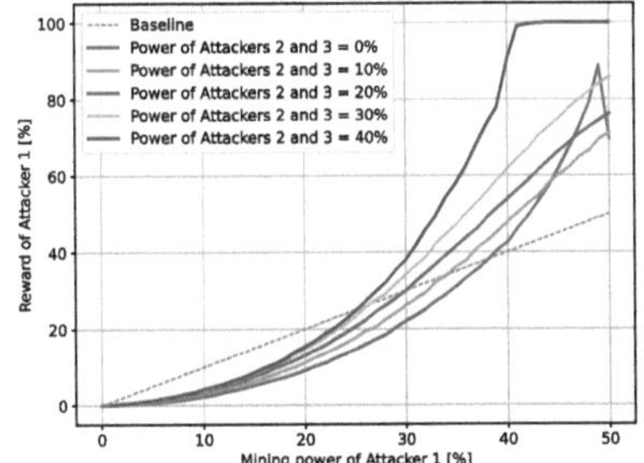

(a) Longest chain rule with 3 attackers.

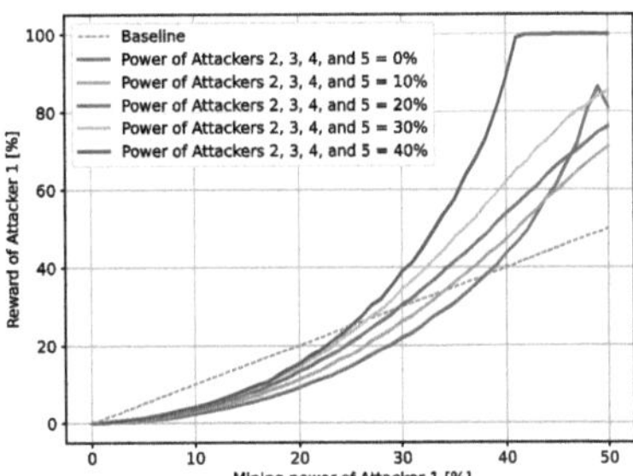

(b) Longest chain rule with 5 attackers.

**Fig. 7.** Analysis of selfish mining on Fruitchain's consensus with multiple attackers. Shows the rewards of the first attacker based on their mining power relative to the other attackers with a longest chain rule for scenarios with 3 and 5 total attackers.

Our experiments with Fruitchain revealed interesting dynamics, especially when considering multiple attackers. In Fig. 6, for all investigated $\gamma \in \{0, 0.5, 1\}$,

---

[5] We note that this phenomenon also occurs in the case of Strongchain.

increasing the other attacker's power causes decrease of Attacker 1' relative revenue $R_1$, but on the other hand, it decreases his profitability threshold. In particular, when Attacker 2 has 0% (in red), Attacker 1 threshold is 38–39% (i.e., as in a single attacker scenario – see Fig. 5). At 20% for Attacker 2, the profitability threshold decreases by several percentage points, and at 40%, Attacker 1 becomes profitable at yet lower $\alpha_1$ until the point where a dominant rival can suppress his revenue (the right-hand drop). In sum, the Attacker 1's threshold depends inversely proportional to the Attacker's 2 mining power until Attacker's 2 thresholds is reached – meaning that Attacker 2 loses more rewards when its mining power grows since he adopts the honest chain or Attacker's 1 chain more often (while he does not know about the bigger Attacker's 1 secret chains).

***Three and Five Attackers.*** This experiment considered multiple attackers, and we fixed the $\gamma$ parameter to 0.5 since it has no impact on the results. The results are depicted in Fig. 7a and Fig. 7b, where we experimented with varying mining power of Attacker 1, while we fixed the mining power of other attackers at $\alpha_i \in \{10, 20, 30, 40\}\%$ We can see here the same pattern as in the previous experiment (see Fig. 6).

The key observation is that a higher number of attackers benefit from the decreased profitability threshold due to multiple attackers. However, increased relative revenue of all attackers holds only until the saturation point is reached when increasing $\alpha$ – i.e., the sum of all relative profits cannot exceed 100% / not all attackers will benefit from the attack.

With Fruitchain the simulation ends when one of the participants' blockchains reaches the target height. Figure 5 shows the result of a single attacker while utilizing the longest chain rule. We also experimented with block reward reduction from 50% to 9.09% (i.e., fruits are more valuable) which made the gap even larger. This reduction also caused the point of highest negative difference to shift from baseline to higher mining power.

## 5   Discussion

The results of our empirical evaluation highlight the varying degrees of resilience that different consensus mechanisms offer against selfish mining. Both Strongchain and Fruitchain provide a measurable improvement over the standard Nakamoto consensus, particularly in a single attacker scenario.

Strongchain consistently demonstrates the highest resistance, with a single-attacker threshold of 46% and a two-attacker threshold of 32%. The core mechanism of the protocol, which incorporates weak headers in chain weight calculations, appears to be highly effective in mitigating the primary selfish mining strategy of orphaning honest blocks. Fruitchain also shows a significant improvement, raising the single attacker threshold to 38%. Our findings indicate that defense capability of Fruitchain and Strongchain does not rely on network assumptions, as the $\gamma$ parameter has little effect. A key finding across all protocols is that as the number of independent attackers increases, the individual mining power required for each to be profitable decreases. However, the inclusive principles in Strongchain and Fruitchain ensure that the profitability thresholds remain considerably higher than in Nakamoto consensus, making collusion a more difficult and less profitable endeavor.

## 6   Conclusion

In this work, we address the persistent threat of selfish mining with a particular focus on the under-researched area of multi-attacker scenarios. We introduced a versatile and extensible simulation framework to conduct a rigorous comparative evaluation of selfish mining resistance across multiple Proof-of-Work consensus protocols. By modeling Nakamoto consensus, Fruitchain, and Strongchain, we were able to validate existing findings and, more importantly, provide novel findings.

Our key findings confirm that both Strongchain and Fruitchain offer substantial improvements over Nakamoto consensus. Strongchain is shown to be the most resilient, increasing the two-attacker profitability threshold from 21% to 32% per attacker. Fruitchain also provided significant defense, raising the single-attacker threshold to 38% and demonstrating that this security is largely independent of network connectivity advantages. Our work provides the empirical multi-attacker thresholds for these advanced protocols, filling a gap in the literature.

This study is subject to certain limitations. The simulation framework abstracts network dynamics into the $\gamma$ parameter, a simplification that facilitates comparison but overlooks the demonstrated impact of block propagation time and network topology on attack profitability [5]. Furthermore, the model does not include transaction fees or accidental forks. While these abstractions are standard and facilitate clear comparison, they represent areas for more detailed future analysis. The nature of our framework paves the way for future research. It can be extended to include other consensus protocols (e.g., Subchain [15]), or different consensual parameters to tweak their security even more, or other attack strategies, such as stubborn mining. A deeper investigation into the economic incentives created by different reward structures, such as fruit and block rewards in Fruitchain, would also be a valuable contribution. We would also like to focus on selfish mining attacks executed on DAG-based protocols (e.g. PHANTOM/GOSTDAG [17], Prism [1]) while assuming transaction fees, which have already been proven to be vulnerable to other incentive-based attacks [13,14].

**Acknowledgment.** This work was supported by the internal Brno University of Technology project FIT-S-23-8151 and funded by the EU NextGenerationEU through the Recovery and Resilience Plan for Slovakia under project No. 09I05-03-V02-00057. The work was also supported by the Chips JU and its members, the DistriMuSe project, Grant Agreement No. 101139769.

# References


1. Bagaria, V., Kannan, S., Tse, D., Fanti, G., Viswanath, P.: Prism: Deconstructing the blockchain to approach physical limits. In: Proceedings of the 2019 ACM SIGSAC Conference on Computer and Communications Security, pp. 585–602. CCS '19, Association for Computing Machinery, New York, NY, USA (2019). https://doi.org/10.1145/3319535.3363213
2. Eyal, I., Gencer, A.E., Sirer, E.G., Van Renesse, R.: {Bitcoin-NG}: A scalable blockchain protocol. In: 13th USENIX symposium on networked systems design and implementation (NSDI 16), pp. 45–59 (2016)
3. Eyal, I., Sirer, E.G.: Majority is not enough: Bitcoin mining is vulnerable. In: Christin, N., Safavi-Naini, R. (eds.) Financial Cryptography and Data Security - 18th International Conference, FC 2014, Christ Church, Barbados, March 3–7, 2014, Revised Selected Papers. Lecture Notes in Computer Science, vol. 8437, pp. 436–454. Springer (2014). https://doi.org/10.1007/978-3-662-45472-5_28
4. Gal, J., Szabo, M.B.: Majority is not needed: a counterstrategy to selfish mining (2023). https://arxiv.org/abs/2304.06313
5. Gervais, A., Karame, G.O., Wüst, K., Glykantzis, V., Ritzdorf, H., Capkun, S.: On the security and performance of proof of work blockchains. In: Proceedings of the 2016 ACM SIGSAC Conference on Computer and Communications Security, pp. 3–16. CCS '16, Association for Computing Machinery, New York, NY, USA (2016). https://doi.org/10.1145/2976749.2978341
6. Kwon, Y., Kim, D., Son, Y., Vasserman, E., Kim, Y.: Be selfish and avoid dilemmas: Fork after withholding (faw) attacks on bitcoin. In: Proceedings of the 2017 ACM SIGSAC Conference on Computer and Communications Security, pp. 195–209. CCS '17, Association for Computing Machinery, New York, NY, USA (2017). https://doi.org/10.1145/3133956.3134019
7. Lewenberg, Y., Sompolinsky, Y., Zohar, A.: Inclusive block chain protocols. In: Böhme, R., Okamoto, T. (eds.) Financial Cryptography and Data Security, pp. 528–547. Springer, Berlin Heidelberg, Berlin, Heidelberg (2015)
8. Marmolejo-Cossío, F.J., Brigham, E., Sela, B., Katz, J.: Competing (semi-)selfish miners in bitcoin. In: Proceedings of the 1st ACM Conference on Advances in Financial Technologies, pp. 89–109. AFT '19, Association for Computing Machinery, New York, NY, USA (2019). https://doi.org/10.1145/3318041.3355471
9. Nakamoto, S.: Bitcoin: A peer-to-peer electronic cash system. online (5 2009). http://www.bitcoin.org/bitcoin.pdf. Accessed 10 Nov 2022
10. Nayak, K., Kumar, S., Miller, A., Shi, E.: Stubborn mining: generalizing selfish mining and combining with an eclipse attack. In: IEEE European Symposium on Security and Privacy, EuroS&P 2016, Saarbrücken, Germany, March 21–24, 2016, pp. 305–320. IEEE (2016). https://doi.org/10.1109/EuroSP.2016.32
11. Pass, R., Shi, E.: Fruitchains: a fair blockchain. In: Schiller, E.M., Schwarzmann, A.A. (eds.) Proceedings of the ACM Symposium on Principles of Distributed Computing, PODC 2017, Washington, DC, USA, July 25–27, 2017, pp. 315–324. ACM (2017). https://doi.org/10.1145/3087801.3087809
12. Perešíni, M., Benčić, F.M., Hrubý, M., Malinka, K., Homoliak, I.: Incentive attacks on dag-based blockchains with random transaction selection. In: 2023 IEEE International Conference on Blockchain (Blockchain), pp. 1–8 (2023). https://doi.org/10.1109/Blockchain60715.2023.00011
13. Perešíni, M., Benčić, F.M., Malinka, K., Homoliak, I.: Dag-oriented protocols phantom and ghostdag under incentive attack via transaction selection strategy (2021). https://arxiv.org/abs/2109.01102

14. Perešíni, M., Hladký, T., Malinka, K., Homoliak, I.: Dag-sword: A simulator of large-scale network topologies for dag-oriented proof-of-work blockchains. In: 2024 57th Hawaii International Conference on System Sciences (HICSS), pp. 5960–5969 (2024). https://doi.org/10.24251/HICSS.2024.716

15. Rizun, P.R.: Subchains: A technique to scale bitcoin and improve the user experience. Ledger **1**(1), 38–52 (2016). https://ledgerjournal.org/ojs/index.php/ledger/article/view/40

16. Sapirshtein, A., Sompolinsky, Y., Zohar, A.: Optimal selfish mining strategies in bitcoin. In: Grossklags, J., Preneel, B. (eds.) Financial Cryptography and Data Security - 20th International Conference, FC 2016, Christ Church, Barbados, February 22–26, 2016, Revised Selected Papers. Lecture Notes in Computer Science, vol. 9603, pp. 515–532. Springer (2016). https://doi.org/10.1007/978-3-662-54970-4_30

17. Sompolinsky, Y., Wyborski, S., Zohar, A.: Phantom ghostdag: a scalable generalization of nakamoto consensus: September 2, 2021. In: Proceedings of the 3rd ACM Conference on Advances in Financial Technologies, pp. 57–70. AFT '21, Association for Computing Machinery, New York, NY, USA (2021). https://doi.org/10.1145/3479722.3480990

18. Szalachowski, P., Reijsbergen, D., Homoliak, I., Sun, S.: Strongchain: Transparent and collaborative proof-of-work consensus. In: Heninger, N., Traynor, P. (eds.) 28th USENIX Security Symposium, USENIX Security 2019, Santa Clara, CA, USA, August 14–16, 2019, pp. 819–836. USENIX Association (2019). https://www.usenix.org/conference/usenixsecurity19/presentation/szalachowski

19. Zhang, M., Li, Y., Li, J., Kong, C., Deng, X.: Insightful mining equilibria. In: Hansen, K.A., Liu, T.X., Malekian, A. (eds.) Web and Internet Economics, pp. 21–37. Springer International Publishing, Cham (2022)

20. Zhang, R., Preneel, B.: Lay down the common metrics: evaluating proof-of-work consensus protocols' security. In: 2019 IEEE Symposium on Security and Privacy, SP 2019, San Francisco, CA, USA, May 19–23, 2019, pp. 175–192. IEEE (2019). https://doi.org/10.1109/SP.2019.00086

21. Zhang, S., Zhang, K., Kemme, B.: Analysing the benefit of selfish mining with multiple players. In: IEEE International Conference on Blockchain, Blockchain 2020, Rhodes, Greece, November 2–6, 2020, pp. 36–44. IEEE (2020). https://doi.org/10.1109/Blockchain50366.2020.00013

22. Zhang, S., Zhang, K., Kemme, B.: A simulation-based analysis of multiplayer selfish mining. In: IEEE International Conference on Blockchain and Cryptocurrency, ICBC 2020, Toronto, ON, Canada, May 2–6, 2020, pp. 1–5. IEEE (2020). https://doi.org/10.1109/ICBC48266.2020.9169446

# EVMpress: Precise Type Inference
# for Next-Generation EVM Decompilation


Jung Hyun Kim[1], Soomin Kim[2], Jaeseung Choi[3],
and Sang Kil Cha[1(✉)]

[1] KAIST, Daejeon, South Korea
{jidoc01,sangkilc}@kaist.ac.kr
[2] KAIST CSRC, Daejeon, South Korea
soomink@kaist.ac.kr
[3] Sogang University, Seoul, South Korea
jschoi22@sogang.ac.kr



**Abstract.** Analyzing EVM bytecode is imperative because nearly 45%
of smart contracts on the Ethereum blockchain lack publicly available
source code. While type inference is pivotal for EVM bytecode analysis,
it remains unsolved because (1) current tools can only handle a subset of
Solidity expressions, and (2) they often produce imprecise results due to
unsound heuristics they employ. Furthermore, there is no comprehensive
dataset with precise ground truth for evaluating EVM type inference,
which hinders the development of new tools and the evaluation of existing
ones. Thus, we propose EVMpress, a novel bytecode analysis framework
that enables accurate type inference for Solidity expressions found in
EVM bytecode. We evaluate EVMpress on the largest-to-date dataset
of EVM bytecode containing more than 370K real-world contracts with
precise ground truth for every function and variable. Our evaluation
results show that EVMpress significantly outperforms existing state-of-
the-art tools in terms of its coverage and accuracy. We publicize our
dataset as well as our implementation of EVMpress to facilitate future
research in EVM bytecode analysis.


## 1 Introduction

Ethereum Virtual Machine (EVM) bytecode analysis is essential for understanding the behavior of smart contracts. Developers deploy smart contracts to the
Ethereum blockchain as EVM bytecode, typically *without* including their source
code. Indeed, nearly 45% of the smart contracts in use do *not* disclose their
source code [6], highlighting the need for EVM bytecode analysis.

Type inference is a crucial step in EVM bytecode analysis as it provides essential information about the types of Solidity expressions, such as functions and
variables. Faulty type inference can yield misleading decompiled code [28,31],
making it much harder to understand smart contracts. Also, a recent study [11]
indicates that type inference affects the readability of decompiled code.

Unfortunately, existing EVM type inference techniques remain *immature* in terms of coverage and accuracy.

First, current EVM type inference techniques can only cover a subset of Solidity expressions. For example, `DeepInfer` [32] can only infer types of public functions, while `VarLifter` [22] can only infer types of global variables. To our knowledge, there is no existing technique that can infer types of private functions.

Second, existing type inference techniques suffer from low accuracy due to the unsound heuristics they employ. For instance, `VarLifter` [22] heuristically considers a single path for each function to infer global variable types, leading to an underestimated result. `Gigahorse` [14] employs several heuristics to identify functions that do not follow the standard function call-return pattern, but these heuristics are often imprecise, leading to both false positives and negatives. Due to the imprecise function identification, `Gigahorse` often fails to recover types of critical functions as our study will show.

To make matters worse, there is no high-quality dataset with precise ground truth for EVM type inference, making rigorous evaluation difficult. Indeed, our preliminary study reveals that approximately 31% of the contracts in the dataset of `VarLifter` [22] are duplicates. Additionally, existing datasets do not provide precise ground truth for private functions and global variables. These issues overestimate the accuracy of existing EVM type inference techniques (see §2.2).

In this paper, we propose `EVMpress` to address all the aforementioned limitations of existing EVM type inference techniques in a unified framework. Specifically, we present a novel design of EVM bytecode analysis framework that enables precise type inference for various kinds of Solidity expressions including public functions, private functions, and global variables. Furthermore, we develop a large-scale dataset with precise ground truth to evaluate our system rigorously.

The key innovation of `EVMpress` is its holistic design that integrates function identification, Control Flow Graph (CFG) recovery, and type inference into a unified static analysis framework. Our design allows us to develop *path-based function identification*, a novel function identification technique that can accurately identify all kinds of functions, including public functions, private functions, as well as intrinsic functions generated by the Solidity compiler. The key insight of path-based function identification is that we can leverage a fundamental characteristic of functions in EVM bytecode: a function always pushes a return address before its entry and pops it after its return, regardless of the path it takes within the function. Therefore, we can always pinpoint a function entry point within a *single* execution path assuming there is a function call in the path. This approach allows us to accurately identify various types of functions, thereby significantly improving the accuracy of type inference.

Additionally, we construct a large-scale dataset with precise ground truth, consisting of 370,745 unique contracts, in order to rigorously evaluate our system. We eliminate duplicate contracts by normalizing EVM bytecode to remove references that can change during compilation and deployment. We also thoroughly build ground truth for function entry points, function types, and variable types with compiler-generated information, such as abstract syntax tree (AST).

**Table 1.** Comparison of the state-of-the-art EVM bytecode analysis tools.

| | Open? | Identification | | | Type Inference | | |
|---|---|---|---|---|---|---|---|
| | | Pub. Func. | Priv. Func. | Glob. Var. | Pub. Func. | Priv. Func. | Glob. Var. |
| Neural-FEBI [15] | ✓[†] | ✓ | ✓ | ✗ | ✗ | ✗ | ✗ |
| Gigahorse [13,14,19] | ✓ | ✓ | ✓ | ✗ | ✓[‡] | ✗ | ✗ |
| SigRec [7] | ✗ | ✓ | ✗ | ✗ | ✓[‡] | ✗ | ✗ |
| DeepInfer [32] | ✓[†] | ✓ | ✗ | ✗ | ✓ | ✗ | ✗ |
| VarLifter [22] | ✓ | ✓ | ✗ | ✓ | ✗ | ✗ | ✓ |
| EVMpress | ✓ | ✓ | ✓ | ✓ | ✓ | ✓ | ✓ |

† ✓ means *partially* available. Neural-FEBI publicize their code and dataset, but not their model parameters. DeepInfer lacks their preprocessing module in their code release.

‡ ✓ indicates *partial* support, e.g., Gigahorse does not infer return types of public functions.

Our evaluation shows that EVMpress can infer types of Solidity expressions from EVM binaries in an accurate and efficient manner. Specifically, we demonstrate that EVMpress can recover the types of previously unhandled private functions with over 96% accuracy. Notably, EVMpress finds 30% more private functions than Gigahorse, while showing 2× more accurate global variable type inference results than VarLifter. Additionally, EVMpress achieves 1.6× faster CFG recovery performance on average than existing techniques, and up to 4× faster on large bytecodes. Our main contributions are:

- We propose path-based function identification technique that enables accurate identification of functions in EVM bytecode.
- We design and implement EVMpress, a unified EVM bytecode analysis framework that incorporates path-based function identification technique.
- We present the largest-to-date dataset of EVM bytecode with precise ground truth for function and variable types, consisting of 370,745 unique contracts.
- We publicize our tool along with our dataset to support open science[1].

## 2   Motivation

In this section, we first discuss the limitation and scope of the current state-of-the-art EVM bytecode analysis tools. We then review the limitation of existing datasets for evaluating EVM bytecode analysis tools, and introduce our new dataset. Finally, we present a preliminary study that we performed with a real-world contract in our dataset to motivate our work.

---

[1] https://github.com/SoftSec-KAIST/EVMpress.

**Table 2.** Comparison of the existing datasets.

| | Open? | # Orig. | # Dedup. | Ground Truth | | | | | |
| --- | --- | --- | --- | --- | --- | --- | --- | --- | --- |
| | | | | Identification | | | Type Inference | | |
| | | | | Pub. Func. | Priv. Func. | Glob. Var. | Pub. Func. | Priv. Func. | Glob. Var. |
| Neural-FEBI [15] | ✓ | 39.0K | 22.5K | ✓ | ✓ | ✗ | ✗ | ✗ | ✗ |
| Gigahorse$_G$ [13] | ✗ | 91.8K | – | – | – | – | – | – | – |
| Gigahorse$_E$ [14] | ✗ | 5.0K | – | – | – | – | – | – | – |
| Gigahorse$_S$ [19] | ✗ | 8.0K | – | – | – | – | – | – | – |
| SigRec [7] | ✗ | 119.1K | – | – | – | – | – | – | – |
| DeepInfer [32] | ✓ | 47.8K | 47.8K | ✓ | ✗ | ✗ | ✓ | ✗ | ✗ |
| VarLifter [21] | ✓ | 34.8K | 23.9K | ✗ | ✗ | ✓ | ✗ | ✗ | ✓ |
| EVMpress | ✓ | 370.7K | 370.7K | ✓ | ✓ | ✓ | ✓ | ✓ | ✓ |

## 2.1 Previous Tools

We studied five state-of-the-art EVM bytecode analysis tools: NeuralFEBI [15], SigRec [7], DeepInfer [32], Gigahorse [13,14,19][2], and VarLifter [21]. Table 1 compares these tools in terms of their features and capabilities. The second column indicates whether tool is publicly available. Note that Neural-FEBI and DeepInfer only partially publicize their source code or model. Columns three to five in Table 1 indicate which Solidity expressions are identified by each tool. Columns six to eight show whether each tool infers the types of the identified expressions. For functions, we distinguish between public and private functions. In EVM, public functions are those declared with the external or public keyword in Solidity. Private functions include those marked as internal or private, as well as compiler-generated intrinsic functions. For variables, we only consider global variables, which are stored in the *storage* area [29], and this is because none of the current tools can recover the types of local variables and extracting ground truth for local variables is challenging.

It is worth noting that none of the tools listed in Table 1 comprehensively recovers all kinds of expression types. Neural-FEBI and Gigahorse are the only tools that identify the locations of private functions, although they do not recover their types. While most tools support recovering parameter types of public functions, only DeepInfer can recover their return types. Rather surprisingly, none of the existing tools can infer the types of private functions, which can significantly limit their usability. We present the first EVM bytecode analysis framework that recovers types for all Solidity expressions listed in the table.

## 2.2 Previous Datasets

Table 2 summarizes the existing datasets used by the EVM bytecode analyzers listed in Table 1. Note that we distinguish the three datasets used by Gigahorse

---

[2] Although Gigahorse [13], Elipmoc [14], and Shrnkr [19] are tools presented in three different papers, they are continuous work on the same framework and share the same codebase. Therefore, we refer to them as Gigahorse for the sake of simplicity.

according to the papers in which they were introduced with the suffixes $G$, $E$, and $S$. The second column specifies dataset availability, revealing that among the seven previously proposed datasets, only three are publicly accessible. The third column presents the original number of contracts reported in the paper. Among public datasets, `DeepInfer`'s was the largest with 47.8K contracts. The fourth column shows the number of deduplicated contracts in each dataset obtained by our deduplication method described in §2.3. Notably, over 30% of the contracts in both the `Neural-FEBI` and `VarLifter` datasets were duplicates, which could substantially distort evaluation results. The rest of the columns summarize what kind of ground truth information is provided in each dataset. We note that none of the publicly available datasets provides comprehensive ground truth. All these limitations summarized in the table motivate us to build a new dataset for EVM bytecode analysis that is (1) publicly available, (2) deduplicated, and (3) contains comprehensive ground truth for every function and variable type.

### 2.3  Our Dataset

We introduce the largest-to-date dataset for EVM bytecode analysis that addresses the aforementioned limitations, following the steps outlined below.

**Contract Collection.** We collected all Ethereum bytecode deployed up to January 2025, which includes 68.7M contracts. We then filtered out self-destructed contracts and contracts with no incoming transactions to retain a meaningful dataset. Next, we selected the contracts whose Solidity source code is available on Etherscan [3] and can be compiled with the Solidity compiler version 0.4.11 or higher. This was because our ground truth generation process requires compiler versions higher than or equal to 0.4.11, the first release that introduces the `--standard-json` option for emitting Abstract Syntax Trees (ASTs). Lastly, we deduplicated the contracts that have identical EVM bytecode. Consequently, we were able to obtain 610K contracts along with their source code.

**Contract Compilation.** Next, we compiled the collected source code from the previous step using the same compiler version and compiler options listed in Etherscan to reproduce the same bytecode deployed on the Ethereum blockchain while obtaining extra data to construct the ground truth. To obtain the extra data, we used the `--standard-json` option. For those compiled with the `--via-ir` option, which does not emit the compiled-generated intrinsic functions into the ASTs, we patched the Solidity compiler to emit them, and later used them to generate the ground truth. This step produces the EVM bytecode, assembly code, and ASTs for each contract.

**Normalization and Deduplication.** Deduplicating contracts by bytecode alone is insufficient, as some differ only in addresses or auxiliary data, which are not relevant to the core execution logic of the contract. Thus, we further

```
1   contract GovernanceRouter {
2     function transferGovernor(uint32 _domain, ...) public {
3       // ...
4       formatTransferGovernor(_domain, ...);
5     }
6     function formatTransferGovernor(uint32 _domain, ...) private {
7       clone(mustBeTransferGovernor(ref(_domain, ...)));
8     }
9     function ref(...) private returns(...) {
10      if (...) { ... }
11      else { ... }
12    }
13    function mustBeTransferGovernor(...) private returns (...) {
14      ...
15    }
16    function clone(...) private returns (...) {
17      ...
18    }
19  }
```

**Fig. 1.** Simplified source code of the `GovernanceRouter` contract, which is located at address `0xfbea6d67ddd90e1f726c2622c6c42b016fdad5a7`.

normalized the contracts in two steps. First, we removed auxiliary data from the bytecode. Next, we found the locations of address references in the bytecode, and zeroed them out to ignore the differences in addresses. As a result, 48.1% of contracts were duplicates, leaving 370K unique contracts.

**Ground Truth Generation.** Finally, we generated the ground truth for each contract using the EVM bytecode, assembly code, and ASTs generated by the compiler. Our ground truth includes (1) function addresses and their signatures, and (2) global variable locations and their types. To locate functions in the EVM bytecode, we analyzed the assembly code, which shows annotated assembly instructions with source code line information. Once we identified the entry point of each function, we checked the corresponding byte offset in the bytecode to obtain the function address. We then extracted from the corresponding AST the function signature, which includes the parameter types as well as the return type. We similarly identified the locations and types of global variables by analyzing the ASTs and the EVM bytecode based on the official documentation of the Solidity compiler [30]. Consequently, we obtained 370,745 unique contracts with the ground truth information for every function and global variable type. To the best of our knowledge, this is the *largest* dataset for EVM bytecode analysis with comprehensive ground truth information.

### 2.4   Motivating Example

Can the new dataset provide new insights into the limitations of existing EVM bytecode analysis tools? As we will show in the evaluation section §4, our dataset reveals that the state-of-the-art EVM bytecode analysis tools exhibit significantly low accuracy in identifying functions. For example, we found that the F1 score of `Gigahorse` in terms of detecting private function is only 71.0%.

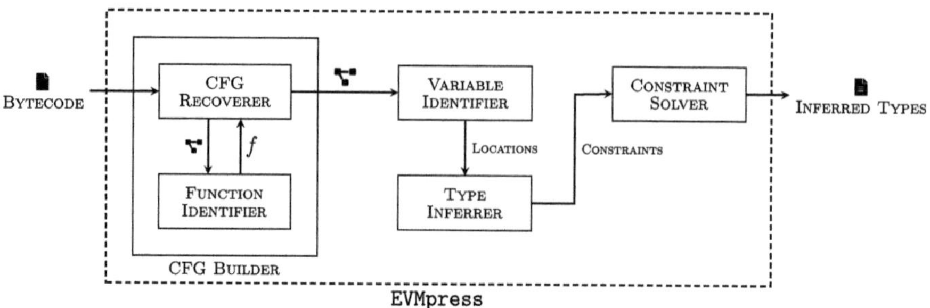


**Fig. 2.** EVMpress architecture.

Figure 1 illustrates one such example, named the GovernanceRouter contract. It includes the formatTransferGovernor function (Line 6), which is called by the transferGovernor function (Line 4). In Line 7, the format-TransferGovernor function calls three private functions in sequence: ref, must-BeTransferGovernor, and clone. Unfortunately, Gigahorse fails to identify the clone function despite the simple structure of the formatTransferGovernor function—no loops nor conditionals. The primary reason for this failure is that Gigahorse requires a function entry point to be reachable from multiple call sites, which is not the case for clone. We note that Gigahorse is prone to such errors because it relies on declarative patterns found in the EVM bytecode to identify functions. This limitation motivates us to develop a unified static analysis framework for EVM bytecode that can procedurally identify functions without relying on such patterns.

## 3   Design

This section presents the design of EVMpress. We first present the overall architecture of EVMpress. We then describe the details of path-based function identification. Finally, we conclude this section by illustrating the overall workflow of EVMpress using a running example.

### 3.1   Overview

Figure 2 shows the overall architecture of EVMpress, which takes in an EVM binary as input, and outputs the inferred types of functions and variables. At a high level, EVMpress runs in four main steps. CFG BUILDER first identifies functions and reconstructs the Control-Flow Graph (CFG) of each function from the given EVM bytecode. Subsequently, VARIABLE IDENTIFIER identifies variables used by each function and returns the locations of the identified variables to TYPE INFERRER. A variable here is any recoverable high-level construct—function parameters, return values, local variables, and global variables. VARIABLE IDENTIFIER identifies variables used by each function and returns their locations to TYPE INFERRER. TYPE INFERRER then collects type constraints for each identified variable and returns them to CONSTRAINT SOLVER. Finally, CONSTRAINT SOLVER solves the constraints and infers the types of each variable and outputs the results.

**CFG Builder** reconstructs the intra-procedural CFG for each function from the given EVM bytecode. It first recursively traverses the control flow of the EVM bytecode starting from the entry point of the contract. Every time a jump instruction is encountered, CFG BUILDER consults with FUNCTION IDENTIFIER to check if the jump instruction is a function call. This is where our path-based function identification comes into play, which enables robust function identification from highly optimized EVM bytecode (§3.2).

**Variable Identifier** analyzes every data access in the CFG and identifies locations of variables used by each function. It returns the location information of identified variables, such as calldata, memory, and storage as well as their addresses or offsets, to TYPE INFERRER.

**Type Inferrer** collects type hints for each identified variable to generate type constraints. Specifically, we analyze variable access patterns by traversing the CFG as in the classic approaches [7, 20]. For instance, when a variable is accessed by applying bit-masking operations, we can infer the bit-width of the variable. Similarly, when a variable is used as a conditional, we can infer that the variable is a boolean type.

**Constraint Solver** solves the type constraints generated by TYPE INFERRER and infers the types of each variable. We use the traditional (naive) bottom-up evaluation to saturate the constraint set [5].

## 3.2   Path-based Function Identification

The complexity of EVM bytecode optimization makes it challenging to identify function entry points, especially for private functions. Recall from §2.4 that previous approaches [13, 14, 19] suffer from both false positives and false negatives when identifying function entry points as they rely on declarative heuristics that are not robust against highly optimized EVM bytecode.

Our technique, on the other hand, leverages the invariant of a function call, which is that there must be a function entry point in any execution path between a return address definition and the corresponding return instruction. Suppose $f$ and $g$ are two functions in a contract where $f$ is a caller of $g$, and $g$ is a complex function containing many execution paths. Let $callsite(f, g)$ be the program point in $f$ where $g$ is called. When $g$ returns to $f$ using a jump instruction, the function entry point of $g$ is always within an execution path between the $callsite(f, g)$ and the return instruction of $g$, no matter which path in $g$ is taken. Therefore, we can simply investigate a single path, instead of all paths, to efficiently identify the function entry point of $g$. Depending on the complexity of $g$, our algorithm can significantly reduce the number of paths to be traversed, thus improving the efficiency of function identification.

At a high level, path-based function identification runs on every jump instruction encountered while recovering the CFGs (CFG BUILDER in Fig. 2).

1. For every jump instruction encountered, we consider it as a potential return instruction $r$ if there is no immediate jump target on top of the stack.
2. For each potential return instruction, we follow the use-def chain to find the definitions of the jump target address.
3. We then extract a random path from the definition to $r$ and traverse it, excluding the first basic block, to identify whether there is a block that can be a function entry point. Specifically, a basic block in the path is a function entry point if it does not satisfy any of the following conditions:
   **C1.** The basic block has been identified as a return point of a function.
   **C2.** The basic block is included in the CFG of another function.
   **C3.** The basic block is a fall-through of another basic block.

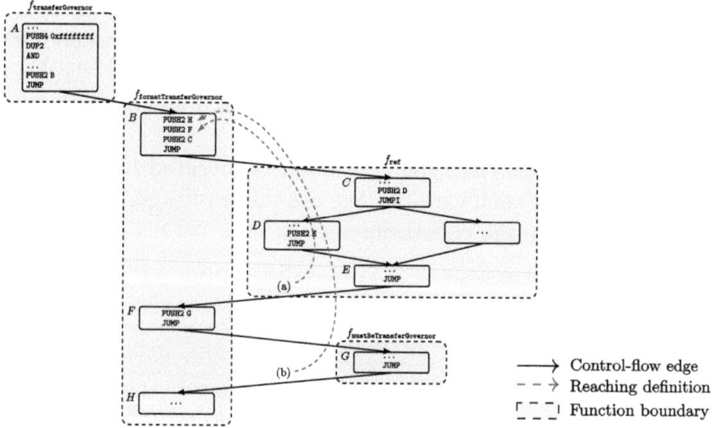


**Fig. 3.** CFG of the `GovernanceRouter` contract shown in Fig. 1.

### 3.3   Running Example

To illustrate how `EVMpress` works, let us consider the same example contract in Fig. 1. We present the corresponding CFG in Fig. 3. We denote each function in Fig. 1 with $f_{name}$, where **name** is the name of the function. Note that we exclude the last function call (of `clone`) to simplify the illustration.

CFG BUILDER starts to analyze the given EVM bytecode. The very first step is to identify public functions by analyzing the function dispatcher located at the beginning of the EVM bytecode. In this example, CFG BUILDER identifies the public function `transferGovernor` defined in Line 2 of Fig. 1. It then starts to disassemble the function to recover the basic block $A$ of the CFG in Fig. 3. When it encounters the jump instruction in $A$, it checks whether there is an *immediate* jump target, which comes from the same basic block, on top of the stack. Since there is a PUSH instruction right before the jump that pushes the address of $B$ onto the stack, we know that this is *not* a returning edge. Therefore, we continue to disassemble the basic block $B$ and perform the same analysis until we reach the basic block $E$, which does not include a push instruction before its jump instruction. At this point, CFG BUILDER follows the use-def chain (the red dotted arrow) of the jump target (a) to know that it jumps to the basic block $F$. Since $E$ does not have an immediate jump target, the jump instruction in $E$ is considered as a potential return instruction.

Recall from §3.2 that we now select a random path from the definition site $B$ to $E$ and traverse it to identify whether there is a function entry point. Note that we have not yet identified any function except transferGovernor, which is a public function. Suppose we selected the path $B \rightarrow C \rightarrow D \rightarrow E$. We then traverse the path, excluding $B$, to check whether there is a basic block that can be a function entry point. The first block to consider is $C$, which does not satisfy any of the conditions listed in §3.2. Therefore, we identify $C$ as a function entry point (of the function ref) and mark all reachable basic blocks from $C$ to $E$ as the CFG of the function.

Similarly, we can detect $f_{\texttt{mustBeTransferGovernor}}$ when we reach the basic block $G$. In this case, the reaching definition of the jump target (b) is at the basic block $B$ because $B$ pushes the address of $H$ onto the stack even before it makes a call to $f_{\texttt{ref}}$. This is so-called Continuation Passing Style (CPS) function call [14], often found in EVM bytecode. Path-based function identification gracefully handles this case by selecting and analyzing a single path from $B$ to $G$. Suppose we selected the path $B \rightarrow C \rightarrow D \rightarrow E \rightarrow F \rightarrow G$. Since $C$, $D$, and $E$ satisfies condition C2, and $F$ satisfies condition C1, we skip them and identify $G$ as a function entry point. We follow the same procedure to identify all the CFGs in the bytecode, and proceeds to the next step, which is variable identification.

VARIABLE IDENTIFIER analyzes the CFGs of the identified functions and identifies variables used by each function. For instance, we can easily detect function parameters by analyzing the stack before making a function call, as our path-based function identification can precisely identify which jump instruction is a function call. In this running example, VARIABLE IDENTIFIER detects that the function transferGovernor passes the first parameter _domain to formatTransferGovernor. Thus, it returns the corresponding stack offset of the parameter to TYPE INFERRER.

Finally, TYPE INFERRER collects type hints for the given parameter _domain of transferGovernor. Specifically, it collects two type hints about the parameter. First, it identifies that transferGovernor computes the logical-and of _domain and a constant value, 0xffffffff $(= 2^{32} - 1)$, which indicates that _domain is a 32-bit number. Furthermore, it realizes that the computed value is never sign-extended with a SIGNEXTEND instruction, which indicates that _domain is an unsigned integer. These two type hints are then passed to CON-

STRAINT SOLVER, which will conclude that _domain is a 32-bit unsigned integer, i.e., uint32.

## 3.4  Implementation

We implemented EVMpress with 10K SLoC of F#. We used B2R2 [16], a binary analysis framework, to disassemble and lift EVM instructions, and implemented CFG BUILDER as a middle-end module in B2R2. CFG BUILDER employs an incremental data-flow analysis [26] to track use-def chains of stack values on-the-fly, enabling it to identify jump targets and recognize patterns of public function entry points. VARIABLE IDENTIFIER uses an Static-Single Assignment (SSA) form of the Control-Flow Graph (CFG), which CFG BUILDER emits, to parse data access instructions (e.g., SLOAD, CALLDATALOAD, MLOAD) and identify variable locations. TYPE INFERRER also operates on an SSA-formed CFG to parse instructions that provide useful type hints (e.g., AND for bit-width, SIGNEXTEND for signed type) and collects constraints over the variables identified by VARIABLE IDENTIFIER (e.g., HasBitWidth(x, 160), UsedAsSigned(y)). We apply a set of rules, including memory aliasing and type inference rules, to propagate constraints until no new ones can be derived for each variable, eventually obtaining constraints that describe variable types (e.g., HasType(x, uint32)).

## 4  Evaluation

In this section, we evaluate EVMpress to answer the following research questions.

**RQ1.** How accurate is EVMpress in terms of function identification, variable identification, and type inference?

**RQ2.** How does EVMpress compare with the state-of-the-art tools in terms of function identification, variable identification, and type inference?

**RQ3.** Does path-based function identification enable efficient function identification?

### 4.1  Experimental Setup

**Comparison Targets.** Recall from §2.1 that only Gigahorse [13,14,19] and VarLifter [22] are fully available, although they do not support all the features that EVMpress supports. Thus, our evaluation focuses on comparing EVMpress with these two tools. We ran Gigahorse with the --disable_inline option, which prevents the default inlining of private functions. We found that this option improves Gigahorse's function identification accuracy by about 10%. Particularly, we used Gigahorse commit 18ce2685 and VarLifter commit 47f9e681 for our evaluation.

**Our Environment.** We conduct our experiments on a server equipped with two 22-core Intel Xeon CPU E5-2699 processors and 512 GB RAM, running Ubuntu 22.04. We use 88 ($= 22 \times 2 \times 2$) virtual cores to run the tools in parallel.

## 4.2   RQ1: Accuracy Evaluation

**Table 3.** Comparison of function identification, variable identification, and type inference accuracy. Bold numbers denote the best results among the tools.

| | Function Identification | | | | | | Variable Identification | | | | | Type Inference | | | | |
| | Public. | | | Private. | | | Public. | | Private. | | Glob. (%) | Public. | | Private. | | Glob. (%) |
| | Prec. (%) | Rec. (%) | F1 (%) | Prec. (%) | Rec. (%) | F1 (%) | Par. (%) | Ret. (%) | Par. (%) | Ret. (%) | | Par. (%) | Ret. (%) | Par. (%) | Ret. (%) | |
|---|---|---|---|---|---|---|---|---|---|---|---|---|---|---|---|---|
| VarLifter | – | – | – | – | – | – | – | – | – | – | 49.4 | – | – | – | – | 48.6 |
| Gigahorse | 94.9 | 99.4 | 97.1 | 78.1 | 65.0 | 71.0 | 82.8 | – | 99.9 | 99.9 | – | 82.8 | – | – | – | – |
| EVMpress | 99.2 | 99.7 | 99.5 | 96.4 | 95.8 | 96.1 | 99.4 | 97.5 | 98.6 | 99.4 | 94.1 | 96.6 | 94.2 | 96.4 | 97.8 | 88.8 |

To measure the accuracy of EVMpress, we ran it on our large-scale dataset introduced in §2.3. The last row of Table 3 shows the results of our evaluation. For function identification, we show precision, recall, and F1-score for both public and private functions. For variable identification and type inference, we show success rates.

Overall, EVMpress demonstrates high accuracy across all metrics, achieving 95% or higher in every case except for global variable type inference. Given that type inference is a challenging task and there are only a few existing tools that support it, 88.8% accuracy for global variable type inference is still a promising result. We further discuss why EVMpress's global variable type inference is not as accurate as the other metrics in §4.3 when we compare the result with that of VarLifter.

## 4.3   RQ2: Comparison with State-of-the-Art Tools

We compared EVMpress with the two state-of-the-art tools, Gigahorse and VarLifter, in terms of function identification, variable identification, and type inference as shown in Table 3. It is important to note that EVMpress is the only tool capable of inferring the types of private functions and the return values of public functions.

EVMpress vs. Gigahorse. EVMpress outperforms Gigahorse in all the metrics, except for private function parameter and return value identification. Although EVMpress shows about 99% of accuracy, Gigahorse achieves slightly higher accuracy for private function parameter and return value. This is simply because Gigahorse recovers significantly fewer private functions than EVMpress—the recall of Gigahorse for private function identification is only 65%. As a result, Gigahorse only recovers types of the most basic private functions and misses many highly optimized ones. This leads to a slightly higher accuracy than EVMpress, but only because it analyzes a much smaller and simpler subset of private functions.

For public functions, both EVMpress and Gigahorse achieved higher than 99% recall in identifying them. However, Gigahorse showed significantly lower precision than EVMpress because it often misidentifies some intrinsic functions as public functions. Although both tools were able to identify most of the public functions, Gigahorse's F1-score for identifying their parameters was only 82.8%, while EVMpress achieved 99.4%. This is because Gigahorse relies on an external database based on the hash of the function signature, which can lead to false negatives if the function signature is not present in the database.

EVMpress vs. VarLifter. EVMpress consistently outperforms VarLifter across all metrics. In particular, EVMpress achieves nearly twice the F1-score for global variable type recovery compared to VarLifter, which only reached 48.6% accuracy. This result is rather surprising, as the accuracy of VarLifter reported in its original paper [22] was 96.2%. There are several reasons for this discrepancy. First, we manually inspected the results of VarLifter and found that it *does not* recover the offset of global variables that have the same slot number. Second, VarLifter had difficulty recovering the types of both the key and value in mapping variables, which are commonly used in real-world contracts. Third, the authors used the highly duplicated dataset and its partial ground truth information (recall from §2.3).

Although EVMpress achieves 88.8% accuracy in global variable type inference, we further analyzed the causes of the remaining errors. We found that EVMpress struggles to distinguish between bool and uint8 types, which have the same sizes and are often used interchangeably in the bytecode. Interestingly, by ignoring the distinction between these two types, we were able to achieve 95% accuracy in global variable type inference.

## 4.4   RQ3: Impact of Path-based Function Identification

**Table 4.** Averaged CFG recovery time and total execution time on our dataset.

|  | CFG Recovery Time | Total Execution Time | Error Rate |
|---|---|---|---|
| Gigahorse | 4.5 s | 4.6 s | 0.04% |
| EVMpress | 2.7 s | 8.3 s | 0.02% |

Recall from §3.2 that path-based function identification is a key component of EVMpress that reduces the number of paths to be analyzed while precisely recovering the CFG. Having established the high accuracy of EVMpress in the previous evaluations, we now assess how path-based function identification specifically improves the runtime performance of EVMpress.

Table 4 shows the averaged time consumption of EVMpress and Gigahorse on our dataset. We exclude VarLifter from this comparison since it does not report CFG recovery time. The last column shows the runtime error rate of each tool. When the tool reaches the timeout, we consider it as a runtime error, too.

Notably, the CFG recovery time of `EVMpress` is nearly 66% faster than it of `Gigahorse`. The difference becomes even more significant on large bytecodes (of top 10K bytecodes by size in our dataset), where `EVMpress` achieves nearly 4× faster code recovery than `Gigahorse`. This result confirms that path-based function identification effectively reduces the number of paths to be analyzed by `EVMpress`, leading to faster CFG recovery.

As the third column of Table 4 shows, the total time consumption of `EVMpress` is slightly higher than that of `Gigahorse`. This slight increase is due to `EVMpress` performing a more comprehensive analysis than `Gigahorse`. Specifically, `EVMpress` recovers additional information such as the types of private function parameters, private function return values, and public function return values, which `Gigahorse` does not support. Nonetheless, `EVMpress`'s total time is comparable to `Gigahorse`, which is a significant achievement, rendering `EVMpress` a practical tool for EVM bytecode analysis.

## 5    Discussion

While `EVMpress` advances the current state of EVM type recovery, it still has several limitations.

**Transient Storage.** Since Solidity 0.8.28, the language supports *transient storage*, a temporary and cheaper storage area. `EVMpress` does not yet support transient storage, but extending our approach to handle it is straightforward since its mechanism is similar to storage area. However, transient storage is not yet common in real-world contracts, and our dataset contains no such contracts.

**Unused Variables.** Our variable identification and type inference rely on the behavioral hints of variables found in EVM bytecode. Therefore, our approach cannot recover the types of variables that are defined but not used in the code. This limitation is common in type inference, and hence, is beyond the scope of this paper.

## 6    Related Work

There are numerous studies on identifying functions in traditional binary code. They often utilize pattern matching [4,17,23], compiler metadata [25], or probabilistic models [18] to identify functions in binary code.

However, it is not feasible to apply these techniques to EVM bytecode as it introduces additional challenges due to the lack of explicit call and return instructions, especially for private functions. `Gigahorse` [13,14] leverage declarative code patterns such as Continuation-Passing Style (CPS) calls to detect private functions, while `Neural-FEBI` [15] employs a deep learning-based approach to identify private functions. On the other hand, `EVMpress` introduces a procedural approach to identify private functions, which is more efficient than declarative approaches and does not require a large training dataset like deep learning-based approaches.

A common approach for inferring public function parameters is to use pre-built databases of known function selectors [1,2,12,13]. While effective, this method cannot be applied to closed-source smart contracts. To address this, `SigRec` [7] symbolically analyzes the prologue of public functions, extracting argument variables and their types by tracking how calldata is loaded into memory. Other tools, such as `VarLifter` [22] and `Crush` [27], focus on recovering types of variables in the EVM storage area, which holds contract assets. However, because these tools are tailored to specific EVM data areas, they lack a unified analysis framework for all variable types. Deep learning-based approaches [32] have also been proposed to recover types of public function parameters and return values, but their effectiveness depends heavily on the quality of training data and they require substantial computational resources. In contrast, `EVMpress` is the first tool to comprehensively recover all types of variables and their types in EVM bytecode, without incurring heavy computational costs.

The rise of DeFi and NFTs highlights the need for scalable EVM bytecode analysis to ensure smart contract security and reliability. Several tools [1,2,9, 10,13,14,24] decompile EVM bytecode into human-readable code to aid manual and automated analysis. Although `EVMpress` is not a decompiler, it can serve as a pre-processor for decompilers as it can recover precisely functions and variables in EVM bytecode. Furthermore, our precise CFG recovery and type inference techniques can benefit vulnerability detection tools that leverage EVM bytecode analysis [8] by providing accurate information about functions and their types.

## 7   Conclusion

In this paper, we studied the current limitations of existing EVM bytecode analysis techniques and proposed a novel framework that addresses these limitations. We also presented the largest dataset for EVM bytecode analysis to date, comprising over 370K unique contracts with precise ground truth. We evaluated our framework on this dataset and demonstrated its effectiveness in recovering types of global variables and functions.

**Acknowledgments.** This work was supported by the Institute of Information & Communications Technology Planning & Evaluation (IITP) grant funded by the Korea government (MSIT) (No.RS-2025-02263143, Development of Cybersecurity Threat Response Technologies for Satellite Ground Stations).

## References


1. Porosity (2017). https://github.com/msuiche/porosity
2. Eveem (2019). https://eveem.org
3. Etherscan (2025). https://etherscan.io/

4. Bao, T., Burket, J., Woo, M., Turner, R., Brumley, D.: ByteWeight: learning to recognize functions in binary code. In: Proceedings of the USENIX Security Symposium, pp. 845–860 (2014)
5. Ceri, S., Gottlob, G., Tanca, L., Ceri, S., Gottlob, G., Tanca, L.: Logic Programming and Databases: an Overview. Springer (1990)
6. Chaliasos, S., Gervais, A., Livshits, B.: A study of inline assembly in solidity smart contracts. In: Proceedings of the ACM SIGPLAN International Conference on Object Oriented Programming Systems Languages & Applications, pp. 1123–1149 (2022)
7. Chen, T., et al.: Sigrec: automatic recovery of function signatures in smart contracts. IEEE Trans. Software Eng. **48**(8), 3066–3086 (2021)
8. Choi, J., Kim, D., Kim, S., Grieco, G., Groce, A., Cha, S.K.: Smartian: enhancing smart contract fuzzing with static and dynamic data-flow analyses. In: Proceedings of the International Conference on Automated Software Engineering, pp. 227–239 (2021)
9. Contro, F., Crosara, M., Ceccato, M., Dalla Preda, M.: Ethersolve: computing an accurate control-flow graph from Ethereum bytecode. In: 2021 IEEE/ACM 29th International Conference on Program Comprehension (ICPC), pp. 127–137. IEEE (2021)
10. Dedaub: Dedaub bytecode decompiler (2025). https://app.dedaub.com/decompile
11. Eom, H., Kim, D., Lim, S., Koo, H., Hwang, S.: R2I: A relative readability metric for decompiled code. In: Proceedings of the 32nd ACM Joint European Software Engineering Conference and Symposium on the Foundations of Software Engineering, pp. 383–405 (2024)
12. Ethervm: Online solidity decompiler (2024). https://ethervm.io/decompile
13. Grech, N., Brent, L., Scholz, B., Smaragdakis, Y.: Gigahorse: thorough, declarative decompilation of smart contracts. In: 2019 IEEE/ACM 41st International Conference on Software Engineering (ICSE), pp. 1176–1186. IEEE (2019)
14. Grech, N., Lagouvardos, S., Tsatiris, I., Smaragdakis, Y.: Elipmoc: Advanced decompilation of ethereum smart contracts. In: Proceedings of the ACM SIGPLAN International Conference on Object Oriented Programming Systems Languages & Applications, pp. 1–27 (2022)
15. He, J., Li, S., Wang, X., Cheung, S.C., Zhao, G., Yang, J.: Neural-FEBI: Accurate function identification in Ethereum virtual machine bytecode. J. Syst. Softw. **199**(C), 1–16 (2023)
16. Jung, M., Kim, S., Han, H., Choi, J., Cha, S.K.: B2R2: Building an efficient frontend for binary analysis. In: Proceedings of the NDSS Workshop on Binary Analysis Research (2019)
17. Kim, H., Lee, J., Kim, S., Jung, S., Cha, S.K.: How'd security benefit reverse engineers? the implication of intel CET on function identification. In: Proceedings of the International Conference on Dependable Systems and Networks, pp. 559–566 (2022). https://doi.org/10.1109/DSN53405.2022.00061
18. Kim, S., Kim, H., Cha, S.K.: FunProbe: Probing functions from binary code through probabilistic analysis. In: Proceedings of the International Symposium on Foundations of Software Engineering, pp. 1419–1430 (2023)
19. Lagouvardos, S., Bollanos, Y., Grech, N., Smaragdakis, Y.: The incredible shrinking context... in a decompiler near you. In: Proceedings of the 30th ACM SIGSOFT International Symposium on Software Testing and Analysis (2025)
20. Lee, J., Avgerinos, T., Brumley, D.: TIE: principled reverse engineering of types in binary programs. In: Proceedings of the Network and Distributed System Security Symposium, pp. 251–268 (2011)

21. Li, S., Su, Z.: Finding unstable code via compiler-driven differential testing. In: Proceedings of the International Conference on Architectural Support for Programming Languages and Operating Systems, pp. 238–251 (2023). https://doi.org/10.1145/3582016.3582053
22. Li, Y., Song, W., Huang, J.: Varlifter: Recovering variables and types from bytecode of solidity smart contracts, pp. 1–29 (2024)
23. Meng, X., Miller, B.P.: Binary code is not easy. In: Proceedings of the international symposium on software testing and analysis, pp. 24–35 (2016). https://doi.org/10.1145/2931037.2931047
24. MrLuit: Evm bytecode decompiler (2018). https://github.com/MrLuit/evm
25. Pang, C., Yu, R., Xu, D., Koskinen, E., Portokalidis, G., Xu, J.: Towards optimal use of exception handling information for function detection. In: Proceedings of the International Conference on Dependable Systems and Networks, pp. 338–349 (2021). https://doi.org/10.1109/DSN48987.2021.00046
26. Pollock, L.L., Soffa, M.L.: An incremental version of iterative data flow analysis. IEEE Trans. Software Eng. **15**(12), 1537–1549 (1989)
27. Ruaro, N., Gritti, F., McLaughlin, R., Grishchenko, I., Kruegel, C., Vigna, G.: Not your type! detecting storage collision vulnerabilities in Ethereum smart contracts. In: Proceeding of Network Distribution System Security Symposium, pp. 1–17 (2024)
28. Schwartz, E.J., Lee, J., Woo, M., Brumley, D.: Native x86 decompilation using semantics-preserving structural analysis and iterative control-flow structuring. In: Proceedings of the USENIX Security Symposium, pp. 353–368 (2013)
29. Team, S.: Introduction to smart contracts (2025). https://docs.soliditylang.org/en/latest/introduction-to-smart-contracts.html
30. Team, S.: Layout of state variables in storage and transient storage (2025). https://docs.soliditylang.org/en/latest/internals/layout_in_storage.html
31. Wiedemeier, J., et al.: PyLingual: Toward perfect decompilation of evolving high-level languages. In: Proceedings of the IEEE Symposium on Security and Privacy, pp. 2976–2994 (2025)
32. Zhao, K., Li, Z., Li, J., Ye, H., Luo, X., Chen, T.: Deepinfer: deep type inference from smart contract bytecode. In: Proceedings of the 31st ACM Joint European Software Engineering Conference and Symposium on the Foundations of Software Engineering, pp. 745–757 (2023)

# 11th Workshop on the Security of Industrial Control Systems and of Cyber-Physical Systems (CyberICPS 2025)

# Salty Seagull: A VSAT Honeynet to Follow the Bread Crumb of Attacks in Ship Networks

Georgios Michail Makrakis[1] , Jeroen Pijpker[1,3] , Remco Hassing[1] ,
Rob Loves[1] , and Stephen McCombie[2(✉)]

[1] Maritime IT Security Research Group, NHL Stenden, Emmen, The Netherlands
`{george.makrakis,jeroen.pijpker,remco.hassing,rob.loves}@nhlstenden.com,`
`j.pijpker@rug.nl`
[2] Maritime IT Security Research Group, NHL Stenden,
Leeuwarden, The Netherlands
`stephen.mccombie@nhlstenden.com`
[3] Department of Computer Science, University of Groningen,
Groningen, The Netherlands

**Abstract.** Cyber threats against the maritime industry have increased notably in recent years, highlighting the need for innovative cybersecurity approaches. Ships, as critical assets, possess highly specialized and interconnected network infrastructures, where their legacy systems and operational constraints further exacerbate their vulnerability to cyberattacks. To better understand this evolving threat landscape, we propose the use of cyber-deception techniques and in particular honeynets, as a means to gather valuable insights into ongoing attack campaigns targeting the maritime sector.

In this paper we present Salty Seagull, a honeynet conceived to simulate a VSAT system for ships. This environment mimics the operations of a functional VSAT system onboard and, at the same time, enables a user to interact with it through a Web dashboard and a CLI environment. Furthermore, based on existing vulnerabilities, we purposefully integrate them into our system to increase attacker engagement. We exposed our honeynet for 30 days to the Internet to assess its capability and measured the received interaction. Results show that while numerous generic attacks have been attempted, only one curious attacker with knowledge of the nature of the system and its vulnerabilities managed to access it, without however exploring its full potential.

**Keywords:** Cybersecurity · Maritime · VSAT · Honeynet

## 1 Introduction

As one of the most integral components of modern maritime, vessels are equipped with a broad array of cyber systems that encompass both information technology (IT) and operational technology (OT), distributed across various operational domains within the ship. These include communication, propulsion and


R. Laborde et al. (Eds.): ESORICS 2025, LNCS 16231, pp. 363–381, 2026.
https://doi.org/10.1007/978-3-032-16089-8_23

machinery control, power management, navigation, and cargo handling systems. Designed to operate with minimal human intervention, these systems aim to optimize vessel performance while ensuring safety and reliability. However, their increasing complexity and interconnectivity introduce a broad attack surface. Many of these systems depend on interconnected devices and digital services which, if compromised, could significantly disrupt vessel functionality and operational continuity [2, 16].

Previous studies have demonstrated that very small aperture terminals (VSATs), satellite-based communication systems commonly deployed to provide Internet connectivity to ships at sea, can be exploited through various attack vectors [21, 37]. Given their exposure and relatively accessible attack surface, VSAT systems are often regarded as a low-hanging fruit for adversaries seeking initial access. Even with IEC 61162-460-compliant segmentation, risks remain due to misconfigured VLANs, weak firewall rules, or unintended network bridging. These gaps can expose critical ship systems to the Internet indirectly via VSAT. Once compromised, VSAT-connected systems may serve as a pivot point for further reconnaissance, service disruption, or intrusion into more critical onboard systems, thus posing a significant risk to maritime cybersecurity [5].

To observe and analyze the behavior of adversaries attempting to exploit digital systems, honeypots and honeynets can be strategically deployed. These cyber-deception systems simulate vulnerable targets, luring attackers into interacting with what they perceive to be legitimate services or devices. During these interactions, valuable insights can be gathered regarding the attacker's movements and techniques. While honeypots are commonly used in traditional IT environments to simulate services (e.g. SSH, HTTP, or FTP), their deployment in cyber-physical systems (CPS), such as those found aboard maritime vessels, presents unique challenges. These challenges stem from the domain-specific nature of the systems involved, which often include proprietary communication protocols and interactions with physical processes.

In this paper, we propose the design and implementation of a VSAT honeynet capable of attracting, recording, and analyzing early-stage interactions from potential attackers targeting shipboard communication systems. To ensure the system's effectiveness and realism, our design is informed by the ICSvertase framework [12], while the implementation is grounded in the characteristics of real-world, Internet-exposed VSAT devices. To enhance the credibility of the simulation, the honeynet integrates a Web dashboard and command line interface (CLI), alongside replayed voyage data, thereby mimicking the operational features of an actual maritime communication system. Stemmed from real-world VSAT vulnerabilities, we purposefully integrate them into our system to increase the chances of attacker interaction.

Based on the specific nature of the system we try to simulate, we aim to answer the following research questions (RQs):

- RQ1: Were there any actors exploiting specific vulnerabilities related to VSAT environments?

– RQ2: What were their interactions with Web dashboard and CLI environments?
– RQ3: Were there any persistence mechanisms attempted?

The collected results from 30 days of deployment indicate that despite the multiple attempts to target the system with generic exploits, only one attacker with knowledge of the nature of the system and its vulnerabilities managed to access it, and perform some familiarization actions inside the environment. Thus, we deduce that specific knowledge is required to meaningfully exploit such systems and gain access to the inner workings of a ship's network. The anonymized raw data to reach to those conclusions are provided in[1].

The rest of the manuscript is organized as follows: preliminary background information is presented in Sect. 2 and related work in Sect. 3, while the design of our system is detailed in Sect. 4. The evaluation of Salty Seagull is described in Sect. 5, followed by the concluding remarks in Sect. 6.

**Ethical Considerations:** The ultimate goal of this research is to improve the security of vessels and their satellite communication systems, by understanding the potential attackers' interactions with them. To this end, all scanning and resources retrieval were conducted via the Shodan and Censys services, without any login attempts or other forms of active interaction with each accessed system.

## 2    Background

In the following, we briefly present the some background information useful to understand the remainder of the paper.

### 2.1    Honeypots and Honeynets

Honeypots are defined by Spitzner as a "security resource whose value lies in being probed, attacked, or compromised" [30]. Conceptually, they function as deliberately vulnerable systems that mimic real services or data to deceive and attract malicious actors. Their core objectives are to divert attackers from critical assets, gather detailed intelligence on adversarial behavior, and engage intruders long enough to monitor and analyze their actions. The origins of honeypots trace back to early deception systems described in Cliff Stoll's *The Cuckoo's Egg* [33] and Bill Cheswick's *An Evening With Berferd* [4], where attackers were lured into controlled environments to better understand their behavior. These foundational works inspired the Honeynet Project [31], which advanced the use of honeypots as tools for studying and defending against cyber threats. When multiple honeypots are deployed and interconnected, they form a honeynet—an architecture that has since evolved into a powerful method for capturing adversarial tactics, techniques, and procedures (TTPs) [19], enhancing both defensive strategies and cyber threat intelligence capabilities.

---

[1] https://doi.org/10.5281/zenodo.15469996.

## 2.2   IoT, IIoT and CPS Honeypots

A plethora of honeypots has been developed and used in the past to acquire information about their respective environments [11,13,14,32]. Well known examples of tools used to create honeypots include Cowrie [20], Conpot [26], Glastopf [27], Dionaea [35], and T-Pot [1]. Honeypots have gained considerable attention in industrial environments due to their potential to attract adversaries, such as ransomware gangs, who target these systems for financial gain or adversaries that aim to inflict denial, manipulation and loss of control, view, and safety [7].

Franco et al. compiled a survey on honeypots deployed in the IoT, industrial IoT, CPS and industrial control systems (ICS) [6]. They categorized the honeypots based on a multitude of parameters such as levels of interactions, roles, and scalability. According to this research a significant challenge in deploying honeypots in such environments arises from their low-interaction nature. Most implementations rely on simplified versions of the targeted systems, often lacking the complex functionality and specific vulnerabilities that would typically exist in fully operational systems. This makes these honeypots relatively easy for attackers to identify, as they do not replicate the nuanced behavior of genuine industrial environments. Consequently, the lack of sophisticated interaction can limit the effectiveness of these honeypots in evading detection and capturing valuable intelligence.

## 2.3   Shipboard Systems and VSAT

In the context of CPS, consider the modern ship, which is equipped with a variety of integrated systems designed to enhance operational efficiency and support the crew. These systems encompass a wide range of functionalities, from autopilot controls to sensors monitoring environmental factors, such as water temperature. An example of shipboard systems can be found in Table 1.

Among the various systems in a ship, the VSAT is particularly relevant to this study. VSAT is part of SATCOM that enables vessels to maintain Internet connectivity while at sea. Another use case is the transmission of fishing yield data to cloud services from fishing vessels [28]. It operates as a two-way satellite ground station, utilizing a dish antenna connected to a gateway that facilitates a wide area network (WAN). VSATs commonly include Web as well as command line interfaces for configuration and maintenance tasks. Despite their importance in maintaining communications, VSAT systems have previously been found vulnerable to cyber threats [17,18]. Exploiting these vulnerabilities could provide adversaries with a potential entry point to breach the internal network of the vessel.

## 3   Related Work

While only a limited number of studies have specifically addressed the development of deception systems for the maritime sector, these efforts have provided valuable insights and influence for the work presented in this paper.

**Table 1.** Examples of Shipboard Systems according to [24].

| System | Components |
| --- | --- |
| Communication | satellite communication (SATCOM) |
| | integrated communication |
| | wireless local area network (WLAN) |
| Propulsion, Machinery, and Power Control | engine governor |
| | fuel oil |
| | alarm monitoring & control |
| | power management |
| | emergency generators and batteries |
| Navigation | electronic chart display and information system (ECDIS) |
| | radio detection and ranging (RADAR) |
| | automatic identification system (AIS) |
| | global positioning system (GPS) |
| | dynamic positioning system (DPS) |
| | global maritime distress and safety system (GMDSS) |
| | voyage data recorder (VDR) |
| | integrated navigation system (INS) |
| Cargo Management | cargo control room (CCR) |
| | ballast water system (BWS) |

Pitropakis et al. [23] proposed a framework named MAINFRAME, which focuses on intrusion detection within maritime vessel networks. Although not a honeynet in the traditional sense, MAINFRAME shares certain characteristics with honeynet systems, most notably, its capability to detect malicious activity and potentially mislead attackers. Designed to be deployed directly within a ship's network, the framework aims to provide early detection of cyber threats. MAINFRAME also remains at the conceptual level, with no publicly documented operational deployment so far.

In a same domain Yigit et al. [38] introduced the TwinPot project, which addresses cybersecurity in the context of seaport infrastructure through the development of a digital twin model. The objective of TwinPot is to create a virtual representation of both the operational and informational systems of a seaport, enabling the simulation and analysis of cyberattacks in a controlled environment. This digital twin functions as an intelligence-gathering tool, designed to enhance situational awareness by identifying potential cyber threats and vulnerabilities. Notably, it incorporates its own detection mechanisms capable of identifying both internal and external attacks. However, the project remains in the conceptual stage, with no known full-scale implementation to date.

Pijpker and McCombie [22] presented a practical approach to maritime cybersecurity through the design of a VSAT-based honeynet intended to capture and analyze cyberattacks targeting vessel networks. In contrast to conceptual frameworks, their work emphasized implementation aspects, offering a detailed blueprint for a honeynet that emulates a shipboard environment. The proposed system will replicate critical maritime components, including AIS and VDR, thereby increasing the realism of the simulated network. To facilitate attacker interaction, the honeynet will incorporate several deliberately exposed entry points, such as Telnet and a web server, enabling the collection of adversarial behavior for further analysis.

The most closely related work to ours is by Brouwer [3], which presents a VSAT honeypot designed to analyze threats in the maritime domain. The honeypot, named HoneyShip, includes a web portal that emulates the management interface of a VSAT system, logging all interactions with it. However, there is no mention of a realistic implementation of the accompanying Telnet service, which could enhance the deception capabilities of the system. Additionally, the study does not specify an important factor for ensuring realism and collecting reliable attack data i.e., the IP address space in which HoneyShip was deployed. Finally, the work includes vulnerabilities such as unauthenticated access to the administrative dashboard (i.e., Menu pages), which could attract bots and web crawlers, potentially skewing the collected data with generic, non-targeted attacks. Nevertheless, we get inspired by this work as we believe that an enhancement will enable more precise data collection, thereby facilitating a solid understanding of the TTPs employed by adversaries targeting shipboard systems.

## 4   System Design

In this section, we first introduce the threat model we operate on, then the main design considerations for our honeynet, and finally the technical aspects of the exposed services and the configuration of the environment.

### 4.1   Threat Model

We assume that malicious actors targeting VSAT systems aim to explore these systems and potentially establish a foothold within the vessel's network. These actors are likely to possess knowledge about the use of VSATs on ships and may have access to documentation that details their operation, which could be either publicly or privately available.

The primary objectives of these attackers include either disabling the VSAT system to create confusion for the crew and passengers, and/or exploiting the system to facilitate lateral movement within the ship's internal network. To achieve these goals, attackers would typically leverage both documented and undocumented vulnerabilities, often after gathering basic information, such as version details or build numbers, through manual or automated scanning techniques. Additionally, we assume that attackers will be able to fingerprint the IP address of the VSAT system to ensure that they are targeting a legitimate system of a ship.

### 4.2   Design Considerations

With regards to the defined threat model, we leveraged the ICSvertase framework [12] to design our honeynet. Although our system is not strictly an ICS honeynet, we utilized the framework to guide our design, aligning it with components from *MITRE ATT&CK® for ICS* and *MITRE Engage_{TM}*. The main key considerations is what adversary behaviors should a honeynet be designed to capture, and the effective capture of them, while at the same time recognize the importance of capturing such behavior as well as, the ways to incentivize an adversary to exhibit such behaviors.

Thus according to the Engage approaches, we aim to *Collect* adversary tools, observe tactics, and other raw intelligence about the adversary's activity, *Detect* adversary activity throughout an environment, *Direct* them towards an intended path and, *Reassure* them that the access to an environment is real by adding authenticity to deceptive components. The mapping of such activities and techniques used are shown in Tables 2 and 3.

**Table 2.** Engage Approaches Activities According to ICSvertase Requirements Analysis.

| Approach | Activity |
| --- | --- |
| Collect | System Activity Monitoring (EAC0003) |
| | Software Manipulation (EAC0014) |
| Detect | Introduced Vulnerabilities (EAC0023) |
| Direct | Introduced Vulnerabilities (EAC0023) |
| Reassure | Information Manipulation (EAC0015) |

Collection of activity logs can reveal adversary activity (EAC0003), while making changes to a system's software properties and functions can achieve a desired effect (reveal deceptive artifacts and systems) (EAC0014). At the same time introduction of vulnerabilities will motivate the adversary to target specific resources (EAC0023) and the concealment and reveal of both facts and fictions will support a deception story (EAC0015).

The corresponding techniques include exploiting CLIs (T0807) for executing commands, using commonly used ports (T0885) to blend in with normal traffic, and leveraging default credentials (T0812) to gain unauthorized access. Adversaries may also restart or shut down devices (T0816) to disrupt operations, exploit vulnerabilities in public-facing applications (T0819) to gain access, and modify system firmware (T0857) for persistence. Finally, the identified techniques involve discovering remote systems (T0846) and gathering information about them (T0888) to facilitate further attacks, as well as using valid accounts (T0859) to maintain access and evade detection.

Based on the above, the design we propose relates to the traditional classification of *medium-interactive honeynets*. The design choices are made based on the assumption that we can acquire more precise results about techniques threat actors might exploit to gain initial foothold to the systems of a vessel. We implement the Web interface of a *Sea Tel VSAT management portal* up to

**Table 3.** ATT&CK Techniques According to ICSvertase Requirements Analysis.

| Technique | Functional Feature | Data Component |
|---|---|---|
| Command-Line Interface (T0807) | Size: single<br>ICS component: Protocols<br>ICS component: OS<br>Logging: file system<br>Logging: processes | Application Log Content<br>Command Execution<br>Process Creation |
| Commonly Used Port (T0885) | Size: single<br>ICS component: OS<br>Logging: processes | Network Traffic Content<br>Network Traffic Flow |
| Default Credentials (T0812) | Size: single<br>ICS component: Protocols | Logon Session Creation<br>Network Traffic Content |
| Device Restart/Shutdown (T0816) | Size: single<br>ICS component: Runtime | Application Log Content<br>Network Traffic Content<br>Network Traffic Flow<br>Device Alarm |
| Exploit Public-Facing Application (T0819) | Size: single<br>ICS component: Protocols<br>ICS component: Runtime | Application Log Content<br>Network Traffic Content |
| System Firmware (T0857) | Size: single<br>ICS component: Runtime<br>ICS component: Bootloader<br>Logging: file system | Application Log Content<br>Firmware Modification<br>Network Traffic Content<br>Device Alarm |
| Remote System Discovery (T0846) | Size: single<br>ICS component: OS<br>Logging: processes | File Access<br>Network Traffic Content<br>Network Traffic Flow<br>Process Creation |
| Remote System Information Discovery (T0888) | Size: single<br>ICS component: OS<br>Logging : processes | File Access<br>Network Traffic Content<br>Network Traffic Flow<br>Process Creation |
| Valid Accounts (T0859) | Size: single<br>ICS component: Protocols | Logon Session Creation<br>Logon Session Metadata<br>User Account Authentication |

a point where a potential attacker can acquire information about the system and to make changes that however do not have any real impact on the system e.g., upload new firmware. The same applies to its accompanied CLI where a variety of commands can be issued with up to two arguments/options following them. While in this study we explore this specific system, we argue that VSAT systems from other vendors might also include similar vulnerabilities that allow an attacker to gain access to a ship's networks.

Given that the vulnerabilities associated with the studied system (CVE-2018-5267, CVE-2018-5266, CVE-2018-5071, CVE-2018-5728) include unauthenticated access to sensitive resources, we deliberately chose not to implement those that could be trivially exploited by automated bots or Web crawlers. Instead, we selectively implemented vulnerabilities related to the use of default credentials and exposure of sensitive information, which are more likely to attract targeted interest from actors with a specific focus on maritime systems and equipment. Importantly, all incoming connections to our system are logged. Therefore, when attempts are made to exploit any of the referenced CVEs, we interpret this as an indication that the adversary has conducted some degree of reconnaissance or prior research upon identifying our system as potentially vulnerable.

The honeynet is composed of three parts:

- The Web service. The service responsible for the front-end and the back-end services of a Sea Tel VSAT.
- The Telnet service. The service that provides a CLI interface used to manage the VSAT.
- The VDRPlayer service. The service that enables the replay of voyage information to enhance deception.

Our system's architecture is shown in Fig. 1. Each of the components incorporates a robust logging system to record attacker trace for further analysis and investigation, based on the aforementioned *MITRE ATT&CK® for ICS Techniques* (provided inside brackets in the following subsections).

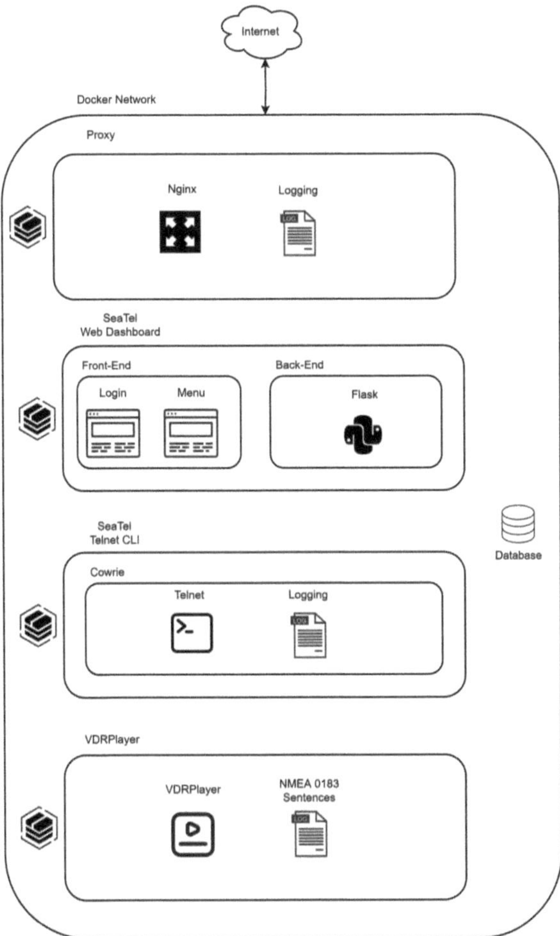


**Fig. 1.** The architecture of the proposed honeynet.

## 4.3   Web Service

The Web service consists of the proxy, the front-end service and the back-end service of the Web management portal of a Sea Tel VSAT. We describe each as follows:

**Proxy.** A minimal configuration of the widely used Nginx proxy is deployed to serve as the entry point to the Web service. This setup allows potential adversaries to perform service discovery [T0846] and attempt to exploit a public-facing application [T0819], in alignment with known adversarial tactics. Nginx was selected due to its built-in support for detailed HTTP request and response logging in JSON format, which facilitates effective data analysis. To enhance the realism of the emulated system, we modified the HTTP response headers to mimic those typically returned by a Sea Tel VSAT.

**Front-End.** The front-end of the system comprises static assets, such as HTML, CSS, and JavaScript files, that are served by the back-end component. The user is first presented with a login page, which acts as the landing interface. Upon successful authentication, the appropriate menu page is displayed based on the user's role. The system defines three distinct user roles: "User", "SysAdmin", and "Dealer", each associated with specific access privileges. Consequently, all front-end resources must be served conditionally [T0859].

For instance, a user with the "User" role is primarily permitted to view operational information related to the satellite and antenna. The "SysAdmin" role provides access to system configuration options and diagnostic functionalities, while the "Dealer" role grants administrative privileges, including system commissioning and firmware updates. An illustrative example of the dashboard accessible to a "SysAdmin" user is presented in Fig. 2.

Those static files, related to the front-end functionality, were cloned from other Internet exposed VSATs as indicated in [3]. Notice, that some of them were needed to be acquired manually so it will not affect the operation of such exposed systems.

**Back-End.** We implemented the back-end of the Web service in Python Flask. Since the majority of the front-end requests to the back-end are performed via the included JavaScript files, we deduced the data and format that the responses of such requests should have. To this end, we implemented the required endpoints to return all the necessary information based on a combination of realistic and random data. Information related to the nature of the ship such as the heading and coordinates, are drawn from the data replayed from the VDRPlayer Service (see Sect. 4.5), while other, such as satellite position and antenna azimuth, are randomly created. At the same time, any changes made via the front-end, are processed and stored in a SQLite database to support the deception narrative.

To avoid the access of our Web-page from bots and spiders, Flask's built-in authentication and authorization mechanisms were used to access each page.

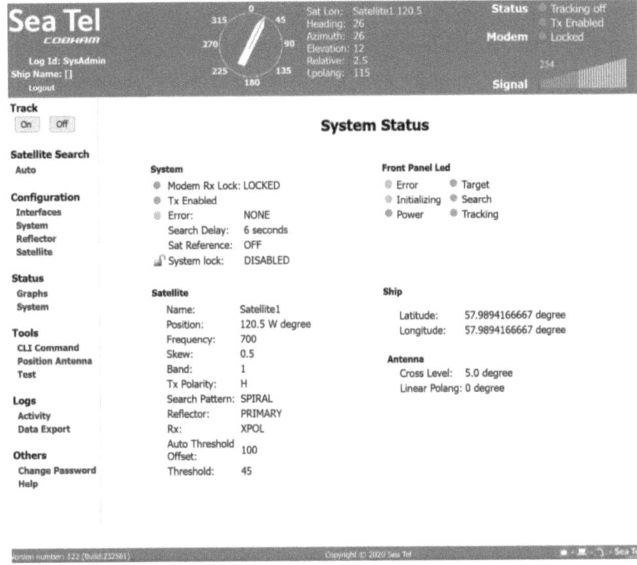


**Fig. 2.** An example of the VSAT menu page for the SysAdmin.

The default credentials [T0812] and roles for each user of the system, are stored in the SQLite database. Those credentials can be changed for each user, by accessing the respective page in the Web UI. File uploads for firmware [T0857] and configuration modifications, are saved to explore the potential of an attacker trying to modify the system and maintaining persistence.

Regarding the integrated CLI menu option [T0807], since the vendor's commands manual for the Web interface was not available anymore in the public domain, we implemented only a subset of the commands that are found when accessing the system via the Telnet service.

## 4.4 Telnet Service

The Sea Tel VSAT system features a CLI for management, which operates on its antenna control unit (ACU) and can be accessed via Telnet [T0807]. Although, not exposed by default, we implement it as such to give the impression of a misconfigured setup. To emulate this functionality, we utilize the widely adopted and academically recognized Cowrie SSH and Telnet honeypot [20]. However, since the VSAT CLI interface includes a distinct set of commands and error messages, it is necessary to customize the default Cowrie setup to better align with the real system [29].

To achieve this, we disabled SSH and implemented a subset of the VSAT CLI commands in Telnet, supporting up to two options for each command. An exception to this rule are commands that were further developed to enhance deception by displaying data from the VDRPlayer service (as detailed in Sect. 4.5) or restarting the system [T0816]. The default credentials used in the Web service are also applied to the Telnet service, ensuring consistency. If credentials are modified in one place, the change propagates due to the shared SQLite database. Furthermore, to improve realism, fake but plausible parameters such as MAC addresses and ship names are incorporated. All interactions with the Telnet service are logged in JSON format for subsequent analysis.

### 4.5  VDRPlayer Service

The voyage data recorder (VDR) is an important component of vessels as it collects and provides forensic evidence in the case of an incident/accident, and monitors system performance. According to Chap. 5, Regulation 20 of IMO's safety of life at sea convention (SOLAS) [10] vessels that utilize VDRs are (a) passenger ships on international voyages, regardless of size and (b) cargo ships of 3,000 gross tonnage and above constructed on or after July 1, 2002. Cargo ships of 3,000 gross tonnage and above constructed before July 1, 2002 are required to have at least a simplified VDR (S-VDR), if engaged on international voyages. A typical VDR system consists of an electronics unit that gathers information such as the vessel's position, heading, speed, navigational chart data, AIS data, RADAR imagery, bridge audio recordings, and rudder movement [8,9]. Commonly it includes two hard drives that mirror each other for redundancy reasons.

By utilizing the open-source VDRPlayer tool [36], we replay such data to the network and feeding them to the back-end and Telnet services. The data are encoded as NMEA 0183 sentences [25], that the Web and Telnet services decode and process the data accordingly. This ensures that an attacker with access to both services receives the same data, making it believable that the system belongs to a genuine vessel. When the feed of the data ends, we repeat the replay to keep a constant feed of data to our honeynet.

### 4.6  Containerization

Each of the aforementioned services is deployed as a Docker container on a rented virtual private server (VPS) from a commercial cloud provider. The deployment is managed using separate docker-compose.yml configuration files, one for the Web service and another for the Telnet service, with the VDRPlayer included in the Web service configuration. These files define how the containers are launched, how logs are stored, and how the services interact within the honeynet.

An internal network is established to create the environment, enabling communication between the back-end, Telnet, and VDRPlayer services. For instance, the VDRPlayer replays NMEA data via UDP, which is consumed by both the back-end and Telnet services. The only externally exposed ports are port 80 for the Nginx proxy and port 23 for the Telnet service (T0885), minimizing the attack surface while preserving the honeynet's intended functionality.

## 5   Evaluation

In this section, we present the experimental setup, analysis of the results from a the deployment of our honeynet for 1 month, and some insights from the identified attacks.

### 5.1   Experimental Setup

To evaluate our system, we deployed it on a commercial VPS by a cloud provider located in Europe. The honeynet was hosted on a virtual machine equipped with 4 GB of RAM and two virtual CPU cores, running Ubuntu 24.04 as the operating system. To emulate the behavior of a VSAT system, only ports 80 (HTTP) and 23 (Telnet) were left open and accessible from the Internet.

Previous studies in the domain of IT, and IoT/IIoT, CPS and ICS honeynets have explored the deployment of multiple instances distributed across various geographic regions [34]. In contrast, our objective is to realistically simulate the environment of a single vessel. Each ship typically has unique attributes, such as name, call sign, and location, making a single-instance deployment more appropriate for deception. This approach increases the likelihood that adversaries perceive our VSAT system as part of a genuine maritime asset.

To further enhance realism and reduce detectability, we channeled our exposed services through IP address blocks leased from a commercial provider offering both IPv4 and IPv6 addresses. This strategy mitigates the risk of our system being flagged as a honeynet based on a reverse lookup or reputation check of the cloud provider's IP space. Specifically, we employed generic routing encapsulation (GRE) to tunnel incoming traffic from the leased IP address to the public IP address of the VPS. Subsequently, internal Linux-based routing forwards the traffic to and from the internal Docker network hosting the containerized honeynet.

### 5.2   Data Analysis

This setup has been running from Apr 3, 2025 to May 3, 2025. In this period, we have gathered around 16 MB logs from the Web service and 22 MB from the Cowrie honeypot, making a total of 175,290 entries. Those entries include attempts to access our honeynet services from 9,054 distinct IP addresses. Table 4 shows the distribution of Web and Telnet connections based on geographical location. In Fig. 3, we see the change in log recorded for the two services per day. It is evident that the Telnet service received more attempts than the Web one.

The limited interaction can be attributed to its accessibility through specific ports or services, reflecting a narrowly defined operational role. The system is highly specialized and typically requires awareness of its existence and an understanding of the operational contexts in which VSATs are deployed to recognize its value or relevance. Its minimal exposure surface, enforced by authentication, further reduces general engagement.

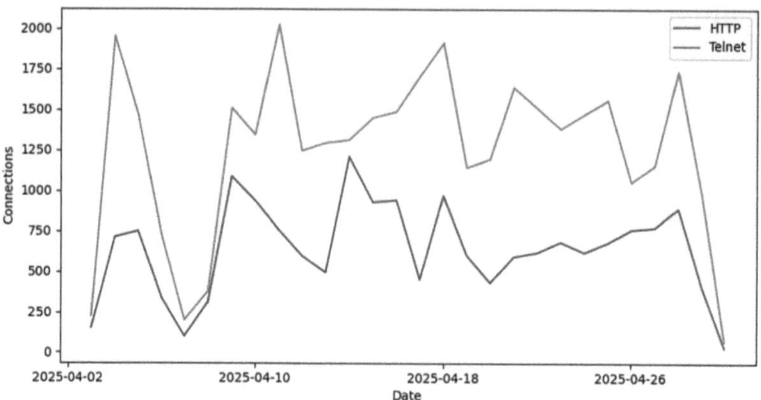

**Fig. 3.** Change in the number of log entries gathered per day.

**Table 4.** Top 20 connections received by geolocation.

| Geolocation 1/2 | Times | Geolocation 2/2 | Times |
| --- | --- | --- | --- |
| China | 31,895 | Indonesia | 1,397 |
| India | 12,570 | United Kingdom | 1,210 |
| USA | 6,080 | Iran | 1,215 |
| The Netherlands | 4,839 | Singapore | 1,106 |
| Russia | 2,910 | Vietnam | 1,097 |
| Taiwan | 2,150 | Bulgaria | 937 |
| South Korea | 2,070 | Argentina | e937 |
| Germany | 1,749 | Japan | 858 |
| Brazil | 1,608 | Sweden | 818 |
| Hong Kong | 1,541 | Türkiye | 492 |

**Table 5.** The 10 most used credential combinations in Telnet.

| Username | Password | Times |
| --- | --- | --- |
| admin | 1234 | 1,178 |
| root | aquario | 1,010 |
| root | admin | 962 |
| root | root | 686 |
| root | (empty) | 670 |
| root | hi3518 | 666 |
| admin | admin | 634 |
| admin | password | 632 |
| ubnt | ubnt | 630 |
| admin | ujMko0admin | 624 |

To answer **RQ1: Were there any actors exploiting specific vulnerabilities related to VSAT environments?**, we search in our logs for (a) access to the Web and Telnet services via the default credentials (CVE-2018-5266) and (b) access to the status of the VSAT via the getSysStatus endpoint without authentication (CVE-2018-5728). Only one such attempt has been recorded in the login page of Web dashboard, with the use of default credentials. On the contrary, generic attempts, with credentials such as those in Table 5, have been logged in the Telnet service.

The role "'User" has been used in one Telnet login attempt, that however had the combination of *"username=User,password=1001"* and *"username=User,password=User"*, which are invalid in the scope of this honeynet. In the attempt to access the Web dashboard, a single IP address used the credential combinations of *"username=(empty),password=(empty)"*, *"username=Dealer,password=seatel2"*, *"username=dealer,password=seatel2"*, *"username=user,password=seatel2"* and *"username=User,password=seatel1"*. Only the last one is a valid combination providing access to the Menu interface of the Web dashboard. The only records for accessing the *getSysStatus* endpoint indicate that those attempts have been made after the authentication, and not with unauthenticated connections by leveraging the vulnerability in CVE-2018-5728.

Among all the requests, we received 19,334 GET and 644 POST actions. Only 8,950 GET and 228 POST requests attempted to access endpoints served by our Web service. Besides those of the single successful login, the majority of the requests revolve mainly around the Login endpoint, which serves the landing page of the VSAT. Many others such as the GET request to */cgi-bin/iptest.cgi?cmd=iptest.cgi&url=%60wget+http%3A%2F%2F209.200.246.240%3A8081%2Fmeow%60&time=%!(NOVERB) HTTP/1.1)*, or the POST one to */cgi-bin/account_mgr.cgi*, indicate generic efforts to exploit potentially vulnerable services.

For **RQ2: What were their interactions with Web dashboard and CLI environments?**, we observe that a number of 196 IP addresses have attempted to access both services. Nevertheless, only logs from the Web dashboard exhibit some form of interaction, after the single successful login recorded. This constitutes of configuring the satellite (*/ConfigSat.html*), setting the antenna parameters (*/cgi-bin/setAntParams*), setting the possition of the ship (*UserShpPosSet.html*) viewing and exporting data from the VSAT (*/Viewlog.html* and */DataExport.html*), and attempting to access the Menu for the "Dealer" (*/MenuDealerGX.html*). Since there are no successful logins to the Telnet service, there are no meaningful interactions that can be correlated between the two honeynet services.

With respect to **RQ3: Were there any persistence mechanisms attempted?**, we argue that a dedicated focus on persistence is necessary because, as demonstrated in past CPS/ICS attacks [15], maintaining persistence enables adversaries to gather intelligence on the targeted environment, develop tailored tooling, and return at will to carry out further attacks or pivot to other systems. This sustained access is especially critical in ICS contexts, where disruption can have significant operational and safety consequences. For our environment, actions such as the change of passwords, configuration or drop of modified firmware did not occur during the data collection period. There was only one attempt, in the Web service, to escalate privileges to the user "Dealer", by attempting to directly access the corresponding Menu page while being authenticated as "User". This lack of usage of persistence mechanisms could be attributed to the fact that, besides the change of the password of the user "User", all the other endpoints that could potentially enable persistence mechanisms to be established, require the user to first be authenticated with a properly privileged account.

Overall, the above indicate only one attack from a curious party that is somewhat familiar with the particular VSAT system and its vulnerabilities, that is still exploring the nature of such systems. In this attack, the actor was knowledgeable about the user roles and their privileges of the VSAT, but only attempted some basic actions via the account with the lowest permissions. We intend to continue collecting data from our honeynet over the course of the next year. This could enrich the answers to the above RQs, and can provide us with a better understanding of any further adversaries that specifically look for and target VSAT systems.

### 5.3   Limitations

In the current implementation, Salty Seagull is limited to the simulation of a VSAT communication system, with no additional shipboard components integrated. Expanding the honeynet to include other critical subsystems, such as propulsion control and navigation systems, along with vulnerabilities that facilitate lateral movement, could significantly enhance the realism and depth of the deception environment. Nevertheless, the present configuration effectively illustrates how the compromise of an insecure communications system could serve as an initial entry point for adversaries targeting maritime assets.

It is important to note that a sophisticated adversary may attempt to cross-reference the replayed VDR information, such as latitude and longitude coordinates, with external maritime tracking data to assess the authenticity of the simulated vessel. As a potential enhancement, future work could involve the integration of live voyage data from operational commercial vessels. However, acquiring such real-time data introduces substantial challenges, particularly concerning privacy regulations and operational security constraints e.g., voice recordings from the bridge might include private conversations, or logged routes, cargo data, and operational practices, are sensitive for competitive reasons.

Finally, we acknowledge that the credibility and discoverability of the honeynet could be further strengthened by situating it within a network infrastructure associated with satellite telecommunications. Deploying the system over low Earth orbit satellite networks, such as Starlink, OneWeb, or Amazon's Project Kuiper, may more convincingly reinforce the perception that the emulated VSAT system belongs to a legitimate maritime platform, thereby improving the effectiveness of the overall deception strategy. Furthermore, this could involve deploying multiple instances across diverse geographic locations, with variations in displayed information. However, this approach is both resource-intensive and logistically complex, as it necessitates collaboration with other researchers to physically deploy and maintain low Earth orbit satellite connectivity in distributed regions worldwide.

## 6    Conclusions

To investigate the threat landscape associated with VSAT systems aboard maritime vessels, we developed a specialized VSAT honeynet designed to attract potential attackers targeting shipboard communication infrastructure. To replicate the operational characteristics of such CPS environments, we implemented both a Web-based dashboard and a CLI, each populated with simulated voyage data. The major findings of this work demonstrate that despite numerous attempts using generic exploits, only a single adversary demonstrated awareness of the system's nature and associated vulnerabilities, successfully gaining access and performing initial reconnaissance within the environment. This suggests that meaningful exploitation of such systems requires specific domain knowledge, underscoring the complexity of compromising a ship's network. Future improvements could include the expansion of the honeynet with more elaborate ship services and components to increase emulation fidelity.

**Acknowledgement.** We sincerely thank the anonymous reviewers for their insightful comments and valuable suggestions. We would like to acknowledge the students participating in the Hack@Sea Minor course in 2024 at NHL Stenden University of Applied Sciences, for their assistance regarding parts of the web development used for this work.

**Data Availability Statement.** The anonymized version of the data collected in this work are made available at https://doi.org/10.5281/zenodo.15469996.

**Disclosure of Interests.** The authors have no competing interests to declare that are relevant to the content of this article.

## References


1. AG, D.T.: T-pot: A multi-honeypot platform. Honeynet Project (2025)
2. Akpan, F., Bendiab, G., Shiaeles, S., Karamperidis, S., Michaloliakos, M.: Cybersecurity challenges in the maritime sector. Network **2**(1), 123–138 (2022). https://doi.org/10.3390/network2010009, https://www.mdpi.com/2673-8732/2/1/9
3. Brouwer, S.: HoneyShip: A Maritime VSAT Honeypot to Collect Cyberattacks and Analyze Threats. Master's thesis, Rijksuniversiteit Groningen, 9712 CP Groningen, Netherlands (2024)

4. Cheswick, B.: An evening with berferd in which a cracker is lured, endured, and studied. In: Proceedings of Winter USENIX Conference, San Francisco, pp. 20–24 (1992)
5. CYDOME: Lab dookhtegan cyber attack on iranian oil tankers disrupts operations. https://cydome.io/lab-dookhtegan-cyber-attack-on-iranian-oil-tankers-disrupts-operations/. Accessed 27 Apr 2025
6. Franco, J., Aris, A., Canberk, B., Uluagac, A.S.: A survey of honeypots and honeynets for internet of things, industrial internet of things, and cyber-physical systems. IEEE Commun. Surv. Tutor. **23**(4), 2351–2383 (2021)
7. Hilt, S., Maggi, F., Perine, C., Remorin, L., Rösler, M., Vosseler, R.: Caught in the act: Running a realistic factory honeypot to capture real threats. Trend Micro Research (2020)
8. IACS: Recommendations on voyage data recorder. https://web.archive.org/web/20230202060115/https://iacs.org.uk/download/1871. Accessed 01 Apr 2025
9. International Maritime Organization (IMO): Resolution MSC.333(90) (Adopted on 22 May 2012): Adoption of Revised Performance Standards for Shipborne Voyage Data Recorders (VDRs). https://wwwcdn.imo.org/localresources/en/OurWork/Safety/Documents/333(90).pdf (2012), iMO: London, UK
10. International Maritime Organization (IMO): International Convention for the Safety of Life at Sea (SOLAS), 1974. International Maritime Organization, London, UK (2021), available online: https://www.imo.org/en/About/Conventions/Pages/International-Convention-for-the-Safety-of-Life-at-Sea-(SOLAS),-1974.aspx
11. Jiang, X., Wang, X.: "out-of-the-box" monitoring of VM-based high-interaction honeypots. In: International Workshop on Recent Advances in Intrusion Detection, pp. 198–218. Springer (2007)
12. Kempinski, S., Ichaarine, S., Sciancalepore, S., Zambon, E.: ICSvertase: A framework for purpose-based design and classification of ICS honeypots. In: Proceedings of the 18th International Conference on Availability, Reliability and Security, pp. 1–10. ACM, Benevento Italy (Aug 2023). https://doi.org/10.1145/3600160.3605020, https://dl.acm.org/doi/10.1145/3600160.3605020
13. Koniaris, I., Papadimitriou, G., Nicopolitidis, P.: Analysis and visualization of ssh attacks using honeypots. In: Eurocon 2013, pp. 65–72. IEEE (2013)
14. Mahmoud, R.V., Pedersen, J.M.: Deploying a university honeypot: A case study. In: CEUR Workshop Proceedings, vol. 2443, pp. 27–38. CEUR Workshop Proceedings (2019)
15. Makrakis, G.M., Kolias, C., Kambourakis, G., Rieger, C., Benjamin, J.: Industrial and critical infrastructure security: technical analysis of real-life security incidents. IEEE Access **9**, 165295–165325 (2021). https://doi.org/10.1109/ACCESS.2021.3133348, https://ieeexplore.ieee.org/document/9638617/
16. Martin, L., Benson, B.: Ics/ot cybersecurity considerations for maritime transportation (2023), https://hub.dragos.com/hubfs/116-Whitepapers/Dragos_WP_ICS_OTCybersecuritMaritimeTransp_Final%20(1).pdf. Accessed 03 Apr 2025
17. MITRE: Cve-2018-5266. https://nvd.nist.gov/vuln/detail/cve-2018-5266. Accessed 03 Apr 2025
18. MITRE: Cve-2018-5267. https://nvd.nist.gov/vuln/detail/cve-2018-5267. Accessed 03 Apr 2025
19. MITRE: MITRE ATT&CK®. https://attack.mitre.org/. Accessed 03 Apr 2025
20. Oosterhof, M.: Cowrie ssh/telnet honeypot. https://github.com/micheloosterhof/cowrie. Accessed 01 May 2025

21. Pavur, J., Moser, D., Strohmeier, M., Lenders, V., Martinovic, I.: A tale of sea and sky on the security of maritime vsat communications. In: 2020 IEEE Symposium on Security and Privacy (SP), pp. 1384–1400. IEEE (2020)

22. Pijpker, J., McCombie, S.J.: A ship honeynet to gather cyber threat intelligence for the maritime sector. In: 2023 IEEE 48th Conference on Local Computer Networks (LCN), pp. 1–6. IEEE (2023)

23. Pitropakis, N., Logothetis, M., Andrienko, G., Stefanatos, J., Karapistoli, E., Lambrinoudakis, C.: Towards the creation of a threat intelligence framework for maritime infrastructures. In: International Workshop on the Security of Industrial Control Systems and Cyber-Physical Systems, pp. 53–68. Springer (2019)

24. Rajaram, P., Goh, M., Zhou, J.: Guidelines for cyber risk management in shipboard operational technology systems. J. Phys.: Conf. Series. **2311**, 012002. IOP Publishing (2022)

25. Raymond, E.S.: Nmea revealed. URL https://gpsd.gitlab.io/gpsd/NMEA.html (2019)

26. Rist, L., Vestergaard, J., Haslinger, D., Pasquale, A., Smith, J.: Conpot ics/scada honeypot. Honeynet Project (conpot. org) (2013)

27. Rist, L., Vetsch, S., Kossin, M., Mauer, M.: Know your tools: Glastopf-a dynamic, low-interaction web application honeypot. Honeynet Project **4**, 2 (2010)

28. Rivieramm: Fishing vessel owners turn to vsat. https://www.rivieramm.com/opinion/opinion/fishing-vessel-owners-turn-to-vsat-35069. Accessed 01 Apr 2025

29. SeaTel: Document ima cli protocol specification. https://www.yumpu.com/en/document/read/50984924/document-ima-cli-protocol-specification-livewire-connections-ltd. Accessed 03 Apr 2025

30. Spitzner, L.: Honeypots: Tracking Hackers. Addison-Wesley Longman Publishing Co., Inc (2002)

31. Spitzner, L.: The honeynet project: trapping the hackers. IEEE Secur. Priv. **1**(2), 15–23 (2003)

32. Srinivasa, S., Pedersen, J.M., Vasilomanolakis, E.: Deceptive directories and "vulnerable" logs: a honeypot study of the ldap and log4j attack landscape. In: 2022 IEEE European Symposium on Security and Privacy Workshops (EuroS&PW), pp. 442–447. IEEE (2022)

33. Stoll, C.: The cuckoo's egg: tracking a spy through the maze of computer espionage. Simon and Schuster (1989)

34. Tambe, A., et al.: Detection of threats to Iot devices using scalable vpn-forwarded honeypots. In: Proceedings of the Ninth ACM Conference on Data and Application Security and Privacy, pp. 85–96 (2019)

35. Tools, D.: Web honeypot. https://github.com/DinoTools/dionaea/. Accessed 01 Apr 2025

36. transmitterdan: Vdrplayer - play voyage data recorder files over ip link., https://github.com/transmitterdan/VDRplayer. Accessed 01 Apr 2025

37. Willbold, J., Schloegel, M., Bisping, R., Strohmeier, M., Holz, T., Lenders, V.: Vsaster: uncovering inherent security issues in current vsat system practices. In: Proceedings of the 17th ACM Conference on Security and Privacy in Wireless and Mobile Networks, pp. 288–299 (2024)

38. Yigit, Y., Kinaci, O.K., Duong, T.Q., Canberk, B.: Twinpot: digital twin-assisted honeypot for cyber-secure smart seaports. In: 2023 IEEE International Conference on Communications Workshops (ICC Workshops), pp. 740–745. IEEE (2023)

# Signals and Symptoms: ICS Attack Dataset From Railway Cyber Range

Anis Yusof[1(✉)] [iD], Yuancheng Liu[2] [iD], Niklaus Kang[2] [iD], Choon Meng Seah[2] [iD], Zhenkai Liang[1] [iD], and Ee-Chien Chang[1] [iD]

[1] School of Computing, National University of Singapore, Singapore, Singapore
{anis,liangzk,changec}@comp.nus.edu.sg
[2] National Cybersecurity R&D Lab, National University of Singapore, Singapore, Singapore
{yc_liu,niklausk,seahcm}@nus.edu.sg

**Abstract.** The prevalence of cyberattacks on Industrial Control Systems (ICS) has highlighted the necessity for robust security measures and incident response to protect critical infrastructure. This is prominent when Operational Technology (OT) systems undergo digital transformation by integrating with Information Technology (IT) systems to enhance operational efficiency, adaptability, and safety. To support analysts in staying abreast of emerging attack patterns, there is a need for ICS datasets that reflect indicators representative of contemporary cyber threats. To address this, we conduct two ICS cyberattack simulations to showcase the impact of trending ICS cyberattacks on a railway cyber range that resembles the railway infrastructure. The attack scenario is designed to blend trending attack trends with attack patterns observed from historical ICS incidents. The resulting evidence is collected as datasets, serving as an essential resource for cyberattack analysis. This captures key indicators that are relevant to the current threat landscape, augmenting the effectiveness of security systems and analysts to protect against ICS cyber threats.

**Keywords:** ICS Dataset · Railway Cyber Range · ICS Cyberattack Simulation

## 1 Introduction

Cyberattack often targets ICS and cause disruptions to industrial operations. This is especially crucial for critical infrastructure, whose operations are vital to society. The impact of an ICS cyberattack could lead to life-threatening situations. One such critical infrastructure is the railway system comprising of interconnected systems and devices across the IT and OT segments. The railway systems has evolved to include complex OT systems to meet the growing demand of mass transportation. While such advancement is targeted to enhance the safety and reliability of railway infrastructure, complex interdependent systems impose a significant cybersecurity challenge in defending and detecting threats. Furthermore, the segmented systems increase the complexity of understanding the malicious behaviors when a cyberattack occurs in railway systems.

© The Author(s), under exclusive license to Springer Nature Switzerland AG 2026
R. Laborde et al. (Eds.): ESORICS 2025, LNCS 16231, pp. 382–402, 2026.
https://doi.org/10.1007/978-3-032-16089-8_24

This raises the need for security analysts to be well equipped so as to promptly react and analyze a cyber incident, minimizing the operational impact without endangering human safety.

Security analysts generally rely on past incidents as a case study to conduct digital forensics and gain a better understanding about existing threats. To improve the overall effectiveness of analysis, one method is to conduct a cyber exercise by simulating various threats in the rail infrastructure [21,24] and assessing their response based on playbook [4]. Some examples of threats include ransomware and Denial of Service (DoS) attacks which disrupt the operational and safety aspect of the infrastructure [10]. Cyber exercise provides a platform for analysts to familiarize themselves with the forensics tools and validate their skillsets. Additionally, any lapses in existing workflow can be detected and rectified, improving the overall communication and coordination across various teams (e.g., management, operators, engineers). However, conducting a cyber exercise is often laborious and costly, requiring significant efforts to realize the simulated threats. Furthermore, the datasets resulting from such cyber exercises are often used within their context and are not made available for future use.

Analyzing real-world cyberattack data extracted from an actual railway system would provide valuable insights. This includes the actual Indicator of Compromise (IoC) and attack patterns observed from the data. However, real-world data are generally unavailable due to security and privacy concerns. Furthermore, conducting a simulated cyberattack on real-world systems to obtain useful data is infeasible due to the associated risks. This includes the risk of operational downtime during a train malfunction and the cascading effect of failures due to other fragile components. To overcome these challenges, one method is to replicate the rail infrastructure as a digital twin. By modeling the railway systems accurately, the digital twin provides a safe and controlled virtual environment for investigation without jeopardizing real-world operations. The digital twin also provides better control and monitoring capabilities, allowing analysts to execute their workflow and assess the impact based on the data extracted from the railway systems. However, developing a digital twin involves significant cost and complexity, further aggravating the challenge of making useful ICS datasets accessible. Despite this, the lack of quality data for ICS cyberattacks limits the understanding of the threat landscape [5,7], hampering the ability to effectively defend against trending attack patterns.

This raises the need to support cyberattack analysis with datasets that are an approximation of real-world attack scenarios which can then be used for various analysis, including tracing attacks, identifying vulnerabilities, and mitigating future risks. However, existing studies has highlighted the need for the simulation testbed to be realistically designed so as to avoid having highly dependent features and experimental artifacts in the generated data [12,18]. In this work, our goal is to generate ICS attack dataset that is useful for various security applications. Specifically, we design two realistic cyberattack scenarios based on attack patterns observed from actual historical ICS cyberattacks. These cyberattack scenarios are customized for a large-scale international cyber exercise organized by a European-based center of excellence specializing in international research, training, and capacity in building cybersecurity and cyber defense. The cyberattack is executed in a railway cyber range, generating relevant evidence which is then collected as a dataset. Additionally, we share the challenges faced in designing the cyberattack scenario and collecting the relevant evidence. To support future research efforts, we collect the evidence as datasets and share them in a public repository.[1] To summarize, the contribution of this work is as follows:

- We share the design of our railway cyber range that enables experimentation with cyberattacks on railway infrastructure.
- We present the design of two cyberattack scenarios that are customized for a large-scale international cyber exercise on ICS.
- We publicly release two ICS attack datasets resulting from the cyberattack scenarios to support future research in this field.

The remainder of this paper is structured as follows. Section 2 introduce the background of ICS cyberattacks and existing works related to this context. Section 3 presents the design of our railway cyber range that is used as the testbed for simulating cyberattacks. Section 4 introduces the methodology of our study in designing the cyberattack scenario and experimentation to extract the relevant evidence. Section 5 empirically evaluates the dataset collected from the cyberattack scenario and presents a case study of analyzing the dataset. Section 6 discuss the challenges of designing ICS attack simulations and the applications of the dataset. Section 7 concludes the paper.

## 2 Background and Related Work

This section provides an overview of the required context by firstly introducing the threat landscape of ICS, then we introduce the related work to establish the context of generating ICS attack datasets.

### 2.1 Threat Landscape

Understanding the threat landscape of critical infrastructure is the key to designing attack scenarios that accurately represent current ICS cyberattacks. Historically, cyberattacks conducted by Advanced Persistent Threats (APT) are known to target industries that are important to national security and the economy. This includes energy facilities, transportation, telecommunications, and healthcare. Consequently, the cyberattacks cause disruptions and potentially allow them to conduct cyber espionage. Despite critical infrastructure being well protected, APT cyberattacks are targeted and highly motivated by their goal, which makes them challenging to detect as they stealthily conduct longitudinal multi-stage attacks on the critical infrastructure [15].

---

[1] https://doi.org/10.5281/zenodo.15536351.

The ICS infrastructure is categorized into IT and OT segments. Based on the operational needs, systems in the OT segment are designed to prioritize high availability and safe operations. Additionally, the systems in ICS are generally isolated and do not provide direct communication with the public [3], thus neglecting the need for security. This effectively reduces the attack surface for critical infrastructure, as public-facing connections provide more opportunities for threat actors to establish a foothold. The systems in the IT segment may need to interact with the OT systems for various functionalities (e.g., remote monitoring and access). Furthermore, this is especially prominent where ICS infrastructure undergoes digital transformation to make it more intelligent, exposing these OT systems to typical IT-related cyber threats. This effectively invalidates existing assumptions where air-gapped OT systems are isolated and inherently secure. As a result, ICS systems are facing an emerging threat originating from the IT segment.

The initial attack vector is a vital entry point for APT to gain an initial foothold into the critical infrastructure. Some of the patterns that are commonly observed for the initial access include supply chain compromise (e.g., Dragonfly APT) and spearphishing (e.g., APT33, APT44). Further aggravating the situation, the connectivity from IT segment has enable existing IT-related threats (e.g., LockBit ransomware campaign) to make their way into critical infrastructure. This suggest the shift of focus of threat actors from achieving financial gain through ransom to causing disruptions on ICS systems. This reflects the consequence of intersecting IT and OT segments, increasing the complexity of detecting and preventing ICS cyberattacks. Concurrently, such complex characteristics of cyberattacks provide the basis for designing realistic attack scenarios.

## 2.2   Related Work

We present two topics that are related to this work, namely existing works that construct a virtual model to simulate ICS infrastructure and works that involves the generation and sharing of ICS-related datasets.

**Virtual Modeling of ICS Infrastructure.** A virtual model of ICS infrastructure serves as a platform for safe experimentation of cyber threats, thus providing a means to obtain insights into ICS cyberattacks. An open-source framework called SCASS [9] provide a means for analysts to construct a customizable and extensible testbed that replicates complex Supervisory Control and Data Acquisition (SCADA) and ICS infrastructure with high fidelity. Similarly, ICSSIM [6] proposes a framework to construct a virtual ICS testbed, and provides a means to deploy them on actual hardware (e.g., physical devices, containerized environments, simulation systems). With a focus on generating data that is appropriate for analysis, an existing work [20] proposes a testbed for repeatable cyberattack simulations aimed at generating useful datasets. Likewise, the Tennessee-Eastman System simulates a chemical process that is modeled after a real industrial operational systems [8], thus enabling the generation of data from attack simulation (e.g., PLC-SAGE [25]). While existing works provide a general platform to simulate ICS cyberattacks, the SAFETY4RAILS project [13] and CaESAR [23] focus on providing a simulation platform for the railway infrastructure. In this work, we propose a railway cyber range that models a railway infrastructure, thus providing a platform to simulate complex ICS cyberattacks, effectively producing indicators that can be extracted as datasets.

**ICS Cyberattack Dataset.** High-quality datasets are essential to facilitate research and analysis of cyberattacks on ICS. To address this, the HAI dataset 1.0 [22] provide a Cyber-Physical Systems (CPS) dataset based on numerous benign and attack scenarios. Similarly, the SWaT [16], WaDi [2], and EPIC [1] datasets are constructed based on ICS-based attack scenarios executed on water treatment, water distribution, and energy control respectively. Additionally, ICS-ADD [14] provides an open-source dataset that contains network traffic captured from ICS systems that are subjected to simulated cyberattacks. Instead of generating datasets from cyberattack simulations, this work [17] proposes a data augmentation approach that leverages existing data to recreate a simulation environment, thus providing a means to produce a realistic synthetic dataset. In this work, we provide railway-specific ICS datasets that are generated based on cyberattack simulation conducted on a railway cyber range.

## 3   Railway Cyber Range

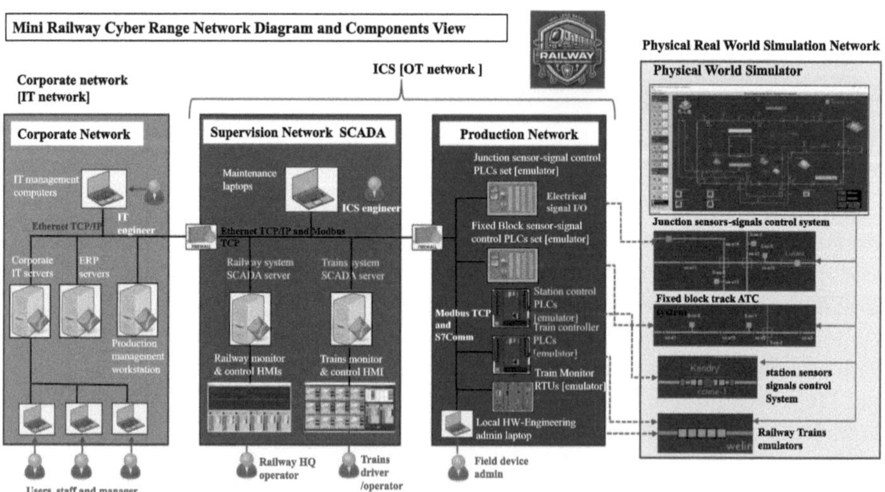


**Fig. 1.** An overview of the railway cyber range

Experimentations enable analysts to gain insights into various cyberattack scenarios across IT and OT systems. To facilitate experiments on a railway infrastructure, we construct a simulated railway IT/OT system as a railway cyber range to conduct cybersecurity experimentation. The railway cyber range models the railway infrastructure and has emerged as a useful mechanism to simulate ICS cyberattack, effectively providing a safe environment for experimentation with cyber threats. As reflected in Fig. 1, the platform consists of four network systems, namely the corporate network, supervision SCADA network, production network, and physical real-world simulation network. The systems in both IT and OT segments serve distinct purposes. The IT segment consists of a corporate network that focuses on business processes (e.g., workstations, web server, business applications). The OT segment consists of both supervision and production networks which control the equipment and operational processes (e.g., sensors, actuators). The real-world network emulates the physical effects that the devices have caused in the real world. This platform is designed as a miniature railway IT/OT system that reflects the fundamental operational logic and is used as a cyber range to conduct cyber exercises.

**IT Systems.** To replicate a realistic IT system in the railway platform, we establish three key components that form the IT system. They consist of IT computing environment, the execution of realistic organizational activities, and conducting attack behaviors. The IT environment simulates a typical corporate network of a railway organization. This environment consists of various business-oriented computing systems such as workstations, firewalls, routers, and switches. Based on real-world computing environment, diverse day-to-day activities from the respective business units are conducted using the IT systems. To generate benign activities on the computing environment and the corresponding network traffic, the activities of railway staff are virtually simulated. This includes actions made by a railway operator, train driver, safety officer, IT support engineer, and administrative officer. In addition to benign behaviors, we simulate the malicious activities to mimic attack scenarios throughout the IT systems. This includes the process of sending phishing emails, conducting False Control Injection (FCI), False Data Injection (FDI), Man-in-the-Middle (MITM), and Distributed Denial of Service (DDoS) attacks.

**OT Systems.** The OT system in the platform replicates the ICS components that control the railway system. The OT environment consists of two networks, namely the SCADA network and the production network. The SCADA network consists of control and monitoring systems. This includes the SCADA historian server that serves as a centralized repository for data collected from SCADA systems. Additionally, this network also contains Human-Machine Interface (HMI) for monitoring and maintenance computers used by system operators and engineers, respectively. The production network contains Field Device Controller (FDC) that simulates a realistic representation of production environment in a railway system. This includes the simulation of Programmable Logic Controller (PLC) and Remote Terminal Unit (RTU) devices.

The ICS components in the OT systems are functionally categorized into two subsystems, namely the railway signaling system and the train control system. The track signaling system simulates the control of track junctions and railway stations. To automate the control of the tracks and junctions, the signaling system reads the simulated electrical signals from the devices in the real-world network. For example, the devices in the real-world network indicate the train's position on the track. This allows the signaling system to control the fixed block signaling, manage passing trains through different track junctions, and guide trains to dock and depart from railway stations.

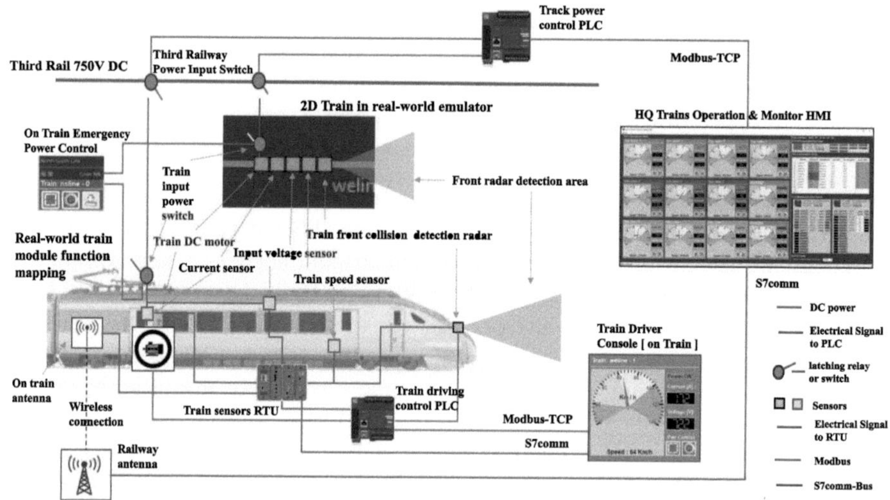


**Fig. 2.** An overview of the train control system

As reflected in Fig. 2, the train control system replicate the train management by simulating the PLC and RTU devices. The PLC devices are used to manage the third rail, train signaling, and collision avoidance mechanisms. Additionally, the RTU devices are used to collect operational sensor data from the train such as throttle and braking, current speed, input voltage, and motor current. This allows the train control system to detect the state of track signals, thus making coordinated decisions for the train to pass through junctions and make a stop at stations. Furthermore, the train control system monitors the train ahead to avoid collision and adheres to the fixed block states of railway tracks. The train control system also communicates with the railway headquarters and provides monitoring and control capabilities on the train driver's console.

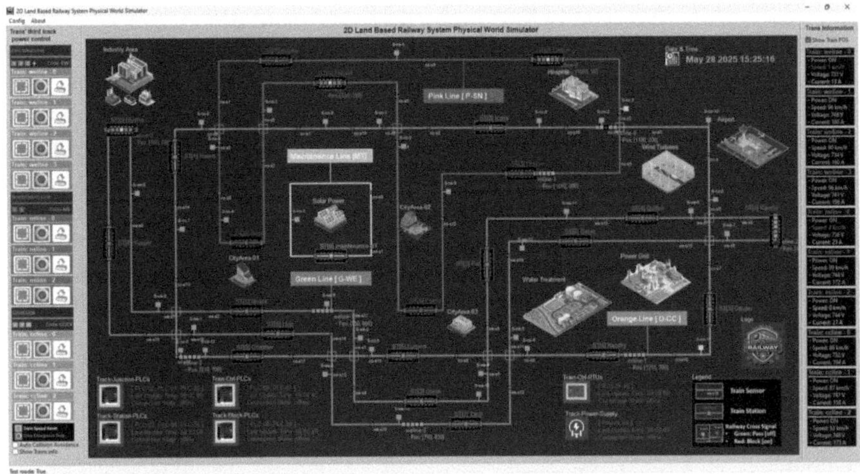

**Fig. 3.** Visualization of the railway cyber range

**Railway Real World Emulation.** The railway trains are simulated based on the interconnected systems across both IT and OT networks. To visualize the train network, we provide a graphical user interface for the users of this platform to monitor and control the system as shown Fig. 3. This includes the visualization of physical real-world scenarios of trains traversing the tracks and docking at stations. The railway emulator features ten trains across four tracks. This includes the simulation of the track signaling system which simulates track junction control and railway stations. By having the visualization, the emulator aims to deliver a realistic and dynamic railway environment that serves as a cyber range to perform experimentation on a railway platform.

## 4 Methodology

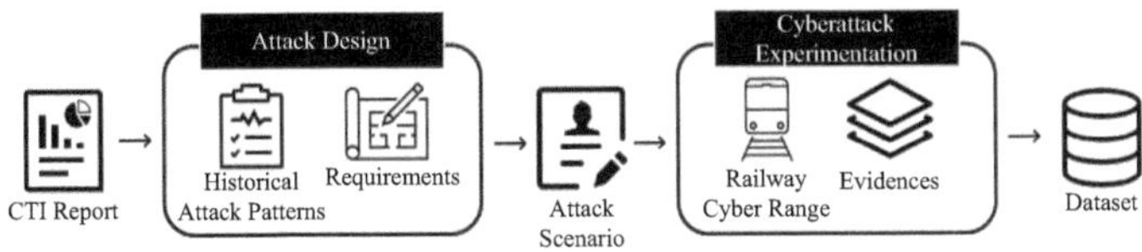



**Fig. 4.** The methodology to construct ICS dataset

To construct a dataset that is representative of ICS attack, we describe the process of designing and executing the attack scenario. As reflected in Fig. 4, this is segregated into two phases. The first phase involves the process of designing the cyberattack while the second phase performs experimentation which orchestrates the cyberattack on the railway cyber range. To conduct attack scenario that are representative of real-world cyberattacks, we utilize the information found from Cyber Threat Intelligence (CTI) reports that describe past incidents. This information is analyzed to identify historical attack patterns that contribute to attack complexity and realism. This leads to the process of collecting the relevant information related to the infrastructure, malware, and activity as a requirement. The outcome of the first phase produces the attack scenario which describes the timeline of the cyberattack. The second phase utilizes the information in the attack scenario to execute the cyberattack on the railway platform. Upon executing the attack scenario, the resulting evidences are extracted from the railway platform. These evidences are collected as a dataset that represents the observations of the ICS cyberattack.

## 4.1   Phase I: Attack Design

To design scenarios with sufficient complexity, it is vital to capture the attack patterns that are observed from existing cyberattacks. We begin by identifying the relevant information with regards to historical attack patterns. To attain a realistic cyberattack, we utilize the observables that are described in CTI reports. This includes information related to the threat actors, the discovered IoC, and the attack activities in terms of Techniques and Procedures (TTPs) that are observed from past cyberattacks. The CTI report describes the overview of the threat actor, stating about their background and motivation behind the attack on the critical infrastructure. Additionally, CTI report describes the IoC that are observed from the cyberattack such as the IP addresses (e.g., communication with Command and Control (C2) server) and file hashes of suspicious artifacts. The TTPs describe the threat actor's behaviors and methods that are observed in the infrastructure. Due to the variety of CTI reports that describe the same cyberattack, the key challenge is to identify non-conflicting information that contributes towards the appearance of indicators in the resulting evidence. Despite this, the information described in CTI report describes complementary aspects of the cyber threat, serving as the basis for designing attack scenarios. This provides a comprehensive understanding of historical ICS cyberattacks, especially for incidents that happen on railway systems.

To design a realizable end-to-end cyberattack, we gather the information about the required components and activities. One challenge is to identify the relevant details from unstructured information, which are then collected as a requirement. There are various types of components that are needed to realize the cyberattack. This includes the process of defining the network segments along with their respective hosts. Additionally, network-related systems (e.g., router, firewall) can be specified to allow or deny access in terms of network connectivity. When the infrastructure is set, the next step is to implement the behavior component which provides interactivity among the systems. The attack behaviors are defined as a sequence of actions to be taken by the threat actor (e.g., running commands, executing malware). To increase the complexity of finding malicious activities, one challenge is to design diverse benign behaviors and include them as part of the requirements. These benign behaviors replicate the day-to-day activities of humans (e.g., administrative staff, technician) that utilize the system. This enhances the realism of the cyberattack as contextually relevant activities are included as part of the design.

Upon integrating the historical attack patterns as part of the requirements, the components are then translated to an attack scenario. This scenario contains information that can be classified into three categories, namely the network segments, hosts, and activities. This contains the technical description about the components that are then used to instantiate cyberattack. For network segments, we define the logical groups of network segments that represent the real-world physical networks (e.g., external network, operations network, physical network). This includes network configurations such as subnets and IP addresses. Additionally, the hosts are defined with configurations related to the operating system (e.g., operating system type and version, credentials) and applications (e.g., productivity software). To simulate the activities, the benign and attack behaviors are chronologically defined as the actions taken by an actor at a specific time (e.g., hacker runs a command to find the credential file at 08:50).

## 4.2   Phase II: Cyberattack Experimentation

To reproduce the attack, the experimentation phase uses the attack scenario to instantiate the cyberattack on a testbed that is connected to the railway cyber range. The testbed provides the means to realize virtual instances in their respective network segments. This enables the simulation of computing infrastructure that is connected to the railway platform. Additionally, the railway platform mirrors the physical railway infrastructure with signaling systems and rolling stocks across different tracks. To simulate the benign and attack activities, we utilize Cluster User Emulation System (CUE) [19] which uses customizable scheduling profiles to generate benign and malicious traffic according to the attack scenario. Overall, the testbed serves as a sandbox for simulation, analysis, and generating data related to both computing and railway infrastructure.

The cyberattack simulation generates the corresponding data that is useful for analysis. To obtain the relevant evidence, we extract the data that is available on the testbed. The key challenge in this phase is to ensure that the resulting indicators are preserved in the extracted data. We utilize `tcpdump` to capture the network traffic in the routers and switches. This provides an overview of internal communications between hosts and communications across network segments. The network traffic is captured in `pcap` format, which is compatible with various network forensic analysis tools (e.g., Wireshark). For system-level evidence, we collect the state of the affected hosts by taking a memory snapshot. The snapshot provides an insight into the attack activities that occurred in the affected hosts (e.g., running processes, loaded libraries, and open sockets) and can be analyzed using memory forensic tools (e.g., Volatility). Additionally, we capture the disk images of the affected hosts. The disk images are captured as E01 format which is widely used in Digital Forensics and Incident Response (DFIR) investigations due to its forensically sound characteristics (i.e., metadata and integrity verification). The evidences are extracted from the testbed and collected as a dataset. The indicators that are captured during the experimentation are useful for analysis as they represent the observations of the simulated cyberattack.

## 5   Experiment

In this section, we design two attack scenarios to simulate ICS cyberattacks that involve the railway cyber range. We then empirically evaluate the evidence that is extracted from the ICS infrastructure. The dataset includes evidence that is appropriate for DFIR analysts to conduct forensics on filesystems, memory, network, and logs.

### 5.1   Scenario For ICS Cyberattack

To demonstrate the usefulness of the datasets, we designed two attack scenarios, namely AS1 and AS2, as described below. These scenarios are designed to simulate end-to-end cyberattack throughout the ICS environment.

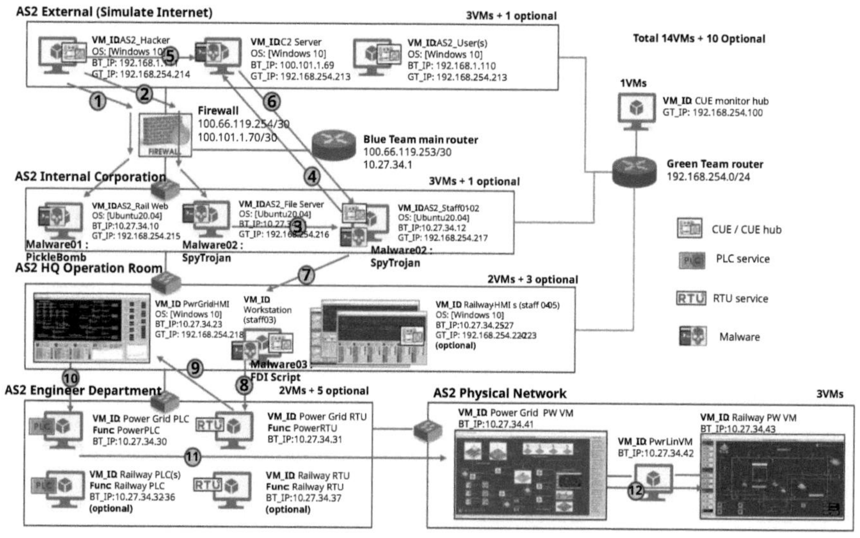


**Fig. 5.** Environment setup and attack path for AS1

**Attack Scenario 1.** – We design the cyberattack scenario named AS1 to demonstrate a multi-stage ICS cyberattack, specifically on a railway infrastructure as reflected in Fig. 5 along with its attack steps as described in Table 1. We studied and implemented the attack patterns (e.g., execution of custom ICS malware) that are commonly observed from ICS cyberattacks conducted by APT groups (e.g., Dragonfly and Allanite APTs). Based on the historical attack patterns, we integrate the patterns as part of the requirements for the AS1 attack scenario. This scenario consists of five network segments, four of which form the internal ICS networks. The first segment is the external network which simulates two hosts from a public network. These hosts are controlled by the threat actor that connects from the internet. The external network is connected to the internal ICS networks through a firewall that filters unauthorized inbound network traffic. The second network segment is the internal corporation network that consists of two hosts used by railway staff. Subsequently, the headquarters operation room network contains four hosts equipped with consoles for real-time control and monitoring by headquarters operators and engineers. This is followed by the maintenance department network which consists of three hosts that manage the diagnostics of the railway infrastructure and rolling stock. The engineer department network consists of three hosts that simulates the PLC which provides functionalities to the railway infrastructure (i.e., train control, station control, and junction control).

**Table 1.** Attack steps for AS1 attack scenario

| Step | Description |
| --- | --- |
| 1 | An insider downloads the spyTrojan malware into a system within the internal corporation network |
| 2 | The malware is disguised as `updateInstaller.exe`, and is received via email and subsequently propagated to other staff members through internal email communication |
| 3 | The hacker executes malicious tasks using the spyTrojan once it is installed |
| 4 | The spyTrojan exfiltrates sensitive information to the C2 server, including user credentials, keystrokes, and screenshots |
| 5 | The spyTrojan securely copies the FCI module to the PLC machine using SCP |
| 6 | The spyTrojan remotely executes the FCI module on the compromised machine using SSH |
| 7 | The FCI module sends the Modbus data readings from the PLC to the C2 server and resolves the FCI attack targets and parameters |
| 8 | The FCI module frequently sends false Modbus TCP coil control commands to the PLC |
| 9 | The PLC disables the collision avoidance control system and triggers an emergency power cutoff to the 'weline01' train |

To simulate the attack activities for AS1, we construct two custom malware as part of the attack steps as described in Table 1. The first malware is *spyTrojan* which is an espionage and delivery toolkit for the threat actor to monitor and transfer data from its victim. The second malware is *FCI module* which monitors and executes Modbus commands base on instructions from the threat actor.

**Attack Scenario 2.** – We introduce the design of the second cyberattack scenario named AS2. To construct a scenario with realistic attack patterns, we refer to a specific APT group called APT44, also commonly known as Sandworm. The APT group has conducted their campaigns since at least 2014 and are known to attack IT and critical infrastructures. In this case, we refer to a specific cyberattack conducted in 2015 that utilized the updated BlackEnergy malware [11] to perform DDoS attack on a power grid, temporarily disrupting the power supply to the public. In AS2, we introduce a new dimension to the ICS control systems by adding a power grid simulation system to the railway system.

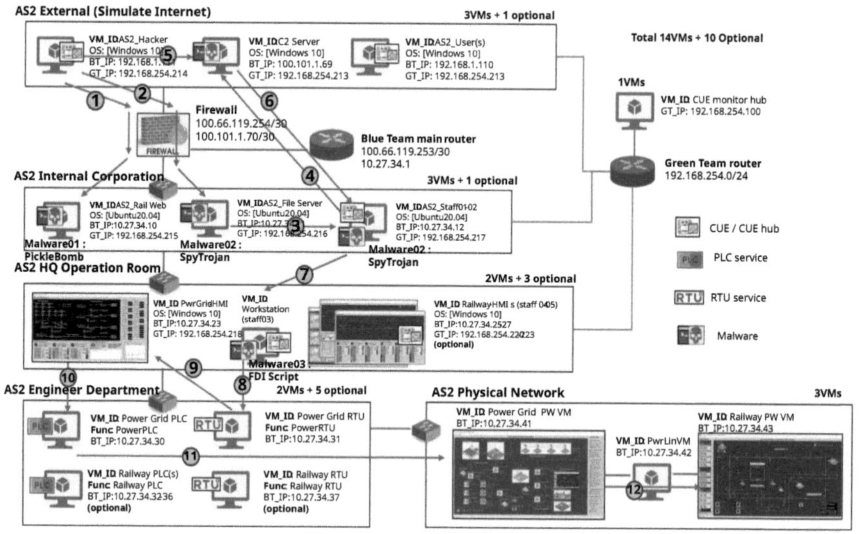


**Fig. 6.** Environment setup and attack path for AS2

The AS2 attack scenario is set up with five network segments in the environment setup as reflected in Fig. 6, along with the attack steps as described in Table 2. The first network segment is the external network which includes hosts (e.g., threat actor, C2 Server, users) that are from a public network. This is followed by the internal corporation network which consists of at least three hosts that simulate the day-to-day activities (e.g., hosting of the railway web application, FTP file sharing, railway officer's routine). This network is isolated from the public and connects through a firewall that restricts unauthorized access, serving as the sole entry point into the critical infrastructure. This network is connected to the headquarters operation network which contains at least two hosts equipped with consoles for control and monitoring by headquarters operators and engineers.

Subsequently, the engineer department network consists of at least two essential hosts, which include the PLC that controls the power breakers for the power grid simulation and RTU that collects power grid operational data. This network is directly connected to the physical network that consists of three major components, namely the power grid simulation, the railway simulation, and the power link. The power grid simulation include hosts that simulate the real world functionalities such as communicating the state of the power breaker to the PLC, generating metering units data, and supplying power to the railway simulation system. The railway simulation consists of hosts that perform railway functionalities, including the railway power distribution system.

**Table 2.** Attack steps for AS2 attack scenario

| Step | Description |
| --- | --- |
| 1 | Threat actor exploits a deserialization vulnerability in the image upload feature within the railway web application, allowing them to execute malicious codes, access sensitive files, and obtain credentials to a FTP file sharing server |
| 2 | Threat actor uses a valid credential to upload a spy trojan disguised as `ZoomMeetingInstaller.exe` in the file sharing server. |
| 3 | Staff synchronizes their local folder with the file sharing server, unknowingly downloaded and executed the disguised spy trojan to start an online meeting. |
| 4 | The spy trojan collects information from the victim and communicates its findings with the C2 server where the threat actor has control using a web interface. |
| 5 | The spy trojan is directed by the C2 server to perform network reconnaissance, stealing sensitive files, and records keystrokes and screen with the goal of finding an IT engineer PC to access SCADA workstation. |
| 6 | The threat actor devises a S7Comm-based FDI attack script based on stolen manual, then utilize the spy trojan to download the script onto the victim to effectively bypass firewall protection |
| 7 | The threat actor uses the stolen credential to transfer the FDI attack script from the IT engineer's PC to the SCADA workstation using SCP, which provides remote access to the SCADA workstation. |
| 8 | The FDI script connects to the RTU and injects false voltage and current data into its memory. |
| 9 | The HMI reads the false RTU values and detected an anomaly, thus triggering the power transformer's automated protection mechanism. |
| 10 | The HMI changes to alert state, temporarily halt PLC auto control and issue the command to turn off circuit breaker to protect the transformer. |
| 11 | The PLC received the Modbus command and turn off the circuit breaker in the power grid physical world simulation. |
| 12 | This causes the railway power outage as the power value drops to zero. |

To execute the cyberattack for AS2, we construct three custom malware as part of the attack steps as described in Table 2. The first malware is *pickle bomb* which is a serialized web shell backdoor that is delivered through an image upload vulnerability. This is used by the threat actor to execute malicious commands on the web server as described in the first attack step. The second malware is *spy trojan* that receives instructions from the C2 server to perform network scan, lateral movement, and file transfers. The third malware is *S7Comm FDI Script* which is used to perform false injection attack at high frequency with the purpose of overwriting the RTU memory.

### 5.2   Dataset Construction

The evidences from the respective attack scenario are extracted from the testbed and collected as a dataset. There are four types of evidence, namely disk image, memory image, network capture, and system-level logs. In addition to the captured dataset, we provide the screen recording of the respective emulators as information that visualizes activities occured during the cyberattack. We also include the Secure Sockets Layer (SSL) key that can be used to decrypt the SSL communication with the C2 server and categorize the SSL key logs as part of the system-level logs.

**Table 3.** Dataset statistics of the respective attack scenario

| | | File System | Memory Image | Network Capture | System Logs |
|---|---|---|---|---|---|
| AS1 | Total Size | 19.63 GB | 7.00 GB | 2.13 GB | ✗ |
| | Indicator Count | 2 | 13 | 14 | ✗ |
| AS2 | Total Size | ✗ | 4.64 GB | 966.77 MB | 352.92 KB |
| | Indicator Count | ✗ | 14 | 8 | 6 |

The dataset statistics of the respective attack scenario are presented in Table 3. The statistics show the total approximate archived file size of the evidence from the respective attack scenarios. Additionally, this includes the minimum amount of indicators that are found from the respective evidence.

The AS1 dataset consists of one disk image, two memory images, and one network dump that is collected across two days. The disk image is taken from the maintenance workstation (i.e., `10.27.34.85`) in the maintenance department network immediately after the `welin01` train has crashed at the end of the attack steps. To capture the state of the affected systems, we take a memory dump from two hosts after the train has crashed, namely the same maintenance workstation and the `staff03` workstation (i.e., `10.27.34.10`) in the internal corporation network. In addition to system-level data, we capture the network traffic from all interfaces firewall and router between 03 April 2024 and 04 April 2024. The captured network traffic consists of all communications between hosts in the internal network and with hosts in the external network. To supplement the dataset, we provide a video that reflects the cyberattack activities that occurred in the `Real World` emulator from the maintenance department network. The system-level logs for AS1 are unavailable.

The AS2 dataset consists of two memory images, one network capture, and one application log. The memory dump is taken from two hosts, namely the `staff01` and `staff03` workstations in the internal corporation network. The network capture consists of network traffic monitored from the main router (i.e., `100.66.119.253/30`). Additionally, we capture the application logs for the railway company's web application. We also provide three videos that show the cyberattack activities that occurred in the `Power Grid HMI` from the internal corporation network and the `Power Grid` as well as `Physical World` from the physical world network. The disk image for AS2 is unavailable.

## 5.3 Case Study: AS2 Attack Scenario

This section conducts a case study of AS2 to showcase the usefulness of the dataset for ICS cyberattack analysis. Based on the attack scenario as described in Sect. 5.1, we analyze the evidence that is extracted from affected hosts and identify the IoC. As described in the attack steps (i.e., Table 2), the threat actor interacts with a public-facing web application and perform a file upload during the early attack stages. The file upload activity is captured in the web application logs, as reflected in Listing 1.1. While the filename `image.txt` appears to be benign, the contents of the uploaded file indicate a resemblance to an encoded text. When the content is decoded using `base64` format, it becomes apparent that it contains malicious code to create a Flask-based web shell written in Python.

```
2025-04-21 08:30:17,481 INFO     File image.txt is uploaded via POST API.
2025-04-21 08:30:17,482 INFO     File Contents=b'gASVfwwAAAAAAACMCGJ1aWx
0aW5zlIwEZXh1Y5ST1FhgDAAAIyBUaGUgYWxsIG1uIG9uZSB2ZXJzaW9uIG9m ...'
```

Listing 1.1. Logs from web application showing file upload

In subsequent attack steps, the trojan (i.e., `ZoomMeetingInstaller.exe`) is executed on the first victim's host. Since the trojan is executed as a process in the memory, the memory image taken from the host of the affected victim captures this IoC. As reflected in Listing 1.2, executing `ZoomMeetingInstaller.exe` results in the creation of process 8340 on the system. This reflects the successful execution of the trojan, allowing the victim to communicate with the C2 server.

```
  PID       PPID        ImageFileName    Offset(V)       Threads     Handles
  ...
  5596      9660        cmd.exe          0xb5884bf39080  1           -
  8340      5596        ZoomMeetingIns   0xb5884b76c080  1           -
  8552      8340        conhost.exe      0xb5884abe1080  4           -
  6640      8340        ZoomMeetingIns   0xb5884abda080  7           -
  ...
```

Listing 1.2. Running processes based on the memory image taken from the first victim

When the installed malware communicates with the C2 server, the captured network traffic contains the network-level IoC that reflects their communication.

Based on Fig. 7, the network packet indicates that the communication contains a suspicious encoded URL string. When the string is decoded, it indicates the intention to exfiltrate the content of `credentials.txt` by using the `cat` command. This reflects the attack steps by collecting sensitive information from the victim and send them to the threat actor.

```
Wireshark · Packet 446779 · 20250421Tcpdump.pcap

> Frame 446779: 625 bytes on wire (5000 bits), 625 bytes captured (5000 bits)
> Linux cooked capture v1
> Internet Protocol Version 4, Src: 100.101.1.150, Dst: 100.66.119.4
> Transmission Control Protocol, Src Port: 50147, Dst Port: 5001, Seq: 1, Ack: 1, Len: 569
> Hypertext Transfer Protocol
∨ HTML Form URL Encoded: application/x-www-form-urlencoded
    ∨ Form item: "cmdContents" = "cat /home/ncl/credentials.txt"
        Key: cmdContents
        Value: cat /home/ncl/credentials.txt
    ∨ Form item: "resultContents" = "/home/ncl/credentials.txt\r\n"
        Key: resultContents
        Value: /home/ncl/credentials.txt\r\n
```

**Fig. 7.** Communication between the victim and the C2 server

We have also included three videos as part of AS2 dataset, showing the failure of the power grid which affects the entire railway infrastructure. This marks the success for the threat actors in reaching their desired goal by causing a disruption to the railway infrastructure according to AS2 attack steps. Based on the forensics performed on the evidences, analysts are able to identify various IoC from system-level and network-level perspectives. This allows analysts to reconstruct the attack sequence based on the discovered indicators, effectively understand the threat actor's behaviors and the motivation behind the cyberattack.

## 6   Discussion

The railway cyber range provides a means for the ICS cybersecurity community to study the impact of various cyberattacks on a railway infrastructure, especially for attacks by APT groups who are known to target other critical sectors (e.g., Dragonfly targeting aviation sectors). However, it is challenging to faithfully replicate the exact attack scenario due to the lack of comprehensive knowledge about the full scale of the cyberattack. Cyberattack sources (e.g., CTI report) consist of indicators observed from the remnants of the attack (e.g., due to obfuscation techniques), which only reflect the observable portion of the complete cyberattack. Furthermore, the exact hardware and program that are used as part of the ICS is not known (e.g., confidentiality reasons), thus limiting the ability to virtually replicate the infrastructure. This raises the need to infer missing information that is required to realize the cyberattack as a simulation without contradicting the current understanding that is described in the CTI report. The observations generated from cyberattack simulations are collected as datasets, making them useful for education and training (e.g., DFIR). This enables users to interact with ICS cyberattack data for hands-on investigation such as discovering IoC to map the attack chain during cyberattack reconstruction, leading to root cause identification.

## 7   Conclusion

This work highlighted the increasing prevalence of cyberattacks on ICS in critical infrastructure, especially in the context of railway systems which cause operational disruptions and potentially life-threatening situations. We emphasized the need to strengthen the cybersecurity posture for critical infrastructure despite the complexity, criticality, and fragility of ICS systems. To address these challenges, the intuition is to realistically simulate cyberattacks on critical infrastructure so as to generate valuable observations that reflect contemporary attack patterns. To enable cyberattack analysis of trending ICS cyberattacks, we construct railway-specific ICS datasets that are generated from our railway cyber range. Specifically, we present the design of cyberattack scenarios based on commonly observed attack patterns from past incidents. The cyberattack scenarios are realized on the railway cyber range to simulate the ICS cyberattack. The data and indicators that result from the cyberattack simulation are extracted as evidence and collected as a dataset. The ICS dataset is publicly shared to facilitate research and analysis in ICS cyberattacks. For future work, we aim to study and compare the impact of cyberattacks on cyber ranges from other critical sectors and generate observations with sector-specific attack indicators.

**Acknowledgments.** This research is supported by the National Research Foundation, Singapore, through the National Cybersecurity R&D Lab at the National University of Singapore under its National Cybersecurity R&D Programme (Award No. NCR25-NCL P3-0001). Any opinions, findings and conclusions or recommendations expressed in this material are those of the author(s) and do not reflect the views of National Research Foundation, Singapore.

# References


1. Ahmed, C.M., Kandasamy, N.K.: A comprehensive dataset from a smart grid testbed for machine learning based cps security research. In: Abie, H., Ranise, S., Verderame, L., Cambiaso, E., Ugarelli, R., Giunta, G., Praça, I., Battisti, F. (eds.) Cyber-physical security for critical infrastructures protection, pp. 123–135. Springer International Publishing, Cham (2021)
2. Ahmed, C.M., Palleti, V.R., Mathur, A.P.: Wadi: a water distribution testbed for research in the design of secure cyber physical systems. In: Proceedings of the 3rd International Workshop on Cyber-Physical Systems for Smart Water Networks, pp. 25–28. CySWATER '17, Association for Computing Machinery, New York, NY, USA (2017). https://doi.org/10.1145/3055366.3055375
3. Akbarzadeh, A., Erdodi, L., Houmb, S.H., Soltvedt, T.G.: Two-stage advanced persistent threat (apt) attack on an iec 61850 power grid substation. Int. J. Inf. Secur. 23(4), 2739–2758 (May 2024). https://doi.org/10.1007/s10207-024-00856-6
4. Allison, D., Smith, P., Mclaughlin, K.: Digital twin-enhanced incident response for cyber-physical systems. In: Proceedings of the 18th International Conference on Availability, Reliability and Security. ARES '23, Association for Computing Machinery, New York, NY, USA (2023). https://doi.org/10.1145/3600160.3600195
5. Conti, M., Donadel, D., Turrin, F.: A survey on industrial control system testbeds and datasets for security research. IEEE Commun. Surv. Tutorials 23(4), 2248–2294 (2021). https://doi.org/10.1109/COMST.2021.3094360
6. Dehlaghi-Ghadim, A., Balador, A., Moghadam, M.H., Hansson, H., Conti, M.: Icssim – a framework for building industrial control systems security testbeds. Comput. Ind. 148, 103906 (2023). https://doi.org/10.1016/j.compind.2023.103906, https://www.sciencedirect.com/science/article/pii/S0166361523000568
7. Dehlaghi-Ghadim, A., Moghadam, M.H., Balador, A., Hansson, H.: Anomaly detection dataset for industrial control systems. IEEE Access 11, 107982–107996 (2023). https://doi.org/10.1109/ACCESS.2023.3320928
8. Downs, J., Vogel, E.: A plant-wide industrial process control problem. Comput. Chem. Eng. 17(3), 245–255 (1993). https://doi.org/10.1016/0098-1354(93)80018-I, https://www.sciencedirect.com/science/article/pii/009813549380018I, industrial challenge problems in process control
9. d'Ambrosio, N., Capodagli, G., Perrone, G., Romano, S.P.: Scass: Breaking into scada systems security. Comput. Secur. 151(C) (Apr 2025). https://doi.org/10.1016/j.cose.2025.104315
10. Fernandes, T., Magalhães, J.P., Alves, W.: Cybersecurity in smart railways: exploring risks, vulnerabilities and mitigation in the data communication services. Green Energy and Intelligent Transportation p. 100305 (2025). https://doi.org/10.1016/j.geits.2025.100305, https://www.sciencedirect.com/science/article/pii/S2773153725000556
11. Firoozjaei, M.D., Mahmoudyar, N., Baseri, Y., Ghorbani, A.A.: An evaluation framework for industrial control system cyber incidents. Int. J. Crit. Infrastruct. Prot. 36, 100487 (2022). https://doi.org/10.1016/j.ijcip.2021.100487, https://www.sciencedirect.com/science/article/pii/S1874548221000718
12. Flood, R., Engelen, G., Aspinall, D., Desmet, L.: Bad design smells in benchmark nids datasets. In: 2024 IEEE 9th European Symposium on Security and Privacy (EuroS&P), pp. 658–675 (2024). https://doi.org/10.1109/EuroSP60621.2024.00042

13. Fraunhofer: Safety4rails eu project. https://safety4rails.eu/ (2020). Accessed 25 May 2025
14. Gaggero, G.B., Armellin, A., Portomauro, G., Marchese, M.: Industrial control system-anomaly detection dataset (ics-add) for cyber-physical security monitoring in smart industry environments. IEEE Access **12**, 64140–64149 (2024). https://doi.org/10.1109/ACCESS.2024.3395991
15. Genge, B., Haller, P., Roman, A.S.: E-aptdetect: Early advanced persistent threat detection in critical infrastructures with dynamic attestation. Appl. Sci. **13**(6) (2023). https://doi.org/10.3390/app13063409, https://www.mdpi.com/2076-3417/13/6/3409
16. Goh, J., Adepu, S., Junejo, K.N., Mathur, A.: A dataset to support research in the design of secure water treatment systems. In: Havarneanu, G., Setola, R., Nassopoulos, H., Wolthusen, S. (eds.) Critical Information Infrastructures Security, pp. 88–99. Springer International Publishing, Cham (2017)
17. Kim, M., Jeon, S., Cho, J., Gong, S.: Data-driven ics network simulation for synthetic data generation. Electronics **13**(10) (2024). https://doi.org/10.3390/electronics13101920, https://www.mdpi.com/2079-9292/13/10/1920
18. Liu, J., Inam, M.A., Goyal, A., Riddle, A., Westfall, K., Bates, A.: What we talk about when we talk about logs: understanding the effects of dataset quality on endpoint threat detection research . In: 2025 IEEE Symposium on Security and Privacy (SP). pp. 112–129. IEEE Computer Society, Los Alamitos, CA, USA (May 2025). https://doi.org/10.1109/SP61157.2025.00112, https://doi.ieeecomputersociety.org/10.1109/SP61157.2025.00112
19. LiuYuancheng: Cluster User Emulation System. https://github.com/LiuYuancheng/Cluster_User_Emulation_System
20. Lo, C., Win, T.Y., Rezaeifar, Z., Khan, Z., Legg, P.: Digital twins of cyber physical systems in smart manufacturing for threat simulation and detection with deep learning for time series classification. In: 2024 29th International Conference on Automation and Computing (ICAC), pp. 1–6 (2024). https://doi.org/10.1109/ICAC61394.2024.10718749
21. Neema, H., Koutsoukos, X., Potteiger, B., Tang, C., Stouffer, K.: Simulation testbed for railway infrastructure security and resilience evaluation. In: Proceedings of the 7th Symposium on Hot Topics in the Science of Security. HotSoS '20, Association for Computing Machinery, New York, NY, USA (2020). https://doi.org/10.1145/3384217.3385623
22. Shin, H.K., Lee, W., Yun, J.H., Kim, H.: HAI 1.0: HIL-based augmented ICS security dataset. In: 13th USENIX Workshop on Cyber Security Experimentation and Test (CSET 20). USENIX Association (Aug 2020), https://www.usenix.org/conference/cset20/presentation/shin
23. Srivastava, K., Köpke, C., Walter, J., Faist, K., Berry, J.M., Porretti, C., Stolz, A.: Modelling and simulation of railway networks for resilience analysis. In: Computer Security. ESORICS 2022 International Workshops: CyberICPS 2022, SECPRE 2022, SPOSE 2022, CPS4CIP 2022, CDT&SECOMANE 2022, EIS 2022, and SecAssure 2022, Copenhagen, Denmark, September 26–30, 2022, Revised Selected Papers, pp. 308–320. Springer-Verlag, Berlin, Heidelberg (2022). https://doi.org/10.1007/978-3-031-25460-4_17

24. Teo, Z.T., et al.: Securerails: Towards an open simulation platform for analyzing cyber-physical attacks in railways. In: 2016 IEEE Region 10 Conference (TENCON), pp. 95–98 (2016). https://doi.org/10.1109/TENCON.2016.7847966
25. Yang, Z., He, L., Cheng, P., Chen, J.: Mismatched control and monitoring frequencies: vulnerability, attack, and mitigation. IEEE Trans. Dependable Secure Comput. **22**(01), 16–33 (Jan 2025). https://doi.org/10.1109/TDSC.2024.3384146, https://doi.ieeecomputersociety.org/10.1109/TDSC.2024.3384146

# Designing and Testing a Low-Cost Electromagnetic Spectrum Attack Threat Monitoring System

Vasileios Andrianopoulos[✉], Panayiotis Kotzanikolaou, and Christos Douligeris

Department of Informatics, University of Piraeus, Piraeus, Greece
vandriano@proton.me, {pkotzani,cdoulig}@unipi.gr

**Abstract.** Electromagnetic spectrum (EMS) attacks aim to exploit vulnerabilities across electromagnetic radiation frequencies to disrupt, control, or intercept communications and operations in cyber-physical systems. This paper presents a low-cost and modular EMS threat monitoring system for real-time detection and visualization of cyber electromagnetic threats. At the hardware layer, the system is built using affordable hardware components such as Software Defined Radio (SDN), Raspberry Pi, and Global Positioning System (GPS) modules. At the software layer, custom Pyhton-based scripts have been developed, capable of both simulating and detecting electromagnetic threats such as GPS spoofing, wireless network impersonation, and signal jamming. For each examined attack, practical mitigation controls applicable for operational deployment are described. The effectiveness and responsiveness of the proposed platform have been demonstrated by conducting controlled experiments in a cyber range environment. Finally, future directions are considered, that may further improve the EMS threat detection capabilities of the proposed platform.

**Keywords:** Cyber Electromagnetic Activities (CEMA) · Electronic Warfare (EW) · Software Defined Radio (SDR) · Electromagnetic Spectrum (EMS) · Global Positioning System (GPS) Spoofing · Signal Jamming · Wireless Threat Detection · Situational Awareness

## 1 Introduction

The enhanced interdependence of cyber and physical systems has brought new challenges for critical infrastructure protection, such as power grids, SCADA (Supervisory Control And Aata Acquisition) systems, and industrial IIoT (Industrial Internet of Things) environments [1]. Since Cyber Physical Systems (CPS)

---

This work has been partly supported by the University of Piraeus Research Center, and by the European Union through the Recovery and Resilience Fund and Greek national funds through the Ministry of Education, Religion and Sports, under the call SUB1.1 SEA Research Excellence Partnerships (project code: YP3-0560811/project name: CoDrones).

usually rely on wireless communications and electromagnetic spectrum (EMS) operations, they are highly vulnerable to electromagnetic threats, i.e., threats that combine both cyber and electromagnetic attack vectors. Typical examples of EMS threats include GPS spoofing, jamming, and Wi-Fi impersonation.

Cyber Electromagnetic Activities (CEMA) include a series of operations that converge cyberspace activities, Electronic Warfare (EW), and spectrum management to dominate the Electro-Magnetic Spectrum (EMS) [2]. Originally developed in a military context, especially by the United States Army [3], CEMA strives to deprive adversaries of accessing the EMS and to maintain operational superiority for friendly forces [4]. EMS comprises the entire spectrum of electromagnetic waves and, due to its ability to propagate, reflect, and penetrate, can be both powerful and vulnerable in critical applications. [5].

CEMA strategies integrate offensive and defensive electronic operations [6, 7]. *Electronic Warfare* (EW) involves: *Electronic Support* (ES) for signal collection, *Electronic Attack* (EA) for jamming and system deception, and *Electronic Protection* (EP) to protect systems from adversaries interference [2]. *Signal intelligence* (SIGINT), specifically *communications intelligence* (COMINT) and *Electronic intelligence* (ELINT), plays an important role in the detection and characterization of threats within the EMS.

The growing convergence of military and civil use of the spectrum, for example, interference between 5G networks and air defense Radio Detection And Ranging (RADAR) systems [8] - reaffirms the application of CEMA concepts outside the war zone. However, while CEMA has been successfully used in military contexts, in civilian/industrial applications (especially in critical infrastructures), awareness of CEMA is underdeveloped and underused [9].

*Motivation.* Monitoring the EM spectrum is becoming more critical as it becomes more congested with Radio frequencies (RF). As an example, Fig. 1 depicts the Greek RF allocation map, generated using the HackRF One [10] Software Defined Radio (SDR) and a spectrum analyzer [11]. The figure shows a waterfall visualization of real-time RF activity in the range of 10 MHz to 6 GHz, having overlaps of signals and spectrum use. It can be observed that the RF allocation map is congested with high and variable usage across services. Unauthorized or hostile use of these frequencies can cause interference, interruption of the services, or security threats.

Since the RF spectrum is susceptible to interference, jamming, and spoofing attacks, there is a need for continuous monitoring of the RF spectrum, especially for critical systems. However, existing monitoring systems are usually expensive and have limited integration capabilities. There is a need for cost-effective solutions that can detect anomalies or attacks while providing timely alerts, in order to maintain situational awareness, quality of communication, and spectrum regulation.

*Contribution.* This paper describes an innovative and low-cost platform for CEMA threat detection and situational awareness. The proposed platform is designed with affordable hardware components as building blocks: in particular,

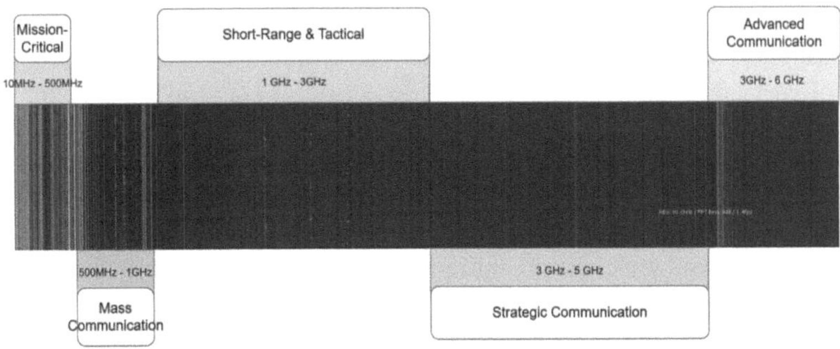


**Fig. 1.** Visual representation of RF allocation map congestion

software-defined radios (HackRF One), GPS receivers (NEO-6M), and embedded controllers (Raspberry Pi). The platform facilitates real-time visualization and automated detection of electromagnetic anomalies. The proposed platform is capable of detecting spoofing, jamming, and network layer impersonation attacks using modular and open-source tools. The system aims to be user-friendly and to provide operational EMS awareness in CPS environments. The main contributions of the paper are:

- A unified **real-time monitoring software** that aggregates EMS monitoring with the physical network status to identify CEMA aware threats.
- **Practical verification** of the system in a cyber range, demonstrating the detection of GPS spoofing, Wi-Fi Evil Twin attacks, and drone command link jamming.
- A **low-cost and extensible** reference design for applied EMS security in critical infrastructure settings.

*Paper Structure.* The paper is structured as follows. Section 2 summarizes the related work, while Sect. 3 presents the proposed EMS threat detection system. Section 4 describes the cyber range environment developed to test the proposed platform, while Sect. 5 describes the attack implementation and testing results. Finally, Sect. 6 concludes this paper and summarizes future work that may extend the threat detection capabilities of the proposed system.

## 2   Related Work

*Wireless Communication Threats in CPS.* Eavesdropping, replay attacks, spoofing, and signal jamming are the main categories of wireless communication threats in CPS [12,13]. For example, in GPS-dependent systems, spoofing attacks can alter location and timing, therefore causing major service interruptions. Wireless jamming with the help of noise amplitude modulation (NAM), compression spectroscopy (CS), or interrupted sampling and repeater (ISR) methods can take down radars, or take control of drones' communication systems [12]. Although these attacks have been extensively studied in the literature, there is a lack of cost-effective solutions for the detection of these attacks in real-time.

*Mitigation Strategies.* Existing mitigation strategies cover a wide range of techniques to respond to electromagnetic, cyber-physical, and hybrid attacks. These comprise of physical-layer defenses, i.e., electromagnetic shielding, frequency hopping, and spread spectrum techniques, in addition to AI-augmented anomaly detection, and spectrum polarimetry, which promise to deliver early threat detection [14][?]. Concerning GPS spoofing, existing mitigation controls include the simultaneous use of multiple Global Navigation Satellite System (GNSS) signals (e.g., Galileo, GLONASS, BeiDou) [16,17], the combination of independent motion-related (e.g. accelerometer- and gyroscope-dependent) [16,17], and signal strength and Doppler filtering, to identify spoofed signal power or irregular Doppler profiles [16,17].

For evil twin Wi-Fi attacks, mitigation controls include the use of the WPA3-compliant (Wi-Fi Protected Access 3 compliant) Simultaneous Authentication of Equals (SAE) protocol, which reduces the risk of offline cracking or downgrading attacks [18,19], the use of 802.11w Protected Management Frames [20,21], and client-side SSID (Service Set Identifier) fingerprinting, by examining previously used SSID profiles (signal strength, channel, MAC address) to warn users for potential anomalies [20,21].

Concerning RF jamming attacks, existing countermeasures include: Frequency Hopping Spread Spectrum (FHSS), which utilizes fast pseudo-random frequency switching of transmitter and receiver to reduce radiation of narrowband jamming [22], control channel redundancy, where a different channel such as LTE (Long-Term Evolution), 5.8 GHz Wi-Fi, or a satellite link enables backup if it is disrupted on 2.4 GHz [23]; Direction-finding and avoidance, where RF triangulation or signal direction estimation may enable the UAVs (Unmanned Aerial Vehicles) to deflect from active jammers [24]; and signal authentication, in which signed control packets or time-locked tokens are used to prevent MitM (Man-in-the-middle attack) injection, even in jammed environments [25].

Despite this progress, most suggested solutions require high-end SDR equipment, or are tailored to military applications that usually do not support scalable modularized platforms to integrate electromagnetic monitoring with classical cybersecurity practices. This paper aims to contribute to this gap by presenting a modular, low-cost EMS threat detection platform validated in a cyber range environment, using open-source software tools and low-cost hardware.

## 3    The Proposed EMS Threat Detection System

The proposed architecture incorporates the use of hardware components, open-source software tools and simulated attack vectors to deliver real-time threat detection and situational awareness across a distributed network of LANs (Local Area Networks).

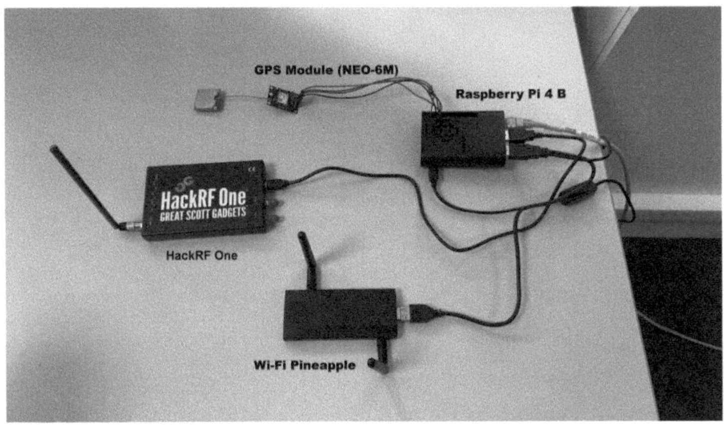


**Fig. 2.** Hardware Component Integration

### 3.1 Hardware Components

The implemented proof-of-concept platform, employs low-cost standard hardware, shown in Fig. 2, selected based on a combination of cost, compatibility with open-source tools, and deployment versatility:

- **SDR Module (HackRF One):** A half-duplex SDR, capable of both signal analysis and active attack simulation (including GPS spoofing and jamming) (10 MHzâĂŞ6 GHz) [10].
- **GPS Module (NEO-6M):** Implements real-time satellite signal reception as well as geolocation through the Universal Asynchronous Receiver/Transmitter (UART) interface to a Raspberry Pi [26].
- **Embedded Controller (Raspberry Pi 4 Model B):** Acts as an embedded controller of SDR, GPS, and WiFi Pineapple [27].
- **WiFi Pineapple** was used as a penetration testing device for wireless attacks such as Evil Twin SSID spoofing, deauthentication, and Man-in-the-middle attack scenarios [28].
- **eStar-Drone-HD-52 Drone and Ground Control System:** were used for testing interference of the control signal and jamming response [29].

### 3.2 Software Stack

The system utilizes various open-source software libraries, for signal generation, analysis, and visualization:

- **GNU Radio Companion:** With GNU Radio, users can make and reuse modular blocks to create radio systems. GNU Radio is usually used with devices like the HackRF to design, test and send data over RF connections. [30].

- **hackrf-spectrum-analyzer:** This is a lightweight Graphical User Interface (GUI) tool that works with the HackRF to display real-time RF spectrum data. It provides a visual representation of the power of signals over frequency, helping detect RF activity or anomalies. [11]
- **gpsd:** gpsd listens to data from the GPS module (such as the NEO-6M), translates it and offers access to it via a local socket [31].
- **gpsmon:** gpsmon displays information from gpsd in a human-friendly way, all in real-time, through the terminal [31].
- **gps-sdr-sim:** The tool gps-sdr-sim allows users to simulate GPS satellite signals. It generates raw data that looks like real GPS signals and these signals can be sent via the HackRF to confuse GPS receivers into thinking they are located elsewhere. [32].
- **Kafka:** A tool for data ingestion and threat visualization in real time [33].
- **Scapy:** Scapy is a Python tool used for creating and analyzing network packets. It can scan and list available Wi-Fi networks by capturing broadcast signals from nearby access points [34].

The Raspberry Pi was utilized to interconnect HackRF, GNU Radio with the spectrum analyzer, the WiFi pineapple, and the NEO-6M GPS module; and the rest of the components were run in virtual machines inside of the cyber range.

### 3.3   Implemented Attack Detection Scripts

To support the platform hardware capabilities for real-time situational awareness, a set of software detection scripts were developed in Python, for each attack scenario. These scripts run on the endpoint devices like Raspberry Pi, allowing centralized, low-overhead anomaly detection without requiring external infrastructure or cloud analytics.

**1) GPS Spoofing Detection:** A Python script was developed to capture real-time GPS data using `gpsd` and analyze spatial-temporal inconsistencies [35]. Three fundamental features were used in the detection logic:

- *Position delta monitoring:* The script calculates the distance between consecutive GPS fixes, using the Haversine formula. When the jump surpasses the specified criteria (e.g., $>100\,$m in $<5\,$s), a spoofing alert is flagged.
- *Fix stability and HDOP evaluation:* Unexpected dips in visibility on the satellite side and peaks of Horizontal Dilution Of Precision (HDOP $> 5.0$) are taken as suspicious spoofing or jamming indicators.
- *Fix mode transitions:* Abrupt changes from a valid 3D fix to "no fix" mode are proposed as a secondary trigger.

Detected anomalies cause immediate alerts that log and optionally include GUI indicators.

**2) Wi-Fi Evil Twin Detection:** For Wi-Fi evil twin detection, a Python script was developed, that sniffs the Wi-Fi management frames and then analyzes SSID / BSSID ( Basic Service Set Identifier) discrepancies [35].

The script performs *SSID fingerprinting*, by storing expected SSIDâĂŞBSSID mappings of trusted networks. It stirs throughout the time, checking for cloned SSIDs, connected to the altered MAC addresses.

**3) Drone Command-Link Jamming Detection:** To detect RF jamming, a lightweight spectrum sensing script was written in Python, using GNU radio [35]. The detection process includes:

- *Fast Fourier transform based spectrum scanning:* Periodic samples of real and imaginary quantities are used to make the corresponding real-time spectral density plots.
- *Noise energy analysis:* The normalized power distribution is analyzed over the defined control band ranges (e.g., $2.4\,\mathrm{GHz}$).
- *Anomaly classification:* If the average energy of either the signal (mean $> 0.7$) or interference (variance $> 3000$) exceeds a pre-defined threshold in successive windows, then jamming is declared.

## 4    Developing a Cyber Range Testing Environment

To test and verify the proposed CEMA thread detection system, a cyber range environment was developed to simulate real-world cyber-physical CEMA attacks and to test the proposed mitigation controls.

*Attack Simulation Support.* The cyber range environment currently supports the simulation of the following attacks: 1) *RF signal live injection and capture,* 2) *GPS spoofing* (including the distorted satellite-transmitted signal), and 3) *Wi-Fi Evil Twin and deauthentication attacks.* However, the system topology is modular and can be scaled to accommodate more sensors, control rooms, simulated attacks or other facilities.

*Cyber Range Platform Architecture.* The cyber range platform is adaptable hybrid simulation platform which could be used for electromagnetic monitoring as well as physical sensor anomaly detection to locate and response to RF-focused attacks such as jamming and spoofing. The platform architecture involves various interconnected LANs, each of which simulates a different operational environment (see Fig. 3). Each LAN is connected with SDN links, which allow communication in both directions and re-propagation of cross-site events. Each subsystem uses lightweight messaging protocols (Kafka) for communication for real-time synchronization and scalability across sites.

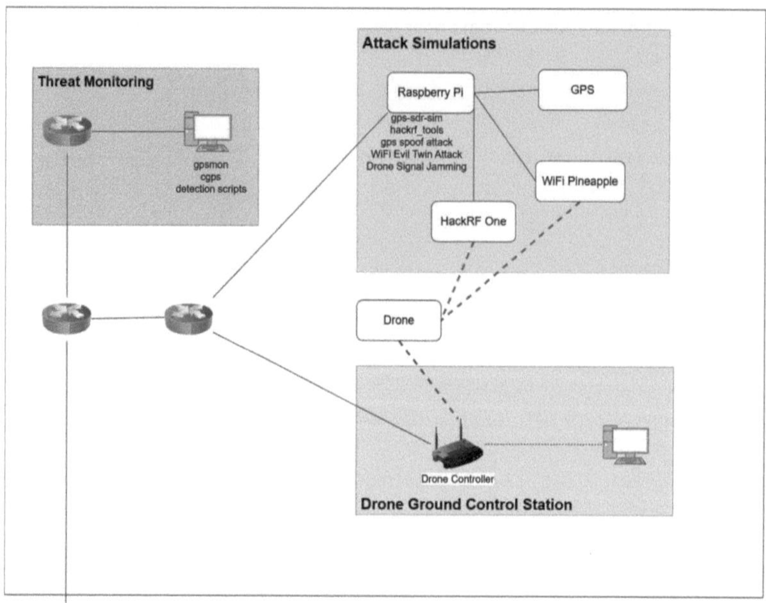


**Fig. 3.** Topology Architecture of Cyber Range Including LAN Segments

- **LAN 1 - Attack Simulations:** Provided with SDR sensors for transmitting and monitoring of RF signals. In our setup, it hosts the HackRF One SDR, the NEO-6M GPS receiver for the EMS transmitting and monitoring, and the Drone Controller. In addition, the Raspberry Pi was used both to execute the attack by executing the necessary tools and to retrieve GPS information during the experiments.
- **LAN 2 - Drone's Ground Control Station:** It serves mission-critical endpoints such as control terminals or drone command centers. From this LAN, an operator can send commands to the Drone Controller via Wi-Fi. In addition, the Wi-Fi Pineapple is implemented for Evil Twin Attack.
- **Threat Monitoring:** This network is used for the overall control, brings EMS and network alert together, decision visualization method. It hosts a central dashboard for the purposes of visualization, alerting, and threat response. In this LAN, Kafka is implemented for data gathering from the other LANs.

*Communication Protocols and Signal Sources.* The system monitors both physical and electromagnetic signals. The physical network components monitored include routers, switches, and end-user equipment. The monitored electromagnetic channels include GPS signals, Wi-Fi traffic, and RF emissions.

*Visualization and Situational Awareness.* Usability is one of the important design goals. The system comes with an easy interface and color-coded, intuitive alerts, i.e., green or white for normal operation; yellow for anomalous/ possibly malicious operation (e.g., low number of satellites, weak signal strength); and red for critical threats identified (e.g., GPS spoofing, Wi-Fi impersonation or drone command link jamming). Every alert is accompanied with metadata (signal strength, timestamp, type of threat) and could include recommended mitigation measures. With this, operators are able to look at a situation and react appropriately.

## 5    Attack Implementation and Testing

To test the effectiveness of the proposed EMS threat detection system, three representative attack scenarios were simulated in the cyber range environment. Such situations aim at common weaknesses in cyber-physical systems: satellite signal spoofing, impersonating a Wi-Fi or electromagnetic jamming of control channels. Each scenario contains threat setup, execution and detect outcomes according to platform sensors and logic.

### 5.1    GPS Spoofing Attack

The goal of this test scenario was to test the capability of the proposed system to detect GPS spoofing attacks, which were simulated via the HackRF One SDR.

**Setup:** As shown in Fig. 2, a Raspberry Pi 4 was connected to a NEO-6M GPS receiver and configured to report real-time satellite data via `gpsd`. The HackRF One SDR device was also connected to the same host to transmit spoofed GPS signals, using the open-source `gps-sdr-sim` tool [32]. The simulation generated in-phase and quadrature (I/Q) data corresponding to a falsified location (Moscow) and transmitted it at the GPS L1 frequency (1.57542 GHz). Then, the I/Q data was generated using the most recent broadcast ephemeris file (brdc1220.25n) retrieved from NASA's database [36].

**Attack Execution:** The `gps-sdr-sim` tool created a 300-second spoofed signal using almanac and ephemeris data.

```
./gps-sdr-sim -b 8 -e brdc1220.25n -l 55.7558,37.6176,156 -o gps.bin -T
    now
```

**Listing 1.1.** Generating GPS spoofed signal coordinates using gps-sdr-sim

Figure 4 explains how validation is carried out. As the HackRF sends out a continuous I/Q signal in the right panel, the real-time GPS feed appears on the left side using `gpsmon`.The falsified location data is highlighted in red, clearly marking the spoofed position.

Further evidence is shown on the geospatial map in Fig. 5 to confirm that GPS spoofing actually took place.

This data was broadcast via HackRF One using the command:

```
hackrf_transfer -t gps_simulation.bin -f 1575420000 -s 2600000 -a 1 -x 47
```

**Listing 1.2.** Sending GPS spoofing signal via HackRF

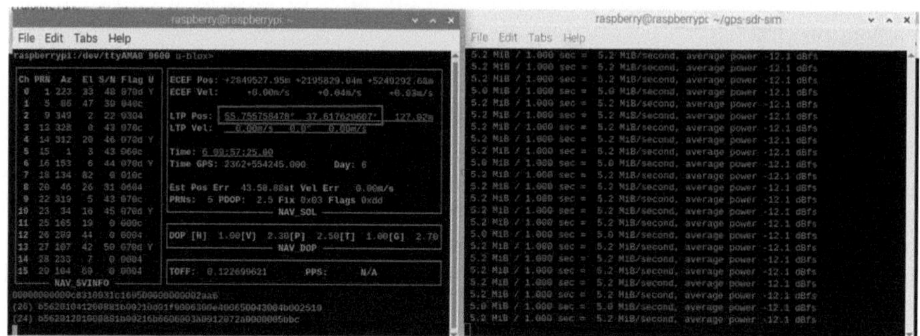

**Fig. 4.** GPS Signal Transmission with HackRF and Reception (spoofed location) confirmed by LTP Pos Value

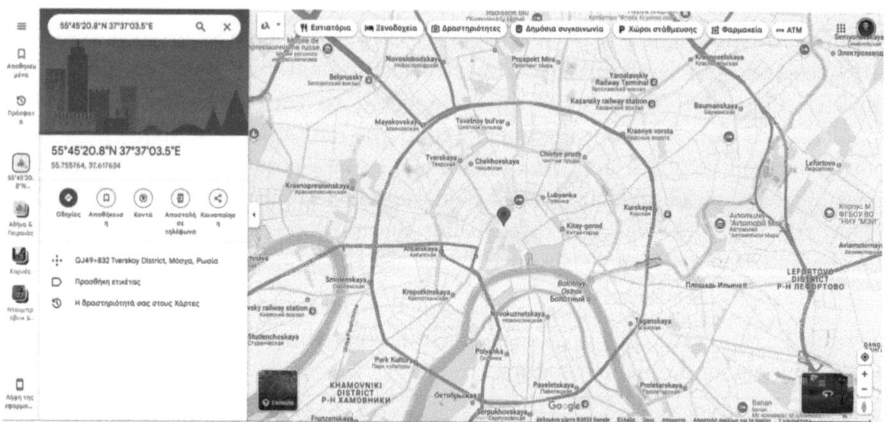

**Fig. 5.** Confirmation of spoofed location on an online map application

**Attack Detection:** The system detected the spoofing activity based on:

- Sudden *positional deviation* between successive GPS position readings. After two fixes have been measured by the order of 5 s in the GPS, the Haversine formula translates their position in latitude-longitude. Any positional jump beyond 100 m in these coordinates is classified as suspicious. This threshold was practically limited to the hardware limitations of the test apparatus and the theoretically anticipated motion trajectory of the device. The delays are made to reduce the repetitive alerts, which are made because of continuous alerts about the spoofing signals hence 10 s cooldown window is given between any two consequent detections.

- A drop or increase in *satellite count and elevated HDOP* (Horizontal Dilution of Precision). A number of four or more satellites must be visible in order to get a reliable 3D fix position. Once the amount of visible satellites drops by a number less than this level or when Horizontal Dilution of Precision (HDOP) rises above 5.0, a warning in the system is given. The use of these indicators, of the number of satellites and the HDOP, becomes a good guide as to signal degradation and possible spoofing interference, where an attacker may have larger relative signal level, but low satellite diversity or imperfect geometric distribution.

- A *stronger signal* at 1.57542 GHz. Although the Python script considered here does not directly measure the amplitude of radio-frequency (RF) signals due to the limitations of the GPSD application programming interface (API), we have been able to indulge in the spoofed GPS signal analysis by charting the spectrum of such signals (using the HackRF One platform and GNU Radio), which came to be well beyond the range of -60 dBm in the L1 band (1.57542 GHz) which is considerably greater in the open-sky context of around -130 dBm. This measurement is a secondary parameter, however, to obtain a final picture further detail in terms of signal strength would require combining with an SDR-based energy detector with capability of measuring spectral power density in real time.

The system was found to be effective in controlled simulations of spoofing, correctly identifying cases of GPS manipulation at low rates of false positives.

Additional proof that spoofing has been effectively detected can be seen in Fig. 6, where the spoofed signal is transmitted continuously by the Hack-RF and it shown on the right panel. In the left section, the script written in python spots any attempt to falsify location data and displays the real-time reaction of the system.

## 5.2  Wi-Fi Evil Twin Attack

In this scenario, a simulated Wi-Fi Evil Twin attack was used to evaluate how well the system could detect any spoofing threats in the wireless area of the drone. The attack was made on the Wi-Fi part of the drone responsible for directly sending live video views and readings to an connected smartphone. With this WiFi channel, users could have a live video feed of the drone's view and control some of its actions.

**Setup:** The attacker cloned a genuine SSID ("eStar-Drone-HD-52") transmitted from the Drone which is near the Attack Simulation LAN using the WiFi

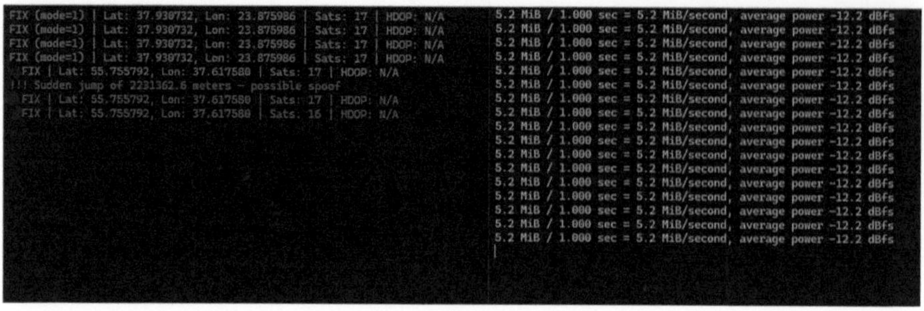

**Fig. 6.** GPS Spoofing Detection via Sudden Location Jump and SDR Signal Transmission

Pineapple device. While advertising the fake SSID, the WiFI Pineapple was at the same time broadcasting deauthentication frames to force clients to disconnect from the real AP (see Fig. 7).

**Attack Execution:** The rogue AP spoofed the SSID of the legitimate access point. The WiFi client (i.e., the drone) trying to reconnect to the WiFi network was redirected to the rogue AP. The connection is being confirmed after DHCP (Dynamic Host Configuration Protocol) server assigned to the operator's end point, an IP in the range 172.16.42.0/24.

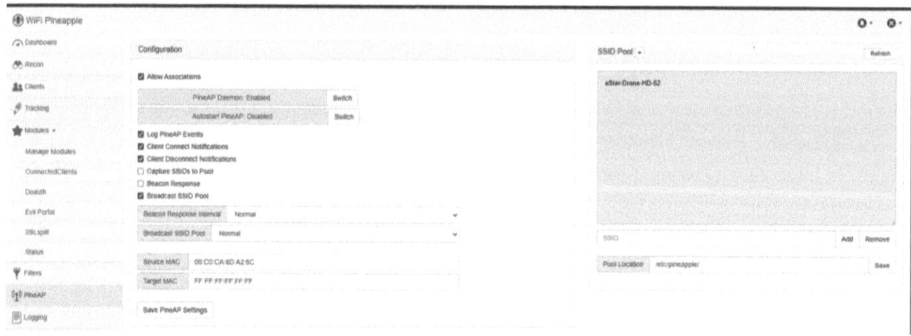

**Fig. 7.** WiFi Pineapple Configuration for Broadcasting the Spoofed «eStar-Drone-HD-52» SSID in an Evil Twin Attack Setup

**Detection:** The Raspberry Pi was running the developed detection script with Scapy, which detected several BSSIDs transmitting the same SSID.

As shown in Fig. 8, the fake SSID is marked in red, indicating that a possibly fake access point is nearby.

```
C:\windows\py.exe

[*] Scanning nearby Wi-Fi networks...

[*] Analysis complete.

[!!!] Potential Evil Twin Detected for SSID 'eStar-Drone-HD-52'
      - BSSID: 64:66:b3:70:de:71
      - BSSID: 64:66:b3:70:de:72
```

**Fig. 8.** Identification of potential Evil Twin Attack on the SSID 'eStar-Drone-HD-52'

### 5.3   Drone Command Link Jamming

In contrast to the previous spoofing scenario, where the attack was directed at the drone's Wi-Fi transmission, this section is focused on targeting the drone's internal control receiver. Specifically, the attack was executed against the 2.4 GHz ISM band, which is commonly used for communication between the drone and the ground controller.

This scenario evaluated the ability of the platform to detect electromagnetic jamming of the control channel. By disrupting the link between the controller and the drone, the attack was aimed at jamming flight commands. The system demonstrated effective detection of this jamming behavior by analyzing the degradation in signal integrity by detecting signal bursts in 2.4 GHz band.

**Setup:** The same drone (EStar Marcopolo-52 HD) with 2.4 GHz control link was used. The HackRF One SDR plugged into the Raspberry Pi on LAN-1, was set up to send noise and tone bursts on the control frequency.

**Execution:** To perform the jamming attack on the drone's control channel, GNU Radio Companion (GRC) is used. A visual programming tool that allows the design of signal processing pipelines known as flowgraphs. These flowgraphs are composed of interconnected blocks that represent signal sources, filters, sinks (outputs), and other processing units. This setup is ideal for creating custom signals in software-defined radio (SDR) applications.

For this purpose, by using the hackrf-spectrum-analyzer it is revealed that the drone's control signal activity is centered around 2.42 GHz. As shown in Fig. 10, the drone's control communication operates within the 2.4 GHz to 2.44 GHz range, a total bandwidth of 40 MHz. However, since HackRF One only covers a 20 MHz bandwidth at a time, it cannot block signals in the entire control band.

To overcome this constraint, a round-robin (circular) jamming approach was implemented. A custom GNU Radio Companion flowgraph was developed to automate this process by generating a noise signal at both 2.41 GHz and 2.43 GHz. In this way, the 2.41 GHz and 2.43 GHz signals were used alternately, which covered all 40 MHz of the control band in two complete sweeps. At 0.5-second intervals, each sub-band was flooded with noise for a short time by continuously changing the center frequency from 2.41 GHz to 2.43 GHz. A random noise source was used to create the jamming signal, which was them sent to the frequency sink for transmission, as shown in Fig. 9. In this way, it was possible to simulate a jamming attack from a full-spectrum interfering signal.

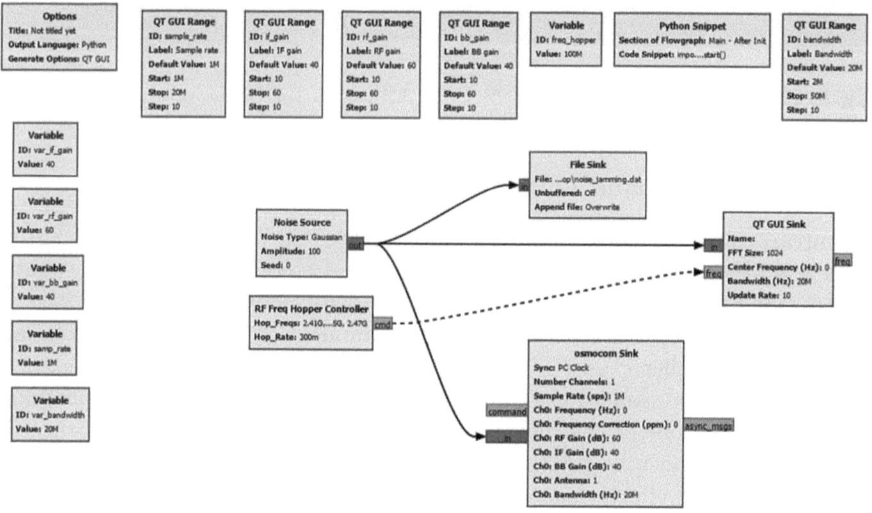


**Fig. 9.** GNU Radio Companion Flowgraph for Jamming at 2.41 GHz and 2.43 GHz

**Detection:** The detection of jamming events in the control band depends on Fast Fourier Transform (FFT) analysis of the captured I/Q data. This analysis transforms raw time-domain signals into the frequency domain using FFT, allowing the visualization of power levels across a range of frequencies. Signal activity, including peaks, interference, and anomalies, becomes visible on the spectrum as it occurs.

The Python script takes as input the incoming I/Q samples and determines their power spectral density. Baseline numbers calculated from the mean and standard deviation of the background spectrum are used to define when the script flags unexpectedly higher power in certain spectral regions. This approach enables the detection of both continuous-wave (CW) jamming and sweeping noise interference, such as that produced by the HackRF One.

Jamming events are indicated in the red area in Fig. 11, where an uncommon accumulation of spectral energy occurs at the drone control frequencies. Although the detection logic is straightforward by design, it works efficiently by setting an optimal noise threshold.

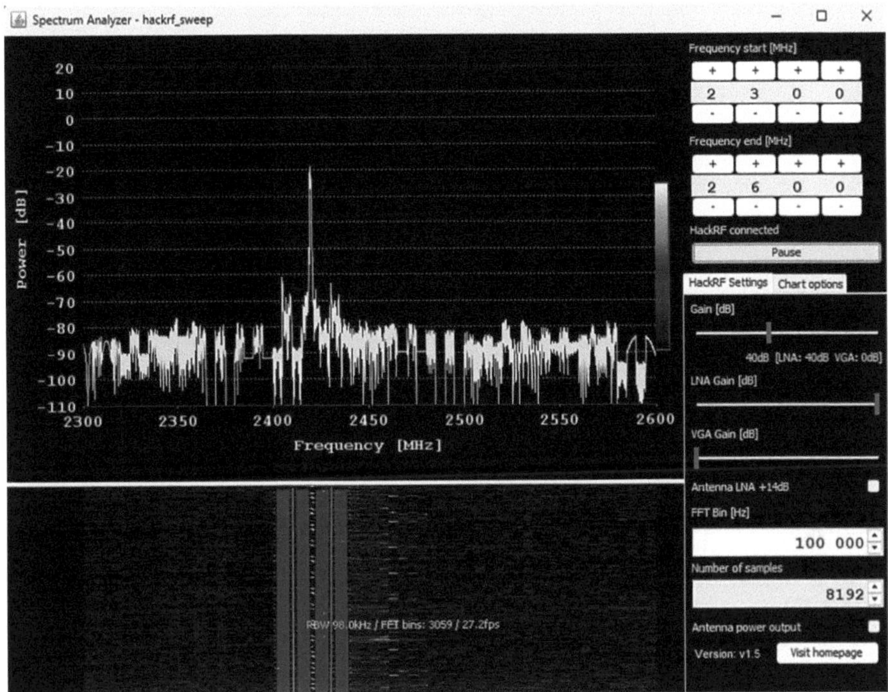


**Fig. 10.** Visualization of Drone's Operation ISM Band Using hackrf-spectrum-analyzer

## 6 Discussion and Future Work

### 6.1 Results and Limitations

The main goal of this work was to demonstrate the plausibility and operational value of cost-effective CEMA threat detection platforms in cyber-physical scenarios. By integrating low-cost hardware with custom Python scripts developed in Python, it was possible to demonstrate in a cyber range environment the effectiveness in detecting GPS spoofing, Wi-Fi Evil Twin, and drone jamming attacks, without the need for cloud processing or enterprise-scale infrastructure. However, the developed proof-of-concept system has several limitations that need to be addressed:

- *Hardware constraints:* Due to the half-duplex operation of the SDR used (HackRF One), it was only possible to analyze half-duplex mode (e.g. The HackRF cannot perform jamming and monitoring simultaneously.). The platform is modular and may easily integrate full-duplex SDRs (such as USRP B210) to increase testing capabilities. Based on the application needs a cost-benefit analysis may indicate the need to extend the SDR capabilities of the platform.
- *Scope is limited to civilian GPS:* Only civilian signals from the Global Navigation Satellite System (GNSS) are studied, and those are in the GPS L1 band.

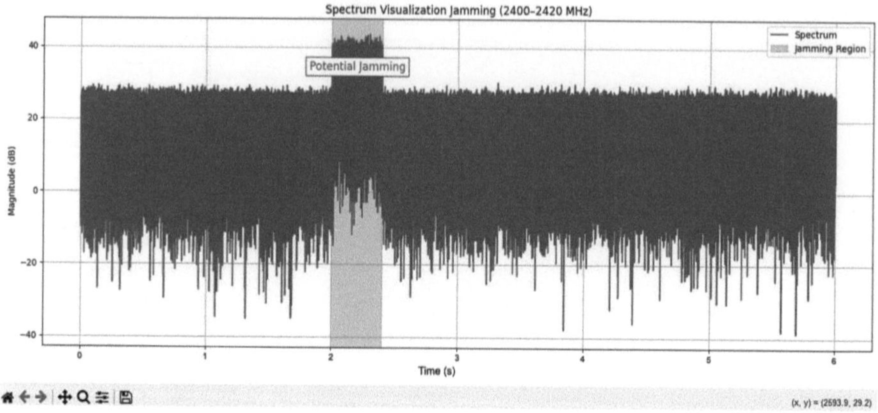



**Fig. 11.** Jamming Detection Plot using the .dat file generated from GNU Radio.

On purpose, the extent of the investigation does not encompass military-grade GPS signals, the most recognizable of which are P(Y)-Code and M-Code, that feature encryption and anti-spoofing functionalities.

- *Spoofing subtlety:* The current GPS spoofing detection is based on sudden changes in position and fix instability. A more advanced attacker may choose gradual drift or multi-path deception for which the signal analysis must be finer grained.

- *Applicability to GNSS Variants:* The platform architecture which is based on software-defined radios (SDRs) and an open source signal-analysis system provides a flexible framework in which detection of GPS spoofing can be generalised to other GNSS constellations such as GLONASS, GALILEO and BeiDou. However these systems operate at different frequencies and may require respective I/Q sample datasets and ephemeris formats, but detection logic (e.g., HDOP analysis, signal power anomalies, and position delta checks) remains applicable with minimal modifications.

- *False positives and usability:* Although detection thresholds were optimized for reliability, there still exist trade-offs between sensitivity and the cognitive burden on the operator. Context-aware filtering and adaptive thresholds are required for long-term deployment. In addition, the proposed spoofing detection system is subject to the quality and the availability of Global Navigation Satellite System (GNSS) signals. In unfavorable situations (e.g. urban canyons, high forest, or in indoors), the GNSS waves experience a significant loss or reflection in the environment, or the waves are blocked. The effects deteriorate the signal strength, increases the horizontal dilution of precision (HDOP) parameters and lowers satellite visibility. This creates the following risks of smuggled alerts or false positives, since the common wear and tear on a signal can look like signals of spoofing. Future versions of the platform may incorporate other localization modes, e.g. Inertial Navigation Systems (INS), dead reckoning, or even vision-based odometry so that the constant position estimation can also be achieved even when no satellites are visible. The hybrid systems would improve reliability of detection in signal-denied (NO-FIX), or degraded environments by combining the GNSS data with logic sensor-fusion techniques.

These challenges notwithstanding, the architecture shows how real-time EMS and cyber-monitoring could be integrated into a practical defense mechanism that protects CPS and critical infrastructures.

## 6.2  Future Work and Extensions

The proposed proof-of-concept system is scalable and can be extended in various ways to increase its detection capabilities and operational trust:

1. *Physical layer authentication through RF fingerprinting and PUFs:* To differentiate the genuine devices from spoofers, the platform may be extended to use RF fingerprinting tools. When used in combination with Physical Unclonable Functions (PUFs), they may provide an additional hardware-based trust layer for drones or SCADA field units.
2. *Efficient GPS spoofing detection method:* A future goal is to add deep learning models for GPS spoofing detection (e.g., [37]). The modularity of the proposed system allows for the deployment of such models at the edge layer (e.g., on Raspberry Pi), enabling real-time inference directly on-site. In the future, the results of capsule models can be tested using real-world GPS databases simulated within the cyber range, as an extra layer of detection on top of the existing spatial-temporal rules.
3. *Differential GPS (D-GPS) integration:* One of the most popular enhancement systems, which may extend positional precision and integrity through distribution of real-time correction signals provided by fixed reference stations is Differential GPS (D-GPS). In the framework of prospective workable EMS detection systems, including D-GPS would presumably impart an increased resistance to spoofing. In particular, it is possible to compare the real-time GPS solution created by a mobile receiver and the solution created with the surrounding base station that is a trusted fixed station of D-GPS. The sources of discrepancy can be discerned with more certainty in the pseudorange measurements or position estimates. The associated relative positioning scheme allows detecting anomalies that does not necessarily relate to signal behavior indicators (e.g. HDOP, signal strength), but also to spatial consistency in a network of trusted nodes. The conceptually is worldly that this combination will aid in developing differential anomaly detection models integrating cooperative localization with error-confinement approaches, e.g., residual analysis, to reinforce spoofing resistance. In addition to this, the use of the D-GPS enables the comparative study between the single-point GNSS receiver and the networked positioning architecture during adversarial environments [38].
4. *Swarm-Based Edge Deployment:* The platform can be extended into mobile swarmable nodes, such as UAVs and ground vehicles thus allowing the spatial coverage of large critical infrastructures. Different nodes may function

as an independent CEMA sensor and contribute to a common distributed threat monitoring system. Triangulation, source localization, and distributed response planning might be supported by collaborative sensing.

# References


1. Bichmou, A., et al.: Physical cyber-security of SCADA systems. In: 2019 IEEE National Aerospace and Electronics Conference (NAECON). Dayton, OH, USA: IEEE, Jul. 2019, pp. 243–248. [Online]. Available: https://ieeexplore.ieee.org/document/9057860/

2. Spezio, A., et al.: Electronic warfare systems. IEEE Trans. Microwave Theor. Techn. **50**(3), 633–644 (Mar 2002). https://ieeexplore.ieee.org/document/989948/

3. Soesanto, S.: A Digital Army: Synergies on the Battlefield and the Development of Cyber-Electromagnetic Activities (CEMA). ETH Zurich, Tech. Rep., Aug. 2021, artwork Size: 36 p. Medium: application/pdf. [Online]. Available: http://hdl.handle.net/20.500.11850/502731

4. Hermon, R., Singh, U., Khatkar, M.: Cyber and Electronic Warfare in Context of Defence Forces in Present Scenario. In: 2023 Second International Conference on Electrical, Electronics, Information and Communication Technologies (ICEE-ICT). Trichirappalli, India: IEEE, Apr. 2023, pp. 1–6. [Online]. Available: https://ieeexplore.ieee.org/document/10157307/

5. Ricciardi, S., Souque, C., et al.: Modern electromagnetic spectrum battlefield: From EMS global supremacy to local superiority. PRISM, vol. 9, no. 3, pp. 122–139, 2021. [Online]. Available: https://www.jstor.org/stable/48640750

6. Nejib, P., Marks, R.: The future of information operations for airborne reconnaissance SIGINT: the Joint Interoperable Operator Network (JION). In: MILCOM 1999. IEEE Military Communications. Conference Proceedings (Cat. No.99CH36341), vol. 2. Atlantic City, NJ, USA: IEEE, 1999, pp. 1378–1382 (1999). [Online]. Available: http://ieeexplore.ieee.org/document/821429/

7. Scorrano, L., Trotta, F., Manna, A., Dinoi, L.: Dual-polarization DF Array for airborne SIGINT in VHF / UHF bands. In: 2014 44th European Microwave Conference. Rome: IEEE, Oct. 2014, pp. 1912–1915. [Online]. Available: http://ieeexplore.ieee.org/document/6986836/

8. Maeng, S.J., Park, J., Guvenç.: Analysis of UAV Radar and communication network coexistence with different multiple access protocols. IEEE Trans. Commun. **71**(11), 6578–6592 (Nov 2023). [Online]. Available: https://ieeexplore.ieee.org/document/10217344/

9. Vasicek, R., Oulehlova, A.: Cyber and electromagnetic activities and their relevance in modern military operations. In: Proceedings of the 31st European Safety and Reliability Conference (ESREL 2021). Research Publishing Services, 2021, pp. 512–519. [Online]. Available: https://rpsonline.com.sg/proceedings/9789811820168/html/231.xml

10. "HackRF One - Great Scott Gadgets." [Online]. Available: https://greatscottgadgets.com/hackrf/one/

11. "pavsa/hackrf-spectrum-analyzer." [Online]. Available: https://github.com/pavsa/hackrf-spectrum-analyzer

12. Zhou, H., Wang, L., Guo, Z.: Recognition of radar compound jamming based on convolutional neural network. IEEE Trans. Aerosp. Electron. Syst. **59**(6), 7380–7394 (Dec 2023). [Online]. Available: https://ieeexplore.ieee.org/document/10158791/

13. Keerthi, C.K., Jabbar, M., Seetharamulu, B.: Cyber Physical Systems(CPS):security issues, challenges and solutions. In: 2017 IEEE International Conference on Computational Intelligence and Computing Research (ICCIC). Coimbatore: IEEE , pp. 1–4 (Dec 2017). [Online]. Available: https://ieeexplore.ieee.org/document/8524312/

14. Alrefaei, F., Alzahrani, A., Song, H., Zohdy, M., Alrefaei, S.: Cyber physical systems, a new challenge and security issue for the aviation. In: 2021 IEEE International IOT, Electronics and Mechatronics Conference (IEMTRONICS). Toronto, ON, Canada: IEEE , pp. 1–5 (Apr 2021). https://ieeexplore.ieee.org/document/9422483/

15. Dayanikli, G.Y.: Electromagnetic Interference Attacks on Cyber-Physical Systems: Theory, Demonstration, and Defense, 8 (2021). [Online]. Available: http://hdl.handle.net/10919/104862

16. Khan, S.Z., Mohsin, M., Iqbal, W.: On GPS spoofing of aerial platforms: a review of threats, challenges, methodologies, and future research directions. PeerJ Comput. Sci. **7**, e507, May 2021. [Online]. Available: https://peerj.com/articles/cs-507

17. Charitou, N.: Understanding and Mitigating GPS Spoofing Attacks in Shipping," Master's thesis, UNIVERISITY OF PIRAEUS, Athens, Greece (Jan 2025). [Online]. Available: https://dione.lib.unipi.gr/xmlui/handle/unipi/17419

18. Chatzisofroniou, G., Kotzanikolaou, P.: Association attacks in IEEE 802.11: Exploiting wifi usability features. In: International Workshop on Socio-Technical Aspects in Security and Trust. Springer, 2019, pp. 107–123 (2019)

19. Chatzisofroniou, G., Kotzanikolaou, P.: Exploiting wifi usability features for association attacks in IEEE 802.11: attack analysis and mitigation controls. J. Comput. Secur. **30**(3), 357–380 (2022)

20. Bauer, K., Gonzales, H., McCoy, D.: Mitigating evil twin attacks in 802.11. In: 2008 IEEE International Performance, Computing and Communications Conference. Austin, TX, USA: IEEE, , pp. 513–516 (Dec 2008). [Online]. Available: http://ieeexplore.ieee.org/document/4745081/

21. Muthalagu, R., Sanjay, S.: Evil twin attack mitigation techniques in 802.11 Networks. Int. J. Adv. Comput. Sci. Appl. **12**(6) (2021)

22. Parlin, K.: Jamming of Spread Spectrum Communications Used in UAV Remote Control Systems (2017)

23. Jung, J., Nag, S., Modi, H.C.: Effectiveness of redundant communications systems in maintaining operational control of small unmanned aircraft. In: 2019 IEEE/AIAA 38th Digital Avionics Systems Conference (DASC). San Diego, CA, USA: IEEE, Sep. 2019, pp. 1–7 (Sept 2019). [Online]. Available: https://ieeexplore.ieee.org/document/9081782/

24. Wei, X., Peng, L., Xu, R., Wang, H.: Jamming avoidance trajectory planning and load balancing user association in mmWave UAV-assisted HetECN. Comput. Netw. **254**, 110820, (Dec 2024). [Online]. Available: https://linkinghub.elsevier.com/retrieve/pii/S1389128624006522

25. Huang, K.-W., Wang, H.-M.: Combating the Control Signal Spoofing Attack in UAV Systems (Apr 2018), arXiv:1804.06562 [cs]. [Online]. Available: http://arxiv.org/abs/1804.06562

26. "NEO-6 series," (June 2015). [Online]. Available: https://www.u-blox.com/en/product/neo-6-series

27. Ltd, R.P.: Buy a Raspberry Pi 4 Model B. [Online]. Available: https://www.raspberrypi.com/products/raspberry-pi-4-model-b/

28. Hak5, "WiFi Pineapple." [Online]. Available: https://shop.hak5.org/products/wifi-pineapple

29. User manual eSTAR Marcopolo-52 HD FPV (English - 98 pages). [Online]. Available: https://www.manua.ls/estar/marcopolo-52-hd-fpv/manual

30. "gnuradio/gnuradio," Apr. 2025, original-date: 2011-12-21T22:05:37Z. [Online]. Available: https://github.com/gnuradio/gnuradio

31. "gpsd / gpsd · GitLab," May 2025. [Online]. Available: https://gitlab.com/gpsd/gpsd

32. Ebinuma, T.:"osqzss/gps-sdr-sim," May 2025, original-date: 2015-06-15T01:03:14Z. [Online]. Available: https://github.com/osqzss/gps-sdr-sim

33. "apache/kafka: Mirror of Apache Kafka." [Online]. Available: https://github.com/apache/kafka

34. "secdev/scapy," May 2025, original-date: 2015-10-01T17:06:46Z. [Online]. Available: https://github.com/secdev/scapy

35. "bandr1ano/cyber-rf-monitoring-tools: Tools for detection and simulation of wireless interference, including GPS spoofing, radar jamming, and Wi-Fi Evil Twin attacks." [Online]. Available: https://github.com/bandr1ano/cyber-rf-monitoring-tools

36. "CDDIS | | Data and Derived Products | GNSS | broadcast ephemeris data." [Online]. Available: https://cddis.nasa.gov

37. Talaei Khoei, T., Al Shamaileh, K., Devabhaktuni, V.K., Kaabouch, N.: Performance analysis of capsule networks for detecting GPS spoofing attacks on unmanned aerial vehicles. Int. J. Inform. Secur. **24**(1), 62 (Feb 2025). [Online]. Available: https://link.springer.com/10.1007/s10207-024-00978-x

38. Shao, M., Sui, X.: Study on differential GPS positioning methods. In: International Conference Computer Science Mechanical Automation (CSMA) 2015, pp. 223–225 (2015)

# Detecting Anomalous Resource Consumption in EdgeAI-Based MQTT Brokers

Phi Tuong Lau[1] and Stefan Katzenbeisser[2]($\boxtimes$)

[1] Ho Chi Minh, Vietnam
[2] Faculty of Computer Science and Mathematics, Passau, Germany
`Stefan.Katzenbeisser@uni-passau.de`

**Abstract.** The integration of IoT and EdgeAI into cyber-physical systems (CPS) is transforming critical infrastructures, including industrial control systems, smart transportation, and smart grids by enabling scalable, real-time, and low-latency operations with enhanced connectivity, but also introduces new security challenges. MQTT, a lightweight messaging protocol widely used in IoT-enabled environments, enables efficient communication but lacks robust security features. Consequently, such critical infrastructures are vulnerable to various attacks such as resource exhaustion and communication disruptions, which can lead to system instability or failures.

In this paper, we present a lightweight anomaly detection model integrated into resource-constrained MQTT brokers operating at the edge. These EdgeAI-based brokers function as standard MQTT brokers while simultaneously performing real-time traffic analysis to detect abnormal resource consumption. For training and evaluation, we construct synthetic datasets that emulate both benign and malicious MQTT traffic, with data categorized into three risk levels: normal, borderline, and anomalous. Our model achieves high detection accuracy and precision (up to 99%) while maintaining a compact memory footprint of approximately 20 KB, underscoring its suitability for deployment on the edge.

**Keywords:** EdgeAI · MQTT · IoT · Anomaly Detection · Resource Consumption · Critical Infrastructures · Cyber-Physical Systems

## 1 Introduction

Anomaly detection is a fundamental technique for identifying deviations from expected behavior and plays a crucial role in securing critical infrastructures such as smart energy grids, smart transportation, and industrial control systems [1–11]. With IoT technologies and edge computing becoming increasingly embedded in cyber-physical systems [5–7] that power critical infrastructures, the demand for lightweight, real-time anomaly detection methods capable of operating reliably in resource-constrained environments is growing.


R. Laborde et al. (Eds.): ESORICS 2025, LNCS 16231, pp. 423–441, 2026.
https://doi.org/10.1007/978-3-032-16089-8_26

MQTT, a widely used communication protocol in IoT-enabled environments, enables efficient, real-time data exchange between distributed devices. However, its lightweight design comes with inherent security limitations such as weak authentication, insufficient access control, and minimal encryption that make it vulnerable to various threats, including DoS attacks, message spoofing, and data manipulation. In a CPS ecosystem, MQTT brokers can be deployed at both the edge and in the cloud to balance low-latency responsiveness with centralized coordination. While cloud-based brokers are susceptible to global disruptions such as data exfiltration or remote service disruption, edge-based brokers are particularly vulnerable to local network intrusions and resource exhaustion.

EdgeAI refers to deploy lightweight machine learning algorithms directly at the edge, allowing for smarter, faster, and more autonomous systems without relying on the cloud for decision-making. This paper introduces a lightweight anomaly detection model integrated into resource-constrained MQTT brokers operating at the edge. Such EdgeAI-based brokers operate as normal MQTT brokers, while simultaneously monitoring real-time MQTT traffic to identify abnormal patterns of resource usage such as spikes in CPU, memory, or network bandwidth consumption that may indicate early warning of DoS attacks or protocol abuse.

The process of our approach includes two main phases. The training process begins with the selection of features extracted from MQTT packet headers, broker status, and client behavior, and the definition of normal and attack patterns, which guides the generation of a synthetic dataset. This synthetic dataset is then refined to eliminate duplicates and prevent data leakage. The refined dataset is used to train an anomaly detection model using TensorFlow, a widely used machine learning framework, particularly for deep neural networks (DNNs). The trained DNN model is subsequently converted to an embedded C code using TensorFlow Lite for Microcontrollers (TFLM) [12], ported to resource-constrained MCUs. At runtime, the converted model is executed on MQTT brokers, where it analyzes incoming messages in real time to monitor system behavior and detect anomalies at the edge.

For evaluation, we measure the performance and runtime overhead of the model in both float and int8 configurations across varying dataset sizes. The int8 model consistently outperforms the float model in terms of accuracy, precision, and F1-score across all datasets. As the dataset size increases, both models maintain stable and high performance with accuracy and precision at 99%. To evaluate the runtime overhead, the models are deployed on Zephyr RTOS [13] running on an ESP32 microcontroller, configured as an edge MQTT broker. Results show that the int8 model achieves consistently lower inference time per message than the float model, while both models consume minimal memory space of around 20KB. However, both models contribute noticeable overhead when comparing the inference time to the total processing time per message.

**Main Contributions.** This paper makes the following contributions:

- We propose a lightweight anomaly detection model built into resource-constrained MQTT brokers, supporting both real-time processing of MQTT messages and anomaly detection (e.g., resource consumption) at the edge.
- We present how synthetic datasets are generated by statistical methods to train the anomaly detection models.
- We evaluate the performance and runtime overhead of the models. The results show that the models consistently maintain high performance across increasing dataset sizes (e.g., accuracy up to 99%), while consuming minimal memory footprint, with a model size of approximately 20 KB.

The remainder of the paper is organized as follows. Section 2 presents background information on MQTT. Section 3 demonstrates how MQTT networks are exposed to security threats. Section 4 introduces our approach for anomaly detection, which is evaluated in Sect. 5. Section 6 reviews related work, and Sect. 7 concludes this paper.

## 2   Background

In cyber-physical systems, data processing is often distributed across multiple layers, each with different resource capabilities. Edge computing refers to the processing of data on local devices such as gateways or routers that have moderate or limited computational power, memory, and storage. These edge devices serve as intermediaries between sensors and the cloud, enabling localized execution of lightweight models. This reduces reliance on cloud services, lowers latency, and improves real-time responsiveness.

MQTT (Message Queuing Telemetry Transport) is a lightweight, publish-subscribe messaging protocol designed for efficient communication in resource-constrained environments, making it widely used in IoT applications. It involves clients that publish messages to topics and brokers that manage the distribution of these messages to subscribers. A message consists of several fields, including the fixed header, which contains the message type and flags; the variable header, which includes information such as the protocol version, client ID, and topic name; and the payload, which carries the actual data being exchanged. The protocol is designed with features like Quality of Service (QoS) levels, message retention, and support for various message types such as CONNECT, PUBLISH, and SUBSCRIBE. These features make MQTT a preferred protocol for IoT applications such as home automation, healthcare, transportation, etc., where real-time communication and control are crucial.

## 3   Threat Scenario

MQTT applications are susceptible to various security weaknesses [14–16] such as lack of authentication, weak encryption, improper access control, weak validation, and misuse of message delivery mechanisms, potentially leading to security threats like DoS. This makes it easy for attackers to intercept, spoof, or manipulate messages.

**Brokers.** Edge brokers running on local edge devices (e.g., gateway) reduce network latency by processing messages near end devices (sensors), even with limited connectivity. Cloud brokers operating on servers offer centralized management and integration with cloud services, making them ideal for global connectivity and remote monitoring. We illustrate the brokers deployed on cloud and edge levels in Fig. 1. The edge brokers communicate with end devices using the MQTT protocol via wireless transmissions such as BLE, WiFi, and ZigBee, while gateways pass messages between networks via a cloud broker.

**Attacker.** Attackers, who often overwhelm the brokers in IoT-enabled critical infrastructures [16], are categorized into cloud and local adversaries. Cloud attackers aim at compromising the centralized cloud broker, disrupting system-wide communication, stealing sensitive data, or injecting malicious commands that affect all connected devices globally. Local attackers, on the other hand, target edge brokers at hubs or gateways, focusing on disrupting or manipulating local communication, such as between sensors and actuators in local areas. They can further be classified into external attackers and internal attackers.

External attackers, who lack authorized access, may exploit weak authentication, unencrypted messages, or open ports to invade cloud or edge brokers. For example, an external attacker could intercept plaintext messages from a cloud broker to steal sensitive data or launch DoS attacks on an edge broker to disrupt a local network. Internal attackers with full authorized access pose a greater threat by bypassing authentication and abusing features (e.g., QoS, retain). Furthermore, attackers can be still legitimate publishers or subscribers who may misuse MQTT operations, resulting in unexpected attacks.

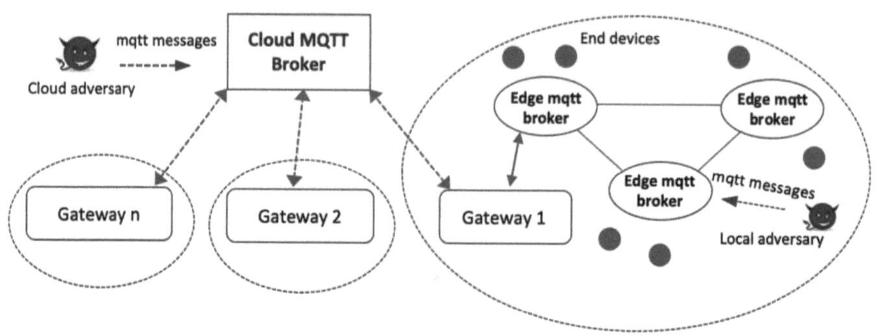


**Fig. 1.** MQTT attacks are launched at cloud and edge brokers.

## 4   Methodology

Anomaly detection for MQTT traffic has commonly been deployed in cloud environments, which offers greater computational power [17–23]. However, local adversaries can launch MQTT attacks by targeting less secure edge brokers as shown in Fig. 1. Such local brokers are executed on resource-constrained edge devices, with limited processing power and memory. In this section, we propose a lightweight anomaly detection model integrated directly into local brokers operating on EdgeAI devices. This enables the local brokers to act as normal brokers, while analyzing MQTT messages in real time and detect anomalous patterns that overwhelm broker resources such as CPU, memory, and network bandwidth, potentially triggering system instability or failures. The pipeline of our methodology is represented in Fig. 2.

The training phase begins with dataset specification, including features, normal and attack patterns, that guide generation of a synthetic dataset. Then, the synthetic dataset is refined to remove duplicates and data leakages. This cleaned dataset is used to train the detection model using TensorFlow, a software library for machine learning and artificial intelligence. This framework can be used across a range of tasks, but is used mainly for training and inference of neural networks, typically DNN models. The DNN-based model is then converted to embedded code (e.g., C/C++) using TensorFlow Lite for Microcontrollers (TFLM) [12], a lightweight version of TensorFlow designed for porting deep learning models to low-cost and low-power MCUs (e.g., ARM Cortex-M, ESP32, RISC-V). In the runtime phase, the converted model is built into MQTT brokers to analyze messages in real time and identify abnormal behavior at the edge.

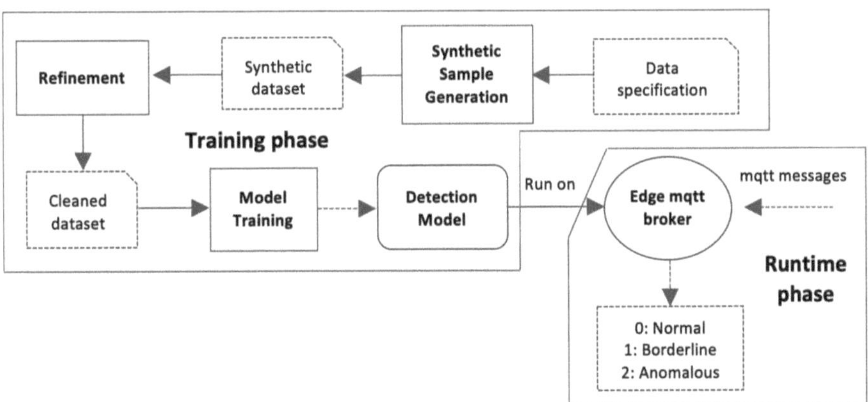


**Fig. 2.** The pipeline of the proposed methodology.

## 4.1   Data Specification

We extract features of the MQTT protocol such as event types, session states, QoS levels, payload sizes, etc., along with their impact on anomalous patterns.

**Anomalous vs Normal.** Anomalous patterns can overwhelm resource-limited brokers at the edge, potentially triggering DoS attacks. These attacks, common in IoT devices, result from excessive resource use and may cause failures or crashes [24, 25]. Resource consumption is influenced by several key factors: processing time, memory usage, and network usage. Processing time refers to the computational power required to execute tasks, while memory usage denotes the amount of RAM or storage used to hold data, configuration settings, and communication buffers. Network usage involves the bandwidth consumed during transmission or reception of messages, resulting in different traffic rates.

In contrast, normal patterns involve typical resource usage that aligns with expected operations and does not strain system resources. For example, in normal operation, QoS levels are efficiently managed, memory usage is optimal, and processing time is kept within acceptable limits. Brokers handle requests, store messages, and maintain subscriptions without significant delays or resource overload. While there may be occasional spikes in resource consumption, these are brief and do not result in lasting disruptions or crashes, maintaining stable operation and responsive communication.

**Feature Selection.** An MQTT packet is structured into three main sections: fixed header, variable header, and payload, each contributing valuable metadata for message analysis. The fixed header includes the control packet type (e.g., CONNECT, PUBLISH), flags like DUP, QoS, and Retain, and the remaining length field, which indicates the size of the packet. The variable header contains fields such as protocol name and version, connect flags (e.g., clean session, will flag), keep alive timer, and packet identifier, which helps track messages in QoS 0, 1 and 2. The payload contains the actual message data in PUBLISH packets or topic filters in SUBSCRIBE packets. In MQTT 3.0, there are 14 control packet types in total, including 7 where clients send messages to the broker (client→broker) and 7 where the broker sends acknowledgments to clients (broker→client). We focus on 3 out of 7 event types where attackers commonly intercept messages to hijack the broker (client→broker): CONNECT initiates a connection, PUBLISH sends data to a topic, and clients use SUBSCRIBE to manage subscriptions and receive messages. Table 1 illustrates the relationships between the event types and their corresponding features.

**Table 1.** Event types and their corresponding features.

| Event | Description | Corresponding features |
| --- | --- | --- |
| CONNECT | A client requests to establish a connection with the broker | Clean Session, Will, Will QoS, Will Retain, Will Payload Size, Keep-Alive, Reconn Frequency, Pending Queue, Retained Queue, Subscription Count |
| PUBLISH | A client sends a message to a specific topic | QoS, Retain, Payload Size, Pending Queue, Retained Queue, Republish Frequency |
| SUBSCRIBE | A client subscribes to one or more topics to receive messages | QoS, Pending Queue, Retained Queue, Subscription Count, Resubscription Frequency |

**Table 2.** Feature description in our dataset.

| Feature | Description | Possible Values |
|---|---|---|
| Event Type | Type of MQTT event | 1 (CONNECT)<br>2 (PUBLISH)<br>3 (SUBSCRIBE) |
| Clean Session | Whether the client starts a fresh session when reconnecting | 0 (False), 1 (True) |
| Keep-Alive | Time interval to keep connection alive | 0 (Short), 1 (Mid), 2 (Long) |
| Will Flag | If the client has a Last Will message. If 0, Will-related fields = -1 | 0 (No), 1 (Yes) |
| QoS/Will QoS | QoS level for messages/Will message. If Will = 0, Will QoS = -1 | 0 (Low), 1 (Mid), 2 (High) |
| Retain/Will Retain | If the broker retain the message/Will message retention. If Will = 0, Will Retain = -1 | 0 (No), 1 (Yes) |
| Payload/Will Payload Size | Size of the message payload/Will message payload. If Will = 0, Will Payload Size = -1 | 0 (Low), 1 (Mid), 2 (High) |
| Reconn Freq. | How often the client reconnects | 0 (Low), 1 (Mid), 2 (High) |
| Pending Queue | Number of pending messages waiting for sending to the client in the broker | 0 (Low), 1 (Mid), 2 (High) |
| Retained Queue | Number of retained messages for a topic in the broker | 0 (Low), 1 (Mid), 2 (High) |
| Subscription Count | Number of active subscription topics for the client | 0 (Low), 1 (Mid), 2 (High) |
| Resubscription Freq. | How often the client resubscribes to topics | 0 (Low), 1 (Mid), 2 (High) |
| Republish Freq. | How often the client republishes to topics | 0 (Low), 1 (Mid), 2 (High) |

We identify 13 relevant features, extracted from MQTT packet headers (e.g., QoS, clean session), broker status (e.g., pending queue), and client behavior (e.g., reconnect frequency) as summarized in Table 2, and discuss how these features affect resource consumption at the CPU, memory, and network levels as follows.

1. **Event type.** Different event types have different impacts on resource consumption. The CONNECT event typically involves authentication, session setup, and establishing communication, which requires more processing time and memory for session storage, especially if Clean Session is set to 0. The PUBLISH event, especially when messages are larger or when higher QoS levels (1 or 2) are involved, can demand more memory for message buffering and increase processing time due to acknowledgments and message delivery confirmation. The SUBSCRIBE event, on the other hand, increases memory

usage as the broker stores active subscriptions, and processing time increases as more frequent resubscriptions occur.

2. **Clean session.** The Clean Session flag controls whether the client starts a new session when it reconnects or reuses an existing one. If Clean Session = 0, the broker needs to maintain state information (such as subscriptions and pending messages) between client disconnections, leading to higher memory consumption and longer processing times to maintain and retrieve session data.

3. **Will flag.** The Will flag indicates whether the client has a *Last Will* message that should be sent if the client unexpectedly disconnects. When the flag is set to 1, the broker must store the will message and check for disconnections, which can lead to a slight increase in memory usage as well as processing time when unexpected disconnections events occur more frequently.

4. **QoS/Will QoS.** The QoS level determines the message delivery guarantee, but its value directly impacts resource consumption. For QoS 1, messages require an acknowledgment, leading to more processing time and slight memory overhead for storing the message until an acknowledgment is received. QoS 2 introduces the highest overhead, as it involves a four-step handshake to guarantee message delivery exactly once, which requires more processing time.

5. **Retain/Will Retain.** The Retain flag determines whether the broker should retain the last message sent on a topic for future subscribers. When set to 1, the broker must store these retained messages and deliver them to new subscribers when they subscribe to the topic, leading to higher memory consumption and processing time. This can also increase network usage for new subscribers since they receive the retained message immediately upon subscription.

6. **Keep-Alive.** The keep-alive setting controls how often the client sends a ping message to the broker to maintain the connection. A short keep-alive interval causes the client to send ping messages more frequently, increasing the processing time for the broker as it must handle these frequent checks. This also slightly increases network usage due to the repeated messages.

7. **Payload/Will Payload size.** The payload size refers to the amount of data in the message being transmitted. For example, a large payload size can cause delays in message transmission, increase latency due to message encryption/decryption (e.g., TLS/SSL), and consume more memory for storing the pending message at brokers. The processing time to encode, send, and decode large messages also increases, as messages are repeated with high frequency.

8. **Reconnection frequency.** The reconnection frequency refers to how often clients reconnect to a broker. A high reconnection frequency increases resource consumption as the broker consumes the overhead of establishing new connections and updating client sessions more frequently. Each reconnection requires re-subscribing to topics, which involves more processing time and memory usage for tracking and managing the active subscriptions. High-frequency reconnections can also introduce more network usage.

9. **Pending queue.** The pending queue indicates how many messages are waiting to be sent to the client. A larger pending queue requires more memory to store these messages until they are delivered. It also increases processing time because the broker must manage and attempt to send each pending message. If the queue becomes very large, the broker will delivery many messages in the queue, resulting in high volume of data being transmitted over network affecting network usage.

10. **Retained queue.** The retained queue indicates the number of messages that the broker stores for a specific topic. A larger retained queue demands more memory for persistent storage, and delivering these messages to new subscribers requires additional processing time. Furthermore, as new subscribers receive all retained messages upon subscriptions, network usage can increase significantly.

11. **Subscription count.** The subscription count represents the number of topics a client is actively subscribed to. A higher subscription count increases memory usage because the broker must maintain a larger list of active subscriptions. It also elevates processing time, as the broker needs to compare each incoming message with all active subscriptions to determine delivery, which in turn can lead to increased network usage due to the higher volume of message delivery.

12. **Resubscription frequency.** The resubscription frequency controls how often the client resubscribes to topics. A high frequency of resubscription increases processing time on the broker, as the broker must re-process the subscription requests. Memory usage can also increase because each resubscription may involve storing additional session information or re-checking subscriptions. Moreover, frequent resubscriptions elevate network usage, as the client and broker must constantly resynchronize their subscription data.

13. **Republish frequency.** The republish frequency indicates how often a client republishes messages to topics. A higher frequency increases the processing time needed to manage these messages and may lead to higher memory consumption, especially when messages are stored in the pending queue using QoS levels 1 or 2. Additionally, frequent republishing can elevate network usage as more messages are transmitted over the network.

Table 3 shows the estimates of the impact scores of the mentioned features on three key resource categories: processing time, memory usage, and network usage. Each feature is assigned an impact score for each resource type based on its relative influence: 1.0 for high impact, 0.5 for medium, and 0.0 for negligible or low impact. The final column, overall impact score, represents the average of the three individual scores, providing a combined measure of the total resource demand of a feature. The impact scores of each feature are heuristic estimates rather than direct experimental data, and help approximate how much each feature might contribute to processing time, memory usage, or network load. However, their actual effects can vary depending on system design and runtime conditions.

**Table 3.** Impact scores of features on resource consumption.

| Feature | Proc. Time | Memory Usage | Network Usage | Overall Score |
|---|---|---|---|---|
| Event Type | ✓ (1.0) | ✓ (1.0) | ✓ (1.0) | 1.00 |
| Clean Session | ✓ (1.0) | ✓ (0.5) | ✓ (0.5) | 0.67 |
| Will Flag | ✗ (0.0) | ✓ (0.5) | ✗ (0.0) | 0.17 |
| QoS/Will QoS | ✓ (1.0) | ✓ (1.0) | ✓ (1.0) | 1.00 |
| Retain/Will Retain | ✓ (1.0) | ✓ (1.0) | ✓ (1.0) | 1.00 |
| Keep-Alive | ✓ (0.5) | ✗ (0.0) | ✓ (1.0) | 0.50 |
| Payload Size/Will Payload Size | ✓ (1.0) | ✓ (1.0) | ✓ (1.0) | 1.00 |
| Reconnection Freq. | ✓ (1.0) | ✓ (1.0) | ✓ (1.0) | 1.00 |
| Pending Queue | ✓ (1.0) | ✓ (1.0) | ✓ (1.0) | 1.00 |
| Retained Queue | ✓ (1.0) | ✓ (1.0) | ✓ (1.0) | 1.00 |
| Subscription Count | ✓ (1.0) | ✓ (1.0) | ✓ (1.0) | 1.00 |
| Resubscription Freq. | ✓ (1.0) | ✓ (1.0) | ✓ (1.0) | 1.00 |
| Republish Freq. | ✓ (1.0) | ✓ (1.0) | ✓ (1.0) | 1.00 |

## 4.2   Sample Collection

Anomaly detection datasets can be generated through physical monitoring or
simulation. Even though physical monitoring collects real-world data, ensuring
authenticity, it is difficult to capture targeted attack patterns and a large volume
of data. Simulations provide controlled environments for large-scale data generation, including rare attack scenarios. However, both methods require further
optimization to reduce their size for deployment in resource-constrained EdgeAI
devices. Moreover, these methods primarily collect packet contents and network
traffic in real-world contexts to extract packet-based and network-based features,
excluding system-level features (e.g., pending queue) and client behavior (e.g.,
republish frequency). Due to the scarcity of labeled real-world MQTT attack
datasets and the limited feature coverage of existing simulations, we adopt a
synthetic dataset approach, which allows controlled variation of MQTT header
features, broker states, and client behaviors.

**Synthetic Dataset Generation.** To simulate diverse MQTT client behavior, we generate a synthetic dataset consisting of three key MQTT event types:
CONNECT, PUBLISH, and SUBSCRIBE. For each event type, an equal number of samples are created across three behavioral classes: normal, borderline,
and anomalous. Each sample includes features with randomized values, selected
from specific ranges tailored to each class. The dataset captures various MQTT
parameters such as session settings, QoS levels, payload sizes, and frequencies of
actions like reconnections and resubscriptions. Additionally, a normalized weight
score is computed for each sample, representing the level of resource consumption. Let $F$ denote the set of all features in a sample, $f_i \in F$ an individual
feature, $v_i$ the value of a feature $f_i$ (see Table 2), $w_i$ the overall score for $f_i$

(see Table 3), and $R \subset F$ the set of relevant features (i.e., $v_i \neq -1$). Then, the normalized weight score (NWS) is given by:

$$\text{NWS} = \frac{\sum_{f_i \in R} w_i \cdot v_i}{|R|}$$

To facilitate the interpretation of samples, we derive severity thresholds from the dataset using quantile analysis. The percentiles method divides the dataset into three segments using the 33rd and 66th percentiles. The 33rd percentile represents the threshold below which one-third of the data points fall (low), and the 66th percentile represents the threshold below which two-thirds of the data points fall (medium). Any data point above the 66th percentile is considered high. We generate synthetic datasets of three different sizes: 900, 4,500, and 45,000 samples and use the quantile analysis with the 33rd and 66th percentiles to label each sample as normal, borderline, or anomalous, indicating the overall resource consumption of a broker.

1. Label 0 (normal) corresponds to low resource usage, reflecting normal behavior that operates efficiently with minimal impact on broker's processing time, memory, and network.
2. Label 1 (borderline) indicates medium resource usage, representing configurations that are still within normal operating conditions but exert a moderate load on the broker. Although not inherently malicious, such behavior may lead to further degradation once the number of reconnections or subscriptions is increased.
3. Label 2 (anomalous) denotes high resource usage, associated with anomalous patterns. These samples are often characterized by high QoS, frequent reconnections or republishing, large payloads, and high numbers of subscriptions or retained messages. Such activity can overload the broker, leading to delayed responses, DoS, or even system crashes, especially in resource-constrained edge devices.

**Refinement.** The synthetic dataset may contain two types of duplicates: exact duplicates, where entries are identical, and semantic duplicates, where entries convey the same meaning but differ in wording or structure. We leverage Min-Hash+LSH [26], an efficient technique for removing duplicate records in a dataset. This tool has been widely adopted by many LLMs such as Qwen, Code-Parrot, SantaCoder, StarCoder, and StarCoder2 to detect and filter potential duplicate data within their pre-training corpora [27]. MinHash generates compact signatures for dataset records, and Locality-Sensitive Hashing (LSH) organizes these signatures into hash buckets, ensuring that only records with high similarity are compared directly. By filtering out redundant entries, this approach enhances dataset quality by preventing overfitting and data leakages in machine learning models.

Table 4 reveals the distribution of data samples, including normal, borderline, and anomalous data after refinement. The synthetic dataset comprises 668, 1,815, and 6,243 samples across three refined sizes. For the smallest set, normal, borderline, and anomalous traffic represent 36%, 34%, and 30%, respectively. In the medium set, these classes account for 47%, 33%, and 20%, while in the largest set, they constitute 61%, 31%, and 8%. No artificial balancing was applied, preserving the dataset's natural distribution, which reflects real-world MQTT traffic where normal patterns dominate and anomalies become increasingly rare as the dataset size grows.

**Table 4.** Distribution of classes across different dataset sizes after refining.

| No. samples | Normal | Borderline | Anomalous |
| --- | --- | --- | --- |
| 668 | 240 (36%) | 224 (34%) | 203 (30%) |
| 1815 | 853 (47%) | 598 (33%) | 363 (20%) |
| 6243 | 3841 (61%) | 1910 (31%) | 491 (8%) |

## 5  Evaluation

The evaluation of our DNN-based detection model, as illustrated in Fig. 2, is conducted in two key parts: model performance and runtime overhead. First, the model performance is assessed using standard metrics such as F1 score, precision, and recall implemented in Python programs run on a computer. We use 80% of the generated dataset for training and 20% for testing. Second, the runtime overhead is evaluated by deploying the trained model on real hardware.

### 5.1  Model Performance

We evaluate key metrics, including accuracy, which measures overall correctness; precision, which indicates the proportion of correctly predicted positives; and recall, which quantifies the ability to detect actual positives. The F1-score balances precision and recall, making it particularly useful for imbalanced datasets. Additionally, we use PR AUC (Precision-Recall Area Under the Curve) to assess the trade-off between precision and recall. Similarly, ROC AUC (Receiver Operating Characteristic Area Under the Curve) measures the model's ability to distinguish between classes by evaluating the true positive rate against the false positive rate. Higher values across these metrics generally reflect better model performance.

In addition, we train an int8 model since integer operations are faster and require less power than floating-point operations on resource-constrained embedded devices. Modern quantization techniques allow the int8 model to maintain accuracy comparable to their float counterparts, enabling efficient deployment of AI models on edge-based MQTT brokers. Tables 5, 6, 7 compare int8 and float32 models across different metrics for three datasets, including 668, 1815, and 6243 samples.

**Table 5.** Comparison of int8 and float32 models (668 instances).

| Metric | Class | int8 | float32 | Diff. | Overall | int8 | float32 | Diff. |
|---|---|---|---|---|---|---|---|---|
| Precision | 0 | 0.9783 | 0.9783 | 0.0000 | Accuracy | 0.9627 | 0.9627 | 0.0000 |
| | 1 | 0.9298 | 0.9298 | 0.0000 | Precision | 0.9639 | 0.9639 | 0.0000 |
| | 2 | 1.0000 | 1.0000 | 0.0000 | | | | |
| Recall | 0 | 0.9375 | 0.9375 | 0.0000 | Recall | 0.9627 | 0.9627 | 0.0000 |
| | 1 | 0.9815 | 0.9815 | 0.0000 | PR AUC | 0.9943 | 0.9971 | +0.0028 |
| | 2 | 0.9688 | 0.9688 | 0.0000 | ROC AUC | 0.9965 | 0.9982 | +0.0017 |
| F1-score | 0 | 0.9574 | 0.9574 | 0.0000 | F1-score | 0.9628 | 0.9628 | 0.0000 |
| | 1 | 0.9550 | 0.9550 | 0.0000 | | | | |
| | 2 | 0.9841 | 0.9841 | 0.0000 | | | | |

**Table 6.** Comparison of int8 and float32 models (1815 instances).

| Metric | Class | int8 | float32 | Diff. | Overall | int8 | float32 | Diff. |
|---|---|---|---|---|---|---|---|---|
| Precision | 0 | 1.0000 | 0.9873 | +0.0127 | Accuracy | 0.9862 | 0.9862 | 0.0000 |
| | 1 | 0.9848 | 0.9848 | 0.0000 | Precision | 0.9863 | 0.9862 | +0.0001 |
| | 2 | 0.9600 | 0.9863 | -0.0263 | | | | |
| Recall | 0 | 1.0000 | 1.0000 | 0.0000 | Recall | 0.9862 | 0.9862 | 0.0000 |
| | 1 | 0.9774 | 0.9774 | 0.0000 | PR AUC | 0.9986 | 0.9994 | -0.0008 |
| | 2 | 0.9730 | 0.9730 | 0.0000 | ROC AUC | 0.9994 | 0.9997 | -0.0003 |
| F1-score | 0 | 1.0000 | 0.9936 | +0.0064 | F1-score | 0.9862 | 0.9862 | +0.0001 |
| | 1 | 0.9811 | 0.9811 | 0.0000 | | | | |
| | 2 | 0.9664 | 0.9796 | -0.0132 | | | | |

**Class-Level Metrics.** The comparison between the int8 and float32 models shows that performance differences at the class level are negligible across all dataset sizes. There are slight variations in some classes for the 1,815-instance dataset. For example, the int8 model achieves a marginally higher Precision for Class 0 (+0.0127) and a slightly lower F1-score for Class 2 (-0.0132).

**Overall Metrics.** The int8 model shows only a very slight difference in Accuracy, Precision, and F1-score compared to the float model across all datasets. However, the float model tends to slightly outperform the int8 model in specific metrics such as PR AUC and ROC AUC. For instance, in 1815 instances, the float model yields a slightly higher PR AUC (+0.0028) and ROC AUC (+0.0017) compared to the int8 model. Nevertheless, these differences are relatively small, indicating that both int8 and float models perform similarly, with slight trade-offs depending on dataset sizes.

**Increasing Sizes.** As the dataset size increases, both the int8 and float models continue to perform well and show stable performance. In the smaller dataset

**Table 7.** Comparison of int8 and float32 models (6243 instances).

| Metric | Class | int8 | float32 | Diff. | Overall | int8 | float32 | Diff. |
|---|---|---|---|---|---|---|---|---|
| Precision | 0 | 1.0000 | 1.0000 | 0.0000 | Accuracy | 0.9984 | 0.9984 | 0.0000 |
| | 1 | 0.9945 | 0.9945 | 0.0000 | Precision | 0.9984 | 0.9984 | 0.0000 |
| | 2 | 1.0000 | 1.0000 | 0.0000 | | | | |
| Recall | 0 | 1.0000 | 1.0000 | 0.0000 | Recall | 0.9984 | 0.9984 | 0.0000 |
| | 1 | 1.0000 | 1.0000 | 0.0000 | PR AUC | 0.9997 | 1.0000 | -0.0003 |
| | 2 | 0.9798 | 0.9798 | 0.0000 | ROC AUC | 0.9999 | 1.0000 | -0.0001 |
| F1-score | 0 | 1.0000 | 1.0000 | 0.0000 | F1-score | 0.9984 | 0.9984 | 0.0000 |
| | 1 | 0.9972 | 0.9972 | 0.0000 | | | | |
| | 2 | 0.9898 | 0.9898 | 0.0000 | | | | |

(668 instances), the models perform almost identically across all metrics. As the dataset grows to 1815 and 6243 instances, the int8 model's performance remains comparable to the float model, with only minor differences observed in some metrics like PR AUC and ROC AUC.

## 5.2    Runtime Overhead

To measure runtime overhead, we integrate the trained models into Zephyr OS [13], a real-time operating system (RTOS) for embedded systems and IoT devices. Zephyr OS supports multiple architectures (ARM, RISC-V, x86, etc.), offers real-time capabilities, and allows direct integration of TFLM models. We build an MQTT network, including an edge-based MQTT broker running on ESP32-S3-DevKitC (520KB RAM, 4 MB Flash) and clients running on a computer for publishing/subscribing messages to the broker.

Table 8 shows differences in terms of model size and runtime overhead between two models across different dataset sizes. The int8 model consistently demonstrates lower inference times per message compared to the float model. For instance, at 663 instances, the inference time for the int8 model is 5.22 ms, while the float model takes 5.67 ms per message. This difference persists across other dataset sizes, with int8 having slightly faster inference times overall. Furthermore, the int8 model is smaller in size, making it more memory-efficient than the float model, which is beneficial for resource-constrained devices. Despite this, both models add significant overhead when considering the inference time relative to the total processing time of each message. However, it is important to note that our research does not optimize the model's responsiveness, as the main focus is on security, and measuring the model performance and runtime overhead.

**Table 8.** Comparison of model size (kilobytes), inference and total processing time (in milliseconds) in both models by analyzing a message across different dataset sizes.

| Dataset Size | Model Size | | Inference Time | | Total Time | | Overhead | |
|---|---|---|---|---|---|---|---|---|
| | int8 | float32 | int8 | float32 | int8 | float32 | int8 | float32 |
| 663 | 19 | 23 | 5.22 | 5.67 | 14.14 | 14.11 | 36.9% | 40.2% |
| 1815 | 19 | 23 | 5.67 | 5.68 | 14.12 | 14.12 | 40.1% | 40.2% |
| 6243 | 19 | 23 | 5.22 | 5.22 | 14.18 | 14.13 | 36.8% | 36.9% |

## 5.3   Discussion

Our evaluation demonstrated the feasibility and effectiveness of deploying anomaly detection models in resource-constrained MQTT brokers running at the edge. The results indicated high accuracy and minimal memory footprint across different dataset sizes, making it suitable for early-stage anomaly detection.

**Limitations.** The datasets are generated using statistical techniques and protocol-level knowledge, which enables controlled and scalable evaluation. However, this method does not fully reflect the behavioral complexity of real-world MQTT traffic. For instance, temporal and sequential patterns such as the timing between events or the order of operations (e.g., CONNECT $\rightarrow$ SUBSCRIBE $\rightarrow$ PUBLISH) are not synthesized in our datasets. In addition, feature values are randomized, which may limit generalization due to class imbalance as indicated in Table 4. Furthermore, our anomaly detection method focuses primarily on resource consumption attacks, but edge brokers are vulnerable to various threats.

**Threats to Validity.** Even though our model can detect resource consumption patterns based on analyzing features, attackers could manipulate timing or order of operations to bypass the detection model. The model may miss such abnormal behavior unless it captures temporal context or state transitions.

Timing attacks in MQTT-based systems involve adversaries initially sending benign or diagnostic packets to measure response times and infer internal states such as CPU load, memory usage, or latency. These leaks expose the broker's real-time resource conditions, allowing attackers to identify periods of elevated vulnerability. Leveraging this insight, they can subsequently dispatch precisely timed malicious packets designed to maximize impact while avoiding inspection of suspicious behavior like repeated subscriptions, republishes, or reconnect attempts as learned by the models.

Event order manipulation is a stealthy evasion strategy in which attackers deliberately reorder legitimate MQTT control messages (e.g., CONNECT $\rightarrow$ SUBSCRIBE $\rightarrow$ PUBLISH $\rightarrow$ UNSUBSCRIBE) and adjust configuration parameters such as the clean session flag or QoS level. Different sequences and settings can trigger varied resource allocation behaviors in brokers. By crafting suspicious yet valid message sequences that lead to disproportionate resource consumption, attackers can send such sequences of messages to overwhelm the system. This strategy can evade detection models, as it does not rely on repeatedly suspicious actions within a short time frame such as republishing, resubscribing, or reconnecting, but instead exploits subtle variations in message order and parameters. Combining these attacks with timing attacks makes them significantly easier to overwhelm edge-based brokers running on resource-constrained MCUs or platforms.

## 6   Related Work

**Anomaly Detection.** Numerous anomaly detection models have been proposed for IoT systems operating in cloud environments [17–23], whereas research on edge-level detection has primarily focused on diverse application domains [1–11,28–30]. Tan et al. [4] proposed a hybrid intrusion detection model for cyber-physical systems by combining signature-based and threshold-based IDS with machine learning techniques to detect known and unknown threats in operational technology networks. Ngo et al. [6] introduced a networking model for CPS to handle edge-assisted authentication, addressing the growing complexity of IIoT security by offloading security operations to edge routers, thereby reducing the burden on resource-constrained devices. Cao et al. [7] implemented ADRIoT, an edge-based anomaly detection framework for IoT networks, targeting malware and zero-day attacks in resource-constrained environments.

EdgeAI devices range from powerful platforms such as Raspberry Pi, NVIDIA Jetson to resource-constrained MCUs like ESP32, nRF5340, STM32. Bratu et al. [28] presented a low-power, compact EdgeAI solution for predictive maintenance using an unsupervised learning algorithm on an ESP32 microcontroller. Sivapalan et al. [29] presented a lightweight neural network combining LSTM and MLP for real-time ECG anomaly detection and power-efficient operation on IoT edge wearable devices. Katariya et al. [30] introduced VegaEdge, a lightweight and efficient EdgeAI solution for real-time vehicle anomaly detection on highways operating on Nvidia's Jetson. Our work proposed a lightweight anomaly detection model that is deployed in edge-based MQTT brokers, running on resource-constrained MCUs to detect abnormal resource consumption.

**Benchmark Datasets.** Several IoT benchmark datasets have been developed for anomaly detection, including RT-IoT2022 (54 MB) [31], MQTT-IoT-IDS2020 (1.65 GB) [32], MQTTSet (10 GB) [33], BoT-IoT (277 MB) [34], and IoT23 (21 GB) [35]. While some datasets like RT-IoT2022 rely on real network traffic, others use simulations. Due to their large size, they are more suited for cloud-based anomaly detection. For MQTT-specific attacks, MQTT-IoT-IDS2020 and MQTTSet are highly relevant to our work. MQTT-IoT-IDS2020 includes 44 MQTT/TCP-based features and covers four attack types: aggressive scanning, MQTT brute-force, Sparta SSH brute-force, and UDP scanning. MQTTSet consists of 33 features for detecting five attack patterns, including flooding DoS, MQTT publish flood, SlowITe, malformed data, and brute-force authentication.

These existing datasets are large and cover various attack patterns, primarily targeting intrusion detection systems and cloud environments. However, they mainly focus on network-based DDoS attacks caused by traffic overload, while overlooking other forms of DoS that stem from excessive resource consumption on resource-constrained systems or devices. In contrast, our dataset is specifically designed for resource-constrained EdgeAI devices running MQTT brokers, with the goal of detecting anomalous resource usage resulting from excessive CPU load, memory consumption, and network usage that could potentially lead to DoS.

## 7    Conclusion

Anomaly detection plays a critical role in ensuring the security, safety, and operational integrity of critical infrastructures powered by CPS, especially at the edge where data is processed near physical devices such as sensors and actuators. The MQTT protocol, a lightweight, real-time communication used widely in IoT-enabled CPS, offers minimal built-in security. Attackers can exploit protocol-level vulnerabilities to trigger excessive resource usage or disrupt communication flows, potentially resulting in disrupting the availability and responsiveness of sensors and actuators.

This paper proposed a lightweight anomaly detection model built into MQTT brokers tailored for resource-constrained EdgeAI, ensuring secure, real-time traffic analysis alongside standard broker processes. We generated synthetic datasets for training the models using key features extracted from MQTT packet headers, broker status, and client behavior. Experimental results demonstrated that the models achieved high accuracy and precision, while maintaining a compact memory footprint, making it a practical and efficient solution for enhancing security at the edge of CPS. Our source code is publicly available for testing and evaluation [36].

## References


1. Fernandes, G., Rodrigues, J.J., Carvalho, L.F., Al-Muhtadi, J.F., Proença, M.L.: A comprehensive survey on network anomaly detection. In: Telecommunication Systems, pp. 447–489 (2019)
2. Altulaihan, E., Almaiah, M.A., Aljughaiman, A.: Anomaly detection ids for detecting dos attacks in Iot networks based on machine learning algorithms. Sensors **24**(2), 713 (2024)
3. Howley E. Yang, X., Schukat, M.: Adt: Time series anomaly detection for cyber-physical systems via deep reinforcement learning. Computers Secur. **141**, 103825 (2024)
4. Tan Q. Jeffrey, N., Villar, J.R.: A hybrid methodology for anomaly detection in cyber–physical systems. Neurocomputing **568**, 127068 (2024)
5. Wang, H., Muñoz-González, L., Eklund, D., Raza, S.: Edge computing for cyber-physical systems: a systematic mapping study emphasizing trustworthiness. ACM Trans. Cyber-Phys. Syst. (TCPS) **6**(3), 1–28 (2022)

6. Ngo, M.V., Chaouchi, H., Luo, T., Quek, T.Q.: Edge-assisted intelligent device authentication in cyber–physical systems. IEEE Internet Things J. **10**(4), 3057–3070 (2022)
7. Cao J. Xiang, X., W. Fan, W.: Secure authentication and trust management scheme for edge ai-enabled cyber-physical systems. IEEE Transactions on Intelligent Transportation Systems (2025)
8. Huč, A., Šalej, J., Trebar, M.: Analysis of machine learning algorithms for anomaly detection on edge devices. Sensors **21**(14), 4946 (2021)
9. Li, R., Li, Q., Zhou, J., Jiang, Y.: Adriot: an edge-assisted anomaly detection framework against Iot-based network attacks. IEEE Internet Things J. **9**(13), 10576–10587 (2021)
10. Liu, Y., et al.: Deep anomaly detection for time-series data in industrial Iot: a communication-efficient on-device federated learning approach. IEEE Internet Things J. **8**(8), 6348–6358 (2020)
11. Rathi, V.K., et al.: An edge AI-enabled Iot healthcare monitoring system for smart cities. Comput. Electr. Eng. **96**, 107524 (2021)
12. Tensorflow lite for microcontrollers. https://github.com/tensorflow/tflite-micro
13. Zephyr rtos. https://github.com/zephyrproject-rtos/zephyr
14. Andy, S., Rahardjo, B., Hanindhito, B.: Attack scenarios and security analysis of MQTT communication protocol in Iot system. In: Proceedings of the 4th International Conference on Electrical Engineering, Computer Science and Informatics (EECSI), pp. 1–6 (2017)
15. Hintaw, A.J., Manickam, S., Aboalmaaly, M.F., Karuppayah, S.: MQTT vulnerabilities, attack vectors and solutions in the internet of things (iot). IETE J. Res. **69**(6), 3368–3397 (2023)
16. Calzarossa, M.C., Zuppelli, M., Caviglione, L., Polisiani, C.C., Guarascio, M.: Improving MQTT security through the generation of malicious test cases. In: Joint National Conference on Cybersecurity (ITASEC and SERICS) (2025)
17. Ciklabakkal, E., Donmez, A., Erdemir, M., Suren, E., Yilmaz, M.K., Angin, P.: Artemis: an intrusion detection system for MQTT attacks in internet of things. In: 2019 38th Symposium on Reliable Distributed Systems (SRDS), pp. 369–3692 (2019)
18. Dikii, D., Arustamov, S., Grishentsev, A.: Dos attacks detection in MQTT networks. Indonesian J. Electr. Eng. Comput. Sci. **21**(1), 601–608 (2021)
19. Alzahrani, A., Aldhyani, T.H.: Artificial intelligence algorithms for detecting and classifying MQTT protocol internet of things attacks. Electronics **11**(22), 3837 (2022)
20. Alaiz-Moreton, H., Aveleira-Mata, J., Ondicol-Garcia, J., Muñoz-Castañeda, A.L., García, I., Benavides, C.: Multiclass classification procedure for detecting attacks on MQTT-IQT protocol. Complexity, (1) 6516253 (2019)
21. Zuhairi, M.F., Ali, S.M., Shahid, Z., Alam, M.M., Su'ud, M.M.: Realtime feature engineering for anomaly detection in Iot based MQTT networks. IEEE Access (2024)
22. Khan, M.A., et al.: A deep learning-based intrusion detection system for MQTT enabled Iot. Sensors **21**(21), 7016 (2021)
23. Ap, H., K.K.: Secure-mqtt: an efficient fuzzy logic-based approach to detect dos attack in MQTT protocol for internet of things. EURASIP J. Wireless Commun. Network. (1), 90 (2019)
24. Lau, P.T., Katzenbeisser, S.: Firmware-based dos attacks in wireless sensor network. In: 6th International Workshop on Attacks and Defenses for Internet-of-Things (ADIoT), pp. 214–232 (2023)

25. Lau, P.T., Katzenbeisser, S.: A protocol fuzzing framework to detect remotely exploitable vulnerabilities in iot nodes. In: IEEE International Conference on Software Testing, Verification and Validation Workshops (ICSTW), pp. 226–234 (2025)
26. Minhash+lsh. https://ekzhu.com/datasketch/lsh.html
27. Zhou, X., et al.: Lessleak-bench: A first investigation of data leakage in LLMs across 83 software engineering benchmarks (2025)
28. Bratu, D.V., Ilinoiu, R.Ş.T., Cristea, A., Zolya, M.A., Moraru, S.A.: Anomaly detection using edge computing ai on low powered devices. In: IFIP International Conference on Artificial Intelligence Applications and Innovations, pp. 96–107 (2022)
29. Sivapalan, G., Nundy, K.K., Dev, S., Cardiff, B., John, D.: ANNet: a lightweight neural network for ECG anomaly detection in Iot edge sensors. IEEE Trans. Biomed. Circuits Syst. **16**(1), 24–35 (2022)
30. Katariya, V., Pazho, A.D., Noghre, G.A., Tabkhi, H.: Vegaedge: edge ai confluence anomaly detection for real-time highway Iot-applications. arXiv preprint arXiv:2311.07880 (2023)
31. Sharmila, B.S., Nagapadma, R.: Quantized autoencoder (qae) intrusion detection system for anomaly detection in resource-constrained iot devices using rt-iot2022 dataset. Cybersecurity **6**(1), 41 (2023)
32. Hindy, H., Bayne, E., Bures, M., Atkinson, R., Tachtatzis, C., Bellekens, X.: Machine learning based iot intrusion detection system: an MQTT case study (mqtt-iot-ids2020 dataset). In: International Networking Conference, pp. 73–84 (2020)
33. Vaccari, I., Chiola, G., Aiello, M., Mongelli, M., Cambiaso, E.: Mqttset, a new dataset for machine learning techniques on MQTT. Sensors **20**(22), 6578 (2020)
34. Koroniotis, N., Moustafa, N., Sitnikova, E., Turnbull, B.: Towards the development of realistic botnet dataset in the internet of things for network forensic analytics: Bot-iot dataset. Futur. Gener. Comput. Syst. **100**, 779–796 (2019)
35. Iot-23 dataset. https://www.stratosphereips.org/datasets-iot23 (2020)
36. Edgeai mqtt broker. https://github.com/phituong/edgeAI-mqtt-broker (2025)

# CRLF: A Sim2Real Reinforcement Learning Environment for Automated IT/OT Pentesting

Marc-Antoine Faillon[1,2]([✉]), Julien Francq[3], Nora Boulahia-Cuppens[1], Frédéric Cuppens[1], and Reda Yaich[2]

[1] Polytechnique Montréal, Montreal, Canada
[2] IRT SystemX, Palaiseau, France
`marc-antoine.faillon@polymtl.ca`
[3] Naval Group, CERT, Paris, France

**Abstract.** Automated penetration testing (pentesting) is crucial to efficiently assess the cybersecurity of infrastructures. It allows to discover attack paths before they are actively exploited, hereby providing a chance to block them. Reinforcement Learning (RL) has demonstrated great promise in academia for cybersecurity, including for automated penetration testing. However, despite encouraging research, market-ready solutions are still limited, potentially due to the difficulty of the Simulation-to-Reality (Sim2Real) transition and the scarcity of appropriate RL environments, especially for industrial infrastructures.

This paper addresses these challenges by first introducing essential features for RL cybersecurity environments. It then presents CRLF (Cyber Reinforcement Learning Framework), a novel environment designed to bridge the Sim2Real gap and support the training of autonomous pentesting agents on both IT and OT infrastructures. CRLF's key features are high fidelity, OT support, user-friendliness via a graphical interface and enhanced agent generalization through a pseudo-random infrastructure generator. Experimental results demonstrate the potential of CRLF to facilitate sophisticated autonomous pentesting for critical ICSs.

**Keywords:** Cybersecurity · Reinforcement Learning · RL Environment · Operational Technology (OT) · Industrial Control Systems (ICSs) · Simulation · Emulation · Pentest · Sim2Real

## 1 Introduction

Cybersecurity of industrial infrastructures is a critical task since most of today's products and services depend directly or indirectly on it. Thus, OT must be highly secured, but it is a challenging task because of the historical background of these infrastructures: they used to be on isolated networks, leading manufacturers to believe security was inherent by design. Nonetheless, some examples such as the well known Stuxnet [17] cyberattack demonstrated the opposite. In addition, with the new capabilities offered by Industry 4.0, OT networks tend to be more and more interconnected to provide additional functionalities such as remote monitoring or predictive maintenance. With the high price of OT components, manufacturers cannot allow to change all their infrastructures at once, which often results in the cohabitation of legacy technologies with state-of-the-art systems.

Securing such heterogeneous systems then becomes significantly challenging. With a mix of new technologies, outdated components and proprietary systems, traditional security tools are difficult to integrate, and specifically tailored systems must be created. Some security providers now propose firewalls or network probes dedicated to OT, but there is still a lack of OT security tools compared to Information Technologies (IT) systems. Another critical aspect of cybersecurity is penetration testing (pentesting). It is a preventive action which relies on cybersecurity experts who try to find vulnerabilities on a target infrastructure so that these vulnerabilities can be reported and patched. However, performing a pentest on OT infrastructures requires specialized experts in both IT and OT since the Industry 4.0 may also integrate IT and cloud systems to the traditional OT networks. Therefore, pentesting such infrastructures requires multidisciplinary pentesters, who can be difficult to find and is often expensive, resulting in pentests being only occasionally performed.

This is why automated pentesting systems start to emerge, in order to provide a cost and time-efficient approach to assess the security level of infrastructures. These systems can be of different types, mainly either based on logical rules or Artificial Intelligence (AI). Even if automated pentesting systems may not yet be as advanced as human pentesters, they show great promises. Logic-driven approaches include attack graphs [30] and attack trees [15], which are formal, structured models used in cybersecurity to analyze and represent potential attack paths against a system. While efficient and popular for IT and OT automated pentesting, their primary drawback lies in their static nature and the expert knowledge often required for generation, as automatic attack graph/tree generation still faces significant challenges, particularly concerning scalability and the ability to accurately reflect dynamic, large-scale networks [16]. A famous rule-based tool for pentesting automation is Caldera [1], which also features dedicated plugins for OT. Caldera provides the ability to design attacker profiles and run them on infrastructures to evaluate their weaknesses or assess defense measures. However, even if Caldera proposes autonomous algorithms that make dynamic choices according to observations, it still operates within a human-defined and relatively static model of actions and impacts.

On the other hand, AI-based systems have the advantage to aim for generalization capabilities, which can facilitate their long term maintenance and propose constant evolution, but they require tailored algorithms and specific data to be trained. Among the AI techniques, Large Language Models (LLMs) and Reinforcement Learning (RL) tend to gain traction for automated pentesting. LLMs due to their broad capabilities, and RL because of its ability to learn to make long-term oriented decisions and its good generalization capabilities. RL is relatively lightweight compared to LLMs, making it easier to train, deploy and adapt. RL is also easier to control in order to ensure no unplanned action is taken. Furthermore, RL does not require a pre-existing dataset to be trained. Instead, its learning process relies on a continuous interaction within a carefully constructed environment that accurately simulates the system to be tested. However, it is crucial to acknowledge that, to the best of our knowledge, automated pentesting systems (whether AI- or rule-based) remain significantly under-represented in the context of Operational Technology (OT) infrastructures.

In order to increase the attraction to such infrastructures, we introduce in this article an environment to train autonomous pentesting agents on both IT and OT infrastructures. In light of RL's advantages for learning complex, long-term strategies in dynamic environments, this environment is designed for RL agents, though it can also accommodate other AI techniques. A key feature of this environment is its ability to facilitate a seamless transition from simulated training environments to realistic testbeds, a step often challenging, and a potential blocking point for the general adoption of RL in cybersecurity.

The remainder of this article is organized as follows: Sect. 2 introduces background on RL and related works, Sect. 3 addresses the challenges inherent in developing efficient RL environments and outlines common challenges, Sect. 4 details the key features of our environment, Sect. 5 presents illustrative scenarios which can be made within the environment, Sect. 6 showcases the experimental results obtained from those scenarios and Sect. 7 concludes.

## 2   Background and Related Works

RL is a type of learning algorithm where an *agent* learns to make decisions by interacting with an *environment*. Unlike supervised learning, RL does not rely on labeled datasets. Instead, the agent selects an *action* from a finite set (hence ensuring it cannot take an unauthorized action) and observes its impact on the environment. This impact is reflected by two pieces of information: (i) an *observation* vector, which translates the actual state of the environment into numeric values, and (ii) a numerical *reward* (or penalty) indicating the desirability of the action taken. This iterative process of actions, observations and rewards continues until a goal is achieved or a maximum number of steps is reached, concluding an *episode*. The agent's objective is to learn an optimal *policy* function that maps states to actions, in order to maximize its cumulative reward over time thanks to a balance between the exploration of new actions or states, and the exploitation of previous knowledge.

RL has been widely investigated in the literature across various domains, including cybersecurity. Its capability to extract the logic of environments and learn successful pseudo-reasoning in order to reach long-term objectives makes it very promising for cybersecurity. However, in order to be efficient in real-world applications, an RL agent must be trained in environments which have high fidelity with respect to the target environment. Furthermore, it must also be

trained with diverse situations in order to allow the agent to accurately determine the impact of each feature, and prevent it from learning biased information.
Consequently, while RL does not require a dataset, its performance is intrinsi-
cally tied to the quality and representativeness of the training environment.

In cybersecurity, RL finds applications in both offensive (penetration testing
or red teaming) and defensive (detection, response, or blue teaming) contexts.
For pentesting, an agent learns to identify and exploit vulnerabilities to achieve
specific objectives within a target infrastructure. For instance, in [11], an agent
is trained specifically to evade Web Application Firewalls (WAF) and in [5] to
perform web attacks. RL agents can also make use of predefined attack graphs
in order to orchestrate an attack [12], or leverage Hierarchical Reinforcement
Learning (HRL) to reduce the action space [32] and divide the task into sub-
objectives [6]. In cyberdefense, agents are trained to detect cyberattacks based on
labeled datasets [10,21] or directly within RL environments [35]. They can also
respond to incidents [8], or proactively protect systems by deploying decoys and
honeypots [33]. Despite promising academic results for cybersecurity within simulated environments, studies exploring RL in real-world settings remain uncommon, and the limited adoption of RL in cybersecurity Commercial-Off-The-Shelf
(COTS) products highlights a critical gap. One of the reasons explaining this
gap may reside in the scarcity of sufficiently accurate, complete and practical RL
environments that facilitate the transition from theoretical models to deployable
solutions (Sim2Real).

For the purpose of this paper, we distinguish between *simulated* and *emulated*
environments. Simulated environments are entirely software-based, so interactions between an agent and the environment are computed programmatically.
While efficient, they risk inaccuracies with real behaviors if every aspect is not
perfectly modeled. Emulated environments, conversely, are built upon real (often
virtualized) infrastructures which guarantees more fidelity. In emulation, primary
challenges reside in (i) keeping good performance in terms of actions per second,
and (ii) accurately translating real-world observations and action impacts into
a format an RL agent can ingest, while avoiding information overload.

Recently, several RL environments started to emerge in order to train various
RL agents for cybersecurity, either for pentesting or defending. Some comprehensive surveys [26,36] detail the challenges of applying RL to cybersecurity and
review a large number of environments. However, among them and in the current literature, there is a significant lack of OT-compatible environments. Some
do exist, but they are mostly focused on power grid system simulation [20] and
emulation [28]. However, the high abstraction level even in the emulated ones,
and specific focus mostly on the bandwidth impact of cyberattacks, make them
not suitable for creating generic pentesting agents. The closest OT environment
to this objective seems to be IPMSRL [34] , which models a maritime platform
with OT components. Nonetheless, its abstraction level is too high to allow the
transition from simulation to reality, and it is not publicly available. Thus, the
most advanced cyber RL environments seem to only target IT infrastructures.
While not focused on OT, the following environment examples represent the

evolution of RL environments for cybersecurity and the most relevant existing work in order to fill the gap between simulation and reality:

**NASim** [29]: One of the earliest and most influential simulated environments, NASim provides an abstract representation of network attack graphs. While excellent for foundational RL research in cybersecurity, its high level of abstraction limits its direct applicability for real-world testing.

**CyberBattleSim** [22]: Developed by Microsoft, it proposes a simulation focused on training red-team agents. It models hosts with services, IP addresses, firewall rules, and credentials. However, actions are purely simulated, and it lacks a direct mechanism to transfer trained agents to real environments. Its simplified networking and limited action space restrict its completeness for complex pentesting scenarios. Our initial experiments with CyberBattleSim, nonetheless, were valuable for understanding RL's potential in pentesting and identifying key challenges like Sim2Real transition and generalization.

**CybORG** [3]: Introduced for the CAGE challenge [2], CybORG is a blue-team oriented environment. It offers a more detailed representation, including process IDs (PID/PPID), user information, network interfaces, and network protocols. While a visualization tool and integration with virtual infrastructures are mentioned, their public availability remains unclear, limiting the ability for external researchers to leverage its full emulation potential.

**NASimEmu** [13]: An extension to NASim, it brings some new features as well as an emulation workflow allowing to test agents on realistic environments. On the emulation side, it makes use of Vagrant and VirtualBox for Virtual Machines (VMs), and a Kali Linux is combined to predefined Metasploit [27] actions for the attacker agent. Key improvements include the possibility of adding some randomness to the scenario generation (e.g., number of hosts, random host configurations). However, it still exhibits limitations, such as simplified firewall rules, lack of specific interface binding for services, and a restrictive approach to host template creation, which prevents the generation of realistic controlled infrastructures. The graphical interface is also limited to basic agent progression visualization.

**PenGym** [24]: This is an emulation-focused environment which uses KVM for virtualization and a NASim scenario to define its infrastructure. Unlike NASimEmu, PenGym targets a training entirely on emulated infrastructures in order to prevent inaccuracies. To do so, it makes use of a combination of cyber tools and Metasploit to perform real actions. A particular aspect of PenGym to still provide an efficient execution time, is its history-mapping of successful actions, significantly reducing execution time by retrieving cached results rather than re-executing actions. However, this approach raises questions about the fidelity of deeper technical information (e.g., active remote shells for pivoting), and its current action space seems limited to SSH bruteforce for exploits, which highly limits the range of possible scenarios.

**CyberWheel** [25]: Designed in order to train and test blue-team agents on both simulated and emulated environments, CyberWheel computes observations based on alerts triggered by real cyber detection tools, such as host and network

Intrusion Detection Systems (IDSs). A deterministic, logic-based attacker agent is included within the environment. This agent has the goal of impacting some servers, and the blue agent must prevent it from succeeding. The blue agent presented in the paper has the goal of deploying decoy hosts in order to lure the attacker. Concerning the emulation process, it makes use of FireWheel [9], a cyber range based on KVM, and it automatically builds real VMs according to the scenario's hosts definitions. While promising, the current lack of results on emulated infrastructures and unclear external usability without FireWheel are drawbacks. Moreover, as primarily designed for blue-team agents, significant work would be required to fine-tune it, especially since only basic actions are implemented yet.

In summary, recent works have led to a greater variety of RL environments for cybersecurity and emulation is gaining more concern. However, no environment seems to be complete enough to train robust, generalizable, and OT-compatible autonomous pentesting agents with a practical Sim2Real pipeline. This identified gap motivated the development of CRLF, which integrates these capabilities.

## 3   Challenges in Designing Efficient RL Cybersecurity Environments

Designing an accurate and efficient RL environment for cybersecurity is a complex task, combining many components that have a direct impact on the effectiveness of autonomous agents. A comprehensive survey [26] has been conducted on the challenge of applying RL to cyberdefense, highlighting the necessity of complete and accurate environments. Such environments must realistically model operating system functionalities, network rules, and crucially for this work, specific OT behaviors. Moreover, to prevent overfitting or underfitting, the environment must offer enough diversity, which means the environment must cover all desired learning aspects. It must also provide randomness to represent the completeness of real-world systems. RL agents can also find and abuse shortcuts, hence it is sometimes required to force agents towards certain paths.

Based on our experience and our literature review, the key challenges in building cyber RL environments allowing a Sim2Real transition include:

- **C1 - Achieving accurate simulation fidelity:** The simulated environment must be accurate enough to represent real-world behaviors without being overly complex, which could impact the performance or alter the agent learning. This involves carefully selecting the level of detail to include, but also to correctly represent the action impacts and IT/OT core component behaviors.
- **C2 - Feature selection and efficient data model:** Defining precisely what information is necessary for the agent to accomplish its task allows to reduce the observation space's dimension. The format and structure given to the data and observations then enable the agent to be more sample-efficient (i.e., it learns from fewer experiments).

- **C3 - Ensuring modularity:** Cybersecurity environments require the ability to be permanently updated to include new behaviors according to state-of-the-art solutions or cyberattacks. A modular data structure is essential to be able to factorize as many situations as possible while still allowing customizations. There are thousands of possible actions and near-infinite combinations of actions and observations; individual handling of each case is impractical.
- **C4 - Bridging the Sim2Real gap:** The transition from simulated training to real-world validation is often challenging. Environments must provide robust mechanisms to easily connect to and interact with emulated or cyber-physical infrastructures. This is particularly vital for OT systems where direct experimentation on live infrastructure carries high risks. Moreover, if possible, RL environments should be independent from emulation technologies in order to support a broader community of researchers who use different tools.
- **C5 - Preventing agents from learning biased information:** An agent that is trained to perform an SSH bruteforce only on Windows hosts will likely learn that SMB or other Windows services are required to perform this attack. This is because it did not encounter enough diverse situations. Its learning is not false, but it is biased by its experience. In a cyber RL environment, RL agents have a lot of possibilities to encounter such situations, and they can overfit on many aspects: HostIDs, IP addresses, processes orders, users names or orders, etc. The environment must be specifically tailored to prevent such aspects in order to optimize the learning process.

# 4   CRLF: Our Proposed Environment Design and Key Features

In this section, we present our Cybersecurity Reinforcement Learning Framework, designed to address challenges (C1-C5) outlined in Sect. 3 and considering them as requirements to be fulfilled. More than just an environment, we refer to CRLF as a *Framework* due to its comprehensive suite of tools, including a Graphical User Interface (GUI) for scenario building, host templating, and agent progression monitoring, as well as its realistic attack modules, full integration with real infrastructures and direct integration with an RL library (RLlib [18]).

## 4.1   Overview and Objectives

Directly training RL agents on emulated infrastructures presents significant challenges, primarily due to the execution time of certain actions (e.g., network scans which can take minutes) and the large number of actions required for an agent to converge (at least 500,000 to 1 million steps in our tests). Therefore, CRLF is designed to provide a simulated training environment, with dedicated connectors to validate trained agents on emulated or real infrastructures. However, in both cases, CRLF's core operations rely on a simulated environment: when connected to a real infrastructure, the connectors translate the information (machine states) into an internal simulated representation of the current infrastructure. This workflow allows the RL agent to receive information consistently, regardless of whether it is operating in simulation or in emulation. The environment is compatible with gymnasium [31], an RL library that provides a standardized API for developing and comparing RL environments and algorithms.

CRLF supports a variety of pentesting objectives beyond simple vulnerability exploitation. Common objectives found in the literature include (i) constructing a kill chain to impact critical services on specific hosts (often servers) or (ii) exploiting as many vulnerabilities as possible. CRLF implements these, but also introduces new objectives. For instance, a ransomware objective aims to encrypt as many hosts as possible (or a specific number). A data leak scenario is also implemented, where the agent must gather particular data types such as industrial blueprints or programs. It is also possible to combine multiple objectives, in order to train agents that can adapt to different goals without requiring retraining for each objective.

A key design choice for CRLF is its focus on black-box pentesting, where agents begin with no prior knowledge of the infrastructure topology or components. An agent starts from a session on its own Kali Linux machine, which is used as a Command-and-Control machine, allowing it to handle multiple remote sessions. This machine is deployed into a target network, and the agent has to explore and expand to fulfill its objective(s). This black-box design makes pentesting significantly harder, but allows trained agents to be deployed instantly on any infrastructure, without requiring prior precise mapping or information.

## 4.2  Feature Selection and Observation Design

The selection of features to implement in the environment and the design of the observation space are critical for the final capabilities of the pentesting agent. We prioritized features that were necessary for a completeness level allowing the agent to complete advanced scenarios such as those presented in Sect. 5, rather than implementing every possible option. Excessive detail can hinder simulation performance and overwhelm the agent, while insufficient detail prevents the extraction of deterministic reasoning. For instance, a simple process listing on a Linux or Windows machine can yield hundreds of results, most of which are irrelevant for an RL agent. Feeding such large, noisy observation spaces (e.g., 1000 processes) can severely impact the learning efficiency. Therefore, we implemented a balanced data structure combined with a filtering mechanism, similar to a whitelist, to retain only the most relevant elements **(C1,2)**.

**Host Representation.** CRLF represents hosts with essential IT and OT characteristics: hostname, network interfaces (IP, gateway, type), users (name, privilege), and files. System information includes architecture and OS. Processes, which are exploitation targets, are detailed with PID, owner, listening interface (for subnet-specific exposure), name, optional credentials, connection states, and application name for grouping (e.g., SCADA software with multiple child processes). An optional configuration file can be defined to detail versions or specific information. An exploration status keeps track of the attacker progress on this host: process/file discovery levels, connection attempts, OT exploration and exploit status. Depending on the observation type, this exploration status may not be required, but experiments demonstrated it seems to help agents to converge faster. This representation is chosen to accurately represent critical elements **(C1)**.

**Observation Types.** CRLF offers a flexible observation mechanism with dynamic length based on scenario hyperparameters (max element counts for networks, hosts, processes, files). However, for most RL algorithms, changes in these hyperparameters typically require agent retraining. Two primary observation structures are provided: classical and hierarchical.

*Classical Observations.* This single flat vector includes global information (objective, progression), network status (discovered, scanned, reachable from pivot), and concatenated observations of every host. Each host observation includes subnetwork IDs (without IPs to prevent overfitting), process identifiers (name ID, port ID, application ID), file details (file type, data type, value contained) and the exploration status. Current privilege level (none, user, admin) of the attacker on this host is provided instead of the list of users to reduce the observation space and prevent overfitting on users. This privilege level is linked to a remote session ID to allow the agent to interact with it. Elements which are below the corresponding hyperparameter limit (e.g., max processes) are 0-padded. This structure was thought in order to reduce the occasions where agents can learn from biased observations and only keep necessary information **(C2,5)**.

*Hierarchical Observations.* Inspired by an approach proposed in a recent work [6] using Hierarchical Reinforcement Learning to reduce the observation and action space dimensions, CRLF also supports hierarchical information. A two-agent system is used with a Master agent which selects a target host from a high-level view of the infrastructure, and then an Exploit Selector agent is focused on choosing the exploit action based only on this host's observation. This HRL approach, named SHiPPO, also introduces a sequential evaluation policy for the Master agent, individually assessing targets instead of using a concatenated vector which reduces the possibilities of overfitting **(C5)**. SHiPPO greatly accelerated our training experiments but required some adaptations such as a *"stuck"* variable to create a communication between the Exploit Selector and the Master to prevent unproductive loops on the same target. This sequential hierarchical observation mechanism is provided to serve as an example to implement new hierarchical algorithms or multi-agent systems.

### 4.3   Action Design

The default CRLF action space is multi-discrete, meaning it consists in a vector of several independent discrete values that must be chosen simultaneously in order to select: a target ID, an action ID, and an optional parameter which depends on actions (e.g., for a bruteforce, it allows to configure the protocol or to choose a credential to connect via SSH). Actually, there is a 4th parameter to define the source session ID, which is internally used but automatically determined by default thanks to logical rules and requirements.

Actions were designed to prioritize modularity in order to provide convenient action additions. They are categorized by impact, drawing from MITRE ATT&CK [23] and Metasploit: *Information Discovery, Remote Execution/Exploits, Auxiliary, Connect, Privilege Escalation, Impact and Persistence.* While similar to MITRE tactics, these categories were designed to gather actions which have similar requirements and observable impacts, so they sometimes differ from the MITRE classification.

Actions are defined in JSON, then translated into YAML for faster loading, and finally integrated into the environment with an action identifier. They include requirements to programmatically determine their success and some metadata that covers: attack outcome (e.g., Information Discovery, Remote Execution), action type (local, remote), source and target requirements (e.g., session type, target process, credentials), scope (host, subnet, user), optional success strings or commands for emulation validation, and Metasploit details (module, payload, parameters). Non-Metasploit actions can also be included thanks to special keywords and formatting, and custom Metasploit modules have been developed to facilitate some behaviors. The design of this precise action data structure facilitates the creation of atomic functions for each requirement and impact combination. It then enables seamless integration of new actions via their JSON representation, without requiring code modifications **(C3)**. A detailed list of actual actions is available in Appendix B.

### 4.4   OT Integration

CRLF is designed to support Industrial Control Systems (ICSs) and Operational Technology (OT) components. We defined specific OS types and interaction rules for PLCs, sensors, actuators and HMIs, which differ from conventional IT systems. Indeed, these systems impose new constraints on the RL agent, such as not being able to employ SSH or execute a .exe file on a PLC **(C1)**. Dedicated network connection types are also implemented to simulate non-Ethernet protocols like Modbus RTU over serial communication, which is critical for legacy industrial systems.

The framework also includes specific objectives and actions for OT environments, enabling agents to be trained on tasks like data exfiltration, critical OT component disruption, or industrial process modification through Modbus command injection. These actions are currently tailored to some software (open source) but they can be extended to other OT platforms and protocols.

## 4.5  Graphical User Interface (GUI)

Most of the recent works provide a graph representation of the infrastructure during evaluation allowing to visualize the red-team agent progression. While this is interesting, multiple functionalities are lacking in order to provide a convenient workspace to cyber researchers. To this end, CRLF features a comprehensive Graphical User Interface, shown in Fig. 1. It allows to visualize the agent progression and also to intuitively build and modify simulated infrastructures. The GUI's builder mode allows to drag-and-drop hosts or network templates, and connect hosts to networks within a few clicks. Clicking on a host displays editable properties via a foldable tree menu, which can also be used to add elements such as users or processes. Hosts, processes, applications (groups of processes) and infrastructures can graphically be saved as templates and then be loaded and deployed again, which greatly improves the workflow of scenario creation by providing modular components **(C3)**.

The runner mode can load RL models (compatible with supported libraries), execute individual steps or a complete episode, while visually displaying the agent's progress (discovered hosts, session levels, discovered processes on host). Manual actions can also be selected to verify their impact, and environment modification during runtime is possible to aid debugging and interactive experiments.

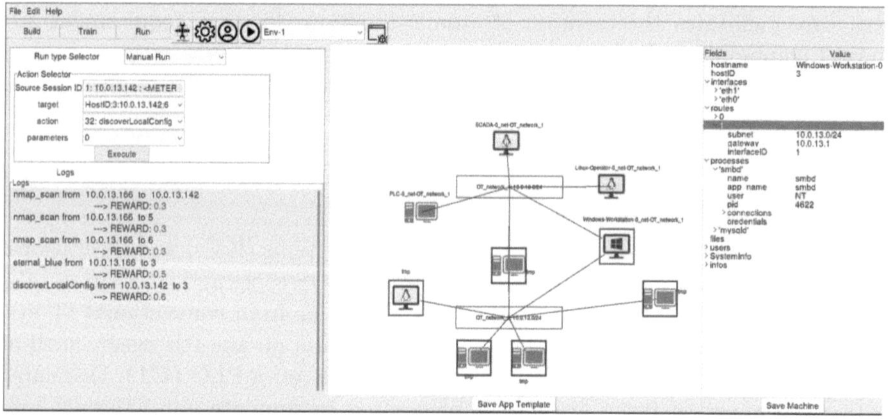

**Fig. 1.** Screen capture of an ongoing infrastructure discovery from the GUI. On the left, manual actions are available. On the right, editable host properties. Hosts framed blue are scanned, green have a user session, and red an administrator session. (Color figure online)

## 4.6  Pseudo-random Infrastructures Generator (PRIG)

Our experiments and current works [26, 34] highlighted the need for improved generalization in RL agents. To this end, we designed a Pseudo-Random Infrastructures Generator (PRIG) to automatically create varying infrastructures, thereby reducing the risk of overfitting. This *pseudo-random* approach, unlike static template sampling, enables to enforce realistic constraints (e.g., no SSH on a PLC, or no'NT SYSTEM' user on Linux - **C1**).

A JSON configuration defines high-level generation rules like the number of networks or vulnerable hosts, as well as more detailed rules like host template mutations. Thus, users can specify host templates they desire in each sub-network, and then override some elements of template hosts to create controlled, randomized infrastructures. For instance, the generator can be configured to select only one out of two available SCADA software instances per infrastructure, ensuring realistic single-SCADA deployments per infrastructure. Optional services like SSH or RDP can be added independently of the SCADA, while an FTP service is consistently present. Such configurations are easily defined within the JSON configuration by combining applications (created with GUI) using AND/OR rules. Then, the final process list is shuffled to mitigate overfitting on processes order.

These rules are defined by the user, hence they can lead to generated infrastructures which are not suitable for training (i.e. there is no valid path to reach the configured objective). To prevent these infrastructures from altering the training performance, infrastructures are saved only if they are successfully validated by a bruteforce agent, which tries every possible action until a goal is reached. In order to maintain the training speed, the infrastructures are pre-generated, validated and exported. Then, users can load, verify, or modify the infrastructures via the GUI before using them for training. A parameter in the global running experiment instructs the environment to shuffle and load these pre-generated infrastructures, and the training will then use each infrastructure sequentially, ensuring a fair representation of each one **(C5)**.

### 4.7   Pipeline to Emulation

In order to support broader compatibility, CRLF does not rely on any specific virtualization or emulation software **(C4)**. The only requirements for integration are a Metasploit installation and access to its Remote Procedure Call (RPC) service to interact with its API. Metasploit has well-defined naming conventions for modules and parameters which facilitates programmatic interaction and also features convenient management of multiple remote sessions. Furthermore, it can be deployed across diverse systems such as cyber ranges, Docker containers, VMs and physical machines.

Once connected to Metasploit's API, CRLF uses dedicated action wrappers in order to format and execute real actions. Then, these wrappers or connectors translate the action result into an internal simulated representation of the infrastructure. Finally, the agent receives the observation computed from the simulated environment (ensuring consistent format) along with the reward. Figure 2 summarizes this workflow. Through this mechanism, security constraints are also implemented to prevent agents from attacking unwanted targets or networks. Thanks to a white and blacklists, discovered IPs can be filtered out before being added to the simulated environment. Thus, the agent has no idea they exist and cannot target them.

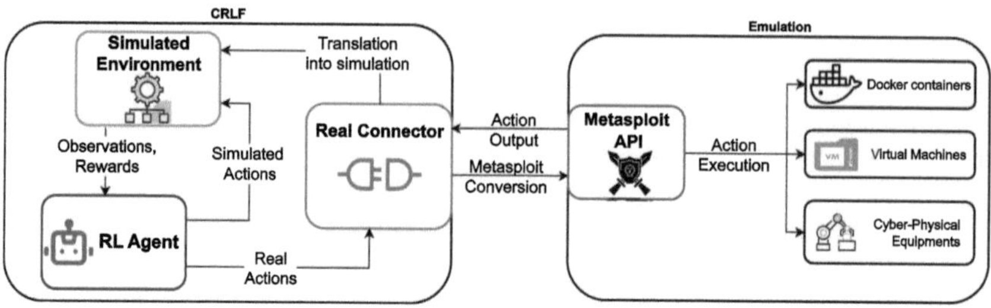


**Fig. 2.** CRLF simulation and emulation workflows.

By combining this pipeline with the GUI, CRLF features the unique capability of effortlessly creating a simulated copy of real environments: manually performing a pentest scenario on a real infrastructure while using the GUI automatically adds hosts and their observed states into the internal simulated representation. Then, the internal state of the simulation can be saved, and loaded again as a simulated infrastructure to serve as a training or validation environment.

## 5  Illustrative Scenarios

This section details a main illustrative scenario showcasing CRLF's features and its potential for training autonomous pentesting agents. It combines both IT and OT capabilities to demonstrate its flexibility and the range of supported pentesting scenarios. The objective is to train an agent on simulated infrastructures, and validate it on a slightly different emulated infrastructure in order to assess its robustness and adaptation capability. To this end, we created 3 variations of our target scenario.

*Scenario 1* instantiates a single simulated infrastructure with 15 hosts. It is built manually via the GUI and serves as a baseline for other scenarios.

*Scenario 2* consists of 10 generated infrastructures, gathering the main properties of the target scenario but also adding new actions which will not be used in the emulation. The goal is to increase the difficulty by presenting more situations to agents, in order to verify if they are still able to reach their objectives. The main variations among those infrastructures are: number of hosts (10−20), topology (repartition of hosts on networks), SCADA software (which impacts the final step of the pentest scenario), processes and vulnerabilities deployed on hosts. The total number of vulnerable hosts remains the same to keep a total reward per episode relatively equivalent, making it easier to compare results.

*Scenario 3* is the final target scenario which serves to validate both the Sim2Real pipeline, as well as the agent's efficiency and capability to generalize to new topologies. It utilizes Factory IO [4], a proprietary emulation software to learn how to program ICSs. It provides a 3D model of industrial premises where the user can deploy cyber-physical components such as robots, sensors and conveyors. Factory IO was chosen for its pre-configured OT devices (i.e. internal logic of robots or sensors is already configured) and its support for external PLC control. However, a significant limitation of Factory IO for cybersecurity studies resides in its aggregation of all devices into a single, large virtual device exposed to the PLC (i.e. even if there are 5 robots, the PLC will only read/write into this single virtual device's registries instead of 5). While it does not impact the PLC logic, it does not provide realistic networking communication and prevents an attacker to perform a Man-in-the-Middle attack between the PLC and a particular component. To overcome this, a custom system was created within a cyber range, pulling sensor data from Factory IO and updating register values on external Docker containers representing Modbus devices. Then, PLCs (Open-PLC) read the sensor data from these containers and send their commands to actuator containers, which are forwarded back to Factory IO to update the emulation. This mechanism enables a relatively realistic OT behavior and network communications to validate RL agents, with a visual feedback for some cyber-attacks. To complete this infrastructure, we deployed on a cyber range a few operator workstations running Windows, a backup server (containing programs, plans and technical documentation), and a SCADA host (ScadaBR) controlling the entire industrial process. A complete view of the topology is shown in Fig. 3, and the Factory IO view in Fig. 4.

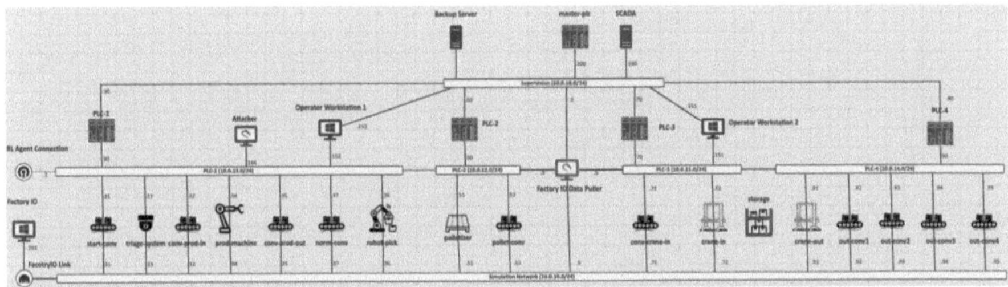

**Fig. 3.** Cyber range view of the infrastructure. Simulation network, at the bottom, is used to interact with Factory IO. Modbus devices are then dispatched on 4 OT networks with 1 PLC per network. Finally, a supervision network gathers at the top a Master PLC, a SCADA host, a backup server and operator workstations.

The main steps of the final scenario are the following:

1. **Reconnaissance Service Discovery:** ARP sweep and port scans.
2. **Initial Compromise:** Exploiting EternalBlue [14] on an operator workstation.
3. **Local Reconnaissance:** Discovering local configs, processes, files and network interfaces, leading to the supervision network discovery.

4. **Network Expansion Pivoting:** Performing ARP sweep from Meterpreter session and auxiliary actions: adding a route, preparing proxychains and port forwarding to use the workstation as a gateway.
5. **Post Reconnaissance:** Port scan in the supervision subnet.
6. **Secondary Compromise:** Exploiting a bruteforceable SSH on the Linux backup server, using acquired credentials.
7. **Credential Discovery:** Local discovery on backup server yielding SCADA service credential from a backup file.
8. **Final Compromise:** Identifying and exploiting a Remote Code Execution (RCE) on ScadaBR (via HTTP), using the acquired credential to gain administrator remote shell.
9. **Disrupting OT services:** Once administrator access to the SCADA is obtained, the agent should kill the SCADA process, encrypt as many hosts as possible, and perform a Modbus command injection to a PLC to alter the industrial routine (set all coils to 0).

**Fig. 4.** Screen capture of the infrastructure running on Factory IO.

This scenario aims to highlight some key features of CRLF: realistic network rules, auxiliary actions (which are often left aside), remote exploits, sessions management, file discovery, credential exploitation, integration of external pentesting tools, interaction with OT components and lastly, transition from simulation to emulation. In a real pentesting scenario, the agent would not perform destructive actions such as the final one. However, it is an interesting capability for pentesting on digital twins or emulated infrastructures in order to highlight the risks of previous vulnerabilities of the kill chain, and for assessing the robustness of recovery plans of industrial infrastructures.

# 6    Experimental Results

This section demonstrates CRLF's main features, Sim2Real capabilities, and support for generalization in OT contexts, rather than rigorously evaluating specific RL algorithms. SHiPPO agents have been trained on either Scenario 1 (SHiPPO-S1) with only one infrastructure, or on Scenario 2 (SHiPPO-S2) on the 10 generated infrastructures. The goal of this experiment is to observe the impact of the PRIG generator on training and prediction performance. RL algorithms were implemented using RLlib [18] and hyperparameter optimization with Tune [19]. Hyperparameters can be found in Appendix A.

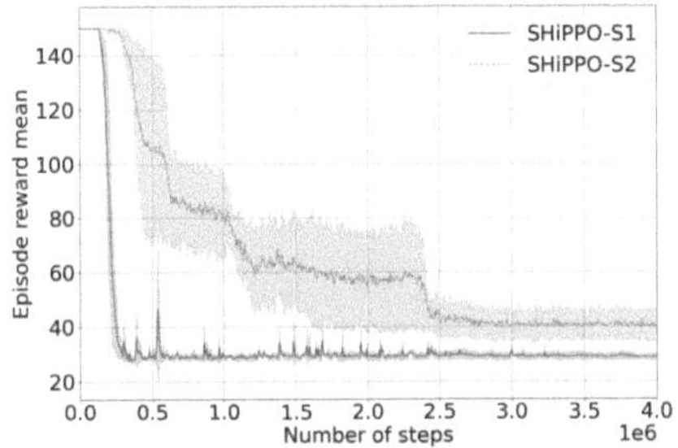
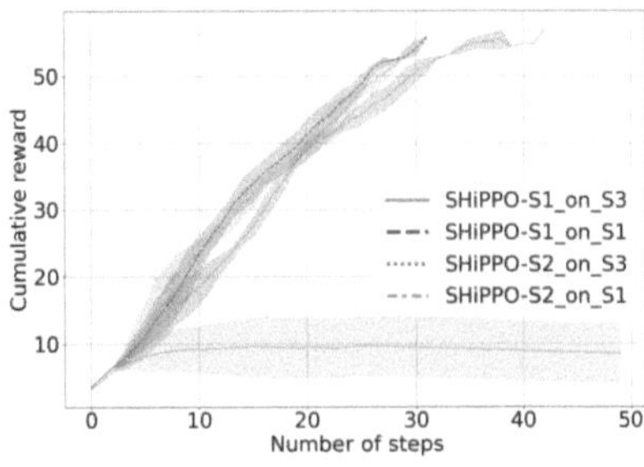

(a) SHiPPO trainings on Scenario 1 and 2          (b) Testing on Scenario 1 and 3

**Fig. 5.** Training progress (a) is represented by the mean number of actions taken per episode, with the goal of reducing it until only necessary actions are chosen (averaged over 5 trainings). Testing results (b) represent the agent's mean rewards during one episode until it reached its objective (averaged from 10 experiments).

## 6.1    Training Performance

As clearly visible in Fig. 5.a, SHiPPO-S2 needed a lot more time to reach decent convergence than SHiPPO-S1. This is expected because of the increased complexity brought by the 10 generated infrastructures of Scenario 2. The agent requires more steps to explore new situations and to learn robust policies allowing it to extract the meaning of each feature and the impact of actions. On the other hand, the training time at equivalent timesteps is roughly equivalent, meaning the PRIG sampling has no negative impact on the execution time.

We chose to display SHiPPO results instead of classical RL algorithms because of SHiPPO's capability to learn faster and generalize better even from a few examples.

## 6.2    Sim2Real Validation and Robustness

Figure 5.b highlights the critical role of diversity when training for generalization. The agent trained only on Scenario 1 performs well on Scenario 1, but very poorly on Scenario 3. After a few successful actions, the lack of diversity in terms of topological networks and host processes makes it unable to adapt to a new instantiation of the scenario, even if it has the exact same actions available during training. Conversely, SHiPPO-S2 shows strong performance: it is as efficient as SHiPPO-S1 on Scenario 1, but also manages to adapt to the emulated Scenario 3 it never faced before.

These results validate the previously defined challenges: (i) the simulation model is *accurate* and *complete* enough to represent such IT/OT scenarios; (ii) the chosen data structure and observations enable efficient training; (iii) modular data models facilitate the integration of new actions and templates; (iv) the Sim2Real pipeline correctly bridges actions to the emulated infrastructure, and effectively translates the emulated states into the simulated environment; and (v) the diversity provided by the PRIG is crucial for robust and adaptable agents. CRLF's simulated environment is openly available on GitHub [7], and the emulation module upon request.

## 7   Conclusion and Future Work

This paper presented essential characteristics for an efficient RL environment dedicated to automated penetration testing, and it introduced CRLF (Cyber Reinforcement Learning Framework). CRLF is an advanced framework to train autonomous pentesting agents, which was designed to facilitate the challenging Sim2Real transition, often preventing theoretical works from being deployed onto real-world infrastructures.

This is achieved by: (i) providing a high-fidelity simulated environment, with efficient information representation; (ii) creating a robust pipeline to seamlessly validate RL agents on emulated or real infrastructures; and (iii) incorporating features to enhance the generalization capabilities of agents by design, like the pseudo-random infrastructure generator and a modular design. A major objective of CRLF is to specifically target Operational Technology (OT) infrastructures, a domain that remains underrepresented in this field. This framework also features a convenient Graphical User Interface (GUI) to build, clone, and modify IT or OT scenarios, allowing researchers to focus more on algorithmic development. Finally, the results presented in this paper demonstrate CRLF's potential to train realistic OT/IT pentesting autonomous agents, thereby paving the way for the emergence of new automated solutions for such infrastructures.

Future work will focus on increasing the number of available actions with a particular focus on broader support for industrial equipments, notably with the integration of specific equipments (e.g., maritime) and protocols. Ultimately, blue-team agent compatibility is also considered in order to allow adversarial training.

**Disclosure of Interests.** The authors have no competing interests to declare that are relevant to the content of this article.

# A   Configuration of Hyperparameters

In Table 1 we show the configuration of the hyperparameters used in our models.

**Table 1.** Hyperparameters configuration

| Hyperparameters | SHiPPO |
|---|---|
| Discount Factor ($\gamma$) | 0.8 |
| Number of Workers | 10 |
| Minibatch Size | 128 |
| Train Batch Size | 4000 |
| Sgd Iterations | 20 |
| Policy Architecture | [256, 256] |
| Entropy Coefficient | 0.0001 |
| Clip Parameter | 0.15 |

# B   List of Implemented Actions

The following actions are used for the experiment presented in the results Sect. 6. Actions are a mix of available Metasploit modules, custom modules developed for this environment, and external tools such as hydra (Table 2).

**Table 2.** Actions and categories

| Categories | Actions |
|---|---|
| Discovery | local ping scan; proxied ARP sweep; TCP scan; local credential finder (Linux & Windows); local discovery (processes, connections, network interfaces); hydra bruteforce; OT application identification |
| Remote Exploits | RCE_ScadaBR; RCE_Ignition; RCE_Bluekeep; IRC backdoor; vsftpd backdoor; DrupalGeddon2; Connect SSH; |
| Auxiliary | add route; proxychains; port-forwarding; upgrade shell to meterpreter; kill windows firewall;"stucked" |
| Impact | encrypt host; encrypt user files; Modbus injection; kill process |
| Privilege Escalation | nmap suid; |

# References


1. Caldera. https://caldera.mitre.org/. Accessed 17 June 2025
2. CAGE Challenge 1. arXiv (2021)
3. Cyber operations research gym. https://github.com/cage-challenge/CybORG (2022). created by Maxwell Standen, David Bowman, Son Hoang, Toby Richer, Martin Lucas, Richard Van Tassel, Phillip Vu, Mitchell Kiely, KC C., Natalie Konschnik, Joshua Collyer
4. Factory i/o. https://factoryio.com/ (2024). Accessed 17 June 2025
5. Amouei, M., Rezvani, M., Fateh, M.: RAT: Reinforcement-learning-driven and adaptive testing for vulnerability discovery in web application firewalls. IEEE Trans. Dependable Secure Comput. **19**(5), 3371–3386 (2021). https://doi.org/10.1109/TDSC.2021.3095417
6. Faillon, M.A., et al.: How to better fit reinforcement learning for pentesting: a new hierarchical approach. In: European Symposium on Research in Computer Security, pp. 313–332. Springer (2024)
7. Faillon, M.A., Francq, J., Boulahia-Cuppens, N., Cuppens, F., Yaich, R.: https://github.com/StuffEngineering/CyberRLFramework.git
8. Foley, M., Hicks, C., Highnam, K., Mavroudis, V.: Autonomous network defence using reinforcement learning. In: Proceedings of the 2022 ACM on Asia Conference on Computer and Communications Security, pp. 1252–1254 (2022)
9. Gabert, K.G., et al.: Firewheel-a platform for cyber analysis. Tech. rep., Sandia National Lab.(SNL-NM), Albuquerque, NM (United States) (2015)
10. Gülmez, H.G., Angın, P.: A study on the efficacy of deep reinforcement learning for intrusion detection. J. Comput. Inform. Sci. (2021)
11. Hemmati, M., Hadavi, M.A.: Using deep reinforcement learning to evade web application firewalls. In: 2021 18th International ISC Conference on Information Security and Cryptology (ISCISC), pp. 35–41. IEEE (2021)
12. Hu, Z., Beuran, R., Tan, Y.: Automated penetration testing using deep reinforcement learning. In: 2020 IEEE European Symposium on Security and Privacy Workshops (EuroS&PW), pp. 2–10. IEEE (2020)
13. Janisch, J., Pevný, T., Lisý, V.: Nasimemu: Network attack simulator & emulator for training agents generalizing to novel scenarios (2023). https://arxiv.org/abs/2305.17246
14. Kao, D.Y., Hsiao, S.C.: The dynamic analysis of wannacry ransomware. In: 2018 20th International Conference on Advanced Communication Technology (ICACT), pp. 159–166. IEEE (2018)
15. Keskin, O.F., Lubja, K., Bahsi, H., Tatar, U.: Systematic cyber threat modeling for maritime operations: attack trees for shipboard systems. J. Marine Sci. Eng. **13**(4), 645 (2025)
16. Konsta, A.M., Lafuente, A.L., Spiga, B., Dragoni, N.: Survey: automatic generation of attack trees and attack graphs. Comput. Secur. **137**, 103602 (2024)
17. Langner, R.: Stuxnet: dissecting a cyberwarfare weapon. IEEE Secur. Priv. **9**(3), 49–51 (2011)
18. Liang, E., et al.: RLlib: Abstractions for distributed reinforcement learning. In: International Conference on Machine Learning (ICML) (2018)
19. Liaw, R., Liang, E., Nishihara, R., Moritz, P., Gonzalez, J.E., Stoica, I.: Tune: A research platform for distributed model selection and training. arXiv preprint arXiv:1807.05118 (2018)

20. Liu, X., Ospina, J., Konstantinou, C.: Deep reinforcement learning for cybersecurity assessment of wind integrated power systems. IEEE Access **8**, 208378–208394 (2020). https://doi.org/10.1109/ACCESS.2020.3038769

21. Lopez-Martin, M., Carro, B., Sanchez-Esguevillas, A.: Application of deep reinforcement learning to intrusion detection for supervised problems. Expert Syst. Appl. **141**, 112963 (2020)

22. Microsoft Defender Research Team: Cyberbattlesim. https://github.com/microsoft/cyberbattlesim (2021), created by Christian Seifert, Michael Betser, William Blum, James Bono, Kate Farris, Emily Goren, Justin Grana, Kristian Holsheimer, Brandon Marken, Joshua Neil, Nicole Nichols, Jugal Parikh, Haoran Wei

23. MITRE Corporation: Mitre att&ck® (2015). https://attack.mitre.org/

24. Nguyen, H.P.T., Chen, Z., Hasegawa, K., Fukushima, K., Beuran, R.: Pengym: Pentesting training framework for reinforcement learning agents. In: ICISSP, pp. 498–509 (2024)

25. Oesch, S., et al.: Towards a high fidelity training environment for autonomous cyber defense agents. In: Proceedings of the 17th Cyber Security Experimentation and Test Workshop, pp. 91–99 (2024)

26. Palmer, G., Parry, C., Harrold, D.J., Willis, C.: Deep reinforcement learning for autonomous cyber defence: A survey. arXiv preprint arXiv:2310.07745 (2023)

27. Rapid7 LLC: Metasploit. https://www.metasploit.com/

28. Sahu, A., Venkatraman, V., Macwan, R.: Reinforcement learning environment for cyber-resilient power distribution system. IEEE Access **11**, 127216–127228 (2023). https://doi.org/10.1109/ACCESS.2023.3282182

29. Schwartz, J., Kurniawati, H.: Autonomous penetration testing using reinforcement learning. arXiv preprint arXiv:1905.05965 (2019)

30. Sunder, G., Colletto, A.S., Raimondi, S., Basile, C., Viticchié, A., Aliberti, A.: Enhancing ot threat modelling: An effective rule-based approach for attack graph generation. In: 2024 4th Intelligent Cybersecurity Conference (ICSC), pp. 142–150 (2024). https://doi.org/10.1109/ICSC63108.2024.10895716

31. Towers, M., et al.: Gymnasium: A standard interface for reinforcement learning environments. arXiv preprint arXiv:2407.17032 (2024)

32. Tran, K., et al.: Deep hierarchical reinforcement agents for automated penetration testing. arXiv preprint arXiv:2109.06449 (2021)

33. Walter, E., Ferguson-Walter, K., Ridley, A.: Incorporating deception into cyberbattlesim for autonomous defense. arXiv preprint arXiv:2108.13980 (2021)

34. Wilson, A., et al.: Multi-agent reinforcement learning for maritime operational technology cyber security. arXiv preprint arXiv:2401.10149 (2024)

35. Wolk, M., et al.: Beyond cage: Investigating generalization of learned autonomous network defense policies. arXiv preprint arXiv:2211.15557 (2022)

36. Yang, W., Acuto, A., Zhou, Y., Wojtczak, D.: A survey for deep reinforcement learning based network intrusion detection. arXiv preprint arXiv:2410.07612 (2024)

# From Words to Wires: Toward Rapid ICS Cyber-Range Construction Using LLMs


Tommy Helland Berg[1], Ahmed Amro[1]([✉]) [iD], Aida Akbarzadeh[1], and Georgios Kavallieratos[1,2] [iD]

[1] Norwegian University of Science and Technology, Gjøvik, Norway
tommyhbe@stud.ntnu.no,
{ahmed.amro,aida.akbarzadeh,georgios.kavallieratos}@ntnu.no
[2] University of Oslo, 2007 Kjeller, Norway
georgios.kavallieratos@its.uio.no



**Abstract.** Industrial Control System (ICS) testbeds are critical for cybersecurity research but typically demand significant time, expertise, and vendor-specific tooling. This paper explores whether Large Language Models (LLMs) can automate the generation of runnable, network-visible ICS simulations from plain-language descriptions. We introduce Words2Wires, a lightweight, LLM-integrated toolchain combining a Lua-based control logic runtime with open-source Modbus/TCP and OPC-UA implementations. Given a simple textual prompt (e.g., describing a tank or traffic light system), the LLM produces control scripts, simulation code, and an OPC-UA tag map. These artefacts are executed directly, without manual edits or formal validation, to yield functioning ICS testbeds in under 90 s per instance. The resulting simulations behave as valid Modbus and OPC-UA devices, respond to HMI inputs, and support basic adversarial scenarios such as discovery, command injection, and denial-of-service. While the generated logic may contain flaws and the process models are simplistic, our results show that LLMs can greatly reduce the effort needed to create ICS testbeds for protocol-centric and exploratory security testing. Though not suitable for high-fidelity simulations, this prompt-to-simulation pipeline is well-suited for cyber ranges, deception systems, and rapid prototyping.

**Keywords:** ICS · LLM · Cyber Range · Simulation · Cybersecurity


## 1 Introduction

Industrial Control Systems (ICS) encompass several types of control systems found in industrial sectors and critical infrastructure [12]. Conducting cybersecurity research on industrial control systems might be inherently dangerous or have serious consequences due to their critical functions and operations. Testbeds could serve as a tool to reduce these threats. The importance of developing security testbeds is highlighted in [17]. However, several challenges may occur due to the oversimplification of the industrial control system. Balancing the need for fidelity and the researcher's goal, testbeds can play a role in cyber deception, vulnerability analysis, educational purposes, testing security mechanisms, threat, and impact analysis.

This paper aims to determine whether the Large Language Model (LLM) generated testbed simulations can achieve sufficient realism to be used for cybersecurity testing and research purposes. The potential gains in efficiency and accuracy are explored considering traditional methods of ICS testbed development. Recent advances in LLMs have shown promising results in code generation for general-purpose programming languages. However, according to Koziolek [13] (2023), it remained unclear how effectively these models can contribute to "control logic engineering"—particularly in Industrial Control Systems. Koziolek's work demonstrated that ChatGPT could generate syntactically correct Structured Text (ST) code (IEC 61131–3) and provide domain-relevant logic, such as working state machines for traffic lights or elevator controls. Additionally, Harter's [10] study explores whether LLMs (e.g., GPT-4) can aid in developing safety-critical embedded software. Results show GPT-4 can help design aircraft HMIs without manual coding, while meeting safety and reliability standards.

Building on these insights, this work investigates the utilisation of LLMs to automate the development and deployment of plausible ICS simulations for cybersecurity research. Building a realistic ICS testbed for cybersecurity research purposes requires significant multi-disciplinary effort [17]. In addition, the cooperation of both IT and automation professionals is needed. This work explores the utilisation of LLMs to automate the Programmable Logic Controller (PLC) component. We scope the LLM's responsibility to configure the PLC for HMI/SCADA connectivity and supply the PLC component with code responsible for either (i) executing I/O operations in an external system or (ii) simulating I/O operations internally. Particularly, this work investigates how LLMs translate high-level process descriptions into working ICS simulations and the application of such simulations in a testbed environment. Overall, the aim is to produce an LLM-driven framework that integrates with existing testbed infrastructure and lowers barriers for security testing in industrial settings.

To the best of our knowledge, a comprehensive framework that enables a user to provide a description of an industrial process scenario and convert this to a ready-to-run ICS testbed component for cybersecurity purposes has yet to be developed.

The proposed framework called `Words2Wires` aims to reduce human labour for use-cases like honeypots, where variation of scenarios would be valuable. In addition, serves as a tool for CTF competitions and educational purposes, demonstrating how simple techniques can affect ICS components via cyber attacks.

The contributions of this work are as follows:

- We review existing developments in applying LLMs to control engineering, including PLC code generation, P&ID interpretation, SCADA/HMI tag synthesis, and protocol emulation.

- We propose `Words2Wires`, a lightweight, cross-platform framework that transforms a plain-language scenario description into a deployable PLC simulation.
- We evaluate the framework across several end-to-end scenarios where the LLM generates both the control logic and the physical process simulation, and a hybrid scenario using an external simulation engine (i.e. Factory IO). Each case is tested for protocol fidelity, responsiveness, and suitability for adversarial experimentation.
- We discuss our findings and the limitations of the proposed framework as bases for future work.

The rest of this paper is structured as follows: Sect. 2 summarise the works related to utilising LLMs in ICS and cybersecurity research in ICS. Section 3 outlines the threat model assumed in this paper. Section 4 introduces the proposed Words2Wires framework for developing ICS testbeds from natural language descriptions. Section 5 documents the experiments conducted for evaluating the framework. Section 6 reflects on the findings in the paper and the identified limitations of the framework. Finally, Sect. 7 concludes the paper.

## 2    Related Work

Design and implementation of a credible ICS testbed requires careful attention to various factors, including simulation fidelity, repeatability, and safe execution. An ICS is not a single unit or device, but a complex ecosystem of hardware and software components used to monitor and control industrial processes. Conti et al. [8] surveyed ICS testbeds and described various devices and their specific roles as foundational components. To effectively simulate an ICS, a test environment must reflect the complexity of real-world industrial automation.

Simulating complex, high-fidelity ICS systems requires domain knowledge of the physical process and how to simulate the physical world.

Cherian et al. [3] described how LLMs make educated guesses based on intuitive physics learned from training data, and argued that complex systems are often too intricate to be learned this way. Even with full physical attributes, simulating realistic system behaviour remains challenging for LLMs. Ali-Dib et al. [2] evaluated state-of-the-art LLMs on PhD-level computational physics problems. As expected, they found limitations in GPT-4, such as incorrect unit handling and a lack of physical justification. However, they argued that combining problem-solving and coding capabilities could one day enable AI to simulate the physical world. Cherian et al. [3] proposed integrating LLMs with physics engines. Tinsel et al. [18] proposed a method to transform user descriptions into processes and machines using LLMs. Their pipeline created simulation models, imported into a factory simulator, demonstrating how LLMs can aid in factory planning and inferring relationships between machines and processes.

Koziolek et al. [13] showed that ChatGPT-4 can generate sophisticated and syntactically correct IEC 61131-3 code from natural language prompts. However, the LLM still had limitations and occasionally generated false answers. Their study investigated how LLMs could assist control engineers in designing control logic for industrial automation. They created 100 prompts across 10 categories covering PLC programming, sequential logic, and interlocks. They noted that in many domains (e.g., rolling mills), control logic involves wiring pre-defined, often proprietary, function blocks with limited custom code. Function block diagrams, ladder logic and sequential function charts require graphical notations which are currently not directly supported by LLMs. Some commercial vendors, such as Beckhoff[1], have integrated an AI assistant within the Twincat Engineering software suite, allowing users to leverage LLMs for tasks such as code generation, completion, and troubleshooting.

By leveraging Piping and Instrumentation Diagrams (PI&Ds), engineers and researchers can better understand industrial operations, aiding in the design of plausible and realistic testbeds for cybersecurity research and industrial process simulation. However, Geng et al. [8] note that physical modelling of industrial processes is often abstracted and simplified. Thus, this paper aims to simulate a plausible industrial control system, and PI&D is one of many sources that could help comprehend the physical process. Koziolek et al. [14] proposed an approach to transform P&IDs into IEC 61131–3 Structured Text using LLMs. Their method uses image recognition to extract relevant data and generate matching control logic, evaluated in three industrial case studies, demonstrating its feasibility. In a related domain, Harter [10] conducted an empirical study on whether LLMs like GPT-4 can assist with embedded software for safety-critical systems. He found GPT-4 could partially support engineers in designing HMIs for aircraft displays without manual coding, while still adhering to safety and reliability requirements. Ma et al. [15] showed how structured prompts can help LLMs to generate SCADA system tags. The authors argue that LLMs can process Structured Text and comprehend complex control logic, making them strong candidates for configuring SCADA system tags. However, standard naming conventions and tag relationships pose challenges, and LLMs are less effective without a predefined, structured prompt optimisation strategy. Using such strategies, the authors were able to enhance accuracy and usability, enabling effective SCADA tag generation.

Fakih et al. [6] presented a pipeline to generate PLC control code with LLMs. They produced Structured Text, applied grammar checks and compilers, and increased the generation success rate from 47% to 72% when tested on a FischerTechnik Manufacturing Testbed. By incorporating user feedback and external verification tools, they refined the model using LoRA[2] fine-tuning combined with prompt engineering techniques. Vasilatos ct al. [19], in their work on *LLM-Pot*, described a system using self-hosted LLMs to provide realistic responses to ICS network protocols and emulate devices with high fidelity. Running on an RTX3090Ti GPU, it achieved  160 ms response times. The authors implemented algorithms that modelled both PLC and physical process behaviour to support

---

[1] https://www.beckhoff.com/en-en/products/automation/twincat-projects-with-ai-supported-engineering/.

[2] LoRA - Low-Rank Adaptation of Large Language Models.

effective model training, successfully deceiving reconnaissance tools like Nmap and Shodan. Heluany et al. [11] introduced DecEPt, a low-interaction honeypot that uses ChatGPT to simulate ICS device responses. Instead of real devices or simulations, DecEPt engages attackers through LLM-generated replies. The authors note that practical deployment would require improvements, such as fine-tuning or adopting specialised LLMs over general ones like ChatGPT.

As our related work highlighted, there are still gaps in integrating LLM-driven control logic generation, simulation, and protocol emulation into a cohesive framework. Therefore, in this paper, we propose a unified solution that transforms plain-language industrial scenarios into runnable ICS testbed components for cybersecurity experimentation.

## 3   Threat Model

This section outlines the threat model assumed in the Words2Wires framework, as illustrated in Fig. 1, including the expected level of adversarial access, the supported objectives, and the defined attack surface.

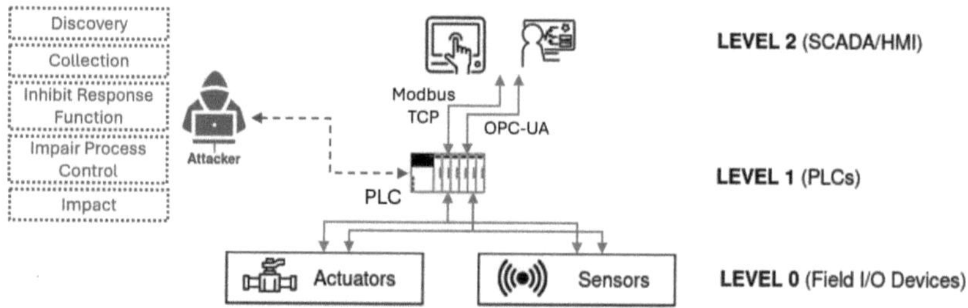


**Fig. 1.** The Assumed Threat Model

### 3.1   Access Level

The access level in the threat model assumes that the attacker has network-level access and can communicate with the PLC over the Internet Protocol (IP). According to the Purdue Model by Williams et al. [20], the PLC resides at Level 1 and is connected to Level 0 (e.g. Sensors and Actuators) and Level 2 (e.g. HMI).

### 3.2   Adversarial Objectives

The supported adversarial objectives in such an environment, as mapped to the MITRE ATT & CK ICS tactics[3], include: **Discovery, Collection, Inhibit Response Function, Impair Process Control**, and **Impact**.

---

[3] https://attack.mitre.org/tactics/ics/.

**Discovery** refers to the adversary identifying and assessing information within the environment to locate potential targets. **Collection** involves the adversary gathering relevant data and domain knowledge about the ICS environment to support their objectives. **Inhibit Response Function** describes attempts by the adversary to prevent safety, protection, quality assurance, or operator intervention functions from responding to failures, hazards, or unsafe states. **Impair Process Control** refers to efforts by the adversary to manipulate, disable, or damage physical process control systems. **Impact** indicates that the adversary is attempting to manipulate, disrupt, or destroy ICS systems, data, or the surrounding environment.

We focus on adversarial behaviours at the protocol and logic layer for a single device (e.g., malformed commands, unauthorised state changes). Physical compromise, supply chain risks, and safety-layer bypasses are considered out of scope.

### 3.3    Attack Surface

The primary attack surface involves two widely used industrial automation protocols: Modbus TCP and OPC-UA, each with specific characteristics and vulnerabilities.

**Modbus TCP** is a network protocol that operates without encryption or authentication. This makes it susceptible to attacks if an adversary gains network access—they can intercept, flood, or inject malicious messages, potentially gaining unauthorised control over physical processes.

**OPC-UA** includes built-in security features such as encryption and authentication. However, for our toolkit, these protections are deliberately disabled to simplify use. This allows attackers to intercept or tamper with messages, which often include descriptive tags that aid in understanding and manipulating process behaviour.

Attack outcomes are typically visible through simulation changes caused by command injections or message flooding—standard ICS attack paths. Despite the simplified environment, the setup remains valuable for instructional purposes. Attackers can perform discovery using tools like `nmap`, inspect commands by querying Modbus registers or OPC-UA tags, and inject commands to observe simulated effects. Actual consequences vary depending on the simulation configuration.

Although the testbed models only a single component (a PLC), it still allows for basic ICS attack demonstrations. We recognise this limitation, as emphasised by Dehlaghi-Ghadim et al. [5], who state that a single-PLC setup is inadequate for analysing attacks targeting PLC-to-PLC communication. However, since this work focuses on evaluating the utility of LLM for ICS cyber range construction, future work will expand the scope to include additional ICS elements.

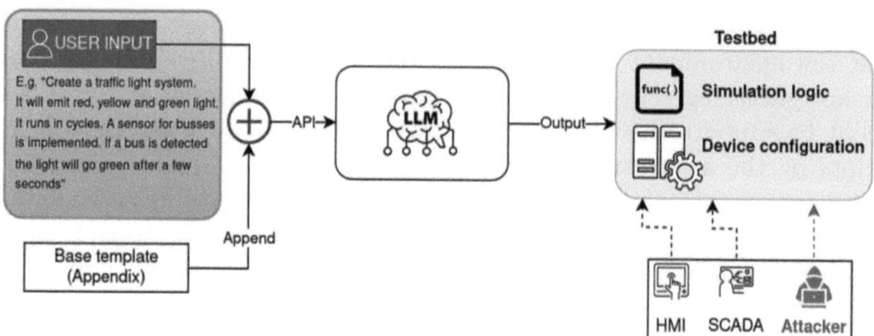


**Fig. 2.** Overview of the proposed Words2Wires framework

# 4    The Words2Wires Framework

Building on the assumption that LLMs are highly capable of generating computer code from natural text, we propose a framework that leverages this capability to bypass the tedious manual work of configuring and programming a PLC for a testbed scenario. At a high level, our system architecture, as shown in Fig. 2 centres around a PLC that exposes industrial automation network protocols. The simulation logic and device configuration are generated using LLMs from a user input in natural language. The outcome logic and configuration are used to create an operational environment able to connect to other ICS components and allow interactive adversarial capabilities.

Rather than addressing a full industrial network, our work is confined to a PLC testbed. However, the testbed is developed to communicate with other ICS components (e.g. HMI) using high-fidelity industrial protocols (Modbus and OPC-UA), allowing it to integrate smoothly with other components in simulated or real ICS environments.

## 4.1    Framework Components

The Words2Wires framework is developed as a toolchain or pipeline of components that, when put together, can be used to deploy an interactive ICS virtual environment. The framework is open-source and hosted online[4]. The components and their interaction with each other are depicted in Fig. 3. Further details of each component and functions are provided hereafter.

**Simulation Generation.** The simulation generation function is developed as a Python script called "getSimulation". The script receives from the user a scenario description (e.g. burner management process). The description is concatenated with a base template including a Lua script template and an LLM prompt template to be sent together to the LLM API (e.g. ChatGPT), which could be hosted

---

[4] https://github.com/tommy-berg/SimplePLC.

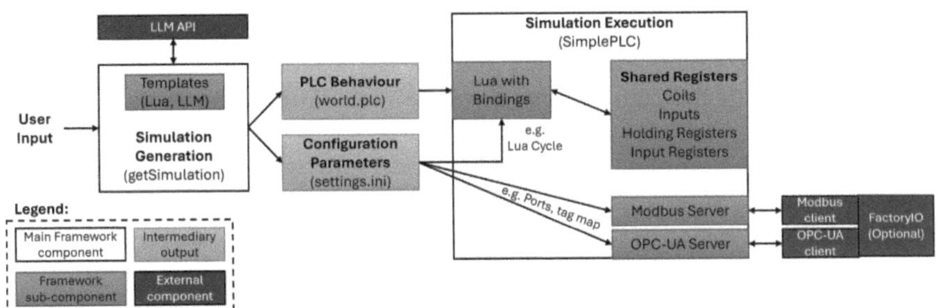


**Fig. 3.** The Words2Wires architecture

online or locally. The Lua template is necessary for the smooth processing of the Lua scripting (discussed later on), while the LLM template defines the expected output from the LLM. The base template defines the following:

- No external dependencies (or libraries in code)
- Use integer-safe logic
- Use our naming convention for SimplePC
- Simulate physical behaviour
- Include safety interlocks (makes the states of two mechanisms dependent on each other. E.g. a valve could be closed if a water pump fails.)
- Deterministic state transitions
- Cause-and-effect-matrix
- Timing of cycle() is 100ms

The script outputs two files, `world.plc` and `settings.ini`, which are later transferred into the simulation execution function (i.e. SimplePLC). The `world.plc` file describes the PLC behaviour (how the system should behave including controling the actuators and sensors in the simulation), while the `settings.ini` describes the environment configuration, such as network addresses, port numbers, and tag map, allowing clients to interface with the PLC over the network.

**Simulation Execution.** A software toolchain called "SimplePLC" has been developed for this framework. The simulation tool was created by combining open-source libraries of industrial automation network protocols with an embedded Lua scripting engine. The simulation tool was created using GitHub CoPilot in Visual Studio and is written in C++ and consists of a single executable. It is available for Windows, macOS and Linux both as pre-built binaries and source code.

Upon startup, the tool reads the `world.plc` and `settings.ini` files. Internally, the simulation maintains a set of in-memory registers. These registers are polled approximately every 100 milliseconds (on a best-effort basis, as the system does not run under a real-time operating system). In each cycle, the tool evaluates the current register values to determine whether any process intervention is necessary. If intervention is required, the relevant memory registers are updated. This loop continues to run until the simulation is terminated.

Our toolchain embeds a Lua runtime. The registers of the toolchain were exposed to Lua, enabling Lua scripts to read and write updates to registers shared by all the components of the toolchain. For fast prototyping, the user can also modify the Lua scripts during runtime and hot reload them to fix logical errors potentially made by the LLM during the Lua control code generation.

While we move away from IEC 61131-3 languages, which are traditionally used for industrial automation, we argue that similar goals can be achieved through alternative methods, such as monitoring network traffic and assessing the attack surface. IEC 61131-3 programs are typically compiled into binary executables, which are then loaded and managed by proprietary PLC runtime environments (e.g. Step7, Studio 5000, or CODESYS). These binaries dictate the scan cycle behaviour of the PLC. For example, OpenPLC uses MATIEC to compile Structured Text into C code, which is then integrated with a runtime and compiled into a final executable. In our implementation, we comparably use Lua scripts, as the component responsible for the scan cycle, similar to how commercial platforms like CODESYS support Python scripting for tasks such as updating libraries, generating code, or dynamically configuring machines.[5].

**Industrial Communication Protocols.** To enable interactive simulation over the network while preserving the protocol fidelity required for cybersecurity analysis, SimplePLC supports two widely used industrial communication standards: Modbus and OPC UA.

Modbus is a well-established open standard developed by Modicon in 1979. It remains widely used in industrial automation today. Originally designed for serial communication, Modbus has since been extended to support encapsulation over TCP/IP networks, commonly referred to as Modbus/TCP.[6].

To implement Modbus support, SimplePLC includes the open-source library libmodbus.[7] Written in C, libmodbus is cross-platform and compatible with Linux, macOS, FreeBSD, and Windows. In the SimplePLC runtime, this library enables the testbed to act as a Modbus server, bridging internal simulation registers with external clients via the Modbus protocol.

OPC UA (Open Platform Communications Unified Architecture) was introduced in 2006 and is standardised under IEC 62541. It functions as middleware, facilitating data exchange between industrial systems and monitoring tools such as HMIs or SCADA systems [9]. According to a survey on ICS testbeds by Conti et al. [4], which analysed 86 testbeds, 39.5% implemented Modbus while only 2.4% used OPC UA—highlighting Modbus's dominance and the relatively limited adoption of OPC UA in experimental environments.

---

[5] https://store.codesys.com/en/3\protect\kern+.1667em\relaxs-systems-python-editor.html.

[6] https://modbus.org/docs/Modbus_Application_Protocol_V1_1b3.pdf.

[7] https://github.com/stephane/libmodbus.

For OPC UA support, SimplePLC integrates open62541,[8], an open-source implementation licensed under the Mozilla Public License v2.0. The library supports the full OPC UA communication stack, including dynamic node management, subscriptions, and encrypted communication.

In this version of SimplePLC, encryption and authentication features of OPC UA were not implemented to simplify the proof-of-concept and introduce information disclosure as a threat vector within the threat model. A basic publish/-subscribe pattern was implemented to allow potential future integration with SCADA or HMI systems. This design decision prioritises threat modelling and proof-of-concept clarity over full implementation of OPC UA security best practices.

The inclusion of high-fidelity industrial communication protocols into the Words2Wires framework supports its integration with a range of software tools that are developed specifically for industrial systems. Among these tools is the Factory I/O[9]. It is a commercial computer software that turns a computer into a PLC training kit, developed by Real Games Unipessoal Lda. It allows the user to control a physical simulation of typical factory scenarios, either by using pre-built scenes or building scenarios.

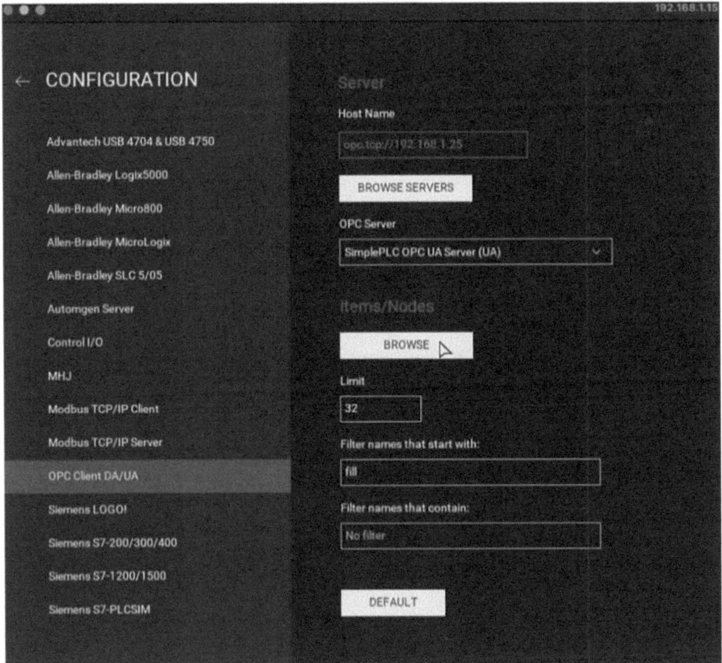

**Fig. 4.** Factory IO Configuration for connecting to the PLC

---

[8] https://www.open62541.org.
[9] https://factoryio.com.

By connecting to our toolset with Factory IO as seen in Fig. 4, we are able to connect our toolset to Factory IO and configure the training PLC software to communicate both via OPC-UA and Modbus protocol. Upon interacting with the simulation in Factory IO, we see the data reflected in Prosys OPC UA Browser when connecting to the same OPC UA server as Factory IO.

**Tag Generation.** The LLM is responsible for generating the PLC device configuration, including tags that can be consumed by HMIs and SCADA systems.

Inspired by the work of Ma et al. [15], we implemented basic SCADA tag generation within our pipeline. This implementation operates in its simplest form: we instruct the LLM to generate a [Tags] section in a configuration file, which is later parsed by our toolchain. The tags are defined as key-value pairs, where the value type indicates the Modbus data type: 0=Coil, 1=DiscreteInput, 2=HoldingRegister, 3=InputRegister. Below is the prompt snippet provided to the LLM after code logic generation:

```
Now generate a corresponding [Tags] section in INI format for Modbus
    mapping.
    Use this format:
    [Tags]
    ; Format: tag_name,modbus_address,type
    ; Types: 0=Coil, 1=DiscreteInput, 2=HoldingRegister, 3=InputRegister
```

These automatically generated tags are compatible with OPC-UA applications. To demonstrate this, we built a simple OPC-UA client. A screenshot of which is shown in Fig. 7 in Sect. 5.3.

By combining these approaches, we demonstrate the potential for dynamically generating HMIs that extend the SimplePLC toolchain. This supports rapid iteration and refinement of simulation environments, paving the way for autonomous, fast-tracked testbeds that go beyond a single PLC setup. Open-source libraries are used to ensure protocol authenticity, but we also perform manual verification to establish a reliable baseline. This enables the LLM to safely configure device types, expose HMI tags, and generate appropriate PLC logic and simulation behavior.

## 5    Evaluation

In this section, we present an empirical evaluation of the Word2Wires framework. The evaluation covers the ability to emulate a range of attacks in the simulated environment using state-of-the-art tools. Additionally, a group of use cases are utilised to evaluate the diversity and fidelity of the simulation scenarios.

### 5.1    Attack Emulation

The range of supported adversarial tactics or objectives in the current version of the Word2Wires framework is discussed in Sect. 3. In this section, we present the conducted experiments for each of them:

**Discovery and Collection.** To verify the ability to conduct network Discovery and Collection techniques, the Nmap[10] tool was used with the modbus-discover plug-in. In addition, the port exposing OPC-UA was included in the mapping. It was verified that by changing the configuration file, we are able to set the device type to our own choosing. This function can be useful in researching deceptive methods where the ICS could pose as a honeypot. However, for this section, we run tests to verify the capabilities of the toolchain.

Nmap scan shown below returned an opcua-tcp server on port 4840 and a Modbus device on port 502.

```
nmap IP_ADD -p 4840,502 --script=modbus-discover
Starting Nmap 7.95 ( \url{https://nmap.org} ) at 2025-04-21 15:02 CEST
Nmap scan report for 192.168.1.154
Host is up (0.00086s latency).


PORT      STATE SERVICE
502/tcp   open  modbus
| modbus-discover:
|   sid 0x1:
|     Slave ID data: \xFA\xFFSimple
|_    Device identification: SimplePLC v.0.1
4840/tcp open  opcua-tcp


Nmap done: 1 IP address (1 host up) scanned in 0.09 seconds
```

**Impact Through Denial-of-Service** To verify the ability to conduct denial of service in the kind of stress-testing to check if several Modbus connections can be handled at once.

Based on the work of Gamess et al. [7], we conduct some evaluations of the modbus implementation. We start by running two concurrent mbpoll[11] to our tool running on a Windows Virtual Machine. We set the polling interval to 100 milliseconds and read 125 registers for each register type. We can verify that we can read from all registers, and two concurrent connections are possible to connect to our tool, as shown below.

```
mbpoll -m tcp -a 1 -r 1 -c 125 -t 0 -l 100 -o 0.01 IP_ADD (Coils)
mbpoll -m tcp -a 1 -r 1 -c 125 -t 1 -l 100 -o 0.01 IP_ADD (Discrete
 inputs)
mbpoll -m tcp -a 1 -r 1 -c 125 -t 3 -l 100 -o 0.01 IP_ADD (Input
 register)
mbpoll -m tcp -a 1 -r 1 -c 125 -t 4 -l 100 -o 0.01 IP_ADD (Holding
 register)
```

Secondly, we implement a program based on Gamess et al. [7] (Fig. 5 in the source). We use a simple program that performs read operations for 100 iterations and prints the response time.

---

[10] https://nmap.org/.
[11] https://github.com/epsilonrt/mbpoll.

Thirdly, we implement a program where we flood the tool with Modbus requests and measure if this changes the response time. We spawn 30 threads polling the Modbus server 224 times per second and measure again. The maximum response time doubled 4 times, and the median response time doubled. The 95th percentile of requests also more than doubled.

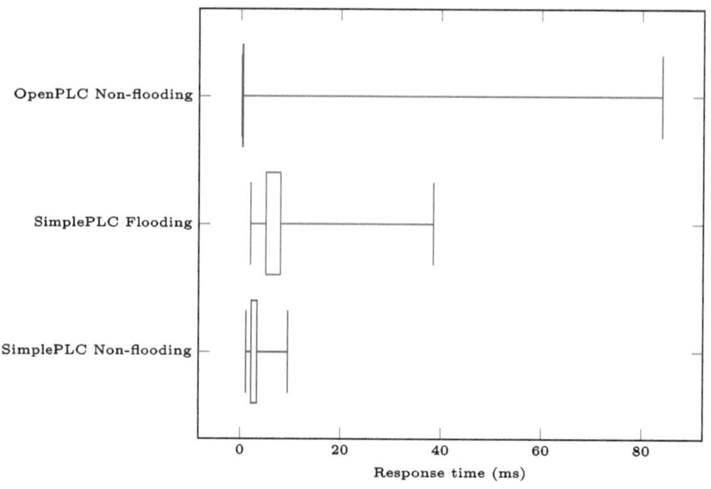

**Fig. 5.** Response time increase due to DDoS emulation

OpenPLC is superior with a median response time of 0.277 milliseconds with 95% of requests being responded within 0.391 milliseconds, compared to SimplePLC median 2.213 milliseconds and 95% within 3.336 milliseconds. However, it was impossible to measure OpenPLC response times during DDoS flooding as the connections timed out before receiving an answer. The same test was performed using mbpoll with the same results. This could be due to how OpenPLC handled multiple connections in their implementation of the libmodbus library.

Although we were unable to completely flood the network using the same tools for our toolchain, the flooding test caused a noticeable increase in Modbus response times, as shown in Fig. 5. Notably, timing degradation and desynchronization in time-sensitive protocols can lead to instability or missed real-time constraints in industrial systems. Similar timing disruptions have been shown to block protection functions in IEC 61850 substations, highlighting the critical role of time integrity in operational safety [1].

**Impair Process Control Through Manipulation of Controls.** Adversaries can disrupt industrial processes by manipulating control elements such as set points, tags, or parameters. In the generated environment by the Words2Wires framework, the attack can be achieved by injecting data into system registers and sending commands through both Modbus and OPC UA protocols.

To verify the capabilities of the OPC UA server, we attempt to connect to our toolkit by using the Prosys OPC UA Browser as shown in Fig. 6.

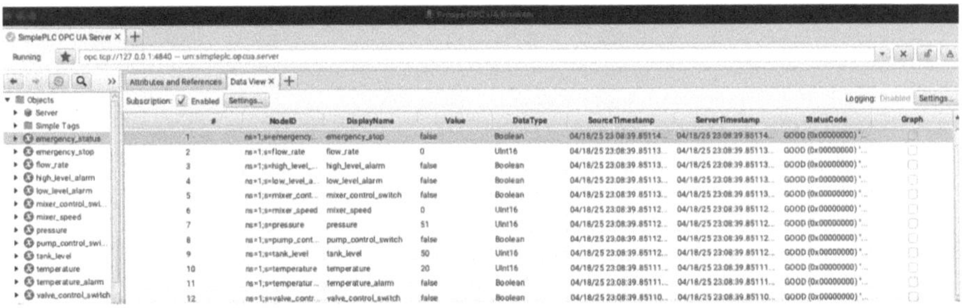

**Fig. 6.** Prosys OPC UA Browser connected to testbed

We successfully connected to the device and identified objects corresponding to our defined tags. These tags, configured as bool or uint16 data types, represent the shared memory area between the Lua engine and the Modbus server. Using the Prosys OPC UA Browser, we verified the ability to write values to the testbed via the OPC UA protocol. The values written through OPC UA were accurately reflected when polling the corresponding Modbus registers. This demonstrates the capability to manipulate the control process, supporting the objective of impairing the physical process control.

### 5.2  Scenario 1: Wastewater Treatment

This scenario demonstrates the ability to generate scenarios related to the wastewater control domain. A detailed, 156-word process prompt based on the real-world description by Ning et al. [16] was used as user input. The prompt outlines a continuous dissolved oxygen (DO) control loop using an aeration tank with feedback from DO sensors and blower actuation. The goal was to assess whether the LLM could generate a closed-loop control system that mimics a realistic industrial treatment process.

***Prompt and Generation***: The prompt was submitted to GPT-4o (temperature 0.7). The model returned 303 lines of Lua, along with a set of 16 OPC UA tags covering binary actuators, alarms, and analogue sensor data (some are shown in Fig. 7). Generation completed in 74 s. SimplePLC compiled and launched successfully on the first attempt. However, one manual edit was required to suppress a logic error, causing the simulation to start in emergency state due to unset blower conditions.

***Functional Behaviour***: Once deployed, the simulation accepted external write requests to setpoints and actuator states. When the pump and valve were enabled, the tank level increased as expected. The blower could be activated,

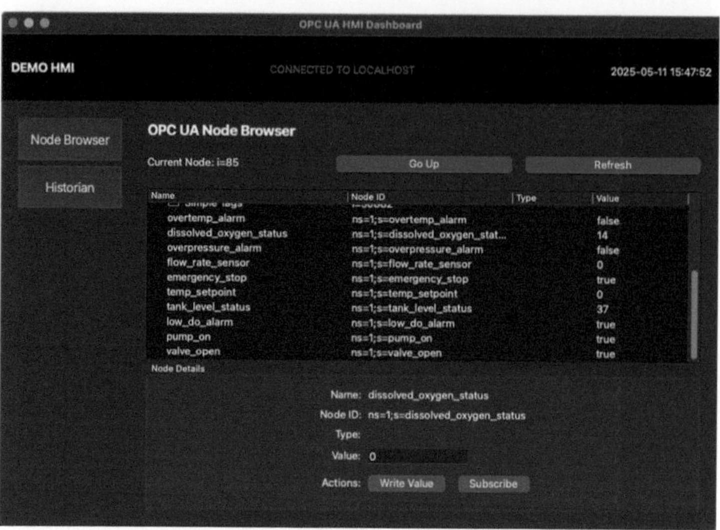

**Fig. 7.** Dissolved oxygen water treatment scenario connected to proof-of-concept HMI client via OPC-UA

and dissolved oxygen values rose to 100% in response. However, temperature remained fixed and temperature-related setpoints had no observable effect. The pressure and flow-rate sensors responded with pseudo-random values but did not correlate with physical inputs. The emergency-stop logic worked correctly and reliably halted all operations.

*Security Exercise*: External commands via Modbus and OPC UA successfully overrode Digital Output (DO) setpoints and blower activation states. Tag coherence across protocols was preserved. Discovery using the nmap script modbus-discover exposed the full device identification, confirming protocol visibility. All injected commands were reflected in the simulation's internal state, satisfying the attackability criterion.

*Observed Flaws*: Although the simulation implements basic DO feedback, the logic lacks robust range checking and shows weak integration between setpoints and sensor simulation. DO rises to 100% regardless of actual flow or pressure values, and temperature control is entirely non-functional. The need for a manual patch to avoid booting in emergency state also highlights how even well-informed prompts can result in brittle control logic.

*Interpretation*: The scene demonstrates that LLMs can produce control logic approximating the structure of an industrial feedback loop when given precise, domain-rich prompts. However, physical realism and inter-variable consistency remain shallow. While this scenario yields usable network behaviour for discovery, collection, and control-injection experiments, it falls short of the behavioural fidelity required for validation of safety-critical automation strategies.

## 5.3  Scenario 2: Factory Conveyor Belt

The development of this scenario includes integration with Factory IO, allowing for visualisation of the industrial scenario and interactions with the industrial process. Additionally, the Scenario Generation script (i.e. getSimulation) discussed in Sect. 4.1 was modified to prompt different LLMs for each scenario, allowing the evaluation of different models for the same experiment. The modified script is called "getLogic" and is available on the project Github repo[12].

**Fig. 8.** Pre-built scenario "From a to B" in Factory IO

The objective of the scene titled "From A to B" (Fig. 8) in Factory I/O is to transport a box until it reaches a sensor. The conveyor belt is activated when Input Register 0 is set to true. When the box reaches the end of the conveyor, the sensor writes a false value to Coil 0. If the conveyor belt is not stopped in time, the box will fall off the end rather than stopping on the belt. To understand how Factory I/O configures this training scenario, the user must examine the scene directly within the application and inspect how sensors and actuators are mapped in the system.

***Prompt and Generation***: ChatGPT-4.1 was prompted using the getLogic.py script, with the following input:

```
Transport a box until it reaches a sensor using a conveyor belt.
The conveyor belt is turned on when input register 0 is set true.
When the box reaches the end of the conveyor belt , the sensor
on the modbus client writes false to coil 0.
```

---

[12] https://github.com/tommy-berg/SimplePLC/blob/main/scripts/getLogic.py.

ChatGPT-4.1 responded with a code snippet, which was then used to generate a PLC logic file. SimplePC was launched on a MacBook Pro, with the GPT-generated content as input. The Windows PC, running Factory I/O with prebuilt scenes, was configured as a Modbus client connected to the SimplePC instance on the MacBook.

***Functional Behaviour***: When the simulation was started, the conveyor belt behaved as expected: it stopped when the box reached the end of the belt. This is exactly what we hoped for, and we were able to complete the PLC training scene with natural language.

***Models Comparison***: Several models were tested, including ChatGPT-3.5-turbo, GPT-4.1, Phi-3, and Qemma-3. However, none of the locally hosted models produced meaningful control logic. For instance, the locally hosted Microsoft Phi-3 model generated invalid Modbus addresses.

While the frontier models (e.g., GPT-4.1) successfully produced valid and executable control logic, smaller local models failed to yield usable results. Human oversight was required to correct or verify outputs in every case.

The control programs from the GPT-generated logic were connected unmodified to Factory I/O. Communication was established via OPC-UA and Modbus TCP/IP, with Factory I/O acting as a Modbus client. Tags were automatically mapped, sensor values were streamed, and actuator commands were correctly processed by the PLC. This confirms that external tools recognise our toolchain as a conventional soft-PLC device.


# 6   Discussion

The proposed approach is characterised by high protocol fidelity since both Modbus TCP and OPC-UA stacks respond correctly to standard discovery tools and support read/write operations. Packet-level traffic is identical to that of real devices, by leveraging open-source protocol libraries and not considering LLM control, unlike the dynamic, LLM-driven simulation in Vasilatos et al. [19]. The LLM is utilised to generate static scenarios, making the prototype suitable for educational purposes. However, the proposed approach is insufficient for high-fidelity research applications such as intrusion detection. This is due to only simulating a single PLC and not a whole ICS environment. Timing and other network artefacts produced by certain PLC devices are probably not transferable. Moreover, LLM-generated control logic exhibits certain limitations. In some cases, the generated programs fail to handle state transitions correctly or do not reflect dynamic changes in system variables. These issues typically arise from shortcomings in prompt design and the absence of runtime validation mechanisms. These limitations stem from prompt design limitations and the lack of runtime validation. The current prompt template poorly generalises to diverse domains like consumer devices or transportation. However, scenario-specific prompt design may improve control accuracy and behavioural realism.

Furthermore, LLMs can generate correct syntactic control programs. However, they lack a comprehensive understanding of physical systems, and hence leads to invalid physical processes. This highlights the gap between syntactic trustworthiness and semantic correctness. Thorough assessment of LLM capabilities requires deeper prompt engineering, potential fine-tuning, and interdisciplinary evaluation by leveraging domain experts in control systems and automation.

This work investigated LLM-generated ICS logic in a simplified testbed featuring a single soft-PLC, unencrypted protocols, and basic adversarial actions. However, further analysis is needed to overcome the following limitations:

- **Use of Lua over IEC 61131-3:** Enables rapid development but lacks deterministic scan cycles and compatibility with industrial standards. Integrating MATIEC could enable Structured Text support and improve interoperability.
- **Simplified physical modelling :** System dynamics are reduced to integer counters, limiting realism.
- **Limited security features:** No authentication, encryption, or role-based access controls, reducing relevance for production environments.
- **Basic threat modeling:** Supports discovery, command injection, and DoS only; no advanced attack simulation.
- **LLM role is static:** Generates control logic but lacks runtime awareness or validation mechanisms.

Despite these constraints, the prototype illustrates that protocol-accurate simulation is feasible using LLMs and prompt templates. This has practical value for education, cyber ranges, and deception systems.

## 7    Conclusions

This paper set out to investigate whether Large Language Models could generate functional, network-visible PLC simulations from concise, plain-English descriptions of industrial processes. The results affirm that LLMs can indeed automate the generation and deployment of industrial control system simulations from high-level prompts, achieving the core objective of the research.

We developed a lightweight toolchain comprising a custom Lua-based soft-PLC capable of Modbus and OPC-UA communication, an LLM prompt template for generating control logic and tag maps, and an automated deployment script requiring no manual intervention. This end-to-end pipeline successfully produced simulations that compile, initialise, and behave as valid networked PLCs, responding appropriately to standard discovery, collection and injection tools. These outcomes demonstrate the feasibility of prompt-driven PLC configuration generation for single-controller ICS security testbeds.

Although the prototype simplifies rapid experimentation in ICS security, it also highlights future challenges. A single controller cannot capture the complexity of multi-stage or lateral-movement attack scenarios. Extending the framework to support coordinated multi-PLC and other ICS components is a logical next step. Moreover, the current simulations rely on approximated rather than physically realistic process models. Integrating a digital twin or lightweight physics engine could improve fidelity and test the LLM's capacity to operate under stricter physical constraints. Finally, incorporating automated verification, perhaps via lightweight formal methods, could improve reliability by catching logical inconsistencies in generated configurations.

In summary, this work demonstrates that LLMs can serve as effective tools for automating the creation of ICS simulations from natural language, offering a foundation for further development toward more complex, realistic, and reliable cyber-physical testbeds.

**Acknowledgments.** This research has been partially co-financed by the European Regional Development Fund of the European Union through the CYBERUNITY project, which has received funding from the European Union, under the Digital Europe grant 101128024.

This research has been partially financed by the European Commission [grant 101120657 "European Lighthouse to Manifest Trustworthy and Green AI" - ENFIELD].

**Disclosure of Interests.** The authors have no competing interests to declare that are relevant to the content of this article.

# References


1. Akbarzadeh, A., Erdodi, L., Houmb, S.H., Soltvedt, T.G., Muggerud, H.K.: Attacking IEC 61850 substations by targeting the PTP protocol. Electronics **12**(12), 2596 (2023)
2. Ali-Dib, M., Menou, K.: Physics simulation capabilities of LLMs. Physica Scripta **99** (2024). https://doi.org/10.1088/1402-4896/ad7a27
3. Cherian, A., Corcodel, R., Jain, S., Romeres, D.: Llmphy: complex physical reasoning using large language models and world models (2024). https://arxiv.org/abs/2411.08027
4. Conti, M., Donadel, D., Turrin, F.: A survey on industrial control system testbeds and datasets for security research. IEEE Commun. Surv. Tutor. **23**(4), 2248–2294 (2021). https://doi.org/10.1109/COMST.2021.3094360
5. Dehlaghi-Ghadim, A., Balador, A., Moghadam, M.H., Hansson, H., Conti, M.: Icssim — a framework for building industrial control systems security testbeds. Comput. Ind. **148**, 103906 (2023). https://doi.org/10.1016/j.compind.2023.103906
6. Fakih, M., Dharmaji, R., Moghaddas, Y., Quiros, G., Ogundare, O., Al Faruque, M.A.: Llm4plc: harnessing large language models for verifiable programming of PLCs in industrial control systems. In: Proceedings of the 46th International Conference on Software Engineering: Software Engineering in Practice, pp. 192–203. ICSE-SEIP '24, ACM (2024). https://doi.org/10.1145/3639477.3639743
7. Gamess, E., Smith, B., Iii, G.: Performance evaluation of modbus TCP in normal operation and under a distributed denial of service attack. Int. J. Comput. Netw. Commun. **12**, 1–21 (2020). https://doi.org/10.5121/ijcnc.2020.12201
8. Geng, Y., Wang, Y., Liu, W., Wei, Q., Liu, K., Wu, H.: A survey of industrial control system testbeds. IOP Conf. Seri. Mater. Sci. Eng. **569**, 042030 (2019). https://doi.org/10.1088/1757-899X/569/4/042030

9. González, I., Calderón, A., Figueiredo, J., Sousa, J.: A literature survey on open platform communications (OPC) applied to advanced industrial environments. Electronics **8**, 510 (2019). https://doi.org/10.3390/electronics8050510

10. Harter, M.: LLM assisted no-code hmi development for safety-critical systems: insights of a short empirical study. In: CENTRIC 2023: The Sixteenth International Conference on Advances in Human-oriented and Personalized Mechanisms, Technologies, and Services. Hochschule RheinMain - University of Applied Sciences, Rüsselsheim (2023)

11. Heluany, J., Amro, A., Gkioulos, V., Katsikas, S.: Interplay of digital twins and cyber deception: unraveling paths for technological advancements. In: Proceedings of the 2024 ACM/IEEE 4th International Workshop on Engineering and Cybersecurity of Critical Systems (EnCyCriS) and 2024 IEEE/ACM Second International Workshop on Software Vulnerability, pp. 20–28 (2024)

12. Initiative, J.T.F.T.: Security and Privacy Controls for Information Systems and Organizations. Tech. Rep. NIST Special Publication 800-53 Rev. 5, National Institute of Standards and Technology (2020). https://doi.org/10.6028/NIST.SP.800-53r5, includes updates as of December 2020

13. Koziolek, H., Gruener, S., Ashiwal, V.: Chatgpt for plc/DCS control logic generation. In: 2023 IEEE 28th International Conference on Emerging Technologies and Factory Automation (ETFA), pp. 1–8 (2023). https://doi.org/10.1109/ETFA54631.2023.10275411

14. Koziolek, H., Koziolek, A.: LLM-based control code generation using image recognition. In: 2024 IEEE/ACM International Workshop on Large Language Models for Code (LLM4Code), pp. 38–45 (2024)

15. Ma, F., Li, D., Liu, Y., Lan, D., Pang, Z.: Step: a structured prompt optimization method for scada system tag generation using LLMs. J. Industr. Inf.Integration **45**, 100832 (2025). https://doi.org/10.1016/j.jii.2025.100832

16. Ning, S., Hong, S.: Programmable logic controller-based automatic control for municipal wastewater treatment plant optimization. Water Pract. Technol. **17** (2021). https://doi.org/10.2166/wpt.2021.121

17. Tao, Y., Xu, W., Li, H., Ji, S.: Experience and lessons in building an ICS security testbed. In: 2019 1st International Conference on Industrial Artificial Intelligence (IAI), pp. 1–6 (2019). https://doi.org/10.1109/ICIAI.2019.8850804

18. Tinsel, E.F., Lechler, A., Riedel, O., Verl, A.: Concept of an initial requirements-driven factory layout planning and synthetic expert verification for industrial simulation based on LLM. In: 2024 IEEE 22nd International Conference on Industrial Informatics (INDIN), pp. 1–6 (2024). https://doi.org/10.1109/INDIN58382.2024.10774366

19. Vasilatos, C., Mahboobeh, D.J., Lamri, H., Alam, M., Maniatakos, M.: Llmpot: dynamically configured LLM-based honeypot for industrial protocol and physical process emulation (2025). https://arxiv.org/abs/2405.05999

20. Williams, T.J.: The purdue enterprise reference architecture. Comput. Ind. **24**(2), 141–158 (1994). https://doi.org/10.1016/0166-3615(94)90017-5, https://www.sciencedirect.com/science/article/pii/016636159490175

# In Numeris Veritas: An Empirical Measurement of Wi-Fi Integration in Industry


Vyron Kampourakis[1]([✉]) [ID], Christos Smiliotopoulos[2] [ID], Vasileios Gkioulos[1] [ID], and Sokratis Katsikas[1] [ID]

[1] Norwegian University of Science and Technology, 2802 Gjøvik, Norway
{vyron.kampourakis,vasileios.gkioulos,sokratis.katsikas}@ntnu.no
[2] University of the Aegean, 83200 Karlovasi, Greece
csmiliotopoulos@aegean.gr



**Abstract.** Traditional air gaps in industrial systems are disappearing as IT technologies permeate the OT domain, accelerating the integration of wireless solutions like Wi-Fi. Next-generation Wi-Fi standards (IEEE 802.11ax/be) meet performance demands for industrial use cases, yet their introduction raises significant security concerns. A critical knowledge gap exists regarding the empirical prevalence and security configuration of Wi-Fi in real-world industrial settings. This work addresses this by mining the global crowdsourced WiGLE database to provide a data-driven understanding. We create the first publicly available dataset of 1,087 high-confidence industrial Wi-Fi networks, examining key attributes such as SSID patterns, encryption methods, vendor types, and global distribution. Our findings reveal a growing adoption of Wi-Fi across industrial sectors but underscore alarming security deficiencies, including the continued use of weak or outdated security configurations that directly expose critical infrastructure. This research serves as a pivotal reference point, offering both a unique dataset and practical insights to guide future investigations into wireless security within industrial environments.

**Keywords:** Industrial Wi-Fi · WiGLE Dataset · Network Mapping · Wireless Security · Critical Infrastructure


## 1 Introduction

At the epicenter of Industry 4.0, industrial systems and Critical Infrastructures (CI) are rapidly integrating modern technologies, including the Internet of Things (IoT) and Industrial IoT (IIoT), Artificial Intelligence (AI) and Machine Learning (ML), and cloud computing and analytics. This convergence is progressively dissolving the traditional air gaps that once characterized Operational Technology (OT) environments. Wireless technologies are no exception, enabling increasingly flexible, agile, and cost-effective operational paradigms,



R. Laborde et al. (Eds.): ESORICS 2025, LNCS 16231, pp. 482–502, 2026.
https://doi.org/10.1007/978-3-032-16089-8_29

crucial for supporting IIoT deployments and enhancing overall flexibility and efficiency [13]. The predominant wireless protocol for Wireless Local Area Networks (WLANs) is IEEE 802.11, universally known as Wi-Fi. The advent of Wi-Fi 6 (802.11ax) and the emerging Wi-Fi 7 (802.11be) has brought significant advancements in throughput, latency, security, and overall performance. These substantial improvements render next-generation Wi-Fi a viable and increasingly attractive solution for meeting the stringent reliability, low-latency, and high-density requirements of mission-critical industrial environments.

However, the integration of Wi-Fi into industrial environments introduces significant security challenges. Unlike formerly isolated Operational Technology (OT) ecosystems, wireless-enabled networks inadvertently extend network access beyond physical perimeters, as Wi-Fi signals can propagate outside facility walls. This expanded attack surface enables adversaries with commodity radio devices to conduct passive reconnaissance, such as wardriving, or to actively attempt unauthorized access from a distance, without ever stepping foot inside the premises [1]. A compelling real-world example occurred in 2022, where threat actors utilized drones equipped with Wi-Fi Pineapple modules to capture employee credentials; subsequent drone deployments actively attempted unauthorized access to a financial firm's internal Wi-Fi network by exploiting signal leakage beyond the building's physical boundaries [7]. Another notable real-world example occurred ahead of Russia's invasion of Ukraine, where Advanced Persistent Threat (APT) actors employed a so-called *nearest neighbor* attack to covertly infiltrate a target organization's internal Wi-Fi. Namely, they compromised adjacent organizations and hijacked dual-homed systems with active Wi-Fi radios, exploiting previously harvested credentials to access enterprise networks without ever being physically present [32]. These incidents powerfully underscore the central problem: as industrial operations become increasingly interconnected via Wi-Fi, are existing security practices adequately protecting these critical networks? Despite these evident risks, there remains a dearth of empirical data and research on the actual prevalence of Wi-Fi in industrial settings and the specific security configurations deployed in the field.

To address this critical gap, this study sets out to investigate the following research question: What is the current state of Wi-Fi deployment and associated security configurations in real-world industrial environments? To do this, we adopt a data-driven approach, leveraging the global crowdsourced WiGLE database [33] as our lens into real-world Wi-Fi usage. The WiGLE platform aggregates publicly submitted, geotagged wireless network metadata, making it an invaluable resource for understanding real-world wireless infrastructure at scale. By systematically identifying Service Set Identifiers (SSIDs) and locations indicative of industrial networks, we gain empirical insight into Wi-Fi's penetration within the industrial domain. Crowdsourced analyses like this are widely recognized and employed in security research, offering scalable and empirical perspectives that are often difficult to obtain through traditional fieldwork [19,26]. Specifically for Wi-Fi, similar methodologies have been successfully applied to assess WLAN abundance and security. For instance, the work in [17] presented a systematic approach for WLAN assessment, validating WiGLE's utility as a comparative baseline. Similarly, the authors in [9] utilized WiGLE-formatted data for wardriving-based security assessments, extracting statistics on encryption types, SSIDs, and vendor distributions. Furthermore, the work in [21] examined global Wi-Fi security trends by incorporating multiple public datasets, including WiGLE.

***Contribution:*** This work provides a timely and multifaceted contribution to the evolving landscape of industrial wireless security, spanning four key areas. We compile and present the first publicly available dataset [11] of 1,087 high-confidence industrial Wi-Fi networks globally. We offer comprehensive statistics on SSID naming conventions, security practices, vendor prevalence, and geospatial distribution within these industrial networks. We highlight and discuss the critical security risks associated with Wi-Fi integration in operationally sensitive industrial environments. We outline actionable best practices designed to enhance the security posture of wireless-enabled industrial systems. Through these contributions, our research establishes a baseline for understanding real-world Wi-Fi integration into industrial infrastructure and aims to stimulate essential future research into its security implications.

The rest of this paper is organized as follows. Section 2 details the data collection framework. Section 3 analyzes the compiled dataset. Section 4 discusses the security implications of Wi-Fi integration in industrial settings. Section 5 outlines best practices for strengthening the security posture of wireless-enabled industrial systems. Section 6 summarizes the study's limitations. The last section concludes and identifies potential avenues for future research.

## 2   Data Collection

To empirically assess global industrial Wi-Fi deployments, we designed and implemented a systematic data collection framework utilizing the WiGLE API [33], as illustrated in Fig. 1.

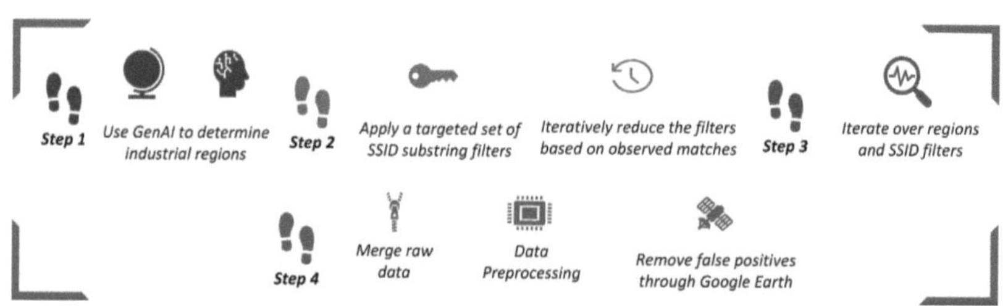


**Fig. 1.** Workflow for identifying industrial wireless networks.

***Step 1 (Region selection):*** Our initial step involved compiling a list of 264 industrially significant regions worldwide. Each region is precisely defined by a geographic bounding box, using latitude and longitude coordinates, as depicted in Fig. 3. Region selection was facilitated by an AI-assisted process utilizing a Large Language Model (LLM), specifically ChatGPT Plus. This LLM leveraged its advanced analytical capabilities to synthesize insights from open-source intelligence, infrastructure datasets, and industrial geography literature, enabling the identification of global hotspots of industrial activity. Our selection criteria prioritized areas with significant manufacturing zones, logistics hubs, industrial ports, and energy infrastructure. To validate the LLM-generated list, we cross-referenced a sample of the selected regions with OpenStreetMap (OSM) and Environmental Systems Research Institute (ESRI) land-cover references [34] and industrial cluster maps [10]. Each selected region was then encoded into a JSON registry, detailing its *code_name*, geographic bounding box (*lat_min*, *lat_max*, *lon_min*, *lon_max*), and a brief justification for its inclusion. The specific prompt used to generate these regions is provided in Prompt 2.

> *Generate a JSON file containing geographic bounding boxes for approximately 200–300 industrially significant cities or regions around the world. Each entry should include the region's name (code_name), latitude and longitude bounds (lat_min, lat_max, lon_min, lon_max), and a brief explanation (reason) of its industrial relevance. The regions should cover diverse countries and industries, including manufacturing, electronics, automotive, and logistics hubs.*

**Fig. 2.** Prompt for generating industrial regions.

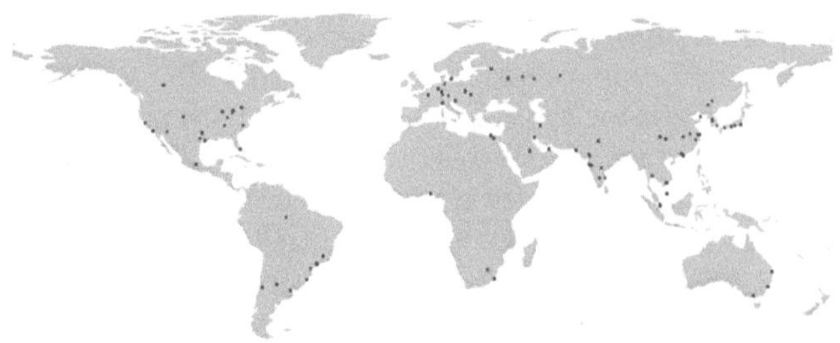

**Fig. 3.** Search regions. The scanned locations cover a geographical area totaling $\approx$ $75.000 km^2$.

***Step 2 (SSID Filtering):*** Subsequently, we employed a targeted set of 24 SSID substring filters to increase the likelihood of identifying industrial wireless networks from the initial regions dataset, acquired in the first step. These filters were meticulously designed to match SSIDs commonly associated with ICS, OT infrastructure, and vendor-specific deployments. Specifically, the list included manufacturer names such as *Siemens*, *Rockwell*, and *Yokogawa*; control system terminology such as *PLC*, *SCADA*, *HMI*, and *Historian*; and infrastructure-related keywords like *substation, power grid,* and *pump station.* The full list of SSID filters is presented in 1. The SSID filters were iteratively refined based on observed matches during the region scanning process. This refinement allowed us to prioritize high-yield filters and eliminate ambiguous or low-signal terms, thereby improving both the precision and efficiency of the data collection pipeline. For instance, filters such as *OPC Server, Historian,* and *General Electric* were eliminated early in the scanning phase due to consistently low or zero match rates across regions. Other filters, like *site* and *HMI* initially yielded high match counts but were discarded at a later stage after closer manual inspection of intermediate results. This inspection revealed their frequent use in non-industrial contexts, significantly reducing their specificity and relevance to the industrial domain.

**Table 1.** SSID substring filters used to identify industrial wireless networks. The character '%' is used as a wildcard. Filters marked with $^{(\dagger)}$ were removed due to near-zero match rates, while those marked with $^{(*)}$ were removed due to a predominant proportion of irrelevant matches.

| ICS/OT Terminology | Infrastructure | Vendors |
|---|---|---|
| %PLC%, %SCADA%, %process%control%$^{(\dagger)}$, %control%system%, %OPC%server%$^{(\dagger)}$, %Historian%$^{(\dagger)}$, %Workstation%, %HMI%$^{(*)}$ | %substation%, %power%grid%, %pump%station%$^{(\dagger)}$, %power%station%$^{(\dagger)}$, %waste%water%$^{(\dagger)}$, %site%$^{(*)}$, %plant%, %PCU%$^{(*)}$ | %Honeywell%, %Schneider%, %Rockwell%$^{(\dagger)}$, %Emerson%Electric%$^{(\dagger)}$, %General%Electric%$^{(\dagger)}$, %Fortinet%, %Yokogawa%, %Siemens% |

***Step 3 (API querying):*** To adhere to WiGLE's daily API request limit (100 requests per day), our collection script iterated through each region-filter pair, paginating results using the API's *searchAfter* parameter. We checkpointed progress with a JSON state file, allowing the resumption of data collection across multiple days. Each successful query returned up to 100 networks per page, which were then stored in structured CSV files, organized by region and filter. Specifically, algorithm 1 presents the approach for collecting Wi-Fi network data using the WiGLE API. The input consists of the list of predefined geographic regions $\mathcal{R}$, as identified in Step 1; a set of SSID-based heuristic filters $\mathcal{F}$ representing industrial naming patterns, as pinpointed in Step 2; and a daily query limit $Q$ imposed by the API. The algorithm begins by initializing the query counter and resuming from previously saved progress, represented by region index $i$, filter index $j$, and the pagination token $s$; in case the query results in more than 100 entries. For each selected region $r_i$ and filter $f_j$, the algorithm performs paginated API queries until no more results are available or the query budget $Q$ is exhausted. Each query returns a batch $\mathcal{B}$ of network metadata, which is appended to an output dataset $\mathcal{D}$. Once all pages for a given region-filter combination are retrieved, the corresponding results $\mathcal{D}_{i,j}$ are saved to a CSV file.

---

**Algorithm 1:** Industrial Wi-Fi Network Collection via WiGLE API

---

**Input**: List of regions $\mathcal{R} = \{r_1, r_2, \ldots, r_n\}$, SSID filters
$\qquad \mathcal{F} = \{f_1, f_2, \ldots, f_m\}$, max queries $Q$
**Output**: CSV files $\mathcal{D}$ containing network scan results

1  Initialize query counter $q \leftarrow 0$;
2  Load progress indices $i \in [1, n]$, $j \in [1, m]$, and search token $s$;
3  **while** $q < Q$ *and* $i \leq n$ **do**
4  $\quad$ Let $r_i$ be the current region and $f_j$ be the current filter;
5  $\quad$ **repeat**
6  $\quad\quad$ Send API query with $(r_i, f_j, s)$;
7  $\quad\quad$ Receive results $\mathcal{B}$ and update $s$;
8  $\quad\quad$ Append $\mathcal{B}$ to dataset $\mathcal{D}$;
9  $\quad\quad$ $q \leftarrow q + 1$;
10 $\quad$ **until** *search token* $s = \emptyset$ *or* $q \geq Q$;
11 $\quad$ Save $\mathcal{D}_{i,j}$ to file;

---

***Step 4 (Data preprocessing):*** The raw scan results were initially stored hierarchically, with each geographic region in a dedicated directory and each SSID filter yielding a separate CSV file. Once the scanning phase was complete, all CSV files were merged into a unified dataset, resulting in 43,188 candidate industrial wireless networks, as detailed in Table 2. We then performed an initial data-cleaning process. This involved deduplication of identical entries, removal of false positives based on keyword heuristics (e.g., *guest, home, cafe*), exclusion of records with invalid or empty location or SSID fields, filtering out networks with last visited timestamps before 2020, and elimination of spatial near-duplicates using a 1 km radius threshold via Haversine distance, which is used for determining distances between points on Earth's surface. Regarding the latter, we acknowledge that distinct WiFi networks with identical SSIDs may exist within 1km in dense industrial areas, leading to false negatives; this threshold was selected to strike a balance between redundant detections and data granularity.

**Table 2.** Dataset reduction process through preprocessing and manual validation. $\Delta$ indicates the number of entries removed at the respective step.

| Stage | Entries | $\Delta$ Entries | Retention Rate | |
| --- | --- | --- | --- | --- |
|  |  |  | Step (%) | Total (%) |
| Raw merged dataset | 43,188 | – | – | – |
| Preprocessed dataset | 11,973 | 31,215 | 27.7% | 27.7% |
| Final dataset | 1,087 | 10,886 | 9.1% | 2.6% |

Observe from Table 2 that this preprocessing step reduced the initial data to 11,973 entries. To further eliminate false positives, we then manually verified the coordinates of each remaining entry using Google Earth. This enabled manual visual verification of the physical context of each wireless network, excluding those located in residential, commercial, or otherwise non-industrial environments. Only networks situated within visible industrial zones, such as factories, substations, energy facilities, or logistics hubs, were retained in the final dataset [11]. Our refined dataset ultimately contained 1,087 high-confidence industrial wireless networks, as also detailed in Table 2. The substantial reduction from the raw dataset can be attributed to multiple factors. Firstly, the raw data contained a large number of duplicate records, likely due to repeated scanning activities, overlapping coverage, or multiple users registering the same Wi-Fi network in the WiGLE database. Secondly, numerous entries were false positives retrieved by the SSID filtering heuristics. Thirdly, several entries lacked valid or complete information, including missing SSIDs, invalid geolocation coordinates, or outdated timestamps predating our threshold year. Finally, during manual verification through Google Earth, a significant number of entries were identified as being situated in residential, commercial, or non-industrial areas.

Nevertheless, the fact that 9.1% of the preprocessed data represent high-confidence industrial networks suggests that systems commonly associated with OT environments are now more frequently exposed to external connectivity. Although this proportion may appear negligible, it is crucial to recognize that our dataset represents only a limited snapshot of the global industrial landscape; the scanned locations cover a constrained geographical area totaling $\approx 75.000 km^2$. Additionally, the heuristic filters employed for SSID selection have inherent limitations, as they may fail to capture networks whose naming conventions do not align with predefined industrial keywords or are expressed in native languages, thus obscuring their identification. Furthermore, a substantial number of additional industrial wireless networks probably exist that were not detected. These might not be registered in public databases such as WiGLE, could be intentionally named using ambiguous or misleading SSIDs to conceal their presence and evade detection, or may be hidden due to private configurations, such as SSID cloaking, a practice that constitutes security by obscurity and should generally be avoided for robust protection. Consequently, the actual extent of wireless network proliferation in industrial settings is likely to be significantly greater than suggested by the available data [13, 16].

## 3   Analysis

We analyzed 1,087 industrial Wi-Fi networks from our dataset [11] to assess their current state. Specifically, we measured the frequency of SSID filters to identify which industrial terms most consistently indicated a relevant network. We also analyzed the distribution of security protocols to evaluate the security practices employed in industrial Wi-Fi deployments and identified the most common hardware vendors by analyzing MAC address prefixes. Finally, we mapped country-level retention rates to reveal regional patterns in industrial Wi-Fi visibility.

## 3.1   SSID Naming Conventions

Figure 4 illustrates the most frequent SSID filters identified in the dataset, revealing common naming conventions in industrial Wi-Fi. PLC leads with 32.0%, followed closely by *plant* at 30.1%. Other notable keywords are *Siemens* (21.2%), *Workstation* (6.1%), *Honeywell* (5.7%), and *SCADA* (4.8%). Keywords with smaller contributions are omitted for improved readability. The prevalence of these terms shows that industrial SSIDs often explicitly refer to OT (e.g., *PLC*, *SCADA*), infrastructure (e.g., plant, workstation), or vendors (e.g., *Siemens*, *Honeywell*).

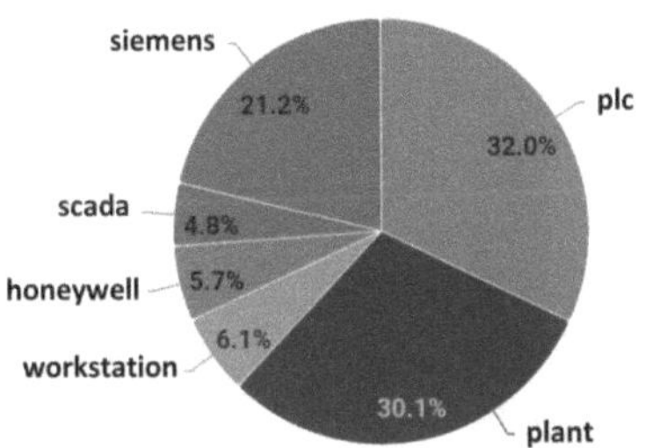


**Fig. 4.** Keyword distribution in the dataset. Keywords representing less than 3% are excluded.

Figure 5 shows satellite imagery of industrial sites where Wi-Fi networks with SSIDs containing keywords like *Siemens*, *SCADA*, *PLC*, and *Plant* were detected. These are not generic or low-sensitivity environments; each location in subfigures 5a to 5d represents a Critical Infrastructure (CI) site. The clear presence of identifiable Wi-Fi infrastructure at these sites indicates that wireless technologies have indeed expanded into sectors traditionally known for tightly controlled networks and securely segregated OT ecosystems. While this direct labeling might be useful for internal management and system identification, it may also suggest a lack of security awareness. For internal operations, descriptive SSIDs can indeed simplify network administration, troubleshooting, and asset tracking. They help personnel quickly identify and connect to the correct network segment, especially in complex industrial facilities with numerous devices and varying access needs. This can improve operational efficiency and reduce human error. However, this convenience comes at a severe security cost. Such naming conventions enable heuristic filtering and facilitate a straightforward classification of industrially-relevant modules, presenting a clear information leakage vector, and exposing system roles and technologies to passive observers. In essence, these SSIDs are broadcasting valuable reconnaissance information to anyone within wireless range, whether they are a casual passerby or a dedicated malicious actor. The same methodology followed in this study can be weaponized by adversaries to quickly identify and target high-value ICS or OT environments. Furthermore, this specific approach to SSID naming highlights a broader issue:

the absence of standardized security guidelines addressing SSID anonymization or the avoidance of disclosing critical system components, roles, or vendor identities.

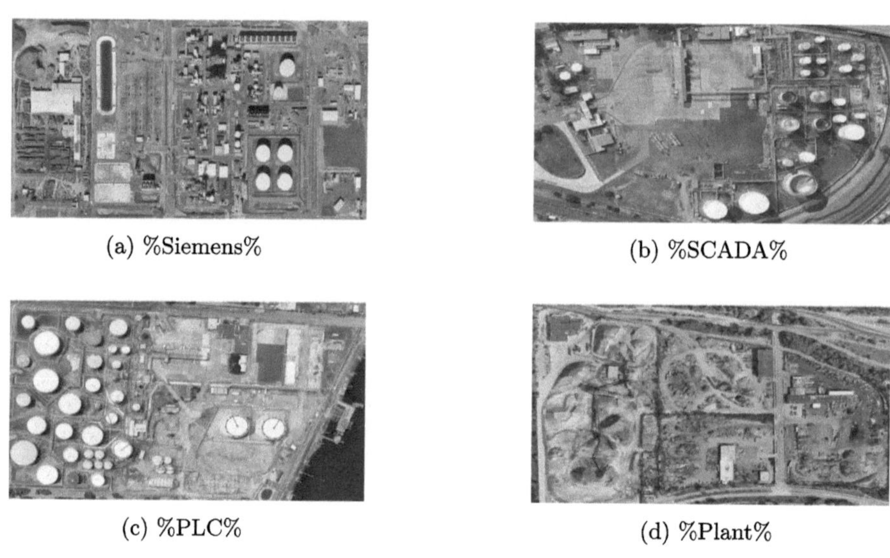

(a) %Siemens%　　　　　(b) %SCADA%

(c) %PLC%　　　　　(d) %Plant%

**Fig. 5.** Screenshots of detected Wi-Fi networks associated with industrial systems.

## 3.2  Security Protocols

Figure 6 illustrates the distribution of security protocols employed by the identified industrial Wi-Fi networks. The vast majority (73.9%) utilize WPA2, while a non-negligible portion still relies on obsolete, less secure protocols: WEP (6.3%) and WPA (5.8%). Interestingly, for 10% of the identified Wi-Fi networks, the security protocol was not registered. This could be attributed to inherent limitations of passive scanning or occasional gaps in metadata collection. Further investigation revealed that all networks identified within Russian territories were reported with an unknown security protocol. This strongly suggests that WiGLE may intentionally suppress encryption information for certain regions, possibly due to security concerns or adherence to local data policies. Finally, the most modern Wi-Fi security certification, WPA3, accounts for a mere 1.9% of deployments, and networks with no security represent 2.0% of the dataset.

Outdated Wi-Fi encryption protocols present serious security vulnerabilities, especially when used in CI environments. For example, the obsolete WEP is highly insecure, relying on short, repeating initialization vectors and a critically flawed implementation of the RC4 cipher [20]. This makes its keys extremely

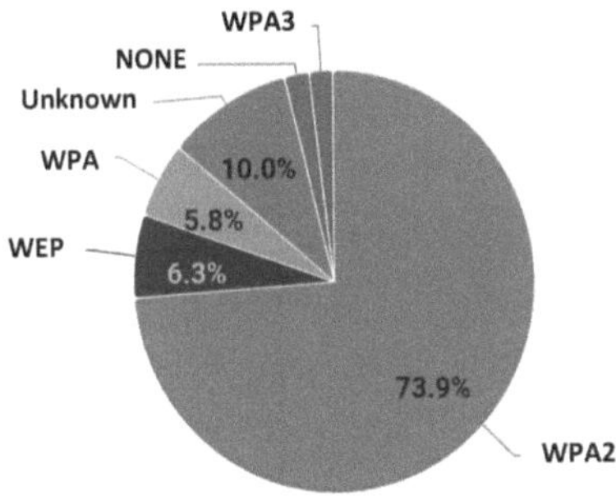


**Fig. 6.** Distribution of Wi-Fi security types in the dataset. Types with less than 3% are not labeled.

vulnerable and easy to crack, often in a matter of seconds with readily available tools. Similarly, WPA also has known weaknesses. While the 4-way handshake itself is openly exchanged during connection, Pre-Shared Key (WPA-PSK) networks are susceptible to offline dictionary/brute-force attacks if a weak passphrase is used. An attacker can capture this handshake and then attempt to crack the passphrase offline without needing further interaction with the network, effectively gaining access. A critical flaw in WPA-PSK is its lack of forward secrecy: if the pre-shared key is ever compromised, all past recorded traffic can be decrypted, as session keys are directly derived from this static key. Beyond passphrase cracking, the Temporal Key Integrity Protocol (TKIP) protocol has also been found partially vulnerable to cryptographic attacks. These vulnerabilities allow attackers to decrypt packets by exploiting weaknesses in TKIP's Message Integrity Code (MIC) and key scheduling, recovering portions of encrypted traffic which, while differing from a full key recovery, still allows for significant information disclosure [25,27]. Furthermore, attackers can inject forged frames by crafting and injecting malicious data packets into a WPA/TKIP network, potentially leading to Denial-of-Service (DoS) or other undesirable actions, even without fully recovering the encryption key. Practical attacks against TKIP have also demonstrated the ability to recover the Michael message authentication key in minutes, enabling further exploitation.

Even WPA2 has been proven vulnerable under certain conditions. A prominent example is the Key Reinstallation Attacks (KRACK) [28,29], which targeted a protocol-level design flaw in the WPA2 4-way handshake. Another notable vulnerability is Kr00k (CVE-2019–15126), which revealed that many Wi-Fi devices implementing WPA2 (and WPA) could transmit certain data frames unencrypted under specific circumstances, such as after disassociation or deauthentication. Furthermore, WPA2-PSK networks, much like their WPA counterparts, remain susceptible to offline dictionary/brute-force attacks if a weak passphrase is used, as the 4-way handshake can be captured and cracked offline. Critically, WPA2-PSK also lacks forward secrecy, meaning that if the pre-shared key is ever compromised, all past recorded encrypted traffic can be decrypted. Moreover, the study in [15] provides a real-world attack dataset against WPA2-

enabled Wi-Fi networks. This dataset highlights vulnerabilities such as the absence of Protected Management Frames (PMF) (an optional feature in WPA2, mandated in WPA3), which enables deauthentication and disassociation attacks leading to DoS. The same work also demonstrates authentication flooding and fake access point injections, often facilitating Man-in-the-Middle (MitM) scenarios. Additionally, it reveals how MAC spoofing and replay attacks exploit insufficient frame protection, further highlighting how active adversaries can interfere with Wi-Fi operations, even without directly breaking cryptographic keys. Altogether, relying on outdated or misconfigured Wi-Fi security (WEP, WPA, or even unpatched WPA2) leaves networks open to well-documented attacks. These range from classic WEP key-cracking tools to sophisticated handshake manipulations, all of which can lead to unauthorized network access and traffic manipulation by a variety of threat actors.

In this context, WPA3 was designed to address many of the inherent flaws of its predecessors. Specifically, for WPA3-Personal, typically used in Small Office/Home Office (SOHO) environments, a key improvement is the Simultaneous Authentication of Equals (SAE), an authentication and key exchange method derived from the Dragonfly Key Exchange (defined in RFC 7664) and incorporated into the IEEE 802.11-2016 and onwards standards. WPA3-Enterprise deployments continue to utilize 802.1X/EAP for authentication. Notably, SAE is resistant to offline dictionary attacks and provides forward secrecy. WPA3 also imposes frame protection through the mandatory use of PMF, introduced with the 802.11w amendment, and mandates the use of modern cryptographic algorithms. However, despite its security enhancements, WPA3 is not without weaknesses. Recent studies have uncovered several critical vulnerabilities in both its design and Access Point (AP) firmware implementations. Importantly, early analyses of SAE revealed protocol-level weaknesses [31], including DoS via resource exhaustion, and downgrade attacks in WPA3's transitional mode, forcing fallback to WPA2. These analyses also exposed side-channel leaks enabling offline password cracking. Subsequent studies demonstrated that WPA3 networks remain vulnerable to various DoS vectors. For instance, an adversary can overload APs by exploiting the CPU-intensive SAE exchange [5], or disrupt communications by injecting spoofed unprotected control frames, such as *Block-Ack* frames [6]. Implementation flaws further compound these issues. The work in [12], for example, exposed numerous bugs in management frame handling code that could be exploited to crash or destabilize devices through fuzzing, even in the presence of WPA3's mandatory PMF mechanism [4]. Even WPA3's newer features have shown vulnerabilities. The SAE-PK mechanism, for instance, can leak its private key if a weak random number generator is used and is susceptible to timeâĂŞmemory trade-off attacks (rainbow tables), allowing efficient offline recovery of the password [30]. Finally, fundamental design oversights in Wi-Fi's frame queuing were found to bypass WPA3 encryption entirely. Specifically, an attacker can trick an AP into sending buffered frames encrypted with an all-zero (null) key or plaintext, and can also force client disconnections via manipulated queue control flags [22].

## 3.3   Vendor Landscape

Analysis of Wi-Fi AP manufacturers revealed prominent vendors, identified by matching the MAC address prefixes (OUIs) of the detected networks with a MAC vendor lookup database [18]. As illustrated in Fig. 7, well-known vendors such as Cisco (5.5%), Netgear (4.6%), and TP-Link (4.0%) appear most frequently in the dataset, indicating a significant footprint in industrial and enterprise wireless infrastructure. Notably, the presence of Siemens AG (3.5%) among the top manufacturers further confirms the dataset's industrial relevance, given Siemens' strong association with automation and control systems. Vendors such as D-Link, Ubiquiti, and Linksys also contribute sizable shares. Interestingly, 24.3% of the identified AP devices are associated with unknown vendors. This suggests that their manufacturers may not be registered in the MAC vendor lookup API, or that the address blocks used are either anonymized, unassigned, or derived from obscure or non-standard hardware sources.

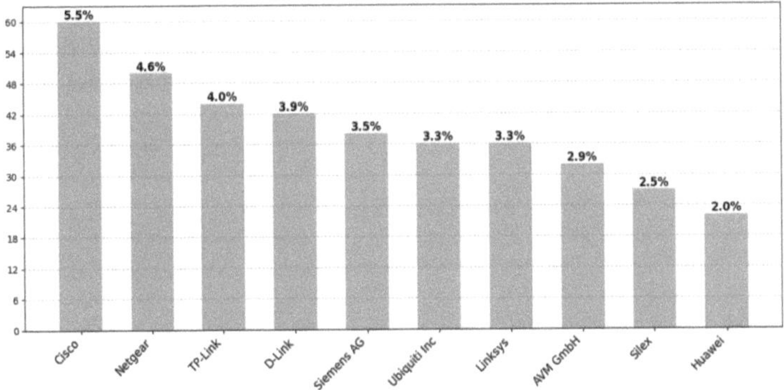


**Fig. 7.** Top 10 AP manufacturers in the dataset.

Interestingly, SOHO vendors like Huawei (2.0%), Xiaomi, and Zyxel are underrepresented in the dataset, suggesting that commodity-grade hardware is – as anticipated – less common in industrial contexts. In contrast, although vendors like Netgear, TP-Link, and D-Link are widely recognized for their SOHO product lines, they also offer a broad range of enterprise-grade APs. This trend reflects a clear preference for more robust, managed, and security-capable hardware in critical environments. Enterprise APs offer crucial advantages over SOHO ones, including centralized management, stronger security features like WPA3-Enterprise, 802.1X authentication, and certificate-based access control, higher reliability under varying workloads, enhanced environmental durability, and long-term firmware support. These features are essential for maintaining security and operational continuity in complex industrial environments. Despite their general scarcity, the presence of SOHO vendors in the dataset suggests that these devices may be frequently repurposed for industrial environments. This could reflect cost-driven decisions, uninformed legacy deployments, or overlay network expansions implemented without centralized oversight. In many cases, such deployments offer short-term convenience but typically lack the hardened security features and lifecycle guarantees of enterprise solutions. This potentially introduces vulnerabilities and increases the risk of misconfiguration, outdated firmware, or insufficient access control, all of which are critical concerns in CI settings.

## 3.4 Geospatial Distribution

Figure 8 illustrates the geospatial distribution of the dataset, with countries shaded based on the percentage of industrial Wi-Fi networks retained after the filtering steps outlined in Sect. 2. The white (unshaded) regions on the map were intentionally omitted from the search due to their relatively lower industrial relevance and WiGLE's daily API request restrictions, as discussed in the data collection process in Sect. 2. We opt to visualize the percentage of retained industrial networks relative to each region's preprocessed data, rather than relative to the absolute count; using global-normalized values would disanalogously highlight countries with larger scan volumes, potentially obscuring insights from smaller or less-scanned regions.

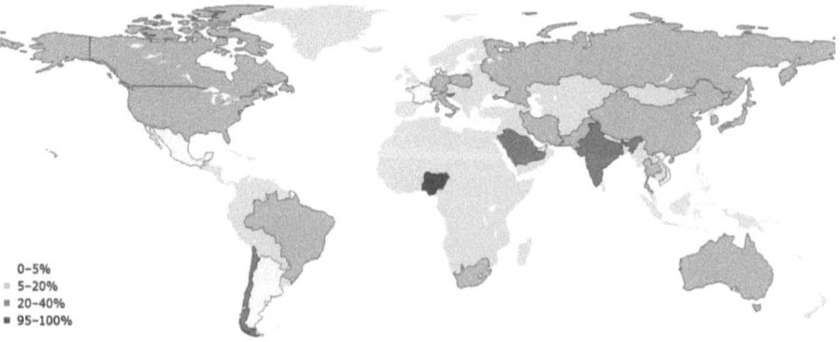


**Fig. 8.** Heatmap of dataset distribution by country. Countries are shaded by the percentage of industrial Wi-Fi networks retained in the final dataset, relative to the preprocessed dataset.

Among the analyzed countries, Nigeria (100%), Saudi Arabia (33.3%), Chile (23.4%), and India (20.6%) show some of the highest retention percentages, all exceeding 20%. This suggests a strong match between their wireless industrial network footprints and the keyword-based filtering heuristics we used. Most of the regions searched, including the United States (9.3%), Brazil (8.1%), Australia (10.4%), and major European and Asian industrial economies, fall within the 5âĂŞ20% range. These moderate retention levels might indicate a broader diversity in SSID naming or a larger proportion of non-industrial networks within the scanned areas. On a positive note, this trend could also suggest more cautious

SSID labeling practices in these regions, discouraging the exposure of sensitive operational details in network identifiers. Finally, a subset of countries, including France (0.3%), Vietnam (1.47%), Argentina (1.97%), Denmark (2.04%), the United Arab Emirates (2.44%), and Mexico (3.09%), display retention percentages below 5%. These results may point to less descriptive SSID conventions in industrial deployments, a lower density of industrial Wi-Fi infrastructure within the scanned regions, or more stringent anonymization practices. Additionally, the use of SSIDs in native languages or non-English scripts could hinder detection by keyword-based filtering heuristics. In some cases, like France, the near absence of identifiable industrial SSIDs may also reflect stricter adherence to operational security policies.

## 4   Security Implications

The integration of Wi-Fi into industrial systems significantly expands the attack surface, and the known wireless vulnerabilities are especially concerning in converged IT/OT environments like ICS and smart manufacturing. For example, in a scenario where factory engineers use Wi-FiâĂŞenabled tablets for Human-Machine Interface/Supervisory Control and Data Acquisition (HMI/SCADA) access, an attacker can remotely crack a weakly protected industrial Wi-Fi network. This allows them to pivot directly into the control system and gain network access to field control devices such as Programmable Logic Controllers (PLC) and Remote Terminal Units (RTU). Even if facilities are well-isolated and segmented, e.g., following the well-known Purdue Enterprise Reference Architecture (PERA), insecure Wi-Fi can still introduce a backdoor. Specifically, corporate or contractor Wi-Fi networks that are bridged (even indirectly) to the plant network become attractive targets. Adversaries can compromise a poorly secured corporate WLAN, subsequently tunneling into the control system environment. Similarly, an initial compromise on the business logistics layer through a wireless link can enable malicious actors to move laterally [24] within the corporate network and eventually reach the lower layers of field control and devices.

Similarly, nearest-neighbor attacks involve exploiting devices or networks located in proximity to industrial sites. In settings like industrial parks, shared facilities, or urban sites, adjacent Wi-Fi networks may expose attack paths. If these neighboring systems are dual-homed, a compromise can serve as a bridge into otherwise segmented environments. Even without direct connections, attackers may leverage signal leakage or misconfigured association behaviors to laterally traverse network boundaries and bypass perimeter defenses. Recall that this tactic was exemplified by the Russian APT28 group during cyber operations linked to the Ukraine invasion, where attackers breached internal networks by first compromising Wi-Fi-connected systems in adjacent offices, exploiting proximity and poor isolation to evade defenses [32].

This is exacerbated by the fact that many industrial protocols such as MODBUS, DNP3, and proprietary fieldbus protocols lack built-in encryption or authentication; they often send commands in cleartext and trust the network's integrity. Consequently, once an attacker is on the ICS network, they can intercept, spoof, or alter control commands and sensor readings with relative ease. For example, an attacker in a MitM scenario could inject false sensor data or send unauthorized control signals, potentially disrupting the physical process. This is because, unlike IT systems which often employ robust transport-layer security, many OT devices still have predictable sequence numbers and other weaknesses that make MitM attacks feasible, meaning that a Wi-Fi MitM can be leveraged to cause real process manipulation. Indeed, even passive eavesdropping on an ICS Wi-Fi network can leak sensitive operational data. For instance, decrypting wireless traffic might reveal sensor measurements or control setpoints that could enable an attacker to perform more damaging actions.

These concerns have not gone unnoticed by leading industrial vendors, many of whom have acknowledged that their products are vulnerable to Wi-FiâĂŞbased attacks [2,23]. For example, Cisco has confirmed that its 829 Industrial Integrated Services Routers and Industrial Wireless 3700 Series APs are susceptible to the KRACK vulnerability [28]. Similarly, Rockwell Automation's Stratix 5100 APs, along with several Siemens product lines such as SCALANCE, SIMATIC, RUGGEDCOM, and SINAMICS, have been identified as affected. In this context, Cisco issued a technical report [8] emphasizing the security risks posed by wireless connectivity in ICS. It outlines how attackers can exploit weaknesses in wireless networks to gain unauthorized access to essential components such as SCADA systems and PLCs, potentially jeopardizing the integrity and reliability of industrial operations. In the same vein, Kaspersky Lab ICS CERT has extensively documented how vulnerabilities in wireless protocols can be exploited in attacks targeting industrial systems [3]. Overall, the security implications of outdated Wi-Fi protections in OT environments extend significantly beyond passive threats like eavesdropping or data theft, as detailed in Sect. 3.2. They introduce the concrete possibility of attackers triggering physical disruptions or safety incidents by exploiting wireless links in converged IT/OT networks. Therefore, safeguarding against these threats necessitates maintaining strong, up-to-date wireless configurations and eliminating deprecated protocols. Put differently, proactively securing wireless communication is a foundational requirement for preserving both operational continuity and the safety of physical processes.

## 5    Best Practices

This section outlines best practices that can be employed to reduce attack surfaces and promote the safe integration of wireless technologies into CI environments, drawing from well-known standards such as NIST SP 800-53, NIST SP 800-82, and IEC 62443.

**Descriptive SSIDs:** Industrial entities should refrain from using SSIDs that could reveal sensitive information like vendor names, component types, or facility identifiers. Instead, they should employ randomized or neutral SSIDs, following anonymization practices to reduce the risk of passive reconnaissance. This approach makes wardriving and other passive surveillance techniques less likely to yield actionable intelligence for adversaries. Such obfuscation aligns with the operational security (OPSEC) measures described in NIST SP 800-53, which aim to minimize information leakage and increase the effort required for network fingerprinting or targeted intrusion attempts.

**Centralized management and monitoring:** Wi-Fi deployments in industrial ecosystems should leverage enterprise-level APs, which typically offer centralized management capabilities. This enables continuous visibility into network operations, facilitates real-time monitoring, and ensures consistent enforcement of security policies across all connected devices. In such industrial settings, where availability is paramount, these features are critical for maintaining compliance, detecting unauthorized access attempts, and promptly isolating compromised network segments. Equally important, integration with Security Information and Event Management (SIEM) modules can further enhance situational awareness and incident response readiness.

**Network segmentation:** Industrial networks should be segmented to isolate OT systems from general IT traffic. This separation minimizes the risk of lateral movement attempts. Even when Wi-Fi connectivity is required in the OT segment it should be provisioned on dedicated, access-controlled Virtual Local Area Networks (VLANs) that enforce strict traffic isolation. Additionally, wirelessly accessible OT-specific segments should be subject to tailored firewall rules, role-based access controls, and continuous monitoring to ensure minimal exposure to the uppermost layers of the corporate network, aligning with security frameworks such as IEC 62443 and NIST SP 800-82, which emphasize defense-in-depth strategies in industrial environments.

**Audits and penetration testing:** Security assessments, including Wi-Fi penetration tests, should be periodically conducted to ensure deployed wireless infrastructure aligns with current security policies and industry standards. Penetration testing can uncover vulnerabilities that may not be evident through routine checks. Additionally, site surveys using spectrum analysis tools can detect unintended signal propagation beyond physical perimeters, mitigating risks such as eavesdropping or unauthorized device associations. These routine assessments also verify that device and firmware hygiene is maintained and deprecated configurations are removed.

**Personnel awareness:** Operators and administrators of industrial systems should undergo targeted training focused specifically on wireless security, with an emphasis on Wi-Fi-related threats. Beyond theoretical knowledge gained from tabletop exercises, organizations should adopt practical training methods, such as cyber ranges [14] and hands-on labs, to simulate real-world attacks. This helps personnel develop the technical skills and situational awareness necessary to identify Wi-Fi-related vulnerabilities. By cultivating wireless-specific expertise, organizations enhance their frontline defenses and ensure that critical systems operators can confidently secure and manage Wi-Fi infrastructure in industrial environments.

**Physical exposure and signal leakage:** Physical security controls and radio containment techniques should be employed to restrict Wi-Fi signal propagation beyond the boundaries of industrial facilities. This includes the use of directional or low-gain antennas, strategic AP placement, and physical barriers. Limited signal leakage minimizes the risk of unauthorized access or passive reconnaissance by adversaries positioned near the facility. In addition, periodic wireless site surveys should be conducted to identify areas of excessive signal bleed or shadow zones, allowing for adjustments that optimize both security and performance.

## 6   Limitations

While the analysis presented in Sect. 3 offers meaningful insights into the state of industrial Wi-Fi deployments and the industry's transition towards IT-based infrastructure, several limitations must be acknowledged. First, the dataset was compiled through a selective and heuristic-based querying process via the WiGLE API, constrained by daily request limits and guided by industrial relevance. Naturally, this approach narrows the scope of coverage, excluding regions deemed less relevant and potentially overlooking industrial deployments that do not match the applied SSID heuristics. Second, the spatial distribution of the data is uneven. Even within countries included in the data collection process, the search was limited to specific cities or known industrial hubs rather than offering national coverage. This localized focus, while useful for targeting high-density industrial zones, limits the generalizability of observed trends and may bias results toward regions with higher visibility, scanning activity, or more extensively documented infrastructure.

Third, the analysis relies heavily on SSID-based heuristics and MAC address prefixes for filtering and vendor classification, respectively. While these techniques are easy to implement, they can also be brittle. Specifically, industrial networks using non-descriptive SSIDs, native language labels, or obfuscated naming schemes may evade detection. Similarly, MAC prefixes from unregistered or ambiguous vendors may be misclassified or excluded. Finally, the collected data reflects only data that has been passively observed and uploaded to WiGLE. This introduces further bias stemming from who performs the data collection, when and where it occurs, what scanning devices are used, and which devices and networks are visible during scanning. Keeping these limitations in mind, the results should be interpreted as indicative of observable trends in industrial Wi-Fi deployment rather than as comprehensive or globally representative findings. Additionally, it is important to emphasize that the core contribution of this paper is not to provide exhaustive global coverage, but rather to demonstrate that Wi-Fi is indeed being integrated into industrial settings in the context of the ongoing IT/OT convergence. In other words, the observed trends and case studies offer empirical evidence that wireless technologies are increasingly present in operational environments traditionally characterized by wired and siloed architectures, even though the findings are shaped by the scope and constraints of the data collection process.

## 7   Conclusions

This work provides the first, to our knowledge, data-driven investigation into the real-world adoption of industrial Wi-Fi deployments using the widely recognized WiGLE database. To achieve this, we applied a thorough data collection and filtering process grounded in SSID keyword heuristics and manual validation, compiling a high-confidence dataset of 1,087 industrial wireless networks distributed across diverse regions. The results successfully substantiate the claim that wireless technologies, particularly Wi-Fi, are increasingly entering formerly air-gapped industrial environments, driven by the demands of Industry 4.0+ and the broader convergence of IT and OT infrastructures. Our analysis uncovered several key insights. First, a substantial number of industrial Wi-Fi networks use descriptive SSIDs that expose vendor names, operational roles, or infrastructure types. This facilitates potential passive reconnaissance and undermines security through information leakage. Second, while the majority of networks adopt WPA2, a concerning minority still rely on obsolete or weak security implementations associated with WEP and WPA. Third, the vendor landscape revealed a mix of enterprise and commodity-grade APs. Finally, the geospatial distribution of networks highlighted region-specific variations in SSID practices and detection visibility, possibly shaped by linguistic, policy, and deployment factors. Beyond empirical observations, this study underscores the broader security implications of deploying Wi-Fi in operationally sensitive environments. Wireless connectivity, while enhancing flexibility and efficiency, also introduces new attack vectors, including reconnaissance for network mapping and vulnerability identification, cyber-physical intrusion into control systems, lateral movement to compromise operational assets, and process disruption with potentially severe consequences for production, safety, and environmental control. These security concerns highlight the urgent need for standardized guidelines and best practices tailored to the unique profile of industrial wireless systems. Looking forward, the dataset and findings presented lay a foundation for future research, including the development of more robust and scalable scanning methodologies that go beyond SSID-based heuristics and the creation of a Wi-Fi-specialized cyber range tailored to industrial use cases.

**Acknowledgments.** This work is supported by the Research Council of Norway through the SFI Norwegian Centre for Cybersecurity in Critical Sectors (NORCICS) project no. 310105 and by the European Union through the Horizon 2020 project PERSEUS (Grant No. 101034240).

# References


1. Abedi, A., Vasisht, D.: Non-cooperative wi-fi localization & its privacy implications. In: Proceedings of the 28th Annual International Conference on Mobile Computing And Networking, pp. 570–582. MobiCom '22, Association for Computing Machinery, New York, NY, USA (2022). https://doi.org/10.1145/3495243.3560530
2. CERT, K.L.I.: Vendors confirm that industrial solutions are vulnerable to krack attacks. https://ics-cert.kaspersky.com/publications/blog/2017/11/15/ics-krack/
3. CERT, K.L.I.: Wpa2 vulnerabilities can be used to attack industrial systems. https://ics-cert.kaspersky.com/publications/blog/2017/10/18/krack/
4. Chatzoglou, E., Kambourakis, G., Kolias, C.: Empirical evaluation of attacks against IEEE 802.11 enterprise networks: the awid3 dataset. IEEE Access 9, 34188–34205 (2021). https://doi.org/10.1109/ACCESS.2021.3061609
5. Chatzoglou, E., Kambourakis, G., Kolias, C.: How is your wi-fi connection today? dos attacks on wpa3-sae. J. Inf. Secur. Appl. 64, 103058 (2022). https://doi.org/10.1016/j.jisa.2021.103058
6. Chatzoglou, E., Kampourakis, V., Kambourakis, G.: Bl0ck: paralyzing 802.11 connections through block ack frames. In: Meyer, N., Grocholewska-Czuryło, A. (eds.) ICT Systems Security and Privacy Protection, pp. 250–264. Springer Nature Switzerland, Cham (2024)
7. DarkReading: airborne drones are dropping cyber-spy exploits in the wild. https://www.darkreading.com/threat-intelligence/drones-cyber-spy-exploits-in-the-wild
8. eBook, C.I.: Industrial cybersecurity: monitoring & anomaly detection. https://www.cisco.com/c/dam/en/us/solutions/internet-of-things/cisco-cyber-vision-ebook.pdf
9. Etta, V.O., Sari, A., Imoize, A.L., Shukla, P.K., Alhassan, M.: [retracted] assessment and test-case study of wi-fi security through the wardriving technique. Mob. Inf. Syst. 2022(1), 7936236 (2022). https://doi.org/10.1155/2022/7936236
10. IAS, R.: Industrial regions: india and the world. https://compass.rauias.com/geography/industrial-regions-india-and-the-world/
11. Kampourakis, V.: Industrial wi-fi networks dataset. https://github.com/byrkam/Industrial_WiFi_dataset
12. Kampourakis, V., Chatzoglou, E., Kambourakis, G., Dolmes, A., Zaroliagis, C.: Wpaxfuzz: sniffing out vulnerabilities in wi-fi implementations. Cryptography 6(4) (2022). https://doi.org/10.3390/cryptography6040053
13. Kampourakis, V., Gkioulos, V., Katsikas, S.: A systematic literature review on wireless security testbeds in the cyber-physical realm. Comput. Secur. 133, 103383 (2023). https://doi.org/10.1016/j.cose.2023.103383
14. Kampourakis, V., Gkioulos, V., Katsikas, S.: A step-by-step definition of a reference architecture for cyber ranges. J. Inf. Secur. Appl. 88, 103917 (2025). https://doi.org/10.1016/j.jisa.2024.103917
15. Kolias, C., Kambourakis, G., Stavrou, A., Gritzalis, S.: Intrusion detection in 802.11 networks: empirical evaluation of threats and a public dataset. IEEE Commun. Surv. Tutorials 18(1), 184–208 (2016).https://doi.org/10.1109/COMST.2015.2402161
16. Li, X., Li, D., Wan, J., Vasilakos, A.V., Lai, C.F., Wang, S.: A review of industrial wireless networks in the context of industry 4.0. Wireless Netw. 23(1), 23–41 (2017). https://doi.org/10.1007/s11276-015-1133-7

17. Lindroos, S., Hakkala, A., Virtanen, S.: A systematic methodology for continuous wlan abundance and security analysis. Comput. Netw. **197**, 108359 (2021). https://doi.org/10.1016/j.comnet.2021.108359, https://www.sciencedirect.com/science/article/pii/S1389128621003479
18. MACVendors: macvendors: find mac address vendors. https://macvendors.com/
19. Mladenov, M., Erdodi, L., Smaragdakis, G.: All that glitters is not gold: uncovering exposed industrial control systems and honeypots in the wild. IEEE European Symposium on Security and Privacy (EuroS&P) (2025)
20. Paterson, K.G., Poettering, B., Schuldt, J.C.N.: Big bias hunting in amazonia: Large-scale computation and exploitation of rc4 biases (invited paper). In: Sarkar, P., Iwata, T. (eds.) Advances in Cryptology - ASIACRYPT 2014, pp. 398–419. Springer, Berlin Heidelberg, Berlin, Heidelberg (2014)
21. Schepers, D., Ranganathan, A., Vanhoef, M.: Let numbers tell the tale: measuring security trends in wi-fi networks and best practices. In: Pöpper, C., Vanhoef, M., Batina, L., Mayrhofer, R. (eds.) WiSec '21: 14th ACM Conference on Security and Privacy in Wireless and Mobile Networks, Abu Dhabi, United Arab Emirates, 28 June - 2 July, 2021, pp. 100–105. ACM (2021). https://doi.org/10.1145/3448300.3468286, https://doi.org/10.1145/3448300.3468286
22. Schepers, D., Ranganathan, A., Vanhoef, M.: Framing frames: Bypassing wi-fi encryption by manipulating transmit queues. In: 32nd USENIX Security Symposium (USENIX Security 23), pp. 53–68 (2023)
23. SecurityWeek: more industrial products at risk of krack attacks. https://www.securityweek.com/more-industrial-products-risk-krack-attacks/
24. Smiliotopoulos, C., Kambourakis, G., Kolias, C.: Detecting lateral movement: a systematic survey. Heliyon **10**(4) (2024).https://doi.org/10.1016/j.heliyon.2024.e26317
25. Tews, E., Beck, M.: Practical attacks against wep and wpa. In: Proceedings of the Second ACM Conference on Wireless Network Security, pp. 79–86. WiSec '09, Association for Computing Machinery, New York, NY, USA (2009).https://doi.org/10.1145/1514274.1514286
26. Tsiatsikas, Z., Karopoulos, G., Kambourakis, G.: Measuring the adoption of TLS encrypted client hello extension and its forebear in the wild. In: Computer Security. ESORICS 2022 International Workshops, pp. 177–190. Springer International Publishing, Cham (2023)
27. Vanhoef, M., Piessens, F.: Practical verification of wpa-tkip vulnerabilities. In: Proceedings of the 8th ACM SIGSAC Symposium on Information, Computer and Communications Security, pp. 427–436. ASIA CCS '13, Association for Computing Machinery, New York, NY, USA (2013). https://doi.org/10.1145/2484313.2484368
28. Vanhoef, M., Piessens, F.: Key reinstallation attacks: forcing nonce reuse in wpa2. In: Proceedings of the 2017 ACM SIGSAC Conference on Computer and Communications Security, pp. 1313–1328. CCS '17, Association for Computing Machinery, New York, NY, USA (2017). https://doi.org/10.1145/3133956.3134027
29. Vanhoef, M., Piessens, F.: Release the kraken: new kracks in the 802.11 standard. In: Proceedings of the 2018 ACM SIGSAC Conference on Computer and Communications Security, pp. 299–314. CCS '18, Association for Computing Machinery, New York, NY, USA (2018). https://doi.org/10.1145/3243734.3243807
30. Vanhoef, M., Robben, J.: A security analysis of wpa3-pk: Implementation and precomputation attacks. In: Pöpper, C., Batina, L. (eds.) Applied Cryptography and Network Security, pp. 217–240. Springer Nature Switzerland, Cham (2024)

31. Vanhoef, M., Ronen, E.: Dragonblood: analyzing the dragonfly handshake of wpa3 and eap-pwd. In: 2020 IEEE Symposium on Security and Privacy (SP), pp. 517–533 (2020). https://doi.org/10.1109/SP40000.2020.00031
32. Volexity: the nearest neighbor attack: how a russian apt weaponized nearby wi-fi networks for covert access. https://www.volexity.com/blog/2024/11/22/
33. WiGLE: Wigle.net: all the networks. found by everyone. https://wigle.net/
34. Yoo, C., Zhou, Y., Weng, Q.: Mapping 10-m industrial lands across 1000+global large cities, 2017–2023. Sci. Data **12**(1), 278 (2025). https://doi.org/10.1038/s41597-025-04604-w

# Using Dual Algorithm Certificates in TLS: Enabling Rapid Transition to Post-Quantum Cryptography with Backward Compatibility


Tobias Frauenschläger[(✉)][iD] and Jürgen Mottok[iD]

Laboratory for Safe and Secure Systems (LaS3), University of Applied Sciences (OTH) Regensburg, Regensburg, Germany
{tobias.frauenschlaeger,juergen.mottok}@oth-regensburg.de



**Abstract.** The deployment of Post-Quantum Cryptography (PQC) is accelerating, particularly within the *Transport Layer Security* (TLS) protocol. However, long device lifetimes and limited update capabilities in domains such as *Operational Technology* (OT) and the *Internet of Things* (IoT) hinder the adoption of PQC-based authentication, as backward compatibility with legacy devices is essential. In this work, we present a transition mechanism based on *dual algorithm certificates*, which embed cryptographic artifacts (public key and signature) of both a traditional and a post-quantum algorithm. We introduce a new negotiation mechanism for the TLS handshake that enables secure and flexible use of such certificates for peer authentication, allowing rapid PQC deployment without sacrificing interoperability. We implemented our mechanism in the WolfSSL and OpenSSL libraries and evaluated it on a resource-constrained microcontroller, demonstrating its viability for constrained OT and IoT environments.



**Keywords:** Post-Quantum Cryptography · Transport Layer Security · PQC Transition · Dual Algorithm Certificate · Backward Compatibility · Operational Technology · Internet of Things


## 1 Introduction

The deployment of *Post-Quantum Cryptography* (PQC) is on the rise. At the time of writing, for example, nearly 40 % of web traffic to the CDN Cloudflare is secured using a PQC key establishment algorithm [9]. PQC algorithms are considered a countermeasure to the threat of quantum computers, which are increasingly becoming attainable [8,17]. Hence, the standardization for PQC algorithms is already in progress for various protocols [25,43,44].

In this work, we focus on the *Transport Layer Security* (TLS) protocol, one of the most widely used protocols to establish secure communication channels, and the authentication part of its handshake, which is based on certificates and


© The Author(s), under exclusive license to Springer Nature Switzerland AG 2026
R. Laborde et al. (Eds.): ESORICS 2025, LNCS 16231, pp. 503–522, 2026.
https://doi.org/10.1007/978-3-032-16089-8_30

private keys within a *Public Key Infrastructure* (PKI). The straightforward transition of peer authentication to PQC is by replacing traditional signatures and keys (based on RSA or ECDSA) with new PQC ones. Unlike cipher suites for transport-layer protection, which are negotiated during the TLS handshake, the cryptographic algorithms used in certificates for authentication are not negotiated and must be supported in advance by both peers. Hence, all participating TLS endpoints within a PKI must support the new PQC algorithms. However, in many domains such as *Operational Technology* (OT) or *Internet of Things* (IoT), devices often feature no or only limited update capabilities, which is especially problematic considering the long mission times of devices in these domains [15]. As a result, the transition to new algorithms is thoroughly delayed to avoid disrupting compatibility with legacy devices.

However, based on the growing threat of quantum computers and also the growing regulatory requirements [27,28], the PQC transition should be carried out sooner rather than later. Consequently, transition mechanisms for such systems are required that support backward compatibility for legacy participants to enable a near-term deployment of PQC. In this paper, we expand on the concept of employing certificates that incorporate two distinct sets of cryptographic algorithms, commonly called *dual algorithm certificates*. To enable their use for peer authentication within the TLS handshake, a negotiation mechanism is required to determine how the two algorithms are utilized. The integration of dual algorithm certificates with such a negotiation mechanism facilitates the seamless deployment of PQC algorithms, ensuring compatibility with peers that lack support. This approach enables a rapid and incremental transition of OT and IoT systems. More specifically, our contributions are as follows:

1. A new negotiation mechanism for the TLS handshake is presented to enable backward-compatible usage of dual algorithm certificates for peer authentication.
2. Improved implementations are described for dual algorithm certificate support in TLS libraries, optimized for resource-constrained devices.
3. A detailed evaluation of the impact on system performance is discussed when deploying such certificates.

The remaining paper is structured as follows. In Sect. 2, we introduce necessary background and related work, with Sect. 3 focusing on dual algorithm certificates in detail. Building on that, Sect. 4 presents our improvements for using dual algorithm certificates with the new negotiation mechanism for PQC transition. Consequently, we describe our implementations in Sect. 5, followed by a discussion of our evaluation on resource-constrained devices in Sect. 6. Finally, the paper is concluded in Sect. 7.

## 2   Fundamentals and Related Work

### 2.1   Authentication in TLS 1.3

TLS 1.3, specified in RFC 8446 [36], follows a so-called *authenticated key exchange* to establish shared session secrets for secure transmission of user data.

After the initial ephemeral key exchange is conducted to generate a shared master secret, peer authentication must be performed to prevent impersonation. TLS supports server-only and mutual authentication through digital certificates. The *authenticated party* presents a certificate chain consisting of an entity certificate and a series of optional intermediate certificates, ultimately leading to a trusted root certificate (not part of the presented chain). The *authenticating party*, on the other hand, requires this root certificate as a *trust anchor* to verify the validity of the presented chain. This root certificate is typically deployed long-term through out-of-band mechanisms to the authenticating party.

To prove ownership of the presented entity certificate, the authenticated party creates a signature over a handshake transcript using its private key. This signature is then transmitted in the `CertificateVerify` message to the peer. The successful verification of this signature by the peer, together with the verification of the certificate chain, completes the one-sided authentication procedure. To trigger mutual authentication, the server sends an additional `CertificateRequest` message to the client.

TLS 1.3 defines two extensions that allow an authenticating party to advertise the list of supported algorithms for signatures in a certificate chain and for the handshake signature (`signature_algorithms`, `signature_algorithms_cert`), identified via standardized *object identifiers* (OIDs). In case the presented lists do not contain one of the algorithms the certificate chain of the authenticated party uses, the handshake is aborted. This leads to the problem that new algorithms for use in certificates can be deployed only when all participating TLS endpoints support them. In systems within domains such as OT or IoT, consisting of devices with long lifetimes of up to several years and simultaneously with no or only limited update capabilities [15], this results in an increasingly slow transition to new algorithms when no backward compatibility is available. Hence, improved transition mechanisms are required.

### 2.2  General Transition to Post-Quantum Cryptography

The transition from traditional cryptography to PQC is currently ongoing for TLS deployments, building on already standardized new algorithms. The integration of these algorithms in their pure form into TLS and PKIs is straightforward in theory: simply replace traditional keys and signatures with PQC ones, as already proposed in the standardization process [16,20,35]. However, the level of confidence in the security of PQC algorithms is currently not as profound as in traditional algorithms. This is exemplified by successful attacks against some PQC candidates [3] or the discussion related to the security strength of some algorithms [2,29]. As a result, current efforts are focused on hybrid deployments, in which a PQC algorithm ("PQ") is combined with a traditional ("T") one to form a "PQ/T" construction [10]. In practice, the integration of such hybrids under elaboration is done similarly to pure algorithms. The PQ/T constructions are handled as new standalone algorithms with unique identifiers for keys and signatures [31,34,43]. As a result, there is no need to alter the TLS messages or their flow. This approach is already widely used [1,7].

In general, the transition mechanisms presented to PQC both via hybrid constructions and in their pure form retain the problem of no backward compatibility for authentication with legacy endpoints without support for the new algorithms. In the literature, it is suggested to divide the effort for the transition to PQC into smaller steps by creating mixed certificate chains in which different algorithms are used for trust anchors and derived certificates [33]. This enables incremental deployment of new algorithms, resulting in smaller upgrades for endpoints that could be deployed more easily. However, even in this approach, all participating endpoints require upgrades to support the new algorithm.

### 2.3  Other Transition Mechanisms with Backward-Compatibility

In addition to the dual algorithm approach, there are other approaches to implement transition mechanisms to PQC for peer authentication within TLS that maintain backward compatibility. They all build upon multiple certificate chains with different algorithms which are used individually or in combination. More detailed descriptions of the different approaches can be found in the works of Scheible [37] and Lytle [26].

The simplest and already practically used approach is to deploy multiple certificate chains to endpoints with different algorithms. The authenticated party selects a suitable chain to use based on the lists within the `signature_algorithms` and `signature_algorithms_cert` extensions provided by the authenticating party. This functionality enables the incremental deployment of new algorithms without losing backward compatibility and without the need to change anything regarding TLS itself. Some TLS implementations already support this approach when provided with multiple chains (e. g., OpenSSL). However, deploying multiple certificate chains for a single endpoint is often considered a non-viable approach due to the increased management effort thereof (e. g., different validity periods, more complex revocation). Furthermore, many resource-constrained embedded devices do not support multiple chain handling, which is, however, the main target group for backward-compatible transition mechanisms. In this concept, hybrid PQ/T setups could be deployed through a chain containing a hybrid algorithm, as described in Subsect. 2.2.

In addition to selecting one of the available chains, there are approaches to using two chains at once. A new RFC draft proposes sending two chains in the TLS handshake [38]. This enables hybrid authentication using both algorithms to create two handshake signatures, which are sent in a new `DualCertificateVerify` message. Backward compatibility is achieved with a custom negotiation mechanism, which is further discussed in Subsect. 3.2. Furthermore, the concept of *nested certificates* has been proposed, which are also called *chameleon certificates* [6]. Instead of two separate certificate chains with two distinct algorithms, a delta is generated between the first and the second. With this delta, the second certificate chain can be recreated from the first one. After recreation, the second chain can be used as normal. The delta is encoded as optional extensions within the first chain, enabling endpoints without support for the feature to simply ignore it. This achieves incremental deployment with backward compatibility. The advantage is that the validation path of a chain within a TLS library is not modified, as the reconstruction logic could be processed externally. The big disadvantage of this approach is the duplicated metadata within the delta. Furthermore, the management disadvantages of multiple chains presented above remain in this design.

Another approach is proposed by Fries and Falk [14], who suggest using *attribute certificates* to attach alternative public keys and signatures to existing entity certificates. This avoids tight coupling between the original certificate and alternative cryptographic material, offering increased flexibility and cryptographic agility. Although this method allows the deployment of PQC alongside traditional algorithms without modifying the original certificate, it lacks any integration with protocols for secure communication. This lack is critical, as incorporating attribute certificates into e. g. TLS would require extensive changes to the protocol and its implementations, making practical adoption significantly more complex compared to the other approaches presented.

Although the discussed approaches offer varying degrees of backward compatibility, they often come with practical limitations such as increased management overhead, lack of TLS integration, or constraints on flexibility. To overcome these challenges, our work builds on the concept of *dual algorithm certificates*, presented in the next section.

## 3   Dual Algorithm Certificates

### 3.1   General Structure

The approach of deploying two distinct public keys and signatures within a certificate to form a *dual algorithm certificate* was originally published as a patent [46] and then specified in an RFC draft [45]. Due to raised problems with the approach (discussed at the end of this subsection), the RFC draft has expired, but the general approach was later formally standardized in the X509 standard [23]. Since 2022, the patent has also been made public without licensing requirements [21,22], allowing for broader adoption. A newer RFC draft [39] builds on this concept and proposes solutions to the problems of the initial approach, discussed below.

The second set of artifacts (i. e., public key and issuer signature) in a dual algorithm certificate is commonly referred to as *alternative*, while the original ones are considered *primary*. For storage, new extensions have been defined for the alternative public key (`SubjectAltPublicKeyInfo`), the alternative signature algorithm (`AltSignatureAlgorithm`), and the alternative signature (`AltSignatureValue`) [23, Chap. 9.8]. To guarantee backward compatibility, the extensions are marked non-critical, resulting in an endpoint without support for the feature ignoring them. This enables the rapid practical deployment of trust anchors and certificate chains with both traditional and PQC algorithms in legacy systems. As a result, legacy endpoints simply ignore the extensions and proceed with the primary artifacts, while capable peers also incorporate the alternative ones, preserving backward compatibility without breaking authentication. Furthermore, compared to chameleon certificates, duplicate information is avoided.

The use of dual algorithm certificates within a PKI closely resembles the deployment of pure certificates. The primary difference is that applications must additionally manage the alternative private key. Likewise, certificate chain verification is extended to include validation of the alternative signature for each certificate. The revocation process for individual certificates remains unchanged. However, the distribution of revocation information through CRLs and OCSP must be extended to incorporate alternative artifacts to ensure PQ/T security.

The dual algorithm approach has already been elaborated on in the literature. Fan et al. [12] extended a certificate authority to support the creation of dual algorithm certificate chains, which have then been used to verify backward compatibility in various deployments and use cases. Furthermore, Bindel et al. [4, 18] presented an integration of the approach in OpenSSL, with a limitation to the creation and verification of dual algorithm certificate chains. Scheible [37] follows a similar approach for the generation of certificate chains but extends it with the practical use of these certificates within the OPC UA protocol. Furthermore, since the patent was dedicated to the public, many tools and libraries have implemented support for the functionality [11, 32, 47].

There are three problems with this approach that stall its adoption, as noted in a "tombstone notice" added to the final revision of the expired RFC draft [45]. The first is related to the general idea of transition mechanisms based on a single certificate chain. When deploying certificates with a second algorithm, its artifacts are always transmitted between peers during the handshake, regardless of whether they are actually used or not. Considering the large sizes of PQC public keys and signatures, this can greatly influence handshake performance in some use cases [40]. For systems like the Web, which are very sensitive to degraded handshake performance but provide thorough update capabilities, this disadvantage may indeed discourage the deployment of dual algorithm certificates. However, for systems with limited update capabilities, this approach could greatly accelerate the PQC transition. Hence, a degraded handshake performance could be considered an acceptable sacrifice for increased security.

The new RFC draft mentioned above [39] improves on this problem by allowing the placement of the alternative artifacts not by value but by reference. This means that the actual artifacts are not placed in the optional extensions, but only a hash of the artifact along with an URI pointing to a location from where the artifact can be retrieved (e. g., an HTTPS server). This reduces the size of the certificate chains as the references are much smaller than the actual PQC artifacts. However, the necessary retrieval of the alternative artifacts to make use of them for authentication introduces a large set of new complexities and potential points of failure into the system (e. g., additional download process, unavailability of download server, more complex parsing), which are avoided in OT and IoT environments. Hence, we consider this by-reference approach not suitable for the use cases focused on in this work.

The other two problems with dual algorithm certificates are related to the implementation of the feature within TLS endpoints. First, the generation and verification of dual algorithm certificates require modifications to the parsing and verification logic of certificates. As this low-level part of software libraries is very susceptible to bugs and vulnerabilities, common practice is to avoid such modifications. However, in Sect. 5, we show that the scope of the required changes is limited, effectively reducing the impact of this constraint. Finally, the main disadvantage of the current specifications and implementations is the lack of negotiation mechanisms to actually use the alternative key of the entity certificate within protocols. As this is a key aspect of the transition to the new algorithm, proposed approaches are discussed in the next subsection.

## 3.2   Dual Algorithm Certificates in Protocols

Scheible demonstrates the use of dual algorithm certificates within the OPC UA protocol to authenticate peers for secure channel establishment [37]. In OPC UA, the client learns about the certificates and other security parameters of the server through the `getEndpoints` mechanism that takes place before an actual handshake [30]. Scheible uses this mechanism to negotiate the algorithm(s) used from a dual algorithm certificate. The server advertises support not only for the primary algorithm of its dual algorithm certificate but also for the PQ/T construction using both algorithms. This enables a capable client to select the hybridization, while a legacy client still uses only the primary. As a result, incremental deployment with backward compatibility is achieved.

For TLS, a similar mechanism is required to use the alternative key for the handshake signature, either instead of the primary one or together with it in a hybrid PQ/T construction. However, to the best of our knowledge, only one approach has been proposed to address this problem directly. A draft specification has been published on the IETF TLS mailing list that defines a *certificate key selection* (CKS) mechanism for TLS [42]. Following the request-response model, the authenticating party advertises a list of CKS options it supports ("only primary", "only alternative", or "both" keys) and the authenticated party returns its selected option. The signature within the CertificateVerify message is then created with the selected algorithm(s). However, the encoding of PQ/T signatures within the CertificateVerify message is not specified. If either endpoint does not support the feature, no CKS selection is negotiated, implicitly indicating that only the primary algorithm is to be used to achieve backward compatibility.

However, the CKS approach has one major disadvantage. The mechanism requires the authenticating party to know the algorithms within the dual algorithm certificate of the authenticated party prior to the actual TLS handshake. Otherwise, the authenticating party cannot properly select the CKS options to advertise, as it does not have prior knowledge of the algorithms contained in the peer's dual algorithm certificate. In practice, this may result in handshake failure followed by retries with different CKS parameters. Furthermore, this approach is contrary to existing TLS negotiation mechanisms (see Subsect. 2.1), as these are based on the advertisement of supported algorithms.

In the already mentioned RFC draft for using two certificate chains in the TLS handshake [38], a negotiation mechanism is presented following the existing scheme to advertise supported algorithms. This could, in theory, also be adapted for dual algorithm certificates. Building upon the existing `signature_algorithm` extension, a new `dual_signature_algorithms` extension is proposed. In it, the algorithms supported within the two signatures of the new DualCertificateVerify message are advertised. The absence of this new extension indicates that the functionality is not supported, resulting in the presentation of only one certificate chain for authentication. Mapping this extension to the dual algorithm certificate case, it could be used to negotiate a PQ/T hybridization in combination with the DualCertificateVerify message. However, the requirement for this new TLS message is the main disadvantage of this approach, as it necessitates extensive changes to the TLS protocol. To address this, we propose a similar but protocol-compliant negotiation mechanism for the TLS handshake that overcomes these limitations without requiring disruptive changes such as new TLS messages.

## 4    Dual Algorithm Negotiation and Transition Framework

### 4.1    Algorithm Selection and Signature Encoding

Instead of the request-response structure of the proposed CKS approach (see Subsect. 3.2), our improved negotiation mechanism to determine how the artifacts of a dual algorithm certificate should be used for peer authentication follows the design of existing TLS negotiation mechanisms. Similarly to the `signature_algorithms` and the introduced `dual_signature_algorithms` extensions, we define a new extension called `dual_alg_signature_algorithms`, sent along in the ClientHello and CertificateRequest messages. It serves two purposes:

1. Its presence indicates that the authenticating party generally supports the dual algorithm certificate functionality.
2. It may contain a list of OIDs for hybrid PQ/T constructions that are supported by the authenticating party for the handshake signature using both algorithms of a dual algorithm certificate.

Explicitly **not** included in the list of this extension are the supported standalone algorithms, as they are already present in the `signature_algorithms` extension. The authenticated party parses the lists of both extensions and determines the key(s) to use for the handshake signature. For this, the following extended selection flow is proposed:

1. Check if one of the advertised hybrid PQ/T constructions within the list of the `dual_alg_signature_algorithms` extension can be realized with the two algorithms of the installed dual algorithm entity certificate.
2. If not, check the `signature_algorithms` list for the primary algorithm and use it when present.

3. If not, scan the `signature_algorithms` list again for the alternative algorithm and use it when present.
4. If not, abort the handshake.

As the selected signature algorithm is encoded in the CertificateVerify message, there is no need for a response message like in the CKS mechanism. The flow presented ensures that hybrid PQ/T constructions are preferred, which are currently considered more secure (see Subsect. 2.2). Furthermore, this approach ensures compatibility with other simultaneous PQC deployment approaches such as PQ/T constructions directly as the sole primary algorithm in certificates [34], since these only use the `signature_algorithms` extension.

The main difference from the approach of the mentioned RFC draft for using two certificate chains in the TLS handshake [38] is the encoding of hybrid PQ/T signatures, avoiding the need for the new DualCertificateVerify message. To maximize compatibility and minimize changes to the TLS protocol, the current message structure is kept as is except for the addition of new extensions and new OIDs. Hence, the PQ/T constructions are encoded as a single signature with a unique new OID. The authenticated party computes both signatures for the handshake transcript and creates the encoded signature for placement in the CertificateVerify message, indicating the PQ/T construction through the algorithm field of the message. The authenticating party splits the two individual signatures and then verifies both using the two public keys from the dual algorithm entity certificate it received prior in the Certificate message.

### 4.2   Algorithm Transition

During the transition to PQC, dual algorithm certificates provide a flexible mechanism for interoperability. Initially, the traditional algorithm ("T") is placed in the primary artifacts, while the post-quantum algorithm ("PQ") is integrated into the alternative artifacts. As devices begin to support the new negotiation mechanism, they negotiate the use of PQ/T constructions and, eventually, PQ-only usage. In such cases, the T algorithm should no longer be advertised in the `signature_algorithms` extension to avoid unnecessary exposure. Our mechanism supports this behavior by prioritizing hybrid constructions or the alternative algorithm. The removal of the T algorithm from advertisement marks a formal step in deprecating its use.

To maintain compatibility with legacy devices lacking support for dual algorithm negotiation, the T algorithm must still be advertised when required. This can be handled dynamically, based on peer capabilities or endpoint-specific policies, enabling interoperability without weakening security for upgraded TLS peers.

If hybrid constructions are deprecated in the future while dual algorithm certificates remain in use, the `dual_alg_signature_algorithms` extension should still be sent containing an empty list. This signals support for the feature and allows the authenticated party to select the alternative algorithm from the `signature_algorithms` list. Omitting the extension entirely would prevent capability detection, potentially causing handshake failures between compatible peers.

For permanently non-upgradable devices, a more efficient deployment strategy involves issuing traditional-only entity certificates in parallel with full dual algorithm chains. This can be achieved by creating a second intermediate CA that omits alternative artifacts, reducing storage, bandwidth, and processing costs for constrained legacy endpoints. Meanwhile, upgraded devices continue to use the full dual algorithm certificate chain to ensure protection against quantum-capable adversaries.

## 4.3  Security Considerations

Building on the deployment considerations above, we now examine the security implications of using dual algorithm certificates with our negotiation mechanism, particularly regarding downgrade attacks and weak non-separability. *Weak non-separability* allows an attacker to strip one part of a hybrid PQ/T signature (with the remaining one still successfully verifying in isolation), but any such modification is detectable through external mechanisms. In contrast, *strong non-separability* prevents this altogether through the hybrid construction itself [5].

Our threat model assumes an attacker capable of breaking the T algorithm, while the PQ algorithm remains secure. All upgraded devices are provisioned with full dual algorithm certificate chains (T as primary, PQ as alternative). Mixed chains may be used for legacy devices, provided that all upgraded devices use full dual algorithm chains. For the TLS key exchange, we assume quantum-secure ephemeral methods (e. g., a PQC key encapsulation mechanism, with or without T hybrids).

TLS connections that still advertise the T algorithm to support legacy peers are vulnerable to impersonation by the attacker in our threat model. However, connections between upgraded peers use either hybrid PQ/T or PQ-only signatures, both secure in our model. The attacker's goal is to downgrade such connections to use only the T algorithm, enabling impersonation again. To achieve this, the attacker might:

1. Strip the `dual_alg_signature_algorithms` extension from the ClientHello or CertificateRequest.
2. Reintroduce the T algorithm into the `signature_algorithms` extension.
3. Strip the PQ portion of the hybrid signature and change the algorithm field in the CertificateVerify message.

However, all these manipulations modify the handshake transcript. Since TLS incorporates transcript hashes in its key schedule to derive session keys, such tampering causes handshake failures unless the attacker can also break the ephemeral key exchange, enabling a full man-in-the-middle attack. Under our assumptions, this is infeasible, and the downgrade attack is detected, achieving weak non-separability for the handshake signature.

For certificate chain verification, we define the following rules to enforce weak non-separability, modified from an initially proposed ruleset by Gladiator [18]:

1. If the issuer certificate contains an alternative public key, the issued certificate **must** include an alternative signature.
2. If a certificate includes an alternative public key, it **must** be issued by a certificate with an alternative public key.

These rules ensure that once an alternative public key is introduced in the chain, all subsequent certificates (including the root) must support the alternative path. Since root certificates are distributed securely out-of-band without attacker modification in our threat model, artifact stripping is detected when verifying the chain with the root. Furthermore, this prevents attackers from constructing malicious traditional-only certificates.

Altogether, our mechanism and validation rules provide handshake and certificate authentication with weak non-separability. Downgrade attempts are detectable and can be suppressed, provided that peers enforce correct algorithm advertisement policies throughout the transition.

## 5    Implementation

To evaluate our improved transition mechanism, we implemented support for dual algorithm certificates in the TLS libraries WolfSSL and OpenSSL to ensure interoperability across a range of systems. WolfSSL was a natural fit for our focus on resource-constrained environments, as it scales from small microcontrollers to enterprise systems. It already included basic support for dual algorithm certificates and the CKS mechanism, which we extended to support our negotiation enhancements. In contrast, OpenSSL was chosen for its widespread use and ease of integration into existing applications.

WolfSSL already supports dual algorithm chain verification and several PQC algorithms, some already optimized for embedded use. However, the existing implementation was not suitable for resource-constrained devices. We reduced both code size and runtime memory usage and removed unnecessary feature dependencies to enable deployment even on small microcontrollers. The resulting optimizations are evaluated in Sect. 6. We also added support for the `dual_alg_signature_algorithms` extension and several hybrid PQ/T signatures in the `CertificateVerify` message. To ensure interoperability, we aligned our signature encoding with that of OpenSSL.

OpenSSL required a broader integration as it lacks native support for dual algorithm certificates. We reused and extended parts of Gladiator's implementation [18] for chain verification, adapting it to current OpenSSL versions and our final extension structure. Supporting all three certificate extensions required updates to OpenSSL's ASN.1 handling. Specifically, the creation and verification of the alternative signature required a new *preTBS* certificate structure that omits both the alternative signature extension and the primary signature algorithm identifier. Since the encoding of our extensions matches standard structures, much of the existing core logic could be reused. For PQC support in OpenSSL, we integrated the `oqs-provider` and `liboqs` libraries from the Open Quantum Safe project, which also provide hybrid PQ/T signature capabilities.

Support for the `dual_alg_signature_algorithms` extension was also added to OpenSSL's handshake logic.

From an application perspective, integration of the new functionality requires only one change: providing the alternative private key alongside the primary one. We introduced a new API method for this purpose, compatible with existing mechanisms and supporting both PEM and DER formats. In WolfSSL, alternative keys can also be sourced from external security tokens such as secure elements or smart cards. While the OpenSSL integration is currently less mature, both implementations are feature-equivalent. Given our focus on deployment in constrained environments such as OT and IoT systems, the WolfSSL implementation forms the basis for our evaluation in the next section.

## 6   Evaluation and Discussion

We evaluated the impact of dual algorithm certificate deployment and implementation, focusing on resource-constrained devices. All setups use a typical three-tier PKI hierarchy (root, intermediate, and entity), common in OT systems [19]. The following algorithms are used as representative configurations:

- Traditional certificate algorithm: `ECC secp384r1` (public key size: 100 byte; private key size: 48 byte; signature size: 104 byte).
- PQC certificate algorithm: `ML-DSA 65` (public key size: 1952 byte; private key size: 4032 byte; signature size: 3309 byte).

Both algorithms target NIST security level 3 (192-bit security), providing a balanced trade-off between size, performance, and security. ECC is used instead of RSA due to its widespread deployment and smaller artifacts. ML-DSA is chosen as a representative PQC algorithm due to its artifact/performance balance [41] and its availability in WolfSSL with low resource optimizations. Other candidates, such as stateful hash-based schemes (e. g., LMS or XMSS), may become more suitable in the future, but were not available for our evaluation.

To isolate the effect of authentication, all measurements use a traditional `ECDHE secp384r1` key exchange, excluding PQC to avoid unrelated overhead. However, in practice, PQC must also be integrated there during full transitions to ensure long-term security.

### 6.1   Generic Parameters

We first assess the generic impact of dual algorithm certificates on object sizes and transmitted data. PQC algorithms substantially increase artifact sizes compared to traditional schemes. Dual algorithm certificates, which combine both, lead to further increases.

Table 1 compares the DER-encoded file sizes of ECC-only, PQC-only, and dual algorithm certificate chains with identical metadata. As shown in the relative columns, dual algorithm chains are nearly 10× larger than ECC-only chains, due to the inclusion of the large PQC public key and signature in each certificate

(e. g., $603 + 1952 + 3309 \approx 5964$). However, compared to PQC-only chains, the increase is marginal ( 5 %), as ECC artifacts contribute little additional size.

Considering that the general transition to PQC is required in any case, upgraded systems and endpoints have to handle much larger chain sizes anyway, rendering the overhead of dual algorithm certificates less detrimental for upgraded endpoints. Only legacy devices are significantly affected negatively during the transition, as they must handle larger chains without utilizing the alternative artifacts(Table 1).

**Table 1.** File sizes for different certificate chains (DER encoded, in bytes)

| Type | ECC-only | PQC-only | Dual Alg. | Rel. ECC | Rel. PQC |
|---|---|---|---|---|---|
| Root | 603 | 5659 | 5964 | 9.89 | 1.0539 |
| Intermediate | 611 | 5667 | 5973 | 9.78 | 1.0540 |
| Entity | 670 | 5725 | 6028 | 9.00 | 1.0529 |
| Private Key | 167 | 4060 | 167 | 1.0 | 1.0411 |
| Alt. Private Key | - | - | 4060 | - | - |
| Total Size | 2051 | 21111 | 22192 | 10.82 | 1.0512 |

During the handshake, the certificate chains are exchanged between peers, so size increases directly translate into higher bandwidth usage, even if the alternative artifacts are unused. Table 2 shows the total number of bytes transmitted for mutually authenticated handshakes with each chain type. When at least one peer does not support dual algorithm certificates ("Dual Alg. (off)" column), the alternative artifacts are unused, wasting bandwidth. However, we believe that for the security benefit of rapid incremental deployment of PQC with backward compatibility, this is acceptable for many use cases and systems. Compared to the PQC-only setup again, dual algorithm certificates result in only a marginal increase (nearly 5 %).

**Table 2.** Number of transmitted bytes during the TLS handshake (in bytes)

| Chain | ECC-only | PQC-only | Dual Alg. (off) | Dual Alg. (on) |
|---|---|---|---|---|
| **Bytes** | 3594 | 30227 | 25007 | 31660 |

## 6.2   Handshake Time

We next evaluate the impact of dual algorithm certificates on TLS handshake duration. Our test setup includes two representative embedded platforms: a Raspberry Pi 4 ("RPi") running Linux (Raspberry Pi OS Lite, Kernel 6.12), and an STM32H743 microcontroller ("MCU", ARM Cortex-M7, 480 MHz) running Zephyr RTOS (v 4.2). These cover a broad spectrum of processing capabilities in embedded systems. Test applications on each device establish a mutually authenticated TLS session, with either peer acting as client or server. After the handshake, the client sends a byte which the server echoes, allowing us to measure the *time-to-first-byte* (TTFB). Each configuration is tested over 1000 runs in an isolated network with a round-trip time of about 0.3 ms.

For each device pairing, we define four test cases with different deployments or capabilities of the TLS endpoints, which are listed below. The resulting median TTFBs are summarized in Table 3.

a) **ECC-only** certificate chain (traditional algorithm).
b) **Dual algorithm** certificate chain, but **without feature support** (legacy devices).
c) **Dual algorithm** chain **with feature support** (upgraded devices).
d) **PQC-only** certificate chain.

**Table 3.** TTFB (median) for the different test cases (milliseconds)

| Test Setup | a) | b) | c) | d) |
|---|---|---|---|---|
| RPi → RPi | 7.593 | 9.769 | 12.025 | 6.433 |
| RPi → MCU | 97.975 | 111.828 | 159.373 | 89.034 |
| MCU → RPi | 99.278 | 111.551 | 166.314 | 93.362 |
| MCU → MCU | 153.675 | 180.366 | 228.567 | 135.284 |

The increase from case a) to b) reflects the additional network overhead caused by larger certificate chains, as already discussed in other work [41]. When dual algorithm features are actually used (case c), further increases result from the additional cryptographic operations (signing and verification). These effects are particularly pronounced on lower-performance devices, as seen in the wider differences in TTFB across setups. Interestingly, case d), representing the PQC-only chain, shows lower TTFBs than case a), despite larger artifacts. This demonstrates the general efficiency of ML-DSA [13] and the high level of optimization in the WolfSSL implementation.

In total, the increased handshake times have to be individually assessed for each system to be deemed acceptable. This is especially relevant considering the more typical long-lived connections of OT and IoT environments, where increased handshake times are often not as problematic [24].

## 6.3   Memory Consumption

We conclude by analyzing the memory overhead introduced by dual algorithm certificates, focusing on the MCU platform, where resource constraints are most critical. We measured stack and heap usage on the MCU acting as a TLS server. The test application logs all memory operations (allocations, frees, and maximum stack usage), covering a full connection lifecycle: endpoint and session creation, handshake, data exchange, termination, and cleanup. As in the previous subsection, we evaluate the four test cases a) to d). The progression of heap usage is shown in Fig. 1.

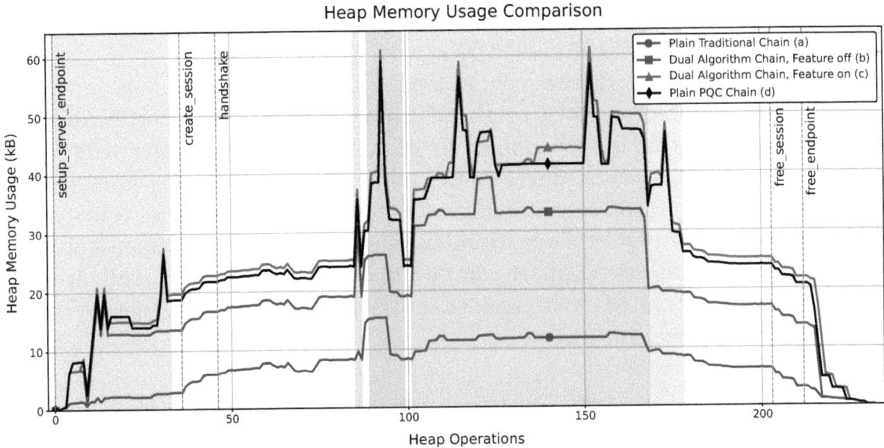


**Fig. 1.** Heap usage progression on the MCU for test cases a) – d), covering a full TLS session lifecycle.

The increase in dynamic memory usage from the deployment of dual algorithm certificates is evident from the offset of cases b) (green) and c) (red) over case a) (blue). The PQC-only case d) (purple) shows only a minor difference from case c) with slightly smaller values, indicating that the majority of the memory overhead arises from handling large PQC artifacts, not from the dual algorithm logic itself.

Five key areas are annotated in Fig. 1. The first on the left (orange) occurs during TLS endpoint creation, where the certificate chain is loaded into memory. The green offset corresponds to the additional PQC artifacts (two public keys and signatures) in the entity and intermediate certificates. Case c) (red) adds the PQC private key and root public key to memory, explaining its further offset. These allocations persist throughout the session.

The second area (blue) reflects a short peak during the construction of the Certificate message, now containing the larger chain. As all test cases b) – d) use large certificates, the peaks are similar. The third area (green) marks the peak during CertificateVerify generation for server authentication. The additional overhead in cases c) and d) is attributable to PQC signing.

The fourth area (purple) corresponds to the handling of the client certificate chain during mutual authentication. Again, the larger PQC artifacts increase memory usage across cases b) – d). In c) and d), three additional peaks appear: two from PQC signature verification and one from storing the client's PQC public key for handshake verification. The final peak in the yellow area marks the actual verification of the client's handshake signature.

Stack usage is comparatively stable. Cases a) – c) show similar peak usage (10264 B for a and b), with only a small increase in case c) to 10368 B. Interestingly, the PQC-only case d) requires significantly less stack space (7084 B), indicating that ECC operations contribute more to peak stack consumption. Furthermore, enabling the dual algorithm feature increases the MCU firmware size by approximately 15 kB (14452 B).

These results support two conclusions. First, both legacy and upgraded devices incur notable memory overhead from dual algorithm certificates. For upgraded devices, this is very similar to what the full PQC deployment would require anyway. For legacy devices, the additional memory use is essentially wasted but may be rated acceptable in many situations given the security benefits of incremental PQC rollout. Second, our measurements demonstrate that dual algorithm certificate support can be implemented efficiently, validating its suitability for constrained environments, and demonstrating the general viability of our transition mechanism.

## 7   Conclusion and Outlook

This work presented a transition mechanism for the TLS protocol that enables rapid deployment of PQC while maintaining backward compatibility with legacy systems, with a particular focus on OT and IoT environments where update capabilities are limited and mission times are long. Building on the concept of dual algorithm certificates, which contain artifacts (public key and signature) of two distinct algorithms, we introduced a TLS-compliant negotiation mechanism for their use in peer authentication (contribution C1). Through implementations in two TLS libraries and a detailed evaluation on a resource-constrained microcontroller, we demonstrated the practical viability of this approach (contributions C2 and C3).

We conclude that dual algorithm certificates, together with our negotiation mechanism, offer a promising path for the incremental deployment of PQC in mixed-system OT and IoT environments. By enabling secure interoperability between upgraded and legacy devices, this approach helps accelerate PQC adoption ahead of regulatory deadlines or the arrival of practical quantum threats.

Future work includes further optimizing performance and memory usage to support even more constrained platforms, expanding integration to additional TLS libraries, and adapting the mechanism for other secure communication protocols (e. g., IPsec) and cryptographic frameworks (e. g., CMS).

**Acknowledgments.** The presented work is part of the research project *KRITIS Scalable Safe and Secure Modules* (KRITISÂşM), which is funded by the Project Management Jülich (PtJ) and the German Federal Ministry for Economic Affairs and Climate Action (BMWK) under funding code 03EI6089A.

# References


1. Anastasova, M., Azarderakhsh, R., Kermani, M.M.: Fully Hybrid TLSv1.3 in Wolf-SSL on Cortex-M4. In: Applied Cryptography and Network Security Workshops, vol. 14586, pp. 376–395. Springer Nature Switzerland, Cham (2024). https://doi.org/10.1007/978-3-031-61486-6_22
2. Bernstein, D.J.: cr.yp.to: 2023.11.25: Another way to botch the security analysis of kyber-512 (2023). https://blog.cr.yp.to/20231125-kyber.html, Accessed 25 Apr 2025
3. Beullens, W.: Breaking rainbow takes a weekend on a laptop. In: Advances in Cryptology – CRYPTO 2022, pp. 464–479. Springer Nature Switzerland, Cham (2022)
4. Bindel, N., Braun, J., Gladiator, L., Stöckert, T., Wirth, J.: X.509-Compliant hybrid certificates for the post-quantum transition. J. Open Source Softw. p. 1606 (2019). https://doi.org/10.21105/joss.01606
5. Bindel, N., Hale, B., Connolly, D., D, F.: Hybrid signature spectrums. Internet-Draft Draft-Ietf-Pquip-Hybrid-Signature-spectrums-07, Internet Engineering Task Force (2025). https://datatracker.ietf.org/doc/draft-ietf-pquip-hybrid-signature-spectrums/07/, Work in Progress
6. Bonnell, C., Gray, J., Hook, D., Okubo, T., Ounsworth, M.: A mechanism for encoding differences in paired certificates. Internet-Draft draft-bonnell-lamps-chameleon-certs-06, Internet Engineering Task Force (2025). https://datatracker.ietf.org/doc/draft-bonnell-lamps-chameleon-certs/06/, Work in Progress
7. Chatziamanetoglou, D., Rantos, K.: On the implementation of x509-compliant quantum-safe hybrid certificates. IST-SET-198-RSY on Quantum Technology for Defence and Security (2023). https://www.sto.nato.int/publications/STO%20Meeting%20Proceedings/STO-MP-IST-SET-198/MP-IST-SET-198-A1-02.pdf
8. Chevignard, C., Fouque, P.A., Schrottenloher, A.: Reducing the number of qubits in quantum factoring. Cryptology ePrint Archive, Paper 2024/222 (2024). https://eprint.iacr.org/2024/222
9. Cloudflare, Inc.: Post-quantum encryption adoption | cloudflare radar. https://radar.cloudflare.com/adoption-and-usage#post-quantum-encryption-adoption, Accessed 12 Mar 2025
10. Driscoll, F., Parsons, M., Hale, B.: Terminology for post-quantum traditional hybrid schemes. Internet-draft, Internet Engineering Task Force (2025). https://datatracker.ietf.org/doc/draft-ietf-pquip-pqt-hybrid-terminology/06/, Work in Progress
11. EJBCA: Preparing for the migration to post-quantum public key algorithms with hybrid certificates (2023), https://www.ejbca.org/resources/preparing-for-the-migration-to-post-quantum-public-key-algorithms-with-hybrid-certificates/, Accessed 23 Apr 2025-04-23
12. Fan, J., et al.: Impact of post-quantum hybrid certificates on PKI, common libraries, and protocols. Int. J. Secure. Network. (2021). https://doi.org/10.1504/IJSN.2021.117887
13. Farisi, M.G.: Post-Quantum digital signatures — the benchmark of ML-DSA Against ECDSA and EdDSA (2025). https://blog.moeghifar.com/post-quantum-digital-signatures-the-benchmark-of-ml-dsa-against-ecdsa-and-eddsa-d4406a5918d9, Accessed 06 Jun 2025

14. Fries, S., Falk, R.: Supporting cryptographic algorithm agility with attribute certificates. Int. J. Adv. Secur. 17 (1& 2) (2024). https://personales.upv.es/thinkmind/dl/journals/sec/sec_v17_n12_2024/sec_v17_n12_2024_8.pdf
15. Garcia-Morchon, O., Kumar, S., Sethi, M.: Internet of things (IoT) security: state of the art and challenges. Request for Comments RFC 8576, Internet Engineering Task Force (2019). https://doi.org/10.17487/RFC8576
16. Geest, D.V., Bashiri, K., Fluhrer, S., Gazdag, S.L., Kousidis, S.: use of the HSS and XMSS hash-based signature algorithms in internet X.509 public key infrastructure. Internet-Draft draft-ietf-lamps-x509-shbs-13, Internet Engineering Task Force (2024). https://datatracker.ietf.org/doc/draft-ietf-lamps-x509-shbs/13/, Work in Progress
17. Gidney, C.: How to factor 2048 bit RSA integers with less than a million noisy qubits (2025). https://doi.org/10.48550/arXiv.2505.15917, arXiv:2505.15917
18. Gladiator, L.: Hybrid certificates in OpenSSL (2019). https://github.com/CROSSINGTUD/openssl-hybrid-certificates/blob/OQS-OpenSSL_1_1_1-stable/HybridCert_technical_documentation.pdf, Accessed 22 Apr 2025
19. Heinl, M.P., Pursche, M., Puch, N., Peters, S.N., Giehl, A.: From standard to practice: towards ISA/IEC 62443-conform public key infrastructures. In: Computer Safety, Reliability, and Security. Springer Nature Switzerland (2023). https://doi.org/10.1007/978-3-031-40923-3_15
20. Hollebeek, T., Schmieg, S., Westerbaan, B.: Use of ML-DSA in TLS 1.3. internet-draft draft-tls-westerbaan-mldsa-00, internet engineering task force (2024). https://datatracker.ietf.org/doc/draft-tls-westerbaan-mldsa/00/, Work in Progress
21. Internet engineering task force: IPR details - ISARA corporation's statement about IPR related to draft-truskovsky-lamps-pq-hybrid-x509 (2022). https://datatracker.ietf.org/ipr/5829/, Accessed 23 Apr 2025
22. ISARA corporation: ISARA dedicates four hybrid certificate patents to the public, easing path to quantum-safe security (2022). https://www.isara.com/company/newsroom/isara-dedicates-four-hybrid-certificate-patents-to-the-public.html, Accessed 23 Apr 2025
23. ITU-T: Recommendation ITU-T X.509 (2019). https://www.itu.int/rec/T-REC-X.509-201910-I/en
24. Kampanakis, P., Childs-Klein, W.: The impact of data-heavy, post-quantum TLS 1.3 on the time-to-last-byte of web connections. In: Proceedings 2024 Workshop on Measurements, Attacks, and Defenses for the Web. Internet Society, San Diego, CA, USA (2024). https://doi.org/10.14722/madweb.2024.23010
25. Kampanakis, P., Stebila, D., Hansen, T.: PQ/T hybrid key exchange in SSH. Internet-Draft draft-ietf-sshm-mlkem-hybrid-kex-02, Internet Engineering Task Force (2025). https://datatracker.ietf.org/doc/draft-ietf-sshm-mlkem-hybrid-kex/02/, Work in Progress
26. Lytle, J.: Performance of hybrid signatures for public key infrastructure certificates. Master's thesis, Naval Postgraduate School (2021). https://apps.dtic.mil/sti/citations/trecms/AD1204814
27. Moody, D., Perlner, R., Regenscheid, A., Robinson, A., Cooper, D.: Transition to post-quantum cryptography standards. Tech. Rep. NIST IR 8547 ipd, National Institute of Standards and Technology, Gaithersburg, MD (2024). https://doi.org/10.6028/NIST.IR.8547.ipd
28. National cyber security centre: timelines for migration to post-quantum cryptography (2025). https://www.ncsc.gov.uk/guidance/pqc-migration-timelines, Accessed 29 Apr 2025

29. National institute of standards and technology (NIST): FAQ on kyber512 (2023). https://csrc.nist.gov/csrc/media/Projects/post-quantum-cryptography/documents/faq/Kyber-512-FAQ.pdf, Accessed 24 Apr 2025

30. OPC foundation: UA part 4: security - 6.1.4 creating a securechannel (2025). https://reference.opcfoundation.org/Core/Part4/v105/docs/6.1.4, Accessed 29 Apr 2025

31. Ounsworth, M., Gray, J., Pala, M., Klaußner, J., Fluhrer, S.: Composite ML-DSA for use in X.509 public key infrastructure and CMS. Internet-Draft draft-ietf-lamps-pq-composite-sigs-07, Internet Engineering Task Force (2025). https://datatracker.ietf.org/doc/draft-ietf-lamps-pq-composite-sigs/07/, Work in Progress

32. Patil, K.: Preparing for the quantum leap with hybrid certificates (2024). https://www.appviewx.com/blogs/preparing-for-the-quantum-leap-with-hybrid-certificates/, Accessed 23 Apr 2025

33. Paul, S., Kuzovkova, Y., Lahr, N., Niederhagen, R.: Mixed certificate chains for the transition to post-quantum authentication in TLS 1.3. In: Proceedings of the 2022 ACM on Asia Conference on Computer and Communications Security, pp. 727–740. ACM (2022). https://doi.org/10.1145/3488932.3497755

34. Reddy, T., Hollebeek, T., Gray, J., Fluhrer, S.: Use of composite ML-DSA in TLS 1.3. internet-draft draft-reddy-tls-composite-mldsa-01, internet engineering task force (2024). https://datatracker.ietf.org/doc/draft-reddy-tls-composite-mldsa/01/, Work In Progress

35. Reddy.K, T., Hollebeek, T., Gray, J., Fluhrer, S.: Use of SLH-DSA in TLS 1.3. internet-draft draft-reddy-tls-slhdsa-01, internet engineering task force (2025). https://datatracker.ietf.org/doc/draft-reddy-tls-slhdsa/01/, Work in Progress

36. Rescorla, E.: The transport layer security (TLS) protocol version 1.3. RFC 8446 (2018). https://doi.org/10.17487/RFC8446

37. Scheible, P.: Quantum resistant authenticated key exchange for OPC UA using hybrid X.509 certificates. Master's thesis, Universitat Politècnica de Catalunya (2020). https://upcommons.upc.edu/handle/2117/191775

38. Shekh-Yusef, R., Tschofenig, H., Ounsworth, M., Sheffer, Y., Reddy.K, T., Rosomakho, Y.: Post-Quantum traditional (PQ/T) hybrid authentication with dual certificates in TLS 1.3. internet-draft draft-yusef-tls-pqt-dual-certs-00, internet engineering task force (2025). https://datatracker.ietf.org/doc/draft-yusef-tls-pqt-dual-certs/00/, Work in Progress

39. Shuzhou, S., He, Y., Lin, H.Y.: Convertible forms with multiple keys and signatures for use in internet X.509 certificates. Internet-Draft draft-sun-lamps-hybrid-scheme-01, Internet Engineering Task Force (2025). https://datatracker.ietf.org/doc/draft-sun-lamps-hybrid-scheme/01/, Work in Progress

40. Sikeridis, D., Kampanakis, P., Devetsikiotis, M.: Assessing the overhead of post-quantum cryptography in TLS 1.3 and SSH. In: Proceedings of the 16th International Conference on emerging Networking EXperiments and Technologies, pp. 149–156. ACM (2020). https://doi.org/10.1145/3386367.3431305

41. Sikeridis, D., Kampanakis, P., Devetsikiotis, M.: Post-Quantum authentication in TLS 1.3: a performance study. In: Proceedings 2020 Network and Distributed System Security Symposium. Internet Society, San Diego, CA (2020). https://doi.org/10.14722/ndss.2020.24203

42. Stapleton, J., Bordow, P., Rao, A., Hu, A., Hook, D., Stevens, S.: TLS certificate key selection (CKS) extension using x.509 hybrid certificates. E-Mail Attachment, IETF Mail Archive (2023). https://mailarchive.ietf.org/arch/msg/tls-reg-review/YleguOWXpJ8FaDisGHAHggNCr1U/, Accessed 22 Apr 2025

43. Stebila, D., Fluhrer, S., Gueron, S.: Hybrid key exchange in TLS 1.3. internet-draft draft-ietf-tls-hybrid-design-12, internet engineering task force (2025). https://datatracker.ietf.org/doc/draft-ietf-tls-hybrid-design/12/, Work in Progress
44. Tjhai, C., Tomlinson, M., Bartlett, G., Fluhrer, S., Geest, D.V., Garcia-Morchon, O., Smyslov, V.: Multiple key exchanges in the internet key exchange protocol version 2 (IKEv2). RFC 9370 (2023). https://doi.org/10.17487/RFC9370
45. Truskovsky, A., Geest, D.V., Fluhrer, S., Kampanakis, P., Ounsworth, M., Mister, S.: Multiple public-key algorithm X.509 certificates. Internet-Draft draft-truskovsky-lamps-pq-hybrid-x509-00, Internet Engineering Task Force (2018). https://datatracker.ietf.org/doc/draft-truskovsky-lamps-pq-hybrid-x509/00/, Expired Internet-Draft
46. Truskovsky, A., Yamada, A., Brown, M.K., Gutoski, G.M.: Using a digital certificate with multiple cryptosystems. Patent (2017). https://patents.google.com/patent/US9660978B1/en, Accessed 23 Apr 2025
47. WolfSSL: The new wolfSSL "experimental" framework – wolfSSL (2024). https://www.wolfssl.com/the-new-wolfssl-experimental-framework/, Accessed 23 Apr 2025

# Secure and Efficient Attribute-Based Signature Scheme for Substation Automation Systems

Mohammed Ramadan$^{(\boxtimes)}$, Moritz Gstür, Pranit Gadekar, Ghada Elbez, and Veit Hagenmeyer

Institute for Automation and Applied Informatics (IAI), Karlsruhe Institute of Technology (KIT), 76344 Eggenstein-Leopoldshafen, Germany
`mohammed.ramadan@kit.edu`

**Abstract.** The recent advancements of digital substations and their integration within modern smart grids have made the security and privacy of communication among the entities a critical requirement. This is especially relevant to access control and authentication processes in substation automation systems. This paper proposes an attribute-based access signature scheme for secure communication in substations' architecture. The proposed scheme provides fine-grained access control, ensuring only authorized entities can sign messages under hybrid attribute-based policies. By employing a certificateless primitive, the system allows efficient signature generation and verification with a semi-trusted third party. Also, key security properties, including unforgeability against chosen-message and collusion attacks, are formally defined and proven, ensuring the scheme's robustness against unauthorized access. The evaluation and discussion show that the scheme supports the delegation of signing authority and enables efficient signatures when required. The proposed construction demonstrates computational efficiency and compatibility with energy systems environments, serving as a secure role/rule-based access control scheme.

**Keywords:** Cryptography · Attribute-based cryptography · Digital signature · Smart grids · Substation automation systems

## 1 Introduction

Modern operational technology (OT) is progressively dependent on information and communication technology (ICT) for the purposes of monitoring and control [1]. Consequently, the similarities between OT and information technology (IT) systems are becoming more pronounced as OT systems incorporate IT advancements. While this convergence offers new opportunities, such as the integration of distributed OT into supervisory control and data acquisition (SCADA) systems, it also presents significant challenges resulting from the heightened reliance on ICT. In the energy-related sector, the infrastructures


R. Laborde et al. (Eds.): ESORICS 2025, LNCS 16231, pp. 523–540, 2026.
https://doi.org/10.1007/978-3-032-16089-8_31

transform from traditional top-down electricity distribution systems to smart grids with bidirectional data and electricity flow [2].

The number of economically or politically motivated adversaries attacking OT systems shows that energy-related critical infrastructures are at risk [3]. Incidents such as Stuxnet [4], Blackenergy [5], Industroyer/CrashOverride [6, 7], and Triton/Trisis [8] indicate that current mitigation approaches might not be appropriate for such critical infrastructures. The realization of national or global smart grids, however, requires appropriate security solutions to safeguard their availability and reliability [9–11]. In this paper, we focus on providing a solution that can be applied to secure the communication in so-called substation automation systems (SAS). A SAS represents the entirety of the communication and control equipment of a substation [12]. A substation is a facility of a high-voltage electricity grid connecting power transmission and distribution lines that use different voltage levels [13]. The tasks of a SAS are time-critical and have to be executed reliably, as the electricity sector and its substations are critical infrastructures.

The IEC 61850 standards series standardize the SAS domain, its components, and occurring message exchanges [14,15]. The goal of the IEC 61850 standards is the seamless communication and interoperability of devices in power utility automation systems. While IEC 61850 focuses on the power system architecture and communication protocols, its scope does not include considerations or solutions regarding information security. To eradicate this flaw, the International Electrotechnical Commission (IEC) created the sixth part of the IEC 62351 standards series [16]. This standard recommends securing SAS protocols by using message authentication to prevent unauthorized information manipulation. For time-critical SAS communication, satisfying confidentiality by using encryption is explicitly not recommended by this standard. Additionally, the eighth part of IEC 62351 provides a role-based access control (RBAC) concept for power systems, including IEC 61850 compliant systems [17]. Figure 1 shows the smart grids (SGs) architecture, which not only interconnects power plants and con-

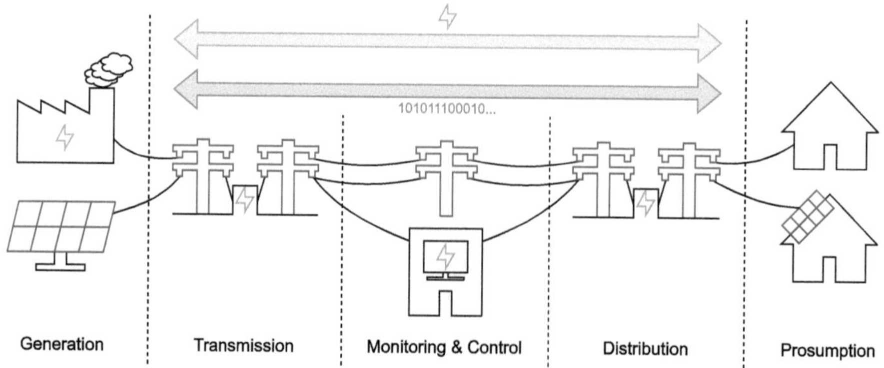


**Fig. 1.** Electricity and data distribution in a smart grid environment.

trol centers, but also integrates prosumers, substations, and other grid-related elements.

## 2   Related Work

**SAS access control.** About authorization and access control, the National Institute of Standards and Technology (NIST) emphasizes the importance of considering physical and logical means for OT security [1]. NIST states that organizations are not limited to a single access control approach, but may instead employ different approaches resulting in higher effectiveness and efficiency. A combination of access control lists (ACL), RBAC, and attribute-based access control (ABAC) is mentioned as an example for achieving the access control requirements of an organization. It is recommended that approaches support the principle of least privilege (PoLP) and separation of duties (SoD).

A review of the existing literature reveals a plethora of access control approaches for smart grid applications, including the following ABAC and RBAC approaches: An access control approach driven by ABAC policies for smart grid systems, including substations, is presented by Ruland and Sassmannshausen [18]. The presented access control approach is realized in the form of an access control firewall. The access control firewall enforces access request decisions based on ABAC policies. A real-time capable ABAC approach is presented by Burmester et al. [19]. The authors propose an extended ABAC model that is based on time-dependent attributes to support availability within the strict time constraints of cyber-physical systems. An IEC 61850 and IEC 62351 compliant RBAC approach for substations is presented by Lee et al. [20]. The approach focuses on session-based access control for TCP/IP communication on the station bus of substations.

The implementation demonstrates the feasibility of RBAC for substations as specified by IEC 62351 [17]. Furthermore, the presented implementation is capable of processing and responding to MMS requests within the 500 millisecond time requirement for type 3 messages (low speed messages) specified by IEC 61850-5 [14]. A distributed RBAC approach for subscription-based remote network services is presented by Ma and Woodhead [21,22]. The authors propose a distributed authentication and role-based authorization framework called distributed role-based access control (DRBAC). The distributed authentication is realized by delegating the authentication of users to their subscribing institutions by issuing authentication delegation certificates. The role-based authorization approach extends traditional RBAC by adding the concept of distributed roles shared by the service provider and service subscribers. A rule-based RBAC policy enforcement approach for smart grid systems is presented by Alcaraz et al. [23]. The presented approach integrates into a smart grid system with a supernode networking architecture. Supernodes are servers at fixed locations responsible for handling data flows of a set of subscribers [24]. The approach is based on a rule-based expert system and a context manager for the analysis of the source, target, and context of a request.

**Attribute-based digital signatures.** The usage of message authentication for SAS protocols, including GOOSE, SV, and MMS, is stipulated by existing standards [16]. Ensuring the integrity and authenticity of control and protection communication without compromising the time criticality is a challenge for SAS security [25]. Public-key cryptography (PKC) was formally recommended to ensure message authentication for different types of SAS communication, including the low-latency protocols Goose and SV. Nowadays, standards recommend the usage of symmetric cryptography, including HMAC-SHA256 and AES-GMAC-128/256, as the feasibility of PKC for time-critical SAS protocols was questioned due to its high computational complexity [25,26].

The emerging attribute-based PKC (AB-PKC) might provide security to distributed or pervasive high-performance systems, as it integrates attribute-based authentication, authorization, and access control [27]. AB-PKC is a generalization of the identity-based PKC (ID-PKC) concept [28,29]. Attribute-based signatures (ABS) integrate attributes into their signing and verification algorithms [30]. Therefore, ABS enables fine-grained ABAC based on anonymously signed messages [31]. In recent years, different types of ABS schemes were proposed in literature [32], including approaches with centralized attribute authority [33], decentralized attribute authorities [34], and server-aided computations [35–38].

**Gaps in the existing literature.** The integration of operational technology (OT) and information technology (IT) in modern substation automation systems reveals significant security issues, especially in access control and authentication for critical infrastructures. Current standards, e.g., IEC 61850 [14], focus on interoperability and overlook essential security measures. Meanwhile, IEC 62351 [17] offers only basic role-based access control (RBAC) and message authentication, which are insufficient for SAS security.

Access control approaches for energy systems, such as access control lists (ACL), role-based access control (RBAC), and attribute-based access control (ABAC), often fail to provide the fine-grained and dynamic authorization needed for real-time operations in resource-constrained environments such as SAS. The functionality of public-key cryptography (PKC) in time-sensitive SAS communications is limited due to its high computational cost, leading to a reliance on symmetric cryptography, which does not support flexible attribute-based policies. Moreover, the above literature proposed some attempts to provide lightweight attribute-based public-key signatures for SAS communications. However, providing hybrid role/rule-based access while meeting the latency and reliability requirements remains largely unaddressed. This reveals a significant gap in developing secure and efficient access control mechanisms to meet the requirements of modern digital substations.

## 2.1   Contributions

The proposed approach is a novel, efficient, and secure attribute-based signature and access control scheme that ensures reliable authentication and fine-grained access control through hybrid role/rule-based access, abbreviated as ABS-SAS. The scheme employs certificateless cryptographic primitives, enabling a secure, lightweight approach through a server-aided verification (SAV) technique. The main contributions in the paper are summarized as follows.

- We propose a hybrid attribute-based and role/rule-based access control signature scheme that utilizes certificateless cryptographic primitives, enabling both secure authentication and fine-grained authorization for SAS entities.
- We propose a server-aided verification technique to offload some parts of the verification process to a semi-trusted server, achieving the lightweight property, which significantly reduces the processing burden on IEDs, thus making it compatible with real-time system requirements.
- We provide a provable security analysis with formal security definitions demonstrating that the proposed scheme is existentially unforgeable under chosen-message attacks (EU-CMA) as well as is resistant to collusion attacks.
- We implement and evaluate the proposed scheme, conducting performance evaluations and comparisons; this proves its efficiency and compatibility with real-world deployment in substation environments.

**Paper Organization.** The remainder of this paper is structured as follows. Section 3 describes the system description, including the system and architecture models, and the security models and definitions. Section 4 introduces the proposed scheme and its detailed construction and algorithms. Section 5 provides security proof and analysis of the proposed scheme, including proofs of resistance to forgery and collusion under some security definitions. Section 6 presents performance evaluation based on complexity analysis, implementation, and comparisons with related schemes, and discussion. Finally, in Sect. 7, we conclude the paper with future research directions.

## 3   Models Descriptions

### 3.1   System Model

A three-layered architecture of an SAS based on IEC 61850 standards is illustrated in Fig. 2. Devices at the bay and process levels, such as intelligent electronic devices (IEDs) and merging units (MUs), may have limitations in computational performance, energy consumption, and communication latency. Additionally, non-resource-constrained devices, like SCADA terminal units or trusted third parties (TTP), can be integrated into the SAS or connected remotely via its gateway. This paper distinguishes two coexisting communication patterns in a SAS, observable in real systems. They differ in quality of service (QoS), including round-trip time (RTT), data transfer time, consistency, and data loss probability. The patterns are defined in our system model as follows.

The first communication pattern is horizontal communication, which occurs between neighboring devices, either directly or through local area networks (LAN). This pattern offers high transfer rates ($> 100$ MBit/s), low latency ($<$

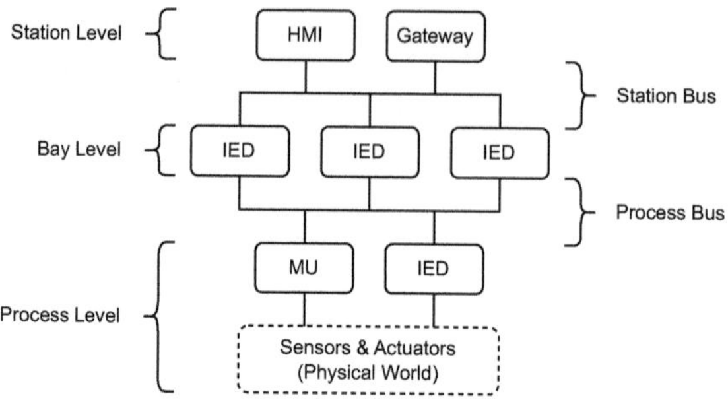


**Fig. 2.** Three-layered architecture of a SAS.

1 ms RTT), and reliable quality of service (QoS). This enables the exchange of time-critical messages, commonly used in multicast/broadcast protocols such as GOOSE and sampled values (SV) [15].

The second communication pattern is vertical communication, also known as uplink/downlink communication, which exchanges messages between non-neighboring devices, typically over wide area networks (WAN). It can be classified as either onsite/offsite or offsite/offsite, depending on the device's location. Due to shared media, vertical communication has higher latency, jitter, and data loss than horizontal communication, leading to reduced QoS predictability and making it impractical for reliable low-latency exchanges. The security requirements for OT systems like SAS differ from traditional IT systems [1]; while IT focuses on preventing unauthorized access and eavesdropping, OT prioritizes system availability and reliability. Therefore, applying IT security approaches to OT may not be effective due to these differences in system characteristics, risks, and priorities.

### 3.2  Security Model

The ABS-SAS scheme satisfies the following security properties:

- *Unforgeability*: to ensure that no adversary can create a valid signature for a message under a policy unless their attribute set satisfies the policy. Formally, unforgeability is defined using a game between a challenger and an adversary.
  - *Setup*: The challenger runs the **Setup** algorithm to generate the public parameters $PK$ and the master secret key $MSK$. The public parameters are given to the adversary, while the $MSK$ is kept secret.
  - *KeyGen*: The adversary can query the **KeyGen** oracle to obtain private keys for sets of attributes of its choice. The challenger responds with the corresponding private keys.
  - *SignQueries*: The adversary can request signatures for messages and policies from the **Sign** oracle. The oracle returns valid signatures if the queried attributes satisfy the signing policy.

- *Forgery*: The adversary outputs a forged signature $(m^*, T^*, \sigma^*)$ for a message $m^*$ and policy $T^*$. The adversary wins if the following conditions hold: The adversary did not request a signature on $(m^*, T^*)$ from the *Sign* queries. The adversary does not possess a private key whose attributes satisfy the policy $T^*$. The verification algorithm accepts $\sigma^*$ as a valid signature under $T^*$.
- *Existential Unforgeability under Chosen-Message Attacks (EU-CMA)*: An adversary $\mathcal{A}$ is given access to public parameters, hash oracles, and a signing oracle. The scheme is secure if $\mathcal{A}$ cannot forge a valid signature $\sigma^*$ for a new message $M^*$ without knowing the signer's full private key. The adversary's advantage in this game is its probability of generating a valid forgery. We say the scheme is *existentially unforgeable* if the adversary's advantage is negligible.
- *Collusion Attacks*: An adversary $\mathcal{A}$ colludes with the KGC and corrupted signers to derive private keys or forge valid signatures. The scheme is secure if such collusion does not compromise honest signers or allow forgery.

## 3.3   Preliminaries

The following notations and cryptographic primitives are utilized within the proposed ABS-SAS scheme. This includes bilinear pairing, hard assumptions that prove the scheme is secure, and the underlying access policy and structure.

- *Bilinear Pairing*: Let $G_1$ and $G_2$ be cyclic groups of prime order $p$, and let $e : G_1 \times G_1 \to G_2$ be a bilinear map with the following properties:
  - *Bilinearity*: $e(g^a, g^b) = e(g, g)^{ab}$ for all $g \in G_1$ and $a, b \in \mathbb{Z}_p$.
  - *Non-degeneracy*: $e(g, g) \neq 1$ for some $g \in G_1$.
  - *Computability*: There is an efficient algorithm to compute $e(g_1, g_2)$ for any $g_1, g_2 \in G_1$.
- *Attributes and Policies*: The following access policy, structure, and attributes are utilized within the scheme constructions.
  - *Attributes*: Each entity in the substation architecture (e.g., SCADA systems, IEDs, operators) is associated with attributes representing their role or access rights.
  - *Access Policies*: The system enforces access control using Boolean formulas on the attributes that combine AND/OR gates, and represented as an access matrix $M$.
  - Define hybrid attributes $\mathcal{R}$ as role-based and $\mathcal{L}$ as rule-based attributes.
  - Define the MSP matrix $\mathbf{I} \in \mathbb{Z}_q^{4 \times 3}$, and it is constructed as follows.

$$\mathbf{I} = \begin{bmatrix} 1 & a_1 & a_1^2 \\ 1 & a_2 & a_2^2 \\ 1 & a_3 & a_3^2 \\ 1 & a_4 & a_4^2 \end{bmatrix}$$

  where $a_1, a_2, a_3, a_4 \in \mathbb{Z}_q^*$ are distinct. Rows 1–2 correspond to $\mathcal{R}$, rows 3–4 to $\mathcal{L}$.

- For attribute set $S \subseteq \mathcal{R} \cup \mathcal{L}$, such that $\mathbf{v} \cdot \mathbf{I} = [1, 0, \ldots, 0]$. For threshold policies, $\mathbf{v}$ exists iff $|S| \geq T_0$.

- *Computational Diffie-Hellman (CDH):* Let $\mathbb{G}$ be a cyclic group of prime order $p$ with generator $g$. Given $(g, g^a, g^b)$ for randomly chosen $a, b \xleftarrow{\$} \mathbb{Z}_p$, it is computationally infeasible for any probabilistic polynomial-time (PPT) adversary to compute $g^{ab}$.
- *Decisional Bilinear Diffie-Hellman (DBDH):* Let $\mathbb{G}$ and $\mathbb{G}_T$ be cyclic groups of prime order $p$, $e : \mathbb{G} \times \mathbb{G} \to \mathbb{G}_T$ a bilinear map, and $g$ a generator of $\mathbb{G}$. Given $(g, g^a, g^b, g^c)$ for random $a, b, c \xleftarrow{\$} \mathbb{Z}_p$ and $T \in \mathbb{G}_T$, it is computationally infeasible to distinguish between $T = e(g, g)^{abc}$ and $T \xleftarrow{\$} \mathbb{G}_T$.
- *Collision-Resistance:* For hash function $\mathcal{H} : \{x\}^* \to \{y\}^\lambda$, it is computationally infeasible to find distinct inputs $x \neq y$ such that $\mathcal{H}(x) = \mathcal{H}(y)$.

## 4    The Proposed ABS-SAS Scheme

The ABS-SAS scheme represents a lightweight attribute-based signature mechanism tailored for smart grid environments. It facilitates dynamic access policies and includes server-aided verification, ensuring secure and efficient communication among various entities. This scheme is aligned with IEC standards and meets SG system and security requirements. The ABS-SAS involves the following entities:

- *STTP*: A semi-trusted entity generating partial private keys.
- *IEDs*: SAS entities/devices signers that generate the designed attribute-based signatures for authentication.
- *PDP*: a verification server assists in verifying signatures.
- *Control Center, e.g., remote access SCADA*: entities that require authentication and verification for access requests.

### 4.1    ABS-SAS: Detailed Construction

- *Setup*:
  - Let $G_1, G_T$ be bilinear groups of prime order $q$, with pairing $e : G_1 \times G_1 \to G_T$, and generator $g \in G_1$.
  - Define the hash functions: $H_1 : \{0, 1\}^* \to G_1$, $H_2 : \{0, 1\}^* \to \mathbb{Z}_q$, $H_3 : G_1 \to \{0, 1\}^*$
  - *STTP* chooses master secret $s \in \mathbb{Z}_q^*$, and computes public master key $P_0 = g^s$.
  - Then, publish $params = (G_1, G_T, e, g, P_0, H_1, H_2, H_3)$.

- *AccessPolicy*:
  - Define the Boolean Policy Mapping; e.g., for a policy $(R_1 \wedge L_1) \vee (R_2 \wedge L_2)$, the MSP matrix will be as follows.

$$\mathbf{I} = \begin{bmatrix} 1 & 1 & 0 \\ 1 & 0 & 1 \\ 0 & 1 & 1 \end{bmatrix}$$

  where Row 1: $R_1 \wedge L_1$, Row 2: $R_2 \wedge L_2$, Row 3: OR gate combining the two AND gates.
  - Define $S = (T_0, N)$ as a threshold policy requiring at least $T_0$ attributes from $\mathcal{R} \cup \mathcal{L}$; such that the attribute set $S \subseteq \mathcal{R} \cup \mathcal{L}$, for all threshold policies.

- *PartialKeyGen*:
  Given identity $ID$ and attribute set $Attr = (t_1, t_2, t_3, ..., t_n)$, $STTP$ computes the partial private key as follows, then sends it to the corresponding entity.

$$Q = H_1(ID \| \text{Attr})$$

$$D = Q^s$$

- *KeyGen*:
  Entities, $IEDs$, select $x \in \mathbb{Z}_q^*$, then compute the key pair as follows.
  Private key $sk = (x, D)$
  Public key $pk = g^x$

- *Sign*:
  To sign a message $M$ under the attributes $Attr$. First, define the signing policy as follows.
  First, bind the following tag.

$$R = H_1(M \| S)$$

Then, compute the following steps.

$$\sigma = D \cdot H_2(R)^x$$

$$C = H_3(\sigma) \oplus H_3(R)$$

Then, output signature as $(\sigma, C)$

- *ServerVerify*:
  $PDP$ receives $(params, pk, M, \sigma)$, and computes the following steps.

$$R = H_1(M \| S)$$

*PDP* verify:

$$e(\sigma, g) \stackrel{?}{=} e(Q, P_0) \cdot e(R, pk)$$

Then, the *PDP* outputs the partial verification and sends it to the end-entity (IEDs/MUs) as $(\sigma, C)$.

- *EntityVerify*:

Recompute:

$$R = H_1(M \parallel S)$$

Then check,

$$C' = H_3(\sigma) \oplus H_3(R) = C$$

Such that: $|S'| \subseteq \mathcal{R} \cup \mathcal{L}$, and $|S'| \geq T_0$

Then, outputs *Valid/Invalid*, and IEDs/MUs accept if the above verifications hold; otherwise, abort.

*Note*: Role-based attributes within SAS may include device roles such as IED, MU, HMI, WAN-Gateway, PDP, and PAP. Additionally, IEC standards define mandatory roles for energy systems, including human roles (e.g., viewer, operator, engineer), as well as some functional roles. Conversely, rule-based attributes in SAS may relate to device characteristics such as IP address, MAC address, and SAS level classifications—namely station, bay, or process—along with bus-affiliation and Network/WAN specifications. Furthermore, rule-based attributes may include communication properties regarding source/destination traffic flow for internet-based connections, commonly referred to as the 5-Tuple (IP address, Port, transport protocol), or for Ethernet traffic flow, the 3-Tuple (MAC address, application protocol, etc.).

## 4.2 Correctness

Given:

$$\sigma = D \cdot R^x = Q^s \cdot R^x$$

Then:

$$\begin{aligned}
e(\sigma, g) &= e(Q^s \cdot R^x, g) \\
&= e(Q, g)^s \cdot e(R, g)^x \\
&= e(Q, P_0) \cdot e(R, pk)
\end{aligned}$$

The above equation holds. Thus, the scheme is consistent.

*Computation-Saving*: To fulfill the SAV property, and the computation analysis presented in Sect. 6, we see that the proposed ABS-SAS scheme reduces the computational cost at the end entity side, and the server carries all the high-computation operations, such as bilinear pairing; such that:

$$\alpha - EntityVerify < \alpha - ServerVerify$$

Thus, ABS-SAS satisfies the SAV property.

## 5   Security Analysis

In this section, we conduct a security analysis of the ABS-SAS scheme within the framework of the random oracle model (ROM), showing that the scheme is secure under the security definitions of existential unforgeability chosen-message attacks (EU-CMA) and demonstrates collusion resistance, considering the hard assumptions stated in the preliminaries. Assume that $A_1$ and $A_2$ are adversaries against EU-CMA and collusion attacks, respectively, while $Ch$ is a Challenger.

**Theorem 1.** The ABS-SAS scheme is secure against existential unforgeability under chosen-message attacks (EU-CMA); if no algorithm exists that can solve the ABS-SAS against the CDH assumption in polynomial time.
**Proof.** The following game for the adversary $A_1$ and the challenger $Ch$ describes the security of EU-CMA.

- *Setup*: The challenger $Ch$ initializes this process by generating the public parameters *params* and the master secret key $s$.
- *Hash-Queries*: This is to query the random oracles $H_1, H_2, H_3$ to include the CDH-based instance $g_1^a$ and $g_1^b$, where $a, b$ are randoms. Thus, $A_1$ is allowed to query the hash functions $H_1, H_2, H_3$ as random oracles, extract the partial private key $ppk$, and request signatures on messages of their choice under any access policy.
- *Sign-Queries*: When the adversary requests a signature on a message $M$ under an access policy $T$, the challenger computes the signature as:

$$\sigma = (Q^a \cdot R)^x$$

Where $h = H_2(M||T)$. The challenger ensures that the signature is valid by simulating the random oracles.
- *Forgery*: Eventually, $A_1$ outputs a forged signature $\sigma^*$ on a message $M^*$ under an access policy $T^*$. $Ch$ extracts the solution to the CDH problem $g_1^{ab}$ from the forged signature by exploiting the structure of the random oracle responses.

- *Analysis*: Forging $\sigma$ requires solving $g^{ab}$ for $I$-mapping-$S$. Considering the boolean operations on $C$ that add negligible computing $\sigma^*$. Thus, the advantage of $A_1$ forging a signature versus solving the CDH problem is negligible, and the ABS-SAS scheme is secure regarding EU-CMA under CDH.

**Theorem 2.** The proposed scheme is secure against collusion attacks under the discrete logarithm assumption and the corresponding access policy.

*Proof.* : The following game for the adversary $A_2$ and the challenger $Ch$ describes the security against collusion attacks.

- *Setup*: The challenger $Ch$ initializes this process by generating the public parameters *params* and the master secret key $s$. $Ch$ also programs the random oracles $H_1, H_2, H_3$ to include the CDH-based instance $g_1^a$ and $g_1^b$, where $a, b$ are randoms. The adversary $A_1$ is allowed to query the hash functions $H_1, H_2, H_3$ as random oracles, extract the partial private key *ppk*, and request signatures on messages of their choice under the access policy $\mathbf{v} \cdot \mathbf{M} = [1, 0, \ldots, 0]$.
- *Hash-Queries*: Same as in *Theorem 1*.
- Access Policy: combining DLP with MSP binding, $A_2$ attempts to compromise $\{sk_i\}$ to satisfy $\mathbf{v} \cdot \mathbf{M} = [1, 0, \ldots, 0]$ for $S^* \not\subseteq \bigcup S_i$, to comprmise the follwoing DLP hard assumption; such that $c_i x_i \equiv x \mod p$.
- Forgery: $A_2$ runs the *Setupt* algorithm to get *params* and can query on *ppk*, $D = Q^s$, then $A_2$ attempts to generate a valid signature as $\sigma = (D \cdot R)^x$. Note that $A_2$ doesn't have access to $x$.

- *Forgery*: in case of $A_2$ Colludes with $\{sk_i\}$; $A_2$ still cannot produce $(\sigma^*, C^*)$ for $S^* \not\subseteq \bigcup S_i$, due to $\sigma^*$ requires solving DLP, and $C^*$ must satisfy $C^* = H_3(\sigma^*) \oplus \tau^*$, where $\tau^*$ depends on $S^*$, and $A_2$ cannot predict $\tau^*$ for unauthorized $S^*$; or extracting $x$ versus. Thus, no polynomial algorithm exists to solve the above equations under the DLP assumption. Thus, the ABS-SAS scheme is secure against collusion attacks.

- *Analysis* The semi-trusted party (PDP) introduces two types of attacks within insider attacks, information leakage, in which a malicious PDP may compromise $\sigma$ through repeated verification queries. The proposed scheme is secure against such an attack via $H_3(\sigma) \oplus H_3(R)$ ensures $\sigma$ remains obscured unless $R$ is known. Another insider attack is a collusion attack, in which PDP may collude with an IED entity. The proposed scheme is still secure against this attack, and PDP cannot forge signatures under the DLP hard assumption; such that $\forall \mathcal{A} \, [\Pr[\text{Extract}_{sk}(ID^*) \mid sk_{IED} \cup sk_{PDP}] \leq \text{negl}(\lambda)]$.

## 6    Perfomance

### 6.1    Complexity Analysis

To evaluate the proposed ABS-SAS within substation environments, we conducted a comprehensive complexity analysis and Python implementation utilizing https://github.com/Jemtaly/pypbc *pycharm/pypbc library*. Table 1 presents a summary of the computational requirements associated with primary operations, benchmarked against a security level of 256 *bits*. The implementation showed high computation cost on modular exponentiations and pairings, which are recognized as the most resource-intensive operations within the proposed attribute-based cryptography primitives. For more details, the code and results of ABS-SAS implementation can be found here https://github.com/Anon94876/ABAC *GitHub*.

**Table 1.** Notations of operations computation complexity (*ms*)

| $Notations$ | $Operations$ | $C_{avg}$ |
|---|---|---|
| $T_1$ | Pairing: $e : G_1 \times G_1 \to G_2$ | 3.7 |
| $T_2$ | Scalar multiplication | 1.6 |
| $T_3$ | Exponentiation $\in \mathbb{Z}_q$ | 2.8 |
| $T_4$ | ECC multiplication | 2 |
| $T_5$ | $H_1 : \{0,1\}^* \to G_1$ | 1.1 |
| $T_6$ | $H_2 : \{0,1\}^* \to Z_q$ | 1 |
| $T_7$ | $H_3 : \{0,1\}^* \to G_1$ | 2.1 |
| $T_8$ | $H_4 : G_2 \to \{0,1\}^*$ | 1.1 |
| Others | e.g. XOR | Omitted |

The absence of pairing-based operations during the verification process significantly decreases computational costs on IEDs and MUs by over 25 % when compared to some other proposed methodologies. However, the pairing-based operations during signing introduce an acceptable level of overhead. This optimization aligns with some standards recommendations related to energy systems, e.g., IEC 62351-6, which specify the need to minimize cryptographic latency for time-sensitive SAS protocols.

We compare ABS-SAS with three state-of-the-art schemes using metrics derived from their proposed approaches, as shown in Table 2 and Fig. 3. Notably, Cui et al. [36] reported 35.3 *ms* latency due to certificate validation—a bottleneck; while ABS-SAS avoids this through its certificateless primitive. Chen et al. [38] has 31.5 *ms* latency but lacked support for hybrid attribute policies. Then, compared to Xiong et al. [37], which has 38.6 *ms* computation cost. Thus, the proposed ABS-SAS approach reduces the computational cost on the end-user side by approximately. 48 % on average.

**Table 2.** Comparison of computation complexity ($ms$)

| Scheme | Ref. [36] | Ref. [37] | Ref. [38] | ABS-SAS |
|---|---|---|---|---|
| Sign | $2T_1 + 2T_2 + 2T_3 + 3T_4 + T_6 + T_8 = 27.1$ | $3T_1 + 2T_2 + T_3 + 5T_4 + 2T_5 = 29.3$ | $2T_1 + 2T_3 + 4T_4 = 23.8$ | $T_3 + 2T_4 + T_6 + T_7 = 11.1$ |
| Verify | $2T_4 + T_5 + T_7 = 8.2$ | $T_1 + T_2 + 2T_4 = 9.3$ | $T_2 + 2T_4 + T_7 = 7.7$ | $2T_7 + T_6 = 5.3$ |
| Total | 35.3 | 38.6 | 31.5 | 16.4 |

## 6.2 Results and Discussion

We evaluated the proposed ABS-SAS scheme using Python, and we observed that single-message signing took about 12 ms per operation, with 90% under 10 $ms$, outperforming Xiong et al. [37], which relies on time-consuming bilinear pairing and exponentiation. While Cui et al. [36] and Chen et al. [38] also aim for lightweight signing, their runtimes are higher due to extra cryptographic operations. ABS-SAS improved the baseline by 31%. Server-aided batch verification of all signatures averaged 5 $ms$, significantly better than Xiong et al.'s 9 $ms$ per signature. ABS-SAS avoids ECC-based operations by using verification actions. Additionally, field data from [20] indicates that 92% of SAS policies have at least 15 attributes, while our scheme keeps latency under 15 $ms$ in 97% of configurations.

Several challenges were identified from the above evaluation, particularly regarding the complexity of policies and their direct impact on latency. For policies that included more than 15 attributes, the verification time increased by 10 $ms$ for each additional attribute. This presents a trade-off that requires careful consideration in practical implementation. In contrast to the traditional role-based access control (RBAC) implementations analyzed by Lee et al. [20], our proposed approach demonstrates a significant performance improvement, specifically a 30% reduction in policy update latency.

The analysis presented above indicates a significant reduction in both computational costs and communication overhead when compared to previously referenced systems. As shown in Fig. 3, 80% of transactions are completed within a time-frame of 12 $ms$, while remaining within the critical 3 $ms$ threshold for protection signals. The advantageous combination of low computational cost, minimized communication overhead, and verifiable security positions ABS-SAS as a highly suitable approach for real-time SAS, including other resource-constrained and wireless-related applications, reducing the trust level on the third-party and ensuring end-to-end security [39]. The server-aided verification technique within the proposed scheme reduces IED overhead by almost half and introduces 0.8 $ms$ network latency. This remains an acceptable margin for non-time-critical MMS messages with approximately 500 $ms$ threshold.

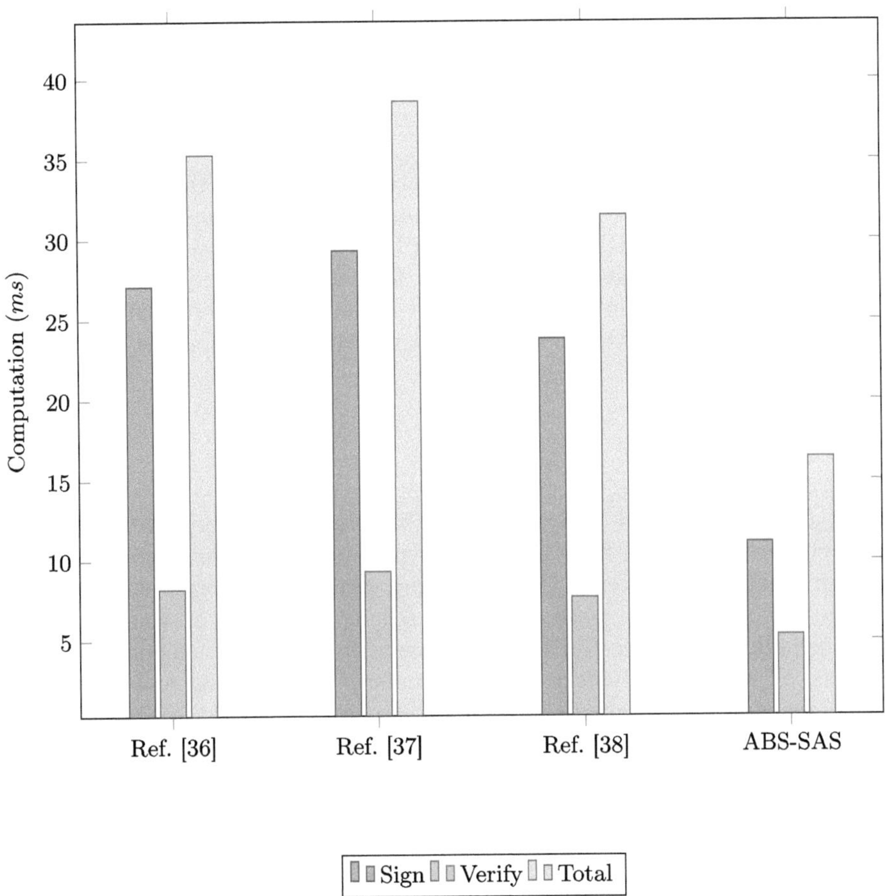


**Fig. 3.** Comparisons of computation complexity.

### 6.3   Future Work

The complexity improvements in the proposed ABS-SAS scheme can be associated with the attribute-driven architecture of the scheme, which enables more context-aware access decisions. Unlike RBAC, which relies on static role assignments and predefined hierarchies, the ABS-SAS dynamically evaluates entities, resources, and attributes at runtime, thereby improving the adaptability in dynamic environments, particularly for operational technology (OT) systems, where access requirements regularly shift based on operational changes and system configurations. Therefore, these findings are in alignment with the recommendations outlined by NIST [40], which highlighted the importance of adopting attribute-based access control (ABAC) models to enhance security, scalability, and flexibility in dynamic and heterogeneous OT environments.

The memory utilization during aggregation exhibited a linear scaling behavior $O(n)$, indicating a need for future research focused on memory-optimized batch processing for large substations. One potential approach to address this challenge is to optimize the overall complexity by utilizing policy compression techniques, which can transform $n$-attribute policies into $O(\log n)$. Also, hardware-based acceleration techniques can be used to offload pairing operations to FPGA co-processors.

For scalability and deployment, and since the storage overhead increases linearly with the batch size $O(n)$, it is feasible to consider edge-tier PDP deployment as a distributed PDP architecture for large-scale substations, such as those with more than 500 IEDs. Another factor for deployment involves using HSM-protected components in a control center as an STTP, along with protected PDPs (e.g., within a DMZ) and IEDs as tamper-resistant modules.

## 7  Conclusion

This paper presents ABS-SAS, a novel attribute-based signature scheme designed for secure, efficient, and fine-grained authentication and access control for substation automation systems. By integrating certificateless cryptographic techniques with server-aided verification, this scheme offers strong security guarantees, including resistance to EU-CMA threats and robustness against collusion attacks, all while complying with IEC standards and meeting real-time operational demands. The evaluation and analysis show that the proposed ABS-SAS is compatible and applicable for next-generation smart grid infrastructures. Our future directions will focus on ensuring dynamic revocation features for access control and post-quantum security, further enhancing the resilience of critical infrastructure security and privacy.

**Acknowledgments.** This work was supported by funding from the topic Engineering Secure Systems of the Helmholtz Association (HGF) and by KASTEL Security Research Labs (structure 46.23.02).

## References

1. Stouffer, K., et al.: Guide to operational technology (OT) security. Technical Report NIST Special Publication 800-82,Rev.3, National Institute of Standards and Technology (2023)
2. Fang, X., Misra, S., Xue, G., Yang, D.: Smart grid – the new and improved power grid: a survey. IEEE Commun. Surv. Tutorials **14**(4), 944–980 (2011)
3. Communications Security Establishment (Canada), issuing body: Cyber threat bulletin: the cyber threat to operational technology. Monograph. December (2021)
4. Barzashka, I.: Are cyber-weapons effective? Assessing Stuxnet's impact on the Iranian enrichment programme. RUSI J. **158**(2), 48–56 (2013)
5. Kozak, P., Ivo, K., Tomas, S.: Industroyer cyber-attacks on Ukraine's critical infrastructure. In: The 2023 International Conference on Military Technologies (ICMT). IEEE, pp. 1–6 (2023)

6. Zinets, N.: Ukraine hit by 6,500 hack attacks, sees russian cyberwar. Reuters (2016)
7. Mekdad, Y., Bernieri, G., Conti, M., El Fergougui, A.: The rise of ICS malware: a comparative analysis. In: Katsikas, S., et al. (eds.) Computer Security. ESORICS 2021 International Workshops. ESORICS 2021. LNCS, vol. 13106, pp. 496–511. Springer, Cham (2022). https://doi.org/10.1007/978-3-030-95484-0_29
8. Johnson, B., Caban, D., Krotofil, M., Scali, D., Brubaker, N., Glyer, C.: Attackers deploy new ICS attack framework "triton" and cause operational disruption to critical infrastructure (2017)
9. Gellings, C.W., Samotyj, M., Howe, B.: The future's smart delivery system. IEEE Power Energ. Mag. $\mathbf{2}(5)$, 40–48 (2004)
10. Yan, Y., Qian, Y., Sharif, H., Tipper, D.: A survey on cyber security for smart grid communications. IEEE Commun. Surv. Tutorials $\mathbf{14}(4)$, 998–1010 (2012)
11. Gopstein, A., Nguyen, C., O'Fallon, C., Hastings, N., Wollman, D. A.: NIST framework and roadmap for smart grid interoperability standards. Technical Report NIST Special Publication 1108r4, National Institute of Standards and Technology (2021)
12. Padilla, E.: Substation automation systems: design and implementation. John Wiley & Sons (2015)
13. Reese, C.D., James V.E.: Handbook of OSHA Construction Safety and Health. CRC Press (2006)
14. Elbaset, A.A., Yehia, S.M., Amer, N.A.E.: IEC 61850 communication protocol with the protection and control numerical relays for optimum substation automation system. J. Eng. Sci. Technol. Rev. $\mathbf{13}(2)$ (2020)
15. International Electrotechnical Commission. IEC 61850-8-1:2011: Communication networks and systems for power utility automation - Part 8-1: Specific communication service mapping (SCSM); Mappings to MMS (ISO 9506-1 and ISO 9506-2) and to ISO/IEC 8802-3 (2017)
16. International Electrotechnical Commission. IEC 62351-6:2020: Power systems management and associated information exchange - Data and communications security - Part 6: Security for IEC 61850 (2020)
17. International Electrotechnical Commission. IEC 62351-8:2020: Power systems management and associated information exchange - Data and communications security - Part 8: Role-based access control for power system management (2020)
18. Ruland, C., Sassmannshausen, J.: Firewall for attribute-based access control in smart grids. In: 2018 IEEE International Conference on Smart Energy Grid Engineering (SEGE). IEEE (2018)
19. Burmester, M., Magkos, E., Chrissikopoulos, V.: T-ABAC: an attribute-based access control model for real-time availability in highly dynamic systems. In: 2013 IEEE Symposium on Computers and Communications (ISCC). IEEE (2013)
20. Lee, B., Kim, D.-K., Yang, H., Jang, H.: Role-based access control for substation automation systems using xacml. Inf. Syst. $\mathbf{53}$, 237–249 (2015)
21. Ma, M., Woodhead, S.: Authentication delegation for subscription-based remote network services. Comput. Secur. $\mathbf{25}(5)$, 371–378 (2006)
22. Ma, M., Woodhead, S.: Constraint-enabled distributed RBAC for subscription-based remote network services. In: The Sixth IEEE International Conference on Computer and Information Technology (CIT'06). IEEE (2006)
23. Alcaraz, C., Lopez, J., Wolthusen, S.: Policy enforcement system for secure interoperable control in distributed smart grid systems. J. Netw. Comput. Appl. $\mathbf{59}$, 301–314 (2016)

24. Samuel, H., Zhuang, W., Preiss, B.: Routing over interconnected heterogeneous wireless networks with intermittent connections. In: 2008 IEEE International Conference on Communications. IEEE (2008)
25. Ishchenko, D., Nuqui, R.: Secure communication of intelligent electronic devices in digital substations. In: 2018 IEEE/PES Transmission and Distribution Conference and Exposition (T&D). IEEE (2018)
26. Elbez, G., Keller, H. B., Hagenmeyer, V.: Authentication of GOOSE messages under timing constraints in IEC 61850 substations. In: Electronic Workshops in Computing. BCS Learning & Development (2019)
27. Hu, V.C.: Overview and considerations of access control based on attribute encryption. Technical Report. US Department of Commerce, NIST Interagency/Internal Report (NISTIR) – 8450, National Institute of Standards and Technology (2023)
28. Sahai, A., Waters, B.: Fuzzy identity-based encryption. In: Cramer, R. (eds.) Advances in Cryptology – EUROCRYPT 2005. EUROCRYPT 2005. LNCS, vol. 3494, pp. 457–473. Springer, Berlin, Heidelberg (2005). https://doi.org/10.1007/11426639_27
29. Goyal, V., Pandey, O., Sahai, A., Waters, B.: Attribute-based encryption for fine-grained access control of encrypted data. In: Proceedings of the 13th ACM conference on Computer and communications security, CCS06. ACM (2006)
30. Li, J., Au, M. H., Susilo, W., Xie, D., Ren, K.: Attribute-based signature and its applications. In:Proceedings of the 5th ACM Symposium on Information, Computer and Communications Security, ASIA CCS '10. ACM (2010)
31. Maji, H.K., Prabhakaran, M., Rosulek, M.: Attribute-based signatures. In: Kiayias, A. (eds.) Topics in Cryptology – CT-RSA 2011. CT-RSA 2011. LNCS, vol. 6558, pp. 376–392. Springer, Berlin, Heidelberg (2011). https://doi.org/10.1007/978-3-642-19074-2_24
32. Oberko, P.S.K., Obeng, V.-H.K.S., Xiong, H., Kumari, S.: A survey on attribute-based signatures. J. Syst. Architect. **124**, 102396 (2022)
33. Gagné, M., Narayan, S., Safavi-Naini, R.: Short pairing-efficient threshold-attribute-based signature. In: Abdalla, M., Lange, T. (eds.) Pairing-Based Cryptography – Pairing 2012. Pairing 2012. LNCS, vol. 7708, pp. 295–313. Springer, Berlin, Heidelberg (2012). https://doi.org/10.1007/978-3-642-36334-4_19
34. Okamoto, T., Takashima, K.: Decentralized attribute-based signatures. In: Kurosawa, K., Hanaoka, G. (eds.) Public-Key Cryptography – PKC 2013. PKC 2013. LNCS, vol. 7778, pp. 125–142. Springer, Berlin, Heidelberg (2013). https://doi.org/10.1007/978-3-642-36362-7_9
35. Ramadan, M., Liao, Y., Li, F., Zhou, S.: Identity-based signature with server-aided verification scheme for 5g mobile systems. IEEE Access **8**, 51810–51820 (2020)
36. Cui, H., Deng, R.H., Liu, J.K., Yi, X., Li, Y.: Server-aided attribute-based signature with revocation for resource-constrained industrial-internet-of-things devices. IEEE Trans. Industr. Inf. **14**(8), 3724–3732 (2018)
37. Xiong, H., Bao, Y., Nie, X., Asoor, Y.I.: Server-aided attribute-based signature supporting expressive access structures for industrial internet of things. IEEE Trans. Ind. Inf, **16**(2), 1013–1023 (2020)
38. Chen, Yu., Li, J., Liu, C., Han, J., Zhang, Y., Yi, P.: Efficient attribute based server-aided verification signature. IEEE Trans. Serv. Comput. **15**(6), 3224–3232 (2022)
39. Ramadan, M., Du, G., Li, F., Xu, C. X.: EEE-GSM: end-to-end encryption scheme over GSM system. Int. J. Secur. Appl., **10**(6), 229–240 (2016)
40. National Institute of Standards and Technology: Personal Identity Verification (PIV) of Federal Employees and Contractors. FIPS 201-3 (2022)

# Author Index


**A**

Abdelrahman, Mostafa  259
Acar, Gunes  188
Ahmad, Shahzad  97
Akbarzadeh, Aida  462
Almeida, Ricardo Lopes  293
Al-Momani, Ala'a  154
Ameh, Jude E.  171
Amro, Ahmed  462
Andrianopoulos, Vasileios  403
Arkhmammadova, Roya  66

**B**

Baiardi, Fabrizio  293
Balenson, David  154
Barker, Ken  206
Berg, Tommy Helland  462
Bistarelli, Stefano  311
Blanco-Justicia, Alberto  32
Borgesius, Frederik Zuiderveen  188
Bösch, Christoph  154
Boulahia-Cuppens, Nora  442
Büchele, Jan  49

**C**

Carle, Georg  259
Cha, Sang Kil  344
Chang, Ee-Chien  382
Chatzigiannis, Panagiotis  242
Choi, Jaeseung  344
Cuppens, Frédéric  442

**D**

Damie, Marc  116
de Montjoye, Yves-Alexandre  16
Domingo-Ferrer, Josep  3, 32
Douligeris, Christos  403
Drăgan, Constantin Cătălin  293
Drechsler, Jörg  137

**E**

Elbez, Ghada  523

**F**

Faillon, Marc-Antoine  442
Fettuh, Tegrid  277
Francq, Julien  442
Frauenschläger, Tobias  503
Frings, Kimberley  188

**G**

Gadekar, Pranit  523
Garg, Sonakshi  137
Gkioulos, Vasileios  482
Glas, Kilian  259
Gnap, Sven  221
Gstür, Moritz  523
Guépin, Florent  16
Gursoy, M. Emre  66

**H**

Hagenmeyer, Veit  523
Hahn, Florian  116
Hassing, Remco  363
Hladký, Tomáš  328
Homoliak, Ivan  328
Hupel, Lars  259

**I**

Ikpehai, Augustine  171

**J**

Jebreel, Najeeb  32

**K**

Kampourakis, Vyron  482
Kang, Niklaus  382
Karame, Ghassan  221
Katsikas, Sokratis  482
Katzenbeisser, Stefan  423

Kavallieratos, Georgios   462
Khalil, Mona   32
Kikuchi, Hiroaki   125
Kim, Jung Hyun   344
Kim, Soomin   344
Kostiainen, Kari   221
Kostkiewicz, Paweł   79
Kotzanikolaou, Panayiotis   403
Krčo, Nataša   16
Kubík, Jakub   328
Kulynych, Bogdan   16
Kutyłowski, Mirosław   79

**L**
Lau, Phi Tuong   423
Lazri, Luigj   49
Le, Duc V.   242
Liang, Zhenkai   382
Liu, Yuancheng   382
Loves, Rob   363
Luchini, Chiara   311

**M**
Maesa, Damiano Di Francesco   293
Makrakis, Georgios Michail   363
Mann, Zoltán Ádám   154
McCombie, Stephen   363
Meeus, Matthieu   16
Minaei, Mohsen   242
Moreno-Sanchez, Pedro   242
Moti, Zahra   188
Mottok, Jürgen   503

**N**
Neunhoeffer, Marcel   137

**O**
Otebolaku, Abayomi   171

**P**
Pape, Sebastian   154
Pavliv, Valentyna   49
Perešíni, Martin   328
Peter, Andreas   116
Petit, Jonathan   154
Pijpker, Jeroen   363

**R**
Raghuraman, Srinivasan   242
Ramadan, Mohammed   523
Ramon, Jan   116
Rass, Stefan   97
Rezabek, Filip   259
Ricci, Laura   293
Rochester, Edward   206

**S**
Santini, Francesco   311
Sastry, Nishanth   293
Seah, Choon Meng   382
Seyedi, Zahra   97
Shenfield, Alex   171
Smiliotopoulos, Christos   482
Sule, Dauda   171

**T**
Tamar, Hosein Madadi   66
Torra, Vicenç   137

**U**
Utz, Christine   188

**W**
Wagner, Isabel   49
Wechta, Gabriel   79

**Y**
Yaich, Reda   442
Yayla, Oğuz   277
Yusof, Anis   382